# Women's Periodicals and Newspapers
from the 18th Century to 1981

*A
Reference
Publication
in
Women's
Studies*

Barbara Haber
*Editor*

# Women's Periodicals and Newspapers
## from the 18th Century to 1981

A union list of the holdings of
Madison, Wisconsin, Libraries

Edited by
### James P. Danky

Compiled by
Maureen E. Hady
Barry Christopher Noonan
Neil E. Strache

In association with the
State Historical Society of Wisconsin

### G.K. HALL & CO.
70 LINCOLN STREET, BOSTON, MASS.

Copyright © 1982 by Dept. of Public Instruction, State of Wisconsin.

All rights reserved. This book, or any part thereof, may not be reproduced by any means, mechanical or electronic, without permission.

**Library of Congress Cataloging in Publication Data**

Hady, Maureen E., 1952—
  Women's periodicals and newspapers from the 18th century to 1981.

  Includes indexes.
  1. Feminism—Periodicals—Bibliography—Union lists. I. Noonan, Barry Christopher. II. Strache, Neil E., 1951—   . III. Danky, James Philip, 1947—   . IV. State Historical Society of Wisconsin. V. Title.
Z7965.H3 1982 [HQ1180] 016.3054'05   82-11903
ISBN 0-8161-8107-1

*This publication is printed on permanent/durable acid-free paper*
MANUFACTURED IN THE UNITED STATES OF AMERICA

Alternative Cataloging in Publication Data:

Danky, James P., 1947-   editor.
  Women's periodicals and newspapers from the 18th Century to 1981: a union list of the holdings of Madison, Wisconsin libraries. Edited by James P. Danky. Compiled by Maureen E. Hady, Barry Christopher Noonan, and Neil E. Strache. Boston, G. K. Hall, in association with the State Historical Society of Wisconsin, 1981.

  1. Women's periodicals--Bibliography--Union lists. 2. Feminist periodicals--Bibliography--Union lists. 3. Union catalogs--Madison, Wisconsin. 4. University of Wisconsin, Madison. Libraries--Catalogs. 5. Wisconsin. State Historical Society--Catalogs. I. Wisconsin. State Historical Society. II. Hady, Maureen E., 1952- compiler. III. Noonan, Barry Christopher, compiler. IV. Strache, Neil E., 1951- compiler. V. Title. VI. Title: Women's periodicals from the 18th Century to 1981. VII. Title: Women's newspapers from the 18th Century to 1981.

050.16 or 301.412'016

*For EJD*

# Contents

Introduction . . . . . . . . . . . . . . . . . . . . . . . . . . ix

How to Use the Bibliography . . . . . . . . . . . . . . . . . xiii

Herstory Holdings . . . . . . . . . . . . . . . . . . . . . . . xv

Indexes Included in this Compilation . . . . . . . . . . . . . xvii

Sources for the Purchase of Microfilm . . . . . . . . . . . . xix

Libraries Included in this Compilation . . . . . . . . . . . . xxi

Alphabetical Listing of Titles . . . . . . . . . . . . . . . . . 1

Geographic Index . . . . . . . . . . . . . . . . . . . . . . . 277

Editors Index . . . . . . . . . . . . . . . . . . . . . . . . . 285

Index of Publishers . . . . . . . . . . . . . . . . . . . . . . 297

Subject Index . . . . . . . . . . . . . . . . . . . . . . . . . 317

Foreign Language Materials Index . . . . . . . . . . . . . . . 333

Catchword and Subtitle Index . . . . . . . . . . . . . . . . . 335

Chronological Index . . . . . . . . . . . . . . . . . . . . . . 341

About the Contributors . . . . . . . . . . . . . . . . . . . . 376

# Introduction

This publication is a guide to the holdings and locations of nearly 1500 periodical and newspaper titles relating to women which were received before July, 1981, in the Library of the State Historical Society of Wisconsin, libraries of the University of Wisconsin-Madison, and other public, academic, and special libraries in the greater Madison area. It includes older titles which have long since ceased publication as well as those still being published. The scope of the guide is broad, including literary, political, and historical journals as well as general newspapers and feature magazines. This guide, the first of its kind published for Madison and perhaps the most extensive ever compiled in the United States, represents many phases of women's thought and action, from the eighteenth century to contemporary titles of the women's movement beginning in the 1960's. The guide was prepared in order to assist faculty and students who found it difficult to use these rich but widely dispersed resources. We hope that this publication will facilitate the use of our collections by scholars and others, locally as well as nationally. It is, we believe, a guide to the strongest collection of women's periodicals and newspapers in North America and truly a national resource.

This bibliography had its origins in 1975, when the first edition of Women's History Resources at the State Historical Society of Wisconsin was published. In the course of constructing this introduction to the vast collections of the Society, the need for improved finding aids, nationally, in the field of women's studies became evident. The three most needed general bibliographies were for books, manuscripts, and periodicals. Over the next few years two of these needs were met. Book materials appropriate for college libraries were described in Esther Stineman and Catherine Loeb's Women's Studies: A Recommended Core Bibliography (Libraries Unlimited, 1979). An additional source, with detailed annotations of books, is Barbara Haber's Women in America: A Guide to Books, 1963-1975 (G.K. Hall, 1978). After many years of work by archivists and librarians around the country led by Andrea Hinding, Women's History Sources (Bowker, 1979) was published, making manuscript collections on women more widely accessible than they had ever been.

A tentative effort at creating a union list of women's periodicals and newspapers began in 1976 when research on the third edition of Women's History Resources was underway. The plan was to include such a union list for the University of Wisconsin-Madison campus, including the State Historical Society of Wisconsin, as an appendix to the pamphlet. Two volunteers from the U. W. Library School, Sarah Pritchard and Ivy Lerner, worked on filling out simple forms and soon uncovered hundreds of currently received and older titles. In addition, many campus librarians contributed their time and reported their holdings. At this point the decision was made to publish the third edition of Women's History Resources without this appendix because of the incomplete nature of the survey and because the appendix would have been far larger than the original pamphlet. This was the first concrete indication of the great size of the collection of women's periodicals and newspapers held on the Madison campus, especially at the State Historical Society's Library. At this juncture the project went into abeyance, as the staff of the Society's Newspapers and Periodicals Unit turned to other bibliographical tasks.

In late 1978 the additional staffing acquired through the Comprehensive Employment and Training Act (CETA) allowed the Unit to begin work on special projects that would not have been possible before. In 1975 Susan Bryl, then Newspapers and Periodicals Librarian at the Society, and Erwin Welsch, Social Studies Bibliographer at the University of Wisconsin-Madison's Memorial Library, compiled and published Black Newspapers and Periodicals... This guide proved most popular and by 1977 it was out of print. As most of the student staff of the unit had not worked towards a publication before, it was decided to revise the Bryl-Welsch bibliography, incorporating the many titles added to the Society's collections. In April, 1979, Black Periodicals and Newspapers: A Union List of the Holdings in Libraries of the University of Wisconsin and the Library of the State Historical Society of Wisconsin, Second Edition, Revised, was published by the Society. This edition was compiled by two undergraduates, Neil E. Strache and Maureen E. Hady, working under the direction of James P. Danky, the Society's Newspapers and Periodicals Librarian. The experience gained through this project led Danky to consider two additional, though potentially smaller, bibliographical projects. The ability of talented students to gather the data accurately was an important development, but so were dissatisfactions with the level of bibliographic description in the second edition of Black Periodicals and Newspapers.

With funds provided by Richard A. Erney through the Director's Fund, Strache and Hady were hired for the summer of 1979 to compile detailed bibliographic data on Hispanic American and Asian American periodicals and newspapers in the Society and on campus. For the Black project the compilers had noted seven separate data points; on the two new endeavors seventeen points were gathered. It was possible to increase the detail because the universe of titles--129 for Hispanics and 104 for Asians--was so much smaller than the over 600 for Blacks. Asian American Periodicals and Newspapers... and Hispanic Americans in the United States: A Union List of Periodicals and Newspapers... were published in November and December, 1979, respectively. Because we had acquired so much more information on each title by reading every issue, the scope and number of indexes could be increased. Black Periodicals and Newspapers... had geographic and subject indexes; the works on Hispanics and Asians added a name index (editors and publishing organizations) and a chronological index. The success of these projects led to discussions about other projects. The most obvious choice was the long-neglected women's periodicals and newspapers project.

At the annual meeting of the American Library Association in Dallas in 1979, Danky was invited to participate in a panel discussion entitled "Women's Collections: Where Are They Going?" The panel was sponsored by the Reference and Adult Services Division of ALA. Other panel members were Barbara Haber of the Schlesinger Library at Radcliffe, Sarah Sherman of Northwestern Univeristy, and Margaret Childs of the National Endowment for the Humanities. In discussing their various interests and ideas, Danky's colleagues impressed upon him the desirability of completing the union list of women's periodicals and newspapers for several reasons. Margaret Childs was interested in the possible development of improved indexing of women's materials and suggested that the union list would help to facilitate such work. Also, Barbara Haber had earlier visited the Society's Library in Madison and refamiliarized herself with the collections in Madison and continued to educate librarians on the lack of access. She was also familiar with compiling bibliographies. In addition to her duties in the Schlesinger Library, Barbara Haber was also field editor for women's studies for the publisher G. K. Hall, and she thought that they might be interested in such a volume. With this encouragement, Danky returned to Madison and began to seek funds for such a project. Coincidentally, Governor Lee S. Dreyfus had just appointed Marlene Cummings as the Governor's Advisor for Women's Initiatives, effective August 1, 1979. This office was to supersede the Commission on the Status of Women which had been disbanded earlier in 1979. Danky requested permission to ask Cummings for funds or sources for funds for such a bibliographic project. She referred him to the Department of Public Instruction's Equal Educational Opportunity Unit. There Danky was referred to Betty Smith of the Sex Equity Project, who tentatively approved the grant request of $4,885.74 on the telephone and actually provided the funds within three weeks. (This must have been one of the fastest granting processes in bureaucratic/academic history!) The original request was for personnel costs to hire Maureen Hady for four months and printing costs to produce 500 copies for statewide distribution. The estimated number of entries was 1300, which is quite close to the final 1460 figure, but the time necessary to complete the work was vastly underestimated. The two most significant errors were in underestimating the complexity of title entries for the Herstory collection and the difficulty of collecting information on important publications held only by small public, school, or special libraries in the area. To complete the bibliography, the staff requested and received an additional $3,000 from the Department of Public Instruction, making the present volume possible.

The labor on this project can be divided and credited quite easily. Maureen Hady did the bulk of the field work in area libraries after she finished surveying the Society's collections. Neil Strache was responsible for properly cataloging, for the first time, the entire Herstory collection, a task those familiar with the set will appreciate. Barry Noonan compiled most of the indexes and supervised the compilation of the others. The improvements in the chronological index are due to Barry's work. The entire manuscript was typed by Marge McGuigan, a most complicated and tedious chore. The editing was done by Jim Danky.

The research into the selection of titles for Women's Periodicals and Newspapers... presented problems not encountered in compiling earlier works on black, Asian American, or Hispanic American publications. The most significant problem involved those titles concerned with "traditional" women's roles or tasks which are open to both sexes today. When the compilers examined the collections of Steenbock Agriculture Library some titles were not included in this volume because they were not edited for women but rather for professionals in fields such as home economics. Forecast for Home Economics and Home Economics Research Journal are two examples. The dramatic change in the composition of nursing professionals in the years since World War II made it inappropriate to include nursing or public health publications such as The American Journal of Nursing or The Public Health Nurse. Thus, despite the predominance of women in the fields of home economics and nursing, the publications devoted to those areas are not included in this bibliography. Researchers interested in examining women's roles in these professions will need to consult appropriate subject bibliographies in agriculture and medicine.

The cooperation of librarians around the Madison area and in other libraries in the United States was essential to this compilation. While the number of libraries and institutions is too extensive to enumerate individually, there are several who provided particular assistance. Ruth Carter, Head of the Serials Unit at the University of Pittsburgh's Hillman Library, graciously provided the local system numbers for Herstory titles that had been entered by the staff at Hillman. Without her assistance the appropriate OCLC records could not have been located. In the tentative investigations made in 1977 several campus librarians provided information about their holdings that greatly aided the staff of the current volume, including Cris Rom, formerly of Memorial Library's Rare Book Room, and now of the Cleveland Institute of Art, and Audrey Orr, the late Director of the Library School Library. During the last two years the encouragement of Linda J. Parker, Women's Studies Librarian-at-Large, University of Wisconsin, and her assistant Catherine Loeb has served to make us work the harder to bring the volume to a conclusion.

Sanford Berman, Head Cataloger of the Hennepin County Library in Edina, Minnesota, and author of The Joy of Cataloging (Phoenix, Arizona, Oryx Press, 1981), reviewed all of the subject focus terms for each entry and generated the Alternative Cataloging in Publication just as he haddone earlier for Asian American Periodicals and Newspapers... and Hispanic Americans in the United States: A Union List of Periodicals and Newspapers...

As we plan to update this list periodically, we would appreciate comments or suggestions for additional information or titles. Please submit them to James P. Danky, Newspapers and Periodicals Librarian, State Historical Society of Wisconsin, 816 State Street, Madison, Wisconsin 53706, telephone (608) 262-9584.

# How to Use the Bibliography

The arrangement of this union list is alphabetical. An explanation of the standard entry format follows:

[1]622 [2]McCalls. [3]1876. [4]Monthly. [5]$9.95 for individuals and institutions. [6]Robert Stein, editor, McCalls, 230 Park Avenue, New York, NY 10017. [7]Business address: Box 10293, Des Moines, IA 50336. [8](212) 551-9430. [9]ISSN 0024-8908, 0197-1255. [10]OCLC 4840517, 1586376, 4410903, 5947724, 5462346, 4171150. [11]LC sc79-5631, sn78-5890. [12]Last issue 196 pages, last volume 2352 pages, [13]size 21 x 27. [14]Line drawings, photographs, some in color, commercial advertising. [15]Indexed: Readers Guide (1952-). [16]Available on microfilm: McP (1960-), UnM (1894-). [17]Previous editors: Otis Lee Wiese, Oct., 1957-Feb., 1959; Herbert R. Mayes, Mar., 1959-Feb., 1962; John Mack Carter, Mar., 1962-Feb., 1965. [18]Subject focus: fashion, beauty care, interior decorating, entertaining, food, fiction. [19]Other holding institutions: AU (ALM), ArAR (AKO), AzFU (AZN), AzLeS (AZS), AzU (AZU), CLobS (CLO), CLU (CLU), CU-UC (UCU), [Pepperdine University, Malibu, CA] (CPE), CSt (Stanford University), CoDU (DVP), WeharU (HRM)

[20]Agric          v.85, n.1-        Periodicals
                  Oct., 1957-       Section

MPL              v.87, n.1-        Literature
                 Jan., 1959-       and Social
                                   Sciences
                                   Section

MATC             Current           Cora Hardy
                 Issues            Library
                 Only

1. Entry number.
2. Title (most recent title in the case of publications with earlier titles).
3. Year(s) title began publication and/or ceased.
4. Frequency (most recent frequency in the case of publications with varying previous schedules).
5. Subscription rates for individuals and institutions (currently published titles only).
6. Current editor and editorial address.
7. Current business address.
8. Telephone number.
9. International Standard Serials Number (ISSN).
10. OCLC, Inc. control number (cataloging record).
11. Library of Congress catalog card number.
12. Number of pages in latest issue and/or volume held on campus.
13. Size of latest issue.
14. Indication if the title contains any of the following: line drawings, photographs, commercial advertising, and if any of these are in color.
15. Indication where the title is indexed and for which period.
16. Indication if the title is available on microfilm and for what period.
17. Previous editors and their tenures.
18. Subject focus.
19. Non-campus library holdings, National Union Catalog symbol (OCLC participant symbol).
20. Campus library holding the title, dates held, location within library.

An indication of language (other than English) and the name of the publishing organization, if distinctive from the title, are also included. After the main alphabetical listing, which contains all of the title variants, there are a number of indexes. The indexes are geographical (alphabetically by state and city, then by title), editors, publishing organizations, subject, catchword, and subtitle index, foreign languages, and chronological.

# Herstory Holdings

[Holdings of the Women's History Research Center's Herstory series arranged by National Union Catalog symbol followed by OCLC symbol, when available]

Herstory I

AJact (AJB), AU (ALM), AzU (AZU), CO [Berkely-Oakland Public Library, Oakland, CA], CDhS [California State College, Dominquez Hills, CA], CLobS (CLO), CLS (CLA), CNoS (CNO), CARcHT [Humbolt State College, Arcata, CA], CWhR [Rio Hondo College, Whittier, CA], CSdS (CDS), CU (CUY), CU-I (CUI), CLU (CLU), CLSU (CSL), [Skyline College, San Bruno, CA], CSf [San Francisco Public Library, San Francisco, CA] Co-U (COP), CoU-DA (COA), CtU (UCW), CtY (YUS), DLC (DLC), FTaFA (FCM), FMFIU (FXN), FTS-M (FHM), FTaSU (FDA), FU (FUG), GDS (EGA), GEU (EMU), GForsT [Tift College, Forsyth, GA], GU-De (GUA), GASU (GSU), HU (HUH), IdBB [Boise State University, Boise, ID], ICharE (IAD), IPfsG (IAF), INS (IAI), IEN [Northwestern University, Evanston, IL], ISS (IAS), ICarbS (SOI), IU (UIU), IMacoW (IAZ), InMuB (IBS), InFW [Fort Wayne Public Library, Fort Wayne, IN], InU (IUL), InLP (IPL), InTI (ISU), InU-SB [Indiana University, South Bend, IN], IaDmD (IOD), KU (KKU), KyHhN (KHN), KyLoU (KLG), LU (LUU), LLafS (LWA), MeU (MEU), MdBMC (MSU), MdStm (MDS), MdBT (TSC), MdU (UMC), MH (HLS), MMeT (TFW), MU (AUM), MiMtpT (EZC), MiEM (EEM), MiPhS (EEC), MiU (EYM), MiDW (EYW), MnSTpeG (MNG), MnMHCL [Hennepin County Library, Edina, MN], MnSCC (MNE), MnStcls (MST), Mt [Montana State Library, Helena, MT], NbOU (MBU), NvU [University of Nevada, Reno, NV], NhD (DRB), NjUpM (NJM), MsSM (MFM), NjN (NPL), NjP (PUL), NjR (NJR), NjWP (NJP), NjTMC [Mercer County Community College, Trenton, NJ], NjJS (NJJ), NmLcU (IRU), NmU (IQU), NmScW (IQW), NA1F (YAH), NBC (VDB), NBu (VHB), NNR (ZXC), NGH (ZEM), NGcCC (VVX), NN (NYP), NFQC (XQM), NBronSL (VVS), NA1U (NAM), NSbSU (YSM), NBrockU (ZBM), NPV (VXW), NSyU (SYB), NBuC (YBM), NBiSU (BNG), NcGU (NGU), NcGU (NGU), NcU (NOC), OCU (CIN), OBgU (BGU), OClCC [Cuyahoga Community College, Cleveland, OH], OU (OSU), OAkU (AKR), OkEdT (OKX), OrU [University of Oregon, Eugene, OR], PAtC (EVI), PP (PLF), PPiC (PMC), PInU (PZI), PSt (UPC), PRosC (RMC), PPT (TEU), PU (PAU), PPiU (PIT), PKuS (KZS), ScU (SUC), SdU (USD), TMM (TMA), TU (TKN), TxDA (IGA), TxLT (ILU), TxSmS (TXI), TxDW (INT), TxClcU [University of Houston, Clear Lake City, TX], TxU (IXA), TxHU (TXH), UU (UUM), VtU [University of Vermont, Burlington, VT], ViRCU (VRC), ViStM (VMB), ViBlbV (VPI), ViPetS (VSC), ViU (VA@), WaOE [Evergreen State College, Olympia, WA], WaU (WAU), WaBeW [Western Washington State College, Bellingham, WA], WaSpW [Whitworth College, Spokane, WA], WMUM (GZN), WMMt [Mount Mary College, Milwaukee, WI], WEU (GZE), WKenU (GZC), AuSU [University of Sydney, Sydney, Australia], ]Murdock University, Western Australia], ]National Library of Australia, Canberra, Australia], CaQMM [McGill University, Montreal, Quebec, Canada], CaOHM [McMaster University, Hamilton, Ontario, Canada], CaNFSM [Memorial University of Newfoundland, St. Johns, Newfoundland, Canada], CaOTMCL [Metropolitan Toronto Central Library, Toronto, Ontario, Canada], CaNSHS [St. Mary's University, Halifax, Nova Scotia, Canada], CaBVaU [University of British Columbia, Vancouver, British Columbia, Canada], CaOW [Windsor Public Library, Windsor, Ontario, Canada], CaSSU [University of Saskatchewan, Saskatoon, Saskatchewan, Canada], CaQmG [Concordia University, Montreal, Quebec, Canada], DnRoU [Roskilde University, Roskilde, Denmark], [Royal Library, Copenhagen, Denmark], [Freie Universitat Berlin, Berlin, Germany], GuaU [University of Guam, Agana, Guam], [Kobe Women's College, Kone Kobe, Japan].

Herstory II

AJact (AJB), AU (ALM), AzU (AZU), CO [Berkeley-Oakland, CA], CLS (CLA), CNoS (CNO), CSdS (CDS), CU (CUY), CU-I (CUI), CLU (CLU), CLSU (CSL), DLC (DLC), CSf [San Francisco Public Library, San Francisco, CA], Co-U (COP), CoU-DA (COA), CtY (YUS), FTaFA (FCM), FMFIU (FXN), FTS-M (FHM), FTaSU (FDA), FU (FUG), GDS (EGA), GForsT [Tift College, Forsyth, GA], GU-De (GUA), GASU (GSU), HU (HUH), IdBB [Boise State University, Boise, ID], INS (IAI), IEN [Northwestern University, Evanston, IL], ISS (IAS), ICarbS (SOI), IU (UIU), InMuB (IBS), InFW [Fort Wayne Public Library, Fort Wayne, IN], InU (IUL), InTI (ISU), KU (KKU), LU (LUU), LLafS (LWA), MdStm (MDS), MdBT (TSC), MH (HLS), MMeT (TFW), MU (AUM), MiMtpT (EZC), MiEM (EEM), MiU (EYM), MiDW (EYW), MnSTpeG (MNG), MnManS (MNM), MnSCC (MNE), MnStcls (MST), Mt [Montana State Library, Helena, MT], NbOU (MBU), NvU [University of Nevada, Reno, NV], NhD (DRB), MsSM (MFM), NjP (PUL), NjWP (NJP), NjTMC [Mercer County Community College, Trenton, NJ], NjJS (NJJ), NmLcU (IRU), NmU (IQU), NBC (VDB), NNR (ZXC), NGcCC (VVX), NBronSL (VVS), NSbSU (YSM), NSyU (SYB), NBuC (YBM), NBiSU (BNG), NcGU (NGU), NcU (NOC), OCU (CIN), OU (OSU), OAkU (AKR), OkEdT (OKX), PAtC (EVI), PP (PLF), PInU (PZI), PSt (UPC), PRosC (RMC), PPT (TEU), PPiU (PIT), PKuS (KZS), ScU (SUC), SdU (USD), TU (TKN), TxLT (ILU), TxDW (INT), TxU (IXA), TxHU (TXH), UU (UUM), VtU [University of Vermont, Burlington, VT], ViRCU (VRC), ViStM (VMB), ViBlbV (VPI), ViPetS (VSC), ViU (VA@), WaOE [Evergreen State College, Olympia, WA], WaU (WAU), WaBeW [Western Washington State College, Bellingham,

## Women's Periodicals and Newspapers

HERSTORY HOLDINGS

Herstory II (continued)

WA], WaSpW [Whitworth College, Spokane, WA], WMUM (GZN), WEU (GZE), WKenU (GZC), AuSU [University of Sydney, Sydney, Australia], [Murdock University, Western Australia], [National Library of Australia, Canberra, Australia], CaQMM [McGill University, Montreal, Quebec, Canada], CaOHM [McMaster University, Hamilton, Ontario, Canada], CaNFSM [Memorial University of Newfoundland, St. Johns, Newfoundland, Canada], CaOTMCL [Metropolitan Toronto Central Library, Toronto, Ontario, Canada], CaNSHS [St. Mary's University, Halifax, Nova Scotia, Canada], CaSSU [University of Saskatchewan, Saskatoon, Saskatchewan, Canada], CaQmG [Concordia University, Montreal, Quebec, Canada], DnRoU [Roskilde University, Roskilde, Denmark], [Freie Universitat Berlin, Berlin, Germany], Kobe Women's College, Kone Kobe, Japan].

Herstory III

AJact (AJB), AU (ALM), AzU (AZU), CO [Berkeley-Oakland Public Library, Oakland, CA], CNoS (CNO), CSdS (CDS), CU (CUY), CU-I (CUI), CLU (CLU), CLSU (CSL), CSf [San Francisco, Public Library, San Francisco, CA], Co-U (COP), CoU-DA (COA), CtY (YUS), DLC (DLC), FTaFA (FCM), FMFIU (FXN), FTS-M (FHM), FTaSU (FDA), FU (FUG), GDS (EGA), GForsT [Tift College, Forsyth, GA], GU-De (GUA), GASU (GSU), HU (HUH), IdBB [Boise State University, Boise, ID], INS (IAI), IEN [Northwestern University, Evanston, IL] (ISS (IAS), ICarbS (SOI), IU (UIU), InMuB (IBS), InU (IUL), InTI (ISU), IaDmD (IOD), KU (KKU),

Herstory III (continued)

KyLoU (KLG), LU (LUU), LLafS (LWA), MdStm (MDS), MdBT (TSC), MH (HLS), MMeT (TFW), MU (AUM), MiMtpT (EZC), MiEM (EEM), MiU (EYM), MiDW (EYW), MnSTpeG (MNG), MnMHCL [Hennepin County Library, Edina, MN], MnManS (MNM), MnSCC (MNE), MnStcls (MST), Mt [Montana State Library, Helena, MT], NbOU (MBU), NvU [University of Nevada, Reno, NV], NhD (DRB), NjP (PUL), NjWP (NJP), NjTMC [Mercer County Community College, Trenton, NJ], NjJS (NJJ), NmLcU (IRU), NmU (IQU), NBC (VDB), NNR (ZXC), NN (NYP), NBronSL (VVS), NA1U (NAM), NSbSU (YSM), NBrockU (ZBM), NBuC (YBM), NBiSU (BNG), NcU (NOC), OCU (CIN), OBgU (BGU), OU (OSU), OAkU (AKR), OkEdT (OKX), OrU [University of Oregon, Eugene, OR], PAtC (EVI), PP (PLF), PPiC (PMC), PInU (PZI), PSt (UPC), PPT (TEU), PPiU (PIT), PKuS (KZS), ScU (SUC), SdU (USD), TU (TKN), TxDW (INT), TxU (IXA), UU (UUM), VtU [University of Vermont, Burlington, VT], ViRCU (VRC), ViStM (VMB), ViBlbV (VPI), ViPetS (VSC), ViU (VA@), WaOE [Evergreen State College, Olympia, WA], WaU (WAU), WaSpW [Whitworth College, Spokane, WA], WMUM (GZN), WMMt [Mount Mary College, Milwaukee, WI], WEU (GZE), WKenU (GZC), AuSU [University of Sydney, Sydney, Australia], [Murdock University, Western Australia], [National Library of Australia, Canberra, Australia], CaQMM [McGill University, Montreal, Quebec, Canada], CaOHM [McMaster University, Hamilton, Ontario, Canada], CaNFSM [Memorial University of Newfoundland, St. Johns, New Foundland, Canada], CaOTMCL [Metropolitan Toronto Central Library, Toronto, Ontario, Canada], CaQmG [Concordia University, Montreal, Quebec, Canada], DnRoU [Roskilde University, Roskilde, Denmark], [Freie Universitat Berlin, Berlin, Germany], [Kobe Women's College, Kone Kobe, Japan].

# Indexes Included in this Compilation

Abstract of Popular Culture. Bowling Green, Ohio: Bowling Green University Popular Press.

Abstracts of English Studies. Boulder, Colorado.

Access Index to Little Magazines. Syracuse, New York: Gaylord Professional Publications.

Alternative Press Index. Baltimore, Maryland: Alternative Press Center.

America: History and Life. Santa Barbara, California: Clio Press for American Bibliographical Center.

American Humanities Index. Troy, New York: Whitston Publishing Co.

Biological & Agricultural Index. New York, New York: H.W. Wilson Co.

Bulletin Signaletiquesociologie. Paris, France: Centre de documentation du C.N.R.S.

Canadian Periodical Index. Windsor, Ontario, Canada: Public Library.

Catholic Periodical & Literature Index. New York, New York: Catholic Library Association, H.W. Wilson Co.

Chicorel Abstracts to Reading and Learning Disabilities. New York, New York: Chicorel Library Publishing Co.

Child Development Abstracts and Bibliography. Washington, District of Columbia: National Research Council.

Contemporary Sociology. Albany, New York: American Sociological Association.

Contents Current Legal Publications. Wilmington, Delaware: Corporation Service.

Cumulative Index to Nursing, Allied Health Literature. Glendale, California: Glendale Adventist Medical Center Publications Service.

Abstracts on Criminology and Penology. Leiden, Netherlands: Criminologica Foundation, University of Leiden, Ministry of Justice and Joint Bureaus for Dutch Children Welfare.

Current Awareness-Library Literature. Framingham, Massachusetts: Goldstein Associates.

Current Contents/Social and Behavioral Sciences. Philadelphia, Pennsylvania: Institute for Scientific Information.

Current Index to Journals in Education (CIJE). New York, New York: CCM Information Sciences.

Development and Welfare Bi-monthly Index. Delhi, India: Documentation Centre, Delhi School of Social Work, University of Delhi.

Education Index. Bronx, New York: H.W. Wilson Co.

Exerpta Medica. Amsterdam, Netherlands.

Family Planning/Population Report. Washington, District of Columbia: Washington Center for Family Planning Program Development, Planned Parenthood-World Population.

Film Literature Index. Albany, New York: Filmdex, Inc.

Historical Abstracts. Santa Barbara, California: Clio Press for American Bibliographical Center.

Hospital Literature Index. Chicago, Illinois: American Hospital Association.

Human Resources Abstracts. Beverly Hills, California: Sage Publications.

Human Sexuality Update. New York, New York: Haworth Press.

Index of American Periodical Verse. Metuchen, New Jersey: Scarecrow Press.

Index to Legal Periodical Literature. Boston, Massachusetts: The Chipman Law Publishing, Co.

Index to Periodicals by and About Blacks. Boston, Massachusetts: G.K. Hall.

International Nursing Index. New York, New York: American Nurses Association, American Journal of Nursing, Co.

Library Literature Index. Bronx, New York: H.W. Wilson Co.

Marriage & Family Review. New York, New York: Haworth Press.

Media Report to Women Index/Directory. Washington, District of Columbia.

Modern Language Association International Bibliography. New York, New York.

New Periodical Index. Boulder, Colorado. Media Works, Ltd.

Philosophers Index. Bowling Green, Ohio: Bowling Green, University.

## Women's Periodicals and Newspapers

INDEXES INCLUDED IN THIS COMPILATION

Pooles Index. Gloucester, Massachusetts.

Psychological Abstracts. Lancaster, Pennsylvania: American Psychological Association.

Psychological Readers Guide. Lausanne, Switzerland: Elsevier Sequoia S.A.

Public Affairs Information Service. New York, New York: H.W. Wilson Co.

Readers Guide to Periodical Literature. Bronx, New York: H.W. Wilson Co.

Referativnyi Zhurnal. Moscow, U.S.S.R.: Vesesoyuznyi Institute Naunchno-Tekhnicheskoi Informatsii.

SIECUS Report. New York, New York: Sex Information and Education Council of the U.S.

Sage Family Studies Abstracts. Beverly Hills, California: Sage Publications.

Social and Behavioral Sciences. New York, New York: Jaques Cattell Press.

Social Science Citation Index. Middlesex, England: Institute for Scientific Information.

Sociologial Abstracts. Brooklyn, New York: Sociologial Abstracts, Inc.

Subject Index to Children's Magazines. Madison, Wisconsin.

Wallace Memorial Library. Rochester, New York: Rochester Institute of Technology.

Women Studies Abstracts. New York, New York: Rush Publishing Co., Inc.

Zeitschrift fuer Kinder und Jugendpsychiatrie. Bern, Switzerland: M. Craig.

# Sources for the Purchase of Microfilm

Association pour la Conservation et la Reproduction
Photographique de la Presse
4 Rue Louvois
Paris 2e, France
ACRPP

Yale University Library
Publications Office
Box 1603A Yale Station
New Haven, CT 06520
(203) 436-3356
CtY

Photoduplication Service
U.S. Library of Congress
Washington, DC 20540
(202) 287-5640
DLC

Greenwood Press
Microform Department
88 Post Road West
Westport, CT 06881
(203) 226-3571
GrP

Women's History Research Center
2325 Oak Street
Berkeley, CA 94708
(415) 548-1770
Herstory

Johnson Associates, Inc.
P.O. Box 1678
165 West Putnam Avenue
Greenwich, CT 06830
(203) 661-7602
JAI

Kraus Microforms
Order Department
Route 100
Milwood, NY 10546
(914) 762-2200
KtO

Microfilming Corporation of America
P.O. Box 10
1620 Hawkins Avenue
Sanford, NC 27330
(919) 775-3456
(800) 334-7510
McA

Microfilm Center of Texas
2043 Empire Central
Dallas, TX 75245
or
P.O. Box 45436
Dallas, TX 75235
(214) 358-5231
McI

McLaren Micropublishing
P.O. Box 972, Station F
Toronto, Ontario, Canada
(416) 461-1627
McL

Micromedia Ltd.
144 Front Street West
Toronto, Ontario, Canada
M5J. 2L7
(416) 593-5211
Telex 065-24668
McM

Micro Photo Division
Bell & Howell Co.
Old Mansfield Road
Wooster, OH 44691
(216) 264-6666
McP

Fairchild Publications on Microfilm, Inc.
7 East 12th Street
New York, NY 10003
(212) 741-4000

Gordon & Breach Science Publishers
One Park Avenue
New York, NY 10016
(212) 689-0360

Pergamon Press
Maxwell House
Fairview Park
Elmsford, NY 10523
(914) 592-7700, Ext. 219

American Jewish Periodical Center
Hebrew Union College, Jewish Institute of Religion
3101 Clifton Avenue
Cincinnati, OH 45220
(513) 221-1875
OCAJ

Ohio Historical Society
1982 Velma Avenue
Columbus, OH 43211
(614) 466-1505
OHi

Perpetual Storage, Inc.
3322 South 300 East
Salt Lake City, UT 84115
(801) 486-3563
OwC

Pennsylvania State Library
Harrisburg, PA 17126
(717) 783-8681
P

## Women's Periodicals and Newspapers

SOURCES FOR THE PURCHASE OF MICROFILM

Research Publications, Inc.
12 Lunar Drive
P.O. Box 3903
Woodbridge, CT 06525
(203) 397-2600
ResP

Brown University
Providence, RI
(401) 863-2515 (Periodicals)
(401) 863-2148 (Archives)
RPB

Newspaper Division
British Library
Colindale Avenue NW9
London, WC1B 3DG England, U.K.
01-200-5515
Uk

University Microfilm, Inc.
300 North Zeeb Road
Ann Arbor, MI 48106
(313) 761-4700
(800) 521-3044
UnM

State Historical Society of Wisconsin
Gifts & Exchanges Librarian
816 State Street
Madison, WI 53706
(608) 262-9583
WHi

World Microfilms Publications
62 Queens Grove
London, NW8 6ER England, U.K.
01-586-3092
WmP

# Libraries Included in this Compilation

Agric — Agriculture Library
Steenbock Memorial Library
University of Wisconsin
550 Babcock Drive
Madison, WI 53706
(608) 262-9635

APL — Applied Population Laboratory
Room 240, Agriculture Hall
University of Wisconsin
1450 Linden Drive
Madison, WI 53706
(608) 262-3029

Art — Kohler Art Library
260 Elvehjem Art Museum
University of Wisconsin
800 University Avenue
Madison, WI 53706
(608) 263-2258

ASP — African Studies Program
Instructional Materials Center
Teacher Education Building
University of Wisconsin
225 North Mills Street
Madison, WI 53706
(608) 263-4750

BAHS — Baraboo Senior High School
Media Center
1201 Draper Street
Baraboo, WI 53913
(608) 356-8536

BEL — Black Earth Public Library
1018 Mills Street
Black Earth, WI 53515
(608) 767-2400

BFL — Brooklyn Free Library
105 North Rutland Street
Box 117
Brooklyn, WI 53521
(608) 455-2951

BHS — Belleville High School Library
101 South Grant Street
Belleville, WI 53508
(608) 424-3371

BML — Bossard Memorial Library
154 North Lexington Street
Spring Green, WI 53588
(608) 588-2335

CFD — Center for Demography Library
Room 3216, Social Science
 Building
University of Wisconsin
1180 Observatory Drive
Madison, WI 53706
(608) 262-2182

CHS — Center for Health Sciences
 Library
University of Wisconsin
1305 Linden Drive
Madison, WI 53706
(608) 262-2371

Coll — College Library
Helen C. White Hall
University of Wisconsin
600 North Park Street
Madison, WI 53706
(608) 262-3245

CFL — Baraboo Public Library
230 Fourth Avenue
Baraboo, WI 53913
(608) 356-6166

CPPL — Cross Plains Public Library
2107 Julius Street
Cross Plains, WI 53528
(608) 798-3881

Crim Just — Criminal Justice Reference and
 Information Center
L140 Law Building
University of Wisconsin
Madison, WI 53706
(608) 262-1499

DFHS — DeForest High School Instructional
 Materials Center
815 Jefferson Street
DeForest, WI 53532
(608) 846-3011

DFPL — DeForest Area Public Library
617 South Main Street
DeForest, WI 53532
(608) 846-5482

DHS — Deerfield High School
300 Simonson Boulevard
Deerfield, WI 53531
(608) 764-5431 Ext. 36

DPIP — Wisconsin Department of Public
 Instruction Library
Room 411, GEF 3
125 South Webster Street
Madison, WI 53702
(608) 266-2529

EC — Edgewood College Library
Regina Hall
855 Woodrow Street
Madison, WI 53711
(608) 257-4861 Ext. 226

EDHS — Edgewood High School Library
 Instructional Materials Center
2219 Monroe Street
Madison, WI 53711
(608) 257-1023 Ext. 35

*Women's Periodicals and Newspapers*

LIBRARIES INCLUDED IN THIS COMPILATION

| | | | |
|---|---|---|---|
| EHS | East High School Instructional Materials Center<br>2222 East Washington Avenue<br>Madison, WI 53704<br>(608) 267-8650 | MAPL | Mazomanie Free Library<br>11 Brodhead Street<br>Mazomanie, WI 53560<br>(608) 795-2544 |
| FPPH | Planned Parenthood of Dane County, Family Planning Library<br>1024 Regent Street<br>Madison, WI 53715<br>(608) 256-7705 | MATC | Madison Area Technical College<br>Cora Hardy Library, Room 139<br>211 North Carroll Street<br>Madison, WI 53703<br>(608) 266-5180 |
| Geology | Geology-Geophysics Library<br>430 Weeks Hall<br>University of Wisconsin<br>Madison, WI 53706<br>(608) 262-8956 | MATC | Madison Area Technical College<br>Technical Center Library<br>211 North Carroll Street<br>Madison, WI 53703<br>(608) 266-5025 |
| Hist | State Historical Society of Wisconsin Library<br>816 State Street<br>Madison, WI 53706<br>(608) 262-3421 | MCL | Marshall Community Library<br>Municipal Building<br>South Pardee Street<br>Box 227<br>Marshall, WI 53559<br>(608) 655-3123 |
| IMC | Instructional Materials Center<br>Teacher Education Building<br>University of Wisconsin<br>225 North Mills Street<br>Madison, WI 53706<br>(608) 263-4750 | Mem | Memorial Library<br>University of Wisconsin<br>728 State Street<br>Madison, WI 53706<br>(608) 262-3193 |
| JR | School of Journalism and Mass Communication Reading Room<br>2130 Vilas Hall<br>University of Wisconsin<br>821 University Avenue<br>Madison, WI 53706<br>(608) 263-3387 | MFHS | McFarland High School Library<br>Instructional Materials Center<br>5101 Farwell Street<br>McFarland, WI 53558<br>(608) 838-3166 |
| | | MGHS | Monona Grove High School Library<br>4400 Monona Drive<br>Monona, WI 53716<br>(608) 222-1291 Ext. 9 |
| LAHS | LaFollette High School Instructional Materials Center<br>700 Pflaum Road<br>Madison, WI 53716<br>(608) 222-0641 | MGN | Maude Webster Middleton Library<br>Madison General Hospital School of Nursing<br>1010 Mound Street<br>Madison, WI 53715<br>(608) 267-6250 |
| Law | Law Library<br>Law Building<br>University of Wisconsin<br>Madison, WI 53706<br>(608) 262-1151 | MHHS | Mount Horeb High School Library<br>305 South 8th Street<br>Mount Horeb, WI 53572<br>(608) 437-5516 |
| Lib Sch | Library School Library<br>Helen C. White Hall<br>University of Wisconsin<br>600 North Park Street<br>Madison, WI 53706<br>(608) 263-2960 | MHL | Methodist Hospital Library<br>309 West Washington Avenue<br>Madison, WI 53703<br>(608) 251-2371 Ext. 3690, 3691 |
| LTC | Land Tenure Center<br>432 Steenbock Library<br>University of Wisconsin<br>Madison, WI 53706<br>(608) 262-1240 | MHPL | Mount Horeb Public Library<br>105 North Grove Street<br>Mount Horeb, WI 53572<br>(608) 437-5021 |

## Women's Periodicals and Newspapers

### LIBRARIES INCLUDED IN THIS COMPILATION

MIMC — Madison Public Schools Professional Library, 545 West Dayton Street, Madison, WI 53703, (608) 266-6188

MIPL — Middleton Public Library, 7426 Hubbard Avenue, Middleton, WI 53562, (608) 831-5564

MMHS — James Madison Memorial High School, 201 South Gammon Road, Madison, WI 53705, (608) 267-6250

MMRL — Municipal Reference Service, Room 103B, City-County Building, 210 Monona Avenue, Madison, WI 53709, (608) 266-6316

MOPL — Monona Public Library, 1000 Nichols Road, Monona, WI 53716, (608) 222-6127

MPL — Madison Public Library, 201 West Mifflin Street, Madison, WI 53703, (608) 266-6300

Music — Mills Music Library, B162 Memorial Library, University of Wisconsin, 728 State Street, Madison, WI 53706, (608) 263-1884, 1885

NFPL — North Freedom Public Library, Box 192, Maple Street, North Freedom, WI 53951, (608) 522-4417

OM — Oscar Mayer & Company Research Department Library, 910 Mayer Avenue, Box 1409, Madison, WI 53701, (608) 241-3311 Ext. 4025

OPL — Oregon Public Library, 219 Park Street, Oregon, WI 53575, (608) 835-3656

Pharmacy — Pharmacy Library, 1136 Chamberlin Hall, University of Wisconsin, 1150 University Avenue, Madison, WI 53706, (608) 262-2894

PPL — Plain Public Library, Plain, WI 53577, (608) 546-4201

R & L — Reference & Loan Library, 2109 South Stoughton Road, Madison, WI 53716, (608) 266-1053

RBR — Memorial Rare Books Room, Memorial Library, Room 443, University of Wisconsin, 728 State Street, Madison, WI 53706, (608) 262-3243

RPL — Reedsburg Public Library, 345 Vine Street, Reedsburg, WI 53959, (608) 524-3316

RVHS — River Valley High School Library, 660 Varsity Boulevard, Spring Green, WI 53588, (608) 588-2554

SAPH — Sauk Prairie High School Library, 213 Maple Street, Sauk City, WI 53583, (608) 643-3336

SCPL — Sauk City Public Library, 515 Water Street, Sauk City, WI 53583, (608) 643-8346

Soc Work — School of Social Work Library, University of Wisconsin, 425 Henry Mall, Madison, WI 53706, (608) 263-3840

SPHS — Sun Prarie Senior High School Library, 220 Kroncke Drive, Sun Prairie, WI 53590, (608) 837-2541 Ext. 327

SPPL — Sun Prairie Public Library, 802 Windsor Street, Sun Prairie, WI 53590, (608) 837-5644

TML — Tripp Memorial Library, 565 Water Street, Prairie du Sac, WI 53578, (608) 643-8318

UWBA — Baraboo Center Library, University of Wisconsin-Baraboo, Sauk County, Box 320, 1006 Connie Road, Baraboo, WI 53913, (608) 356-8351 Ext. 49, 51

## Women's Periodicals and Newspapers
### LIBRARIES INCLUDED IN THIS COMPILATION

| | | | |
|---|---|---|---|
| UW Co-op | University Center for Cooperatives, Room 524<br>University of Wisconsin<br>610 Langdon Street<br>Madison, WI 53706<br>(608) 262-3251, 3332, 3981 | WDHS | Health & Social Services Library<br>Room 743, State Office Building<br>1 West Wilson Street<br>Madison, WI 53702<br>(608) 266-7473 |
| UW Ext | Extension Library<br>104 Extension Building<br>University of Wisconsin<br>432 North Lake Street<br>Madison, WI 53706<br>(608) 262-3340 | WHS | West High School Instructional Materials Center<br>30 Ash Street<br>Madison, WI 53705<br>(608) 267-7001 Ext. 53<br>(608) 267-7094 Ext. 54 |
| VHS | Verona High School Instructional Materials Center<br>300 Richard Street<br>Verona, WI 53593<br>(608) 845-6452 | Wom Ed Res | Women's Education Resources<br>Room 428 Lowell Hall<br>University of Wisconsin<br>610 Langdon Street<br>Madison, WI 53706<br>(608) 262-2576 |
| VPL | Verona Public Library<br>101 East Harriet Street<br>Verona, WI 53593<br>(608) 845-7180 | Wom St | Women's Studies Program<br>Women's Studies Research Center<br>209 North Brooks Street<br>Madison, WI 53706<br>(608) 263-4703, 4704 |
| WAPL | Waunakee Public Library<br>401 West Second Street<br>Waunakee, WI 53597<br>(608) 849-4217 | WSLL | State Law Library<br>State Capitol<br>Madison, WI 53702<br>(608) 266-1424 |
| WCTR | Center for Film and Theater Research<br>Room 6039 Vilas Communications Hall<br>University of Wisconsin<br>821 University Avenue<br>Madison, WI 53706<br>(608) 262-9706, 0585 | | |

# Alphabetical Listing of Titles

AAUW Journal. Concord, NH, Washington, DC

   see The Graduate Woman. Washington, DC

1 A.A.W.C.J.C. Newsletter. 1974//? Unknown. Last issue 19 pages. Line drawings. Available on microfilm: Herstory. Published by the American Association of Women in Community and Junior Colleges, Phoenix, AZ. Subject focus: education, community colleges, junior colleges.

   Hist     v.1, n.3;     Microforms
             May, 1974     Her. 3, R 1

2 ACDS Newsletter. 1969-1971//? Irregular. OCLC 2256889. Last issue 2 pages. Line drawings. Available on microfilm: Herstory. Published by the Association for Children Deprived of Support, Northridge, CA. Title varies: as CDS Newsletter, July, 1969-June, 1970. Editor: Jean Temple. Subject focus: child support, child welfare, divorce, legal services, family services.

   Hist     [July, 1969-     Microforms
             Sep./Oct., 1971]     Her. 1, R 13

3 AERA * Women's Caucus Newsletter. 1973//? Irregular. Last issue 7 pages. Line drawings. Available on microfilm: Herstory. Published by the Women's Caucus of the American Educational Research Association, San Francisco, CA. Title varies: as Task Force on the Status of Women in Education, Feb., 1973. Editor: Noele Krenkel. Subject focus: law, educational research.

   Hist     v.1, n.1-2;     Microforms
             Feb.-Mar./Apr.,     Her. 2, R 1
             1973
             v.1, n.3;     Her. 2 UP, R 1
             Sep./Oct., 1973

AFSC Women's Newsletter. San Francisco, CA

   see American Friends Service Committee Women's Newsletter. San Francisco, CA

AFSCME Bulletin. Berkeley, CA

   see Employee Press. Berkeley, CA

4 A.F.W. Newsletter. 1973-1974//? Unknown. Last issue 6 pages. Line drawings. Available on microfilm: Herstory. Published by the Association of Faculty Women, University of Wisconsin, Madison, WI. Subject focus: education, college teachers.

   Hist     Sep., 1973,     Microforms
             Jan./Spring, 1974     Her. 3, R 1

5 AFW/UCW Newsletter. 1975-1976//? Bi-monthly. Last issue 4 pages, size 22 x 28. Published by the Association of Faculty Women and University Community Women, Madison, WI. Subject focus: affirmative action in education, college teachers.

   Wom St     Nov., 1975-Mar.,     Reading Room
               1976

   Wom Ed     Dec., 1975     Circulation
   Res

ALA/SRRT Task Force Status of Women in Librarianship Newsletter. Chapel Hill, NC

   see ALA/SRRT Task Force on Women Newsletter. Seattle, WA

6 ALA/SRRT Task Force on Women Newsletter. 1970-1974//? Monthly. OCLC 2257110. Last issue 6 pages. Line drawings. Available on microfilm: Herstory. Published by American Library Association Social Responsibility Round Table, Seattle, WA. Title varies: as ALA/SRRT Task Force, Status of Women in Librarianship Newsletter, Aug., 1970-Apr., 1971. Place of Publication varies: Chapel Hill, NC, Aug., 1970-Apr., 1971; West Lafayette, IN, Feb., 1972-June, 1973. Subject focus: wages, Equal Rights Amendment, librarians, sexism in employment, women's studies, child care.

   Hist     v.1, n.1-3;     Microforms
             Aug., 1970-Apr.,     Her. 1, R 13
             1971

|  |  |  |
|---|---|---|
|  | v.1, n.4-v.2, n.6;<br>Feb., 1972-June,<br>1973 | Her. 1 UP, R 1 |
|  | v.3, n.1-6;<br>Oct., 1973-June,<br>1974 | Her. CUP, R 1 |

ASPO Newsletter. Berkeley, CA

    see ASPO News Bay Area Chapter.
    Berkeley, CA

7  ASPO News Bay Area Chapter. 1966-1974//? Irregular. Last issue 9 pages. Line drawings, photographs, commercial advertising. Available on microfilm: Herstory. Published by the American Society for Psycho-Prophylaxis in Obstetrics, Berkeley, CA. Title varies: as ASPO Newsletter, July, 1966-Jan., 1967? Editors: Connie Matteson and Gaylynn Zerkel, Nov., 1966-Feb./Mar., 1968; Janet Gibson, Apr./May, 1968-Jan./Feb., 1969; Ann Minogue, Mar./Apr.-Oct./Nov., 1969; Donna Brown, Dec., 1969/Jan./Feb.-Oct./Nov., 1970; Marcha Fox, Jan./Feb.-Fall, 1972; Nancy Alexander, Winter, 1972-May/June, 1973. Subject focus: Lamaze technique, childbirth education, natural childbirth.

| Hist | v.1, n.1?-v.8, n.3;<br>July, 1966-<br>May/June, 1973 | Microforms<br>Her. 2, R 1 |
|---|---|---|
|  | v.8, n.4-v.9, n.2;<br>Fall, 1973-?, 1974 | Her. 2 UP, R 1 |

8  AWIS. Newsletter of the Association of Women in Science. 1971-1973//? Quarterly. ISSN 0098-6267, 0160-256X. OCLC 1834127, 2258036. LC 74-647243, sc79-4458. Last issue 8 pages. Line drawings. Available on microfilm: Herstory. Published by the Association of Women in Science, New York, NY/San Diego, CA. Subject focus: scientists, Equal Rights Amendment, human rights. Other holding institutions: [Congressional Research Service, Washington, DC] (CRS), DLC (DLC).

| Hist | v.1, n.1;<br>Summer, 1971 | Microforms<br>Her. 1, R 13 |
|---|---|---|
|  | v.1, n.2;<br>Autumn, 1971 | Her. 1, Add. |
|  | v.1, n.2-v.2, n.4;<br>Autumn, 1971-<br>Summer, 1973 | Her. 1 UP, R12 |

9  AWP Newsletter (St. Louis Edition). 1971//? Irregular. OCLC 2258037. Last issue 10 pages. Line drawings. Available on microfilm: Herstory. Published by the Association for Women in Psychology, St. Louis, MO. Editor: Leigh Marlowe. Subject focus: psychologists, psychotherapy.

| Hist | Apr.-July/Aug.,<br>1971 | Microforms<br>Her. 1, R 13 |
|---|---|---|

10  La Abogada Internacional. 1953. Unknown. ISSN 0567-5111. OCLC 4596201. Last issue 47 pages. Line drawings, photographs. Available on microfilm: Herstory (1965, 1968, 1970). Published by the International Federation of Women Lawyers, New York, NY. Editor: Mithan J. Lam. Subject focus: international law, lawyers, United Nations. In Spanish (20-40%).

| Hist | v.13, n.1, v.14,<br>n.1, v.15, n.1;<br>Spring, 1965,<br>Spring, 1968,<br>Spring, 1970 | Microforms<br>Her. 2, R 1 |
|---|---|---|

11  La Abogada Newsletter. 1964-1973//? Irregular. OCLC 3829394. Last issue 20 pages. Line drawings, photographs. Available on microfilm: Herstory (1965-1973). Published by the Internation Federation of Women Lawyers, New York, NY. Editors: Mithan J. Lam, Oct., 1965-Dec., 1968/Jan., 1969; Beng H. Oen, Sep., 1969-Oct., 1971; Eileen Mitchell Thomas, Mar., 1972-Apr., 1973. Subject focus: international law, lawyers, United Nations. In French (5-10%), in Spanish (5-10%).

| Hist | v.2, n.3-v.8, n.2;<br>Oct., 1965-Apr.,<br>1973 | Microforms<br>Her. 2, R 1 |
|---|---|---|

12  Abortion Rights Council of Minnesota. 1972. Bi-monthly. Susan Bidwell, editor, Abortion Rights Council of Minnesota, 111 East Franklin Avenue, #273, Minneapolis, MN 55404, (612) 874-9134. OCLC 2255200. Last issue 4 pages, last volume 24 pages, size 28 x 23. Line drawings. Available on microfilm: WHi (1975-). Frequency varies: monthly, May, 1975-Dec., 1977. Subject focus: pro-abortion, National Abortion Rights Action League, politics. Other holding institutions: [University of Minnesota Union List, Minneapolis, MN] (MUL).

| Hist | May, 1975- | Circulation |
|---|---|---|

13  Act N.O.W. 1969-1973//? Irregular. OCLC 2256897. Last issue 8 pages, last volume 68 pages. Available on microfilm: Herstory. Published by the Chicago Chapter, National Organization for Women. Editors: Irene Repa, Dec., 1970?-Jan., 1972; Barbara Ayukawa, Oct., 1972-June, 1973; Sharon Romjue, July-Oct., 1973. Subject focus: sexism, health, Equal Rights Amendment, pro-abortion.

| | | |
|---|---|---|
| Hist | v.1, n.1-v.3, n.8; Feb.1, 1969-Aug., 1971 | Microforms Her. 1, R 17 |
| | v.2, n.11, v.3, n.9; Dec., 1970, Sep., 1971 | Her. 1 Add. |
| | v.3, n.10-v.5, n.6; Oct., 1971-June, 1973 | Her. 1 UP, R 8 |
| | v.5, n.7-10; July-Oct., 1973 | Her. CUP, R 3 |

Action Bulletin. Washington, DC

see WILPF Legislative Bulletin. Washington, DC

14 L'Action Feminine. 1909-1915//. Bi-monthly. OCLC 5782152. Last issue 24 pages, last volume 84 pages. Line drawings, commercial advertising. Available on microfilm: ResP. Published by the Conseil National des Femmes Francaises, Paris, France. Subject focus: pro-suffrage, France, rights. In French (100%). Other holding institutions: MH (HLS), TxDW (IWU).

| | | |
|---|---|---|
| Mem | v.1, n.1-v.7, n.40; Feb.1, 1909-Sep. 10, 1915 | Microforms |

15 Action for Children. 1971?-1974//? Quarterly. OCLC 2263650. Last issue 4 pages. Line drawings. Available on microfilm: Herstory. Published by the Action Coordinating Council for Comprehensive Child Care, Los Angeles, CA. Title varies: as The Lobbyist, Summer, 1971-1st Quarter, 1972. Subject focus: child care, day care, Equal Rights Amendment, child welfare, child advocacy.

| | | |
|---|---|---|
| Hist | Summer, 1971 | Microforms Her. 1, R 16 |
| | 1st quarter, 1972-2nd quarter, 1973 | Her. 1 UP, R 1 |
| | 3rd quarter, 1973-2nd quarter, 1974 | Her. CUP, R 1 |

Action Memo. Washington, DC

see WILPF Legislative Bulletin. Washington, DC

16 Action N.O.W. 1969-1974//? Monthly. OCLC 2265291. Last issue 8 pages, last volume 94 pages. Line drawings, photographs, commercial advertising. Available on microfilm: Herstory. Published by the National Organization for Women, Orange County Chapter, Santa Ana, CA. Title varies: as N.O.W. News, Aug., 1969-June, 1970; as Orange County Chapter N.O.W. Newsletter, July, 1970-June, 1973. Place of publication varies: Fullerton, CA, Aug., 1969-June, 1973. Editors: Jean Chamberlain, Aug., 1969-?; Karen Armeson, Ezelda García, Annette Sooci, ?-June, 1973; Karen Armeson, July, 1973-June, 1974. Subject focus: rights, pro-abortion, sexism, Equal Rights Amendment, media.

| | | |
|---|---|---|
| Hist | v.1, n.1-v.2, n.9; Aug., 1969-Sep., 1970 | Microforms Her. 1, R 19 |
| | v.2, n.12-v.4, n.6; Dec., 1971-June, 1973 | Her. 1 UP, R10 |
| | July, 1973-June, 1974 | Her. CUP, R 4 |

17 Action N.O.W. 1971-1974//? Irregular. Last issue 8 pages. Line drawings. Published by the Snohomish County Chapter, National Organization for Women, Lynnwood, WA. Place of publication varies: Mount Lake Terrace/Seattle, WA, Oct., 1971-Apr., 1973. Subject focus: pro-abortion, news, politics, employment, discrimination, calendar of events, bibliographies, sexism, Equal Rights Amendment, rights.

| | | |
|---|---|---|
| Hist | v.1, n.1-3; Apr.,-Aug., 1971 | Microforms Her. 1, R 20 |
| | v.1, n.4, 6-19; Oct., 1971, Feb., 1972-Apr., 1973 | Her. 1 UP, R 11-12 |
| | v.2, n.2-v.4, n.2; July, 1973-June, 1974 | Her. CUP, R 5 |

18 Action Social de la Femme. 1902-1940. Irregular. Last issue 44 pages, last volume 224 pages. Line drawings, commercial advertising. Available on microfilm: DLC. Published by Action Social de la Femme et Association du Livre Francais, Paris, France. Title varies: as L'Action Sociale de la Femme. Revue Mensuelle, Apr., 1902-July/Aug., 1914. Subject focus: France, rights. In French (100%).

| | | |
|---|---|---|
| Mem | v.1, n.[1]-v.[40], n.1; Apr. 10, 1902-Jan./May, 1940 | Microforms |

L'Action Sociale de la Femme. Revue Mensuelle.
Paris, France

   see Action Sociale de la Femme.
   Paris, France

The Activist. Washington, DC

   see The Vocal Majority. Washington, DC

19  The Advocate. 1886. Monthly. $5 for individuals and institutions. Catherine McCracken, editor, The Advocate, Rte. 4, Tudor Addition, Columbus, IN 42701, (812) 376-0382. Business address: RR 1, Milo, IA 50166, (515) 942-7146. Last issue 32 pages, size 16 x 23. Line drawings, photographs. Published by the United Society of Friends Women, Columbus, OH. Subject focus: Quakers, human services, missions, child care.

| Hist | v.93, n.7, | Circulation |
|---|---|---|
|  | v.95, n.2- |  |
|  | July/Aug., 1977, |  |
|  | Feb., 1979- |  |

20  Advocates for Women Newsletter. 1972//? Unknown. Last issue 6 pages. Line drawings, photographs. Available on microfilm: Herstory. Published by the Advocates for Women, San Francisco, CA. Editor: Sandy Dobkowski. Subject focus: business, employment, affirmative action.

| Hist | v.1, n.1; | Microforms |
|---|---|---|
|  | Dec., 1972 | Her. 2, R 7 |

21  Aegis: Magazine on Ending Violence Against Women. 1974. Bi-monthly. $8.75 for individuals, $20 for institutions ($10 for individuals, $25 for institutions outside North America). Aegis, P.O. Box 21033, Washington, DC 20009. (202) 543-5580. OCLC 4649349. Last issue 60 pages, last volume 328 pages, size 21 x 18. Line drawings, photographs, commercial advertising. Self-indexed. Published by the National Communication Network, Feminist Alliance Against Rape, Alliance Against Sexual Coercion, Washington, DC. Title varies: as Feminist Alliance Against Rape Newsletter, Spring, 1976-May/June, 1977; as FAAR News, July/Aug., 1977-Jan., Feb., 1978; as FAAR & NCN: A Newsletter of the Feminist Alliance Against Rape and the National Communications Network, July/Aug., 1978; absorbed National Coalition Against Domestic Violence News, July/Aug., 1978. Subject focus: rape prevention, sexual harassment, lobbying, family violence, women's shelters, battered women, self defense. Other holding institutions: CLU (CLU), CU-UC (UCU), FTS (FHM), OU (OSU), WU (GZM).

| Hist | v.3, n.2- | Circulation |
|---|---|---|
|  | Spring, 1976- |  |
| Coll | Current Issues | Women's |
|  | Only | Reading Area |

22  Africa Woman. 1975. Monthly. $18 for individuals and institutions. Austa Uwechue, editor, Africa Woman, Kirkman House, 54a Tottenham Court Road, London, England, W1P OBT. Telephone 01 637-9341/8. Business address: Chase Manhattan Bank, 2291 Broadway, New York, NY 10021. ISSN 0308-5821. OCLC 2908009. LC 76-961223. Last issue 66 pages, size 22 x 27. Line drawings, photographs, some in color, commercial advertising. Published by the Africa Journal Ltd. Previous editor: Raph Uwechue, Oct./Nov., 1975. Subject focus: profiles, Africa, literature, fashion, arts. Other holding institutions: AzU (AZU), CLU (CLU), DLC (DLC), GA (GAP), InU (IUL), MNS (SNN), [University of Minnesota Union List, Minneapolis, MN] (MUL), NcD (NDD), NFQC (XQM), ODaWU (WSU), TxU (IXA).

| Mem | n.20- | Periodicals |
|---|---|---|
|  | May/Apr., 1979- | Room |
| ASP | n.1, 5- | Circulation |
|  | Oct./Nov., 1975, |  |
|  | July/Aug., 1976- |  |

23  The Agitator. 1869//. Weekly. Last issue 8 pages, last volume 272 pages. Line drawings, commercial advertising. Available on microfilm: ResP (1869). Published by The Agitator, Chicago, IL. Subject focus: pro-suffrage, fiction, poetry, rights. Other holding institutions: MCR-S (Schlesinger Library on the History of Women in America, Radcliffe College Cambridge, MA), TxDW (IWU).

| Mem | v.1, n.1-34; | Microforms |
|---|---|---|
|  | Mar. 13 -Nov. 6, |  |
|  | 1869 |  |

24  Ain't I A Woman? 1970-1974//. Irregular. ISSN 0044-6939. OCLC 2221525. Last issue 12 pages, last volume 64 pages. Line drawings, photographs. Self-indexed at end of each volume. Available on microfilm: WHi, Herstory (1970-1973). Published by the AIAW Collective, Iowa City, IA. Subject focus: lesbians, sexism, racism, child care, poetry. Other holding institutions: MCR-S (Schlesinger Library on the History of Women in America, Radcliffe College, Cambridge MA), [University of Minnesota Union List, Minneapolis MN] (MUL), NFQC (XQM), NSbSU (YSM), [Pittsburgh Regional Library Union List] (QPR).

| Hist | v.1, n.1-v.4, n.2; | Microforms |
|---|---|---|
|  | June 26, 1970- |  |
|  | May, 1974 |  |

|   |   | v.1, n.1-v.2, n.2;<br>June 26, 1970-<br>Aug. 27, 1971 | Her. 1, R 1 |
|---|---|---|---|
|   |   | v.1, n.1-v.3, n.4;<br>June 26, 1970-<br>June 22, 1973 | Her. 1 UP, R 1 |
|   | Mem | [v.1, n.3-v.3, n.5];<br>[July 24, 1970-<br>July 20, 1973] | Microforms |

25 Akamai Sister. 1970//? Monthly? OCLC 5652191, 2257101. Last issue 2 pages. Line drawings. Available on microfilm: Herstory. Published by Hawaii Women's Liberation, Honolulu, HI. Subject focus: lobbying, Asian Americans, consumer education.

|   | Hist | v.1, n.1,3;<br>July, Oct., 1970 | Microforms<br>Her. 1, R 1 |
|---|---|---|---|
|   |   | v.1, n.2;<br>Aug., 1970 | Her. 1, Add. |

26 Albatross. 1974. Irregular. $7 for individuals and institutions. Stacey M. Fairchild, editor, Albatross, P.O. Box 2046, Central Station, East Orange, NJ, 07019. Last issue 50 pages, size 22 x 28. Line drawings, photographs, commercial advertising. Subject focus: lesbianism, fiction, poetry, comics.

|   | Mem | Oct., 1975- | Periodicals Room |
|---|---|---|---|

27 Alert. 1975//? Bi-monthly. Last issue 4 pages, size 22 x 28. Photographs. Published by Women's Lobby, Inc., Washington, DC. Editor: Nancy Canblath. Subject focus: lobbying.

|   | Wom Ed Res | v.1, n.3;<br>May/June, 1975 | Circulation |
|---|---|---|---|

28 Alert-Federation of Organizations for Professional Women. 1972-1974//? Quarterly. Last issue 4 pages. Line drawings. Available on microfilm: Herstory (1973-1974). Published by the Federation of Organizations for Professional Women, Washington, DC. Editor: Jane Aufenkamp. Subject focus: professionals, career development, education, employment.

|   | Hist | v.2, n.1-3;<br>Fall, 1973-<br>Summer, 1974 | Microforms<br>Her. 3, R 1 |
|---|---|---|---|

29 Alert; Women's Legislative Review. 1972-1974//? Irregular. Last issue 4 pages, size 29 x 43 (varies). Line drawings, photographs, commercial advertising. Available on microfilm: Herstory. Published by Alert, Inc., Middletown, CN. Subject focus: affirmative action, employment, lobbying.

|   | Hist | [v.1, n.8-v.2, n.5];<br>[June, 1973-<br>July, 1974] | PAM 74-3319 |
|---|---|---|---|
|   |   | v.1, n.1-8;<br>Dec., 1972-<br>June, 1973 | Microforms<br>Her. 2, R 1 |
|   |   | v.1, n.9-v.2, n.4;<br>July/Aug., 1973-<br>June/July, 1974 | Her. 2 UP, R1 |

Alliance Link. Chicago, IL

see The Link. Chicago, IL

Alliance News. Chicago, IL

see The Link. Chicago, IL

30 Amazon: A Midwest Journal for Women. 1972. Irregular. $3 for individuals, $10 for institutions. Amazon: A Midwest Journal for Women, 2211 East Kenwood, Milwaukee, WI 53211. Last issue 32 pages, last volume 144 pages, size 42 x 29. Line drawings, photographs, commercial advertising. Available on microfilm: Herstory (1972-1974), WHi (1972-). Published by the Amazon Collective, Milwaukee, WI. Subject focus: gay rights, pro-abortion, health, poetry, lesbians, feminism.

|   | Mem | v.1, n.1-<br>June?, 1972- | Microforms |
|---|---|---|---|
|   | Hist | v.2, n.1-<br>May?, 1973- | Microforms |
|   |   | v.1, n.1-v.2, n.1;<br>June?, 1972-<br>June, 1973 | Her. 2, R 1 |
|   |   | v.2, n.3-v.3, n.2;<br>July/Aug., 1973-<br>June, 1974 | Her. 2 UP, R1 |

The Amazon-Nation Newsletter. Chicago, IL

see Cries from Cassandra. Chicago, IL

31 Amazon Quarterly. 1972-1975//. Quarterly. OCLC 2750571. Last issue 72 pages, size 18 x 22. Line drawings, photographs. Available on microfilm: UnM (1973-1975). Published by Amazon Quarterly, Somerville, MA. Place of publication varies: Oakland, CA, Spring? 1972-Spring?, 1973. Subject focus: poetry, lesbians, art, literature. Other holding

institutions: MCR-S (Schlesinger Library on the History of Women in America, Radcliffe College, Cambridge, MA), [University of Minnsota Union List, Minneapolis, MN] (MUL), WaU (WAU).

| RBR | v.1, n.2, 4-v.2, n.2; Spring, 1972, Summer, 1972- Fall, 1973 | Circulation |

32  American Association of University Women Madison Branch Bulletin. 1937? 9 times a year. Editor: Kathy Norderhaug, American Association of University Women Madison Branch Bulletin, 2708 Regent Street, Madison, WI 53705. Last issue 8 pages, last volume 72 pages, size 22 x 28. Line drawings. Published by: Madison Branch AAUW, Madison, WI. Previous editor: Lynn Doelle, Sep., 1977-May, 1978. Subject focus: lobbying, college teachers, education.

| Hist | v.41, n.1- Sep., 1977- | Circulation |
| EC | Current Issues Only | Circulation |

33  The American Baptist Woman. 1957? Tri-annual. $3.25 for individuals and institutions. Janice Bailey, editor, The American Baptist Woman, Valley Forge, PA 19481. ISSN 0191-0183, OCLC 1624319, LC sc79-2652. Last issue 48 pages, last volume 150 pages, size 22 x 28. Line drawings, photographs. Published by the American Baptist Woman Leaders, Valley Forge, PA. Subject focus: Baptists. Other holding institutions: MNtcA (BAN), [University of Minnesota Union List, Minneapolis, MN] (MUL), MBTI (BTI), [Pittsburgh Regional Library Union List, Pittsburgh, PA] (QPR).

| Hist | v.12, n.2- Apr., 1968- | BX/6201/A4 |

34  The American Club Woman. 1898-1899//? Weekly. Last issue 8 pages, size 28 x 40. Line drawings, photographs, commercial advertising. Published by the American Club Woman, Milton, WI. Editor: Alice S. Blount. Subject focus: clubs, Federated Clubs in America.

| Hist | v.2, n.1; Nov. 23, 1899 | PAM 76-3698 |

American Cookery.  Boston, MA (1914-1944); New York, NY (1944-1947)

see Better Food.  New York, NY

35  American Fabrics and Fashions. 1946. Quarterly. $48 for individuals and institutions. Dr. George Linton, E.S. Katz, John G. Stiller, Margaret Walch, and Martha Welch de Llosa, editors, American Fabrics and Fashions, 24 East 38th Street, New York, NY 10016. (212) 683-2755. ISSN 0002-8371, 0091-0864. OCLC 1479831, 1775524, 4055682, 5631350, 5631377. LC 48-11592, sn79-8345. Last issue 106 pages, size 37 x 27. Line drawings, photographs, some in color, commercial advertising. Indexed in: American Fabrics Magazine Index (1946-1965). Available on microfilm: UnM (1946-1976). Published by Doric Publishing, Inc. Subject focus: fashion, clothes, fabrics. Other holding institutions: AU (ALM), ArAT (AKH), ArSsJ (AKK), ArU (AFU), AzFU (AZN), AzTeS (AZS), CLU (CLU), CLobS (CLO), CSS (CSA), CU-UC (UCU), DLC (DLC), DeU (DLM), FMFIU (FXG), GASU (GSU), IPB (IBA), [Indiana Union List of Serials, Indianapolis, IN] (ILS), InLP (IPL), InU (IUL), KLindB (KFB), KSteC (KKQ), LU (LUU), MNS (SNN), DNAL (AGL), MiAdC (EEA), MiEM (EEM), MiMtpT (EZC), [University of Minnesota Union List, Minneapolis, MN] (MUL), MnSU (MNP), MoU (MUU), NcGU (NGU), NbU (LDL), NjLincB (BCC), NmLvH (NMH), [New York State Union List, Albany, NY] (NYS), NA1fC (YDM), NBu (VHB), [Western New York Library Resources Council, Buffalo, NY] (VZX), NFQC (XQM), NIC (COO), NOneoU (ZBM), NP1aU (YPM), [Central New York Library Resources Council, Syracuse, NY] (SRR), OAU (OUN), OAkU (AKR), OBgU (BGU), OCU (CIN), OC1 (CLE), OC1W (CWR), OKentU (KSU), OO (OBE), OU (OSU), OYU (YNG), OkU (OKU), PIm (IMM), PMi1S (MVS), PPD (DXU), PPi (CPL), PPiAC (AIC), PPiC (PMC), [Pittsburgh Regional Library Center - Union List, Pittsburgh, PA] (QPR), ScRhW (SWW), ScU (SUC), SdsiPA (SDA), TColIsM (TMS), TMurS (TXM), TxArU (IUA), TxBe1M (MHB), [AMIGOS Union List of Serials, Dallas, TX] (IUC), TxDW (IWU), TxLT (ILU), TxNacS (TXK), ViBlbv (VPI), ViW (VWM), WaU (WAU), WMUW (GZN), WMenU (GZS).

| MATC | Jan., 1954- | Cora Hardy Library |
| MPL | Sep., 1965- | Business & Science Section |
| UWBA | Apr., 1968- | Circulation |
| LAHS | Current Issues Only | Circulation |

36  American Friends Service Committee Women's Newsletter. 1972-1974//? Irregular. Last issue 10 pages. Line drawings. Available on microfilm: Herstory. Published by the American Friends Service Committee, San Francisco, CA. Title varies: as AFSC Women's Newsletter, Mar.-Nov., 1972. Subject focus: child care, poetry, human rights, rights, sexism.

| Hist | v.1, n.1-8; | Microforms |

## Women's Periodicals and Newspapers

|  | Mar., 1972-<br>June, 1973 | Her. 2, R 1 |
|---|---|---|
|  | v.2, n.9-10?;<br>Oct./Nov., 1973-<br>Feb./Mar., 1974 | Her. 2 UP, R1 |

37  American Girl. 1920-1979//. Monthly. ISSN
0002-8630. OCLC 1479932, 1579654. LC
sn78-1902. Last issue 42 pages, last volume
504 pages, size 21 x 28. Line drawings, photographs, some in color, commercial advertising.
Indexed in: Subject Index to Children's Magazines. Published by The Girl Scouts of the
U.S.A., New York, NY. Editors: Esther R. Bien,
Jan., 1965-Apr., 1967; Pat di Sernia, May,
1967-June, 1972; Cleo Paturis, July, 1972-
July, 1979. Subject focus: Girl Scouts, voc-
ational guidance, beauty care, fashion, art,
food, poetry. Other holding institutions:
FBoU (FGM), GA (GAP), [Indiana Union List of
Serials, Indianapolis, IN] (ILS), MiDW (EYW),
[University of Minnesota Union List, Minnea-
polis, MN] (MUL), NhP1S (PSM), NmLvH (NMH),
N (NYG), [New York State Union List, Albany,
NY] (NYS), [Western New York Library Resources
Council, Buffalo, NY] (VZX), [Central New
York Library Resources Council, Syracuse,
NY] (SRR), OCo (OCO), OTU (TOL), OY (YMM),
OkT (TUL), OKTU (OKT), PPi (CPL), [Pittsburgh
Regional Library Center - Union List, Pitts-
burgh, PA] (QPR), TxAu (TXG), [AMIGOS Union
List of Serials, Dallas, TX] (IUC), TxDN
(INT), TxDW (IWU), WFon (WIF), WGR (GZG),
[Arrowhead Library System, Janesville, WI]
(WIJ).

| MPL | v.48, n.1-v.62,<br>n.7;<br>Jan., 1965-<br>July, 1979 | Children's<br>Room |
|---|---|---|
| PPL | v.54, n.1-v.62,<br>n.7;<br>Jan., 1971-<br>July, 1979 | Circulation |
| RPL | v.53, n.1-v.62,<br>n.7;<br>Jan., 1970-<br>July, 1979 | Circulation |
| DFHS | v.57, n.9-v.62,<br>n.7;<br>Sep., 1974-<br>July, 1979 | Circulation |
| MGHS | v.53, n.3-v.62,<br>n.7;<br>Mar., 1970-<br>July, 1979 | Circulation |
| DFPL | v.53, n.1-v.55<br>n.12, v.57, n.1-<br>v.62, n.7;<br>Jan., 1970-Dec.,<br>1972, Jan., 1974- | Circulation |

|  |  | July, 1979 |  |
|---|---|---|---|
| IMC | v.53, n.1-v.57,<br>n.12;<br>Jan., 1970-<br>Dec., 1974 |  | Circulation |
| BFL | v.58, n.1-v.62,<br>n.7;<br>Jan., 1975-<br>July, 1979 |  | Circulation |
| MHPL | v.54, n.1-v.62,<br>n.7;<br>Jan., 1971-<br>July, 1979 |  | Circulation |
| SPPL | v.57, n.1-v.62,<br>n.7;<br>Jan., 1974-<br>July, 1979 |  | Circulation |
| MFHS | v.56, n.1-v.62,<br>n.7;<br>Jan., 1973-<br>July, 1979 |  | Circulation |
| SCPL | v.54, n.1-v.62,<br>n.7;<br>Jan., 1971-<br>July, 1979 |  | Circulation |

38  American Home. 1928-1978//. Monthly. ISSN
0002-8789. OCLC 1479980. LC 29-30019. Last
issue 88 pages, last volume 1238 pages, size
28 x 33 (varies). Line drawings, photographs,
some in color, commercial advertising. Indexed in: Reader's Guide to Periodical Literature, Biological and Agricultural Index
(1928-1942), index also available from publisher. Available on microfilm: UnM, McP
(1973-1978). Published by American Home Publishing Co., Inc., New York, NY. Editors:
Ellen D. Wagner, Oct., 1928-May, 1930;
Reginald Townsend, June, 1930-Oct., 1932;
Jean Austin, Dec., 1932-Feb., 1959; John M.
Carter, Mar., 1959-Aug., 1960; Hubbard H.
Cobb, Sep., 1960-Aug., 1969; Fred Smith, Sep.,
1969-Nov., 1973; Betty Klarnet, Dec., 1973-
Apr., 1975; Margaret E. Happel, May-Aug.,
1975; Helene Brown, Sep., 1975-May, 1976;
Nancy Love, June, 1976-Feb., 1978. Subject
focus: fashion, food, sewing, entertaining,
interior decoration, home economics, garden-
ing. Other holding institutions: AU (ALM),
ArAO (AKO), ArRuA (AKP), ArU (AFU), AzFU
(AZN), AzTeS (AZS), AzU (AZU), CChiS (CCH),
CLobS (CLO), COFS (COF), DI (UDI), DeU (DLM),
FBoU (FGM), FMFIU (FXG), GA (GAP), IPB (IBA),
[Indiana Union List of Serials, Indianapolis,
IN] (ILS), InNomanC (IMN), InU (IUL), KMK
(KKS), KPT (KFP), KSteC (KKQ), LU (LUU), DNAL
(AGL), MdBU (BAL), MiAdC (EEA), MiEM (EEM),
MiKW (EXW), MiMarqN (EZN), MiMtpT (EZC),
[University of Minnesota Union List, Minnea-
polis, MN] (MUL), MnNC (MNN), MsToT (TGC),
NcEUcE (NPE), NcRS (NRC), NbU (LDL), NmLcU

(IRU), NmU (IQU), N (NYG), [New York State Union List, Albany, NY] (NYS), NIC (COO), NOneoU (ZBM), NR (YQR), NStC (VYS), [Central New York Library Resources Council, Syracuse, NY] (SRR), NUtSU (YTM), O (OHI), OAkU (AKR), OBgU (BGU), OCl (CLE), OCo (OCO), OAU (OUN), ODa (DMM), OKentU (KSU), OO (OBE), OTU (TOL), OY (YMM), OkS (OKS), OkT (TUL), PCLS (REC), PCalS (CSC), PInU (PZI), PPD (DXU), PPi (CPL), PPiAC (AIC), [Pittsburgh Regional Library Center - Union List, Pittsburgh, PA] (QPR), ScCleW (SEA), ScRhW (SWW), TCollsM (TMS), TMurS (TXM), TxAbH (TXS), TxAu (TXG), TxBelM (MHB), TxCM (TXA), TxDN (INT), TxDW (IWU), [AMIGOS Union List of Serials, Dallas, TX] (IUC), TxLT (ILU), TxNacS (TXK), Vi (VIC), [Emery & Henry College, Emory, VA] (VEH), WFon (WIF), WGR (GZG), WGrU (GZW), [Arrowhead Library System, Janesville Public Library, Janesville, WI] (WIJ), WMUW (GZN), WMenU (GZS).

| | | |
|---|---|---|
| Agric | v.1, n.1-v.82, n.2; Oct., 1928- Feb., 1978 | Circulation |
| MPL | v.25, n.12-v.81, n.2; Dec., 1953- Feb., 1978 | Literature and Social Sciences Section |
| SPPL | Jan., 1971- Feb., 1978 | Circulation |
| MMHS | Jan., 1971- Feb., 1978 | Circulation |
| DFHS | Sep., 1974- Feb., 1978 | Circulation |
| MFHS | Jan., 1974- Feb., 1978 | Circulation |
| MCL | Jan., 1976- Feb., 1978 | Circulation |
| UWBA | May, 1968- Dec., 1973 | Circulation |
| WHS | Sep., 1973- Feb., 1978 | Circulation |
| BFL | Jan., 1975- Feb., 1978 | Circulation |
| VHS | Sep., 1969- Feb., 1978 | Circulation |
| TML | Jan., 1974- Feb., 1978 | Circulation |
| MGHS | Nov., 1969- Feb., 1978 | Circulation |

39 American Home Magazine. 1897-1898//. Monthly. Last issue 50 pages, last volume 300 pages. Line drawings, commercial advertising. Available on microfilm: ResP. Published by the American Fashion Company, Chicago, IL. Subject focus: home economics, fashion, poetry, fiction. Other holding institutions: NN (NYP), TxDW (IWU).

| | | |
|---|---|---|
| Mem | v.1, n.1-v.3, n.1; Jan., 1897- Jan., 1898 | Microforms |

40 The American Jewess. 1895-1899//. OCLC 5785268. Last issue 64 pages, last volume 320 pages. Line drawings, photographs, commercial advertising. Available on microfilm: ResP (1895-1898), J. Published by Rosa Sonneschein Co., Chicago, IL. Editor: Rosa Sonneschein. Subject focus: Judaism, music, fiction, Jews. Other holding institutions: IC (CGP), MoK (KCP), TxDW (IWU).

| | | |
|---|---|---|
| Mem | v.1, n.1- v.7, n.5; Apr., 1895- Sep., 1898 | Microforms |

41 The American Journal of Eugenics. 1907-1910. Last issue 56 pages, last volume 392 pages. Line drawings, commercial advertising. Available on microfilm: ResP. Published by the American Journal of Eugenics, Chicago, IL. Editor: Moses Harman. Subject focus: eugenics. Other holding institutions: MU (AUM), TxDW (IXU).

| | | |
|---|---|---|
| Mem | v.1, n.1-v.3, n.7/8; July, 1907- Jan./Feb., 1910 | Microforms |

The American Kitchen Magazine. Boston, MA

    see Everyday Housekeeping. Boston, MA

The American Kitchen Magazine and Culinary Topics. Boston, MA

    see Everyday Housekeeping. Boston, MA

American Legion Auxiliary. Lincoln, NE

    see The Legion Auxiliary Star. Lincoln, NE

The American Legion Auxiliary Bulletin. Indianapolis, IN

    see The National News. Indianapolis, IN

42  The American Negro Woman. 1974//? Unknown. Last issue 4 pages. Line drawings. Available on Microfilm: Herstory. Published by the American Negro Woman, Cleveland, OH. Subject focus: Equal Rights Amendment, Afro-Americans, sexism, racism, lobbying, pro-abortion.

    Hist    v.1, n.1;    Microforms
            Mar., 1974    Her. 3, R 1

43  American Society for Public Administration-Task Force on the Status of Women and Minorities-Bay Area. 1973//? Unknown. Last issue 3 pages. Line drawings. Available on microfilm: Herstory. Published by the American Society for Public Administration, Kensington/Oakland, CA. Subject focus: minorities.

    Hist    Mar. 21, 1973    Microforms
                          Her. 2, R 1

            Sept. 19, 1973    Her. 2 UP, R 1

44  The American Suffragette. 1909-1911. Monthly. Last issue 36 pages, last volume 242 pages. Line drawings, photographs, commercial advertising. Available on microfilm: ResP. Published by the National Progressive Woman Suffrage Union, New York, NY. Subject focus: suffrage. Other holding institutions: MCR-S (Schlesinger Library on the History of Women in America, Radcliffe College, Cambridge, MA), NN (NYP), TxDW (IWU).

    Mem    v.1, n.1-v.2,    Microforms
            n.7;
            June, 1909-
            Mar./Apr., 1911

45  American Woman. 1892?-1916?//. Monthly. Last issue 22 pages, last volume 264 pages, size 26 x 39. Line drawings, photographs, commercial advertising. Published by the American Woman, Augusta, ME. Editor: Agnes Cuyler Stoddard. Subject focus: home economics, beauty care, health, fashion, arts, crafts, sewing.

    Agric    v.25, n.8-    Circulation
            v.26, n.8;
            Jan.-Dec., 1916

46  And Ain't I A Woman! 1970-1974//? Irregular. OCLC 2257505. Last issue 24 pages, last volume 136 pages. Line drawings, photographs. Available on microfilm: Herstory. Published by Women's Liberation, Seattle, WA. Subject focus: education, day care, pro-abortion, family, welfare, labor unions, radical feminism, Equal Rights Amendment.

    Hist    v.1, n.1-v.2, n.2;    Microforms
           Mar., 1970-    Her. 1, R 13
           July, 1971

           v.3, n.5, v.4,    Her. CUP, R 1
           n.1-2;
           July 20, 1973,
           ?-May, 1974

And N.O.W...Trenton. Trenton, NJ

    see Trenton N.O.W. Trenton, NJ

47  "....& Nothing Less". 1970-1974//? Monthly. OCLC 2265292. Last issue 10 pages. Line drawings. Available on microfilm: Herstory. Published by the St. Louis Chapter, National Organization for Women, St. Louis, MO. Title varies: as N.O.W. Newsletter, Oct., 1970-Dec., 1972; as St. Louis N.O.W., Jan.-June, 1973. Frequency varies: irregular, Oct., 1970-Apr., 1973. Editors: Kathy Kane and Kathy O'Malley, June, 1973-Jan., 1974; Patricia C. Krauska, Feb.-June, 1974. Subject focus: lobbying, Equal Rights Amendment, day care, media, pro-abortion.

    Hist    Oct., 1970-    Microforms
           Aug., 1971;    Her. 1, R 19

           Nov., 1970, June,    Her. 1, Add.
           Sep., 1971;

           Feb., 1972-    Her. 1 UP, R11
           June, 1973;

           July, 1973-    Her. CUP, R 5
           June, 1974;

48  Androgyny. 1973-1974//? Monthly. Last issue 3 pages. Line drawings. Available on microfilm: Herstory. Published by the Northern Nevada Chapter, National Organization for Women, Sparks, NV. Editors: Pamelia deGaines, Nov.-Dec., 1973; Ann Rusnak and Joan Fuetsch, Jan.-Apr., 1974; Ann Rusnak, May-June, 1974. Subject focus: Equal Rights Amendment, lobbying.

    Hist    v.1, n.2-v.2, n.5;    Microforms
           Nov., 1973-    Her. 3, R 3
           June, 1974

49  Anne Arundel N.O.W. News. 1972-1974//? Monthly. Last issue 10 pages. Line drawings, commercial advertising. Available on microfilm: Herstory. Published by the Anne Arundel County Chapter, National Organization for Women, Annapolis, MD. Subject focus: media, pro-abortion, Equal Rights Amendment, lobbying.

    Hist    v.1, n.1-11;    Microfilm
           July, 1972-    Her. 2, R 9
           June, 1973

           v.1, n.12-v.2,    Her. 2 UP, R6
           n.11;
           July, 1973-
           June, 1974

50  AnNOWncments. 1973-1974//? Unknown. Last issue 6 pages. Line drawings. Available on microfilm: Herstory. Published by the Midland Chapter, National Organization of Women, Midland, MI. Subject focus: Equal Rights Amendment, pro-abortion.

| Hist | v.2, n.6; June, 1973 | Microforms Her. 2, R 11 |
| --- | --- | --- |
|  | v.2, n.7- v.3, n.6; July, 1973- June, 1974 | Her. 2 UP, R 7 |

51  Another Mother for Peace. 1967-1974//? Irregular. ISSN 0003-5181. OCLC 2257574. Last issue 4 pages. Line drawings, photographs. Available on microfilm: Herstory. Published by Another Mother for Peace, Beverly Hills, CA. Subject focus: peace movement, lobbying, nuclear power. Other holding institutions: CLU (CLU), CU-UC (UCU), [University of Minnesota Union List of Serials, Minneapolis, MN] (MUL), NFQC (XQM), OAkU (AKR), [Pittsburgh Regional Library, Pittsburgh, PA] (QPR), [Western New York Library Resources Council, Buffalo, NY] (VZX).

| Hist | [Aug., 1967- June, 1971] | Microforms Her. 1, R 13 |
| --- | --- | --- |
|  | [Oct., 1971- Mar., 1973] | Her. 1 UP, R 1 |
|  | [May-Winter, 1974] | Her. CUP, R 1 |

52  Anti-Polygamy Standard. 1880-1883//. Monthly. OCLC 5787095. LC 20-23060. Last issue 8 pages, last volume 88 pages. Line drawings, commercial advertising. Available on microfilm: ResP; OcW. Published in Salt Lake City, UT. Subject focus: polygamy. Other holding institutions: NN (NYP), TxDW (IWU).

| Hist | v.1, n.1-v.3, n.11-12; Apr., 1880- Feb.-Mar., 1883 | Room 225 |
| --- | --- | --- |
| Mem | v.1, n.1-v.3, n.11-12; Apr., 1880- Feb.-Mar., 1883 | Microforms |

53  The Anti-Suffragist. 1908-1912//. Quarterly. Last issue 8 pages, last volume 16 pages. Available on microfilm: ResP (1908-1912); McA (1908-1912). Published by the Anti-Suffragist, Albany, NY. Editor: Mrs. Winslow Crannell. Subject focus: anti-suffrage. Other holding institutions: NN (NYP).

| Mem | v.1, n.1-v.4, n.2; July, 1908-Apr., 1912 | Microforms |
| --- | --- | --- |

54  Antioch College Newsletter. 1969//? Unknown. OCLC 2257596. Last issue 12 pages. Available on microfilm: Herstory. Published by Antioch Women's Liberation, Yellow Springs, OH. Subject focus: rights.

| Hist | ?, 1969 | Microforms Her. 1, R 13 |
| --- | --- | --- |

55  APHRA. 1969. Quarterly. OCLC 5964004. Last issue 72 pages, last volume 285 pages, size 17 x 22. Line drawings, photographs. Available on microfilm: Herstory (1969-1974); UnM (1969-1976). Published by Aphra, Inc., New York, NY. Editor: Elizabeth Fisher. Subject focus: art, literature. Other holding institutions: CSt (Stanford University), MCR-S (Schlesinger Library on the History of Women in America, Radcliffe College, Cambridge, MA), NNU (ZYU).

| Hist | v.1, n.1-v.2, n.4; Fall, 1969- Autumn, 1971 | Microforms Her. 1, R 5 |
| --- | --- | --- |
|  | v.3, n.1-v.4, n.3; Winter, 1971/1972- Summer, 1973 | Her. 1 UP, R1 |
|  | v.4, n.4-v.5, n.2; Fall, 1973- Spring, 1974 | Her. CUP, R1 |
| MPL | Spring/Summer, 1976- | Literature and Social Science Section |
| Coll | v.6, n.1-3/4; Winter, 1971/1972- Summer, 1973 | Women's Reading Area |

56  The Applecart. 1972-1974//? Monthly. Last issue 4 pages. Line drawings. Available on microfilm: Herstory. Published by the Central Savannah River Area Chapter, National Organization for Women, Augusta, GA. Subject focus: lobbying, feminism, consciousness raising, poetry.

| Hist | v.1, n.6-9; Mar.-June, 1973 | Microforms Her. 2, R 9 |
| --- | --- | --- |
|  | v.1, n.10-v.2, n.5; July, 1973- May, 1974 | Her. 2 UP, R6 |

57  Aradia. 1971//? Unknown. OCLC 2257651. Last issue 6 pages. Line drawings. Available on microfilm: Herstory. Published by the Pittsburgh Radical Women's Union, Pittsburgh, PA. Subject focus: media, rape, radical feminism.

Hist    Oct., 1971    Microforms
Her. 1, R 13

Archiv fuer Frauenkunde und Eugenetik.
   Berlin, West Germany

   see Archiv fuer Frauenkunde und
      Konstitutions-forschung. Berlin,
      West Germany

58  Archiv fuer Frauenkunde und Konstitutions-forschung. Irregular. 1914-1933//. OCLC 1481954, 5868635, 5868735, 5868832. Last issue 122 pages, last volume 218 pages. Line drawings. Each issue self-indexed. Available on microfilm: ResP. Published by: Aertzlichen Gesellschaft fuer Sexualwissenschaft und Konstitutions-forschung, Berlin, Germany. Title varies: as Archiv fuer Frauenkunde und Eugenetik, Mar. 25, 1914-Nov., 1923. Editor: Dr. Max Hirsch. Subject focus: sexuality, health. In German (100%). Other holding institutions: [University of Minnesota Union List, Minneapolis, MN] (MUL), NN (NYP), TxDW (IWU), ViBlbv (VPI).

Mem   v.1, n.1-v.19,   Microforms
n.2-3;
Mar. 25, 1914-
Aug., 1933

59  Archon. 1934?-1978//? Semi-annual. OCLC 6678289. Last issue 64 pages. Line drawings, photographs, some in color, commercial advertising. Published by the Zeta Phi Beta Sorority, Inc., Indianapolis, IN. Place of publication varies: Galesburg, IL, Dec., 1951-?; Oakland, CA, Dec., 1962-June, 1963; Miami, FL, Dec., 1966-June, 1968. Editors: Marie Nero Tarver, Dec., 1951; Mary Theriot Williams, Dec., 1962-June, 1963; Marian H. Shannon, Dec., 1966-June, 1968; Effie B. Burford, Dec., 1968-Dec., 1978. Subject focus: education, Afro-Americans, sororities.

Hist   v.17, n.2, v.27,   Circulation
n.2, v.28, n.3,
v.29, n.2,5,
v.30, n.1-3, v.31,
n.1, v.32, n.2;
Dec., 1951,
Dec., 1962,
June, 1963,
Dec., 1966,
June, 1968,
Spring/Summer,
1975-July, 1976,
Fall/Winter, 1977,
Dec., 1978

60  Arizona Women's Political Caucus. 1972-1974//? Irregular. Last issue 4 pages. Line drawings, photographs. Available on microfilm: Herstory. Published by the Arizona Women's Political Caucus, Phoenix, AZ. Subject focus: child care, lobbying, Equal Rights Amendment.

Hist   v.1, n.1-v.2, n.2;   Microforms
Feb., 1972-             Her. 2, R 12
Mar., 1973

      v.2, n.7, v.3,    Her. 2 UP, R9
n.1;
July, 1973,
Apr., 1974

61  Around and About N.O.W. 1973?-1974//? Irregular. Last issue 6 pages. Line drawings. Available on microfilm: Herstory. Published by the Great Falls/Missoula Chapter, National Organization for Women, Great Falls/Missoula, MT. Editor: Dawn Gregg. Subject focus: pro-abortion, Equal Rights Amendment, feminism.

Hist   Nov., 1973-   Microforms
Feb., 1974      Her. 3, R 13

Artemis... for Enterprising Women.
   New York, NY

   see Enterprising Women. New York, NY

62  Arthur's Home Magazine. 1843-1898//. Monthly. OCLC 1514338, 5919129, 5919274, 5919162, 5919209, 5919094. Last issue 110 pages, last volume 576 pages, size 17 x 25. Line drawings, some in color, commercial advertising. Indexed: self-indexed, (1855-1895). Available on microfilm: UnM (1852-1897). Published by Arthur's Home Magazine, Philadelphia, PA. Title varies: as Arthur's Ladies' Magazine, Nov., 1844; as Arthur's Home Magazine, Mar., 1855-June, 1869; Arthur's Lady's Home Magazine, Jan., 1871-Nov., 1872; as Arthur's Illustrated Home Magazine, Jan., 1874-Dec., 1885. Editors: T.S. Arthur, Nov., 1844-Dec., 1855; T.S. Arthur and Virginia F. Townsend, Jan., 1857-June, 1871. Subject focus: fiction, poetry, fashion, arts, crafts, music. Other holding institutions: MCR-S (Schlesinger Library on the History of Women in America, Radcliffe College, Cambridge, MA).

Hist   v.2, n.5,[v.5,   AP83/AR7
n.3-v.65, n.6;]
Nov., 1844, [Mar.,
1855-June, 1895]

Arthur's Illustrated Home Magazine.
   Philadelphia, PA

   see Arthur's Home Magazine.
      Philadelphia, PA


Arthur's Ladies' Magazine. Philadelphia, PA

*Women's Periodicals and Newspapers*

    see <u>Arthur's Home Magazine</u>.
        Philadelphia, PA

<u>Arthur's Lady's Home Magazine</u>.
    Philadelphia, PA

    see <u>Arthur's Home Magazine</u>.
        Philadelphia, PA

63  <u>As We See It N.O.W</u>. 1970-1974//? Irregular. OCLC 2257805. Line drawings. Available on microfilm: Herstory. Published by the Michigan Chapter, National Organization for Women, Detroit, MI. Editor: Patricia R. Widmayer, May, 1970?-May, 1973. Subject focus: pro-abortion, lobbying, Equal Rights Amendment, feminism, day care, child care.

| Hist | v.1, n.1-v.2, n.5;<br>May, 1970-<br>Aug./Sep., 1971 | Microforms<br>Her. 1, R 18 |
|---|---|---|
| | v.2, n.6-v.4, n.5;<br>Oct., 1971-<br>May, 1973 | Her. 1 UP, R 9 |
| | v.4, n.6/7-v.5, n.6;<br>June/July, 1973-<br>June, 1974 | Her. CUP, R 3 |

64  <u>Asian Women</u>. 1971//? Unknown. OCLC 2257823. Last issue 144 pages. Line drawings, photographs. Available on microfilm: Herstory. Published by the Asian Women of University of California, Berkeley, CA. Subject focus: art, education, college students, Asian Americans.

| Hist | ?, 1971 | Microforms<br>Her. 1, R 5 |
|---|---|---|

65  <u>Asian Women's Center Newsletter</u>. 1973-1974//? Irregular. Last issue 16 pages. Line drawings, photographs. Available on microfilm: Herstory. Published by the Y.W.C.A. of Los Angeles, Los Angeles, CA. Subject focus: drug abuse, health, poetry, Asian Americans, centers, college students.

| Hist | Mar.-Summer, 1973 | Microforms<br>Her. 2, R 1 |
|---|---|---|
| | Nov., 1973-<br>May, 1974 | Her. 2 UP, R 1 |

<u>Association of American Colleges Project on the Status and Education of Women</u>.
    Washington, DC

    see <u>On Campus with Women</u>.
        Washington, DC

<u>The Association Monthly</u>. New York, NY

    see <u>The Woman's Press</u>. New York, NY

66  <u>Association for Women in Mathematics Newsletter</u>. 1971-1974//? Irregular. Last issue 11 pages. Line drawings. Available on microfilm: Herstory. Published by the Association for Women in Mathematics, Washington, DC. Editor: Mary W. Gray, May, 1971-June, 1973? Subject focus: education, employment, lobbying, affirmative action, mathematicians.

| Hist | v.1, n.1?-v.3, n.4;<br>May, 1971-<br>June, 1973 | Microforms<br>Her. 2, R 1 |
|---|---|---|
| | v.3, n.5-v.4, n.4;<br>Sep., 1973-<br>June, 1974 | Her. 2 UP, R1 |

67  <u>Association for Women in Psychology Newsletter</u>. 1971-1973//? Bi-monthly. Last issue 8 pages. Line drawings. Available on microfilm: Herstory. Published by the Association for Women in Psychology, New York, NY. Editor: Leigh Marlowe. Subject focus: psychologists.

| Hist | Sep./Oct., 1971-<br>May/June, 1973 | Microforms<br>Her. 1 UP, R1 |
|---|---|---|

68  <u>Association for Women in Psychology Newsletter. (San Francisco Edition)</u>. 1973-1974//? Bi-monthly. Last issue 8 pages. Line drawings. Available on microfilm: Herstory. Published by the Association for Women in Psychology, San Francisco, CA. Editor: Leigh Marlowe. Subject focus: psychologists, psychotherapy.

| Hist | July/Aug., 1973-<br>May/June, 1974 | Microforms<br>Her. CUP, R1 |
|---|---|---|

69  <u>Association of American Colleges-Project on the Status and Education of Women</u>. 1972-1973//? Monthly? Last issue 12 pages. Available on microfilm: Herstory. Published by the Association of American Colleges, Washington, DC. Subject focus: child care, minorities, affirmative action in education, sexism in education, college students.

| Hist | Feb., 1972-<br>June 19, 1973 | Microforms<br>Her. 2, R 1 |
|---|---|---|

70  <u>Association of American Law Schools Newsletter</u>. 1900-1973//? Tri-annual. Last issue 4 pages. Available on microfilm: Herstory. Published by the Association of American Law Schools, Executive Directors Office, Washington, DC. Subject focus: law schools, lawyers.

## Women's Periodicals and Newspapers

    Hist    v.72, n.1-v.73,    Microforms
             n.2;                         Her. 2, R 1
             Feb. 29, 1972-
             Apr. 30, 1973

71    Association of Libertarian Feminists. 1976. Irregular. $5 for individuals and institutions. Association of Libertarian Feminists, 225 Lafayette Street, Room 1212, New York, NY. (212) 927-9788. Last issue 8 pages, size 18 x 22. Subject focus: rights, libertarian feminism.

    Hist    n.1-                       Circulation
             Feb., 1976-

72    Association of Married Women. 1973//? Unknown. Last issue 3 pages. Line drawings, photographs. Available on microfilm: Herstory. Published by the Association of Married Women, Arlington, VA. Subject focus: crimes against women, missing persons, child welfare, wives.

    Hist    June, 1973         Microforms
                                         Her. 2, R 1

73    Association to Repeal Abortion Laws Newsletter. 1969-1970//? Irregular. OCLC 2257897. Last issue 2 pages. Available on microfilm: Herstory. Published by the Association to Repeal Abortion Laws, San Francisco, CA. Subject focus: rape, anti-abortion, unwed mothers.

    Hist    [Nov. 25, 1969-    Microforms
             Aug. 26, 1970]     Her. 1, R 13

74    At the Berkeley Community Y.W.C.A. 1973-1974. Quarterly. Last issue 4 pages. Line drawings. Available on microfilm: Herstory. Published by the Berkeley Community Y.W.C.A., Berkeley, CA.

    Hist    Fall, 1973-       Microforms
             Summer, 1974     Her. 2 UP, R 3

    Atlanta N.O.W. News.   Atlanta, GA

        see Atlanta NOW News.   Atlanta, GA

75    Atlanta NOW News. 1976-1980//. Monthly. $5 for individuals and institutions. Last issue 12 pages, size 14 x 22. Line drawings. Published by the Atlanta Chapter, National Organization for Women, Atlanta, GA. Title varies: as Atlanta N.O.W. News, July, 1977-June, 1978. Subject focus: pro-abortion, feminism, rights, lesbians.

    Hist    July, Oct.-       Circulation
             Dec., 1977,

             Feb.-July, Oct.,
             1978-Aug., 1980

76    Atlanta Women's Club Bulletin. 1973-1974//? Irregular. Last issue 2 pages. Line drawings. Available on microfilm: Herstory. Published by the Atlanta Women's Club, Atlanta, GA. Editor: Mrs. LeRoy H. Fargason. Subject focus: clubs.

    Hist    Jan.-May, 1973    Microforms
                                       Her. 2, R 2

             Oct.-Nov., 1973,   Her. 2 UP, R1
             Feb., 1974

77    Aurora. 1971-1972//? Irregular. OCLC 2257960. Last issue 48 pages. Line drawings, photographs, commercial advertising. Available on microfilm: Herstory. Published by the Rockland County Feminists, Suffern, NY. Subject focus: poetry, history, day care, health, self-help, feminism. Other holding institutions: MCR-S (Schlesinger Library on the History of Women in America, Radcliffe College, Cambridge, MA).

    Hist    v.1, n.1;         Microforms
             June, 1971       Her. 1, R 5

             v.1, n.2;         Her. 1 UP, R1
             Winter, 1971

             v.1, n.3-4;       Her. CUP, R1
             ?, 1972

78    Auxiliary News. 1923-1926//? Monthly. Last issue 6 pages, size 23 x 28. Published by the American Legion Auxiliary, Burlington, VT. Subject focus: clubs.

    Hist    [v.2, n.5-v.4,    F836/8A51A/VT
             n.5;]
             [Apr., 1924-
             Jan., 1926]

    The Auxiliary Newsletter.   Manitowoc, WI,
        Green Bay, WI

        see Wisconsin Hospital Association
            Auxiliaries.   Milwaukee, WI

79    Awake & Move. 1971//. Bi-monthly. OCLC 2258035. Last issue 4 pages, size 30 x 43. Line drawings. Available on microfilm: Herstory. Published by the Philadelphia Women's Liberation Center, Philadelphia, PA. Subject focus: rights, child care, workers, radical feminism.

    Hist    v.1, n.3-5;       Pam 72-43
             June-Oct., 1971

*Women's Periodicals and Newspapers*

|   |   |
|---|---|
| v.1, n.1-4; Jan./Feb.-July, 1971 | Microforms Her. 1, R 1 |
| v.1, n.5; Oct., 1971 | Her. 1 UP, R 1 |

Awareness. Moscow, ID

see Women's Center Newsletter. Moscow, ID

80  Badger Briefs. 1932. Quarterly. $2.50 for individuals and institutions. Pat Manske, editor, Badger Briefs, Route 1, Box 73A, Amherst, WI 54406. OCLC 5509577. Last issue 16 pages, last volume 48 pages, size 22 x 28. Line drawings, photographs. Published by the Wisconsin State Division, American Association of University Women, Amherst, WI. Place of publication varies: Wausau, WI, Oct., 1968-July, 1971; Janesville, WI, Oct., 1971-July, 1973; Manitowoc, WI, Oct., 1973-Apr., 1977. Previous editors: Mrs. Gerald H. Teletzke, Oct., 1968-July, 1969; Mrs. Robert W. Dean, Oct., 1969-July, 1971; Mrs. Walter Nickol, Oct., 1971-July, 1973; Joan Dramm, Oct., 1973-Apr., 1977. Subject focus: rights, college teachers, continuing education, lobbying.

Hist    v.24, n.1-    Circulation
        Oct., 1968-

81  Baldwin Street Gallery Newsletter. 1972//? Monthly? Last issue 6 pages. Line drawings. Available on microfilm: Herstory. Published by the Baldwin Street Gallery, Toronto, Ontario, Canada. Subject focus: poetry, photography, art.

Hist    Mar.-Apr., 1972    Microforms
                           Her. 2, R 2

The Ballot Box. Toledo, OH

see The National Citizen and Ballot Box. Syracuse, NY

82  Battle Acts. 1970-1974//? Irregular. OCLC 2258192. Last issue 32 pages, last volume 56 pages, size 22 x 28. Line drawings, photographs, commercial advertising. Available on microfilm: Herstory. Published by Women of Youth Against War and Fascism, New York, NY. Editors: Laurie Fierstein, Nov.-Dec., 1970; Sue Davis, Laurie Fierstein, and Emily Hanlon, Feb.-June/July, 1971; Sue Davis and Emily Hanlon, Aug./Sep., 1971-Summer, 1973; Sue Davis and Kathy Durkin, Aug., 1974. Subject focus: rights, poor people, radical feminism, workers, peace movement, health, aging. Other holding institutions: MCR-S (Schlesinger Library on the History of Women in America, Radcliffe College, Cambridge, MA).

| Hist | v.1, n.1-v.4, n.1; Nov., 1970-Aug., 1974 | JX/1901/B3 |
|---|---|---|
|   | v.1, n.1-7; Nov., 1970-Aug./Sep., 1971 | Microforms Her. 1, R 5 |
|   | v.1, n.8-v.2, n.5; Oct./Nov., 1971-Aug./Sep., 1972 | Her. 1 UP, R 1 |
|   | v.3, n.2, v.4, n.1; Summer, 1973, Aug., 1974 | Her. CUP, R 1 |

83  Battle-Axe, and Weapons of War. 1837-1840//. Irregular. OCLC 5870526. Last issue 8 pages, last volume 32 pages. Available on microfilm: ResP. Published by Battle-Axe, and Weapons of War, Philadelphia, PA. Editor: Theophilus Ransom Gates. Subject focus: religion. Other holding institutions: NN (NYP), TxDW (IWU).

Mem    v.1, n.1-4;    Microforms
       July, 1837-
       Aug., 1840

84  Bay Area Women's Liberation Newsletter. 1971//? OCLC 2258196. Last issue 6 pages. Available on microfilm: Herstory. Published by Bay Area Women's Liberation, San Francisco, CA. Subject focus: pro-abortion, child care, Afro-Americans, gay rights, feminism.

Hist    n.1;           Microforms
        Jan., 1971     Her. 1, R 13

85  Beach Cities N.O.W. 1973-1974//? Monthly. Last issue 5 pages. Line drawings. Available on microfilm: Herstory. Published by the Beach Cities Chapter, National Organization for Women, Manhatten, CA. Subject focus: marriage, media, lobbying, feminism.

Hist    v.1, n.6-v.2, n.6;    Microforms
        Nov., 1973-           Her. 3, R 2
        June, 1974

86  La Belle Assemblée, or Court and Fashionable Magazine. 1806-1832?//. Monthly. OCLC 1519474. Last issue 64 pages, last volume 292 pages. Line drawings, commercial advertising. Each volume self-indexed. Available on microfilm: ResP, UnM. Published by George B. Whittaker, London, England. Subject focus: fashion, France, upper classes. Other holding institutions: FGULS (FUL), MB (Boston Public Library), MNS (SNN), [University of Minnesota Union List, Minneapolis, MN] (MUL), OO (OBE), TxDW (IWU).

*Women's Periodicals and Newspapers*

| | | |
|---|---|---|
| Mem | n.1-53, [n.s.] n.1-195, [3rd ser.] 1-90; Feb., 1806- June, 1832 | Microforms |

87  Belles and Bars. 1973-1974?//. Irregular. Last issue 8 pages, size 22 x 28. Line drawings. Published by the Louisiana Correctional Institution for Women, St. Gabriel, LA. Subject focus: minorities, prisoners, law.

| | | |
|---|---|---|
| Crim Just | v.1, n.1-6 Oct., 1973- July, 1974 | Circulation |

88  Berk County Chapter-N.O.W. 1973-1974//? Monthly. Last issue 2 pages. Line drawings. Available on microfilm: Herstory. Published by the Berk County Chapter, National Organization for Women, Reading, PA. Subject focus: pro-abortion, feminism, lobbying, Equal Rights Amendment.

| | | |
|---|---|---|
| Hist | Dec., 1973- Feb., 1974 | Microforms Her. 3, R 2 |

Berkeley-East Bay Branch Newsletter. Berkeley, CA

see Women's International League for Peace and Freedom, Berkeley-East Bay Branch Newsletter. Berkeley, CA

89  Berkeley/Oakland Women's Union Newsletter: A Socialist-Feminist Organization. 1973-1974//? Unknown. Last issue 24 pages. Line drawings. Available on microfilm: Herstory. Published by the Berkeley/Oakland Women's Union, Berkeley, CA. Subject focus: labor unions, prison reform, pro-abortion, media, socialist feminism.

| | | |
|---|---|---|
| Hist | v.2, n.3-4; Feb.-June?, 1974 | Microforms Her. 3, R 1 |

90  Berkeley Women's Liberation Newsletter. 1969-1970//? Irregular. OCLC 2258270. Last issue 6 pages. Line drawings. Available on microfilm: Herstory. Published by Berkeley Women's Liberation, Berkeley, CA. Subject focus: history, research, workers, feminism.

| | | |
|---|---|---|
| Hist | May 15, 1969- Apr. 3, 1970 | Microforms Her. 1, R 13 |

91  Best Friends. 1971?-1973//? Unknown. OCLC 2258285. Last issue 112 pages. Line drawings. Available on microfilm: Herstory. Published by the Best Friends Poetry Collective, Albuquerque, NM. Editor: Sharon Barba. Subject focus: poetry, art.

| | | |
|---|---|---|
| Hist | n.1?; ?, 1971 | Microforms Her. 1, R 5 |
| | n.2; Summer, 1972 | Her. 1 UP, R1 |
| | n.3; ?, 1973 | Her. CUP, R 1 |

92  Better Food. 1895-1947?// 10 times a year. OCLC 4781150, 1716625. LC 16-509*. Last issue 66 pages, last volume 602 pages, size 22 x 30. Line drawings, photographs, some in color, commercial advertising. Self-indexed (1912-1947). Published by Whitney Publications, New York, NY. Title varies: as Boston Cooking School Magazine, June/July, 1912-May, 1914; American Cookery, June/July, 1914-May, 1946. Place of publication varies: Boston, MA, June/July, 1912-Apr., 1944. Editors: Janet McKenzie Hill, June/July, 1912-May, 1920; Robert B. Hill, Dec., 1931-Dec., 1932; Imogene Wolcott, June/July, 1942-Mar., 1944; Sally Larken and Dorothy S. Towle, Apr.-Aug., 1944; Eleonora Borzilleri, Sep., 1944-June, 1945; Hugh Darby, Sep., 1945-May, 1947. Subject focus: cooking, home economics, food, interior decoration, fiction, poetry. Other holding institutions: AzTeS (AZS), DeU (DLM), [Indiana Union List of Serials, Indianapolis, IN] (ILS), [University of Minnesota Union List, Minneapolis, MN] (MUL), [New York State Union List, Albany, NY] (NYS), NIC (COO), OBgU (BGU), TxBelM (MHB).

| | | |
|---|---|---|
| Agric | v.17, n.1- v.52, n.9 June/July, 1912- May, 1947 | Circulation |

93  Better Homes and Gardens. 1922. Monthly. $10 for individuals and institutions. James A. Autry, editor, 1716 Locust Street, Des Moines, IA 50336. ISSN 0006-0151. OCLC 1519682. LC 27-6944. Last issue 230 pages, last volume 1740 pages, size 21 x 27. Line drawings, photographs, some in color, commercial advertising. Self-indexed 1922-1928; Readers Guide 1930-. Available on microfilm: UnM (1922-), McP (1960-), McI (1960-). Title varies: as Fruit, Garden and Home (July, 1922-July, 1924). Previous editors: E.T. Meredity, Aug., 1922-May, 1929; Elmer T. Peterson, June, 1929-Sep., 1937; Frank W. McDonough, July, 1938-Apr., 1950; J.E. Ratner, May, 1950-Nov., 1952; Hugh Curtis, Dec., 1952-June, 1960; Bert Dieter, July, 1960-June, 1967; Jim Riggs, July, 1967-Aug., 1970. Subject focus: health, gardening, crafts, food, interior decoration, entertaining, travel. Other holding institutions: AU (ALM), [Alabama Public Library Service, Montgomery, AL] (ASL), ArAO (AKO), ArRuA (AKP), ArU (AFU), AzFU (AZN), AzTeS (AZS), CLU (CLU), [Pepperdine University, Malibu, CA] (CPE), CU-UC (UCU), COU-DA (COA), CtY (YUS), DeU (DLM), FBoU (FGM), FJUNF (FNP),

FMFIU (FXG), GA (GAP), IGreviC (IAG), InLP (IPL), InU (IUL), KLindB (KFB), KPT (KFP), KSteC (KKQ), KyU (KUK), [Boston State College Library, Boston, MA] (BST), MMeT (TFW), MdStm (MDS), MiEM (EEM), MiLC (EEL), MiMtpT (EZC), [University of Minnesota Union List, Minneapolis, MN] (MUL), MoKU (UMK), MoSMa (MVC), MoSpE (MOE), MsToT (TGC), NcEUcE (NPE), NcRS (NRC), NcWlSB (NVS), NdU (UND), NbRS (RRS), NbU (LDL), NjLincB (BCC), NmLcU (IUR), NmLvH (NMH), [New York State Union List, Albany, NY] (NYS), NBmK (VZK), NBP (VZQ), [Western New York Library Resources Council, Buffalo, NY] (VZX), NGenoU (YGM), NIC (COO), NOneoU (ZBM), N (NYG), NR (YQR), NSyU (SYB), [Central New York Library Resources Council, Syracuse, NY] (SRR), OAk (APL), OAkU (AKR), OBgU (BGU), OCedC (CDC), OCl (CLE), OC1W (CWR), OCo (OCO), OKentU (KSU), O (OHI), OO (OBE), OTU (TOL), OY (YMM), OkTahN (OKN), OkTOR (OKO), OkT (TUL), PAnL (LVC), PCLS (REC), PCalS (CSC), PInU (PZI), PPD (DXU), PPiAC (AIC), PPiC (PMC), PPi (CPL), [Pittsburgh Regional Library Center-Union List, Pittsburgh, PA] (QPR), ScRhW (SWW), TCollsM (TMS), TMurS (TXM), TxAbH (TXS), TxBelM (MHB), TxCM (TXA), TxDW (IWU), [AMIGOS Union List of Serials, Dallas, TX] (IUC), TxEU (TXU), TxHU-D (THD), TxNacS (TXK), [Emory & Henry College, Emory, VA] (VEH), ViRCU (VRC), WA (WIQ), WFon (WIF), WGR (GZG), [Arrowhead Library System, Janesville Public Library, Janesville, WI] (WIJ), WMaPI-RL (GZR), WMenU (GZS), WMUW (GZN).

| | | |
|---|---|---|
| Agric | v.1, n.1-<br>July, 1922- | Circulation |
| MPL | Jan. 19, 1939- | Circulation |
| MHHS | Jan., 1971- | Circulation |
| WHS | Mar., 1968- | Circulation |
| PPL | Jan., 1971- | Circulation |
| WAPL | Sep., 1973- | Circulation |
| MOPL | Jan., 1970- | Circulation |
| DFPL | Jan., 1974- | Circulation |
| OM | Current Issues Only | Circulation |
| SCPL | Jan., 1970- | Circulation |
| DFHS | Aug., 1974- | Circulation |
| MAPL | Current Issues Only | Circulation |
| OPL | Current Issues Only | Circulation |
| MCL | Jan., 1971- | Circulation |
| R & L | May, 1967- | Circulation |
| MGHS | Jan., 1966-1967,<br>Feb., 1969- | Circulation |
| VPL | Jan., 1965- | Circulation |
| MIPL | Jan., 1973- | Circulation |
| BFL | Jan., 1975- | Circulation |
| SPPL | Jan., 1971- | Circulation |
| RPL | Jan., 1970- | Circulation |
| BEL | Current Issues Only | Circulation |
| BHS | May, 1971- | Circulation |
| BML | Current Issues Only | Circulation |
| TML | Jan., 1960- | Circulation |
| MFHS | Jan., 1973- | Circulation |
| MHPL | Jan., 1968- | Circulation |
| DHS | Current Issues Only | Circulation |
| EC | Current Issues Only | Circulation |
| LAHS | Jan., 1971- | Circulation |
| EHS | Mar., 1971- | Circulation |
| VHS | Jan., 1967- | Circulation |
| MMHS | Jan., 1968- | Circulation |
| BAHS | Jan., 1971- | Circulation |
| CFL | Jan., 1971- | Circulation |
| CPPL | Current Issues Only | Circulation |
| EDHS | Sep., 1966- | Circulation |
| SAPH | Current Issues Only | Circulation |
| MMRL | Jan., 1966- | Circulation |
| SPHS | Jan., 1966- | Circulation |

94  Bibliothek der Frauenfrage. 1888-1893//. Irregular. Last issue 84 pages. Available on microfilm: ResP. Editor: Mrs. J. Kettler. Published in Weimar, Germany. Subject focus: education, employment. In German (100%). Other holding institutions: NNC (Nolan, Norton & Co., Inc., Lexington, MA).

| | | |
|---|---|---|
| Mem | n.1-22;<br>?, 1888-?, 1893 | Microforms |

95  Big Mama Rag. 1973. Monthly. $6 for individuals, $12 for institutions. Big Mama Rag, 1724 Gaylord Street, Denver, CO 80206. OCLC 2778484. Last issue 20 pages, size 43 x 29. Line drawings, photographs, commercial advertising. Indexed in the Alternative Press Index (1973-). Available on microfilm: Herstory (1972-1974). Published by Big Mama Rag, Inc., Denver, CO. Subject focus: pro-abortion, health, lesbians, workers, gay rights, feminism. Other holding institutions: CLU (CLU), COU-DA (COA), CU-UC (UCU).

| Hist | v.6, n.6-; June, 1978- | Circulation |
| --- | --- | --- |
|  | v.1, n.1-2; ?, 1973 | Microforms Her. 2, R 2 |
|  | v.1, n.4-v.2, n.8; ? -June, 1974 | Her. 2 UP, R 1 |

96  Birth and the Family Journal. 1974. $10 for individuals, $12 for institutions. Madeline H. Shearer, editor, Birth and the Family Journal, 110 El Camino Real, Berkeley, CA 94705. OCLC 2105394, 1590122, 1578507, 4680560. Last issue 84 pages. Line drawings, photographs, commercial advertising. Indexed in: Current Contents/Social and Behavioral Sciences, Social Science Citation Index, Cumulative Index to Nursing, Allied Health Literature, International Nursing Index. Abstracted in: Exerpta Medica, Psychological Abstracts. Published by International Childbirth Education Association and American Society for Psychoprophylaxis in Obstetrics, Berkeley, CA. Subject focus: pregnancy, childbirth education, childbirth. Other holding institutions: AzFU (AZN), AzTeS (AZS), ClobS (CLO), CSdS (CDS), CU-US (UCU), DAU (EAU), DCU (DCU), DNLM (NLM), GASU (GSU), GStG (GPM), GVaS (GYG), IaDL (IOH), IaDuU (IOV), MiEM (EEM), [University of Minnesota Union List, Minneapolis, MN] (MUL), MnStjos (MNF), MoU (MMU), MWMU (WQM), NcCU (NKM), NCortU (YCM), NGcA (VJA), NNR (ZXC), NNU (ZYU), NTRS (ZRS), [Central New York Library Resources Council, Syracuse, NY] (SRR), OAkU (AKR), OBgU (BGU), OClW-H (CHS), ODaWU (WSU), OkS (OKS), OrU-M (OHS), OSteC (STU), PCW (UWC), PPiD (DUQ), PPJ (TVJ), PU-Med (PAM), TCollsM (TMS), TCU (TUC), [AMIGOS Union List of Serials, Dallas, TX] (IUC), TxDW (IWU), TMurS (TXM), ViRCU (VRC), WU (GZM), Wu-M (GZH), WyU (WYU).

| MGN | v.5, n.4, v.7, n.1- Winter, 1978, Spring, 1980- | Circulation |
| --- | --- | --- |

97  The Birth Control Review. 1917-1940?// Monthly. OCLC 4687088, 1536495. LC 69-11320. Last issue 16 pages, last volume 226 pages. Line drawings, photographs, some in color, commercial advertising. Self-indexed. Published by The American Birth Control League, Inc., New York, NY. Editors: Margaret Sanger, Jan., 1917-Feb., 1929; Mary Sumner Boyd and Annie G. Porritt, Mar.-May, 1929; Stella Hanau, June, 1929-June, 1937; Mabel Travis Wood, Oct., 1937-Oct., 1939; Mrs. Leopold K. Simon, Nov., 1939-Jan., 1940. Subject focus: birth control. Other holding institutions: AzTeS (AZS), CtU-H (UCH), CU-UC (UCU), InU (IUL), MCR-S (Schlesinger Library on the History of Women in America, Radcliffe College, Cambridge, MA), [University of Minnesota Union List, Minneapolis, MN] (MUL), MNS (SNN), MnStcls (MST), [Central New York Library Resources Council, Syracuse, NY] (SRR), NSbSU (YSM), OYU (YNG), PCalS (CSC), [Pittsburgh Regional Library Center-Union List, Pittsburgh, PA] (QPR), [AMIGOS Union List of Serials, Dallas, TX] (IUC), TxLT (ILU).

| Mem | [v.1, n.1-v.27, n.7; (n.s.) v.1, n.1-v.24, n.3]; [Feb., 1917-Jan., 1940] | Microforms |
| --- | --- | --- |

98  Birthright. 1972?//. Last issue 12 pages. Line drawings. Available on microfilm: Herstory. Published by Birthright, Tampa, FL. Subject focus: poetry, consciousness raising.

| Hist | v.1, n.2-5; ?, 1972 | Microforms Her. 2, R 2 |
| --- | --- | --- |

99  Bitch. 1970//? Unknown. OCLC 2258371. Last issue 3 pages. Line drawings, photographs. Available on microfilm: Herstory. Published by Bitch, Milwaukee, WI. Subject focus: pro-abortion, rights.

| Hist | n.1; ?, 1970 | Microforms Her. 1, R 1 |
| --- | --- | --- |

100  Biweekly News Letter. 1917//. Bi-weekly. Last issue 8 pages, size 14 x 22. Line drawings, photographs. Published by the National League for Woman's Service, New York, NY. Subject focus: World War I, war work.

| Hist | v.2, n.6-7; July 1- Sep. 1/15, 1917 | F836/8N26B (Cutter) |
| --- | --- | --- |

101  Black Maria. 1971-1977//. Quarterly. ISSN 0045-222X. OCLC 2786249. LC sc77-1275. Last issue 60 pages, last volume 216 pages, size 16 x 22. Line drawings, photographs, commercial advertising. Available on microfilm: Herstory (1971-1974). Published by the Black Maria Collective, River Forest/Chicago, IL. Subject focus: poetry, fiction. Other holding institutions: CtY (YUS), CSt (Stanford University), MCR-S (Schlesinger

Library on the History of Women in America, Radcliffe College, Cambridge, MA), [University of Minnesota Union List of Serials, Minneapolis, MN] (MUL), NGenoU (YGM), NTRS (ZRS), RPB (RBN), [AMIGOS Union List of Serials, Dallas, TX] (IUC), WMUW (GZN).

| | | |
|---|---|---|
| Hist | v.1, n.1-v.2, n.1/2; Dec., 1971- Spring/Summer, 1973 | Microforms Her. 2, R 2 |
| | v.2, n.3-4; Winter, 1973- Spring, 1974 | Her. 2 UP, R 1 |
| RBR | v.1, n.4-v.3, n.3; Winter, 1973- ?, 1977 | Circulation |

102 Bloodroot. 1976. Tri-annual. $6 for individuals and institutions. Joan Eades, Linda Ohlsen and Dan Eades, editors, Bloodroot, P.O. Box 891, Grand Forks, ND. ISSN 0161-2506. OCLC 3880428. Last issue 72 pages, size 15 x 23. Line drawings. Published by Bloodroot, Inc., Grand Forks, ND. Frequency varies: semi-annual, Fall, 1976-Fall, 1978. Previous editors: Candy Dostert, Fall, 1976; Joan Eades, Spring, 1977; Joan Eades and Linda Ohlsen, Fall, 1977-Fall, 1978. Subject focus: poetry, fiction, interviews. Other holding institutions: [University of Minnesota Union List of Serials, Minneapolis, MN] (MUL), NTRS (ZRS).

| | | |
|---|---|---|
| RBR | n.1- Fall, 1976- | Circulation |

Bloomington Women's Liberation Newsletter. Bloomington, IN

see Front Page. Bloomington, IN

103 Blue Triangle News. 1917-1920//. Weekly. OCLC 1536615. LC 21-8866. Last issue 4 pages, size 22 x 28. Line drawings, photographs. Published by the Y.W.C.A. War Work Council, New York, NY. Title varies: as Y.W.C.A. Bulletin War Work Council, Nov. 1-17, 1917; as War Work Bulletin, Nov. 30, 1917-Sep. 19, 1919. Subject focus: World War I, war work. Other holding institutions: [University of Minnesota Union List of Serials, Minneapolis, MN] (MUL).

| | | |
|---|---|---|
| Hist | n.5-98; Nov. 1, 1917- Sep ?, 1920 | F83756/+Y78 |

104 B'nai B'rith Women's World. 1952-?//? Monthly. Last issue 8 pages, size 22 x 28. Photographs. Published by the B'nai B'rith Women's Supreme Council, Mount Morris, IL. Editor: Mrs. Maurice Turner. Subject focus: Israel, Jews, clubs, Judaism.

| | | |
|---|---|---|
| Hist | v.2, n.9; Mar., 1953 | Pam 72-301 |

105 Body Fashions/Intimate Apparel. 1973. $15 for individuals and institutions. Mimi Finkel, editor, Body Fashions/Intimate Apparel, 757 Third Ave., New York, NY 10017. Business address, 1 East First Street, Duluth, MN 55802. ISSN 0360-3520. OCLC 2244083. LC 75-648053. Last issue 26 pages, size 22 x 28. Line drawings, photographs, some in color, commercial advertising. Published by Harcourt Brace Jovanovich Merchandising Publications, New York, NY. Subject focus: fashion, fabrics, sewing, clothes. Other holding institutions: DLC (DLC), [University of Minnesota Union List of Serials, Minneapolis, MN] (MUL), NcRS (NRC), OCl (CLE), [AMIGOS Union List of Serials, Dallas, TX] (IUC).

| | | |
|---|---|---|
| MATC | Current Issues Only | Cora Hardy Library |

Le Bon Ton: Journal des Modes, Literature, et Beaux Arts. Paris, France

see Le Bon Ton and Le Moniteur de la Mode. New York, NY

106 Le Bon Ton and Le Moniteur de la Mode. 1834-1890//. Monthly. OCLC 5870293. Last issue 14 pages, last volume 168 pages. Line drawings, commercial advertising. Available on microfilm: ResP. Published by S.T. Taylor, New York, NY. Title varies: as Le Bon Ton: Journal des Modes, Literature, et Beaux Arts, Sep. 1, 1852-Oct. 28, 1872. Place of publication varies: Paris, France, Sep. 1, 1852-Oct. 28, 1872. Frequency varies: weekly, Sep. 1, 1852-Oct. 28, 1872. Subject focus: fashion, literature, theatre, art. In French (100%). Other holding institutions: CtY (YUS), PSt (UPM), TxDW (IWU).

| | | |
|---|---|---|
| Mem | yr.18, v.2, n.9- yr.36, v.2, n.11, yr.37, v.1, n.1- yr.38, v.2, n.4, yr.39, n.1-12; Sep. 1, 1852- Sep. 15, 1870, Mar. 8, 1871- Oct. 28, 1872, Jan.-Dec., 1890 | Microforms |

107 The Bond of Kappa Epsilon. 1938? Irregular. Julie Jensen, editor, The Bond of Epsilon, P.O. Box 11, Boonville, MO 65233. Last issue 4 pages, last volume 24 pages, size 22 x 28. Line drawings, photographs. Published by the Kappa Epsilon, National Pharmacy Fraternity

for Women, Boonville, MO. Previous editors: Dr. Ester J.W. Hal, Winter, 1961; Lauretta E. Fox, 1962; Joanne B. Benson, Summer, 1963-Spring, 1969; Charla Leibenguth, Winter, 1969-Spring, 1973; Nancy Starnes, Winter, 1973-Spring, 1974; Metta Lou Henderson, Winter, 1975/1976; Ginger Brewer, Fall, 1976/1977; Metta Lou Henderson, Feb., 1977; Ginger Brewer, Apr.-Winter, 1977/1978. Subject focus: sororities, pharmacists.

| | | |
|---|---|---|
| Pharmacy | v.29?,n.2, v.32, n.1- Apr., 1957/1958, Winter, 1961- | LT/B64/K14 |

108. Booklegger Magazine. 1973-1978//? Irregular. ISSN 0092-7686. OCLC 1791024. LC 74-640095. Last issue 76 pages, last volume 200 pages, size 18 x 25. Line drawings, commercial advertising. Indexed in: Alternative Press Index; Library Literature Index; Women's Studies Abstracts. Published in San Francisco, CA. Subject focus: alternative literature, librarians, non-sexist children's materials. Other holding institutions: [Alabama Public Library Service, Montgomery, AL] (ASL), ArCCA (AKC), AU (ALM), AzFU (AZN), AzTeS (AZS), CLobS (CLO), CLSU (CSL), CtY (YUS), [Congressional Research Service, Washington, DC] (CRS), DLC (DLC), ICI (IAH), InU (IUL), LU (LUU), MBNU (NED), MdBJ (JHE), MiAdC (EEA), MiEM (EEM), MiMtpT (EZC), [University of Minnesota Union List of Serials, Minneapolis, MN] (MUL), MMiltC (CUM), MWelC (WEL), NhD (DRB), NBu (VHB), [New York State Union List, Albany, NY] (NYS), NFQC (XQM), [Central New York Library Resources Council, Syracuse, NY] (SRR), NGcA (VJA), NGenoU (YGM), NIC (COO), NOneoU (ZBM), NcGU (NGU), NjTS (NJT), O (OHI), OU (OSU), OKentU (KSU), OTU (TOL), OkT (TUL), PBm (BMC), [Pittsburgh Regional Library Center Union List, Pittsburgh, PA] (QPR), TCollsM (TMS), TNJ (TJC), [AMIGOS Union List of Serials, Dallas, TX] (IUC), TxDW (IWU), [Emory & Henry College, Emory, VA] (VEH), WMaPI-RL (GZR), WMUW (GZN).

| | | |
|---|---|---|
| Mem | v.1,n.1-v.4,n.17; Nov./Dec., 1973- Summer, 1978 | AP/B7258/M191 |
| Lib Sch | v.1,n.1-v.3,n.16; Nov./Dec., 1973- Autumn, 1976 | Periodicals Section |

109. Born a Woman. 1971//? Unknown. Last issue 38 pages. Line drawings, photographs. Available on microfilm: Herstory. Published by Born A Woman, Los Angeles, CA. Subject focus: Equal Rights Amendment.

| | | |
|---|---|---|
| Hist | n.1; Fall/Winter, 1971 | Microforms Her. 2, R 2 |

Boston Cooking School Magazine. Boston, MA

see Better Food. New York, NY

Boston Weekly Magazine. Boston, MA

see Weekly Magazine and Ladies' Miscellany. Boston, MA

110. Boulder N.O.W. 1971-1974//? Irregular. Last issue 4 pages. Line drawings. Available on microfilm: Herstory. Published by the Boulder Chapter of the National Organization for Women, Boulder, CO. Subject focus: education, sexism, media, consciousness-raising, Equal Rights Amendment, lobbying, feminism.

| | | |
|---|---|---|
| Hist | Jan., 1971- May/June, 1973 | Microforms Her. 2, R 9 |
| | Aug., 1973- June, 1974 | Her. 2 UP, R6 |

111. Boxcar. 1977-1981//. Irregular. Last issue 20 pages, size 45 x 29. Line drawings, photographs, commercial advertising. Published by the Women's Itinerant Hobo's Union, San Francisco, CA. Subject focus: travel, poetry, fiction, hobos.

| | | |
|---|---|---|
| Hist | n.1-5; June, 1977- Winter, 1980-1981 | Microforms |

112. Branching Out. 1973-1980//. Irregular. ISSN 0382-5264. OCLC 2305910. LC cn76-301221. Last issue 48 pages, last volume 192 pages, size 22 x 27. Line drawings, photographs, commercial advertising. Indexed in the Canadian Periodical Index. Available on microfilm: McM; Herstory. Published by the New Women's Magazine Society, Edmonton, Alberta, Canada. Previous editors: Susan McMaster, Mar./Apr.-Sep./Oct., 1974; Susan McMaster and Sharon Batt, Nov./Dec., 1974-Mar./Apr., 1975; Sharon Batt, June/July, 1975-1980. Subject focus: law, fiction, poetry. Other holding institutions: CaOONL (NLC), CU-UC (UCU), CtY (YUS), OU (OSU), [AMIGOS Union List of Serials, Dallas, TX] (IUC), TxDW (IWU).

| | | |
|---|---|---|
| Mem | v.1,n.1- v.7, n.2; Dec., 1973- 1980 | AP/B815/O94 |
| Hist | v.1, n.1-2; Dec., 1973- June/July, 1974 | Microforms Her. 3, R 1 |

113 <u>Bread & Roses</u>. 1977-1980//. Quarterly. ISSN 0197-5927. Last issue 46 pages, size 28 x 22. Line drawings, photographs, commercial advertising. Editor: Annabel Kendall. Subject focus: rights, literature, law, interviews, feminism.

| | | |
|---|---|---|
| Hist | v.1,n.1-v.2,n.3; Sep., 1977- Autumn, 1980 | Circulation |
| Coll | v.1,n.1-v.2,n.3; Sep., 1977- Autumn, 1980 | Women's Reading Area |
| Wom St | v.1,n.1-v.2,n.3; Sep., 1977- Autumn, 1980 | Reading Room |
| MPL | v.1,n.1-v.2,n.3; Sep., 1977- Autumn, 1980 | Literature and Social Science Section |

114 <u>Bread and Roses Newsletter</u>. 1970-1971//? Irregular. OCLC 2258576. Last issue 8 pages. Line drawings. Available on microfilm: Herstory. Published by Bread and Roses, Cambridge/Boston, MA. Subject focus: gay liberation, collectives, Black Panthers, peace movement.

| | | |
|---|---|---|
| Hist | Oct., 1970 | Microforms Her. 1, R 13 |
| | Apr., 1970- Jan., 1971 | Her. 1, Add. |

115 <u>Bread and Roses Newsletter</u>. 1971?// Semi-monthly. Last issue 6 pages. Line drawings. Available on microfilm: Herstory. Published by Women's Liberation, Glebe, Australia. Subject focus: employment, feminism, rights.

| | | |
|---|---|---|
| Hist | n.4-5; Sep./Oct.- Nov./Dec., 1971 | Microforms Her. 2, R 2 |

116 <u>Breakthrough</u>. 1970. Irregular. Breakthrough, 926 J Street, Room 1506, Sacramento, CA. Last issue 12 pages, size 22 x 28. Photographs. Published by the National Association of Commissions for Women, Sacramento, CA. Place of publication varies: New York, NY, Mar., 1971-May, 1972; Washington, DC, Dec., 1972-Apr., 1977. Subject focus: rights, employment, commissions on women.

| | | |
|---|---|---|
| Wom Ed Res | Mar., 1971- | Circulation |

117 <u>Breakthrough</u>. 1969-1974//? Irregular. Last issue 4 pages. Line drawings, photographs. Available on microfilm: Herstory. Published by the Interstate Association of Commissions on the Status of Women, New York, NY. Editor: Dr. Emily Taylor. Subject focus: rights, lobbying, commissions on women.

| | | |
|---|---|---|
| Hist | v.3, n.1-4; Mar., 1972- May, 1973 | Microforms Her. 2, R 2 |
| | v.4, n.1-6; Sep., 1973- Apr., 1974 | Her. 2 UP, R1 |

118 <u>Breff</u>. 1976. Irregular. Breff, Department of French and Italian, University of Wisconsin-Madison, Madison, WI 53706. Last issue 10 pages, size 22 x 28. Subject focus: research, women's studies. In French (95%).

| | | |
|---|---|---|
| Wom St | n.1- May, 1976- | Reading Room |

119 <u>Bride's</u>. 1933? Bi-monthly. $8 for individuals and institutions. Barbara D. Tober, editor, Bride's, 350 Madison Avenue, New York, NY 10017. Business address: P.O. Box 5200, Boulder CO 80323. ISSN 0161-1992, 0006-9795. OCLC 3877103, 1537069. LC sc78-848. Last issue 278 pages, size 22 x 29. Line drawings, photographs, some in color, commercial advertising. Available on microfilm: McP (1973-), UnM (1934-). Published by The Condé Nast Publications, Inc. Subject focus: interior decoration, beauty care, weddings, fashion, travel. Other holding institutions: GA (GAP), [University of Minnesota Union List, Minneapolis, MN] (MUL), [Western New York Library Resources Council, Buffalo, NY] (VZX), NSyU (SYB), [Central New York Library Resources Council, Syracuse, NY] (SRR), OkT (TUL), PIm (IMM), [Pittsburgh Regional Library Center-Union List, Pittsburgh, PA] (QPR), TxBelM (MHB), [AMIGOS Union List of Serials, Dallas, TX] (IUC), TxLT (ILU), WA (WIQ).

| | | |
|---|---|---|
| MPL | v.45, n.1- Feb./Mar., 1978- | Literature and Social Sciences Section |
| SAPH | Current Issues Only | Circulation |
| MCL | v.42, n.1- Feb./Mar., 1975- | Circulation |
| OPL | Current Issues Only | Circulation |
| DHS | Current Issues Only | Circulation |

| | | |
|---|---|---|
| BML | Current Issues Only | Circulation |

The Bridge. Boston, MA

see Speakout News Views. Boston, MA

120 Briefs. Footnotes on Maternity Care. 1937. 10 times a year. $4 for individuals and institutions. Martin Kelly, editor, Briefs. Footnotes on Maternity Care, 6900 Grove Road, Thorofare, NJ 08086. Business address: Maternity Center Association, 48 East 92nd Street, New York, NY 10028. OCLC 1537080. Last issue 16 pages, last volume 162 pages. Line drawings, photographs, commercial advertising. Published by Charles B. Slack, Inc., Thorofare, NJ. Previous editor: Horace H. Hughes, Jan., 1968-Feb., 1972. Subject focus: pediatrics, pregnancy, health. Other holding institutions: AAP (AAA), AzFU (AZN), AzTeS (AZS), CChiS (CCH), CU-UC (UCU), ICL (IAL), ICSX (ICS), [Indiana Union List of Serials, Indianapolis, IN] (ILS), KPT (KFP), KU (KKU), KyRE (KEU), KyU (KUK), MBU (BOS), MH (HUL), MWMU (WQM), [University of Minnesota Union List, Minneapolis, MN] (MUL), NbKS (KRS), NhMSA (SAC), NCorniCC (ZDG), NGcA (VJA), NNR (ZXC), [Central New York Library Resources Council, Syracuse, NY] (SRR), NUtSU (YTM), OAkU (AKR), OC1W-H (CHS), OCU-M (MXC), ODaWU (WSU), OkTOR (OKO), OrU-M (OHS), PCW (UWC), PPiAC (AIC), PPiCa (CRC), PPiD (DUQ), [Pittsburgh Regional Library Center-Union List, Pittsburgh, PA] (QPR), PPiU (PIT), PPJ (TVJ), ScU (SUC), TCollsM (TMS), [AMIGOS Union List of Serials, Dallas, TX] (IUC), TxDW (IWU), TxLT (ILU), TxNacS (TXK), TxU (IXA), ViNO (VOD).

| | | |
|---|---|---|
| MGN | v.32, n.1-<br>Jan., 1968- | Circulation |
| MHL | v.33, n.1-<br>Jan., 1969- | Circulation |

121 The Bright Medusa. 1976-1977// Quarterly. OCLC 4139314. Last issue 44 pages, size 16 x 22. Line drawings. Published by the Bright Medusa Press, Berkeley, CA. Editor: Nancy Stockwell. Subject focus: art, poetry, fiction. Other holding institutions: [University of Minnesota Union List of Serials, Minneapolis, MN] (MUL).

| | | |
|---|---|---|
| RBR | v.1, n.1-2;<br>Fall, 1976-<br>Spring, 1977 | Circulation |

122 Bristol Women's Liberation Group Newsletter. 1971-1972//? Irregular. OCLC 2258590. Last issue 6 pages. Line drawings. Available on microfilm: Herstory. Published by the Bristol Women's Liberation Group, Bristol, England. Subject focus: pro-abortion, gay liberation, birth control.

| | | |
|---|---|---|
| Hist | Mar?, June?,<br>Aug?, 1971 | Microforms<br>Her.1, R 13 |
| | Sep., 1971 | Her. 1, Add. |
| | Oct., Dec.,<br>1971/Jan., 1972 | Her. 1 UP, R1 |

123 Broadsheet. 1972-1974//? Irregular. Last issue 12 pages. Line drawings, photographs, commercial advertising. Available on microfilm: Herstory. Published by the Auckland Women's Liberation, Auckland 3, New Zealand. Subject focus: rights, employment, interviews, health, child care, pro-abortion, lobbying.

| | | |
|---|---|---|
| Hist | n.1-10;<br>July, 1972-<br>June, 1973 | Microforms<br>Her. 2, R 2 |
| | n.11-19;<br>July, 1973-<br>May, 1974 | Her. 2 UP, R1 |

124 Broadside. 1973//? Unknown. Last issue 16 pages. Line drawings, photographs, commercial advertising. Available on microfilm: Herstory. Published by Broadside, Berkeley, CA. Subject focus: midwifery, interviews, child care, Equal Rights Amendment, prisoners.

| | | |
|---|---|---|
| Hist | v.1, n.1;<br>Feb. 16, 1973 | Microforms<br>Her. 2, R 2 |

125 Broadside. 1970-1971//? Monthly. OCLC 2636877. Last issue 10 pages. Line drawings, photographs. Available on microfilm: Herstory. Published by the American Broadside Corporation, New York, NY. Editor: Holly Mouer. Subject focus: employment, rights. Other holding institutions: MCR-S (Schlesinger Library on the History of Women in America, Radcliffe College, Cambridge, MA), NFQC (XQM), NSbSU (YSM), OKentU (KSU), WMUW (GZN).

| | | |
|---|---|---|
| Hist | v.1, n.1-4;<br>Oct., 1970-<br>Jan., 1971 | Microforms<br>Her. 1, R 1 |

126 The Broadside. 1970-1971//? Irregular. OCLC 2258632. Last issue 16 pages. Line drawings. Available on microfilm: Herstory. Published by the Houston Chapter, National Organization for Women, Houston, TX. Editors: Helen Cassidy and Laura Douglas. Subject focus: child care, pro-abortion, birth control, sexism, lobbying, feminism.

| | | |
|---|---|---|
| Hist | Sep., 1970? | Microforms<br>Her. 1, Add. |

## Women's Periodicals and Newspapers

        v.2, n.4-7;      Her. 1, R 18
        Apr.-Sep., 1971

127  Bronx-N.O.W. Newsletter. 1972//? Monthly. Last issue 7 pages. Line drawings. Available on microfilm: Herstory. Published by the Bronx Chapter, National Organization for Women, Bronx, NY. Subject focus: lobbying, feminism.

    Hist     v.1, n.1-2;     Microforms
             Aug.-Sep., 1972   Her. 2, R 9

128  Brooklyn N.O.W. News. 1971-1974//? Monthly. OCLC 2264702. Last issue 14 pages. Line drawings. Available on microfilm: Herstory. Published by the Brooklyn Chapter, National Organization for Women, Brooklyn, NY. Title varies: as Newsletter, Aug.-Oct., 1971. Subject focus: welfare, education, health, employment, child care, sexism, feminism.

    Hist     Aug.-Sep., 1971   Microforms
                             Her. 1, R 1

            Oct?, 1971        Her. 1 UP, R 8

            Nov?, 1971        Her. 1, Add.

            v.3, n.1-v.4, n.6;  Her. CUP, R 3
            Aug., 1973-
            June, 1974

129  Broomstick. 1978. Monthly. $7.50 for individuals, $15 for institutions. Broomstick, 3543 18th Street, San Francisco, CA 94110. (415) 431-6944. Last issue 24 pages, size 22 x 28. Line drawings. Published by the Options for Women Over Forty, San Francisco, CA. Subject focus: seniors, poetry, middle age.

    Hist     Dec., 1978-      Circulation

130  Buffalo N.O.W. Newsletter. 1970-1971//? Monthly. OCLC 2265295. Last issue 4 pages. Line drawings. Available on microfilm: Herstory. Published by the Buffalo Chapter, National Organization for Women, Buffalo, NY. Subject focus: pro-abortion, education, child care, employment, feminism.

    Hist     v.1, n.3, v.2,   Microforms
            n.2-5;              Her. 1, R 17
            Sep. 1, Nov. 1,
            1970-Apr., 1971

            v.3, n.1;         Her. 1, Add.
            Sep., 1971

131  Build! 1965-1967//? Irregular. Last issue 10 pages, last volume 18 pages, size 22 x 28. Line drawings. Published by the National Federation of Republican Women, Washington, DC. Subject focus: lobbying, Republican party.

    Hist     v.1, n.19-v.3,   Pam 2263
            n.43;
            Mar., 1965-
            May, 1967

Bulletin.  San Francisco, CA

    see San Francisco Branch Women's International League for Peace & Freedom. San Francisco, CA

132  Bulletin. 1909-1913//? Irregular. Last issue 4 pages, size 15 x 23. Line drawings. Published by the Illinois Association Opposed to the Extension of Suffrage to Women, Chicago, IL. Subject focus: anti-suffrage, marriage, family.

    Hist     n.1-20;         KWZ/+I29
            Sep., 1909-      (Cutter)
            Nov., 1913

133  Bulletin. 1923-1924//? Monthly. Last issue 1 page, size 36 x 22. Published by the Department Headquarters of the American Legion Auxiliary, Edwardsville, IL. Subject focus: clubs.

    Hist     n.3-4;          F836/8A5IA/
            Dec. 4, 1923-   ILL.(Cutter)
            Jan. 4, 1924

134  Bulletin. 1923-1926//? Irregular. Last issue 2 pages, size 22 x 36. Published by the American Legion Auxiliary of North Dakota, Fargo, ND. Subject focus: clubs.

    Hist     n.39/40, 85-127;  F836A/8A51A/
            Jan. 19, 1924,    N.D.(Cutter)
            July 30, 1925-
            May 26, 1926

135  Bulletin. 1923-?//. Unknown. Last issue 2 pages, size 22 x 37. Published by the American Legion Auxiliary Department of Utah, Kaysville, UT. Subject focus: clubs.

    Hist     n.1/2;           F836/8A51A/
            Nov. 19, 1923    UTAH(Cutter)

136  Bulletin. 1939-1955//. Monthly. Last issue 3 pages. Line drawings. Available on microfilm: WHi (1939-1955). Published by the New York Women's Trade Union, New York, NY. Title varies: as League Bulletin, Dec., 1939-May, 1950. Subject focus: labor unions.

    Hist     Dec., 1939-      Microforms
            Feb., 1955

137 The Bulletin. 1928-1934?//. Monthly. Last issue 24 pages, last volume 132 pages, size 18 x 25. Line drawings, photographs, commercial advertising. Published by the American Women's Club of Paris, Inc., Paris, France. Editor: L.E. Frederickson. Subject focus: poetry, history, interviews, clubs, fiction.

    Mem    [v.2, n.5-v.8, n.4];    AP/A5194/O97
              [Mar., 1929-Jan., 1934]

Bulletin. Rawlins, WY

    see News Bulletin. Rawlins, WY

138 Bulletin. 1969//? Unknown. OCLC 2269630. Last issue 2 pages. Line drawings, photographs. Available on microfilm: Herstory. Published by the Women's International League for Peace and Freedom, Seattle Branch, Seattle, WA. Editor: Alice Franklin Bryant. Subject focus: peace movement.

    Hist    Oct., 1969    Microforms
                            Her. 1, R 22

139 Bulletin. 1923-?//. Irregular. Last issue 1 page, size 22 x 28. Published by the American Legion Auxiliary, Topeka, KS. Subject focus: clubs.

    Hist    [n.1-15];    F836/8A51A/KANS
              [Jan. 13, 1923-  (Cutter)
              Mar. 15, 1924]

140 Bulletin Abolitionniste. 1902-1928?//. Monthly. OCLC 1772830. LC 10-4494. Last issue 40 pages, last volume 440 pages. Line drawings. Available on microfilm: ResP. Published by Fédération Abolitionniste Internationale, Geneva, Switzerland. Subject focus: prostitution, alcoholism. In French (100%). Other holding institutions: [University of Minnesota Union List, Minneapolis, MN] (MUL), TxDW (IWU).

    Mem    v.1, n.1-n.247;    Microforms
              Jan., 1902-
              Nov./Dec., 1928

141 Le Bulletin Continental. 1875-1901. Monthly. Last issue 8 pages, last volume 104 pages. Available on microfilm: ResP. Published by Fédération Britannique, Continentale, et Generale, Geneva, Switzerland. Subject focus: prostitution. In French (100%). Other holding institutions: NN (NYP).

    Mem    v.1, n.1-v.26, n.12;    Microforms
              Dec. 15, 1875-
              Dec., 1901

Bulletin of the Inter-Municipal Committee for Household Research. New York, NY

    see Bulletin of the Inter-Municipal Research Committee. New York, NY

142 Bulletin of the Inter-Municipal Research Committee. 1904-1906//? Monthly. Last issue 12 pages, last volume 144 pages. Available on microfilm: ResP. Published by Inter-Municipal Research Committee. Title varies: as Bulletin of the Inter-Municipal Committee Household Research, Nov., 1904-Oct., 1905. Subject focus: homemakers. Other holding institutions: MCR-S (Schlesinger Library on the History of Women in America, Radcliffe College, Cambridge, MA).

    Mem    v.1, n.1-v.2, n.8;    Microforms
              Nov., 1904-May, 1906

Bulletin of the International Council of Social Democratic Women. London, England

    see ICSDW Bulletin. London, England

143 Bulletin. International Council of Women. (English Edition). 1923?-?//. Monthly. Last issue 8 pages, size 23 x 31. Published by the International Council of Women, Paris, France. Editor: Gertrud M. Gunther. Subject focus: international relations, disarmament.

    Hist    v.10, n.5;    KW/+8IN
            Jan., 1932    (Cutter)

144 Bulletin, Milwaukee Section. NCJW. 1943-1978//? Irregular. OCLC 4731618. Last issue 6 pages. Line drawings, photographs, commercial advertising. Available on microfilm: WHi (1943-1978). Published by the National Council of Jewish Women, Milwaukee WI. Title varies: as Milwaukee Section Bulletin, National Council of Jewish Women, Feb., 1943-Dec., 1966; as National Council of Jewish Women, Milwaukee Section Bulletin, Feb., 1967-Jan., 1972; as National Council of Jewish Women Bulletin, Milwaukee Section, Feb., 1972-June, 1976. Editors:Mrs. Robert Hindin, Dec., 1946; Mrs. Mel Marshall, Oct., 1951-Sep., 1953; Mrs. Harold A. Watkins, Oct., 1953-Apr., 1954; Mrs. William Goodsitt, Oct., 1954-Mar., 1957; Mrs. Robert Fairman, Oct., 1957-May, 1958; Mrs. Ernest Lane, Aug., 1958-Mar., 1960; Mrs. Robert F. Kahn, Sep., 1960-Jan., 1962; Mrs. Harold Albert, Apr.-Sep., 1962; Mrs. John Atkins and Mrs. Maurice Rubinstein,

Oct., 1962-May, 1963; Mrs. Sidney Hack and Mrs. Maurice Rubenstein, Aug., 1963; Mrs. Sidney Hack and Mrs. Robert Mann, Sep., 1963-Mar., 1965; Mrs. Sidney Hack and Mrs. Martin Warshaw, Apr.-Oct., 1965; Mrs. Martin Warshaw and Mrs. Stephen Bailie, Dec., 1965-Aug., 1966; Mrs. Martin Tenenbaum, Oct., 1966-Sep., 1967; Mrs. Victor Matles, Nov., 1967-Mar., 1968; Mrs. Lawrence Bilansky, Sep., 1968-Dec., 1973. Subject focus: Jews, clubs.

| Hist | Feb., Oct., 1943, Apr., Oct., 1944, Mar., 1945, Apr., Dec., 1946, Oct., 1951-Apr., 1978 | Microforms |

Bulletin of the International Socialist Women's Secretariat. London, England

see ICSDW Bulletin. London, England

145 Bulletin of the Pennsylvania League of Women Voters. 1921-?//. Monthly. Last issue 24 pages, size 31 x 23. Line drawings, photographs, commercial advertising. Published by the Pennsylvania League of Women Voters, Philadelphia, PA. Editors: Thomas J. Walker and Harriet L. Hubbs. Subject focus: politicians, politics.

| Hist | v.4, n.4; Apr., 1924 | KWZ/PE. (Cutter) |

146 Bund Deutscher Frauenvereine. 1895-1905//. Irregular. Last issue 42 pages, size 11 x 18. Commercial advertising. Available on microfilm: McA. Published by the Bund Deutscher Frauenvereine, Frankenburg, Saxony. Place of publication varies: Breslau, Germany, 1895; Leipzig, Germany, 1898?, Dresden, Germany, 1904. Subject focus: Germany, family, children, history. In German (100%).

| Mem | n.1-7; 1895, 1898?, 1899, 1900, 1900, 1904, 1905 | Microforms |

147 Business Woman's Magazine. 1914-1915?// Unknown. OCLC 5791266. Last issue 52 pages, last volume 208 pages. Line drawings, photographs, commercial advertising. Available on microfilm: ResP (1914-1915). Published by Mail Order News Corporation, Newburgh, NY. Editor: Helen G. Ruttenber. Subject focus: wages, labor unions, professionals, business. Other holding institutions: NN (NYP), TxDW (IWU).

| Mem | v.1, n.1-v.3, n.4; Oct., 1914-Dec., 1915 | Microforms |

148 Butterick Sewing World. 1978. Quarterly. $5 for individuals and institutions. Butterick Sewing World, 161 6th Avenue, New York, NY 10013. OCLC 6149057. Last issue 72 pages, last volume 288 pages. Line drawings, photographs, some in color. Published by Butterick Fashion Marketing Co., New York, NY. Subject focus: sewing, crafts. Other holding institutions: NBu (VHB).

| DHS | Current Issues Only | Circulation |

149 CAP Alert. 1978. Monthly. $15 for individuals and institutions. CAP Alert, 310 First Street S.E., Washington, DC 20003. Last issue 4 pages size 22 x 28. Published by the National Federation of Republican Women, Comprehensive Advocacy Program, Washington, DC. Subject focus: lobbying, Republican party.

| Hist | v.1, n.1- Oct. 4, 1978- | Circulation |

150 CCWHP Newsletter. 1970. Irregular. $9 for individuals and institutions. CCWHP Newsletter, Mounted Route #8, Box 373, Plattsburgh, NY 12901. OCLC 4310125, 4459888. Last issue 8 pages, size 22 x 28. Line drawings. Available on microfilm: Herstory (1971-1974). Published by the Coordinating Committee on Women in the Historical Profession. Title varies: as Coordinating Committee on Women in the Historical Profession (Current Research on the History of Women), Mar.-Sep., 1971. Place of publication varies: Chicago, IL/Iowa City, IA, Spring, 1970-Sep., 1971; Stanford, CA, Mar., 1972-May, 1973; Woodside, CA, Oct., 1973-Jan., 1977; New York, NY, May, 1977-June, 1978. Subject focus: historians, women's studies, history, research. Other holding institutions: [New York Union List of Serials, Albany, NY] (NYS).

| Hist | v.1, n.1-v.2, n.1; Spring, 1970-Mar., 1971 | Microforms Her. 1, R 14 |
| | v.2, n.2-3; Mar.-Sep., 1971 | Her. 1, Add. |
| | v.2, n.4-v.4, n.2; Mar., 1972-May, 1973 | Her. 1 UP, R2 |

        v.4, n.3-v.5, n.2;   Her. CUP, R 1
        Oct., 1973-
        Apr., 1974

        v.4, n.3-         Circulation
        Oct., 1973-

151   CCWHP Research Bulletin. 1971-1976//. Semi-annual. OCLC 4310125. Last issue 17 pages, size 22 x 28. Available on microfilm: WHi (1971-1976). Published by the Coordinating Committee on Women in the Historical Profession, New Albany, IN. Title varies: as Coordinating Committee on Women in the Historical Profession, Sep., 1971-Mar., 1974. Subject focus: research, women's studies, history.

    Hist     n.1-10;        Microforms
               Sep., 1971-
               Mar., 1976

CDS Newsletter. Northridge, CA

   see ACDS Newsletter. Northridge, CA

152   CFM Report. 1971?-1973//? Irregular. Last issue 4 pages, last volume 58 pages. Line drawings, photographs. Available on microfilm: Herstory. Published by the Comisión Femenil Mexicana, Los Angeles, CA. Title varies: as Comisión Femenil Mexicana Report, ?-Mar., 1972. Subject focus: Hispanics, child care, rights, sex education, pro-abortion, women's centers, politics, Chicanas.

    Hist     v.1, n.1-v.2, n.3;   Microforms
               1971?-May, 1973    Her. 2, R 3

153   CGHW Newsletter. 1975. Quarterly. $9 for individuals and institutions. Nupur Chaudhuri, editor, CGHW Newsletter, Mounted Route #8, Box 373, Plattsburgh, NY 12901. Last issue 22 pages, last volume 108 pages, size 14 x 22. Published by the Conference Group in Women's History, Plattsburgh, NY. Title varies: as Conference Group in Women's History Newsletter, Dec., 1975-May, 1979. Previous editors: Marlene Stein Wortman, Dec., 1975; Marlene Stein Wortman, Nupur Chaudhuri and Peter Tyor, May, 1976-June, 1977. Subject focus: research, history.

    Hist     v.1, n.1-      Circulation
               Dec., 1975-

154   CHOICE-Concern for Health Options, Information, Care, and Education. 1974-?//. Monthly. Last issue 8 pages. Line drawings. Available on microfilm: Herstory. Published by CHOICE, Philadelphia, PA. Subject focus: health, lobbying, pro-abortion, education, family planning, community health planning.

    Hist     v.1, n.1-2;      Microforms
               May-June, 1974

155   CLUW News. 1975. Quarterly. $5 for individuals, $10 for institutions. CLUW News, 15 Union Square, New York, NY 10003. (212) 677-5764. Last issue 6 pages, last volume 22 pages, size 22 x 28. Line drawings, photographs. Published by the Coalition of Labor Union Women, New York, NY. Place of publication varies: Detroit, MI, Winter, 1975-Spring, 1977. Subject focus: labor unions, workers, occupational health and safety.

    Hist     v.1, n.1-       Circulation
               Winter, 1975-

    Wom Ed  v.1, n.2, v.2, n.1- Circulation
    Res      Summer, 1975,
               Winter, 1976-

A CORPAS Communication. Honolulu, HI

   see Human Equality. Honolulu, HI

156   CPGA Women's Caucus Newsletter. 1974-?//. Monthly. Last issue 4 pages. Line drawings. Available on microfilm: Herstory. Published by the California Personnel Guidance Association Women's Caucus/Affiliated Association of California Personnel Guidance Association, Fullerton, CA. Editor: Viviann P. Prescott Subject focus: self-help, vocational guidance, counselors.

    Hist     v.1, n.3-4;      Microforms
               Apr.-May, 1974   Her. 3, R 1

157   CSAC News. 1973-1974?//. Irregular. OCLC 2908963. Last issue 2 pages. Line drawings. Available on microfilm: Herstory. Published by the Chicana Service Action Center, Los Angeles, CA. Editor: Vera Carreon. Subject focus: counseling, education, employment, Hispanics, Chicanas.

    Hist     n.5-6, 11-12;    Microforms
               Oct.-Nov., 1973,   Her. 3, R 1
               Apr.-May/June,
               1974

158   CSW News. 1972-1974. Weekly. Last issue 2 pages. Line drawings. Available on microfilm: Herstory. Published by the Pennsylvania Commission on the Status of Women, (Office of the Governor), Harrisburg, PA. Editor: Ann Gropp. Subject focus: education, rights, lobbying, commissions on women.

    Hist     Apr. 20, 1972-   Microforms
               June 20, 1973    Her. 2, R 3

*Women's Periodicals and Newspapers*

        July 10, 1973-    Her. 2 UP, R 2
        June 10, 1974

159  The CSW Report. 1972-1974//? Monthly. Last issue 2 pages. Line drawings. Available on microfilm: Herstory. Published by the Pennsylvania Commission on the Status of Women, Harrisburg, PA. Frequency varies: weekly, Sep. 18, 1972-Aug. 13, 1973. Editor: Ann Gropp. Subject focus: lobbying, politics, commissions on women offenders, sexism.

    Hist      Sep. 18, 1972-    Microforms
                June 25, 1973     Her. 2, R 3

                v.2, n.1-v.3, n.2;  Her. 2 UP, R 2
                July 2, 1973-
                June, 1974

160  CWIC Clearinghouse on Women's Issues in Congress. 1974-1980//? Irregular. Last issue 24 pages, last volume 228 pages, size 22 x 28. Published by Karen Colaianni Johnson, Silver Spring, MD. Title varies: as Congressional Clearinghouse on Women's Rights, Jan. 11, 1977-June 11, 1979. Previous editors: Carol Forbs, Jan. 11,-Aug. 8, 1977; Linda Lipsen, Aug. 15, 1977-Aug. 14, 1978; Karen Colaianni Johnson, Aug.22, 1978-Mar., 1980. Subject focus: lobbying.

    Hist      v.3, n.1-v.6,     Circulation
                n.3?;
                Jan. 11, 1977-
                Mar., 1980

161  CWLU News. 1970-1971//. Unknown. Last issue 10 pages, size 22 x 28. Line drawings. Published by Chicago Women's Liberation Union, Chicago, IL. Subject focus: rights, poetry.

    Hist      Mar. 22, Oct.,    Pam 74-3288
                1970, July, 1971

162  CWSS Newsletter. 1971-1974//? Irregular. OCLC 2260056, 3949955, 3102111. Last issue 6 pages. Line drawings. Available on microfilm: Herstory. Published by the Center for Women's Studies and Services, San Diego, CA. Subject focus: prison reform, welfare. Other holding institutions: [New York State Union List of Serials, Albany, NY] (NYS).

    Hist      v.1, n.1-4;       Microforms
                Apr.-Sep., 1971   Her. 1, R 14

                v.1, n.5-19;     Her. 1 UP, R 2
                Oct., 1971-
                June, 1973

                July, 1973-      Her. CUP, R 1
                June/July, 1974

163  Calafia Clarion. 1973//? Irregular. Last issue 2 pages. Line drawings, commercial advertising. Available on microfilm: Herstory. Published by Nancy Breitinger, Santa Monica, CA. Title varies: as Calafia Faire News, Aug. 8, 1973.

    Hist      n.1-2;           Microforms
                Aug. 8-Oct. 27,   Her. 3, R 1
                1973

Calafia Faire News.  Santa Monica, CA

    see Calafia Clarion.  Santa Monica, CA

164  Calgary Women's Newspaper. 1975. Monthly. $5 for individuals and institutions. Calgary Women's Newspaper, c/o YMCA, 320 Fifth Avenue S.E., Calgary, Alberta, Canada, T2G 0E5.(403) 262-1873. ISSN 0702-9241. OCLC 3436755. LC cn77-33384. Last issue 12 pages, size 43 x 29. Line drawings, photographs, commercial advertising. Published by the Calgary Status of Women Action Committee, Calgary, Alberta, Canada. Subject focus: rights, politics, workers, health. Other holding institutions: CaCONL (NLC).

    Hist      v.3, n.9-        Circulation
                Oct., 1977-

165  California Apparel News. 1945. Weekly. $25 for individuals and institutions. Richard Leivenberg, editor, California Apparel News, 945 S. Wall Street, Los Angeles, CA 90015. (213) 626-0411. Business addresses: 110 W. 40th Street, Suite 1404, New York, NY 10018, (212) 221-8288; 139 Arcade, 350 North Orleans, Chicago, IL 60654. (312) 670-2230; 250 Spring Street N.W. Atlanta, GA 30303. ISSN 0008-0896. OCLC 3981423. Line drawings, photographs, some in color, commercial advertising. Published by California Fashion Publications, Inc., Los Angeles, CA. Subject focus: fashion, clothes, garment industry, fabrics. Other holding institutions: NjLincB (BCC), ScU (SUC), [AMIGOS Union List of Serials, Dallas, TX] (IUC), TxDN (INT).

    MATC      Current Issues    Cora Hardy
                Only               Library

166  California Division-American Association of University Women. 1970-1972//? Irregular. Last issue 4 pages. Line drawings, photographs. Available on microfilm: Herstory. Published by the California Division of the American Association of University Women, San Jose, CA. Editor: Mrs. Irene Lovewell. Subject focus: education, professionals, employment, career development.

    Hist      v.3, n.2-3;     Microforms
                Jan.-Mar., 1972   Her. 2, R 2

167 California N.O.W. 1973-1974//? Irregular. Last issue 3 pages. Line drawings. Available on microfilm: Herstory. Published by the San Diego Chapter, National Organization for Women, San Diego, CA. Subject focus: education, poor people, feminism.

Hist     Aug. 8, 1973-     Microforms
         May 5, 1974      Her. 2 UP, R 6

168 California N.O.W.-Educational Task Force. 1973-1974//? Unknown. Last issue 3 pages. Line drawings. Available on microfilm: Herstory. Published by the National Organization for Women, California Educational Task Force, La Mesa, CA. Editor: Sheila Moramarce. Subject focus: education, feminism, lobbying.

Hist     v.1, n.4;     Microforms
         Jan., 1974     Her. 3, R 3

169 The California N.O.W. Newsletter. 1973//? Irregular. Last issue 2 pages. Line drawings. Available on microfilm: Herstory. Published by the Statewide National Organization for Women, Los Angeles, CA. Subject focus: education, children's literature, lobbying, feminism.

Hist     n.1-2;     Microforms
         Mar. 3-     Her. 2, R 9
         May 1, 1973

170 California Service Worker. 1973//? Unknown. Last issue 3 pages. Line drawings, photographs. Available on microfilm: Herstory. Published by the Western Service Workers Association, Sacramento, CA. Subject focus: wages, welfare, workers, employment.

Hist     v.1, n.6;     Microforms
         Dec. 28, 1973    Her. 3, R 1

171 California Women. 1977? Irregular. California Women, 926 J. Street, Room 1506, Sacramento, CA, 95814. (916) 445-3173. ISSN 0193-7618. OCLC 3622816. LC sc79-3441. Last issue 16 pages, size 22 x 28. Photographs. Published by the California Commission on the Status of Women, Sacramento, CA. Subject focus: rights, pro-abortion, affirmative action, workers, commissions on women. Other holding institutions: IDeKN (JNA), [New York State Union List of Serials, Albany, NY] (NYS), TxL (IXA).

Wom Ed Res     Feb., 1977-     Circulation

Call to Action.     Jacksonville, FL

     see WM-Jacksonville Women's Movement. Jacksonville, FL

172 Call to Women. 1965-1970//? Monthly. OCLC 2258891. Last issue 8 pages. Line drawings. Available on microfilm: Herstory. Published by the Liaison Committee for Women's Peace Groups, Chingford, England. Subject focus: politics, peace movement, child welfare.

Hist     n.41;     Microforms
         May, 1966     Her. 1, Add.

         n.42, 82-83;     Her. 1, R 13
         June, 1966,
         Feb.-Mar., 1970

173 Calyx. 1976. Tri-annual. $10 for individuals and institutions. Barbara Baldwin, Margarita Donnelly and Meredith Jenkins, editors, Calyx, Route 2, Box B, Corvallis, OR 97330. ISSN 0147-1627. OCLC 3114927. LC 77-649570. Last issue 64 pages, last volume 184 pages, size 18 x 20. Line drawings, photographs. Subject focus: poetry, fiction, art. Other holding institutions: COFS (COF), DLC (DLC), FU (FUG), [New York State Union List of Serials, Albany, NY] (NYS), NIC (COO), WaU (WAU).

RBR     v.1, n.1-     Circulation
        June, 1976-

174 Camera Obscura. A Journal of Feminism and Film Theory. 1976. Tri-annual. $9 for individuals, $18 for institutions. Camera Obscura, Box 4517, Berkeley, CA 94704. OCLC 4818143. LC sc79-4979. Last issue 152 pages, size 14 x 22. Line drawings, photographs. Indexed in: Abstract of Popular Culture, Film Literature Index. Subject focus: films, feminism, interviews. Other holding institutions: CSt (Stanford University), GEU (EMU), InIU (IUP), MH (HLS,HUL), NBrockU (XBM), NNU(EMU).

Wom St     n.1-     Reading
         Fall, 1976-    Area

175 Campus N.O.W. News. 1969//? Unknown. OCLC 2265293. Last issue 2 pages. Available on microfilm: Herstory. Published by the Clark Campus Chapter, National Organization for Women, Worcester, MA. Editor: Debbie Vollmer. Subject focus: college students, education, feminism.

Hist     Apr. 24, 1969     Microforms
                             Her. 1, R 17

176 Canadian Newsletter of Research on Women/Recherches sur la Femme-Bulletin d'Information Canadien. 1972. Tri-annual. Margrit Eichler, Patricia Carter, Marylee Stephenson and Jennifer L. Newton, editors, Canadian Newsletter of Research on Women, Department of Sociology, Ontario Institute for Studies in Education, 252 Bloor Street West, Toronto,

Ontario, Canada, M5S 1V6. ISSN 0319-4477. OCLC 1941051, 3382041. LC cn76-319628. Last issue 165 pages, last volume 461 pages, size 22 x 28. Line drawings. Indexed: self-indexed, (1972-1977). Available on microfilm: Herstory (1972-1974). Place of publication varies: Waterloo, Ontario, Canada, May, 1972-May, 1974. Previous editors: Margrit Eichler, Marylee Stephenson, and Patricia Carter, Feb.-Oct., 1976. Subject focus: women's studies, research, education. Other holding institutions: AzTeS (AZS), CaOONL (NLC), CArcHT (CHU), CChiS (CCH), CSt (Stanford University), CLU (CLU), CSdS (CDS), CtY (YUS), CU-UC (UCU), HU (HUH), IaScB (IOB), InLP (IPL), IU (UIU), KMK (KKS), MBU (BOS), [University of Minnesota Union List of Serials, Minneapolis, MN] (MUL), MnStpeG (MNG), MnU (MNU), MoU (MUU), MWelC (WEL), [New York State Union List of Serials, Albany, NY] (NYS), NGcA (VJA), NIC (COO), NRU (RRR), PPiU (PIT).

| Hist | v.1, n.1-2, v.2, n.1-2; May-Oct., 1972, Feb.-May, 1973 | Microforms Her. 2, R 2 |
|---|---|---|
| | v.2, n.3-v.3, n.2; Oct., 1973-May, 1974 | Her. 2 UP, R 1 |
| Wom St | v.5, n.1-v.6, n.3; Feb., 1976-Oct., 1977 | Reading Room |
| Mem | v.1, n.1-v.6, n.3; May, 1972-Oct., 1977 | AP/C212/N48 |
| Wom Ed Res | v.1, n.2, v.2, n.2-3; Oct., 1972, May-Oct., 1976 | Circulation |

177   Cape Cod Women's Liberation Newsletter. 1972-1973//? Irregular. Last issue 28 pages. Line drawings. Available on microfilm: Herstory. Published by the Cape Cod Women's Liberation, East Sandwich, MA. Subject focus: politics, poetry, education, media, art, health, feminism.

| Hist | v.1, n.1-3, v.2, n.2; June-Oct. 14, 1972, June?, 1973 | Microforms Her. 2, R 2 |
|---|---|---|
| | v.2, n.3; Aug., 1973 | Her. 2 UP, R 1 |

178   Capitol Alert. 1971-1974//? Irregular. OCLC 2258987. Last issue 6 pages, last volume 84 pages. Line drawings. Available on microfilm: Herstory. Published by Legislative Committee, Sacramento Chapter, National Organization for Women, Sacramento, CA. Editor: Cathy MacMillan. Title varies: as N.O.W. Capitol Alert, Feb. 19-Dec. 20, 1971. Subject focus: Equal Rights Amendment, lobbying, politics, pro-abortion, feminism, rights.

| Hist | v.1, n.1-12; Feb. 19-Sep. 1, 1971 | Microforms Her. 1, R 19 |
|---|---|---|
| | v.1, n.14-v.3, n.8; Oct. 11, 1971-June 19, 1973 | Her. 1 UP, R 2 |
| | v.3, n.9-v.4, n.4; July, 1973-May, 1974 | Her. CUP, R 1 |
| | v.1, n.10; July 9, 1971 | Pam 74-3313 |

179   Capitol: Woman. 1973-1974//? Irregular. Last issue 2 pages. Line drawings, photographs. Available on microfilm: Herstory. Published by the House Committee on Constitutional Revision and Women's Rights, Lansing, MI. Subject focus: research, rights, law.

| Hist | v.1, n.2-3?; May 15-June, 1973 | Microforms Her. 2, R 2 |
|---|---|---|
| | v.1, n.4-v.2, n.2; July, 1973-June, 1974 | Her. 2 UP, R2 |

180   Carousel. 1968-1969?// Irregular. Last issue 24 pages. Line drawings, photographs, commercial advertising. Published by Carousel Inc., New York, NY. Editors: Lucy Ames, Fred Ames, and Frederic A. Birmingham. Subject focus: family, fashion, beauty care, celebrities, homemakers.

| Hist | v.1, n.1, v.2, n.1; Dec. 22, 1968, ?, 1969? | Pam 79-1944 |
|---|---|---|

181   Carry On. 1922. Quarterly. $6 for individuals and institutions. Gladys V. Bull, editor, Carry On, 306 E. Simmons Street, Galesburg, IL 61401. Business address, 3000 Farnam Street, Omaha, NB 68131. OCLC 2255627. LC 28-8269. Last issue 24 pages, last volume 120 pages, size 23 x 15. Photographs. Published by the Women's Overseas Service League, Galesburg, IL. Place of publication varies: Boston, MA, Jan.-May, 1922; Indianapolis, IN, May, 1923-Nov., 1930. Previous editors: Mrs. L.W. Fleming, Jan.-May, 1922; A. Grace Hawks, May, 1923-Aug., 1930; Ruth M. McClelland, Nov., 1930-Augs., 1939; Mrs. George T. Moore, Nov., 1939-Oct., 1942; Miss Mildred Eakes, Apr., Aug., 1943-Aug., 1945; A. Grace Hawks, Nov., 1945-Feb., 1953. Subject focus: soldier services. Other holding institutions: [Indiana Union List of

*Women's Periodicals and Newspapers*

Serials, Indianapolis, IN] (ILS), [University of Minnesota Union List of Serials, Minneapolis, MN] (MUL), OC1 (CLE).

| Hist | v.1, n.1-2, v.2, n.2,4, v.3, n.1-3; v.4, n.1- Jan.-May, 1922, May, Nov., 1923, Feb.-Aug., 1924, Feb., 1925- | D/570/A15/W65 (Cutter) |
|---|---|---|

182  Cassandra. 1967-1968//? Unknown. OCLC 2259022. Last issue 8 pages. Line drawings. Available on microfilm: Herstory. Published by the Women's Coordinating Committee, Pittsburgh, PA. Subject focus: peace movement, fascism, politics.

| Hist | v.1-2; Nov.-Dec., 1967/ Jan., 1968 | Microforms Her. 1, R 14 |
|---|---|---|

183  Catalyst. 1970-1971//? Irregular. OCLC 2259031. Last issue 3 pages. Line drawings. Available on microfilm: Herstory. Published by the Women's International League for Peace and Freedom, Fresno Branch-W.I.L.P.F., Fresno, CA. Subject focus: peace movement, ecology.

| Hist | v.1, n.1-2? Feb., 1970- Mar., 1971 | Microforms Her. 1, R 22 |
|---|---|---|

Catholic Junior Leagues of Wisconsin. Fond du Lac, WI

see The Mantle. Eau Claire, WI

184  Caucus for Women in Statistics. 1972-1974//? Irregular. Last issue 10 pages. Line drawings. Available on microfilm: Herstory. Published by the Caucus for Women in Statistics, Philadelphia, PA. Subject focus: career development, statisticians, Equal Rights Amendment.

| Hist | v.1, n.1-4? Jan.-June, 1972, Jan.-Mar., 1973 | Microforms Her. 2, R 2 |
|---|---|---|
|  | v.2, n.4, v.3,n.1, v.4, n.1-3; July, Oct., 1973, Feb.-Apr., 1974 | Her. 2 UP, R2 |

185  Caucus of Women in History Newsletter. 1971-1974//? Irregular. OCLC 2259050. Last issue 6 pages. Available on microfilm: Herstory. Published by the Caucus of Women in History of the Southern Historical Association, Chapel Hill, NC. Place of publication varies: Atlanta, GA, Apr., 1971. Subject focus: history, historians.

| Hist | v.1, n.1; Apr., 1971 | Microforms Her. 1, R14 |
|---|---|---|
|  | v.1, n.2-v.3, n.1; Nov. 8, 1971- May, 1973 | Her. 1 UP,R2 |
|  | v.3, n.2-v.4, n.2; Oct., 1973- May, 1974 | Her. CUP,R1 |

186  Ce Que Nous Les Femmes, Nous Pensons. 1971//? Last issue 20 pages. Available on microfilm: Herstory. Published by Ce Que Nous Les Femmes Nous Pensons, Brussels, Belgium. Subject focus: health. In French (100%).

| Hist | ?, 1971 | Microforms Her. 2, R 2 |
|---|---|---|

187  Center for Continuing Education of Women Newsletter. 1970-1978//? Irregular. Last issue 12 pages, size 22 x 28. Line drawings, photographs. Published by the University of Michigan, Ann Arbor, MI. Editor: Dorothy McGuigan. Subject focus: research, continuing education.

| Wom St | Fall, 1972, Summer, 1974, Spring, 1975- Summer, 1977, Summer, 1978 | Circulation |
|---|---|---|

188  Central Connecticut N.O.W. Newsletter. 1971-1974//? Irregular. Last issue 3 pages. Available on microfilm: Herstory. Published by the Central Connecticut Chapter, National Organization for Women, West Hartford, CT. Editors: D. Gibbs, Aug.-Dec., 1973; Ann Havriluk, Jan.-May, 1974. Subject focus: pro-abortion, rights, feminism.

| Hist | Nov., 1971- June, 1973 | Microforms Her. 1 UP,R8 |
|---|---|---|
|  | July, 1973- May, 1974 | Her. CUP,R 3 |

The Century Club Advance. Dayton, OH

see Woman's Welfare. Dayton, OH

189  Challenge. 1972. Monthly. $7.50 for individuals and institutions. Challenge, 310 First Street, S.E., Washington, DC 20003. (202) 484-6670. Last issue 8 pages, size 22 x 28. Line drawings, some in color, photographs. Published by the National Federation of Republican Women, Washington, DC. Title varies: as Winning Spirit, Jan., 1976-Dec., 1977. Subject focus: Republican Party.

| | | |
|---|---|---|
| Hist | v.1, n.1-<br>Feb., 1972- | Circulation |

A Change is Going to Come.   San Francisco, CA

   see Change; a Working Woman's Newspaper.   San Francisco, CA

190  Change; A Working Woman's Newspaper. 1970-1973//? Irregular. OCLC 2259156. Last issue 8 pages, size 30 x 44. Line drawings, photographs. Available on microfilm: Herstory. Published by Waller Press, San Francisco, CA. Title varies: as A Change is Going to Come, Jan.-Oct., 1971. Subject focus: radical feminism, employment, rights.

| | | |
|---|---|---|
| Hist | v.1, n.6-7. v.2, n.1, 3-7, v.3, n.2; July/Aug.-Sep./Oct., 1971, Feb./Mar., May-Oct./Nov., 1972, Apr./May, 1973 | Pam 72-1283 |
| | v.1, n.1-7; Jan.-Sep./Oct., 1971 | Microforms Her. 1, R 1 |
| | v.1, n.8-v.3, n.2; Nov., 1971-Apr./May, 1973 | Her. 1 UP, R2 |

191  The Changing Woman. 1971-1974//? Irregular. Last issue 8 pages. Line drawings, photographs, commercial advertising. Available on microfilm: Herstory. Published by the Women's Editorial Collective/The Changing Woman, Inc., Portland, OR. Subject focus: poetry, pro-abortion, satire, politics, food, health, child care.

| | | |
|---|---|---|
| Hist | v.1, n.1-v.2, n.5/6; Oct. 15, 1971-Apr. 20, 1973 | Microforms Her. 2, R 2-3 |
| | v.2, n.7-16; Sep. 7, 1973-June 8, 1974 | Her. 2 UP, R 2 |

Channel "C" N.O.W. Newsletter.   Cleveland, OH

   see Women Unite N.O.W.   Cleveland, OH

192  The Channel. 1950? 10 times a year. Mrs. Ronnie Millard, editor, The Channel, 13313 East 53rd Street, Kansas City, MO 64133. Last issue 8 pages, last volume 64 pages, size 22 x 28. Line drawings, photographs. Published by the National Women's Army Corps, Veterans Association, Kansas City, MO. Place of publication varies: Coral Gables, FL, Feb.-Dec, 1972/Jan., 1973; Sun City, AZ, Sep., 1974-July/Aug., 1976; Cleveland, OH, Sep., 1976-July/Aug., 1978. Previous editors: Marie Gallager, Feb.-Dec., 1972/Jan., 1973; Mrs. Ronnie Millard, Feb., 1973-July/Aug., 1974; Jean J. Merritt, Sep., 1974-July/Aug., 1976; Veronica Mazurech, Sep., 1976-July/Aug., 1978. Subject focus: veterans, WACs.

| | | |
|---|---|---|
| Hist | v.23, n.1-<br>Feb., 1972- | Circulation |

Chapter News.   Clifton, NJ

   see N.O.W. News.   Passaic, NJ

193  Chapter News-Essex County. 1971-1973//? Monthly. Last issue 10 pages. Line drawings. Available on microfilm: Herstory. Published by the Essex County Chapter, National Organization for Women, Maplewood, NJ. Title varies: as Essex County Chapter Newsletter, Nov., 1971-Apr., 1972. Place of publication varies: South Orange, NJ, Nov., 1971-June, 1973. Subject focus: feminism, education, Equal Rights Amendment.

| | | |
|---|---|---|
| Hist | Nov., 1971-<br>June, 1973 | Microforms Her. 2, R 10 |

194  China's Women/Chung-hua fu nü. 1950-1976//? Monthly. ISSN 0529-5688. OCLC 1554573. LC cgr64-916. Last issue 32 pages, last volume 384 pages, size 19 x 26. Line drawings, photographs, some in color. Published by the Chinese Women's Anti-Agression League, Taipei, Taiwan, China. Subject focus: rights, family, child rearing, health, fiction. In Chinese (100%). Other holding institutions: [University of Minnesota Union List of Serials, Minneapolis, MN] (MUL), [New York State Union List of Serials, Albany, NY] (NYS), NIC (COO).

| | | |
|---|---|---|
| Mem | v.21, n.2-v.26, n.12; Feb., 1970-Dec., 1975 | AP/C5589/<br>H8736 |

195  The Chisholm Trail. 1972//? Unknown. Last issue 3 pages. Line drawings, commercial advertising. Available on microfilm: Herstory. Published by the Research Committee of the San Francisco Regional Headquarters, Shirley Chisholm for President Campaign Committee, San Francisco, CA. Subject focus: politics, Shirley Chisholm.

| | | |
|---|---|---|
| Hist | v.1, n.2;<br>Mar. 25, 1972 | Microforms Her. 2, R 3 |

196 Chomo-Uri. 1974-1979//. Tri-annual. Last issue 76 pages, last volume 220 pages. Line drawings, photographs. Indexed: Index of Periodical Verse (1974-1979). Published by Chomo-Uri, Amherst, MA. Subject focus: poetry, fiction, art.

| RBR | v.1, n.1-v.4, n.1; Spring, 1974- Summer, 1979 | Circulation |

197 Christian Lady's Magazine. 1834-1848//. Semi-annual. Last issue 576 pages, last volume 576 pages. Line drawings. Each volume self-indexed. Available on microfilm: ResP. Published by R.B. Seeley and W. Burnside, London, England. Editor: Charlotte Elizabeth. Subject focus: etiquette, poetry, biographies, Christianity. Other holding institution: NN (NYP).

| Mem | v.1-19; Jan., 1834- June, 1848 | Microforms |

198 Chrysalis. 1976-1980//. Quarterly. ISSN 0197-1867, 0197-1859. OCLC 3128311. LC 79-643087. Last issue 128 pages, last volume 494 pages, size 20 x 28. Line drawings, photographs. Published by Chrysalis, Los Angeles, CA. Editor: Kirsten Grimstad, 1977-Apr., 1980. Subject focus: feminism, law, literature, health, sports, poetry. Other holding institutions: AzTeS (AZS), CArcHT (CHU), CSt (Stanford University), CChiS (CCH), CLobS (CLO), CLU (CLU), CtY (YUS), DLC (DLC), FJK (FJS), FTS (FHM), ICharE (IAD), IU (UIU), KMK (KKS), KyU (KUK), MBE (ECL), MH (HLS), MH (HUL), MiMtpT (EZC), MnDuU (MND), MNS (SNN), MnU (MNU), [University of Minnesota Union List of Serials, Minneapolis, MN] (MUL), [New York Union List, Albany, NY] (NYS), [Central New York Library Resources Council, Syracuse, NY] (SRR), NA1U (NAM), NBu (VHB), NcCU (NKM), NbU (LDL), NcU (NOC), NdU (UND), NFOC (XQM), NGcA (VJA), NGenoU (YGM), NhD (DRB), NIC (COO), NII (XIM), NmU (IQU), NPurU (ZPM), NSbSU (YSM), NSyU (SYB), OCU (CIN), PPiU (PIT), PPT (TEU), PSt (UPM), [AMIGOS Union List of Serials, Dallas, TX] (IUC), TxCM (TXA), TxU (IXA), TxShA (IAU), ViNO (VOD), ViU (VA@), WMUW (GZN).

| Wom St | v.1, n.4-10; ?, 1977-Apr., 1980 | Reading Room |
| Mem | v.1, n.1-10; ?, 1976-Apr., 1980 | AP/C558/LA |
| MPL | n.1, 3, 5-10; ?, 1976-Apr., 1980 | Literature and Social Sciences Section |

199 Chung Kuo Fu Nü. 1979. Monthly. Chung Kuo Fu Nü, 50 Teng Shih Kuo, Peking, People's Republic of China. OCLC 4329111. LC c64-234. Last issue 48 pages, size 19 x 26. Line drawings, photographs, some in color. Subject focus: politics, health, medicine, marriage, family, nutrition, fiction, rights, education, child care. In Chinese (100%).

| Mem | n.2- Feb., 1979- | AP/C5594/K95 |

200 Church Women's United Newsletter. 1973. Mary Jane Esser, editor, Church Women's United Newsletter, Church Women United in Madison, Inc., 3910 Mineral Point Road, Madison, WI 53705. Last issue 4 pages, size 35 x 22. Line drawings. Subject focus: ecumenism, Church of Christ, UNICEF.

| MPL | Oct., 1973- | Literature and Social Sciences Section |

201 Church Women United, State News. 1960-1973?// 10 times a year. Last issue 4 pages, last volume 40 pages. Line drawings, photographs. Available on microfilm: Herstory. Published by Church Women United of Southern California-Southern Nevada, Whittier, CA. Title varies: as The State Church Woman, Jan., 1965; as The State U.C.W. News, Feb., 1965-Dec., 1967; as State Church Women United News, Jan. 1, 1968-May 1, 1969. Place of publication varies: San Diego, CA, Jan., 1965; Riverside, CA, Feb., 1965-Feb., 1969. Editors: Mrs. Gene D. Shapley, Jan., 1965; Mrs. Edgar R. Dyer, Feb., 1965-Feb., 1969; Mrs. Clarence Spanks, Mar., 1969-Nov., 1973. Subject focus: Church of Christ, health, self-help.

| Hist | v.22, n.1-v.31, n.6; Jan., 1965- June, 1973 | Microforms Her. 2, R 3 |
| | v.31, n.7-9; Sep.-Nov., 1973 | Her. 2 UP,R2 |

202 Church Work. 1885-1889?//. Monthly. OCLC 1554680. Last issue 32 pages, last volume 364 pages. Available on microfilm: ResP. Published by Church Work Association, New York, NY. Editor: Mrs. A.T. Twing. Subject focus: church workers. Other holding institutions: MBTI (BTI), [University of Minnesota Union List, Minneapolis, MN] (MUL), NNC (Columbia University), OCl (CLE), TxDW (IWU).

| Mem | v.1, n.1-v.4, n.12; Nov., 1885- Oct., 1889 | Microforms |

*Women's Periodicals and Newspapers*

Cincinnati Chapter Newsletter. Cincinnati, OH

    see N.O.W. News. Cincinnati, OH

203 The Circle. 1973-1974//? Monthly. Last issue 30 pages. Line drawings, commercial advertising. Available on microfilm: Herstory. Published by the Sister for Homophile Equality (S.H.E.), Wellington, New Zealand. Subject focus: poetry, lesbians, gay rights.

| Hist | Dec., 1973- June, 1974 | Microforms Her. 3, R 1 |

204 La Citoyenne. 1881-1890//? Monthly. Last issue 4 pages. Line drawings, commercial advertising. Published by La Citoyenne, Paris, France. Frequency varies: weekly, Feb. 13, 1881-July, 1889. Editors: Hubertine Auclert, Feb. 13, 1881-May, 1888; Maria Martin, June, 1888-Dec., 1890. Subject focus: pro-suffrage, rights. In French (100%).

| Mem | n.1-165; Feb. 13, 1881- Dec., 1890 | Microforms |

205 City Wide Women's Liberation Newsletter. 1968-1969//? Irregular. OCLC 5121888. Last issue 2 pages. Line drawings. Available on microfilm: Herstory. Published by the City Wide Women's Liberation, New York, NY. Title varies: as The Newsletter, Apr., 1968-May ?, 1969. Subject focus: pro-abortion, theatre, pornography, health, day care.

| Hist | May 14, 1969 | Microforms Her. 1, R 17 |
| | Apr., 1968, May, Nov., 1969 | Her. 1, Add. |

206 The Clarion. 1970-1972//. Irregular. Last issue 18 pages, size 22 x 28. Line drawings, photographs. Published by the California Institution for Women, Frontera, CA. Editor: Pat Sabella. Subject focus: prisoners, art, law, poetry.

| Crim Just | Mar., 1970- Jan./Feb., 1972 | Circulation |

207 Claudia. 1965. Monthly. OCLC 6924717. Last issue 122 pages, last volume 1368 pages, size 23 x 31. Line drawings, photographs, some in color, commercial advertising. Published by Editorial Mex Ameris S.A., Mexico City, Mexico. Editors: Mely Perales, Beatriz Marti, and Bona Campillo. Subject focus: art, fiction, cooking, fashion, biographies. In Spanish (100%). Other holding institutions: [AMIGOS Union List of Serials, Dallas, TX] (IUC).

| WHS | [v.10, n.113- v.13, n.168] [Feb., 1975- Sep., 1979] | Foreign Language RMC |

208 Clearinghouse for Feminist Media. 1972-1974//? Irregular. ISSN 0319-6925. OCLC 2443341. LC cn76-30856. Last issue 10 pages. Line drawings. Available on microfilm: Herstory. Published by the Clearinghouse for Feminist Media, Ancaster, Ontario, Canada. Editor: Lorna Marsden. Subject focus: literature, media. Other holding institutions: CaCONL (NLC).

| Hist | v.1, n.1-3, v.2, n.1; Jan. 20, 1972?- Apr., 1972, Feb., 1973 | Microforms Her. 2, R 3 |
| | v.2, n.2-3; Oct., 1973- June, 1974 | Her. 2 UP, R2 |

209 Clearinghouse International Newsletter. 1976-1977//. Monthly. OCLC 2307641. Last issue 6 pages, size 22 x 28. Published by Women's Forum Clearinghouse International of the Eleanor Association, Chicago, IL. Editor: Dorothy L. Madsen. Subject focus: career development, rights, employment, wages, vocational guidance. Other holding institutions: [University of Minnesota Union List, Minneapolis, MN] (MUL).

| Wom Ed Res | v.2, n.17, 19; June, Aug., 1977 | Circulation |

210 The Cleveland Feminist. 1973-1974//? Monthly. Last issue 42 pages. Line drawings, photographs, commercial advertising. Available on microfilm: Herstory. Published by Infinity Publishing Company, Cleveland, OH. Subject focus: politics, divorce, marriage, Equal Rights Amendment, lobbying, feminism.

| Hist | v.1, n.1-5; Aug., 1973- Jan., 1974 | Microforms Her. 3, R 1 |

The Clubwoman GFWC. Washington, DC

    see General Federation Clubwoman. Washington, DC

211 The Club Woman. 1897-1904//? Monthly. ISSN 0016-6537. OCLC 1554967. Last issue 64 pages. Line drawings, commercial advertising. Available on microfilm: GrP (1897-1904). Published by the General Federation of

Women's Clubs, The National Congress of Mothers, and the United States Daughters of 1812, New York, NY. Place of publication varies: Boston, MA, Oct., 1897-June/July, 1903. Editors: Helen M. Winslow, Oct., 1897-May, 1903; Dore Lyon, Sep., 1903-Oct., 1904. Subject focus: clubs, fiction, poetry. Other holding institutions: CSt (Stanford University), CPT (CIT), CtY (YUS), InU (IUL), MdFreH (HCF), MeB (BBH), [University of Minnesota Union List, Minneapolis, MN] (MUL), MNS (SNN), NmLcU (IRU), OC1W (CWR), OCU (CIN), [Pittsburgh Regional Library Center-Union List, Pittsburgh, PA] (QPR), PPi (CPL), ViU (VA@).

| | | |
|---|---|---|
| Hist | [v.1, n.1-v.12, n.12] [Oct., 1897- Oct., 1904] | Microforms |

212 <u>Coaching: Women's Athletics</u>. 1975. 5 times a year. $14.95 for individuals and institutions. Patsy Neal, editor, Coaching: Women's Athletics, P.O. Box 867, Wallingford, CN 06492. ISSN 0145-9562, 0145-9570, 0160-2624. OCLC 2254702, 2843108, 2957304. LC 77-640350, 77-640352, 78-640691. Last issue 82 pages, last volume 418 pages, size 20 x 28. Line drawings, photographs, some in color, commercial advertising. Indexed: Education Index (1975-). Published by Intercommunications, Inc., Wallingford, CN. Previous editors: William J. Burgess, Jan./Feb., 1977-Mar./Apr., 1979. Subject focus: sports, coaching. Other holding institutions: ArCCA (AKC), ArStC (ASU), ArU (AFU), AzTeS (AZS), CStbW (CWS), DeU (DLM), DLC (DLC), FBoU (FGM), FU (FUG), GU (GUA), HY (HUH), IaCfT (NIU), IaDL (IOH), IaWavU (IOW), ICharE (IAD), InU (IUL), IU (UIU), KWS (KKX), KyRE (KEU), MiAC (EZA), MiAdC (EEA), [Michigan Library Consortium, Detroit, MI] (TQE,TQF), MiEM (EEM), MiHolH (EXH), MiMtpT (EZC), [University of Minnesota Union List, Minneapolis, MN] (MUL), MnManS (MNM), MNQ (MNQ), MnStjos (MNF), MnStpeG (MNG), MnU (MNU), MoSMa (MVC), MoSW (WTU), MoU (MUU), MWelC (WEL), MWP (WPG), NbKS (KRS), NCH (YHM), NCortU (YCM), NEE (VXE), [Central New York Library Resources Council, Syracuse, NY] (SRR), NGenoU (YGM), NII (XIM), NjParB (BER), NOneoU (ZBM), NOsU (YOM), OKentU (KSU), OTU (TOL), [Pepperdine University, Malibu, CA] (CPE), [Pittsburgh Regional Library Center-Union List, Pittsburgh, PA] (QPR), PPiU (PIT), [AMIGOS Union List of Serials, Dallas TX] (IUC), TNJ (TJC), TxDN (INT), TxShA (IAU), TxDW (WU), ViBlbv (VPI), ViU (VA@), WaU (WAU).

| | | |
|---|---|---|
| IMC | v.3, n.3- Jan./Feb., 1977- | Periodicals Section |

213 <u>Coalition Newsletter</u>. 1970-1971//? Monthly. OCLC 2259493. Last issue 16 pages. Line drawings, photographs. Available on microfilm: Herstory. Published by the Women's Liberation Coalition of Michigan, Detroit, MI. Subject focus: pro-abortion, day care, politics, employment, poetry, lobbying, workers.

| | | |
|---|---|---|
| Hist | v.1, n.1, 6- v.2, n.9; Feb., Aug., 1970- Sep., 1971 | Microforms Her. 1, R 22 |
| | Oct., 1971? | Her. 1 UP, R18 |

214 <u>Co-ed</u>. 1956. 10 times a year. $3.25 for individuals and institutions. Kathy Goglick, editor, Co-ed, 50 West 44th Street, New York, NY 10036. ISSN 0009-9724. OCLC 1554970. LC 57-34506. Last issue 64 pages, last volume 702 pages, size 21 x 27. Line drawings, photographs, some in color, commercial advertising. Available on microfilm: UnM (1969-); McP (1974-). Published by the Home Economics Division of Scholastic Magazines, Inc., New York, NY. Subject focus: fashion, health, beauty care, interior decoration, fiction. Other holding institutions: ABAU (ABC), ArU (AFU), AzFU (AZN), CChiS (CCH), CLobS (CLO), CtS (FEM), FBoU (FGM), FMFIU (FXG), FTaSU (FDA), GA (GAP), IPB (IBA), [Indiana Union List of Serials, Indianapolis, IN] (ILS), KLindB IKFB), KSteC (KKQ), LLcM (LHA), MiAdC (EEA), MiDW (EYW), [University of Minnesota Union List, Minneapolis, MN] (MUL), NcEUcE (NPE), NcGU (NGU), NbKS (KRS), NbU (LDL), NmLcU (IRU), NmLvH (NMH), [New York State Union List, Albany, NY] (NYS), NFQC (XQM), NIC (COO), NOneoU (ZBM), NR (YQR), OAkU (AKR), OAU (OUN), OBgU (BGU), OC1U (CSU), OCo (OCO), OKentU (KSU), O (OHI), OTU (TOL), OU (OSU), OY (YMM), OYU (YNG), PPD (DXU), PPi (CPL), [Pittsburgh Regional Library Center-Union List, Pittsburgh, PA] (OPR), ScU (SUC), TCollsM (TMS), TxAu (TXG), TxBelM (MHB), TxDW (IWU), [AMIGOS Union List of Serials, Dallas, TX] (IUC), TxLT (ILU), TxNacS (TXK), ViBlbv (VPI), ViPetS (VSC), WA (WIQ), WFon (WIF), [Arrowhead Library System, Janesville Public Library, Janesville, WI] (WIJ), WMenU (GZS), WMUW (GZN).

| | | |
|---|---|---|
| IMC | v.22, n.1- Sep., 1976- | Periodicals Section |
| Agric | Current Issues Only | Periodicals Section |
| MPL | Current Issues Only | Literature and Social Sciences Section |
| WHS | v.20, n.1- Jan., 1974- | Circulation |
| MFHS | v.20, n.1- Jan., 1974- | Circulation |

| | | |
|---|---|---|
| MMHS | v.20, n.1-<br>Jan., 1974- | Circulation |
| DFPL | v.21, n.1-<br>Jan., 1975- | Circulation |
| R&L | v.19, n.9-v.24,<br>n.6;<br>Oct., 1973-<br>June, 1978; | Circulation |

215 A Cold Day in August. 1972-1974//? Irregular. OCLC 2307415. Last issue 26 pages. Line drawings, commercial advertising. Available on microfilm: Herstory. Published by the Baltimore Women's Liberation, Baltimore, MD. Subject focus: politics, poetry, law, media, pro-abortion, self-help, feminism.

| | | |
|---|---|---|
| Hist | n.1-9;<br>Mar., 1972-<br>June, 1973 | Microforms<br>Her. 2, R 3 |
| | n.10-18;<br>July, 1973-<br>June, 1974 | Her. 2 UP, R 2 |

216 Collective for Woman. 1972-1974//? Irregular. Last issue 10 pages. Line drawings. Available on microfilm: Herstory. Published by the Collective for Woman, Dunedin, New Zealand. Subject focus: pro-abortion, politics, rights, child care, education.

| | | |
|---|---|---|
| Hist | n.1-28;<br>Mar. 5, 1972-<br>June 30, 1973 | Microforms<br>Her. 2, R 3 |
| | n.29-45;<br>July 13, 1973-<br>June 1, 1974 | Her. 2 UP, R 2 |

217 College Park: Women's Studies Newsletter. 1974//? Monthly. Last issue 4 pages. Line drawings. Available on microfilm: Herstory. Published by Women's Studies-University of Maryland, College Park, MD. Editor: Susan Cardinale. Subject focus: research, professionals, women's studies.

| | | |
|---|---|---|
| Hist | v.1, n.1-2;<br>Jan.-Feb., 1974 | Microforms<br>Her. 3, R 1 |

College Settlements Association Quarterly.
New York, NY

   see Intercollegiate Community Service Quarterly. New York, NY

218 The Colonial Courier. 1956. Tri-annual. $2 for individuals and institutions. Mrs. Ray Emerson Slocum, editor, The Colonial Courier, 2205 Massachusetts Avenue, N.W., Washington, DC 20008. ISSN 0010-1435. OCLC 5274151. Last issue 52 pages, last volume 124 pages, size 15 x 22. Photographs. Published by the National Society Daughters of American Colonists, Washington, DC. Place of publication varies: Wellsboro, PA, Feb., 1956-Feb., 1965; Barre, VT, May, 1965-Aug., 1968. Frequency varies: quarterly, Feb., 1956-Feb., 1971. Previous editors: Mrs. William C. Langston, Feb., 1956-Feb., 1961; Mary C. Cameron, May, 1961-Aug., 1964; Ethel Duke Barrows, Aug., 1965-Feb., 1968; Mrs. J.M.H. Fitzgerald, May, 1968-Feb., 1971; Leonore M. Mills, Winter-Fall, 1978. Subject focus: history, genealogy, clubs. Other holding institutions: [Central New York Library Resources Council, Syracuse, NY] (SRR), RhI (RHI), WyU (WYU).

| | | |
|---|---|---|
| Hist | v.1, n.1-v.15,<br>n.4, v.22, n.3-<br>Feb., 1956-<br>Feb., 1971,<br>Winter, 1978- | E/186.99/D3/<br>C6 |

219 The Coming Nation. 1907-1914//? Monthly. OCLC 3930151, 2716186. Last issue 8 pages, last volume 78 pages, size 22 x 28. Line drawings, photographs, commercial advertising. Available on microfilm: WHi (1907-1913); GrP (1907-1914). Published by Socialist Woman Publishing Company, Chicago, IL. Title varies: as The Socialist Woman, June, 1907-Feb., 1909; as The Progressive Woman, Mar., 1909-Oct., 1913. Place of publication varies: Girard, KS, Aug., 1908-Apr., 1911. Editors: Josephine Conger-Kancko, June, 1907-June/July, 1913; Josephine Conger-Kancko and Barnet Braverman, Aug.-Sep., 1913; Barnet Braverman, Nov., 1913-July, 1914. Subject focus: pro-suffrage, socialist feminism. Other holding institutions: CSt (Stanford University), CCU (CIN), CtY (YUS), InU (IUL), [University of Minnesota Union List, Minneapolis, MN] (MUL), MdFreH (HCF), MeB (BBH), MNS (SNN), PPiU (PIT).

| | | |
|---|---|---|
| Hist | v.1, n.1-<br>[n.s.] v.1, n.8;<br>June, 1907-<br>July, 1914 | HWS/"7C733<br>(Cutter) |

220 Coming Out. 1972//? Unknown. Last issue 14 pages. Line drawings, photographs. Available on microfilm: Herstory. Published by Coming Out, Oberlin, OH. Subject focus: sexism, racism, sexuality, pro-abortion, workers.

| | | |
|---|---|---|
| Hist | v.1, n.1;<br>Dec., 1972 | Microforms<br>Her. 2, R 3 |

Comisión Femenil Mexicana Report. Los Angeles, CA

   see CFM Report. Los Angeles, CA

221 Comment on Research/Action About Wo/men. 1969-1978//. Tri-annual. Last issue 8 pages, size 29 x 44. Line drawings, photographs. Published by the Office of Women in Higher Education, Washington, DC. Place of publication varies: Cambridge, MA, Spring, 1974. Frequency varies: quarterly, Spring, 1974-Fall, 1976. Subject focus: rights, research.

| Wom Ed Res | v.8, n.3, v.9, n.4, v.10, n.3; Spring, 1974, Fall, 1976, Mar., 1978 | Circulation |

222 Commission on the Status of Women-District of Columbia. 1974//? Irregular. Last issue 4 pages. Line drawings. Available on microfilm: Herstory. Published by the Commission on the Status of Women, Washington, DC. Editor: Mrs. Mary Dublin Keyserling. Subject focus: education, housing, offenders, commissions on women, law.

| Hist | Feb. 19, Mar. 11, May, 1974 | Microforms Her. 3, R 1 |

223 Commission on the Status of Women Newsletter. 1973-1974//? Monthly. Last issue 4 pages. Line drawings, photographs. Available on microfilm: Herstory. Published by the Commission on the Status of Women, Sacramento, CA. Editor: Pamela Faust. Subject focus: rights, commissions on women, law, Equal Rights Amendment.

| Hist | July, 1973- May, 1974 | Microforms Her. 3, R 1 |

The Common Cause. Manchester, England

   see The Woman's Leader. Manchester, England

224 Common Ground. 1976. Irregular. $5 for individuals, $10 for institutions. Kim Gehrke, editor, Common Ground, 2211 E. Kenwood Blvd., Milwaukee, WI 53211. (414) 964-6117. OCLC 5381855. Last issue 12 pages, size 22 x 28. Line drawings. Published by the Women's Coalition, Inc., Milwaukee, WI. Subject focus: rights, politics, battered women. Other holding institutions: WMUW (GZN).

| Hist | Jan./Feb., 1978- | Circulation |

225 Common Sense. 1972-1974//? Monthly. Last issue 10 pages. Line drawings, photographs. Available on microfilm: Herstory. Published by the Women's Advisory Group to the Bonneville Power Administration, Portland, OR. Frequency varies: irregular, May 12, 1972- Apr?, 1973. Editors: Anne Gibson and Camilla Downing, May 12, 1972-June, 1973; Ruth Aldridge and Maxine Replogle, July, 1973-June, 1974. Subject focus: employment, career development.

| Hist | v.1, n.1-v.2, n.5; May 12, 1972- June, 1973 | Microforms Her. 2, R 3 |
| | July, 1973- June, 1974 | Her. 2 UP, R2 |

The Common Woman is the Revolution. Berkeley, CA

   see Common Woman. Berkeley, CA

226 Common Woman. 1971//? Irregular. OCLC 5339343. Last issue 12 pages. Line drawings, photographs. Available on microfilm: Herstory. Published by the Common Woman Collective, Berkeley, CA. Title varies: as The Common Woman is the Revolution, Feb. 12-Apr., 1971. Subject focus: rights, radical feminism, peace movement.

| Hist | v.1, n.1-4; Feb. 12-Apr. 14, 1971 | Microforms Her. 1, R 1 |
| | v.1, n.5; Apr. 29, 1971 | Her. 1 UP, R2 |

227 Common Woman. 1977//? Semi-annual. Last issue 40 pages, last volume 84 pages, size 22 x 29. Line drawings, photographs, commercial advertising. Published by the Common Woman Collective, New Brunswick, NJ. Subject focus: poetry, interviews, art.

| RBR | v.1, n.1-2; Spring-Fall, 1977 | Circulation |

228 Communication and Services Newsletter-Women's Task Force Newsletter. 1975? Irregular. $7 for individuals and institutions. Communication and Services Newsletter, 786 E. Seventh Street, St. Paul, MN 55106. Last issue 4 pages, size 22 x 28. Line drawings. Published by the Association of Halfway House Alcoholism Programs of North America, Inc., St. Paul, MN. Subject focus: alcoholism, halfway houses.

| Crim Just | Dec., 1975- | Circulation |

229 Community Women's Centre Newsletter. 1974//? Monthly. Last issue 14 pages. Line drawings, commercial advertising. Available on microfilm: Herstory. Published by the Community Women's Centre, Regina, Saskatchewan,

Canada. Subject focus: health, poetry, self-help, legal services.

    Hist        Jan.-June, 1974        Microforms
                                            Her. 3, R 1

230  Concerns. 1971. Quarterly. $10 for individuals and institutions. Elizabeth Meese, editor, Concerns, University of Alabama, University, Alabama 35486. OCLC 2259670. Last issue 14 pages. Line drawings. Available on microfilm: Herstory. Published by the Women's Caucus for Modern Languages, Modern Language Association, West Lafayette, IN. Place of publication varies: Charleston, IL, Mar. 15-July 15, 1971. Subject focus: employment, linguists, sexism in employment.

    Hist      v.1, n.1-3;        Microforms
              Mar. 15-July 15,    Her. 1, R 16
              1971

            v.1, n.4;         Her. 1 UP, R 6
            Oct./Nov., 1971

            v.2, n.1-2,      Her. CUP, R 7
            v.3, n.1;
            Apr.-Oct., 1972,
            Apr., 1973

231  Conditions. 1977. Semi-annual. $8 for individuals, $15 for institutions. Conditions, P.O. Box 56, Van Brunt Station, Brooklyn, NY. ISSN 0147-8311. OCLC 3232386. LC 77-641895. Last issue 208 pages, size 14 x 22. Line drawings, photographs, commercial advertising. Indexed in: Alternative Press Index (1977-). Subject focus: poetry, fiction, lesbians, songs. Other holding institutions: CGraD (DNU), DLC (DLC), FU (FUG), [University of Minnesota Union List, Minneapolis, MN] (MUL), MSHM (MTH), NALU (NAM), NjMD (DRB), NTRS (ZRS), OO (OBE), OU (OSU), TxU (IXA).

    RBR       n.1-               Circulation
            Spring?, 1977-

    Wom St    n.1-              Reading Room
            Spring?, 1977-

232  Conejo Valley Chapter Newsletter. 1972-1973//? Irregular. Last issue 8 pages. Line drawings. Available on microfilm: Herstory. Published by the Conejo Valley Chapter, National Organization for Women, Thousand Oaks, CA. Title varies: as N.O.W. What?, Sep., 1972. Subject focus: employment, education, politics, Equal Rights Amendment, lobbying, feminism.

    Hist      v.1, n.3-8;        Microforms
            Sep., 1972-       Her. 2, R 10
            June, 1973

Conference Group in Women's History Newsletter. Plattsburgh, NY

    see CGHW Newsletter. Plattsburgh, NY

233  Congress to Unite Women. 1969-1970//? Unknown. OCLC 2259721, 4668901. Last issue 6 pages. Line drawings. Availebel on microfilm: Herstory. Published by the Congress to Unite Women, New York, NY. Subject focus: politics, law, children, child care, education.

    Hist     Nov., 1969,      Microforms
           Nov., 1970       Her. 1, R 14

Congressional Clearinghouse on Women's Rights. Washington, DC

    see CWIC Clearinghouse on Women's Issues in Congress. Washington, DC

234  Congresswoman Bella Abzug Reports. 1971-1972//? Irregular. Last issue 2 pages. Line drawings, photographs. Available on microfilm: Herstory. Published by Bella Abzug Reports, Washington, DC. Subject focus: politics, legislators, politicians, law, feminism.

    Hist     v.1,n.1-v.2,n.1;    Microforms
           June, 1971-
           June, 1972

235  Connecticut N.O.W. Newsletter. 1969//? Irregular. OCLC 2259727. Last issue 4 pages. Line drawings, photographs. Published by Connecticut Chapter, National Organization for Women, Elmwood, CT. Subject focus: sexism, lobbying, feminism.

    Hist     v.1, n.1-2;      Microforms
           June-Nov., 1969  Her. 1, R 17

236  Connecticut Woman. 1973//? Unknown. Last issue 4 pages. Line drawings, photographs. Available on microfilm: Herstory. Published by Connecticut Woman, Bristol, CT. Subject focus: biographies, health.

    Hist     n.3;              Microforms
           Sep., 1973      Her. 3, R 1

237  Connections. 1970-1973//? Irregular. OCLC 2259743. Last issue 4 pages. Line drawings. Available on microfilm: Herstory. Published by Connections Guidance Center, San Francisco, CA. Subject focus: rights, prison reform, prisoners, petry, California Prisoners Union (CPU), child care, welfare. Other holding institutions: [New York State Union List, Albany, NY] (NYS).

| | Hist | v.1, n.1-v.2, n.3; May 26, 1970- Oct. 13, 1971 | Microforms Her. 1, R 14 |
|---|---|---|---|
| | | v.2, n.3-v.3, n.5; Oct. 13, 1971- May, 1973 | Her. 1 UP, R2 |
| | | July, Dec., 1973 | Her. CUP, R 1 |

The Conquest Magazine and the Federation Bulletin. Boston, MA

    see General Federation of Women's Clubs Magazine. Boston, MA

238   Consciousness Up. 1974//? Unknown. Last issue 3 pages. Line drawings. Available on microfilm: Herstory. Published by Consciousness Up, Smithtown, Long Island, NY. Subject focus: consciousness raising.

| | Hist | v.1, n.1; Mar., 1974 | Microforms Her. 3, R 1 |
|---|---|---|---|

239   Continuing Comment. 1972-1974//? Quarterly. Last issue 10 pages. Line drawings, photographs. Available on microfilm: Herstory. Published by the National Coalition for Research on Women's Education and Development, Cambridge, MA. Editor: Jo Hartley, Fall, 1973-Spring, 1974. Subject focus: education, professionals, politics, career development.

| | Hist | v.6, n.3, v.7, n.1-4; Apr./June, Fall, 1972- Summer, 1973 | Microforms Her. 2, R 4 |
|---|---|---|---|
| | | v.8, n.1-3; Fall, 1973- Spring, 1974 | Her. 2 UP, R2 |

240   Continuing Currents. 1970-1973//? Irregular. Last issue 8 pages, last volume 64 pages. Line drawings, photographs. Available on microfilm: Herstory. Published by Continuing Education for Women, University of Hawaii, Honolulu, HI. Title varies: Woman Talk, Feb., 1970. Editor: Penny Pagliaro. Subject focus: child care, media, professionals, continuing education, Equal Rights Amendment.

| | Hist | v.1, n.1-v.4, n.1; Feb., 1970- Jan./Feb., 1973 | Microforms Her. 2, R 4 |
|---|---|---|---|

241   Continuing Education for Women Newsletter. 1974//? Irregular. OCLC 1781973. Last issue 4 pages. Line drawings. Available on microfilm: Herstory. Published by Continuing Education and Extension, University of Minnesota, Minneapolis, MN. Subject focus: continuing education.

| | Hist | v.1, n.4-5; Mar.-May, 1974 | Microforms Her. 3, R 1 |
|---|---|---|---|

242   Continuing Education for Women-Temple University. 1973-1974//? Unknown. Last issue 6 pages. Line drawings. Available on microfilm: Herstory. Published by the Office of Continuing Education for Women, Temple University, Philadelphia, PA. Editors: Lois Casey, Summer, 1973; Vicki Madrid and Carol Morrissy, Summer, 1974. Subject focus: continuing education, students.

| | Hist | v.3, n.4; Summer, 1973 | Microforms Her. 2, R 4 |
|---|---|---|---|
| | | v.4, n.3; Summer, 1974 | Her. 2 UP, R2 |

243   Continuing Education for Women-University of Delaware. 1972-1973//? Quarterly? Last issue 2 pages. Line drawings. Available on microfilm: Herstory. Published by the National University Extension Association, University of Delaware, Newark, DE. Subject focus: continuing education.

| | Hist | n.1-4; June, 1972- Feb., 1973 | Microforms Her. 2, R 4 |
|---|---|---|---|

244   Contra Costa N.O.W. Newsletter. 1972-1974//? Irregular. Last issue 2 pages. Line drawings. Available on microfilm: Herstory. Published by the Contra Costa County/Diablo Valley Chapter, National Organization for Women, Walnut Creek, CA. Subject focus: lobbying, Equal Rights Amendment, feminism.

| | Hist | July, 1972- June/July, 1973 | Microforms Her. 2, R 10 |
|---|---|---|---|
| | | Sep.-Oct., 1973, Jan., 1974 | Her. 2 UP, R6 |

245   Convenience Magazine. 1931//? Monthly. Last issue 48 pages, size 15 x 22. Line drawings, photographs, commercial advertising. Published by Convenience Publications, Chicago, IL. Title varies: Racine Convenience; a Magazine Devoted To Modern Home Progress (cover title). Subject focus: fiction, home economics.

| | Hist | v.7, n.4-5, v.9, n.2-5; ?, 1931? | Pam 68-2536 |
|---|---|---|---|

Coordinating Committee on Women in the Historical Profession (Current Research on the History of Women. Chicago, IL/Iowa City, IA

see CCWHP Newsletter. Woodside, CA

246  Cosmopolitan. 1886. Monthly. $21 for individuals and institutions. Helen Gurley Brown, editor, Cosmopolitan, 224 West 57th Street, New York, NY. ISSN 0010-9541. OCLC 4930714, 1770745. LC sc79-3411, sn78-6225. Last issue 352 pages, last volume 4224 pages, size 20 x 27. Line drawings, photographs, some in color, commercial advertising. Indexed: self-indexed (1886-1915); Readers Guide (1900-); Access Index (1975-). Available on microfilm: McP (1886-1900); UnM (1886-). Published by the Hearst Corporation, New York, NY. Place of publication varies: Rochester, NY, Mar., 1886-Feb., 1887. Previous editors: John Brisben Walker, Jan., 1889-May, 1905; H.P. Burton, Jan., 1932-Mar., 1942; Frances Whiting, Apr., 1942-Jan., 1946; Arthur Gordon, Apr., 1946-Nov., 1948; Herbert R. Mayes, Dec., 1948-Apr., 1951; John O'Connell, May, 1951-Apr., 1959; Robert Atherton, May, 1959-June, 1965. Subject focus: fashion, interior decorating, beauty care, clothes, fiction, food. Other holding institutions: AzFU (AZN), AzU (AZU), CSt (Stanford University), CLU (CLU), CU-UC (UCU), FBoU (FGM), GA (GAP), GAuA (GJG), [Indiana Union List of Serials, Indianapolis, IN] (ILS), InLP (IPL), IPB (IBA), KyRE (KEU), KyU (KUK), MCR-S (Schlesinger Library on the History of Women in America, Radcliffe College, Cambridge, MA), MBE (ECL), MiLC (EEL), [University of Minnesota Union List, Minneapolis, MN] (MUL), MNS (SNN), MsU (MUM), N (NYG), NbKS (KRS), NcRS (NRC), [New York State Union List, Albany, NY] (NYS), [Western New York Library Resources Council, Buffalo, NY] (VZX), [Central New York Library Resources Council, Syracuse, NY] (SRR), NjLincB (BCC), NOneoU (ZBM), NR (YQR), O (OHI), OAU (OUN), OCo (OCO), OkAdE (ECO), OkT (TUS), [Pittsburgh Regional Library Center-Union List, Pittsburgh, PA] (QPR), TMurS (TXM), [AMIGOS Union List of Serials, Dallas, TX] (IUC), TxAu (TXG), TxCM (TXA), TxLT (ILU), ViNO (VOD), [Emory and Henry College, Emory, VA] (VEH), ViRU (VRU), [Arrowhead Library System, Janesville Public Library, Janesville, WI] (WIJ), WMUW (GZN).

| Mem | v.1, n.1-<br>Mar., 1886- | AP/C8346 |
| MPL | v.88, n.8-<br>Aug., 1973 | Literature and Social Sciences Section |
| SPPL | v.89, n.8-<br>Aug., 1974- | Circulation |

| BML | Current Issues Circulation Only |

Coordinating Committee on Women in the Historical Profession. New Albany, IN

see CCWHP Research Bulletin. New Albany, IN

247  Council for Women's Equality Newsletter. 1971//? Irregular. OCLC 2259852. Last issue 8 pages. Line drawings. Available on microfilm: Herstory. Published by the Council for Women's Equality, Portland, OR. Subject focus: education, child care, employment, politics, National Organization for Women.

| Hist | v.1, n.1-4;<br>Jan.-<br>June 25, 1971 | Microforms<br>Her. 1, R 14 |

248  Council News. 1968-1971//. 5 times a year. Last issue 4 pages, last volume 16 pages, size 36 x 28. Photographs. Published by the National Council of Jewish Women, New York, NY. Frequency varies: bi-monthly, Jan.-Sep., 1968. Editors: Naomi Volberg, June, 1968-Feb., 1969; Irma Krents, June, 1969; Dr. Ruth Altman, Oct., 1969-Sep., 1971. Subject focus: Israel, Jews, Judaism, clubs.

| Hist | v.1, n.1-v.4, n.1;<br>Jan., 1968-<br>Sep., 1971 | Pam 71-701 |

The Council Woman. New York, NY

see NCJW Journal. New York, NY

249  Country Women. 1973-1980//. 5 times a year. ISSN 0199-1361. OCLC 3804478, 4172430. LC sn79-19329. Last issue 64 pages, size 21 x 27. Line drawings, photographs. Available on microfilm: Herstory (1973-1974); CtY (1973-1977). Published by Country Women, Albion, CA. Subject focus: rural life, child rearing, consciousness raising, art, employment, homesteading, poetry. Other holding institutions: CLU (CLU), CU-UC (UCU), KMK (KKS), MiEM (EEM), [University of Minnesota Union List, Minneapolis, MN] (MUL), MH (HUL), MnStpeG (MNG), [Central New York Library Resources Council, Syracuse, NY] (SRR), NOneoU (ZBM), OU (OSU), [AMIGOS Union List of Serials, Dallas, TX] (IUC), TxDW (IWU), WMUW (GZN).

| Hist | v.1, n.1-6;<br>?, 1973-? | Microforms<br>Her. 2, R 4 |
|      | n.7-10;<br>July, 1973-<br>Apr., 1974 | Her. 2 UP, R2 |

| | Wom St | n.19-24;<br>Mar., 1976-<br>Apr., 1977 | Reading Room |
|---|---|---|---|
| | Mem | v.1, n.3-25;<br>?, 1973-Sep., 1977 | AP/C8564/W872 |

250   Cowrie. 1973-1974//. Irregular. Last issue 6 pages. Line drawings. Available on microfilm: Herstory. Published by the Community of Women, New York, NY. Title varies: as The Udder Side, Apr., 1973. Subject focus: poetry, lesbians.

| | Hist | v.1, n.1-2;<br>Apr.-June, 1973 | Microforms<br>Her. 2, R4, 16 |
|---|---|---|---|
| | | v.1, n.3-v.2, n.1;<br>Oct., 1973-<br>Apr., 1974 | Her. 2 UP, R 2 |

Coyote.   San Francisco, CA

   see Coyote Howls.   San Francisco, CA

251   Coyote Howls. 1973-1979//. Irregular. Last issue 16 pages, size 44 x 29. Line drawings, photographs, commercial advertising. Available on microfilm: Herstory (1973). Published by Coyote Howls, San Francisco, CA. Title varies: as Coyote, May 1-July ?, 1973. Editor: Margo Saint James. Subject focus: prostitution, rights, lesbians, Equal Rights Amendment.

| | Hist | May 1, 13,<br>July 4, 1973 | Microforms<br>Her. 2, R 4 |
|---|---|---|---|
| | | July ?, 1973 | Her. 2 UP, R 2 |
| | | v.4, n.2, v.5,<br>n.1-2, v.6, n.1;<br>Autumn, 1977,<br>Spring-Fall, 1978,<br>Spring, 1979 | Circulation |

252   Cries from Cassandra. 1973//? Irregular. Last issue 7 pages. Line drawings. Available on microfilm: Herstory. Published by the Amazon-Nation, Chicago, IL. Title varies: as The Amazon-Nation Newsletter, Feb./Mar., 1973. Editor: Betty Peters. Subject focus: lesbians satire, poetry.

| | Hist | v.1, n.2-3;<br>?-Feb./Mar., 1973 | Microforms<br>Her. 2, R 1 |
|---|---|---|---|
| | | [n.s.] v.1, n.1;<br>June, 1973 | Her. 2, R 4 |

253   Cry Out. 1971-1973//? Irregular. Last issue 2 pages. Line drawings. Available on microfilm: Herstory. Published by the Roanoke Valley Women's Coalition, Roanoke, VA. Subject focus: Equal Rights Amendment, rape, employment, poetry.

| | Hist | n.25-31;<br>Aug. 10, 1972-<br>June, 1973 | Microforms<br>Her. 2, R 4 |
|---|---|---|---|
| | | n.32;<br>July 28, 1973 | Her. 2 UP,R2 |

254   Czechoslovak Woman. 1954-?//. Quarterly. ISSN 0011-4677. OCLC 2260067. Last issue 24 pages. Line drawings, photographs. Available on microfilm: Herstory (1970-1971). Published by Czechoslovak Women's Council, Prague, Czechoslovakia. Editor: Božena Holečková. Subject focus: fashion, art, health, employment.

| | Hist | 4 issues<br>1970?-1971? | Microforms<br>Her. 1, R 6 |
|---|---|---|---|

255   D.A.R. News Letter. 1928-?//. Irregular. Last issue 3 pages, size 22 x 28. Published by Betty Allen Chapter, Daughters of the American Revolution, Northampton, MA. Title varies: as News Letter, Sept. 27, 1928. Editor: Elaine G. Eastman. Subject focus: national security, clubs.

| | Hist | n.2-7;<br>Sep. 27, 1928-<br>Apr. 6, 1929 | E.F./+8D24/<br>Mass AL<br>(Cutter) |
|---|---|---|---|

Daily Breakthrough.   Houston, TX

   see Houston Breakthrough.   Houston, TX

256   Daisy. 1975. 9 times a year. $7.50 for individuals. Elisabeth Brower, editor, Daisy, 830 Third Avenue, New York, NY 10022. Business address: P.O. Box 2465, Boulder, CO 80302. ISSN 0162-573X. OCLC 4177894. LC sn78-6330. Last issue 32 pages. Line drawings, photographs, some in color. Published by: Girl Scouts of the U.S.A., New York, NY. Subject focus: Girl Scouts, fiction, crafts, food. Other holding institutions: [University of Minnesota Union List, Minneapolis, MN] (MUL), WA (WIQ), WFon (WIF), [Arrowhead Library System, Janesville Public Library, Janesville, WI] (WIJ).

| | MPL | v.3, n.1-<br>Jan., 1977- | Childrens<br>Room |
|---|---|---|---|

257   Damesweekblad Voor Indie. 1906-1910?//. Weekly. Last issue 16 pages, last volume 432 pages. Line drawings, commercial advertising. Available on microfilm: ResP (1906-1910).

Published by N.V. Soerabayasch Handelsblad en Deukkeryen, Soerabaja, Dutch Indies. Editor: T. terHorst-de Boer. In Dutch (100%). Other holding institutions: NN (NYP).

| Mem | v.1, n.1-v.4, n.27; July 18, 1906- Jan. 13, 1910 | Microforms |

258 Damskii Zhurnal. 1823-1833//. Weekly. Last issue 16 pages, last volume 160 pages. Line drawings. Available on microfilm: IDC. Published in Moscow, U.S.S.R. Editor: Count P.I. Shalikov. Frequency varies: bi-monthly, 1827-1828. Subject focus: fiction, criticism, fashion, humor, poetry. In Russian (100%).

| Mem | v. 17-44; 1827-1833 | Microforms |

Dane County Women's Political Caucus. Madison, WI

see Wisconsin Women's Political Caucus/ Dane County Newsletter. Madison, WI

259 Daughters of America. 1886-1894?//. Monthly. OCLC 5794100. Last issue 16 pages, last volume 192 pages. Line drawings, commercial advertising. Available on microfilm: ResP (1886-1894). Published by True and Company, Augusta, ME. Subject focus: biographies, fiction, fashion, home economics. Other holding institutions: DLC (DLC), TxDW (IWU).

| Mem | v.1, n.1-v.8, n.7; Dec., 1886- July, 1894 | Microforms |

260 Daughters of the American Revolution Magazine. 1892. 10 times a year. $5 for individuals and institutions. Mary Rose Hall, editor, Daughters of the American Revolution Magazine, Administration Building, 1776 D Street, N.W., Washington, DC 20006. ISSN 0011-7013. OCLC 2446314, 4762286, 4770841, 1565978, 1589148, 1780257, 4563445. LC sc79-3260, sn78-1128. Last issue 92 pages, last volume 1196 pages, size 21 x 29. Line drawings, photographs, commercial advertising. Self-indexed; also available from publisher, (1867-). Available on microfilm: UnM (1892-). Published by the Daughters of the American Revolution, Washington, DC. Subject focus: history, genealogy, clubs. Other holding institutions: ArU (AFU), AU (ALM), AzTeS (AZS), CLU (CLU), CtY (YUS), CU-UC (UCU), FF1BL (FBR), FO (ORL), FT (TNH), [Indiana Union List of Serials,Indianapolis, IN] (ILS), InLP (IPL), InU (IUL), KLindB (KFB), KSteC (KKQ), [Frostburg State College Library, Frostburg, MD) (MFS), MBNU (NED), MBU (BOS), MdStm (MDS), Me (MEA), [University of Minnesota Union List, Minneapolis, MN] (MUL), MNS (SNN), MnHi (MHS), MoS (SVP), MsU (MUM), NbKS (KRS), NbU (LDL), NcRS (NRC), [Western New York Library Resources Council, Buffalo, NY] (VZX), [Central New York Library Resources Council, Syracuse, NY] (SRR), NGH (ZEM), NIC (COO), NOneoU (ZBM), NR (YQR), NStC (VYS), O (OHI), OCedC (CDC), OKentU (KSU), OC1W (CWR), OkT (TUL), OLoR (LXP), OY (YMM), PPD (DKU), PEr (FPL), PPi (CPL), PPiAC (AIC), PPiCC (HHC), PPiD (DUQ), PPiU (PIT), [Pittsburgh Regional Library Center-Union List, Pittsburgh, PA] (QPR), Rhi (RHI), ScRhW (SWW), TxAbH (TXS), TxCM (TXA), TxDN (INT), TxDW (IWU), [AMIGOS Union List of Serials, Dallas, TX] (IUC), TxEU (TXU), TxLT (ILU), TxNacS (TXK), TxShA (IAU), TxU (IXA), [Emory & Henry College, Emory, VA] (VEH), [Arrowhead Library System, Janesville Public Library, Janesville, WI] (WIJ, WLacU (GZU), WMUW (GZN).

| Hist | v.1, n.1- July, 1892- | E/202.5/A112 |
| MPL | Current Issues Only | Literature and Social Science Section |

261 Dayton Women's Liberation. 1970-1974//? Monthly. OCLC 2269633. Last issue 10 pages. Line drawings, photographs, commercial advertising. Available on microfilm: Herstory. Published by Dayton Women's Liberation, Dayton, OH. Editor: Sherrie Holmes. Subject focus: media, day care, National Organization for Women, pro-abortion, rights, health, poetry, biographies, lobbying.

| Hist | v.1, n.1-v.2, n.1; Aug., 1970- Sep., 1971 | Microforms Her. 1, R 22 |
| | v.2, n.3-v.3 n.8?; [Nov., 1971- June, 1973] | Her. 1 UP, R3 |
| | July, 1973- June, 1974 | Her. CUP, R 1 |

262 Deaconess Annals. 1930-1974//. Semi-annual. OCLC 5526038. Last issue 12 pages, last volume 24 pages, size 13 x 21. Line drawings, photographs. Published by the Lutheran Deaconess Motherhouse, Milwaukee, WI. Frequency varies: quarterly, Apr., 1930-Jan./Mar., 1965; tri-annual, Fall, 1965-Fall, 1966. Editors: Sister Magdalene Krebs, Apr., 1948-Jan./Mar., 1965; Rev. H.A. Flessners, Fall, 1965-? Subject focus: Lutherans, hospital services. Other holding institutions: [University of Minnesota Union List, Minneapolis,

MN] (MUL).

Hist  v.1, n.1-v.45, n.2; Apr., 1930-Winter, 1974  BX/8001/D4

The Deaconess Movement. Des Moines, IA

    see The Journey. Des Moines, IA

263 Definitely Biased. 1973-1974//? Monthly. Last issue 10 pages. Line drawings. Available on microfilm: Herstory. Published by Definitely Biased, Santa Cruz, CA. Title varies: as The Santa Cruz Women's Center Newsletter, Feb.-June, 1973; as Women's Center Newsletter, July-Nov., 1973. Subject focus: rape, women's studies, politics, poetry, consciousness raising, self-help, National Organization for Women, psychotherapy, women's centers, feminism.

Hist  Feb.-June, 1973  Microforms Her. 2, R 14

    July, 1973-Apr., 1974  Her. 2 UP, R2

264 Delta. 1976? 7 times a year. Deborah J. Peaks, editor, Delta, 1707 New Hampshire Avenue N.W., Washington, DC 20009. Last issue 16 pages, size 21 x 28. Line drawings, photographs. Published by Delta Sigma Theta, Inc., Washington, DC. Previous editors: Norliskia A. Jackson, Summer, 1976; Marshallay Brown-Rowe, Summer, 1976-Apr., 1978. Subject focus: sororities, career development, Afro-Americans.

Hist  Summer, 1976-  Circulation

265 The Delta Kappa Gamma Bulletin. 1935?-1974//? Quarterly. ISSN 0011-8044. OCLC 1566125. LC 56-43740. Last issue 64 pages, last volume 256 pages, size 14 x 22. Line drawings, photographs. Published by the Delta Kappa Gamma Society, Austin, TX. Editor: Isabel C. Kerner. Subject focus: teachers, sororities, education, poetry. Other holding institutions: ArU (AFU), AzFU (AZN), AzTeS (AZS), CLavC (CLV), CLU (CLU), CU-UC (UCU), DHU (DHU), FBoU (FGM), FJUNF (FNP), [Indiana Union List of Serials, Indianapolis, IN] (ILS), IC (CGP), InU (IUL), KLindB (KFB), KSteC (KKQ), MBU (BOS), MiAdC (EEA), MiDW (EYW), MiMtpT (EZC), MWelC (WEL), [University of Minnesota Union List, Minneapolis, MN] (MUL), NBmK (VZK), NCorniCC (ZDG), NcRS (NRC), [Central New York Library Resources Council, Syracuse, NY] (SRR), NGcA (VJA), NNepaSU (ZLM), NOneoU (ZBM), OCedC (CDC), OkAdE (ECO), OKentU (KSU), OkTOR (OKO), OkU (OKU), OYU (YNG), PPiU (PIT), [Pittsburgh Regional Library Center-Union List, Pittsburgh, PA] (QPR), ScRhW (SWW), TCollsM (TMS), TMurS (TXM), TNJ (TJC), [AMIGOS Union List of Serials, Dallas, TX] (IUC), TxAbH (TXS), TxBelM (MHB), TxDaB (IDA), TxDW (IWU), TxLT (ILU), TxSmS (TXI), ViRCU (VRC), ViRU (VRU), WMaPI-RL (GZR), WMUW (GZN), WvBeC (WVB).

IMC  v.39, n.2-v.41, n.1; Winter, 1973-Fall, 1974  Periodicals Section

DPIP  1970-1974?  Circulation

The Democratic Bulletin. Washington, DC

    see The Democratic Digest. Washington, DC

266 The Democratic Digest. 1926-1960?//. Irregular. Last issue 28 pages, last volume 168 pages, size 18 x 28. Line drawings, photographs. Available on microfilm: McP (1953-1960). Published by the Democratic National Committee, Women's Division, Washington, DC. Title varies: as The Democratic Bulletin, Jan., 1930-Sep., 1933. Editors: Evelyn C. Condon, Jan., 1930-Nov., 1932; Helen K. Essary, Sep., 1933-Jan., 1941; Virginia Rishel, Feb.,1941-June, 1945; Dorothy Felker Girton, July, 1945-Aug./Sep., 1952. Subject focus: Democratic Party, politicians.

Hist  v.5, n.1-v.29, n.7; Jan., 1930-Aug./Sep., 1952  JK/2311/D3S

267 Denver Women's Newsletter. 1970?//. Last issue 9 pages. Line drawings. Available on microfilm: Herstory. Published by Denver Women's Liberation, Denver, CO. Subject focus: rights, health, pro-abortion.

Hist  May, 1970  Her. 1, Add.

Designer. New York, NY

    see The Designer and the Woman's Magazine. New York, NY

268 The Designer and the Woman's Magazine. 1894-1926?//. Monthly. Last issue 70 pages, last volume 350 pages. Line drawings, photographs, some in color, commercial advertising. Available on microfilm: ResP (1895-1926). Published by Standard Fashion Co., 342 W. 14th Street, New York, NY. Title varies: as The Standard Delineator of Fashions, Fancy Work, and Millinery, May, 1895-Mar., 1896; Standard Designer, Apr., 1896-July, 1898; Designer, Aug., 1898-Apr., 1920. Subject focus: fashion, fabrics, clothes, home economics, fiction.

Other holding institution: DLC (DLC).

| Mem | May, 1895- Oct., 1926 | Microforms |

269 Dialogue; a Newsletter for Cornell Women at Work. 1974-? Monthly. Last issue 12 pages, size 22 x 28. Published by the University Personnel Service at Cornell, Ithaca, NY. Editors: Cecilia Urin, Aug. 28, 1974-July 2, 1975; Deborah MacInnes, Aug. 27, 1975; Willda Shaw Jackson, Jan. 7, 1976; Deborah MacInnes and Cecilia Urin, Jan. 28, 1976; Sandra Klingle, May 27, 1976; Sandra Eells Kling, June 30, 1976. Subject focus: workers.

| Hist | v.1, n.1, 5, v.2, n.6, 8, 11-v.3, n.1, 6; Aug. 28, Dec. 28, 1974, July 2, Aug. 27, Nov. 25, 1975-Jan. 28, June 30, 1976 | Pam 76-1287 |

270 The Diana and Ladies' Spectator. 1822//? Weekly. Last issue 8 pages. Available on microfilm: UnM (1822). Published by the Diana and Ladies' Spectator, Boston, MA. Editor: Mrs. M.L. Rainsford. Subject focus: fiction, poetry, religion, biographies, music.

| Hist | v.1, n.1-4; Oct. 1-26, 1822 | Microforms |

Die Deutsche Haus Frau. Milwaukee, WI

see Die Haus Frau. Milwaukee, WI

271 Distaff. 1973-1975//. Monthly. OCLC 4365066. Last issue 24 pages. Line drawings, photographs. Available on microfilm: Herstory. Published by the New South Feminist Press, Inc., New Orleans, LA. Editors: Mary Gehman and Donna Swanson. Subject focus: rights, National Organization for Women, employment, pro-abortion, art, politics, health, poetry. In Spanish (5%).

| Hist | v.1, n.1-5; Feb.-June, 1973 | Microforms Her. 2, R 4 |
| | v.1, n.6-v.2, n.4; July, 1973- Apr., 1974 | Her. 2 UP, R2 |
| | v.2, n. 8-v.3, n.6; Dec., 1974- July, 1975 | Microforms |
| Mem | v.2, n.3, 8, v.3, n.1, 3-6; Mar., Aug., 1974, Jan., Mar.-July, 1975 | Microforms |

Do It N.O.W.. Madison, WI

see Equality N.O.W., Madison, WI

272 Do it NOW. 1968-1977//? Irregular. ISSN 0149-4740. OCLC 3494944, 2319299. LC sn78-4689. Last issue 8 pages, size 22 x 28. Line drawings, photographs. Available on microfilm: McP (1976-1977). Published by the National Organization for Women, Washington, DC. Place of publication varies: Chicago, IL, Mar., 1971-Sep./Oct., 1975. Editors: Joan Nicholson, Oct./Nov., 1972-June, 1973; Diane Terry, July, 1973-May/June, 1974; Bernice Fiedlander, July/Aug.-Sep./Oct., 1975; Pat Anderson, Mar.-July, 1976. Subject focus: rights, Equal Rights Amendment, feminism, lobbying, politics. Other holding institutions: CLU (CLU), CU-UC (UCU), [Bureau of the Census, Washinton, DC] (CBU), IaDmG (IWG), ICMR (IBF), MiEM (EEM), [University of Minnesota Union List, Minneapolis, MN] (MUL), NBrockU (XBM), [Western New York Library Resources Council, Buffalo, NY] (VZX), PBL (LYU), [AMIGOS Union List of Serials, Dallas, TX] (IUC), TxDW (IWU).

| Hist | [Mar., 1971- Mar., 1977] | Pam 76-1147 |
| Wom Ed Res | Mar., 1973- Aug., 1977 | Circulation |

273 Dokumente der Frau. 1899-1902//? Semi-monthly. Last issue 32 pages, last volume 344 pages, size 14 x 25. Commercial advertising. Indexed: self-indexed. Published by the Dokumente der Frau, Vienna, Austria. Editor: Maria Lang. Subject focus: rights, marriage, law, poetry. In German (100%).

| Hist | v.1, n.1-v.7, n.12; Mar. 8, 1899- Sep. 8, 1902 | AP/D6574 |

274 Dolla Mina. 1971//? Unknown. Last issue 58 pages. Line drawings, photographs. Available on microfilm: Herstory. Published by the Dolla Mina, Amsterdam, Holland. Subject focus: education, rights, sex education, sexism, unwed mothers, child care. In Dutch (50%).

| Hist | n.1-2; ?, 1971 | Microforms Her. 2, R 4 |

275 Dorcas Magazine of Woman's Handi-Work. 1884-1885//? Monthly. Last issue 26 pages, last volume 290 pages, size 15 x 23. Line drawings, commercial advertising. Published in New York, NY. Editor: Laura B. Starr. Subject focus: arts, crafts.

| Hist | v.1, n.1-v.2, n.12; Jan., 1884- Dec., 1885 | AP83/.D07 (Cutter) |

## Women's Periodicals and Newspapers

276 <u>Downtown Women's News</u>. 1975. Monthly. Last issue 4 pages, size 29 x 43. Line drawings, photographs, commercial advertising. Published by Women Organized for Employment, San Francisco, CA. Editor: Cathy Shufro. Subject focus: workers, sexism in employment.

    Hist      v.2, n.1-4;      Pam 75-3203
              Jan.-Apr., 1976

              v.6, n.10-       Circulation
              Nov., 1980-

<u>ERA Monitor</u>. Sacramento, CA

    see <u>Equal Rights Monitor</u>. Sacramento, CA

277 <u>The ERA Times</u>. 1978. Monthly. $5 for individuals and institutions. The ERA Times, P.O. Box 308, Madison, WI 53701. Last issue 4 pages, size 22 x 18. Line drawings. Available on microfilm: WHi. Published by The Madison Coalition for the ERA, Madison, WI. Subject focus: Equal Rights Amendment.

    Hist      v.2, n.1-        Circulation
              Oct., 1979-

278 <u>Earth's Daughters</u>. 1971. $4.75 for individuals, $9 for institutions. Judith Kerman, editor, Earth's Daughters, P.O. Box 41, Station H, Buffalo, NY 14214. ISSN 0163-0989. OCLC 2260537. LC sn79-4559. Last issue 70 pages, size 18 x 25. Line drawings, photographs, commercial advertising. Available on microfilm: Herstory (1971-1972). Subject focus: poetry, art. Other holding institutions: [University of Minnesota Union List, Minneapolis, MN] (MUL), NTRS (ZRS), [Pittsburgh Regional Library Center-Union List, Pittsburgh, PA] (QPR), PInU (PZI), PPiU (PIT), TxDW (IWU), WMUW (GZD).

    Hist      v.1, n.1-2;      Microforms
              Feb.-Sep., 1971   Her. 1, R 6

              v.1, n.3;        Her. 1 UP, R3
              Apr., 1972

    RBR       v.1, n.1-        Circualtion
              Feb., 1971-

279 <u>East Bay Feminists Newsletter</u>. 1970//? Irregular. OCLC 2260549. Last issue 4 pages. Line drawings. Available on microfilm: Herstory. Published by the East Bay Feminists, Berkeley, CA. Subject focus: self-defense, feminism, self-help.

    Hist      n.1-3;          Microforms
              June 10-       Her. 1, R 14
              July 18, 1970

280 <u>East Bay Women for Peace Newsletter</u>. 1962. Monthly. OCLC 2269600. Last issue 6 pages, size 22 x 36. Line drawings, photographs. Available on microfilm: Herstory (1962-1974). Published by the East Bay Women for Peace, Berkeley-Oakland Women for Peace, Berkeley, CA 94704. Title varies: as Women for Peace Newsletter, Oct., 1962-June, 1973. Frequency varies: irregular, Oct., 1962-Dec., 1970. Previous editors: Charity Hirsch, Oct., 1962-June, 1972; Charity Hirsch and Judy Abel, July, 1972; E. Salkind and T. Mandel, Aug., 1972; Judy Abel, Sep., 1972-Mar., 1973; Evelyn Velson, Apr., 1973-Mar., 1974; Libby Mines, Jan., 1979; Edith Laub, Feb./Mar.-Apr., 1979; Libby Mines, May, 1979-Mar., 1980; Evelyn Velson, May/June, 1980; Ellen B. Holzman, Nov., 1980-. Subject focus: rights, ecology, draft, peace movement, nuclear power.

    Hist      [Oct., 1962-    Microforms
              Sep., 1971]     Her. 1, R 23

              Oct., 1971-     Her. 1 UP, R3
              June, 1973

              July, 1973-     Her. CUP, R2
              Mar., 1974

              v.40, n.22-     Circulation
              Jan., 1979-

281 <u>Echo of Sappho</u>. 1972-1974//? Irregular. OCLC 2320647. Last issue 32 pages. Line drawings, photographs, commercial advertising. Available on microfilm: Herstory. Published by the Sisters for Liberation, Brooklyn, NY. Frequency varies: bi-monthly, June/July-Nov./Dec., 1972. Subject focus: lesbians, gay rights, Afro-Americans, media.

    Hist      v.1, n.1-4;      Microforms
              June/July, 1972-?. Her. 2, R 4
              1973

              v.1, n.5;        Her. 2 UP, R3
              Summer/Fall, 1973

282 <u>Ecumenical Women's Center</u>. 1972-1974//? Irregular. OCLC 1781878. Last issue 8 pages. Line drawings. Available on microfilm: Herstory. Published by the Ecumenical Women's Center, Chicago, IL. Editor: Rev. Floria Mikkelson. Subject focus: religion, employment, ecumenism.

    Hist      v.2, n.4-9;      Microforms
              Dec., 1973-     Her. 3, R 1
              May/June, 1974

283 <u>The Education of Women</u>. 1958-1961//. Irregular. ISSN 0422-6607. OCLC 1774724. Last issue 4 pages, size 22 x 28. Published by the American Council on Education, Commission on the Education of Women, Washington, DC. Subject

focus: students, continuing education. Other holding institutions: [Indiana Union List of Serials, Indianapolis, IN] (ILS), [University of Minnesota Union List, Minneapolis, MN] (MUL).

| Wom Ed Res | [n.4-12;] [Dec., 1958- Mar., 1961] | Circulation |

284 <u>Educational Horizons</u>. 1921. Quarterly. $8 for individuals, $10 for institutions. Linda Clark Dague, editor, Educational Horizons, 4101 East Third Street, Box A850, Bloomington, IN 47402. ISSN 0013-175X, 0070-914X. OCLC 1567586, 2124697, 3067681. LC sc77-1189, 79-648770. Last issue 72 pages, last volume 212 pages, size 17 x 26. Line drawings, photographs. Indexed: Current Index to Journals in Education, (1923-); Education Index (1923-). Available on microfilm: UnM. Published by the Pi Lambda Theta, Bloomington, IN. Title varies: as Pi Lambda Theta Journal, Oct., 1934-Fall, 1952. Place of publication varies: Menasha, WI, Oct., 1934-Summer, 1972. Previous editors: Genevieve Knight Bixler, Oct., 1934-May, 1937; Ethel Marie Falk, Oct., 1937-Oct., 1940. Helen B. Warrin, Oct., 1941-Dec., 1945; Virginia Lee Block, Mar., 1946-Dec., 1949; Beulah Benton Tatum, Mar., 1950-Summer, 1951; Gladys A. Coryell, Fall, 1951-Fall, 1953; M. Virginia Biggy, Fall, 1954-Summer, 1961; Miriam M. Bryan, Fall, 1961-Fall, 1964; Wilma A. Bailey, Winter, 1964-Fall, 1970; Miriam M. Bryan, Fall, 1971-Winter, 1973/1974. Subject focus: education, teachers. Other holding institutions: AU (ALM), ArAT (AKH), ArLUA (AKU), ArSeH (AHS), ArU (AFU), AzFU (AZN), AzTeS (AZS), CLavC (CLV), CLU (CLU), [Pepperdine University, Malibu, CA] (CPE), DLC (DLC), FBoU (FGM), FJUNF (FNPO), FMFIU (FXG), FMU (FQG), GAuA (GJG), GU (GUA), ICL (IAL), ICRC (IAR), IPB (IBA), IOC (IBQ), InIU (IUP), InLP (IPL), InMerL (ILC), InU (IUL), InWhC (ICC), KHayF (KFH), KyMurT (KMS), LMN (LNE), MBU (BOS), MNS (SNN), MdBJ (JHE), MiDW (EYW), MiLC (EEL), MiMtpT (EZC), [University of Minnesota Union List of Serials, Minneapolis, MN] (MUL), MnStcls (MST), MsU (MUM), [New York State Union List, Albany, NY] (NYS), [Western New York Library Resources Council, Buffalo, NY] (VZX), NCortU (YCM), NGenoU (YGM), NIC (COO), NNU (ZYU), NOneoU (ZBM), NSbSU (YSM), NSyU (SYB), NFQC (XQM), [Central New York Library Resources Council, Syracuse, NY] (SRR), NbU (LDL), NbKS (KRS), NcElcE (NEP), NcRS (NRC), NmU (IQU), OAU (OUN), OAkU (AKR), OC1U (CSU), OkU (OKU), OKentU (KSU), OKTU (ODT), OTU (TOL), PCW (UWC), PInU (PZI), [Pittsburgh Regional Library Center-Union List, Pittsburgh, PA] (QPR), PPiD (DUQ), PPiU (PIT), PU (PAU), TGaV (TVS), TMurS (TXM), TNJ (TJC), [AMIGOS Union List of Serials, Dallas, TX] (IUC), TxDN (INT), TxDW (IWU), TxH (TXN), TxHU (TXH), TxLT (ILU), TxLarU (TLS), TxLoL (TLT), TxU (IXA), ViRCU (VRC), ViU (VA@), WMUW (GZN), WaU (WAU),

WeharU (HRM).

| Mem | v.13, n.1- Oct., 1934- | Circulation |
| MIMC | Sep., 1968- | Circulation |
| DPIP | Feb., 1969- | Circulation |
| IMC | Jan., 1954- | Circulation |
| R&L | Sep., 1963- Sep. 1969- | Circulation |

285 <u>Effe</u>. 1973-1977//? Monthly. OCLC 4080671. Last issue 48 pages, size 21 x 29. Line drawings, photographs, commercial advertising. Available on microfilm: Herstory (1973). Published by the Edizioni Cooperative Effe, Societa Concessioni Pubblicitarie, Rome, Italy. Place of publication varies: Milan, Italy, Nov., 1973. Editor: Sara Marino. Subject focus: rights, politics, health, employment, childbirth. Other holding institution: CLU (CLU). In Italian 100%).

| Hist | n.1; Nov., 1973 | Microforms Her. 3, R 1 |
| Wom St | v.2, n.3, v.4, n.11, v.5, n.7/8; Mar., 1974, Nov., 1976, Aug., 1977 | Reading Room |

286 <u>El Paso N.O.W.</u>. 1973//? Monthly. Last issue 10 pages. Line drawings. Available on microfilm: Herstory. Published by the El Paso County Chapter, National Organization for Women, Colorado Springs, CO. Subject focus: feminism, politics, education, Equal Rights Amendment.

| Hist | n.1-3; Apr.-June, 1973 | Microforms Her. 2, R 10 |

287 <u>Electra</u>.1971//? Unknown. OCLC 2260708. Last issue 6 pages. Available on microfilm: Herstory. Published by the National Organization for Women, Image of Women National Task Force Committee, Rochester Image Committee, Rochester, NY. Subject focus: legislation, children, media, feminism, education.

| Hist | v.1; Nov., 1971 | Microforms Her. 1, R 17 |

288 <u>Eliza Cook's Journal</u>. 1849-1854?//. Weekly. OCLC 1567792, 4751624. LC cau07-731. Last issue 16 pages, last volume 416 pages. Indexed: each volume self-indexed. Available on microfilm: ResP (1849-1854). Published by John Owen Clarke, London, England. Editor: Eliza Cook. Subject focus: biographies,

fiction, poetry. Other holding institutions: [Indiana Union List of Serials, Indianapolis, IN] (ILS), [University of Minnesota Union List, Minneapolis, MN] (MUL), OCl (CLE).

| Mem | n.1-286; May 5, 1849- Oct. 21, 1854 | Microforms |

289 Elizabeth Blackwell's Women's Health Center Newletter. 1974//? Unknown. Last issue 3 pages. Line drawings. Available on microfilm: Herstory. Published by the Elizabeth Blackwell's Women's Health Center, Minneapolis, MN. Subject focus: health.

| Hist | May, 1974 | Microforms Her. 3, R 1 |

290 Elle. 1970//. Irregular. OCLC 2260729. Last issue 12 pages. Available on microfilm: Herstory. Published by Etats Generaux de la Femme Conference, Versailles, France. Subject focus: politics, health, education, marriage, law, workers.

| Hist | Nov.20-22, 1970 | Microforms Her. 1, R 6 |

291 Elle. Unknown. Semi-monthly. Editor: Elaine Victor, Elle, 6 Rue Ancelle, 9252 Nevilly s/Serne Cedex, Paris, France. Business address: 90 Rue de Flandre, 75943 Paris, France. ISSN 0013-6298. OCLC 2260728, 1606372. Last issue 166 pages, last volume 3984 pages, size 23 x 30. Line drawings, photographs, some in color, commercial advertising. Published by France Editions et Publications SA, Paris, France. Subject focus: beauty care, fashion, health, food. In French (100%). Other holding institutions: AU (ALM), AzFU (AZN), [Pepperdine University, Malibu, CA] (CPE), FSpE (FEC), GA (GAP), [Indiana Union List of Serials, Indianapolis, IN] (ILS), MiMtpT (EZC), [University of Minnesota Union List, Minneapolis, MN] (MUL), NDeUA (XDM), NhMSA (SAC), NOneoU (ZBM), OU (OSU), PClvU (URS), PPD (DXU), PPiU (PIT), ScRhW (SWW), TxDW (IWU), TxNacS (TXK), TMurS (TXM), TxShA (IAU), ViRCU (VRC).

| MPL | Current Issues Only | Literature and Social Sciences Section |

292 The Emancipator. 1935-1948//. Irregular. OCLC 1567816. Last issue 8 pages, size 22 x 29. Line drawings, photographs. Published by the International Ladies Garment Workers Union, Milwaukee, WI. Frequency varies: bi-monthly, June 1-Nov. 15, 1936; Dec., 1937-Dec., 1944; Feb., 1945-Dec., 1947. Editors: Moiree Compere, Sep. 10, 1935-July, 1937; Herman Schendel, Aug., 1937-Feb., 1938. Subject focus: labor unions, AFL-CIO, garment industry.

| Hist | Sep. 10, 1935, Apr. 15, 1936- Fall, 1948 | HFBC6/IN8/7E5 (Cutter) |

293 Emergency Librarian. 1974. Bi-monthly. $12 for individuals, $15 for institutions. Carol-Ann Haycock and Ken Haycock, editors, Emergency Librarian, P.O. Box 46258, Station G, Vancouver, British Columbia V6R4GO. Business address: Dyad Services, P.O. Box 4696 Station D, London, Ontario N5W 5L7. ISSN 0315-8888. OCLC 1780152. LC cn76-308823. Last issue 22 pages, last volume 152 pages, size 21 x 27. Line drawings, photographs, commercial advertising. Indexed: Current Awareness Library Literature. Available on microfilm: McL. Published by the Ontario Arts Council, Vancouver, British Columbia, Canada. Previous editors: Barbara Clubb, Phyllis Jaffe and Sherrill Cheda, Apr., 1974-Feb., 1975; Phyllis Jaffe and Sherrill Cheda, Apr./June-Nov./Dec., 1975. Subject focus: librarians, non-sexist childrens materials, alternative literature, rights. Other holding institutions: CaOONL (NLC), CLU (CLU), In (ISL), KyU (KUK), LU (LUU), MBE (ECL), MdBU (BAL), MiAaW (EYA), MiAdC (EEA), [University of Minnesota Union List, Minneapolis, MN] (MUL), MnU (MNU), NBronSL (VVS), NBu (VHB), [Western New York Library Resources Council, Buffalo, NY] (VZX), NGenoU (YGM), PPD (DXU), PPiU (PIT), [Pittsburgh Regional Library Center-Union List, Pittsburgh, PA] (QPR), RPSL (RDS), TNJ (TJC), [AMIGOS Union List of Serials, Dallas, TX] (IUC), TxDN (INT), ViRCU (VRC), WMUW (GZN).

| Mem | v.1, n.3- Feb., 1974- | AP/E529/L694 |
| Lib Sch | v.1, n.1- Jan., 1974- | Periodicals Section |
| R&L | v.2, n.3- June/July, 1975- | Circulation |
| Hist | v.4, n.4- Mar./Apr., 1977- | Circulation |

294 Employee Press. 1967-1974//? Monthly. OCLC 2260738. Last issue 8 pages, last volume 90 pages. Line drawings, photographs. Available on microfilm: Herstory. Published by Clerical Technical and Professional Employees, AFSCME Local 1695, University of California, Berkeley, CA. Title varies: as AFSCME Bulletin, May 16, 1967. Subject focus: labor unions, AFL-CIO.

| Hist | v.1, n.1-v.5, n.10; May 16, 1967- Sep., 1971 | Microforms Her. 1, R 1 |

|   |   |   |
|---|---|---|
|  | v.7, n.6-v.8, n.6; July, 1973- June, 1974 | Her. CUP, R 2 |

295 The English Woman's Journal. 1858-1864//. Monthly. Last issue 144 pages, last volume 432 pages. Line drawings, commercial advertising. Available on microfilm: McP, ResP, (1050-1063). Published by the English Woman's Journal Company, Ltd., London, England. Subject focus: fiction, poetry, rights, suffrage. Other holding institutions: MCR-S (Schlesinger Library on the History of Women in America, Radcliffe College, Cambridge, MA), NNC (Columbia University).

|   |   |   |
|---|---|---|
| Mem | v.1, n.1-v.8, n.78; Mar. 1, 1858- Aug. 1, 1864 | Microforms |
|  | v.1, n.1-v.7, n.66; Mar. 1, 1858- Aug. 1, 1863 | Microforms |

296 The Englishwoman's Magazine and Christian Mothers' Miscellany. 1846-1854//? Monthly. Last issue 56 pages, last volume 760 pages, size 13 x 22. Line drawings. Indexed: self-indexed (1850-1854). Published by The Englishwoman's Magazine, London, England. Editor: Mrs. Milner. Subject focus: Christianity, biographies, history, education, poetry.

|   |   |   |
|---|---|---|
| Mem | v.4, n.1-v.9, n.12; Jan., 1850- Dec., 1854 | AP/E588/2 |

297 The Englishwoman's Review of Social and Industrial Questions. 1866-1910//. Quarterly. OCLC 4566108. Last issue 106 pages, last volume 252 pages. Available on microfilm: McA. Published by Williams and Norgate, London, England. Editors: Emilia J. Boucherett, 1866-1882; Caroline A. Biggs, 1883-1889; Helen Blackburn and Antoinette M. Mackenzie, 1890-Jan., 1903; Antoinette M. Mackenzie, Apr., 1903-July, 1910. Subject focus: history. Other holding institutions: CSt (Stanford University), DGW (DGW), NhC (DRB), NR (YQR), NSyU (SYB).

|   |   |   |
|---|---|---|
| Mem | v.1, n.1-v.41, n.3; Oct., 1866- July, 1910 | Microforms |

298 Enlace. 1967-1976//. Irregular. ISSN 0425-0702. OCLC 1961154. LC 76-641224, sc76-142. Last issue 54 pages, size 21 x 27. Line drawings. Published by the Organization of American States, Inter-American Commission of Women, General Secretariat, Washington, DC. Subject focus: rights, South America. Other holding institutions: AzTeS (AZS), AzU (AZU), CtY (YUS), DLC (DLC), MiU (EYM), NbU (LDL), PPiU (PIT), TNJ (TJC).

|   |   |   |
|---|---|---|
| Mem | [n.1-28]; [Feb., 1967- June, 1976] | AP/E5882 |

299 Enough. 1970//? Unknown. OCLC 2260770. Last issue 54 pages. Line drawings. Available on microfilm: Herstory. Published by Bristol Women's Liberation, Bristol, England. Editors: Monica Sjoo, Pat Van Twest, and Beverly Skinner. Subject focus: family, single parents, pro-abortion, poetry, workers, feminism.

|   |   |   |
|---|---|---|
| Hist | n.1-3; ?, 1970 | Microforms Her. 1, R 6 |

300 Enterprising Women. 1975-1977//. 11 times a year. ISSN 0199-1124. OCLC 5639579, 3341456. LC sn79 19300. Last issue 8 pages, size 22 x 28. Line drawings. Published by Artemis Enterprises, Inc., New York, NY. Title varies: as Artemis for Enterprising Women, Sep.-Oct., 1976. Editor: Ava Stern. Subject focus: business. Other holding institutions: DLC (DLC), InLP (IPL), [University of Minnesota Union List, Minneapolis, MN] (MUL), NhD (DRB), NIC (COO), OrSaW (OWS).

|   |   |   |
|---|---|---|
| Coll | v.2, n.1-v.3, n.4; Sep., 1976- Dec., 1977 | Women's Reading Area |

301 Equal Rights. 1923-1954//? Bi-monthly. OCLC 1568143. LC 24-12668. Last issue 8 pages, last volume 25 pages, size 30 x 22. Line drawings, photographs, commercial advertising. Available on microfilm: DLC, McA. Published by the National Woman's Party, Washington, DC. Place of publication varies: Baltimore, MD, Feb. 17, 1923-Dec. 29, 1934. Frequency varies: weekly, Feb. 17, 1923-Dec. 29, 1934; semi-monthly, Feb. 15, 1934-May 1, 1939; monthly, June, 1939-Dec., 1944. Editors: Edith Houghton Hooker, Feb. 17, 1923-Dec. 29, 1934; Emily Perry, Feb. 15, 1935-Dec., 1936; Helen Hunt West, Jan. 15, 1937-May, 1940; Anna Kelton Wiley, Oct., 1940-Nov./Dec., 1945; Anne Carter, Jan./Feb., 1947-Mar./Apr., 1951; Dorothy M. Russell, May/June, 1951; Virginia Starr Freedom, July/Aug., 1951-May/June, 1953; Dr. Florence A. Armstrong, Sep.-Dec., 1953; Anne Carter, Oct.-Nov., 1954. Subject focus: rights, politics, history. Other holding institutions: CSt (Stanford University), MCR-S (Schlesinger Library on the History of Women in America, Radcliffe College, Cambridge, MA), [University of Minnesota Union List, Minneapolis, MN] (MUL), MNS (SNN), OAkU (AKR), OKentU (KSU), [Pittsburgh Regional Library Center-Union List, Pittsburgh, PA] (QPR),

PPi (CPL), WMUW (GZN).

| Hist | v.1, n.1-v.40, n.2; Feb. 17, 1923- Nov., 1954 | Microforms |
| --- | --- | --- |
|  | v.1, n.1-v.40, n.2; Feb. 17, 1923- Nov., 1940 | KWZ/"7E64/ Cutter |

302 Equal Rights; Independent Feminist Weekly. 1935-1936//. Weekly. OCLC 2704179. LC 42-47052. Last issue 8 pages, last volume 344 pages, size 34 x 25. Photographs. Available on microfilm: McA, GrP. Published by Equal Rights, Inc., Baltimore, MD. Editor: Edith Houghton Hooker. Subject focus: rights, workers, biographies, personal histories. Other holding institutions: CSt (Stanford University), MeB (BBH), MdBt (TSC), MdFreH (HCF), NmLcU (IRU), OCU (CIN), PPiU (PIT).

| Hist | v.1, n.1-[n.s.] v.2, n.43; Jan. 5, 1935- Dec. 26, 1936 | KWZ/"7E637 (Cutter) |
| --- | --- | --- |

303 Equal Rights Monitor. 1975-1976//? Irregular. OCLC 3404006. Last issue 20 pages. Line drawings, photographs, commercial advertising. Published by the Equal Rights Project, Sacramento, CA. Title varies: as ERA Monitor, Dec. 10, 1975-Feb. 26, 1976. Subject focus: rights, Equal Rights Amendment. Other holding institutions: CLU (CLU), [Congressional Research Service, Washington, DC] (CRS), GAuA (GJG), GU (GUA), IU (UIU), MWelC (WEL), [University of Minnesota Union List, Minneapolis, MN] (MUL), NIC (COO), [New York State Union List, Albany, NY] (NYS), TxCM (TXA), ViBlbv (VPI), ViRCU (VRC), WMUW (GZN).

| Hist | v.1, n.2-3, v.2, n.2-5, 7-8, 10; Dec. 10-24, 1975, Jan. 21-Apr., June-July, Sep./Oct., 1976 | Circulation |
| --- | --- | --- |

304 Equal Times. 1976. Bi-weekly. $8 for individuals, $12 for institutions. Eunice West, editor, Equal Times, 235 Park Square Building, Boston, MA 02116. Last issue 24 pages, size 29 x 40. Line drawings, photographs, commercial advertising. Subject focus: rights, politics, law.

| Coll | Current Issues Only | Women's Reading Area |
| --- | --- | --- |

305 Equal Times. 1973?-1974//? Unknown. Last issue 2 pages. Line drawings. Available on microfilm: Herstory. Published by the Capitol Hill Women's Political Caucus, Washington, DC. Subject focus: politics, employment, lobbying, education.

| Hist | n.7-13; July?, 1973- Jan?, 1974 | Microforms Her. 3, R 1 |
| --- | --- | --- |

306 Equality N.O.W. 1972. Monthly. $5 for individuals and institutions. Chi McIntyre, editor, Equality N.O.W., P.O. Box 2512, Madison, WI 53701. Last issue 8 pages, size 22 x 28. Line drawings. Available on microfilm: Herstory (1972-1974). Published by the National Organization for Women, Madison Chapter, Madison, WI. Title varies: as Do it N.O.W., Oct., 1972-June, 1973. Frequency varies: irregular, Oct., 1972-Jan., 1973. Previous editors: Claudia Vlisides, July, 1973-July, 1974; Patricia Wilson, Oct., 1975; Pamela Pierson, Dec., 1976; Joan Babcock, Jan.-June/July, 1977. Subject focus: feminism, rights, gay rights, pro-abortion, Equal Rights Amendment.

| Hist | v.2, n.6- July, 1973- | Circulation |
| --- | --- | --- |
|  | v.1, n.1?-v.2, n.5; Oct., 1972- June, 1973 | Microforms Her. 2, R 11 |
|  | v.2, n.6-v.3, n.5; July, 1973- May, 1974 | Her. 2 UP, R7 |
| Wom St | [v.5, n.3-v.8, n.12] [Mar., 1976- Feb., 1978] | Reading Room |
| MPL | v.5, n.7- July, 1976- | Literature and Social Sciences Section |
| Wom Ed Res | v.2, n.7- Aug., 1973- | Circulation |

307 Essecondsex. 1971-1973//? Irregular. OCLC 2260827. Last issue 8 pages. Line drawings. Available on microfilm: Herstory. Published by the North Shore/Essex County Chapter, National Organization for Women, Beverly/Rockport, MA. Subject focus: pro-abortion, day care, politics. Other holding institution: MCR-S (Schlesinger Library on the History of Women in America, Radcliffe College, Cambridge, MA).

| Hist | v.1, n.2-4; Jan. 15-May, 1971 | Microforms Her. 1, R 18 |
| --- | --- | --- |
|  | v.2, n.1-v.3, n.3; Nov., 1971- Mar./Apr., 1973 | Her. 1 UP, R11 |

308 **Essence.** 1970. Monthly. $9 for individuals and institutions. Marcia Ann Gillespie, editor, Essence, 1500 Broadway, New York, NY. ISSN 0014-0880. OCLC 5862139, 5146827, 1568247. LC 71-24303. Last issue 116 pages, size 20 x 27. Line drawings, photographs, some in color, commercial advertising. Indexed: Index to Periodicals by and about Negroes; Access Index. Available on microfilm: UnM. Published by Essence Communications, Inc., New York, NY. Subject focus: fashion, beauty care, health, food, fiction, Afro-Americans. Other holding institutions: AU (ALM), ArU (AFU), ArStC (ASU), AzTeS (AZS), AzU (AZU), CLU (CLU), CLSU (CSL), CSt (Stanford University), CtY (YUS), [Congressional Research Service, Washington, DC] (CRS), DI (UDI), DLC (DLC), FBoU (FGM), FJUNF (FNP), FPeU (FWA), GASU (GSU), ICarE (IAD), IPB (IBA), InAndC (INA), [Indiana Union List of Serials, Indianapolis, IN] (ILS), InIU (IUP), InLP (IPL), InU (IUL), KYBB (KBE), KyDC (KCC), KyRE (KEU), KyU (KUK), LHS (LSH), MCR-S (Schlesinger Library on the History of Women in America, Radcliffe College, Cambridge, MA), MiEM (EEM), MiDW (EYW), MiLC (EEL), MiMtpT (EZC), MnStjos (MNF), [University of Minnesota Union List, Minneapolis, MN] (MUL), MoU (MUU), MsU (MUM), MWelC (WEL), NBu (VHB), NCH (YHM), NNR (ZXC), NOneoU (ZBM), NSyU (SYB), NR (YQR), NRU (RRR), NSbSU (YSM), [New York State Union List, Albany, NY] (NYS), [Central New York Library Resources Council, Syracuse, NY] (SRR), NbU (LDL), NcD (NDD), NcDurC (NCX), NcRS (NRC), NcU (NOC), NhD (DRB), NjLincB (BVV), NmLcU (IRU), NmLvH (NMH), OAkU (AKR), OAU (OUN), OBgU (BGU), OC1U (CSU), OCo (OCO), OCU (CIN), OKentU (KSU), OTU (TOL), OU (OSU), OY (YMM), OkLC (OKC), OkT (TUL), PCa1S (CSC), PP (PLF), PPiAC (AIC), PPiC (PMC), PPiU (PIT), [Pittsburgh Regional Library Center-Union List, Pittsburgh, PA] (QPR), ScRhW (SWW), ScU (SUC), TMurS (TXM), [AMIGOS Union List of Serials, Dallas, TX] (IUC), TxAm (TAP), TxArU (IUA), TxCM (TXA), TxDN (INT), TxDW (IWU), TxLT (ILU), TxNacS (TXK), ViRCU (VRC), ViRU (VRU), WaU (WAU), WMUW (GZN).

| Coll | Current Issues Only | Ethnic Collection |
| Mem | v.2, n.2- June, 1971- | AP/E785/N |
| MPL | v.2, n.3- July, 1971- | Literature and Social Science Section |
| MATC | Current Issues Only | Cora Hardy Library |
| SPPL | Mar., 1972- | Circulation |

Essex County Chapter Newsletter. South Orange, NJ

see Chapter News - Essex County. Maplewood, NJ

309 **Et Ta Soeur?** 1973//? Unknown. Last issue 12 pages. Line drawings, photographs. Available on microfilm: Herstory. Published by Et Ta Soeur, Brussels, Belgium. Subject focus: anti-abortion. In French (100%).

| Hist | ?, 1973 | Microforms Her. 2, R 4 |

Euterpeiad, or, Musical Intelligencer. Boston, MA

see The Euterpeiad; or, Musical Intelligencer, and Ladies Gazette. Boston, MA

310 **The Euterpeiad; or, Musical Intelligencer, and Ladies Gazette.** 1820-1831//? Bi-weekly. OCLC 3325664, 748446, 3610896, 1774744. LC 65-23385, 78-641503. Last issue 20 pages, last volume 204 pages. Line drawings. Available on microfilm: UnM. Published by T. Badger, Boston, MA. Title varies: as Euterpeiad, or, Musical Intelligencer, Apr. 1, 1820-Mar. 17, 1821. Frequency varies: weekly, Apr. 1, 1820- Mar. 31, 1821. Editor: John R. Parker. Subject focus: music. Other holding institutions: AU (ALM), AMobu (ACM), ArAO (AKO), ATrT (ADA), CCC (HDC), CCotS (CSO), CLO (CCO), CLU (CLU), CsjU (CSJ), CtNIC (CTL), CU-Riv (CRU), CWhC (CWC), DHU (DHU), DLC (DLC), DeU (DLM), DSI (SMI), FTaSU (FDA), GAuA (GJG), GVaS (GYG), IaDmD (IOD), ICharE (IAD), IDfT (ICT), IU (UIU), ILocL (ICX), InCW (IWC), InLP (IPL), InND (IND), InNomanC (IMN), [Indiana Union List of Serials, Indianapolis, IN] (ILS), InU (IUL), KHayF (KFH), KU (KKU), KWiU (KSW), KyLoU (KLG), MdBt (TSC), MeB (BBH), MEU (MEU), MiD (EYP), MiU (EYM), MNS (SNN), MOMARYu (MNW), MoSp (MOS), MoSW (WTU), MWelC (WEL), NA1f (YAH), NA1U (NAM), NbOU (NBU), NBrockU (XBM), NbU (LDL), NBu (VHB), NCRM (NMC), NcDaD (NNM), NcRSA (NRA), [New England College, Henniker, NH] (NEC), NjGbS (NJG), NmLcU (IRU), NNC-T (VVT), NOneoU (ZBM), NOsU (YOM), NSbSU (YSM), OAkU (AKR), OC (OCP), OCanM (MAL), OGraD (DNU), OOC (OBM), OrPU (OUP), OSW (WIT), PManM (MAN), PP (PLF), PPi (CPL), PPLas (LAS), PPiU (PIT), PSe1S (SUS), RPRC (RCM), TMurS (TXM), TY (TKN), TxAbH (TXS), TxDN (INT), TxHTSU (TXT), TxHU (TXH), TxViHU (TXV), TxWB (IYU), WaU (WAU), WEU (GZE), WOshU (GZO).

| Hist | v.1, n.1-v.3, n. 19; Apr. 1, 1820- Mar., 1823 | Microforms |

311  Eve. 1958//? Unknown. Last issue 66 pages. Line drawings, photographs. Available on microfilm: Herstory. Published by Eve, Enthusiasts' Publications, Inc., Playa del Rey, CA. Editor: Jane Morrison. Subject focus: poetry, fiction, humor.

| Hist | v.1, n.1; Apr., 1958 | Microforms Her. 2, R 4 |

312  The EVE News. 1970-1974//? Irregular. OCLC 2260924. Last issue 5 pages. Line drawings. Available on microfilm: Herstory. Published by Newark State College, Union, NJ. Title varies: as News from EVE, Nov./Dec., 1970. Subject focus: vocational guidance, education, career development, employment.

| Hist | v.1, n.1-3; Nov./Dec., 1970- Sep., 1971 | Microforms Her. 1, R 14 |
| | n.4-7; Jan., 1972- Jan., 1973 | Her. 1 UP, R3 |
| | n.8-11; Sep., 1973- Summer, 1974 | Her. CUP, R2 |

313  Every Woman's Center Newsletter. 1972-1974//? Monthly. Last issue 4 pages. Line drawings. Available on microfilm: Herstory. Published by Everywoman's Center, Division of Continuing Education, University of Massachusetts, Amherst, MA. Subject focus: continuing education, education, women's studies, pro-abortion, employment, health, women's centers, Equal Rights Amendment.

| Hist | v.1, n.1-4; Nov., 1972- May, 1973 | Microforms Her. 2, R 4 |
| | v.2, n.5-v.3, n.6; July, 1973- June, 1974 | Her. 2 UP, R3 |

314  Everyday Housekeeping. 1894-1907//. Monthly. OCLC 1780267, 1605505, 1752220. Last issue 32 pages, last volume 158 pages. Line drawings, photographs, commercial advertising. Self-indexed at end of each volume. Available on microfilm: ResP. Published by New England Kitchen Publishing Co., Boston, MA. Title varies: as The New England Kitchen Magazine, Apr., 1894-Aug., 1895; as the American Kitchen Magazine, Sep., 1895-Mar., 1901; as The American Kitchen Magazine and Culinary Topics, Apr., 1901-Jan., 1902; as American Kitchen Magazine, Feb., 1902-Mar., 1903; as Home Science Magazine, Apr., 1903-June, 1905; as Modern Housekeeping, Aug., 1905-Jan., 1906. Editors: Anna Barrows and Estelle M.H. Merrill. Subject focus: cooking, gardening, home economics. Other holding institutions: IPB (IBA), MCR-S (Schlesinger Library on the History of Women in America, Radcliffe College, Cambridge, MA), MNS (SNN), [University of Minnesota Union List, Minneapolis, MN] (MUL), MnSU (MNP), NN (NYP), OCl (CLE), TxDW (IWU).

| Mem | v.1, n.1-v.24, n.4; Apr., 1894- Dec., 1907 | Microforms |
| Agric | v.1, n.1-v.21, n.3; Apr., 1894- July, 1904 | Periodicals Section |

315  Everywoman. 1970-1972//. Monthly. Last issue 38 pages. Line drawings, photographs, commercial advertising. Indexed: Alternative Press Index. Available on microfilm: WHi, UnM, Herstory. Published by Everywoman Newspaper, Los Angeles, CA. Subject focus: rights, health, law, history, fiction, poetry. Other holding institutions: MCR-S (Schlesinger Library on the History of Women in America, Radcliffe College, Cambridge, MA).

| Hist | v.1, n.1-v.3, n.4; May 8, 1970- May, 1972 | Microforms |
| | v.1, n.1-v.2, n.13; May 8, 1970- Sep. 10, 1971 | Microforms Her. 1, R 1 |
| | v.2, n.14-v.3, n.4; Oct. 1, 1971- May, 1972 | Her. 1 UP, R 3-4 |
| Wom Ed Res | v.1, n.4, v.2, n.7, v.3, n.3; July 10, 1970, Dec. 17, 1971, Mar., 1972 | Circulation |

316  Everywoman. 1973//? Unknown. Last issue 20 pages. Line drawings, photographs, commercial advertising. Available on microfilm: Herstory. Published by Everywoman, Omaha, NB. Subject focus: population, reproduction, satire, poetry, consumer education.

| Hist | v.1, n.3; Nov./Dec., 1973 | Microforms Her. 3, R 1 |

317  Exchange. 1969. Quarterly. $5 for individuals and institutions. Sister Ann McCullough, editor, Exchange, Sinsinawa, WI 53824. Last issue 32 pages, last volume 118 pages, size 22 x 28. Line drawings, photographs. Published by Sinsinawa Publications, Sinsinawa, WI. Previous editors: Sister Jean Derus, Mar./Apr.,

1969-May, 1972; Sister Mary Paynter, Oct., 1972-Sep., 1973; Sister Joan Leonard, Nov./Dec., 1973-May/June, 1974. Subject focus: religious education, Catholic Church.

Hist     v.1, n.1-     BX/4337.4/E9
         Mar./Apr., 1969-

318   The Executive Woman. 1973-1974//? Monthly. OCLC 2826490. Last issue 6 pages. Line drawings, photographs, commercial advertising. Available on microfilm: Herstory. Published by the Sandra Brown Publishing Co., New York, NY. Editor: Shelley Gross, Sep., 1973-Apr., 1974. Subject focus: business, career development, executives, employment, wages. Other holding institutions: CLU (CLU), [Congressional Research Service, Washington, DC] (CRS), DME/DAS (OLA), FMFIU (FXG), LLafS (LWA), [Central New York Library Resources Council, Syracuse, NY] (SRR), NhD (DRB), NSbSU (YSM), [AMIGOS Union List of Serials, Dallas, TX] (IUC), TNJ (TJC), WMUW (GZN).

Hist     v.1, n.1-8;     Microforms
         Sep., 1973-     Her. 3, R 1
         Apr., 1974

319   Exponent II. 1974. Quarterly. $3.50 for individuals and institutions. Nancy T. Dredge, editor, Exponent II, Box 37, Arlington, MA 02174. Last issue 20 pages, last volume 80 pages, size 45 x 29. Line drawings, photographs. Published by the Mormon Sisters, Inc., Arlington, MA. Previous editors: Claudia L. Bushman, July, 1974-Dec., 1975; Nancy T. Dredge, Grethe B. Peterson, and Laurel T. Ulrich, June-Sep., 1976. Subject focus: Mormons, workers, health, education, child care.

Hist     v.1, n.1-     Circulation
         July, 1974-

FAAR & NCN.   Washington, DC

    see Aegis.   Washington, DC

FAAR News.   Washington, DC

    see Aegis.   Washington, DC

FEPC News.   San Francisco, CA

    see News from FEPC.   San Francisco, CA

F.E.W.'s News and Views.   Washington, DC

    see News News and Views from Federally Employed Women.   Washington, DC

320   FLQ Newsletter. 1970?//? Unknown. OCLC 2261149. Last issue 8 pages. Available on microfilm: Herstory. Published by the Women's Collective Front de Liberation des Femmes Quebeçoises, Montreal, Quebec, Canada. Subject focus: education, day care, pro-abortion, research, French-Canadians.

Hist     ?, 1970     Microforms
         Her. 1, R 15

321   FS Feminist Studies. 1972. Quarterly. $12 for individuals, $20 for institutions. Claire D. Moses, editor, FS Feminist Studies, University of Maryland, College Park, MD 20742. ISSN 0046-3663. OCLC 3371391, 1632609. LC sc76-192, 78-645276. Last issue 232 pages, size 16 x 23. Line drawings, photographs, commercial advertising. Indexed in: America: History and Life; Historical Abstracts; Modern Language Association International Bibliography; Philosophers Index; Sociologial Abstracts; Women Studies Abstracts; Bulletin Signaletiquesociologie, Psychological Abstracts. Available on microfilm: UnM, Herstory (1972). Published by Feminist Studies, Inc., College Park, MD. Place of publication varies: New York, NY (1972-1973?). Subject focus: history, law, women's studies. Other holding institutions: AU (ALM), AAP (AAA), ABAU (ABC), ArStC (ASU), ArU (AFU), AzFU (AZN), AzTeS (AZS), [Pepperdine University, Malibu, CA] (CPE), CLobS (CLO), CLU (CLU), COLH (COL), CtW (WLU), CtY (YUS), DeU (DLM), DLC (DLC), DSI (SMI), FJUNF (FNP), FMFIU (FXN), FPeU (FWA), FU (FUG), GASU (GSU), GEU (EMU), GU (GUA), ICI (IAH), IGK (IBK), [Indiana Union List of Serials, Indianapolis, IN] (ILS), InLP (IPL), InU (IUL), KPT (KFP), KYBB (KBE), KyU (KUK), MCR-S (Schlesinger Library on the History of Women in America, Radcliffe College, Cambridge, MA), MA (AMH), MAH (HAM), MBNU (NED), MBTI (BTI), MBU (BOS), MdBJ (JHE), MH (HLS), MH (HUL), MH-AH (BHA), MiMtpT (EZC), [University of Minnesota Union List, Minneapolis, MN] (MUL), MNS (SNN), MnStpeG (MNG), MNtcA (BAN), MnU (MNU), MoSW (WTU), MoU (MUU), MoWgT/MoWgW (ELW), MWelC (WEL), NBC (VDB), NbKS (KRS), NBu (VHB), NbU (LDL), NcCU (NKM), NcGU (NGU), NCH (YHM), NCortU (YCM), NcRS (NRC), NcWsW (EWF), NDFM (VZE), NdU (UND), [New York State Union List, Albany, NY] (NYS), [Western New York Library Resources Council, Buffalo, NY] (VZX), [Central New York Library Resources Council, Syracuse, NY] (SRR), NFQC (XQM), NGcCC (VVX), NGenoU (YGM), NhD (DRB), NIC (COO), NmLcU (IRU), NNCU-G (ZGM), NNepaSU (ZLM), NOneoU (ZBM), NPV (VXW), NRU (RRR), NSbSU (YSM), NSyU (SYB), OAkU (AKR), OAU (OUN), OGK (KEN), OkU (OKU), OMC (MRC), OO (OBE), OTU (TOL), OU (OSU), PBL (LYU), PBm (BMC), [Pittsburgh Regional Library Center-Union List, Pittsburgh, PA] (QPR), PNwC (WFN), PP (PLF), PPiU (PIT), PSC (PSC), PU (PAU), TMurS (TXM), TNJ (TJC), [AMIGOS Union List of Serials, Dallas, TX] (IUC), TxCM (TXA), TxDN (INT), TxDW (IWU), TxHR (RCE), TxLT (ILU),

*Women's Periodicals and Newspapers*

TxU (IXA), ViRCU (VRC), ViW (VWM), VtMiM (MDY), WeharU (HRM), WMUW (GZN), WyU (WYU).

| Coll | Current Issues Only | Women's Reading Area |
|---|---|---|
| Mem | v.1, n.1-3; Summer, 1972-Spring, 1973 | Microforms |
|  | v.2, n.1-Summer?, 1974- | AP/F1095/S105 |
| Wom St | v.2, n.2/3-?, 1975- | Reading Room |
| Hist | v.1, n.1-2; Summer-Fall, 1972 | Microforms Her. 2, R 5 |

322 <u>Familia-Newsletter of Experimental and Communal Family-Oriented People</u>. 1973//? Unknown. Last issue 24 pages. Line drawings. Commercial advertising. Available on microfilm: Herstory. Published by Familia, Kingston, NY. Subject focus: poetry, communes, alternative lifestyles, fiction.

| Hist | n.4; Sep., 1973 | Microforms Her. 3, R 1 |
|---|---|---|

323 <u>Family Circle</u>. 1932. 17 times a year. Arthur Hettich, editor, Family Circle, 488 Madison Avenue, New York, NY 10022. ISSN 0014-7206. OCLC 4178274, 1775561. LC 43-37919, sn78-5303. Last issue 232 pages, last volume 2784 pages, size 21 x 28. Line drawings, photographs, some in color, commercial advertising. Available on microfilm: McA (1974-1978). Published by Family Circle, Inc., New York, NY. Frequency varies: monthly, Jan., 1971-Dec., 1976; 13 times a year, Jan.-Dec., 1977; 14 times a year, Jan.-Dec., 1978. Subject focus: crafts, health, beauty care, food, gardening, fashion, interior decoration, personal finance. Other holding institutions: KyRE (KEU), [University of Minnesota Union List, Minneapolis, MN] (MUL), NCortU (YCM), [Pittsburgh Regional Library Center-Union List, Pittsburgh, PA] (QPR), TxAbH (TXS), [Arrowhead Library System, Janesville Public Library, Janesville, WI] (WIJ), WM (GZD).

| Agric | [v.78, n.1-10], 12-[Jan.-Oct.], Dec., 1971- | Periodicals Section |
|---|---|---|
| MPL | [v.26, n.1-v.78, n.12], v.79, n.1-[Jan., 1953-Dec., 1971], Jan., 1972- | Business and Sciences Section |
| MOPL | Jan., 1975- | Circulation |
| MCL | Jan., 1975- | Circulation |
| OM | Current Issues Only | Circulation |
| BML | Current Issues Only | Circulation |

324 <u>Familyculture</u>. 1896-1897?//. Monthly. Last issue 12 pages, last volume 144 pages. Line drawings, commercial advertising. Available on microfilm: ResP. Published by Familyculture, Boston, MA. Editor: Mary Traffarn Whitney. Subject focus: spirituality, family, poetry. Other holding institution: MB (Boston Public Library).

| Mem | v.1, n.1-12; Mar., 1896-Feb., 1897 | Microforms |
|---|---|---|

325 <u>The Family in Historical Perspective</u>. 1972//? Unknown. Last issue 14 pages. Line drawings. Available on microfilm: Herstory. Published by the Newberry Library, Cambridge, MA. Subject focus: family, history.

| Hist | n.1; Spring, 1972 | Microforms Her. 2, R 4 |
|---|---|---|

326 <u>Family Planning Digest</u>. 1972-1975?//. Bi-monthly. ISSN 0046-3213. OCLC 1295989, 1774913. LC 72-623449. Last issue 16 pages, last volume 112 pages, size 22 x 27. Photographs. Self-indexed by volume. Published by Department of Health, Education and Welfare, Health Medical Service Administration, Bureau of Community Health Service, New York, NY. Editor: Lynn C. Landman. Subject focus: pregnancy, birth control, family planning. Other holding institutions: ArU (AFU), FGULS (FUL), FJUNF (FNP), [Indiana Union List of Serials, Indianapolis, IN] (ILS), MBNU (NED), MChB (BXM), MiAdC (EEA), [University of Minnesota Union List, Minneapolis, MN](MUL), MWelC (WEL), NBu (VHB), NGenoU (YGM), [New York State Union List, Albany, NY] (NYS), [Central New York Library Resources Council, Syracuse, NY] (SRR), NIC (COO), NOneoU (ZBM), OAkU (AKR), OClW (CWR), OClW-H (CHS), OCH (HUC), [State Library of Ohio Catalog Center, Columbus, OH] (SLC), Ok (OKD), OKentU (KSU), OKTU (OKT), OrU-M (OHS), OTMC (MCL), PP (PLF), PPiU (PIT), TxAbH (TXS), [AMIGOS Union List of Serials, Dallas, TX] (IUC), TxShA (IAU), [U.S. Government Printing Office-Serials, Alexandria, VA] (GPA), WaU (WAU), WKenU (GZP), WMUW (GZN).

| CFD | v.1, n.1-v.3, n.7; Jan., 1972-Jan., 1975 | Circulation |
|---|---|---|
| WDHS | v.1, n.1-v.3, n.7; Jan., 1972-Jan., 1975 | Circulation |

| | | | |
|---|---|---|---|
| MPL | v.2, n.1-v.3, n.7; Jan., 1973-Jan., 1975 | Circulation | |

327  Family Planning Perspectives. 1969. Irregular. Richard Lincoln, editor, Family Planning Perspectives, 515 Madison Avenue, New York, NY 10022. ISSN 0014-7354. OCLC 829761, 1568797. LC 72-620943. Last issue 64 pages, last volume 376 pages, size 22 x 27. Line drawings, photographs, some in color, commercial advertising. Published by Alan Guttmacher Institute, New York, NY. Frequency varies: irregular, Spring-Oct., 1969; bi-monthly, Jan., 1970-. Subject focus: family planning, birth control, pregnancy, pro-abortion, sexuality. Other holding institutions: AU (ALM), ArU (AFU), AzTeS (AZS), AzU (AZU), [California State University, Dominguez Hills, Carson, CA] (CDH), CChiS (CCH), [Pepperdine University, Malibu, CA] (CPE), CSUuP (CPS), [Congressional Research Service, Washington, DC] (CRS), DHU (DHU), DLC (DLC), DeU (DLM), FJUNF (FNP), GASU (GSU), IaDmD (IOD), ICI (IAH), INS (IAI), [Indiana Union List of Serials, Indianapolis, IN] (ILS), InU (IUL), InU-M (IUM), InIU (IUP), KPT (KFP), KyRE (KEU), LNX (LNX), LU (LUU), LU-L (LUL), MBU (BOS), MBNU (NED), MH (HUL), MMeT (TFW), MWMU (WQM), [Frostburg State College Library, Frostburg, MD] (MFS), MiAdC (EEA), NuDW (ETW), MiEM (EEM), MiGrC (EXC), MiMtpT (EZC), [University of Minnesota Union List, Minneapolis, MN] (MUL), MnSU (MNP), MsU (MUM), NcCU (NKM), NcRS (NRC), NbOB (BTC), NbU (LDL), NuNCM (NJN), [New York State Union List, Albany, NY] (NYS), NCortU (YCM), NFQC (XQM), NIC (COO), N (NYG), NNepaSU (ZLM), NPurU (ZPM), NEE (VXE), NNR (ZXC), NSbSU-H (VZB), NSchU (ZWU), [Central New York Library Resources Council, Syracuse, NY] (SRR), O (OHI), OAkU (AKR), OAU (OUN), OBgU (BGU), [Raymond Walters General and Technical College Library, Blue Ash, OH] (ORW), OC1U (CSU), OC1W-H (CHS), [State Library of Ohio Catalog Center, Columbus OH] (SLC), OCU-M (MXC), ODaWU-H (WSM), OKentU (KSU), OTMC (MCL), OU (OSU), OrSaW (OWS), OrU-M ((OHS), PBm (BMC), PManM (MAN), PPD (DXU), [Pittsburgh Regional Library Center-Union List, Pittsburgh, PA] (QPR), PPiU (PIT), PPiU-L (PLA), ScCleU (SEA), ScRhW (SWW), TNJ (TJC), TxBelM (MHB), [School of Aerospace Medicine, Brooks AFB, TX] (TBM), TxCM (TXA), [AMIGOS Union List of Serials, Dallas, TX] (IUC), TxDN (INT), TxNacS (TXK), TxShA (IAU), TxSmS (TXI), ViRCU (VRC), ViNO (VOD), WGrU (GZW), WeharU (HRM), [Arrowhead Library System, Janesville Public Library, Janesville, WI] (WIJ), WMenU (GZS), WMUW (GZN).

| | | | |
|---|---|---|---|
| WSLL | v.7, n.1- Jan./Feb., 1975- | Circulation | |
| FPPH | v.5, n.1- Jan./Feb., 1973- | Circulation | |
| MMRL | v.2, n.1- Jan./Feb., 1970- | Circulation | |
| Soc Work | v.1, n.1- Spring, 1969- | Circulation | |
| IMC | v.2, n.1- Jan./Feb., 1970- | Circulation | |
| CFD | v.1, n.1- Spring, 1969- | Circulation | |
| APL | v.4, n.1- Jan./Feb., 1972- | Circulation | |

328  Family Planning/Population Reporter. 1972. $25 for individuals. Patricia Donovan, editor, Family Planning/Population Reporter, 1220 19th Street NW, Washington, DC 20036. ISSN 0090-0923. OCLC 1784698. Last issue 16 pages, last volume 56 pages, size 22 x 27. Line drawings. Published by Alan Guttmacher Institute, New York, NY. Subject focus: birth control, family planning, population policy. Other holding institutions: ArU (AFU), [Pepperdine University, Malibu, CA] (CPE), CtW (WLU), CtY (YUS), DLC (DLC), [Congressional Research Service, Washington, DC] (CRS), FGULS (FUL), FU-L (FUB), FTaSU-L (FSL), GAuA (GJG), InU (IUL), [Indiana Union List of Serials, Indianapolis, IN] (ILS), MBNU (NED), MiDW (EYW), MiMtpT (EZC), [St. Louis University Law Library, St. Louis, MO] (SLU), [Washington University Law Library, St. Louis, MO] (WUL), NA1LS (YZA), NFQC (XQM), NSbSU-H (VZB), [Central New York Library Resources Council, Syracuse, NY] (SRR), O (OHI), OAkU (AKR), OAU (OUN), OKentU (KSU), OkU (OKL), OrU-M (OHS), P (PHA), PPiU (PIT), [AMIGOS Union List of Serials, Dallas, TX] (IUC), ViRCU (VRC), ViRU (VRU), VtU (VTU).

| | | | |
|---|---|---|---|
| CFD | v.1, n.1- Dec., 1972- | Circulation | |
| SWL | v.3, n.4-v.4, n.2; June, 1974-May, 1975 | Circulation | |
| WSLL | v.2, n.1- Jan., 1973- | Circulation | |
| WDHS | v.1, n.1-v.4, n.1; Dec., 1972-Feb., 1975 | Circulation | |

329  Far and Near. 1890-1894?//. Monthly. Last issue 12 pages, last volume 144 pages. Line drawings, commercial advertising. Available on microfilm: ResP. Published by The Critic Company, New York, NY. Editor: Maria Bowen Chapin. Subject focus: working women, clubs, workers. Other holding institution:RPB (RBN).

| | | | |
|---|---|---|---|
| Mem | n.1-48; Nov., 1890-Oct., 1894 | Microforms | |

330 Farm Wife News. 1971. Bi-weekly. $11.95 for individuals and institutions. Ann Kaiser, editor, Farm Wife News, P.O. Box 643, Milwaukee, WI. Business address, P.O. Box 572, Milwaukee, WI 53201. ISSN 0196-190X. OCLC 1279408. LC sc79-4228. Last issue 48 pages. Line drawings, photographs, some in color. Subject focus: farm life, wives, self-reliance, crafts. Other holding institutions: INS (IAI), DNAL (AGL), [University of Minnesota Union List, Minneapolis, MN] (MUL), [New York State Union List, Albany, NY] (NYS), NIC (COO), [Arrowhead Library System, Janesville Public Library, Janesville, WI] (WIJ).

| OPL | Current Issues Only | Circulation |
|---|---|---|

331 The Farmer's Wife. 1857-1939//? Monthly. OCLC 1568937. LC 56-49142. Last issue 52 pages, last volume 690 pages, size 35 x 26. Line drawings, photographs, some in color, commercial advertising. Published by the Farmer's Wife, St. Paul, MN. Editor: Dan A. Wallace. Subject focus: fiction, food, health, child care, crafts, farm life, wives, fashion. Other holding institutions: FU-A (FUA), FGULS (FUL), [University of Minnesota Union List, Minneapolis, MN] (MUL), [New York State Union List, Albany, NY] (NYS), NIC (COO).

| Agric | v.25, n.1-v.30, n.12; June, 1922-Dec., 1927 | Periodicals Section |
|---|---|---|

The Federation Bulletin. Boston, MA

see General Federation of Women's Clubs Magazine. Boston, MA

332 Feelings. 1971//? Unknown. OCLC 2261060. Last issue 40 pages. Line drawings, photographs. Available on microfilm: Herstory. Published by Women's Liberation, Brooklyn, NY. Subject focus: poetry, art, feminism.

| Hist | n.1; ?, 1971 | Microforms Her. 1, R 6 |
|---|---|---|

333 Female Liberation Newsletter. 1971//? Bi-weekly. OCLC 1569087, 3648674. Last issue 3 pages, last volume 36 pages. Line drawings, photographs. Available on microfilm: Herstory. Published by the University of California, Berkeley, CA. Frequency varies: weekly, Feb. 3-Mar. 3, 1971. Subject focus: women's studies, art, literature, pro-abortion, child care, labor unions, sexism, feminism.

| Hist | v.1, n.1-v.2, n.1; Feb. 3-Sep. 29, 1971 | Microforms Her. 1, R 14 |
|---|---|---|
| | v.2, n.2; Oct. 20, 1971 | Her. 1 UP, R4 |

334 Female Liberation Newsletter. 1970-1974//? Irregular. Last issue 8 pages. Line drawings, photographs, commercial advertising. Available on microfilm: Herstory. Published by the Boston/Cambridge Female Liberation, Cambridge, MA. Place of publication varies: Boston, MA, Dec., 1970-Mar. 12, 1973. Subject focus: day care, history, poetry, pro-abortion, self-defense, lesbians, feminism. Other holding institution: MCR-S (Schlesinger Library on the History of Women in America, Radcliffe College, Cambridge, MA).

| Hist | Dec., 1970-Sep. 27, 1971 | Microforms Her. 1, R 14 |
|---|---|---|
| | Oct. 4, 1971-June 25, 1973 | Her. 1 UP, R4 |
| | July 16, 1973-Mar. 4, 1974 | Her. CUP, R 2 |

335 Female Liberation Newsletter. 1969-1971//. Irregular. OCLC 2261067, 1569088. Last issue 18 pages. Line drawings. Available on microfilm: Herstory. Published by the Twin Cities Female Liberation Communication Center (TCFLCC), Minneapolis, MN. Subject focus: poetry, feminism, pro-abortion.

| Hist | n.1-30; Nov.11, 1969-Aug./Sep., 1971 | Microforms Her. 1, R 15 |
|---|---|---|
| | n.31; Nov., 1971 | Her. 1 UP, R4 |

336 The Female Spectator. 1746//? Semi-monthly? OCLC 655385. LC 29-25499. Last issue 40 pages, last volume 255 pages. Self-indexed in each volume. Published by Mrs. Eliza Heywood, Dublin, Ireland. Editor: Mary Priestly. Subject focus: middle class women, etiquette. Other holding institutions: CChiS (CCH), CLS (CLA), CNoS (CNO), CSS (CSA), DeU (DLM), DGU (DGU), IBloW (ICO), IWW (ICW), MWalB (MBB), NcGU (NGU), NPV (VXW), OAU (OUN), OTU (TOL), OWilmC (WMC), TxArU (IUA), TxU (IXA).

| Mem | v.1-4; 1746 | AP/F329 |
|---|---|---|

337 Female Studies. 1970. Irregular. Female Studies, P.O. Box 334, Old Westbury, NY 11568. OCLC 2480579, 2374363. LC 76-365622, 76-365623. Last issue 244 pages, size 22 x 28. Published by the Feminist Press, Old Westbury, NY. Place of publication varies: Pittsburgh, PA, Sep., 1970-Spring?, 1972; Old Westbury, NY, Fall?, 1972; Philadelphia, PA,

Spring?, 1975. Editors: Sheila Tobias, Sep., 1970; Florence Howe, ?, 1971; Florence Howe and Carol Ahlum and Blanche Glassman, Dec., 1971; Rae Lee Siporin, ?, 1972; Nancy Hoffman, Cynthia Secor, and Adrain Tinsley, ?, 1972; Sarah Slavin Schramm, Spring?, 1975; Sidonie Cassirer, Fall?, 1975; Deborah Silverton Rosenfelt, Winter, 1975. Subject focus: women's studies, feminism, art, biographies. Other holding institutions: AAP (AAA), AJacT (AJB), AzTeS (AZS), [California State University, Hayward, CA] (CSH), CSt (Stanford University), [University of Bridgeport, Bridgeport, CT] (UBM), CoCC (COC), CoGrU (COV), CSS (CSA), CtNIC (CTL), CtU (UCW), CtW (WLU), CU-Riv (CRU), DAU (EAU), DGW (DGW), DLC (DLC), FMFIU (FXG), FTS (FHM), FU (FUG), IaDaMC (IOR), IaDmG (IWG), InMuB (IBS), InNdS (ISN), InRE (IEC), InU (IUL), INS (IAI), IPfsG (IAF), IRivfR (IBE), ISS (IAS), KSteC (KKQ), KWiU (KSW), KyLoU (KLG), KyRE (KEU), LU (LUU), MdFreH (HCF), MeB (BBH), MeU-P (PGP), MiAllG (EXG), MiHolH (EXH), MiKW (EXW), MiMtpT (EZC), MiU (EYM), MiYEM (EYE), MLowU (ULS), MMeT (TFW), MnMoU (MNX), MNoeS (STO), MnSH (MHA), MnWinoCT (MNZ), MoStcL (MOQ), NBC (VDB), NBiSU (BNG), NbU (LDL), NBwU (BUF), NcBoA (NJB), NcGU (NGU), NCH (YHM), NcRM (NMC), NcRS (NRC), NcU (NOC), NFredU (XFM), NGenoU (YGM), NjJS (NJJ), NjR (NJR), NjUN (NJK), NNF (VYF), NOwU (ZOX), NPV (VXW), NSsS (VZS), NSyOC (VOC), NWhpG (VZW), OCU (CIN), OGK (KEN), OkS (OKS), OOxM (MIA), OWoC (WOO), OYesA (ANC), OYU (YNG), PAtM/PAtC (EVI), PMilS (MVS), PPCoC (PDC), PSrS (SRS), PSt (UPM), RPRC (RCM), TxDW (IWU), TxU-Da (ITD), ViNO (VOD), ViRCU (VRC), VtMiM (MDY), VtU (VTU), WMM (GZQ), WOshU (GZO).

| Coll | n.1-<br>Sep., 1970- | REF/HQ/1111<br>F4/2 |
| --- | --- | --- |
| Wom St | n.1-<br>Sep., 1970- | Reading Room |
| Mem | n.1-<br>Sep., 1970- | HQ/1111/F4 |

338  Femina. 1960. Bi-monthly. Vimla Patil, editor, Femina, Dr. D.N. Road, Bombay, India 400 001. OCLC 1327320, 1643136. LC sa65-5934, sar65-5934. Last issue 72 pages, size 25 x 33. Line drawings, photographs, some in color, commercial advertising. Published by the Times of India Press, Bombay, India. Previous editors: Dr. K.D. Jtangiani, Jan. 13, 1967-Mar. 16, 1973. Subject focus: rural life, workers, working women, health, fiction, film reviews. Other holding institutions: FJUNF (FNP), FGULS (FUL), [Indiana Union List of Serials, Indianapolis, IN] (ILS), [Central New York Library Resources Council, Syracuse, NY] (SRR).

| Mem | v.8, n.1-<br>Jan. 13, 1967- | AP/F3305 |
| --- | --- | --- |

339  Femina Illustration. 1901-1956//. Monthly. OCLC 1588614. LC 52-10464. Last issue 122 pages, last volume 1232 pages, size 24 x 32. Line drawings, photographs, some in color, commercial advertising. Published by Femina-Illustration, Paris, France. Title varies: as Le Nouveau Femina, Mar., 1954-Mar., 1956. Editors: Helene Gordon-Lazareff, Mar., 1954-Jan., 1956; Michele Rosier, Feb.-Nov., 1956. Subject focus: fashion, travel, interior decoration, beauty care, art, science, fiction, sports. In French (100%). Supplement: see Femina Theatre. Other holding institutions: AzTeS (AZS), DeU (DLM), FGULS (FUL), GASU (GSU), [University of Minnesota Union List, Minneapolis, MN] (MUL), OAkU (AKR), OCl (CLE) OO (OBE), [Pittsburgh Regional Library Center -Union List, Pittsburgh, PA] (QPR), PPi (CPL), TxLT (ILU).

| Mem | Mar., 1954-<br>Nov., 1956 | AP/F331 |
| --- | --- | --- |

340  Femina Theatre (Supplement to Femina Illustration). 1956//. Monthly. OCLC 1588614. LC 52-10464. Last issue 34 pages, size 17 x 26. Photographs. Subject focus: plays. In French (100%).

| Mem | Mar.-Nov., 1956 | AP/F332 |
| --- | --- | --- |

341  Feminary. 1970. Tri-annual. $6.50 for individuals, $13 for institutions. Feminary, Box 954, Chapel Hill, NC 27514. Last issue 36 pages, last volume 192 pages, size 17 x 21. Line drawings, photographs. Title varies: as Feminist Newsletter, Mar. 24, 1974. Frequency varies: bi-weekly, Mar. 24, 1974-Nov. 21, 1976. Subject focus: lesbians, poetry, law, fiction, rights, health, sports.

| Mem | v.9, n.1-<br>Spring, 1978- | Periodicals<br>Room |
| --- | --- | --- |
| | v.5, n.6, 20,<br>v,8, n.4?;<br>Mar. 24, Oct. 6,<br>1974-Dec., 1977 | Microforms |

342  Feminine Focus. 1964? Monthly during academic year. $5 for individuals and institutions. Glenda Earwood, editor, Feminine Focus, Box 2, 2401 Virginia Avenue, N.W., Washington, DC 20037. Last issue 6 pages, size 22 x 28. Line drawings. Published by the Intercollegiate Association for Women Students, Washington, DC. Subject focus: education, political status, women's studies, college students, vocational guidance.

| | | |
|---|---|---|
| Hist | v.14, n.2, v.16, n.1- Oct., 1977, Sep., 1979- | Circulation |

343 Feminine Focus. 1965-1972//? Irregular. OCLC 2261068. Last issue 8 pages. Line drawings, photographs. Available on microfilm: Herstory. Published by the Intercollegiate Association of Women Students, Lansing, MI. Subject focus: education, employment, college students.

| | | |
|---|---|---|
| Hist | v.2-v.7; Mar., 1966- Mar., 1971 | Microforms Her. 1, R 15 |
| | n.1-2, 4; Nov.-Dec., 1971, Feb./Mar., 1972 | Her. 1 UP, R 4 |

344 Feminine Vignettes of the Netherlands. 1948?-1972//? Semi-monthly. Last issue 6 pages, last volume 144 pages, size 22 x 28. Line drawings. Published by Press and Culture Sections of the Netherlands Consulante General, New York, NY. (Also San Francisco, CA, and Holland, MI). Editor: Henreitte Van Nierop. Subject focus: cooking, Netherlands.

| | | |
|---|---|---|
| UW Ext | v.23, n.17-v.25, n.24; Sep. 1, 1970- Dec. 15, 1972 | Circulation |

345 Feminist. 1972-1973//? Monthly. Last issue 8 pages. Line drawings, commercial advertising. Available on microfilm: Herstory. Published by Women's Liberation, Delaware County, Wallingford, PA. Subject focus: feminism, law, consciousness raising.

| | | |
|---|---|---|
| Hist | v.1, n.5-v.2, n.4; Oct., 1972- Apr., 1973 | Microforms Her. 2, R 4 |

Feminist Allaince Against Rape Newsletter.
    Washington, DC

    see Aegis. Washington, DC

346 Feminist Art Journal. 1972-1977//. Quarterly. ISSN 0300-7014. OCLC 1775351. LC 76-647396. Last issue 54 pages, last volume 208 pages, size 20 x 29. Line drawings, photographs, commercial advertising. Available on microfilm: UnM, Herstory (1972-1974). Published by the Feminist Art Journal Inc., Brooklyn, NY. Editors: Patricia Mainardi, Irene Moss and Cindy Nemser, Spring, 1973; Cindy Nemser, Fall, 1973-Summer, 1977. Subject focus: art, interviews, feminism, poetry, theatre. Other holding institutions: AAP (AAA), ArU (AFU), AzTeS (AZS), AzU (AZU), CSt (Stanford University), CLobS (CLO), CLU (CLU), DeU (DLM), DLC (DLC), DLC (NSD), DSI (SMI), FMFIU (FXG), GASU (GSU), IaCfT (NIU), InND (IND), InU (IUL), KyLoU (KLG), MBU (BOS), MdBJ (JHE), MiD (EYP), MiEM (EEM), MNS (SNN), MnStjos (MNF), [University of Minnesota Union List, Minneapolis, MN] (MUL), MWelC (WEL), NAlfC (YDM), NBrockU (XBM), NCaS (XLM), NcGU (NGU), NCortU (YCM), NcWsW (EWY), [New York State Union List, Albany, NY] (NYS), [Central New York Library Resources Council, Syracuse, NY] (SRR), NhD (DRB), NIC (COO), NPV (VXW), NRU (RRR), NSbSU (YSM), OAkU (AKR), OAU (OUN), OC1U (CSU), OCo (OCO), OkS (OKS), OO (OBE), OU (OSU), PPiU (PIT), [Pittsburgh Regional Library Center-Union List, Pittsburgh, PA] (OPR), TU (TKN), [AMIGOS Union List of Serials, Dallas, TX] (IUC), TxDN (INT), WM (GZD), WMUW (GZN).

| | | |
|---|---|---|
| Art | v.1, n.1-v.6, n.2; Apr., 1972- Summer, 1977 | +AP/+F3324/ A78 |
| Coll | v.4, n.3-v.6, n.2; Fall, 1975- Summer, 1977 | Women's Reading Area |
| Wom St | v.5, n.1-2, v.6, n.2; Spring-Summer, 1976, Summer, 1977 | Reading Room |
| MPL | v.1, n.1-v.6, n.2; Apr., 1972- Summer, 1977 | Art Section |
| Hist | v.1, n.1-2, v.2, n.1-2; Apr.-Fall, 1972, Winter-Spring, 1973 | Microforms Her. 2, R 4 |
| | v.2, n.3-v.3, n.2; Fall, 1973- Spring, 1974 | Her. 2 UP, R3 |

347 Feminist Bulletin. 1971. Irregular. $3 for individuals and institutions. Lisa Cobbs, editor, Feminist Bulletin, 908 F Street, San Diego, CA 92101. Last issue 4 pages, last volume 64 pages, size 22 x 18. Line drawings. Published by the Center for Women's Studies and Services, San Diego, CA. Subject focus: rights, education, pro-abortion, lesbians, feminism.

| | | |
|---|---|---|
| Hist | v.7, n.3, 6- May, Nov., 1977- | Circulation |

348 The Feminist Bulletin. 1973-1974//? Irregular. Last issue 8 pages. Line drawings, photographs, commercial advertising. Available on microfilm: Herstory. Published by the Feminist Bulletin, Scarborough, NY. Editor: Jody Israel. Subject focus: poetry, law, lobbying, feminism, rights.

| | Hist | July/Aug., 1973- June, 1974 | Microforms Her. 3, R 1 |

349 Feminist Coalition Newsletter. 1974//? Monthly? Last issue 4 pages. Line drawings. Available on microfilm: Herstory. Published by the Rutgers University Feminist Coalition, New Brunswick, NJ. Subject focus: feminism.

| | Hist | n.1-2; Mar. 25- Apr. 25, 1974 | Microforms Her. 3, R 2 |

350 Feminist Collections: Women's Studies Library Resources in Wisconsin. 1980. Quarterly. Gratis to individuals and institutions. Linda Parker and Catherine Loeb, editors, Feminist Collections: Women's Studies Library Resources in Wisconsin, Women's Studies Librarian-at-Large, University of Wisconsin System, 112A Memorial Library, 728 State Street, Madison, WI 53706. (608) 263-5754. OCLC 6467769. Last issue 18 pages, last volume 120 pages, size 28 x 23. Available on microfilm: WHi. Subject focus: women's studies, library resources, feminism, research. Other holding institution: WMUW (GZN).

| | Hist | v.1, n.1- Feb., 1980- | Circulation |

351 Feminist Communication Collective. 1967-1974//? Monthly. ISSN 0319-8766, 0024-5860. OCLC 2009595, 1605850. LC cn76-308915, cn76-308922. Last issue 23 pages. Line drawings. Available on microfilm: Herstory. Published by the Feminist Communication Collective, Montreal, Quebec, Canada. Frequency varies: bi-monthly, Oct./Nov., 1973. Editors: Mona Forrest and Hilary Dickinson. Subject focus: poetry, rape, employment, feminism, communications. Other holding institutions: CaOONL (NLC), OKentU (KSU), NSbSU (YSM).

| | Hist | v.1, n.5-v.2, n.3; Oct./Nov., 1973- Apr., 1974 | Microforms Her. 3, R 2 |

352 The Feminist Connection. 1980. Monthly. $7.50 for individuals and institutions. Annie Laurie Gaylor, editor, The Feminist Connection, P.O. Box 429, Madison, WI 53701. (608) 238-3338. Last issue 20 pages, size 41 x 29. Line drawings, photographs, commercial advertising. Available on microfilm: WHi. Subject focus: feminism, politics, atheism.

| | Hist | v.1, n.1- Sep., 1980- | Circulation |

353 Feminist Forum. 1972-1974//? Irregular. Last issue 6 pages. Line drawings. Available on microfilm: Herstory. Published by the YWCA of Tacoma and Pierce Counties, Tacoma/Gig Harbor, WA. Subject focus: education, health, pro-abortion, National Women's Political Caucus, employment, poetry, feminism, lobbying.

| | Hist | v.1, n.1-6; Dec., 1972- June 30, 1973 | Microforms Her. 2, R 4 |
| | | v.1, n.7-v.2, n.2; Aug. 18, 1973- Apr. 29, 1974 | Her. 2 UP, R3 |

354 Feminist Journal. 1970//? Irregular. OCLC 1569091. Last issue 18 pages. Line drawings. Available on microfilm: Herstory. Published by Women Unlimited, Minneapolis/St. Paul, MN. Subject focus: feminism.

| | Hist | v.1, n.1-3; Mar.-Sep., 1970 | Microforms |

355 Feminist Media Project Newsletter. 1973-1974//? Last issue 12 pages. Line drawings. Available on microfilm: Herstory. Published by the Feminist Media Project Newsletter, Washington, DC. Subject focus: media, feminism, communications.

| | Hist | Aug., 1973, Feb., 1974 | Microforms Her. 3, R 2 |

356 Feminist News. 1972-1973//. Irregular. Last issue 2 pages. Line drawings. Available on microfilm: Herstory. Published by the Feminist News Women's Center, California State University, Sacramento, CA. Subject focus: welfare, consciousness raising, racism, self-defense, lesbians, poetry, feminism, lobbying.

| | Hist | v.1, n.9-v.2, n.3; Jan. 17-May, 1973 | Microforms Her. 2, R 4 |

Feminist Newsletter. Chapel Hill, NC

   see Feminary. Chapel Hill, NC

357 Feminist Party. 1973-1974//? Quarterly. Last issue 4 pages. Line drawings. Available on microfilm: Herstory. Published by the Feminist Party, San Francisco, CA. Editor: Flo Kennedy. Subject focus: media, employment, political parties, Equal Rights Amendment.

| | Hist | Fall, 1973- Mar., 1974 | Microforms Her. 3, R 2 |

358 Feminist Party News. 1972//? Monthly. Last issue 3 pages. Line drawings. Available on microfilm: Herstory. Published by the Feminist Party, New York, NY. Subject focus: femi-

nism, political parties, pro-abortion, employment.

    Hist        May-June, 1972      Microforms
                                                Her. 2, R 4

359  Feminist Party of Canada News/Nouvelles. 1979. $1 for seniors, students, disabled, welfare, single parents, $5 for individuals and institutions. Feminist Party of Canada/Parti Feministe du Canada, Box 5717, Station 'A', Toronto, Ontario, Canada M5W 1A0. (416) 960-3427. Last issue 8 pages, last volume 20 pages, size 28 x 23. Line drawings. Available on microfilm: WHi. Published by Feminist Party of Canada/Parti Feministe du Canada, Toronto, Ontario, Canada. Subject focus: political parties, feminism, rights. In French (40%).

    Hist        v.1, n.1-          Circulation
                July, 1979-

360  The Feminist Voice. 1971-1972//. Monthly. OCLC 2261071. Last issue 20 pages. Line drawings, photographs. Available on microfilm: Herstory. Published by the Feminist Voice Collective, Chicago, IL. Subject focus: feminism, rights, poetry, pro-abortion, art, fiction, photography, lesbians, lobbying.

    Hist        v.1, n.1;          Microforms
                Aug. 26, 1971      Her. 1, R 2

              v.1, n.2;          Her. 1, Add.
              Sep., 1971

              v.1, n.3-v.2, n.2;  Her. 1 UP, R 4
              Nov., 1971-
              Oct., 1972

361  Feminist Women's Health Center Report. 1974//? Unknown. Last issue 16 pages. Line drawings, photographs. Available on microfilm: Herstory. Published by the Feminist Women's Health Center, Los Angeles, CA. Editor: Francie Hornstein. Subject focus: health, pro-abortion, self-help, feminism.

    Hist        Apr., 1974         Microforms
                                          Her. 3, R 2

362  The Feminist Writers' Guild/Milwaukee Chapter Newsletter. 1980? Irregular. $10 for individuals and institutions, $5 for low income. Feminist Writers' Guild, Milwaukee Chapter, 3223 North 40th Street, Milwaukee, WI 53216. Last issue 2 pages, size 21 x 28. Line drawings. Published by the Feminist Writers' Guild, Milwaukee Chapter, Milwaukee, WI. Subject focus: writers, poets.

    Hist        June, July, 1980,  Circulation
              Feb., 1981-

Feminist for Life. Columbus, OH

    see Sisterlife. Columbus, OH

363  Feminists Women's Health Centers. 1974. Unknown. Last issue 1 page. Line drawings. Available on microfilm: Herstory. Published by the Women's Choice Clinic, Oakland, CA. Subject focus: feminism, clinics, health.

    Hist        Feb. 12, 1974      Microforms
                                         Her. 3, R 2

La Femme de l'avenir; apostolat des femmes. Paris, France

    see La Femme Nouvelle. Paris, France

La Femme Libre; Apostolat des Femmes. Paris, France

    see La Femme Nouvelle. Paris, France

364  La Femme Nouvelle. 1832-1834//. Irregular. Last issue 16 pages, last volume 184 pages. Line drawings. Available on microfilm: McA. Published by Bureau de la Tribune des Femmes, Paris, France. Title varies: as La Femme Libre, v.1, n.1-2; Le Femme de l'avenir, v.1, n.[3]. Subject focus: pro-suffrage. In French (100%).

    Mem        v.1, n.1-v.2,     Microforms
              n.[11];
              1832?-Apr., 1834

La Femme Nouvelle; Affranchisement des Femmes. Paris, France

    see La Femme Nouvelle; Tribune des Femmes. Paris, France

La Femme Nouvelle; Apostolat des Femmes. Paris, France

    see La Femme Nouvelle, Tribune des Femmes. Paris, France

365  51%: A Paper of Joyful Noise for the Majority Sex. 1972-1974//? Monthly. Last issue 16 pages. Line drawings, photographs, commercial advertising. Available on microfilm: Herstory. Published by 51% Publications, Lomita, CA. Editors: Midge Lennert and Norma Wilson. Subject focus: poverty, poetry, art, satire.

    Hist        v.1, n.1-12;       Microforms
              July, 1972-        Her. 2, R 5
              June, 1973

|   |   |   |
|---|---|---|
|   | v.2, n.1-9;<br>July, 1973-<br>June, 1974 | Her. 2 UP, R 3 |

366 Focus. 1968-1971//. Irregular. Last issue 28 pages, last volume 194 pages, size 22 x 28. Line drawings, photographs. Published by the National Federation of Republican Women, Washington, DC. Title varies: as NFRW Focus '68, Feb.-Nov./Dec., 1968. Editors: Elizabeth Fielding, Feb.-July, 1968; Mrs. Gladys O'Donnell, Jan.-Nov./Dec., 1971. Subject focus: political parties, Republican Party.

|   |   |   |
|---|---|---|
| Hist | v.1, n.1-v.4, n.9;<br>Feb., 1968-<br>Nov./Dec., 1971 | JK/2351/F6 |

367 Focus. 1970. Bi-monthly. $8 for individuals and institutions. Focus, 1511 Massachusetts Avenue, Cambridge, MA 02138. (617) 661-3633 or (617) 259-0063. OCLC 2261157. Last issue 14 pages, last volume 84 pages, size 18 x 22. Line drawings, photographs, commercial advertising. Available on microfilm: Herstory (1970-1974). Published by the Boston Daughters of Bilitis, Cambridge, MA. Title varies: as The Maiden Voyage, June/July, 1970-Mar., 1971. Subject focus: lesbians, poetry, gay rights.

|   |   |   |
|---|---|---|
| Mem | v.1, n.3-<br>Feb., 1970- | AP/F6522/B |
| Hist | v.1, n.7, 12-v.3, n.9;<br>June/July, Dec., 1970-<br>Sep., 1971 | Microforms<br>Her. 1, R 6 |
|   | July, 1973-<br>Apr., 1974 | Her. CUP, R 1 |

368 Focus on Women. 1975. Tri-annual. Anne Banks, editor, Focus on Women, 9 Hamilton Hall, Montana State University, Bozeman, MT 59717. (406) 944-2012. Last issue 4 pages, size 22 x 28. Line drawings, photographs. Published by Montana State University, Bozeman, MT. Subject focus: women's studies.

|   |   |   |
|---|---|---|
| Wom Ed Res | Autumn, 1976- | Circulation |

369 Focus on Women. 1972-1973//? Irregular. Last issue 2 pages. Line drawings. Available on microfilm: Herstory. Published by the YWCA Women's Center, Orange, NJ. Title varies: as Women's Center News, June 1, 1972. Subject focus: lobbying, Equal Rights Amendment.

|   |   |   |
|---|---|---|
| Hist | v.1, n.1-2, v.2 n.1-3;<br>June 1-Nov., 1972,<br>Jan.-June, 1973 | Microforms<br>Her. 2, R 5 |

Folklore Feminists Communication. Austin, TX; Baton Rouge, LA; Santa Fe, NM

see Folklore Women's Communication. Ft. Collins, CO

370 Folklore Women's Communication. 1973. Tri-annual. $6 for individuals, $7.50 for institutions. Kathleen Manley and Carol Mitchell, editors, Folklore Women's Communication, English Department, Colorado State University, Ft. Collins, CO 80523. ISSN 0093-8475, 0160-9831. OCLC 1791804, 3795482. LC 74-641188, 78-642248. Last issue 36 pages, size 22 x 28. Line drawings. Title varies: as Folklore Feminists Communication, Fall, 1973-Fall, 1977. Place of publication varies: Austin, TX, Fall, 1973-Spring, 1974; Baton Rouge, LA, Fall, 1974-Fall, 1977; Santa Fe, NM, Spring, 1978-Spring, 1979. Subject focus: women's studies, folklore. Other holding institutions: CtY (YUS), DLC (DLC), InU (IUL).

|   |   |   |
|---|---|---|
| Hist | n.1-<br>Fall, 1973- | Circulation |

Food and Health Education. Floral Park, NY

see The Home Economist and the American Food Journal. New York, NY

371 Foote and Schoe. 1973?//? Unknown. Last issue 8 pages. Line drawings. Available on microfilm: Herstory. Published by the Women's Liberation Center, Norwalk, CT. Subject focus: feminism, satire.

|   |   |   |
|---|---|---|
| Hist | ?, 1973 | Microforms<br>Her. 2, R 5 |

372 The Forerunner. 1909-1916//. Monthly. OCLC 1569743, 4731348. LC 11-16588. Last issue 28 pages, last volume 336 pages. Line drawings, commercial advertising. Available on microfilm: GrP. Published by The Charlton Co., New York, NY. Editor: Charlotte Gilman. Subject focus: rights, socialism, history, fiction, poetry. Other holding institutions: CSt (Stanford University), CLobS (CLO), FGULS (FUL), [Indiana Union List of Serials, Indianapolis, IN] (ILS), InU (IUL), MCR-S (Schlesinger Library on the History of Women in America, Radcliffe College, Cambridge, MA), MeB (BBH), MnStcls (MST), MnStpeG (MNG), [University of Minnesota Union List, Minneapolis, MN] (MUL), NPV (VXW), OAkU (AKR), OC1W (CWR), OKentU (KSU), PPiU (PIT), ScRhW (SWW), TxEU (TXU), TxLT (ILU).

|   |   |   |
|---|---|---|
| Hist | v.1, n.1-v.7, n.12;<br>Nov., 1909-<br>Dec., 1916 | Microforms |

| | | |
|---|---|---|
| Mem | v.1, n.1-v.7, n.12; Nov., 1909- Dec., 1916 | AP/F7157 |

373  The Forum. 1972-1974//? Monthly. Last issue 8 pages. Line drawings. Available on microfilm: Herstory. Published by the Genesee Valley Chapter, National Organization for Women, Rochester, NY. Title varies: as The Genesee Valley N.O.W. Forum, Feb., 1972-?, 1973; as The N.O.W. Forum, ?, 1973-Mar., 1974. Subject focus: law, feminism, lobbying, rights.

| | | |
|---|---|---|
| Hist | Feb., 1972-?, 1973 | Microforms Her. 2, R 10 |
| | July, 1973- June, 1974 | Her. 2 UP, R 6 |

374  Forward. 1921. 5 times a year. $1.50 for individuals and institutions. Merry Mason Whipple, editor, Forward, 625 W. Washington Avenue, Madison, WI 53703. Last issue 4 pages, last volume 20 pages, size 22 x 28. Photographs, commercial advertising. Published by the League of Women Voters of Wisconsin, Inc., Madison, WI. Place of publication varies: Milwaukee, WI, June, 1922-Sep., 1941. Frequency varies: monthly, June, 1921-Feb., 1931; 10 times a year, Mar./Apr., 1931-Sep./Oct., 1942; 8 times a year, Nov., 1942-June, 1953; bi-monthly, Jan., 1954-Jan., 1959; semi-monthly, Jan. 23, 1959-May 14, 1973; bi-monthly, July 27, 1973-June 25, 1975. Previous editors: Ruth Hamilton, June, 1922-Apr., 1924; Edna Wright, June, 1924-Nov., 1925; Helen J. Baldauf, Dec., 1925-Mar., 1926; Mrs. William H. Mayhew, Aug., 1927-May, 1937; Mrs. F.A. Marshall, Aug., 1937-May, 1952; Mrs. J.J. Cates, June-Nov., 1952; Mrs. Howard Dahl, Jan., 1953-May, 1954; Mrs. Bernard Porsak, July, 1954-July, 1956; Mrs. Charles Melicher, Sep., 1956-Jan., 1959; Mrs. Vernon Carstensen, Jan. 23, 1959-Sep., 1961; Mrs. Willard Hurst, Nov., 1961-Sep., 1962; Mrs. Harold L. Nelson, Nov., 1962-July, 1964; Mrs. Bruce H. Westly, Sep., 1964-May, 1966; Mrs. Orvin Helstad, Sep., 1966-July, 1968; Ms. Bruce H. Westly, Sep., 1968-May, 1969; Patricia Georgeson, July 15, 1969-July 30, 1971; Mrs. Ray Evert, Sep. 24, 1971-May 14, 1973; Anne Annesen, July 27, 1973; Sonia Porter, Sep. 27, 1973-May 31, 1974; Randa Keener, Sep. 30, 1974-Mar. 28, 1975; Karen Gochberg, June 25, 1975-Jan. 17, 1977. Subject focus: law, lobbying.

| | | |
|---|---|---|
| Hist | [June, 1921- Mar., 1922], [n.s.] v.1, n.1- [June, 1921- Mar., 1922], June, 1922- | F902/7F7 (Cutter) |

| | | |
|---|---|---|
| MPL | v.52, n.1- Mar., 1973- | Literature and Social Sciences Section |
| R&L | Jan., 1961- | Circulation |
| UWBA | July, 1972- | Circulation |

Four Lights. Philadelphia, PA

  see Peace & Freedom. Philadelphia, PA

375  The 4th World. 1971?//? Unknown. OCLC 2261276. Last issue 24 pages. Line drawings, photographs. Available on microfilm: Herstory. Published by Fourth World Publications, Oakland, CA. Subject focus: poetry, minority women, rights, self-help, photography.

| | | |
|---|---|---|
| Hist | v.1, n.1; June 22, 1971 | Microforms Her. 1, R 2 |

376  Fownes Street Journal. 1972//? Monthly. Last issue 10 pages. Line drawings. Available on microfilm: Herstory. Published by the Fownes Street Journal, Dublin, Ireland. Subject focus: poetry, prostitution, birth control, venereal disease, employment.

| | | |
|---|---|---|
| Hist | v.1, n.1-5; May-Sep., 1972 | Microforms Her. 2, R 5 |

377  Fox Valley/Elgin N.O.W. 1973//? Unknown. Last issue 10 pages. Line drawings. Available on microfilm: Herstory. Published by the Fox Valley/Elgin Chapter, National Organization for Women, Elgin, IL. Subject focus: media, education, pro-abortion, art, consciousness raising, Equal Rights Amendment, feminism.

| | | |
|---|---|---|
| Hist | v.1, n.1; Oct., 1973 | Microforms Her. 3, R 3 |

378  Frank Leslie's Ladies' Journal. 1871-1881//? Weekly. Last issue 16 pages, last volume 352 pages. Line drawings, commercial advertising. Self-indexed (1872-1880). Available on microfilm: DLC. Published in New York, NY. Editor: Miriam F. Leslie. Subject focus: fashion, fiction, poetry, sewing.

| | | |
|---|---|---|
| Mem | v.1, n.1-v.20, n.516; Nov. 18, 1871- Oct. 1, 1881 | Microforms |

379  Frank Leslie's Lady's Magazine. 1854-1882//? Monthly. OCLC 1570068. Last issue 74 pages, last volume 216 pages, size 20 x 30. Line drawings, some in color. Self-indexed (1861-1865). Available on microfilm: DLC (1857-

1882). Published in New York, NY. Title varies: as Frank Leslie's Monthly, Jan., 1861-Dec., 1862. Subject focus: fiction, poetry, art, crafts, home economics, cooking. Other holding institutions: MCR-S (Schlesinger Library on the History of Women in America, Radcliffe College, Cambridge, MA), MnSM (MAC) [University of Minnesota Union List, Minneapolis, MN] (MUL), NCorniCC (ZDG), [Pittsburgh Regional Library Center-Union List, Pittsburgh, PA] (QPR), PPi (CPL), PPiU (PIT).

    Hist        v.8, n.1-v.16,    AP83/FR8L
                n.3;
                Jan., 1861-
                Mar., 1865


Frank Leslie's Monthly.   New York, NY

    see Frank Leslie's Lady's Magazine.
    New York, NY


380   Frankly Female. 1973//? Unknown. Last issue 6 pages. Line drawings. Available on microfilm: Herstory. Published by the Office of Special Services, University of Tennessee, Knoxville, TN. Editor: Barbara Hutchinson. Subject focus: poetry.

    Hist        Summer, 1973    Microforms
                                     Her. 2, R 5


381   Fraternally Yours, Zenska Jednota. 1911? Monthly. $2.50 for individuals and institutions. Dolores J. Soska, editor, Fraternally Yours, Zenska Jednota, 24950 Chagrin Blvd., Cleveland, OH 44122. Last issue 24 pages, size 29 x 21. Line drawings, photographs. Published by the First Catholic Slovak Ladies Association, Cleveland, OH. Subject focus: Catholic Church. In Slovine (5%).

    Hist        v.61, n.1, v.62,   Circulation
                v.3-7, v.63, n.11-
                Aug., Dec., 1976-
                Apr., 1977,
                Aug., 1978-


382   Die Frau. 1893-1944//. Monthly. Last issue 64 pages, last volume 768 pages, size 18 x 27. Line drawings, commercial advertising. Indexed: Memorial Library, AP/F845/INDEX. Available on microfilm: McA (1893-1920). Published by Die Frau, Berlin, Germany. Editor: Helene Lange. Subject focus: rights, women's movement, working women. Other holding institution: CSt (Stanford University).

    Mem        Apr., 1910-      AP/F845
                Jan., 1911


383   Frauen und Arbeit. 1949-1978//? Monthly. Last issue 16 pages, last volume 206 pages, size 17 x 24. Line drawings, photographs. Published by Deutscher Gewerkshaftsbund, Dusseldorf, West Germany. Editor: Maria Weber. Subject focus: labor unions, rights, law, employment, working women. In German (100%).

    Mem        [v.11, n.1-v.21,   AP/F846/A6513
                n.10]
                [Jan., 1958-
                Oct., 1978]


384   Die Frauenbewegung. 1895-1919//. Semi-monthly. Last issue 4 pages, last volume 134 pages. Line drawings, commercial advertising. Self-indexed. Available on microfilm: McA. Published by W. & S. Loewenthal, Berlin, Germany. Editors: Minna Cauer and Lily von Gizycki, Jan.-Dec., 1895; Minna Cauer, Jan., 1896-Dec., 1919. Subject focus: family, history. In German (100%).

    Mem        v.1-25;           Microforms
                Jan. 1, 1895-
                Dec. 15, 1919


385   Frauenbildung; Zeitchrift fuer die gesamten Interessen des weiblichen Unterrichtswesens. 1902-1923//. Irregular. Last issue 40 pages, last volume 116 pages. Available on microfilm: McA. Published by B.G. Leubner, Leipzig, Germany. Editor: Dr. Jacob Wychgram. Subject focus: education. In German (100%).

    Mem        v.1-22;           Microforms
                1902-1923


386   Frau und Frieden. 1952-1973//? Monthly. Last issue 12 pages. Line drawings, photographs. Available on microfilm: Herstory. Published by Frau und Frieden, Essen, Germany. Subject focus: peace movement, West German Women for Peace and Freedom, economics, consumerism. In German (100%).

    Hist        v.20, n.9;       Microforms
                Sep., 1971      Her. 2, R 5

                v.22, n.7-9;     Her. 2 UP, R3
                July-Sep., 1973


387   Frauen-Spiegel. 1840-1841//? Quarterly. Last issue 304 pages. Commercial advertising. Available on microfilm: ResP. Published by the Reichenbach Brothers, Leipzig, Germany. Editor: Louise Marezall. Subject focus: fiction, poetry, biographies. In German (100%). Other holding institution: MBCo (Countway Library of Medicine, Harvard University).

*Women's Periodicals and Newspapers*

    Mem      v.1-v.4,         Microforms
               [n.s.] v.1-2;
               1840-1841

388  Frauen Zeitung. 1973//? Unknown. Last issue 18 pages, line drawings, photographs. Available on microfilm: Herstory. Published in Alicenster, Germany. Subject focus: pro-abortion, lobbying, law, "Action 218", birth control, health. In German (100%).

    Hist     Oct., 1973     Microforms
                                   Her. 3, R 2

389  Frauen-Zukunft. 1910-1911//? Monthly. Last issue 96 pages, last volume 542 pages. Line drawings, commercial advertising. Available on microfilm: ResP. Published in Munich-Gruenwald, Bavaria, Germany. Editors: Gabriele von Lieben, Meta Hammerschlag, and Hanns Dorn. Subject focus: history. In German (100%). Other holding institutions: MCR-S (Schlesinger Library on the History of Women in America, Radcliffe College, Cambridge, MA), NN (NYP).

    Mem      v.1, n.1-v.2, n.6;  Microforms
               ?, 1910-?, 1911

390  Free and Proud. 1969//? Unknown. OCLC 2261319. Last issue 6 pages. Line drawings. Available on microfilm: Herstory. Published by The Women's Liberation and Gay Liberation, Tallahassee, FL. Subject focus: peace movement, feminism, gay rights.

    Hist     ?, 1969         Microforms
                                   Her. 1, R 15

The Free Enquirer. Albuquerque, NM

    see NOW Newsletter. Albuquerque, NM

Free Woman. San Francisco, CA

    see Woman N.O.W.. San Francisco, CA

391  The Freedom Press. 1973-1974//? Monthly. Last issue 6 pages. Line drawings, commercial advertising. Available on microfilm: Herstory. Published by The Rochester Chapter, National Organization for Women, Rochester, MN. Editor: Virginia Grabowski. Subject focus: Equal Rights Amendment, employment, politics, rape, feminism.

    Hist     v.1, n.3-v.2, n.6;  Microforms
           Dec., 1973         Her. 3, R 3
           June, 1974

392  The Freewoman. 1911-1912//. Last issue 8 pages, last volume 408 pages. Line drawings, commercial advertising. Available on microfilm: ResP. Published by Stephan Swift and Co., Ltd., London, England. Editors: Dora Marsden and Mary Gawthorpe. Subject focus: sexuality, eugenics. Other holding institution: MCR-S (Schlesinger Library on the History of Women in America, Radcliffe College, Cambridge, MA).

    Mem      v.1, n.1-v.2,     Microforms
            n.47;
            Nov. 23, 1911-
            Oct. 10, 1912

Free Women's Collective Newsletter. Storrs, CT

    see Sister News. Storrs, CT

393  From N.O.W. On. 1973-1974//? Irregular. Last issue 6 pages. Line drawings. Available on microfilm: Herstory. Published by the Montgomery Chapter, National Organization for Women, Montgomery, AL. Editors: Mary B. Weidler and Brenda Lazin. Subject focus: lobbying, Equal Rights Amendment, health, pro-abortion, rape.

    Hist     v.1, n.8-21;      Microforms
           Oct. 22, 1973-    Her. 3, R 3
           June 18, 1974

394  From N.O.W. On. 1972-1974//? Irregular. Last issue 8 pages. Line drawings, photographs. Available on microfilm: Herstory. Published by the Montgomery County Chapter, National Organization for Women, Rockville, MD. Title varies: as Womb at the Top, Jan., 1972. Editor: Joanne Weiss, Dec., 1973-June, 1974. Subject focus: health, feminism, lobbying, Equal Rights Amendment, education, religion.

    Hist     v.1, n.1-12;      Microforms
           Jan., 1972-       Her. 2, R 11
           Apr., 1973

           July, 1973-       Her. 2 UP, R7
           June, 1974

395  From the Bench of the Women's Athletic Association of San Jose. 1972-1973//? Irregular. Last issue 10 pages. Line drawings, photographs, commercial advertising. Available on microfilm: Herstory. Published by the Women's Athletic Association of San Jose, San Jose, CA. Editors: Dot James and Mary Adams. Subject focus: sports.

    Hist     v.1, n.1-v.2, n.1;  Microforms
           Mar., 1972-       Her. 2, R 5
           Feb., 1973

396  La Fronde. 1897-1929//. Daily. Last issue 4 pages. Line drawings, commercial advertising.

Available on microfilm: ACRPP. Published in Paris, France. Editor: Marguerite Durand, Dec. 9, 1897-Dec. 31, 1926. Subject focus: rights, socialism. In French (100%).

| Mem | [Dec. 9, 1897-May 4, 1929] | Microforms |

397 Front Page. 1970-1974//? Irregular. OCLC 2258403. Last issue 18 pages. Line drawings, photographs. Available on microfilm: Herstory. Published by the Bloomington Women's Liberation, Bloomington, IN. Title varies: as Bloomington Women's Liberation Newsletter, Oct. 13, 1970-Apr 14, 1972. Subject focus: poetry, day care, history, self-defense, health, feminism, birth control.

| Hist | Jan. 8, 1970-Oct., 1971 | Microforms Her. 1, R 13 |
| | Nov., 1971-June 12, 1973 | Her. 1 UP, R4 |
| | Jan., Mar., Mar. 31, 1974 | Her. CUP, R 2 |

398 Frontiers; A Journal of Women Studies. 1975. Tri-annual. Frontiers: A Journal of Women Studies, Women Studies Program, Hillside Court 104, University of Colorado, Boulder, CO 80309. $11 for individuals, $18 for institutions. ISSN 0060-9009. OCLC 2586280. LC sc78-317. Last issue 76 pages, last volume 246 pages, size 22 x 28. Line drawings, photographs, commercial advertising. Indexed: Women Studies Abstracts; American Humanities Index; Human Resources Abstracts; Historical Abstracts. Subject focus: sports, women's studies, motherhood. Other holding institutions: AAP (AAA), AzTeS (AZS), CArcHT (CHU), CSt (Stanford University), CLO (CCO), CLobS (CLO), CLU (CLU), COFS (COF), COU-DA (COA), CtY (YUS), FSpE (FEC), FTS (FHM), FU (FUG), HU (HUH), INS (IAI), IU (UIU), KMK (KKS), KPT (KFP), MBTI (BTI), MH (HLS, HUL), MH-AH (BHA), MNS (SNN), MiKW (EXW), MnU (MNU), [University of Minnesota Union List, Minneapolis, MN] (MUL), MnStjos (MNF), MnStpeG (MNG), MoU (MUU), [New York State Union List, Albany, NY] (NYS), NIC (COO), NPV (VXW), NTRS (ZRS), NbU (LDL), NcCU (NKM), NhD (DRB), NmLcU (IRU), NmU (IQU), OC1U (CSU), OkTahN (OKN), PBL (LYU), PPiU (PIT), RPB (RBN), TxCM (TXA), ViNO (VOD), WKenU (GZP), WMUW (GZN).

| Mem | v.1, n.1-Fall, 1975- | AP/F93575/B |
| Coll | Current Issues Only | Women's Reading Area |
| Wom St | v.2, n.1-v.3, n.3; Spring, 1977-Fall, 1978 | Reading Room |

Fruit, Garden, and Home. Des Moines, IA

see Better Homes and Gardens. Des Moines, IA

399 Full Moon. 1972//? Unknown. Last issue 24 pages. Line drawings, photographs. Available on microfilm: Herstory. Published by the Valley Women's Center, Northampton, MA. Subject focus: welfare, population policy, poetry, self-defense, pro-abortion, day care, sexism in education, peace movement.

| Hist | v.1, n.1-2; ?, 1972 | Microforms Her. 2, R 5 |

400 The Furies. 1972-1973//. Bi-monthly. ISSN 0046-5305. OCLC 2334944. Last issue 12 pages, last volume 124 pages. Line drawings, photographs, commercial advertising. Available on microfilm: WHi, Herstory. Published in Washington, DC. Frequency varies: irregular, Jan.-Fall, 1972. Subject focus: lesbians, rights, literature, poetry, self-defense, feminism, art, satire. Other holding institution: MCR-S (Schlesinger Library on the History of Women in America, Radcliffe College, Cambridge, MA).

| Hist | v.1, n.1-v.2, n.3; Jan., 1972-May/June, 1973 | Microforms Her. 2, R 5 |
| | v.1, n.1-v.2, n.3; Jan., 1972-May/June, 1973 | Microforms |

401 Gallery of Fashion. 1794-1801//. Monthly. OCLC 1570389. Last issue 8 pages, last volume 80 pages. Line drawings, some in color. Available on microfilm: ResP. Published by W. Bulmer & Co., London, England. Subject focus: fashion. Other holding institutions: [University of Minnesota Union List, Minneapolis, MN] (MUL), NN (NYP), PSt (UPM).

| Mem | v.1-v.7; Apr., 1794-May, 1801 | Microforms |

402 Garment Worker. 1958-1975//. Bi-monthly. OCLC 4414290. Last issue 8 pages. Photographs. Available on microfilm: WHi (1972-1974). Published by the Central Pennsylvania District International Ladies' Garment Workers Union, Harrisburg, PA. Editor: Bonnie Segal, Oct., 1972-Dec., 1974/Jan., 1975. Subject focus: AFL-CIO, labor unions, garment industry, lobbying.

| Hist | v.15, n.8, v.16, n.4, v.17, n.1; Oct., 1972, Aug., Dec., 1974/Jan., 1975 | Microforms |

403 The Gay Blade. 1971-1974//? Irregular. Last issue 10 pages. Line drawings, photographs, commercial advertising. Available on microfilm: Herstory. Published by D.Y.K. Enterprises, Washington, DC. Subject focus: gay rights, employment, lesbians.

| Hist | v.3, n.9-v.4, n.8; June, 1972- May, 1973 | Microforms Her. 2, R 5 |
| --- | --- | --- |
|  | v.4, n.11-v.5, n.6; Aug., 1973- Mar., 1974 | Her. 2 UP, R 3 |

404 Gay People and Mental Health: A Monthly Report. 1972//? Monthly. Last issue 4 pages. Line drawings. Available on microfilm: Herstory. Published by Gay People and Mental Health, Minneapolis, MN. Editors: Cindy Hanson and John Preston. Subject focus: lesbians, mental health, counseling.

| Hist | v.1, n.1-3; Oct.-Dec., 1972 | Microforms Her. 2, R 5 |
| --- | --- | --- |

405 Gay Teacher's News. 1973//? Unknown. Last issue 2 pages. Line drawings. Available on microfilm: Herstory. Published by the Chicago Gay Teachers Union, Chicago, IL. Subject focus: lesbians, education, gay teachers.

| Hist | v.1, n.1; Winter, 1973 | Microforms Her. 3, R 2 |
| --- | --- | --- |

406 Gay Women's Newsletter. 1972-1973//? Irregular. Last issue 2 pages. Line drawings. Available on microfilm: Herstory. Published by Gay Women's Newsletter, Champaign, IL. Subject focus: lesbians.

| Hist | Nov. 15, 1972- Jan. 20, 1973 | Microforms Her. 2, R 5 |
| --- | --- | --- |

407 Gayly Forward. 1972?//? Unknown. Last issue 4 pages. Line drawings. Available on microfilm: Herstory. Published by Gayly Forward, Seattle, WA. Subject focus: counseling, poetry, lesbians, mental health.

| Hist | ?, 1972 | Microforms Her. 2, R 5 |
| --- | --- | --- |

408 General Bulletin. 1920-1927//? Monthly. Last issue 9 pages, size 22 x 28. Line drawings. Published by the American Legion Auxiliary, Department of Minnesota, Minneapolis, MN. Subject focus: clubs.

| Hist | [v.4, n.2-v.6, n.2;] [Sep. 24, 1923- Feb. 21, 1927] | F836/8A51A/ Minn (Cutter) |
| --- | --- | --- |

The General Federation Bulletin. Boston, MA

see General Federation of Women's Clubs Magazine. Boston, MA

409 General Federation Clubwoman. 1920. Monthly except in summer. $3 for individuals and institutions. Eve Singer, editor, General Federation Clubwoman, 1734 N Street N.W., Washington, DC 20036. ISSN 0016-6537. OCLC 2251401, 4714828, 4251697. LC sn78-208. Last issue 24 pages, last volume 164 pages, size 29 x 21. Line drawings, photographs, commercial advertising. Published by General Federation of Women's Clubs, Washington, DC. Title varies: as The Clubwoman GFWC., Oct., 1930-Aug., 1941. Previous editors: Vella Alberta Winner, Oct., 1930-June, 1941; Eleanor Meyer, July, 1941-Feb., 1942; Vella Alberta Winner, Mar.-Oct., 1942; Sara W. Whitehurst, Nov., 1942-June, 1944; Alice C. Weitz, Sep., 1944-June, 1947; Mildred White Wells, Sep., 1947-Dec., 1949; Mary McGinn Taylor, Sep., 1957-June, 1969; Mary Kathleen Taylor, Sep., 1969-Sep., 1976; Margaret W. Sullivan, Jan./Feb.-Sep., 1979. Subject focus: lobbying, clubs, human services. Other holding institutions: [University of Minnesota Union List, Minneapolis, MN] (MUL), [Western New York Library Resources Council, Buffalo, NY] (VZX), OkT (TUL), WM (GZD).

| Hist | [v.50, n.7-v.55, n.1] v.57, n.5- [Mar., 1972- Sep., 1976] Jan./ Feb., 1979- | Circulation |
| --- | --- | --- |
| R&L | v.11, n.4-v.12, n.6, v.14, n.7- v.29, n.9, v.37, n.6-v.56, n.3; Oct., 1930- Dec., 1931, Jan., 1934- Dec., 1949, Sep, 1957-Nov., 1977 | Circulation |

410 General Federation Magazine. 1903?-1919//? Monthly. Last issue 40 pages, size 23 x 30. Commercial advertising. Published by the General Federation of Women's Clubs, New York, NY. Editors: Harriet Bishop Waters, May, 1914; Helen Louise Johnson, Nov., 1917-Dec., 1919. Subject focus: art, lobbying, education, home economics, literature, music, public health, government workers, clubs. Other holding institution: NN (NYP).

| | | |
|---|---|---|
| Hist | v.12, n.5, v.16, n.8-v.17, n.9, v.18, n.10; May, 1914, Nov., 1917- Sep., 1918, Dec., 1919 | KW/8W87/G (Cutter) |

411 Genesis III. 1971-1974//? Bi-monthly. ISSN 0360-3601. OCLC 1635813, 5954137. LC sc75-2. Last issue 4 pages. Line drawings. Available on microfilm: Herstory. Published by the Philadelphia Task Force on Women in Religion, Philadelphia, PA. Editor: Nancy Krody. Subject focus: religion, rights. Other holding institutions: DLC (NSD), GEU (EMU), MBTI (BTI), MBU-T (BZM), MCE (BPS), MH-AH (BHA), MSohG (BCT), NcWfSB (NVS), WMUW (GZN).

| | | |
|---|---|---|
| Hist | v.1, n.1-3; May/June- Sep./Oct., 1971 | Microforms Her. 1, R 15 |
| | v.1, n.4-v.2, n.7; Nov./Dec., 1971- May/June, 1973 | Her. 1 UP, R5 |
| | v.3, n.2-v.4, n.2; July/Aug., 1973- June/July, 1974 | Her. CUP, R 2 |

412 General Federation of Women's Clubs Magazine. 1903-1920//. Monthly. OCLC 6246369, 5794178, 2446875. Last issue 50 pages, last volume 202 pages. Line drawings, commercial advertising. Available on microfilm: ResP. Published by the State Federation of Women's Clubs, New York, NY. Title varies: as The Federation Bulletin, Nov., 1903-Apr., 1910; as The Conquest Magazine and the Federation Bulletin, May, 1910; as The General Federation Bulletin, June, 1910-Dec., 1912. Place of publication varies: Boston, MA, Nov., 1903-May, 1910; Troy, NY, June, 1910-Dec., 1916. Editors: May Alden Ward and Helen A. Whittier, Nov., 1903-May, 1910; Harriet Bishop Waters, June, 1910-Dec., 1916; Maryot Holt Dey, Jan.-Sep., 1917; Helen Louise Johnson, Oct., 1917-June, 1920. Subject focus: clubs. Other holding institutions: PSt (UPM), TxDW (IWU).

| | | |
|---|---|---|
| Mem | v.1, n.1-v.19, n.6; Nov., 1903- June, 1920 | Microforms |

The Genesee Valley N.O.W. Forum. Rochester, NY

    see <u>The Forum</u>. Rochester, NY

The Gentlewoman. London, England

    see <u>The Gentlewoman and Modern Life</u>. London, England

413 The Gentlewoman and Modern Life. 1890-1926//? Weekly. Last issue 32 pages, last volume 966 pages. Line drawings, photographs, commercial advertising. Self-indexed at end of each volume. Available on microfilm: ResP. Published by the Gentlewoman and Modern Life, London, England. Title varies: as The Gentlewoman, Jan. 5, 1901-Jan. 2, 1926. Subject focus: poetry, fiction, fashion, biographies. Other holding institution: NN (NYP).

| | | |
|---|---|---|
| Mem | n.548-1883; Jan. 5, 1901- Aug. 7, 1926 | Microforms |

414 Geographers for Women's Achievement Newsletter. 1972-1973//? Irregular. Last issue 3 pages. Line drawings. Available on microfilm: Herstory. Published by the Department of Geography, Syracuse University, Syracuse, NY. Subject focus: employment, career development, professionals, research.

| | | |
|---|---|---|
| Hist | v.1, n.1-2; Nov., 1972- Apr., 1973 | Microforms Her. 2, R 5 |

415 Gerwerkschaftliche Frauenzeitung. 1916-1922//? Bi-weekly. Last issue 8 pages, last volume 192 pages, size 24 x 33. Published by Gewerkschaftliche Frauenzeitung, Berlin, Germany. Subject focus: working women, workers, rights, war work. In German (100%).

| | | |
|---|---|---|
| Mem | v.7, n.1-25; Jan. 11- Dec. 13, 1922 | +AP/+G3932 |

416 Giustizia. 1919. Monthly. $2 for individuals and institutions. Lino Manocchia, editor, Giustizia, 1710 Broadway, New York, NY 10019. ISSN 0195-3729. OCLC 5460457. LC sn79-8716. Last issue 12 pages, last volume 154 pages, size 39 x 29. Line drawings, photographs. Available on microfilm: KtO (1919-1946). Published by the International Ladies' Garment Workers' Union, New York, NY. Subject focus: labor unions, garment industry, AFL-CIO. In Italian (100%).

| | | |
|---|---|---|
| Hist | v.59, n.10- Oct., 1977- | Circulation |

417 Give a Sister a Lift. 1973//? Unknown. Last issue 18 pages. Line drawings. Available on microfilm: Herstory. Published by the Planted Breast Collective, Santa Cruz, CA. Subject focus: poetry, lesbians, pro-abortion, sexuality, health.

| | | |
|---|---|---|
| Hist | n.1-2; ?, 1973 | Microforms Her. 2, R 5 |

418 Glamour. 1903. Monthly. $10 for individuals and institutions. Ruth Whitney, editor, Glamour, 350 Madison Avenue, New York, NY 10017. Business address: P.O. Box 5203, Boulder, CO 80302. ISSN 0017-0747. OCLC 1751250, 5259082. LC 43-33892, sn79-7438. Last issue 214 pages, size 20 x 28. Line drawings, photographs, some in color, commercial advertising. Indexed: Access Index. Available on microfilm: UnM (1939-); McP (1973-). Published by Condé Nast Publications, New York, NY. Subject focus: beauty care, fashion, health, food, travel, interior decoration. Other holding institutions: ArAO (AKO), AzFU (AZN), AzTeS (AZS), [Pepperdine University, Malibu, CA] (CPE), CLU (CLU), CSUuP (CPS), COFS (COF), DLC (DLC), FJF (FJK), GA (GAP), GVaS (GYG), IDeKN (JNA), IPB (IBA), LHS (LSH), MCR-S (Schlesinger Library on the History of Women in America, Radcliffe College, Cambridge, MA), [University of Minnesota Union List, Minneapolis, MN] (MUL), MNS (SNN), MWP (WPG), NcRS (NRC), NjLincB (BCC), [Central New York Library Resources Council, Syracuse, NY] (SRR), [Western New York Library Resources Council, Buffalo, NY] (VZX), NR (YQR), OAU (OUN), OCl (CLE), OkLC (OKC), OkT (TUL), OSteC (STU), OY (YMM), [Pittsburgh Regional Library Center-Union List, Pittsburgh, PA] (QPR), PCoR (ROB), PPD (DXU), ScRhW (SWW), [AMIGOS Union List of Serials, Dallas, TX] (IUC), TxDW (IWU), TxAm (TAP), TxBelM (MHB), TxSmS (TXI), [Arrowhead Library System, Janesville Public Library, Janesville, WI] (WIJ).

| | | |
|---|---|---|
| MPL | v.72, n.2- Oct., 1974- | Literature and Social Science Section |
| MATC | Current Issues Only | Cora Hardy Library |
| MHHS | v.71, n.1- Jan., 1973- | Circulation |
| EHS | Current Issues Only | Circulation |
| CFL | Current Issues Only | Circulation |
| BML | Current Issues Only | Circulation |
| SPHS | Current Issues Only | Circulation |
| MMHS | Mar., 1970- | Circulation |
| MFHS | Jan., 1974- | Circulation |
| MCL | Jan., 1974- | Circulation |
| UWBA | Jan., 1969- | Circulation |
| OPL | Jan., 1969- | Circulation |
| MGHS | Feb., 1973- | Circulation |

419 Glos Polek. 1910? Semi-monthly. Helena Zielinska, editor, Glos Polek, 205 S. Northwest Hwy.,Parkridge, IL 60068. ISSN 0199-0462. OCLC 5537512. LC sn79-7943. Last issue 12 pages, last volume 288 pages, size 29 x 38. Line drawings, photographs. Published by the Polish Women's Alliance of America, Parkridge, IL. Subject focus: Polish Americans, Catholic Church, clubs. In Polish (75%).

| | | |
|---|---|---|
| Hist | v.72, n.10- May 19, 1977- | Circulation |

Godey's Lady's Book. Philadelphia, PA

see Godey's Magazine. Philadelphia, PA

Godey's Lady's Book and Magazine. Philadelphia, PA

see Godey's Magazine. Philadelphia, PA

420 Godey's Magazine. 1830-1898//? Monthly. OCLC 2133694, 5112741. LC 46-40247. Last issue 112 pages, last volume 688 pages, size 15 x 24. Line drawings, photographs, some in color, commercial advertising. Indexed: Poules Index. Available on microfilm: McP, UnM. Published by the Godey Company, Philadelphia, PA. Title varies: as The Lady's Book, Jan., 1836-Dec., 1839; as Godey's Lady's Book, Jan., 1840-Dec., 1858; as Godey's Lady's Book and Magazine, Jan., 1859-Oct., 1892. Editors: Sarah J. Hale, Lydia H. Sigourney and Louis A. Godey, Jan., 1840-Dec., 1842; Sarah J. Hale, Morton Mc Michael and Louis Godey, Jan., 1843-Dec., 1846; Sarah J. Hale and Louis Godey, Jan., 1847-Dec., 1877. Subject focus: fiction, poetry, fashion, art, crafts. Other holding institutions: AU (ALM), ArCCA (AKC), ArLUA (AKU), ArU (AFU), AzTeS (AZS), [Long Beach Public Library, Long Beach, CA] (CLB), CtHT (TYC), [University of Bridgeport, Bridgeport, CT] (UBM), CSdS (CDS), DeU (DLM), DSI (SMI), InU (IUL), IPB (IBA), [North Central Kansas Library, Manhattan, KS] (KKM), KGbLS (KKV), MCR-S (Schlesinger Library on the History of Women in America, Radcliffe College, Cambridge, MA), MiRochOU (EYR), MiSW (EZW), [University of Minnesota Union List, Minneapolis, MN] (MUL), NcCU (NKM), NCortU (YCM), [Central New York Library Resources Council, Syracuse, NY] (SRR), NGenoU (YGM), NII (XIM), NNepaSU (ZLM), NOneoU (ZBM), NR (YQR), NSbSU (YSM), OAkU (AKR), OClW (CWR), ODa (DMM), ODentU (KSU), OO (OBE), PCarlD (DKC), PIm (IMM), PPCHC (CHE), ScRhW (SWW), [AMIGOS Union List of Serials, Dallas, TX]

(IUC), TxDa (IGA), TxShA (IAU), WM (GZD).

| Hist | [v.12, n.1-v.137, n.818]; [Jan., 1836-Aug., 1898] | AP83/G05 |

421 <u>Gold Flower</u>. 1971-1979//. Bi-monthly. OCLC 1605397. Last issue 23 pages, last issue 90 pages, size 22 x 28. Line drawings, photographs, commercial advertising. Available on microfilm: Herstory (1971-1974), WHi. Published by Gold Flower, Minneapolis, MN. Frequency varies: monthly, Nov., 1971-Aug., 1976. Subject focus: rights, pro-abortion, child care, lesbians, feminism, gay rights, poetry.

| Hist | v.1, n.1-v.6, n.1; Nov., 1971-Apr./May, 1979 | Microforms |
| | v.1, n.1-v.2, n.1; Nov., 1971-Mar., 1973 | Her. 2, R 5 |
| | v.2, n.4-11; July, 1973-Mar., 1974 | Her. 2 UP, R3 |

422 <u>Gold Star Mother</u>. 1948? Bi-monthly. $1.15 for individuals and institutions. Ruth Frye, editor, Gold Star Mother, 2128 LeRoy Place, N.W., Washington, DC 20008. OCLC 5533096. Last issue 8 pages, last volume 40 pages, size 37 x 29. Line drawings, photographs. Published by American Gold Star Mothers, Inc., Washington, DC. Frequency varies: monthly, Nov., 1968-Apr., 1974. Previous editors: Marie A. Kittredge, Nov., 1968-July, 1971; Mary Kelly, Aug., 1971-June, 1972; Marie Hart, July, 1972-May/June, 1974; Regina Wilk, Sep./Oct., 1974-Jan./Feb., 1977. Subject focus: motherhood, veterans. Other holding institution: [University of Minnesota Union List, Minneapolis, MN] (MUL).

| Hist | v.21- Nov., 1968- | Circulation |

423 <u>Good Housekeeping</u>. 1885. Monthly. $15.97 for individuals and institutions. John Mack Carter, editor, Good Housekeeping, 959 Eighth Avenue, New York, NY. Business address: P.O. Box 10055, Des Moines, IA 50350. ISSN 0017-209X. OCLC 1605243, 2497043. LC 08-37003. Last issue 302 pages, last volume 3600 pages, size 20 x 28. Line drawings, photographs, some in color, commercial advertising. Self-indexed (1903-1913), Readers Guide (1909-). Available on microfilm: UnM. Published by the Hearst Corporation, New York, NY. Place of publication varies: Springfield, MA, Jan., 1905-Dec., 1910. Previous editors: William Frederick Bigelow, Feb., 1925-June, 1937; Herbert R. Mayes, July, 1942-Jan., 1959; Wade H. Nichols, Feb., 1959-May, 1975. Subject focus: food, parenting, interior decoration, beauty care, fashion, needlework, health, fiction. Other holding institutions: AU (ALM), ArAO (AKO), ArU (AFU), AzFU (AZN), AzTeS (AZS), AzU-L (AZL), [Pepperdine University, Malibu, CA] (CPE), CSt (Stanford University), CLU (CLU), CoDU (DVP), COU-DA (COA), CtY (YUS), [Congressional Research Service, Washington, DC] (CRS), DLC (DLC), DNAL (AGL), FJUNF (FNP), GA (GAP), [Indiana Union List of Serials, Indianapolis, IN] (ILS), InU (IUL), IPB (IBA), KSteC (KKQ), [Frostburg State College Library, Frostburg, MD] (MFS), MiAdC (EEA), MiLC (EEL), MiMtpT (EZC), MnStjos (MNF), [University of Minnesota Union List, Minneapolis, MN] (MUL), MNS (SNN), NbU (LDL), NBu (VHB), NbKS (KRS), NcEUcE (NPE), NCortU (YCM), NcRS (NRC), NcWfSB (NVS), [New York State Union List, Albany, NY] (NYS), [Central New York Library Resources Council, Syracuse, NY] (SRR), NhPlS (PSM), NIC (COO), NjLincB (BCC), NmLcU (IRU), NmLVH (NMH), NR (YQR), NNR (ZXC), NOneoU (ZBM), NSyU (SYB), OAkU (AKR), OCedC (CDC), OGK (KEN), OCl (CLE), OC1U (CSU), OC1W (CWR), OCo (OCO), OKentU (KSU), OkTOR (OKO), OkT (TUL), O (OHI), OO (OBE), [Wood County District Public Library, Bowling Green, OH] (OWC), OLanU (OUL), OTU (TOL), OY (YMM), PCalS (CSC), PCLS (REC), PCoR (ROB), [Pittsburgh Regional Library Center-Union List, Pittsburgh, PA] (QPR), PIm (IMM), PNwC (WFN), PPD (DXU), PPiAC (AIC), PPi (CPL), Sc (DSC), ScRhW (SWW), [AMIGOS Union List of Serials, Dallas, TX] (IUC), TCollsM (TMS), TMurS (TXM), TxAbH (TXS), TxBelM (MHB), TxDaB (IDA), TxDN (INT), TxDW (IWU), TxEU (TXU), TxLT (ILU), ViRCU (VRC), [Emory and Henry College, Emory, VA] (VEH), [Arrowhead Library System, Janesville Public Library, Janesville, WI] (WIJ), WMaPI-RL (GZR), WMUW (GZN), WM (GZD).

| Agric | [v.40, n.1-v.88, n.12], v.89, n.3- [Jan., 1905-Dec., 1953], Mar., 1954- | Periodicals Section |
| MPL | v.65, n.1- Jan., 1930- | Literature and Social Science Section |
| MATC | Current Issues Only | Cora Hardy Library |
| MHHS | v.104, n.1- Jan., 1969- | Circulation |
| PPL | v.106, n.1- Jan., 1971- | Circulation |
| EHS | v.105, n.1- Jan., 1970- | Circulation |

| | | | | | | |
|---|---|---|---|---|---|---|
| VHS | v.104, n.1-<br>Jan., 1969- | Circulation | | DFHS | v.109, n.9-<br>Sep., 1974- | Circulation |
| MMHS | v.104, n.1-<br>Jan., 1969- | Circulation | | MHPL | v.102, n.1-<br>Jan., 1967- | Circulation |
| BAHS | v.106, n.1-<br>Jan., 1971- | Circulation | | BHS | v.106, n.7-<br>July, 1971- | Circulation |
| TML | v.89, n.1-<br>Jan., 1954- | Circulation | | SAPH | Current Issues<br>Only | Circulation |
| DHS | Current Issues<br>Only | Circulation | | BML | Current Issues<br>Only | Circulation |
| CPPL | Current Issues<br>Only | Circulation | | VPL | v.104, n.1-<br>Jan., 1969- | Circulation |
| OPL | Current Issues<br>Only | Circulation | | SCPL | v.103, n.11-<br>Nov., 1968- | Circulation |
| MCL | v.106, n.1-<br>Jan., 1971- | Circulation | | | | |
| WHS | v.104, n.1-<br>Jan., 1969- | Circulation | | | | |
| WAPL | v.108, n.6-<br>June, 1973- | Circulation | | | | |
| MOPL | v.105, n.1-<br>Jan., 1970- | Circulation | | | | |
| DFPL | v.106, n.1-<br>Jan., 1971- | Circulation | | | | |
| CFL | v.109, n.1-<br>Jan., 1974- | Circulation | | | | |
| MFHS | v.107, n.1-<br>Jan., 1972- | Circulation | | | | |
| OM | Current Issues<br>Only | Circulation | | | | |
| MAPL | Current Issues<br>Only | Circulation | | | | |
| NFPL | Current Issues<br>Only | Circulation | | | | |
| MGHS | v.97, n.1-<br>Jan., 1962- | Circulation | | | | |
| MIPL | v.108, n.1-<br>Jan., 1973- | Circulation | | | | |
| BFL | v.110, n.1-<br>Jan., 1975- | Circulation | | | | |
| SPPL | v.105, n.1-<br>Jan., 1970- | Circulation | | | | |
| RPL | v.105, n.1-<br>Jan., 1970- | Circulation | | | | |
| BEL | Current Issues<br>Only | Circulation | | | | |

424 Goodbye to All That. 1970-1973//? Monthly. OCLC 2261582. Last issue 16 pages. Line drawings, photographs, commercial advertising. Available on microfilm: WHi, Herstory (1970-1971). Published by San Diego Women/ Goodbye to All That, San Diego, CA. Frequency varies: bi-weekly, Sep. 15, 1970-Sep. 15, 1972. Subject focus: rights, radical feminism, child care, health, women's studies, fiction, poetry.

| | | |
|---|---|---|
| Hist | n.1-40;<br>Sep. 15, 1970-<br>June, 1973 | Microforms |
| | n.1-15;<br>Sep. 15, 1970-<br>June 2, 1971 | Her. 1, R 2 |
| | n.16-17;<br>June-July, 1971 | Her. 1, Add. |
| | n.19-27;<br>Oct., 1971-<br>May 24, 1972 | Her. 1 UP, R5 |

425 The Graduate Woman. 1882. Bi-monthly. $8 for individuals and institutions. Patricia Jenkins, editor, The Graduate Woman, 2401 Virginia Avenue N.W., Washington, DC 20037. (202) 785-7727. ISSN 0161-5661. OCLC 5177672, 3958255. LC 79-642675, sn78-389. Last issue 64 pages, last volume 112 pages, size 22 x 28. Line drawings, photographs, some in color, commercial advertising. Indexed: Education Index (1929-); Public Affairs Information Service. Available on microfilm: UnM. Published by the American Association of University Women, Washington, DC. Title varies: as Journal of the American Association of University Women, Oct., 1921-Oct., 1961; as AAUW Journal, Jan., 1962-Apr., 1978. Place of publication varies: Ithaca, NY, Oct., 1921-Oct., 1923; Concord, NH, Jan., 1924-June, 1926; Baltimore, MD, Oct., 1926-June,

1930; Menasha, WI, Oct., 1930-June, 1934; Concord, NH, Oct., 1934-May, 1970. Frequency varies: quarterly, Oct., 1921-May, 1970; 7 times a year, Oct., 1970-Nov., 1977. Previous editors: Gertrude S. Martin, Oct., 1921-July, 1922; Louise Fitch, Oct., 1922; Mina Kerr, Jan.-Oct., 1925; Eleanore Boswell, Jan., 1926-Oct., 1927; Belle Rankin, Jan., 1928-Oct., 1929; Ruth Wilson Tryon, Oct., 1930-May, 1955; Elizabeth Phinney, Oct., 1955-May, 1968; Betty Williams, Oct., 1968-May, 1972; Pat Kresge, Aug., 1972-Mar., 1973; Jean Fox, Apr., 1973; Pat Kresge, Aug., 1973-Aug., 1975; Jean Fox, Oct., 1975-Jan., 1977. Subject focus: employment, career development, professionals. Other holding institutions: AAP (AAA), AJacT (AJB), ArCCA (AKC), ArStC (ASU), ArU (AFU), AU (ALM), CLO (CCO), CLobS (CLO), CLSU (CSL), CLU (CLU), COFS (COF), COU-DA (COA), CSfU (CUF), CStbW (CWS), DeU (DLM), DGW (DGW), DLC (DLC), FBoU (FGM), FJUNF (FNP), FOFT (FTU), FMFIU (FXG), FMFIU (FXN), FTaSU (FDA), GASU (GSU), GMIW (GGC), GStG (GPM), GU (GUA), GVaS (GYG), IaCfT (NIU), IaDL (IOH), IaWavU (IOW), ICharE (IAD), ICRC (IAR), IDeKN (JNA), InLP (IPL), InND (IND), INS (IAI), InU (IUL), InWhC (ICC), IRA (ICY), IU (UIU), KHayF (KFH), KLindB (KFB), KSteC (KKQ), KYBB (KBE), KyU (KUK), LLafS (LWA), LNT (LRU), LNU (LNU), MBU (BOS), MBNU (NED), MChB (BXM), MCM (MYG), MdBJ (JHE), MdStm (MDS), MiAdC (EEA), MiDU (EYU), MiDW (EYW), MiEM (EEM), MiGrC (EXC), MiHM (EZT, MiHolH (EXH), MiKW (EXW), MiMtpT (EZC), MiU (EYM), MiYEM (EYE), [University of Minnesota Union List, Minneapolis, MN] (MUL), MH (HUL), MH-Ed (HGM), MnManS (MNM), MnStjos (MNF), MWalB (MBB), MWelC (WEL), MWP (WPG), NA1U (NAM), NBrockU (XBM), NBronSL (VVS), NBuC (YBM), NbWayS (WAY), NCaS (XLM), NcDaD (NNM), NcGA (NQA), NcLS (NSP), NCortU (YCM), NcRS (NRC), [New York State Union List, Albany, NY] (NYS), [Western New York Library Resources Council, Buffalo, NY] VZX), [Central New York Library Resources Council, Syracuse, NY] (SRR), NEE (VXE), NFredU (XFM), NFQC (XQM), NGcA (VJA), NGH (ZEM), NIC (COO), NII (XIM), NmLcU (IRU), NmLvH (NMH), NNU (ZYU), NOneoU (ZBM), NONEOH (VZH), NOsU (YOM), NPLEP (VZU), NPotU (ZQM), NSbSU (YSM), NSchU (ZWU), NTRS (ZRS), OAkU (AKR), OBgU (BGU), OC1U (CSU), OC1W (CWR), OCU (CIN), ODaWU (WSU), OGK (KEN), OkTahN (OKN), OKTU (OKT), OMC (MRC), OOxM (MIA), OTMC (MCL), OTU (TOL), OU (OSU), OrFR (ORC), PAnL (LVC), PBbS (PBB), PBL (LYU), PC1vU (URS), PCoR (ROB), PCW (UMC), PE1C (ELZ), PG1B (BEA), PHC (HVC), [Pittsburgh Regional Library Center-Union List, Pittsburgh, PA] (QPR), PNwc (WFN), PPD (DXU), PPiC (PMC), PPiU (PIT), PPJ (TVJ), PSC (PSC), ScRhW (SWW), ScU (SUC), SdB (SDB), TCU (TUC), TMurS (TXM), [AMIGOS Union List of Serials, Dallas, TX] (IUC), TxBelM (MHB), TxCM (TXA), TxDaU (IVD), TxDN (INT), TxDW (IWU), TxLT (ILU), TxNacS (TXK), TxSmS (TXI), TxU (IXA), [Emory and Henry College, Emory, VA] (VEH), ViNO (VOD), ViRCU (VRC), ViU (VA@), ViW (VWM), VtU (VTU), WGrU (GZW), WKenU (GZP), WMUW (GZN), WyU (WYU).

| | | |
|---|---|---|
| Mem | v.15, n.1-v.63, n.4; Oct., 1921-May, 1970 | AP/A1029 |
| | v.64, n.1- Oct., 1970- | Microforms |
| EC | Current Issues Only | Circulation |
| IMC | [Jan., 1971-Dec., 1972] | Circulation |

426 The Grail. 1971//? Unknown. Last issue 4 pages. Line drawings, photographs. Available on microfilm: Herstory. Published by The Grail, Grailville, Loveland, OH. Subject focus: International General Assembly of the Grail, religion.

| | | |
|---|---|---|
| Hist | Aug., 1971 | Microforms Her. 2, R 5 |

427 Grist. 1975-1978//. Semi-annual. Last issue 8 pages, last volume 16 pages, size 29 x 45. Line drawings, photographs. Published by Grist Press, Cambridge, MA. Subject focus: poetry.

| | | |
|---|---|---|
| RBR | v.1, n.1-v.4, n.1; Spring, 1975-Spring, 1978 | Circulation |

428 Groupe de Recherche et d' Information Feministes. 1973. Quarterly. Jacquelene Aubenas Françoise Collin, editor, Groupe de Recherche et d' Information Feministes, Rue Henry Van Zuylen 59, 1180 Brussels, Belgium 374 9704. Last issue 192 pages, size 18 x 23. Frequency varies: 5 times a year, ?. 1973-Oct., 1976. Subject focus: religion, feminism, interviews. In French (100%).

| | | |
|---|---|---|
| Mem | n.1-?, 1973- | Periodicals Room |

429 Guter Rat; Verlag fuer die Frau. 1979? Monthly. Anneliese Zulgervitz, editor, Guter Rat Verlag fuer die Frau, 701 Liepzig, Leninstrasse 16, East Germany. Last issue 32 pages, size 24 x 31. Line drawings, photographs, some in color, commercial advertising. Subject focus: home economics, interior decoration, health, food, crafts. In German (100%).

| | | |
|---|---|---|
| Mem | Jan., 1979- | Periodicals Room |

430 HRW Newsletter. 1966-1978//? Irregular. OCLC 2262056. Last issue 8 pages, size 22 x 28. Line drawings, photographs. Available on microfilm: Herstory. Published by Human Rights for Women, Inc., Washington, DC. Title varies: as Newsletter-Human Rights for Women, Feb., 1970-Sep., 1971. Subject focus: lobbying, rights, legal services, sexism, educational research, discrimination.

| Hist | Feb., 1970-Sep., 1971 | Microforms Her. 1, R 15 |
| --- | --- | --- |
| | Feb., 1972-Feb., 1973 | Her. 1 UP, R5 |
| | Sep., 1971, Feb., 1972, Nov., 1974, Spring, 1978, Fall, 1978 | Pam 72-1709 |

431 HWRM Newsletter, (Harrisburg Women's Rights Movement). 1972-1973//? Irregular. Last issue 12 pages. Line drawings, commercial advertising. Available on microfilm: Herstory. Published by the Harrisburg Women's Center, Harrisburg, PA. Subject focus: child care, health, sexism, lobbying.

| Hist | Nov., 1972-June, 1973 | Microforms Her. 2, R 5 |
| --- | --- | --- |
| | July-Dec., 1973 | Her. 2 UP, R3 |

Hadassah Headlines and Chapter Instructions. New York, NY

    see Hadassah Headlines. New York, NY

432 Hadassah Headlines. 1941-1965//? Monthly. OCLC 4434042. Last issue 8 pages. Line drawings, photographs. Available on microfilm: WHi. Published by Hadassah, the Women's Zionist Organization of America, Inc., New York, NY. Title varies: as Hadassah Headlines and Chapter Instructions, Mar., 1941. Editor: Hortense L. Amram, Mar., 1941. Subject focus: Zionism, health, Jews, education, Judaism, lobbying.

| Hist | [Mar., 1941-June, 1965] | Microforms |
| --- | --- | --- |

433 Hadassah Newsletter. 1920?-1974//. Monthly. OCLC 4434053. Last issue 32 pages. Line drawings, photographs, commercial advertising. Available on microfilm: WHi (1930-1965), UnM (1972-1974), OCAJ (1920-1933, 1956-1967). Published by Hadassah, The Woman's Zionist Organization of America, New York, NY. Editors: Julliet N. Benjamin, Nov./Dec., 1932-Oct., 1937; Mrs. David de Sola Pool, Nov., 1938-Mar., 1943; Sulamith Schwartz, Apr., 1943; Jesse Zel Lurie, Nov., 1949-Feb., 1965. Subject focus: Zionism, Jews, Judaism.

| Hist | [v.11, n.7-v.46, n.6]; [July/Aug., 1930?-Feb., 1965] | Microforms |
| --- | --- | --- |

434 Half of Brooklyn Newsletter. 1971//? Irregular. Last issue 6 pages. Line drawings. Available on microfilm: Herstory. Published by Half of Brooklyn, Brooklyn, NY. Subject focus: birth control, rights, pro-abortion, health.

| Hist | v.1, n.4, 10; Jan., July, 1971 | Microforms Her. 2, R 5 |
| --- | --- | --- |

435 The Hand. 1970-1973//? Irregular. OCLC 2261734. Last issue 11 pages, size 22 x 28. Available on microfilm: Herstory. Published by the Slippery Rock Women's Liberation, Slippery Rock, PA. Title varies: as Lysistrata, Oct./Dec., 1970; as The Hand that Rocks the Rock, Mar., 1971-Oct., 1972. Subject focus: education, pro-abortion, child care, art, teaching, stereotypes, feminism, sexism.

| Hist | v.1, n.1-v.2, n.5; Oct?, 1970-July, 1971 | Microforms Her. 1, R 15 |
| --- | --- | --- |
| | v.3, n.1-v.4, n.5; Oct., 1971-Mar., 1973 | Her. 1 UP, R5 |
| | [v.2, n.4-v.4, n.5]; [Apr., 1971-Mar., 1973] | Pam 73-1078 |

The Hand that Rocks the Rock. Slippery Rock, PA

    see The Hand. Slippery Rock, PA

436 Happenings. 1969?-1970//. Quarterly. Last issue 68 pages, size 14 x 22. Line drawings. Published by the Maryland Correctional Institution for Women, Jessup, MD. Editor: Virginia Kees. Subject focus: prisoners, religion, poetry, fiction, recreation.

| Crim Just | Fall, 1969-Summer, 1970 | Circulation |
| --- | --- | --- |

437 Harbor-South Bay Chapter Newsletter. 1972-1974//. Monthly. Last issue 4 pages. Line drawings. Available on microfilm: Herstory. Published by the Harbor-South Bay Chapter, National Organization for Women, San Pedro, CA. Title varies: as Newsletter, Nov., 1972-June, 1973. Subject focus: feminism, rape,

Equal Rights Amendment, education, lobbying, stereotypes.

| Hist | Nov., 1972– June, 1973 | Microforms Her. 2, R 10 |
| --- | --- | --- |
|  | July, 1973– May, 1974 | Her. 2 UP, R 6 |

438 <u>Harper's Bazaar</u>. 1867. Monthly. $12 for individuals and institutions. Anthony T. Mozzola, editor, Harper's Bazaar, 717 Fifth Avenue, New York, NY 10022. Business address: P.O. Box 10081, Des Moines, IA 50350. ISSN 0017-7873. OCLC 1639362, 4663223. LC 08-37002. Last issue 262 pages, last volume 2072 pages, size 20 x 28. Line drawings, photographs, some in color, commercial advertising. Indexed: Readers Guide (1900–). Available on microfilm: UnM (1868–); McP (1868–1906). Published by the Hearst Corporation, New York, NY. Title varies: as Harper's Bazar, May 20, 1867–Oct., 1929. Frequency varies: weekly, Jan. 20, 1883–Apr. 27, 1901. Previous editors: Carmel Snow, Jan., 1953–Dec., 1957; Nancy White, Jan., 1958–Jan., 1972; James Brady, Feb.–Dec., 1972. Subject focus: fashion, beauty care, health, travel. Other holding institutions: AU (ALM), ArU (AFU), AzFU (AZN), AzTeS (AZS), AzU (AZU), CLobS (CLO), CLU (CLU), CSt (Stanford University), DAU (EAU), DLC (DLC), DeU (DLM), FGULS (FUL), FJUNF (FNP), FMFIU (FXG), GA (GAP), IPB (IBA), KSteC (KKQ), KyRE (KEU), KyU (KUK), LLafS (LWA), MCR-S (Schlesinger Library on the History of Women in America, Radcliffe College, Cambridge, MA), MWelC (WEL), MiEM (EEM), MiMtpT (EZC), [University of Minnesota Union List, Minneapolis, MN] (MUL), MnStjos (MNF), MsU (MUM), [New York State Union List, Albany, NY] (NYS), [Western New York Library Resources Council, Buffalo, NY] (VZX), NIC (COO), NOneoU (ZBM), NR (YQK), NSbSU (YSM), [Central New York Library Resources Council, Syracuse, NY] (SRR), NSyU (SYB), NbKS (KRS), NbU (LDL), NcCU (NKM), NcRS (NRC), NjLincB (BCC), NmLcU (IRU), NmLvH (NMH), NmU (IQU), O (OHI), OAkU (AKR), OCl (CLE), OC1U (CSU), OClW (CWR), OCo (OCO), OCU (CIN), OKentU (KSU), OO (OBE), OU (OSU), OY (YMM), OYU (YNG), OkT (TUL), PCalS (CSC), PCor (ROB), PPD (DXU), [Pittsburgh Regional Library Center-Union List, Pittsburgh, PA] (QPR), PIm (IMM), PP (PLF), PPi (CPL), PPiAC (AIC), ScRhW (SWW), TMurS (TXM), [AMIGOS union List of Serials, Dallas, TX] (IUC), TxAbH (TXS), TxBelM (MHB), TxDN (INT), TxDW (IWU), TxE (TXP), TxLT (ILU), TxU (IXA), ViRCU (VRC), [Arrowhead Library System, Janesville Public Library, Janesville, WI] (WIJ), WM (GZD), WMUW (GXN).

| Agric | v.1, n.1–v.15, n.1; Nov. 2, 1867– Jan., 1882 | Microforms |
| --- | --- | --- |
|  | v.16, n.1–v.43, n.11, v.86, n.1– Jan. 20, 1883– Nov., 1909, Jan., 1953– | Periodicals Section |
| Hist | v.1, n.1–v.46, n.12; Nov. 2, 1867– Dec., 1912 | Microforms |
|  | [v.48, n.1–v.62, n.12]; [July, 1913– Dec., 1928] | TT/500/"H3 |
| MPL | v.35, n.26–v.49, n.12, v.98, n.1– July, 1900– Dec., 1914, Jan., 1962– | Literature and Social Science Section |
| MATC | Current Issues Only | Cora Hardy Library |
| RPL | v.107, n.1– Jan., 1971– | Circulation |
| BML | Current Issues Only | Circulation |
| SPHS | v.111, n.12– Dec., 1975– | Circulation |
| EHS | v.111, n.9– Sep., 1975– | Circulation |
| UWBA | v.109, n.1– Jan., 1973– | Circulation |
| MCL | Current Issues Only | Circulation |
| SPPL | v.109, n.1– Jan., 1973– | Circulation |
| MFHS | v.109, n.1– Jan., 1973– | Circulation |
| VPL | v.110, n.1– Jan., 1974– | Circulation |

439 <u>Die Hausfrau</u>. 1904. Monthly. $7 for individuals and institutions. Josef Edelmann, editor, Die Hausfrau, 1517 Fullerton Avenue, Chicago, IL 60614. (312) 935-8780. ISSN 0017-842X. OCLC 3058772, 6476359. LC 08-9290. Las Last issue 58 pages, last volume 116 pages. Line drawings, photographs, commercial advertising. Available on microfilm: ResP (1904-1928). Published by Die Hausfrau Inc., Chicago, IL. Title varies: as Die Deutsche Hausfrau, Sep., 1904–Oct., 1918. Place of publication varies: Milwaukee, WI, 1904-1950. Subject focus: home economics, wives, fashion, fiction, poetry, family, crafts. In German (100%). Other holding institutions:

# AMAZON
## Milwaukee's Feminist Press
Volume 7 No. 6 OCT/NOV 1979    50¢

## TAKE BACK THE NIGHT!

### October 19, 1979

*Amazon* 7, no. 6 (October–November 1979).  ©1979 by *Amazon: Milwaukee's Feminist Press.*

*American Baptist Woman* 25, no. 2 (Spring 1981).

# Big Mama Rag

*a feminist newsjournal*

Big Mama Rag
1724 Gaylord St.
Denver, CO 80206

Bulk Rate
U.S. Postage
PAID
Denver, CO
Permit No. 1512

July, 1981   Vol.9 No.7

Colorado    50¢
Elsewhere   55¢

## Social Service Cuts Approved

*Defense Spending Highest In History*

Today, America's largest defense budget was passed in the senate. Proponents are confident that this action will turn the tide in foreign policy. Citing the need for an increased military presence in the international arena, they expressed hopes that the U.S. will once again be first in the arms race...

> What are you fighting for?
> It's not my security.
> It's just an old war,
> Not even a cold war...
> What are you dying for?
> It's not my reality.
>
> — Marianne Faithfull
> "Broken English"

**Middle Eastern Women**

**Feminist Projects in Conflict:**
- Woman to Woman
- Sage

**Combatting Liberal Feminism**

*Millions To The Military*

*Women and Children First*

*Budget Cutbacks To Hit Millions*

As President Reagan's economic plans are put into action, the poor will be hardest hit. And the largest grouping of poor people is comprised of women. Therefore, it is estimated that women will suffer most from recent cutbacks, especially those who are single parents receiving aid from state or federal agencies...

*Big Mama Rag* 9, no. 7 (July 1981).

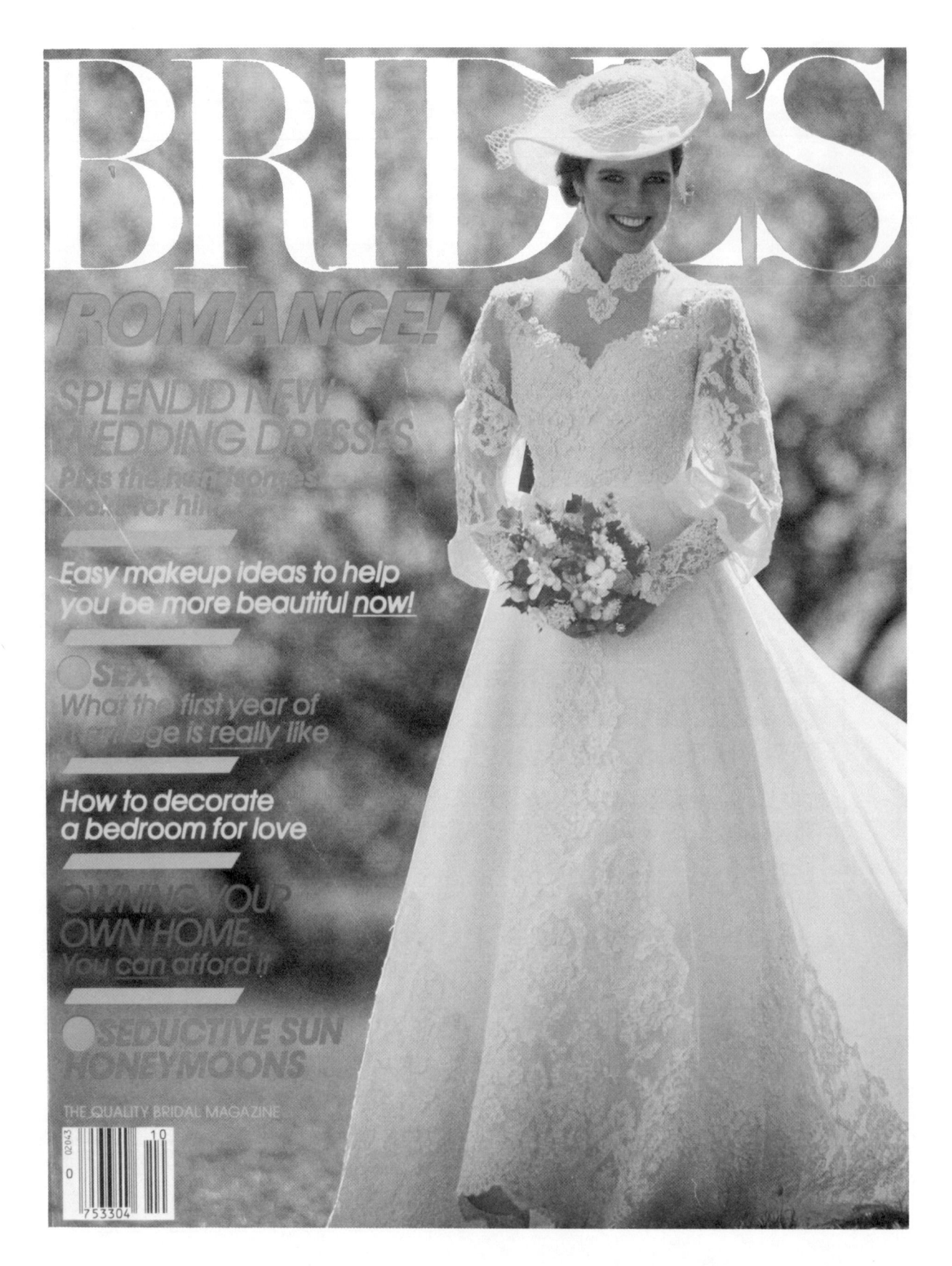

*Brides*, October–November 1981. Reprinted from *Brides*. ©1981 by the Conde Nast Publications, Inc.

# BROOMSTICK

## BY, FOR, & ABOUT WOMEN OVER FORTY

Vol. III, no. 9      SEPTEMBER 1981      $1.25

*Broomstick* 3, no. 9 (September 1981).

*Calyx* 5, nos. 2–3 (October 1980).

*Conditions: Seven.* Cover artist: Jaune Quick-to-See Smith.

*Equal Times* 5, no. 95 (September 1–14, 1980). ©1980 by Equal Times, Inc.

*Farm Wife News* 11, no. 7 (July 1981).

*Femina*, March 23–April 7, 1981.

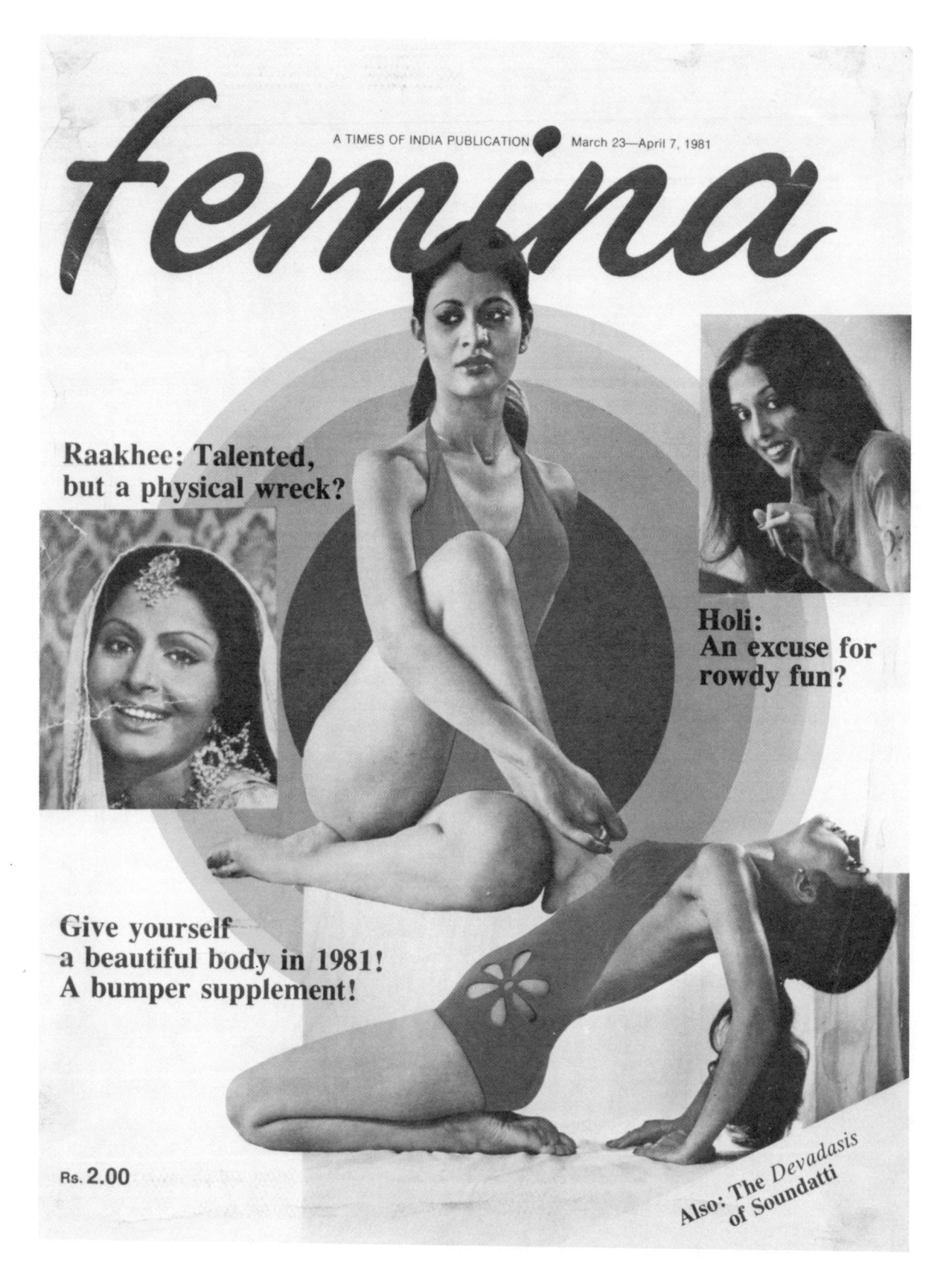

*Feminary* 10, no. 2 (1981).

*Feminist Studies* 5, no. 1 (Spring 1979).

# FOLKLORE WOMEN'S COMMUNICATION

3. THE SCORPION SQUARE DESIG

1. THE MENHADI (MYRTLE) PLANT

2. THE PEACOCK POT

NUMBER 20                                                                                     WINTER 1980

*Folklore Women's Communication* 20 (Winter 1980). ©1980 by Carol Mitchell and Kathleen Manley.

*GFWC Clubwoman* 59, no. 9 (May 1981).

*Giustizia* 61, no. 7 (July 1979).

*Glamour*, June 1981. Courtesy *Glamour*. ©1981 by the Conde Nast Publications, Inc.

*International Women's Tribune Center, Inc. Newsletter 9 (April 1979).*

[University of Minnesota Union List, Minneapolis, MN] (MUL), NN (NYP), OC1W (CWR), OkTOR (OKO), PBL (LYU), ViBlbv (VPI).

| | | |
|---|---|---|
| Mem | v.1, n.1-v.25, n.2; Sep., 1904- Dec., 1928 | Microforms |
| Hist | v.2, n.7-v.12, n.11, v.17, n.4-5,7, v.20, n.6, 9-v.21, n.2, v.23, n.5-8,11, v.26, n.2; Sep., 1905- Dec., 1910, Jan.-Feb., Apr., 1921-Apr., July, 1924-Dec., 1925, Mar.-May, Sep., 1927- Dec., 1929 | Circulation |

440 Headquarters News. 1934-1940//? Quarterly. Last issue 6 pages, last volume 20 pages, size 21 x 14. Published by the National Woman's Relief Corps, Buffalo, KS. Place of publication varies: Scranton, PA, Jan. 1-July 6, 1934; Appleton, WI, Oct. 1, 1934-Apr., 1935; Parkersburg, IA, Oct. 15, 1935-July 20, 1937; Portland, OR, Jan. 5-Nov. 4, 1938. Editors: Bernice Collins Ludwick, Oct. 10, 1939-July 10, 1940. Subject focus: clubs.

| | | |
|---|---|---|
| Hist | v.1, n.1-v.7, n.4; Jan. 1, 1934- July 10, 1940 | F8345/G75/WH (Cutter) |

Headquarters Newsletter. New York, NY

    see National Suffrage News. New York, NY

441 Healthright. 1975. Quarterly. $7.50 for individuals, $15 for institutions. Carla Cassler and Andrea Boroff Eagan, editors, Healthright, 41 Union Square, Rooms 206-8, New York, NY 10003. Last issue 24 pages, size 22 x 28. Line drawings, photographs. Published by Healthright Inc., New York, NY. Subject focus: health.

| | | |
|---|---|---|
| Coll | Current Issues Only | Women's Reading Area |

The Heathen Woman's Friend. Boston, MA

    see Woman's Missionary Friend. Boston, MA

442 Hecate. 1975. Semi-annual. $5 for individuals, $10 for institutions. Carole Ferrier, editor, Hecate, P.O. Box 99, St. Lucia, Brisbane, Queensland 4067, Australia. ISSN 0311-4198. OCLC 2530248. Last issue 104 pages, size 14 x 22. Line drawings, photographs, commercial advertising. Indexed in: Women Studies Abstracts. Subject focus: socialism, radicalism, poetry, art. Other holding institution: CSt (Stanford University).

| | | |
|---|---|---|
| Coll | Current Issues Only | Women's Reading Area |

443 Her/Milwaukee. 1974//. Monthly. Last issue 16 pages. Line drawings, photographs, commercial advertising. Available on microfilm: WHi. Published by Darlex Corp., Milwaukee, WI. Editor: Marion McBride. Subject focus: employment, fashion, volunteer work, home economics, personal finance.

| | | |
|---|---|---|
| Hist | v.1, n.1-3; Feb.-Apr., 1974 | Microforms |

444 Her Own Right. 1970-1971//? Unknown. OCLC 2261868. Last issue 8 pages. Line drawings. Available on microfilm: Herstory. Published by the Women's Liberation Coalition, New Orleans, LA. Subject focus: rights, law, health, Afro-Americans, feminism.

| | | |
|---|---|---|
| Hist | Dec., 1970, Feb., 1971 | Microforms Her. 1, R 15 |

445 Here and N.O.W. 1972-1974//? Irregular. Last issue 4 pages. Line drawings. Available on microfilm: Herstory. Published by the Santa Cruz Chapter, National Organization for Women, Santa Cruz, CA. Editors: Linda Milton, Jan./Feb., 1972-Dec., 1973; Sheila Stromwasser and Louanne Klein, Feb.-June, 1974. Subject focus: child care, education, employment, Equal Rights Amendment, lobbying, feminism.

| | | |
|---|---|---|
| Hist | Jan./Feb., 1972- June, 1973 | Microforms Her. 2, R 12 |
| | July, 1973- June, 1974 | Her. 2 UP, R8 |

446 Here and N.O.W. 1972-1974//? Irregular. Last issue 8 pages. Line drawings. Available on microfilm: Herstory. Published by the New Orleans Chapter, National Organization for Women, New Orleans, LA. Subject focus: Equal Rights Amendment, affirmative action, feminism, employment, lobbying, satire.

| | | |
|---|---|---|
| Hist | Nov., 1972- June, 1973 | Microforms Her. 2, R 11 |
| | Aug., 1973- June, 1974 | Her. 2 UP, R7 |

447 Here and N.O.W. 1970-1974//? Monthly. OCLC 2261878. Last issue 12 pages. Line drawings. Available on microfilm: Herstory. Published

by the Greater Kansas City Chapter, National Organization for Women, Kansas City, MO. Editor: Marianne Evans, Jan., 1973-June, 1974. Subject focus: feminism, education, employment, pro-abortion, Equal Rights Amendment, lobbying, sexism.

| Hist | Dec., 1970-Sep., 1971 | Microforms Her. 1, R 18 |
|---|---|---|
| | Oct., 1971-June, 1973 | Her. 1 UP, R 9 |
| | July, 1973-June, 1974 | Her. CUP, R 4 |

448 <u>Heresies</u>. 1977. Quarterly. $15 for individuals, $24 for institutions. Heresies, P.O. Box 766 Canal Street Station, New York, NY 10013. Business address: 225 Lafayette Street, New York, NY 10012. ISSN 0146-3411. OCLC 2917688. LC sc77-704. Last issue 128 pages, size 22 x 28. Line drawings, photographs, some in color, commercial advertising. Indexed: Alternative Press Index. Published by Heresies Collective Inc., New York, NY. Subject focus: feminism, art, lesbians, poetry. Other holding institutions: AzTeS (AZS), AzU (AZU), CArcHT (CHU), CLobS (CLO), CSt (Stanford University), CtY (YUS), DeU (DLM), FTS (FHM), IU (UIU), InU (IUL), KMK (KKS), KyU (KUK), MBTI (BTI), MH (HLS, HUL), MiEM (EEM), MiMtpT (EZC), [University of Minnesota Union List, Minneapolis, MN] (MUL), NA1fC (YDM), NIC (COO), NOneoU (ZBM), NSbSU (YSM), NSyU (SYB), NcU (NOC), NhD (DRB), OO (OBE), OU (OSU), PLF (LFM), PSC (PSC), TxDN (INT), ViBlbv (VPI), ViNO (VOD), ViU (VA@), WaU (WAU), WMUW (GZN), WyU (WYU).

| Art | v.1, n.4-Winter, 1978- | Circulation |
|---|---|---|
| Wom St | v.1, n.3, 6-Fall, 1977, Spring, 1979- | Reading Room |

<u>Her-self</u>. Ann Arbor, MI

   see <u>Herself: Community Women's Newspaper</u>. Ann Arbor, MI

449 <u>Herself: Community Women's Newspaper</u>. 1972-1977//. Monthly. OCLC 4459043. Last issue 16 pages, last volume 108 pages. Line drawings, photographs, commercial advertising. Available on microfilm: Herstory. (1972-1974); WHi, UnM. Published by Herself Inc., Ann Arbor, MI. Title varies: as Her-self, Apr., 1972-June, 1973. Subject focus: rights, gay rights, health, fiction, poetry, art, music. Other holding institution: MCR-S (Schlesinger Library on the History of Women in America, Radcliffe College, Cambridge, MA).

| Hist | v.1, n.1-v.5, n.6; Apr., 1972-Dec., 1976/Jan., 1977 | Microforms |
|---|---|---|
| | v.1, n.1-v.2, n.3; Apr., 1972-June, 1973 | Microforms Her. 2, R 6 |
| | v.2, n.4-v.3, n.2; June, 1973-May, 1974 | Her. 2 UP, R3 |

450 <u>Hertha</u>. 1914. Bi-monthly. OCLC 1588910. Last issue 30 pages, last volume 255 pages. Line drawings, photographs, commercial advertising. Available on microfilm: Herstory. Published by the Fredrika Bremer Association, Stockholm, Sweden. Subject focus: career development, employment, fashion, law, child care, art. In Swedish (100%).

| Hist | v.58, n.5; ?, 1969 | Microforms Her. 1, R 6 |
|---|---|---|
| | v.58, n.6-v.60, n.5; ?, 1970-?, 1973 | Her. 1 UP, R5 |
| | v.60, n.6-v.61, n.2, 5-6; June, 1973-Feb., May-June, 1974 | Her. CUP, R 2 |

451 <u>Hetbladuandollemina</u>. 1969//? Unknown. OCLC 2261886. Last issue 18 pages. Line drawings. Available on microfilm: Herstory. Published by Dollemina of Antwerp, Antwerp, Belgium. Subject focus: rights, self-help, sexism, lobbying. In Dutch (100%).

| Hist | n.1; Fall, 1969 | Microforms Her. 1, R 6 |
|---|---|---|

452 <u>Highschool Women's Newsletter</u>. 1972//? Unknown. Last issue 18 pages. Line drawings. Available on microfilm: Herstory. Published by the High School Women's Group, Mill Valley, CA. Subject focus: poetry, high school students.

| Hist | Fall, 1972 | Microforms Her. 2, R 6 |
|---|---|---|

453 <u>Hijas de Cuantemoc</u>. 1971//? Unknown. Last issue 12 pages. Line drawings. Available on microfilm: Herstory. Published in Long Beach, CA. Subject focus: poetry, Chicanas. In Spanish (10%).

| Hist | ?, 1971 | Microforms Her. 2, R 6 |
|---|---|---|

The Home Economist. Floral Park, NY and
New York, NY

see The Home Economist and the American
Food Journal. New York, NY

454 The Home Economist and the American Food Journal. 1906-1928//? Monthly. ISSN 0193-1792, OCLC 1479876. LC 08-4162. Last issue 32 pages, last volume 372 pages, size 22 x 29. Line drawings, photographs, commercial advertising. Published by the American Food Journal Inc., New York, NY. Title varies: as Food and Health Education, Jan.-Sep., 1927; as The Home Economist, Oct., 1927. Place of publication varies: Floral Park, NY, Jan. 27-Aug., 1928. Editors: Winifred Stuart Gibbs, Jan., 1927-Jan., 1928; Jessie A. Knox, Feb.-Dec., 1928. Subject focus: home economics, food, health, clothing. Other holding institutions: DLC (DLC), [Indiana Union List of Serials, Indianapolis, IN] (ILS), InLP (IPL), InU (IUL), [University of Minnesota Union List, Minneapolis, MN] (MUL), [New York State Union List, Albany, NY] (NYS), NIC (COO), OBgU (BGU), OKentU (KSU), OCl (CLE), OClloyd (OLM), PIm (IMM), [AMIGOS Union List of Serials, Dallas, TX] (IUC), TxDN (INT).

Agric    v.5, n.1-v.6,    Periodicals
       n.12;           Section
       Jan., 1927-
       Dec., 1928

Home Science Magazine. Boston, MA

see Everyday Housekeeping. Boston, MA

455 Home Science Magazine and Motherhood. 1894-1906//? Monthly. OCLC 1752220. Last issue 30 pages, last volume 142 pages, size 16 x 24. Line drawings, photographs, commercial advertising. Self-indexed (1894). Published in Boston, MA. Title varies: as The New England Kitchen, Apr., 1894-Aug., 1985; as The American Kitchen Magazine, Sep., 1895-Mar., 1903; as Home Science Magazine with Motherhood, Apr., 1903-Apr., 1904. Editors: Anna Barrows and Estelle M.H. Merrill. Subject focus: food, health, motherhood, parenting, home economics. Other holding institutions: [University of Minnesota Union List, Minneapolis, MN] (MUL), MnSU (MNP).

Agric    v.1, n.1-v.21,    Periodicals
       n.3;            Section
       Apr., 1894-
       July, 1904

Home Science Magazine with Motherhood.
Boston, MA

see Home Science Magazine and Motherhood. Boston, MA

456 The Home-Maker. 1888-1893//? Monthly. Last issue 110 pages, last volume 230 pages, size 17 x 25. Line drawings, photographs. Self-indexed. Available on microfilm: ResP. Published by the Home-Maker Co., New York, NY. Subject focus: health, child care, fashion, gardening, home economics, fiction, poetry. Other holding institutions: MCR-S (Schlesinger Library on the History of Women in America, Radcliffe College, Cambridge, MA), NN (NYP).

Agric    v.2, n.1-6;     Periodicals
       Apr.-Sep., 1889    Section

Mem     v.1, n.1-v.10, n.2;   Microforms
       Oct., 1888-
       May, 1893

457 House Beautiful. 1896. Monthly. $11.97 for individuals and institutions. Joann R. Barwick, editor, House Beautiful, 717 5th Avenue, New York, NY 10022. Business address: 9598th Avenue, New York, NY 10019. ISSN 0018-6422. OCLC 1752321. LC 12-16046. Last issue 182 pages. Line drawings, photographs, some in color, commercial advertising. Available on microfilm: UnM. Published by the Hearst Corp., New York, NY. Subject focus: home economics, interior decoration. Other holding institutions: AU (ALM), ArAO (AKO), ArU (AFU), AzFU (AZN), AzTeS (AZS), CLU (CLU), [Pepperdine University, Malibu, CA] (CPE), COFS (COF), COU-DA (COA), CtY (YUS), DLC (DLC), DNAL (AGL), DeU (DLM), FBoU (FGM), FMFIU (FXG), GA (GAP), ICI (IAH), IDeKN (JNA), IPB (IBA), IRA (ICY), KSteC (KKQ), KyDC (KUK), MH (HUL), MNS (SNN), MWelC (WEL), MWP (WPG), [University of Minnesota Union List, Minneapolis, MN] (MUL), MiGrC (EXC), MiMtpT (EZC), MoSMa (MVC), [New York State Union List, Albany, NY] (NYS), NCorniCC (ZDG), NIC (COO), NGcCC (VVX), NOneoU (ZBM), NPV (VXW), NR (UQR), NSbSU (YSM), NSyU (SYB), NbKS (KRS), NbU (LDL), NcRS (NRC), NmLcU (IRU), NmLvH (NMH), O (OHI), OAkU (AKR), OAU (OUN), OC1U (CSU), OC1W (CWR), OCo (OCO), OKentU (KSU), OkT (TUL), OkTOR (OKO), OLanU (OUL), OTU (TOL), OU (OSU), OY (YMM), OYU (YNG), [Pittsburgh Regional Library Center-Union List, Pittsburgh, PA] (QPR), PCalS (CSC), PCLS (REC), PNwC (WFN), PPD (DXU), PPi (CPL), PPiAC (AIC), PPiC (PMC), PPiCC (HHC), ScRhW (SWW), TCollsM (TMS), TMurS (TXM), TxAbH (TXS), TxBelM (MHB), TxCM (TXA), [AMIGOS Union List of Serials, Dallas, TX] (IUC), TxDN (INT), TxDW (IWU), TxEU (TXU), TxLarU (TLS), [Emory and Henry College, Emory, VA] (VEH), ViRCU (VRC), [Arrowhead Library System, Janesville Public Library, Janesville, WI] (WIJ), WM (GZD), WMUW (GZN).

MATC    v.120, n.4-    Cora Hardy
       Apr., 1971-     Library

| | | |
|---|---|---|
| BML | Current Issues Only | Circulation |
| SPPL | Jan., 1971- | Circulation |
| MMHS | Jan., 1969-Dec., 1973 | Circulation |
| OM | Current Issues Only | Circulation |
| TML | Jan., 1969- | Circulation |
| MGHS | Jan., 1969- | Circulation |
| SCPL | Jan., 1971- | Circulation |
| MIPL | Jan., 1973- | Circulation |
| MOPL | Jan., 1973- | Circulation |
| DFPL | Jan., 1971- | Circulation |
| CFL | Jan., 1974- | Circulation |
| MFHS | Jan., 1973- | Circulation |
| SPHS | Jan., 1971- | Circulation |
| EHS | Jan., 1974- | Circulation |
| RPL | Jan., 1970- | Circulation |
| UWBA | May, 1968- | Circulation |
| DFHS | Aug., 1974- | Circulation |
| MCL | Jan., 1971- | Circulation |
| MPL | Jan., 1920- | Circulation |

458  The Household: A Monthly Journal Devoted to the Interests of the American Housewife. 1868-1887//? Monthly. Last issue 28 pages, last volume 380 pages, size 26 x 38. Line drawings, commercial advertising. Published in Battleboro, VT. Editor: George E. Crowell. Subject foucs: food, health, poetry, fiction, parenting, home economics, wives, interior decoration.

| | | |
|---|---|---|
| Agric | [v.5, n.1-v.20, n.12]; [Jan., 1872-Dec., 1887] | Periodicals Section |

459  The Household Monthly. 1858-1860//? Monthly. OCLC 1586523. Last issue 94 pages, last volume 574 pages. Line drawings. Each issue self-indexed. Available on microfilm: ResP. Published in Boston, MA. Editor: Nathan F. Bryant. Subject focus: fiction, poetry, children's literature, fashion, biographies. Other holding institution: ICN (IBV).

| | | |
|---|---|---|
| Mem | v.1, n.1-v.3, n.6; Oct., 1858-Mar., 1960 | Microforms |

460  Houston Breakthrough. 1976-1981//. Monthly. ISSN 0273-7450. OCLC 6440968. LC sn80-2694. Last issue 28 pages, size 41 x 29. Line drawings, photographs, commercial advertising. Available on microfilm: WHi (1977-1981). Published by Breakthrough Publisheding Company, Houston, TX. Title varies: as Daily Breakthrough, Nov. 18-20, 1977. Frequency varies: bi-monthly, July/Aug. and Dec./Jan.; daily, Nov. 18-20, 1977. Editors: Janice Blue, Gabrielle Cosgriff and David Crossley, Apr./May, 1980; Janice Blue, Gabrielle Cosgriff, David Crossley and Victoria Smith, June, 1980; Janice Blue, Gabrielle Cosgriff, David Crossley, and Morris Edelson, July/Aug., 1980; Janice Blue, Gabrielle Cosgriff, Nov.-Dec., 1980/Jan., 1981. Subject focus: rights, alternative press. Other holding institutions: [AMIGOS Union List of Serials, Dallas, TX] (IUC), TxDW (IWU).

| | | |
|---|---|---|
| Hist | [Nov. 18, 1977], v.5, n.3-10; [Nov. 18, 1977], Apr.1-Dec., 1980/Jan., 1981 | Circulation |

461  How's N.O.W. 1970-1974//? Irregular. OCLC 2269465. Last issue 12 pages. Line drawings. Available on microfilm: Herstory. Published by the Western Connecticut Chapter National Organization for Women, Bridgeport, CT. Title varies: as Western Connecticut N.O.W. Newsletter, Sep., 1970-Nov., 1973. Place of publication varies: Stratford, CT, Sep., 1970-Nov., 1973. Frequency varies: monthly, Sep., 1970-Nov., 1973. Editors: Eileen Sarkissian and Bonnie Geriak, Oct., 1971-Aug., 1972; Eileen Sarkissian, Sep., 1972-Sep., 1973; Kasey Jones, Nov., 1973-Apr., 1974. Subject focus: lobbying, pro-abortion, education, child care, feminism.

| | | |
|---|---|---|
| Hist | Sep., 1970-Aug., 1971 | Microforms Her. 1, R 17 |
| | Oct., 1971-June, 1973 | Her. 1 UP, R12 |
| | July-Sep., Nov., 1973, Apr., 1974 | Her. CUP, R6 |

462  Human Equality. 1969-1972//? Irregular. Last issue 2 pages. Line drawings. Available on microfilm: Herstory. Published by the Committee Opposing Racist Practice and Sentiments, Honolulu, HI. Title varies: as A CORPAS Communication, Aug. 12, 1969-Aug. 12, 1970.

Editor: Ann Snyder Moser. Subject focus: racism, lobbying, Black Panthers, poverty.

| | | |
|---|---|---|
| Hist | v.1, n.1-v.2, n.28; Aug. 12, 1969- Dec., 1972 | Microforms Her. 2, R 6 |

463 Hysteria. 1970-1971//? Irregular. OCLC 2262085. Last issue 4 pages, size 28 x 43. Photographs. Available on microfilm: Herstory. Published by the Women's Liberation Media Center, Cambridge, MA. Subject focus: sex roles, fiction, poetry, media, stereotypes. Other holding institution: MCR-S (Schlesinger Library on the History of Women in America, Radcliffe College, Cambridge, MA).

| | | |
|---|---|---|
| Hist | n.1-6; Oct. 9, 1970- July, 1971 | Microforms Her. 1, R 2 |
| | n.6; July, 1971 | Pam 72-1301 |

464 IAWS. 1963-1969//? Quarterly. OCLC 2262095. Last issue 12 pages. Line drawings. Available on microfilm: Herstory. Published by the Intercollegiate Association of Women Studies, East Lansing, MI. Subject focus: education, college students, women's studies.

| | | |
|---|---|---|
| Hist | v.6, n.1; Fall, 1969 | Microforms Her. 1, R 6 |

465 ICSDW Bulletin. 1955-1978//. Monthly. LC 60-38668. Indexed at end of each volume. Published by International Council of Social Democratic Women, London, England. Title varies: as Bulletin of the International Socialist Women's Secretariat, Jan.29-June 11, 1955; Bulletin of the International Council of Social Democratic Women, Aug. 13, 1955-Dec., 1969. Frequency varies: monthly, Jan. 29, 1955-Dec., 1972; bi-monthly, Jan./Feb., 1973-Nov./Dec., 1978. Editor: Vera Matthias, Sep./Oct., 1977-Nov./Dec., 1978. Subject focus: international relations, education, political parties, socialism, politicians.

| | | |
|---|---|---|
| Mem | v.1, n.1-v.24, n.26; Jan. 29, 1955- Nov./Dec., 1978 | Microforms |

466 Illinois Association Opposed to Woman Suffrage Bulletin. 1909-1913//. Irregular. Last issue 4 pages, size 23 x 15. Available on microfilm: McA. Published by the Illinois Association Opposed to Woman Suffrage, Chicago, IL. Subject focus: anti-suffrage.

| | | |
|---|---|---|
| Hist | [n.1-20]; [Sep., 1909- Nov., 1913] | KWZ/I.29/ Oversize (Cutter) |

467 The Illustrated Household Magazine. 1878-1881//? Monthly. Last issue 16 pages, size 34 x 46. Line drawings, commercial advertising. Published in Portland, ME. Editor: George Stinsen. Subject focus: literature, art, science, agriculture, home economics, fashion.

| | | |
|---|---|---|
| Hist | v.3, n.2-v.4, n.3; Feb., 1880- Mar., 1881 | AP/2/"I38 |

468 Image of Women Task Force. 1971//? Unknown. Last issue 4 pages. Line drawings. Available on microfilm: Herstory. Published by the Eastern Massachusetts Chapter, National Organization for Women, Martha's Vineyard Task Force on the Image of Women, Martha's Vineyard, MA. Title varies: as Newsletter, Sep., 1971. Subject focus: media, feminism, stereotypes.

| | | |
|---|---|---|
| Hist | Sep., 1971 | Microforms Her. 1, R 18 |
| | Nov., 1971 | Her. 1 UP, R9 |

469 In Touch. 1973-1974//? Irregular. Last issue 4 pages. Line drawings. Available on microfilm: Herstory. Published by the New Jersey State Commission on Women, Dept. of Community Affairs, Trenton, NJ. Editor: Lois Joice. Subject focus: law, research, commissions on women.

| | | |
|---|---|---|
| Hist | v.1, n.1-3; Sep., Dec., 1973, May, 1974 | Microforms Her. 3, R 2 |

In Transit. Madison, WI

see Women's Transit Home Companion. Madison, WI

The Independent Woman. New York, NY

see National Business Woman. Washington, DC

470 Indiana Abortion Law Repeal Coalition Newsletter. 1971//? Unknown. OCLC 2262248. Last issue 5 pages. Available on microfilm: Herstory. Published by the Indiana Abortion Law Repeal Coalition, Bloomington, IN. Subject focus: pro-abortion, lobbying.

## Women's Periodicals and Newspapers

    Hist     Aug. 2, 1971     Microforms
                                        Her. 1, R 5

471   Indianapolis Women's Liberation Newsletter. 1970-1972//? Monthly. OCLC 2262258. Last issue 12 pages. Line drawings, photographs. Available on microfilm: Herstory. Published by Indianapolis Women's Liberation, Indianapolis, IN. Subject focus: ecology, child care, self-defense, poetry, lobbying, peace movement, feminism, Equal Rights Amendment.

    Hist     v.1, n.1-12;     Microforms
              Oct., 1970-      Her. 1, R 16
              Sep., 1971

              v.2, n.1-9?;     Her. 1 UP, R5
              Sep., 1971-
              June, 1972?

472   IndiaNOWpolis Woman. 1972-1974//? Monthly. Last issue 8 pages. Line drawings. Available on microfilm: Herstory. Published by the Indianapolis Chapter, National Organization for Women, Indianapolis, IN. Title varies: as N.O.W. Newsletter, Nov., 1972-July, 1973; as N.O.W. Knows, Aug.-Dec., 1973. Subject focus: satire, feminism, lobbying, Equal Rights Amendment.

    Hist     Nov., 1972-      Microforms
              June, 1973;      Her. 2, R 10

              June, 1973-      Her. 2 UP, R6
              June, 1974;

473   The Indian's Friend. 1888-1951//? Bi-monthly. OCLC 1753048, 5206941. Last issue 8 pages, last volume 56 pages. Commercial advertising. Available on microfilm: DLC (1888-1940). Published by the Women's National Indian Association, New York, NY. Place of publication varies: Philadelphia, PA, Mar., 1888-Jan., 1902; Hartford, CT, Feb., 1902-Aug., 1906. Frequency varies: monthly, Mar., 1888-Dec., 1914. Editors: Mrs. A.S. Quinton, Feb., 1897-Dec., 1901; Marie E. Ives Humphrey, Jan., 1902-Dec., 1906; T.C. Marshall, Feb., 1907-Dec., 1914; John W. Clark, Jan., 1915-Mar., 1927. Subject focus: Native Americans. Other holding institutions: AzTeS (AZS), CtY (YUS), [University of Minnesota Union List, Minneapolis, MN] (MUL), OkS (OKS).

    Hist     v.1, n.1-v.52,   Microforms
              n.1;
              Mar., 1888-
              Jan., 1940

474   Industrial Facts. 1918//? Weekly. Last issue 4 pages, size 18 x 25. Published by the Industrial Committee of the War Work Council of the Young Women's Christian Association, New York, NY. Subject focus: work, working women, workers, World War I, war.

    Hist     v.1, n.1;       .F83756/YW
              Sep. 28, 1918   (Cutter)

475   Inside/Outside. 1974-1977//. Bi-monthly. Last issue 6 pages, last volume 16 pages, size 22 x 28. Line drawings, photographs. Published by the Pennsylvania Program for Women and Girl Offenders, Inc., Philadelphia, PA. Editors: Carole Rosen Horwitz and G. Ellen Michaud. Subject focus: prisoners, criminal justice system, prison reform, offenders, rape.

    Crim Just  v.2, n.1-v.4, n4;  Circulation
                 Mar., 1975-
                 Aug., 1977

    Coll      v.1, n.1-v.4, n.4;  Circulation
              Oct., 1974-
              Aug., 1977

    R&L       v.2, n.1-v.4, n.4;  Circulation
              Mar., 1975-
              Aug., 1977

476   The Insider. 1976//. Monthly. Last issue 18 pages, size 22 x 28. Line drawings. Published by the Correctional Institution for Women, Clinton, NJ. Editor: Dorothy Tombs. Subject focus: poetry, prisoners, fiction, health.

    Crim Just  July-Aug., 1976   Circulation

477   The Institute for the Study of Women in Transition Newsletter. 1975-1977//. Bi-monthly. Last issue 12 pages, size 22 x 28. Line drawings, commercial advertising. Published by the Institute for the Study of Women in Transit, Portsmouth, NH. Subject focus: research, education, aging, rights.

    Wom St   v.1, n 3, v.2,    Reading Room
              n.1-2, v.3, n.1;
              Dec., 1975,
              Mar.-Nov., 1976,
              Feb., 1977

478   The Intellectual Regale; or Ladies' Tea Tray. 1814-1815//? Weekly. Last issue 6 pages, last volume 946 pages. Line drawings. Self-indexed. Available on microfilm: UnM. Published in Philadelphia, PA. Editor: Mrs. Carr. Subject focus: fiction, poetry.

    Hist     v.1, n.1-v.2,    Microforms
              n.33;
              Mar. 19, 1814-
              Dec. 30, 1815

479   Inter-American Commission of Women Informational Bulletin. 1970-1977//. Monthly. OCLC 2255729. Last issue 8 pages, size 22 x 28.

Published by the Organization of American States-Office of the General Secretariat, Washington, DC. Subject focus: rights, law, Latin America, commissions on women. Other holding institution: [University of Minnesota Union List, Minneapolis, MN] (MUL).

| Mem | n.61-91; Apl., 1974- Feb., 1977 | AP/I613/C73 |

480   Intercollegiate Community Service Quarterly. 1915-1919//? Quarterly. OCLC 5791106. Last issue 24 pages, last volume 68 pages. Available on microfilm: ResP. Published by the College Settlements Association, New York, NY. Title varies: as College Settlements Association Quarterly, Sep., 1915-Apr., 1917. Subject focus: social work. Other holding institutions: MCR-S (Schlesinger Library on the History of Women in America, Radcliffe College, Cambridge, MA), TxDW (IWU).

| Mem | v.1, n.1-v.4, n.3; Sep., 1915- Apr., 1919 | Microforms |

481   International Altrusan. 1924. Eleven times a year. $3.25 for individuals and institutions. Susan Britton, editor, International Altrusan, 8 S. Michigan Avenue, Chicago, IL 60603. (312) 236-5894. OCLC 1640802. Last issue 20 pages, last volume 174 pages, size 28 x 22. Line drawings, photographs. Published by International Association of Altrusan Clubs, Chicago, IL. Title varies: as The National Altrusian, Sep., 1927-June, 1935. Place of publication varies: Shreveport, LA, Sep., 1927-Aug./Sep., 1930; Phoenix, AZ, Oct., 1930-May, 1932; Lincoln, NB, Sep., 1932-Sep., 1941; Mendota, IL, Oct., 1941-June, 1957; Rockford, IL, Sep., 1957-June, 1977. Frequency varies: monthly (bi-monthly in summer), Sep., 1927-Nov., 1933; 10 times a year, Dec., 1933-Sep., 1955. Previous editors: Mary Virginia Saunders, Sep., 1927-Aug./Sep., 1930; C. Louise Boehringer, Oct., 1930-May, 1932; Mary Margaret Kern, Sep., 1932-Oct., 1938; Ruth Lemmer Manlove, Nov., 1938-July, 1943; Lucille Hecht, Nov., 1943-June, 1977; Diana Wendt, Sep., 1977-Sep., 1978. Subject focus: clubs. Other holding institutions: [Indiana Union List of Serials, Indianapolis, IN] (ILS), LNU (LNU), [University of Minnesota Union List, Minneapolis, MN] (MUL), NmLcU (IRU), OkT (TUL), TxLT (ILU), TxNacS (TXK), WFon (WIF), WM (GZD).

| Hist | v.5, n.1- Sep., 1927- | HQ/1101/I47 |

482   International Feminist League of Hong Kong Newsletter. 1973-1974//. Monthly. Last issue 12 pages. Line drawings. Available on microfilm: Herstory. Published by the International Feminist League of Hong Kong, Aberdeen, Hong Kong. Subject focus: poetry, sexism, law, sterilization, pro-abortion, feminism.

| Hist | v.1, n.11, v.2, n.2-6; Dec., 1973- Feb.-June, 1974 | Microforms Her. 3, R 2 |

483   International Journal of Women's Studies. 1978. Bi-monthly. $22.50 for individuals, $30 for institutions. Sherri Clarkson, editor, International Journal of Women's Studies, Suite 201, 1538 Sherbrooke Street West, Montreal, Quebec, Canada. ISSN 0703-8240. OCLC 3797270. LC cn78-30307. Last issue 603 pages, size 19 x 28. Line drawings. Published by Eden Press Women's Publications, Inc., Montreal, Quebec, Canada. Subject focus: professionals, history, women's studies, literature. Other holding institutions: AzTeS (AZS), CArcHT (CHU), CChiS (CCH), CLO (CCO), CLSU (CSL), CLU (CLU), CLobS (CLO), COFS (COF), CtY (YUS), DAL (ARL), DGW (DGW), FJUNF (FNP), FMFIU (FXN), FOFT (FTU), FTS (FHM), FU (FUG), GASU (GSU), GEU (EMU), IDeKN (JNA), InIU (IUP), InU (IUL), IObT (IDI), KMK (KKS), ISteC (KKQ), KyLoU (KLG), LHS (LSH), LLafS (LWA), MA (AMH), MBTI (BTI), MChB (BXM), MH (KLS, HUL), MeB (BBH), MiDU (EYU), MiDW (EYW), MiEM (EEM), MiHolH (EXH), MiKW (EXW), MiMtpT (EZC), [University of Minnesota Union List, Minneapolis, MN] (MUL), MnStpeG (MNG), MnU (MNU), MWelC (WEL), NA1U (NAM), NBrockU (XBM), NBronSL (VVS), NCH (YHM), NDFM (VZE), [New York State Union List, Albany, NY] (NYS), [Central New York Library Resources Council, Syracuse, NY] (SRR), NFQC (XQM), NIC (COO), NNJJ (VVJ), NNU (ZYU), NPurMC (VYE), NPV (VXW), NSbSU (YSM), NTRS (ZRS), NbU (LDL), NcD (NDD), NcU (NOC), NcWfSB (NVS), NcWsW (EWF), NdU (UND), OBgU (BGU), OCU (CIN), OGK (KEN), OKU-M (OKH), OO (OBE), OU (OSU), PCW (UWC), PEL (LAF), PU (PAU), TNL (TJC), [AMIGOS Union List of Serials, Dallas, TX] (IUC), TxCM (TXA), ViFerF (VFC), ViU (VA@), ViNO (VOD), ViRCU (VRC), ViRU (VRU), ViRUT (VUT), WMUW (GZN), WaU (WAU).

| Coll | Current Issues Only | Women's Reading Area |
| Wom St | v.1, n.1- Jan./Feb., 1978- | Reading Room |
| Mem | v.1, n.1- Jan./Feb., 1978- | AP/I616/J92 |

484   The International Woman Co-Operator. 1945-1962//? Bi-monthly. Last issue 6 pages, last volume 18 pages, size 19 x 25. Photographs. Published by the International Cooperative Women's Guild, London, England. Subject focus: human rights, education, health care,

pro-suffrage.

Mem  [v.1, n.3-v.5, n.6], v.6, n.2-v.18, n.3; [May, 1945-Nov., 1949], Mar., 1950-May, 1962    AP/1616/W872

485  The International Woman Suffrage News. (English Edition). 1907-1918//? Monthly. Last issue 16 pages, size 33 x 24. Line drawings, commercial advertising. Published by the International Woman Suffrage Alliance, London, England. Subject focus: pro-suffrage.

Hist  v.12, n.9; June 1, 1918    KWZ/+IN (Cutter)

486  International Women's Tribune Centre, Inc., Newsletter. 1976. Irregular. $3 for individuals and institutions. Ann S. Walker, editor, International Women's Tribune Centre, Inc., Newsletter, 305 E. 46th Street, Sixth Floor, New York, NY 10017. (212) 421-5633. Last issue 32 pages, size 21 x 28. Line drawings. Title varies: as International Women's Year Tribune Project Newsletter, Jan./Feb., 1977-Jan., 1978. Subject focus: technology, rural women, agriculture, United Nations.

LTC  n.3- Jan./Feb., 1977-   Periodicals Section

487  International Women's Year/Année Internationale de la Femme. 1974-1975//. Unknown. Last issue 12 pages, size 22 x 28. Photographs. Published by the International Women's Year Secretariat, Ottawa, Ontario, Canada. Subject focus: law, rights. In French (50%).

Wom Ed Res  v.2, n.7-8; Sep.-Oct./Nov., 1975    Circulation

International Women's Year Tribune Project Newsletter. New York, NY

see International Women's Tribune Centre, Inc., Newsletter. New York, NY

488  Irregular Periodical: Newsletter of the Bread and Roses Women's Health Center. 1979. Quarterly. $3 for individuals and institutions. Carolyn Keith, editor, Irregular Periodical: Newsletter of the Bread and Roses Women's Health Center, 238 West Wisconsin Avenue, Suite 700, Milwaukee, WI 53203. (414) 278-0260. OCLC 6342902. Last issue 8 pages, size 32 x 24. Line drawings, photographs. Available on microfilm: WHi (1979-). Subject focus: health, pro-abortion, motherhood, feminism, psychology. Other holding institution: WMUW (GZN).

Hist  v.1, n.1- Fall, 1979-   Circulation

489  ISHTAR Newsletter. 1973-1974//? Irregular. ISSN 0382-0149. OCLC 2627689, 2627695. LC cn76-31906. Last issue 7 pages. Line drawings. Available on microfilm: Herstory. Published by the Ishtar Women's Resource Centre and Transition House, Aldergrove, British Columbia, Canada. Subject focus: rape, child care, self-help. Other holding institution: CaOONL (NLC).

Hist  July, 1973- June, 1974    Microforms Her. 3, R 2

490  Issues in Health Care of Women. 1978. Bimonthly. $20 for individuals and institutions. Carol Ann McKenzie and Sarah D. Cohn, editors, Issues in Health Care of Women, 1221 Avenue of the Americas, New York, NY 10020. ISSN 0161-5246. OCLC 3967714, 5739410, 5804662, 5258848, 5258857, 5655510. LC sc80-801, sn79-2027. Last issue 64 pages, size 15 x 22. Line drawings. Published by McGraw-Hill, College Division, New York, NY. Subject focus: health, medicine, nutrition, pre-natal care. Other holding institutions: CLU (CLU), CLobS (CLO), CSfU (CUF), DNLM (NLM), HU (HUH), [University of Minnesota Union List, Minneapolis, MN] (MUL), NGcA (VJA), NcU-H (NOH), NhMSA (SAC), PSt (UPM), PU-Med (PAM), [AMIGOS Unon List of Serials, Dallas, TX] (IUC), TxDW (IWU), TxHMC (TMC), ViRCU (VRC).

CHS  v.1, n.1- ?, 1978-   Circulation

491  It Ain't Me Babe. 1970-1971//? Monthly. OCLC 2262810. Last issue 32 pages, size 17 x 24. Line drawings. Available on microfilm: Herstory. Published by the Women's Liberation Basement Press, Last Gasp Ecofunnies, Berkeley, CA. Subject focus: comics, satire. Other holding institution: MCR-S (Schlesinger Library on the History of Women in America, Radcliffe College, Cambridge, MA).

Hist  v.1, n.1-v.2, n.1; Jan. 15, 1970- Apr., 1971    Microforms Her. 1, R 2

July, 1970    Pam 70-789

492 Ivy Leaf. 1954? Five times a year. $2 for individuals and institutions. Ivy Leaf, 5211 S. Greenwood Avenue, Chicago, IL 60615. ISSN 0021-3276. OCLC 4086637. LC sn78-1177. Last issue 44 pages, last volume 212 pages, size 28 x 22. Line drawings, photographs. Published by the Alpha Kappa Alpha Sorority, Chicago, IL. Previous editor: Ernestine Green, Summer, 1976-Summer, 1978. Subject focus: sororities, education, Afro-Americans.

    Hist    v.52, n.2, 4,    Circulation
            v.54, n.3-
            Summer,
            Winter, 1976,
            Fall, 1977-

493 JSAC Grapevine. 1969-1972//? Monthly. ISSN 0364-4103. OCLC 2363567. LC sn78-4436. Last issue 6 pages. Line drawings. Available on microfilm: Herstory (1972). Published by the Joint Strategy and Action Committee, Inc., New York, NY. Editor: Sheila Collins. Subject focus: human rights, lobbying, religion. Other holding institutions: MBTI (BTI), MBU-T (BZM), NSufR (VVR), NcRS (NRC), [Pittsburgh Regional Library Center-Union List, Pittsburgh, PA] (QPR), PPiPT (PKT), TNJ (TJC), [AMIGOS Union List of Serials, Dallas, TX] (IUC).

    Hist    v.4, n.2;    Microforms
            July, 1972    Her. 2, R 6

494 Jeannette Rankin Brigade Newsletter. 1967?-1971//? Unknown. OCLC 2262899. LC sc80-56. Last issue 2 pages. Line drawings. Available on microfilm: Herstory. Published by the Jeannette Rankin Brigade, San Francisco, CA. Subject focus: peace movement.

    Hist    [1967?-1970?]    Microforms
                              Her. 1, R 16

495 The Jewish Woman. 1921-1931//. Quarterly. OCLC 1585518. Last issue 18 pages, last volume 192 pages, size 19 x 28. Line drawings, photographs. Published by the National Council of Jewish Women, New York, NY. Editor: Estelle M. Sternberger. Subject focus: Jews, Judaism, clubs, education. Other holding institutions: [University of Minnesota Union List, Minneapolis, MN] (MUL), [Pittsburgh Regional Library Center-Union List, Pittsburgh, PA] (QPR), PPi (CPL).

    Hist    [v.1, n.1-v.11,    F8399JE/8C85J
            n.2];              (Cutter)
            [Oct., 1921-
            Oct., 1931]

496 Journal des Dames. 1810//. Monthly. Last issue 40 pages, last volume 450 pages. Available on microfilm: UnM. Published by Journal des Dames, New York, NY. Editor: Dr. Francis Durand. Subject focus: fiction, poetry, history. In French (100%).

    Hist    v.1, n.1-v.2,    Microforms
            n.12;
            Jan.-Dec., 1810

Journal of the American Association of University Women. Ithaca, NY; Concord, NH; Baltimore, MD; Menasha, WI

    see The Graduate Woman. Washington, DC

497 Journal of the American Medical Women's Association. 1946-1974//? Monthly. Last issue 48 pages, last volume 568 pages, size 20 x 29. Line drawings, photographs, some in color, commercial advertising. Available on microfilm: UnM. Published by the American Medical Women's Association Inc., New York, NY. Title varies: as Journal of the American Medical Women's Association, Apr., 1946-Dec., 1969; as The Woman Physician, Jan., 1970-Jan., 1972. Place of publication varies: Nashville, TN, Apr., 1946-Dec., 1969; Paterson, NJ, Jan., 1970-Dec., 1972. Editors: Elise S. L'Esperance, Apr., 1946-Dec?, 1947; Ada Chree Ried, Jan., 1950-Dec., 1952; M. Eugenia Geib, Jan., 1953-Dec., 1955; Naomi M. Kanof, Mar., 1972-Dec., 1974. Subject focus: medicine, professionals, health care, doctors.

    CHS    v.1, v.1-v.29,    Q/7AM364/J
           n.12;
           Apr., 1946-
           Dec., 1974

498 Journal of Women's Studies in Literature. 1979. Quarterly. $15 for individuals, $20 for institutions. Sherri Clarkson, editor, Journal of Women's Studies in Literature, 1538 Sherbrooke St. West, Suite 201, Montreal, Quebec, Canada H3G 1L5. ISSN 0707-1981. OCLC 4719202. LC cn79-39032. Last issue 272 pages, size 15 x 23. Published by Eden Press Women's Publications, Inc., Montreal, Quebec, Canada. Indexed in American Humanities Index.

Subject focus: literary criticism, women's studies. Other holding institutions: AzTeS (AZS), COLH (COL), FTS (FHM), InU (IUL), KMK (KKS), KyLoU (KLG), MBU (BOS), MChB (BXM), MH (HLS, HUL), MiDW (EYW), MiMtpT (EZC), MnStpeG (MNG), NBronSL (VVS), NCH (YHM), [Central New York Library Resources Council, Syracuse, NY] (SRR), NTRS (ZRS), NhD (DRB), [AMIGOS Union List of Serials, Dallas, TX] (IUC), TxDW (IWU), TxNacS (TXK), ViBlbv (VPI), WaU (WAU), WyU (WYU), CaOONL (NLC).

    Wom St    v.1, n.1-    Reading Room
              Winter, 1979-

499 The Journey. 1970-1974//? Quarterly. Last issue 6 pages. Line drawings. Available on

microfilm: Herstory. Published by the Deaconess Movement, Des Moines, IA. Title varies: as The Deaconess Movement, Mar. 4, 1970. Subject focus: Cahtolic Church, ecumenism, sexism, Catholic Theological Society.

| Hist | v.1, n.1-v.4, n.2; Mar. 4, 1970- Summer, 1973 | Microforms Her. 2, R 6 |
|---|---|---|
|  | v.4, n.3, 11-12; Fall, 1973, Winter- Summer, 1974 | Her. 2 UP, R 3 |

500 Joyous Struggle. 1972-1977//. Monthly. Last issue 8 pages. Line drawings. Available on microfilm: Herstory. Published by the Women's Coordinating Center, University of New Mexico, Albuquerque, NM. Subject focus: pro-abortion, consciousness raising, sexism in education, rape, family planning.

| Hist | Apr. 15, Nov. 15, 1972, June, 1973 | Microforms Her. 2, R 6 |
|---|---|---|
|  | July, Sep., Nov., 1973 | Her. 2 UP, R 3 |

501 Judy. 1919//. Monthly. Last issue 32 pages. Available on microfilm: ResP. Published by Judy Inc., New York, NY. Editors: Mary Carolyn Davies, Phyllis Duganne, Miriam Gerstle, Anne Heredeen, Margaret Sangster, Betty Shannon, Brenda Ueland, Katharine Hilliker, Mary Kennedy, Margaretta Van Rensellaer Schuyler. Subject focus: fiction, poetry, plays, humor. Other holding institution: MCR-S (Schlesinger Library on the History of Women in America, Radcliffe College, Cambridge, MA).

| Mem | v.1, n.1-3; June-Aug., 1919 | Microforms |
|---|---|---|

502 Jugoslavenska Zena. 1917-1918//? Monthly. Last issue 44 pages, last volume 516 pages, size 17 x 25. Published in Zagreb, Yugoslavia. Editor: Zofka Kreder Demetrovie. Subject focus: law, socialism, rights, fiction, poetry, health, working women. In Serbo-Croatian (100%).

| Mem | v.2, n.1-12; Jan.-Dec., 1918 | AP/J93651/Z54 |
|---|---|---|

503 The Junior League Fogcutter. 1970-1973//? Unknown. Last issue 12 pages. Line drawings, commercial advertising. Available on microfilm: Herstory. Published by the Junior League of San Francisco, CA. Editor: Anne Stratford. Subject focus: professionals, drug abuse, art, fashion, clubs.

| Hist | v.3, n.7; Feb., 1973 | Microforms Her. 2, R 6 |
|---|---|---|

504 Just Like a Woman. 1970//? Unknown. OCLC 2263141. LC sc80-519. Last issue 3 pages. Line drawings. Available on microfilm: Herstory. Published by the Atlanta Women's Liberation, Atlanta, GA. Subject focus: feminism, education, poetry.

| Hist | v.1, n.1; Oct. 10, 1970 | Microforms |
|---|---|---|

505 Justice. 1919. Monthly. $2 for individuals and institutions. Meyer Miller, editor, Justice, 1710 Broadway, New York, NY 10019. (212) 265-7000. ISSN 0022-7013. OCLC 2277370. LC sn78-4132. Last issue 16 pages, last volume 288 pages, size 29 x 37. Line drawings, photographs, commercial advertising. Available on microfilm: OCAJ (1919-1955). Published by the International Ladies Garment Workers Union, New York, NY. Place of publication varies: New York, NY, Jan. 18, 1919-July 13, 1928; Jersey City, NJ, July 27, 1928-Dec. 15, 1971; Stamford, CT, Jan. 1-Dec. 15, 1972; Plainfield, NJ, Jan. 1-15, 1973. Frequency varies: weekly, Jan. 18, 1919-June 29, 1928; semi-monthly, July 13, 1928-Jan. 15, 1979. Editors: S. Yanofsky, Jan. 18, 1919-Dec. 18, 1925; Max D. Danish, Dec. 25, 1925-Feb. 22, 1929; A. Rosebury, Apr. 26-May 10, 1929; Dr. B. Hoffman, May 24, 1929-Nov. 21, 1930: Max D. Danish, Dec. 5, 1930-June 11, 1951; Leon Stein, June 15, 1951-Sep. 1, 1976; Michael Pollack, Sep. 15, 1976-June 1, 1978. Subject focus: labor unions, AFL-CIO, working women, garment industry. In Russian (5%). Other holding institutions: AU (ALM), [Congressional Research Service, Washington, DC] (CRS), DLC (DLC), [Western New York Library Resources Council, Buffalo, NY] (VZX), NIC (COO), OKentU (KSU), PPD (DXU), WM (GZD).

| Hist | v.1, n.1- Jan. 18, 1919- | Microforms |
|---|---|---|
|  | v.18, n.1-24; Jan. 1-Dec. 15, 1926 | Ask at Room 225 |

506 Justicia. 1919. Monthly. $2 for individuals and institutions. Tony Laspier, editor, Justicia, 1710 Broadway, New York, NY 10012. (212) 265-7000. ISSN 0022-7013. OCLC 2277370. LC sn78-4132. Last issue 12 pages, size 30 x 37. Line drawings, photographs, commercial advertising. Published by the International Ladies' Garment Workers Union, New York, NY. Subject focus: AFL-CIO, labor unions, garment industry. In Spanish (100%). Other holding institutions: AU (ALM), [Congressional Research Service, Washington, DC] (CRS), [Western New York Library Resources Council, Buffalo, NY] (VZX), NIC (COO), OKentU (KSU),

PPD (DXU), WM (GZD).

Hist    v.60, n.1-    Circulation
Jan., 1978-

507 KU Commission on the Status of Women-Career Newsletter. 1973-1974//? Irregular. Last issue 2 pages. Line drawings. Available on microfilm: Herstory. Published by the Commission on the Status of Women, University of Kansas, Lawrence, KS. Subject focus: employment, career development, wages, professionals.

Hist    Nov., 1973,    Microforms
Mar.-Apr., 1974    Her. 3, R 1

508 Kaliflower. 1970?-1971//? Unknown. OCLC 2263156. Last issue 10 pages. Line drawings. Available on microfilm: Herstory. Published by the Virgin's Liberation Front, San Francisco, CA. Subject focus: travel, communes, cooperatives.

Hist    v.3, n.11;    Microforms
July 15, 1971    Her. 1, R 16

509 The Kansas Legionette. 1925. Monthly. ISSN 0199-0764. OCLC 5574857. LC sn79-7956. Last issue 12 pages, size 22 x 28. Line drawings, photographs. Published by the American Legion Auxiliary, Dept. of Kansas American Legion, Topeka, KS. Editors: Ida M. Walker, Jan., 1926-June, 1928; Lulu V. Faulkner, July, 1928-Dec., 1940. Subject focus: clubs.

Hist    [v.1, n.6-v.5,    F836/7K16
n.12];    (Cutter)
[Jan., 1926-
Dec., 1940]

510 The Kappa Beta Pi Quarterly. 1916-1973//? Quarterly. OCLC 2027389. Last issue 30 pages, last volume 172 pages, size 17 x 25. Photographs, commercial advertising. Published by the Kappa Beta Pi Legal Sorority, Lansing, MI. Editors: Lorraine A. Kulpa. Subject focus: lawyers. Other holding institutions: DUSC (LAW), MCR-S (Schlesinger Library on the History of Women in America, Radcliffe College, Cambridge, MA), NbU (LDL), [Ohio Northern University Law Library, Ada, OH] (ONL), PPiU (PIT), [AMIGOS Union List of Serials, Dallas, TX] (IUC).

Law    v.55, n.1-v.56,    Periodicals
n.4;    Section
Spring, 1971-
Winter, 1972/1973

511 Keeping in Touch. 1958-1962//? Monthly. Last issue 3 pages, size 28 x 21. Published by the Woman's Activities Dept., AFL-CIO, Committee on Political Education, Washington, DC. Subject focus: labor unions.

Hist    n.3-5, 7, 10;    Pam 72-588
Sep. 1, 1958-
May 15, July 18,
Oct. 15, 1962

512 The Keystone. 1899-1913//? Monthly. OCLC 2704190. LC 08-19674. Last issue 12 pages, last volume 124 pages. Line drawings, commercial advertising. Available on microfilm: GrP. Published by the South Carolina Federation of Women's Clubs, Charleston, SC. Editors: Ida Marshall Lining, June, 1899-June, 1900; Ida Marshall Lining and Mary B. Poppenheim, July-Nov., 1900; Laura B. Poppenheim, Dec., 1900-May, 1903; Mary B. Poppenheim, June, 1903-June, 1913. Subject focus: clubs, fiction, poetry. Other holding institutions: AU (ALM), CSt (Stanford University), CCC (HDC), CtY (YUS), InU (IUL), MdFreH (HCF), MeB (BBH), [University of Minnesota Union List, Minneapolis, MN] (MUL), NmLcU (IRU), OCU (CIN), PPiU (PIT).

Hist    v.1, n.1-v.14,    Microforms
n.9;
June, 1899-
June, 1913

513 Killer Dyke. 1971-1972//? Unknown. OCLC 2263231. LC scg0-543. Last issue 16 pages. Line drawings, photographs. Available on microfilm: Herstory. Published by: the Feminist Lesbian Intergalactic Party, Chicago, IL. Subject focus: FLIPPIES, feminism, gay rights, lesbians, rights, political parties.

Hist    v.1, n.1;    Microforms
Sep., 1971    Her. 1, R 2

v.2, n.2;    Her. 1 UP, R5
July, 1972

514 Kinesis. 1972. Monthly. $8 for individuals, $15 for institutions. Kinesis, 1090 West 7th Avenue, Vancouver, British Columbia, Canada V6H 1B3. Last issue 24 pages, last volume 296 pages, size 43 x 29. Line drawings, photographs. Published by Vancouver Status of Women, Vancouver, British Columbia, Canada. Subject focus: rights, child care, health, pro-abortion, lesbians, gay rights, law.

Hist    v.6, n.6-    Circulation
May, 1977-

515 Kinswomen. Southern Illinois Women's Newsletter. 1973//? Monthly. Last issue 6 pages, size 22 x 36. Published by Kinswomen, Murphysboro, IL. Subject focus: rights, poetry, feminism, lobbying.

| | | | | | |
|---|---|---|---|---|---|
| Hist | v.1, n.9-10;<br>May-June, 1973 | Pam 74-1937 | | July, 1973-<br>May, 1974 | Her. CUP, R2 |
| | | | | v.5, n.1, v.7, n.2-<br>Jan./Feb., 1974,<br>June, 1976- | Circulation |

516 <u>The Kitchen Garden</u>. 1881-1888//? Bi-monthly. Last issue 8 pages, last volume 48 pages, size 19 x 26. Line drawings. Published by The Kitchen Garden, Cincinnati, OH. Subject focus: home economics, poetry.

| | | | | | |
|---|---|---|---|---|---|
| | | | Coll | Current Issues<br>Only | Women's<br>Reading Area |
| Agric | v.1, n.1-v.5, n.6;<br>Oct. 20, 1881-<br>Sep., 1888 | Periodicals<br>Section | Wom Ed<br>Res | v.6, n.6;<br>Sep., 1975 | Circulation |

<u>Know News</u>. Pittsburgh, PA

   see <u>Know, Inc.</u>, Pittsburgh, PA

517 <u>Kitsap County NOWsletter</u>. 1971-1974//? Irregular. Last issue 4 pages. Line drawings. Available on microfilm: Herstory. Published by the Kitsap County Chapter, National Organization for Women, Poulsbo, WA. Subject focus: feminism, lobbying, Equal Rights Amendment, politics.

520 <u>Kvennabladid</u>. 1895-1920//. Monthly. OCLC 2251466. Last issue 6 pages, last volume 94 pages. Available on microfilm: ResP (1895-1919). Published by Kvennabladid, Rey Iceland. Editor: Breit Bjarnjedinsdottir. Subject focus: home economics. In Icelandic (100%). Other holding institutions: MH (HLS), [University of Minnesota Union List, Minneapolis, MN] (MUL).

| | | |
|---|---|---|
| Hist | v.1, n.1-v.2, n.6;<br>Nov., 1971-<br>June, 1973 | Microforms<br>Her. 2, R 10 |
| | v.2, n.7-v.3, n.4;<br>July, 1973-<br>Apr., 1974 | Her. 2 UP, R7 |

| | | |
|---|---|---|
| Mem | v.1, n.1-v.25,<br>n.12;<br>Feb. 21, 1895-<br>Dec. 31, 1919 | Microforms |

518 <u>Knitgoods Workers Voice</u>. 1938. Bi-monthly. Gratis for individuals and institutions. Sylvia F. Grugett, editor, Knitgoods Workers Voice, 519 8th Avenue, New York, NY 10018 and 300 Wyckoff Avenue, Brooklyn, NY 11385. (212) 497-5393. Last issue 8 pages, size 31 x 23. Line drawings, photographs. Available on microfilm: WHi (1980-).Published by Knitgoods Workers' Union, International Ladies Garment Workers Union, Local 155, AFL-CIO. Subject focus: labor unions, AFL-CIO, garment industry, clothes. In Spanish 10%.

521 <u>Kvindebrevet</u>. 1978. Monthly. Helle Stief, editor, Kvindebrevet, Nyhaven 61, 1051 Copenhagen, Denmark, 01-131819. Last issue 8 pages, last volume 56 pages, size 22 x 28. Line drawings. Previous editors: Jette Rantorp, Jan.-Oct., 1978; Lise-Lotte Hartwig, Nov., 1978-Apr., 1979. Subject focus: women's movement, music, art, literature. In Danish (100%).

| | | |
|---|---|---|
| Hist | v.42, n.3-<br>June, 1980- | Circulation |

| | | |
|---|---|---|
| Mem | v.1, n.1-<br>Jan., 1978- | Periodicals<br>Room |

519 <u>Know Inc</u>. 1970. Irregular. $6 for individuals and institutions. OCLC 5073429, 4408939. LC sc80-903. Last issue 14 pages, size 22 x 28. Line drawings, photographs, commercial advertising. Available on microfilm: Herstory (1970-1974). Published by Know Inc., Pittsburgh, PA. Title varies: as Know News, Sep. 27, 1970-June, 1973. Subject focus: child care, women's studies, employment, feminism, Equal Rights Amendment.

522 <u>Kvinden og Samfundet</u>. 1885-1899//? Monthly. Last issue 16 pages, last volume 168 pages, size 13 x 22. Line drawings, photographs. Available on microfilm: McA. Published by Kvinden og Samfundet, Copenhagen, Denmark. Subject focus: pro-suffrage, education, employment, biographies. In Danish (100%).

| | | |
|---|---|---|
| Mem | v.1, n.1-v.15,<br>n.9;<br>Jan., 1885-<br>Sep., 1899 | AP/K983/S187 |

| | | |
|---|---|---|
| Hist | Sep. 27, 1970-<br>July 15, 1971 | Microforms<br>Her. 1, R 16 |
| | May, 1971 | Her. 1, Add. |
| | Oct., 1971-<br>June, 1973 | Her. 1 UP, R 5 |

523 <u>Kvinder</u>. 1977. Bi-monthly. Kvinder, Vestergade 10 A 4 Sal. 1456, Copenhagen, Denmark. Telephone: (01) 15 79 99. Last issue 30 pages, size 22 x 29. Line drawings, photographs, some in color. Subject focus: birth control,

poetry, seniors, art. In Danish (100%).

Mem   n.24-   AP/K984/C
      Feb./Mar., 1979-

L.A. Women's Center Newsletter. Los Angeles, CA

see Sister. Venice, CA

L.A. Women's Liberation Newsletter. Los Angeles, CA

see Sister. Venice, CS

524  LfSC-Librarians for Social Change. 1972-1974//? Unknown. OCLC 5285054, 3807176. Last issue 24 pages. Line drawings. Available on microfilm: Herstory (1973). Published by Librarians for Social Change, Brighton, Sussex, England. Subject focus: librarians, consciousness-raising.

Hist   ?, 1973;   Microforms
                  Her. 3, R 2

525  The Labor Pains Newsletter. 1973-1974//? Irregular. Last issue 16 pages. Line drawings, photographs. Available on microfilm: Herstory. Published in Cambridge, MA. Subject focus: child care, education, media.

Hist   n.1;              Microforms
       June 6, 1973      Her. 2, R 6

       n.2-5;            Her. 2 UP, R 3
       Sep. 20, 1973-
       June 7, 1974

526  Labor Woman. 1913-1971? Monthly. Last issue 12 pages, size 21 x 27. Line drawings, photographs. Published by The Labour Party, London, England. Editor: Mary E. Sutherland, Jan., 1936-Dec., 1960. Subject focus: labor unions, workers, socialism, consumer protection, homemakers, children.

Mem    v.24, n.1-v.61,   AP/L125/W872
       Jan., 1936-
       Sep., 1971

527  Ladder. 1956-1972//. Bi-monthly. ISSN 0023-7108. OCLC 2263409. Last issue 56 pages, last volume 336 pages, size 14 x 21. Line drawings, photographs, commercial advertising. Indexed: in Alternative Press Index (1970-1972). Available on microfilm: UnM, Herstory. Published by the Daughters of Bilitis, Kansas City, MO. Place of publication varies: San Francisco, CA, Jan., 1957-Apr./May, 1970. Frequency varies: monthly, Jan., 1957-Sep., 1968. Editors: Ann Ferguson, Oct.-Dec., 1956, Phyllis Lyon, Jan., 1957-June, 1960; Del Martin, July, 1960-Feb., 1963; Barbara Gittings, Mar., 1963-Dec., 1966; Helen Sanders, Jan., 1967-Aug., 1968; Gene Damon, Sep., 1968-Aug./Sep., 1972. Subject focus: lesbians, poetry, literature, art, film reviews. Other holding institutions: AzTeS (AZS), MBU (BOS), MCR-S (Schlesinger Library on the History of Women in America, Radcliffe College, Cambridge, MA), [University of Minnesota Union List, Minneapolis, MN] (MUL), NFQC (XQM), NbU (LDL), PPiU (PIT), WMUW (GZN).

Hist   v.1, n.1-v.15,   Microforms
       n.11/12;         Her. 1, R7-8
       Oct., 1956-
       Aug./Sep., 1971

       v.16, n.1/2-11/12;   Her. 1 UP, R6
       Oct./Nov., 1971-
       Aug./Sep., 1972

RBR    v.1, n.4-v.16,   Circulation
       n.11/12;
       Jan., 1957-
       Aug./Sep., 1972

528  Ladies' Afternoon Visitor. 1806-1807//. Weekly. OCLC 3810212, 1755430. LC mic56-4624. Last issue 16 pages, size 27 x 35. Line drawings. Available on microfilm: UnM. Published in Boston, MA. Title varies: as Ladies' Visitor, Dec. 4, 1806. Subject focus: biographies, fiction, poetry. Other holding institutions: NTR (YRM), NcWsW (EWF), OAkU (AKR), OYU (YNG), [AMIGOS Union List of Serials, Dallas, TX] (IUC), WMUW (GZN).

Hist   v.1, n.1-13;   Microforms
       Dec. 4, 1806-
       Feb. 28, 1807

       v.1, n.1-13;   AP/2/"B8416
       Dec. 4, 1806-
       Feb. 28, 1807

529  The Ladies' Cabinet of Fashion. 1832-1870?//. Monthly. OCLC 1755432. Last issue 112 pages, last volume 112 pages, size 12 x 19. Line drawings, some in color. Self-indexed: (1840-1844). Available on microfilm: ResP (1832-1861). Published by E. Henderson, London, England. Editors: Margaret De Courcy and Beatrice De Courcy, Jan., 1833-Dec., 1835. Title varies: as Ladies Cabinet of Fashion, Music & Romance, Jan., 1832-June, 1852. Subject focus: fashion, music, poetry. Other holding institutions: CtY (YUS), [Indiana Union List of Serials, Indianapolis, IN] (ILS), [University of Minnesota Union List, Minneapolis, MN] (MUL), NNC (Columbia University), OCl (CLE), TxDW (IWU).

| | | | | | | |
|---|---|---|---|---|---|---|
| Mem | [v.2, n.1-(n.s.) v.2, n.12]; [Jan., 1833- Dec., 1844] | AP/L1548/C115 | | Agric | [v.9, n.1-v.16, n.1] [Nov., 1880- Jan., 1887] | Periodicals Section |
| | v.1, n.1-v.18, n.6; Jan., 1832- July, 1861 | Microforms | | Mem | v.3, n.25-v.16, n.1; Jan., 1874- Jan., 1887 | Microforms |

The Ladies' Cabinet of Fashion, Music & Romance. London, England

see The Ladies' Cabinet of Fashion. London, England

530 The Ladies' Companion. 1828-1844//?. Monthly. Last issue 44 pages, last volume 300 pages, size 16 x 25. Line drawings. Self-indexed (1840-1844). Published in New York, NY. Subject focus: literature, poetry, fiction, art, music. Other holding institution: MCR-S (Schlesinger Library on the History of Women in America, Radcliffe College, Cambridge, MA).

| | | |
|---|---|---|
| Hist | v.13; v.16-21; May-Oct., 1840; Nov., 1841- Oct., 1844 | AP83/LA13 |

531 Ladies Delight Magazine. 1967-1968//. 7 times a year. ISSN 0458-6131. OCLC 3355627. Last issue 58 pages, size 22 x 28. Line drawings, photographs. Published by LDM Publications, Houston, TX. Frequency varies: bi-monthly, July/Aug.-Nov./Dec., 1967. Editor: Nola S. Carroll. Subject focus: poetry, fiction, hobbies, astrology. Other holding institution: [University of Minnesota Union List, Minneapolis, MN] (MUL).

| | | |
|---|---|---|
| RBR | v.1, n.1-v.2, n.4; July/Aug., 1967- Jan./Feb., 1968 | Circulation |

532 The Ladies' Floral Cabinet. 1872-1887//? Monthly. Last issue 30 pages, last volume 336 pages, size 27 x 35. Line drawings, commercial advertising. Self-indexed (1875-1877). Available on microfilm: ResP. Published in New York, NY. Editor: Henry T. Williams. Subject focus: flower arrangement, gardening, home economics, crafts, music. Other holding institutions: CtY (YUS), MCR-S (Schlesinger Library on the History of Women in America, Radcliffe College, Cambridge, MA).

| | | |
|---|---|---|
| Hist | v.3, n.25-v.6, n.72; Jan., 1874- Dec., 1877 | AP83/LA132 |

533 The Ladies' Garment Worker. 1910-1918//. Monthly. OCLC 5807510, 2704314. LC 12-51. Last issue 34 pages, last volume 382 pages, size 17 x 25. Photographs. Available on microfilm: GrP, WHi (1910-1913). Published by The International Ladies' Garment Workers' Union, New York, NY. Editor: John A. Dyche, June, 1911-June, 1914. Subject focus: garment industry, labor unions, AFL-CIO. In Italian (30%) (1910-1911); Yiddish (30-50%) (1910-May, 1917). Other holding institutions: CSt (Stanford University), CtY (YUS), InU (IUL), MNS (SNN), MdFreH (HCF), MeB (BBH), [University of Minnesota Union List, Minneapolis, MN] (MUL), NIC (COO), NmLcU (IRU), OCU (CIN), PPiU (PIT).

| | | |
|---|---|---|
| Hist | v.1, n.1-v.4, n.12; Apr. 1, 1910- Dec., 1913 | Microforms |
| | v.5, n.1-v.9, n.12; Jan., 1914- Dec., 1918 | HFBC6/IN8/7L1 (Cutter) |

534 Ladies' Home Journal. 1883. Monthly. $7.97 for individuals. Lenore Hershey, editor, Ladies' Home Journal, 641 Lexington Avenue, New York, NY 10022. Business address: P.O. Box 1697, Des Moines, IA 50340. ISSN 0023-7124. OCLC 2896794, 1624448. LC ca14-832, cau14-382. Last issue 172 pages, last volume 2184 pages, size 20 x 28. Line drawings, photographs, some in color, commercial advertising. Indexed: in Reader's Guide (1900-). Available on microfilm: McP (1960-), UnM (1884-), McI (1960-). Published by LHJ Publishing Inc., New York, NY. Title varies: as Ladies' Home Journal and Practical Housekeeper, Dec., 1887-Nov., 1888. Place of publication varies: Philadelphia, PA, Dec., 1887. Previous editors: Mrs. Louisa Knapp, Dec., 1887-Dec., 1888; Edward W. Bok, Jan., 1890-Dec., 1919; H.O. Davis, Jan.-June, 1920; John E. Pickett, July-Nov., 1920; Burton W. Currie, Jan., 1921-Jan., 1928; Loring A. Schuller, Feb., 1928-Sep., 1935; Bruce and Beatrice Gould, Oct., 1935-Sep., 1961; Curtis Anderson, Oct., 1961-June, 1963; Hubbard H. Cobb, July, 1963-Oct., 1963; Thomas Davis, Nov., 1963-Mar., 1965; John Mack Carter, Apr., 1965-Dec., 1973. Subject focus: fashion, beauty care, health, food, entertaining, fiction. Other holding institu-

tions: AU (ALM), ArAO (AKO), ArU (AFU), AzFU (AZN), AzTeS (AZS), CLS (CLA), CLU (CLU), [Pepperdine University, Malibu, CA] (CPE), CoDU (DVP), CtS (FEM), CtY (YUS), [Congressional Research Service, Washington, DC] (CRS), DLC (DLC), DNAL (AGL), DeU (DLM), FBoU (FGM), FJUNF (FNP), FM (DZM), GA (GAP), GASU (GSU), [Indiana Union List of Serials, Indianapolis, IN] (ILS), IPB (BA), InU (IUL), KLindB (KFB), KSteC (KKQ), KyDC (KCC), KyU (KUK), LLcM (LHA), MMeT (TFW), MNS (SNN), MCR-S (Schlesinger Library on the History of Women in America, Radcliffe College, Cambridge, MA), [University of Minnesota Union List, Minneapolis, MN] (MUL), MiEM (EEM), MiLC (EEL), MiMtpT (EZC), MsU (MUM), [New York State Union List, Albany, NY] (NYS), [Western New York Library Resources Council, Buffalo, NY] (VZX), NBu (VHB), NCortU (YCM), NGcCC (VVX), NGenoU (YGM), NIC (COO), NNR (ZXC), NOneoU (ZBM), NR (YQR), NSbSU (YSM), NSyU (SYB), NbU (LDL), NbKS (KRS), NcCU (NKM), NcEUcE (NPE), NcRS (NRC), NcWfSB (NVS), NjLincB (BCC), NmLcU (IRU), NmLvH (NMH), O (OHI), OO (OBE), OAU (OUN), OC1 (CLE), OC1U (CSU), OCedC (CDC), OKentU (KSU), OTU (TOL), OU (OSU), OkLC (OKC), OkT (TUL), OkTOR (OKO), PAnL (LVC), PCoR (ROB), PIm (IMM), [Pittsburgh Regional Library Center-Union List, Pittsburgh, PA] (QPR), PPD (DXU), ScRhW (SWW), TCollsM (TMS), TMurS (TXM), TxAbH (TXS), TxBelM (MHB), TxCM (TXA), TxDaB (IDA), [AMIGOS Union List of Serials, Dallas, TX] (IUC), TxDN (INT), TxDW (IWU), TxNacS (TXK), [Emory & Henry College, Emory, VA] (VEH), ViRCU (VRC), ViRU (VRU), [Arrowhead Library System, Janesville Public Library, Janesville, WI] (WIJ), WM (GZD), WMUW (GZN), WeharU (HRM).

| | | |
|---|---|---|
| Agric | v.5, n.1-12, v.7, n.1- Dec., 1887- Nov., 1888, Dec., 1889- | Periodicals Section |
| Mem | Current Issues Only | Periodicals Room |
| MPL | v.16, n.12- Dec., 1898- | Literature and Social Science Section |
| MATC | Current Issues Only | Cora Hardy Library |
| MHHS | Jan., 1972- | Circulation |
| MIPL | Jan., 1973- | Circulation |
| EHS | Jan., 1970- | Circulation |
| MOPL | Jan., 1974- | Circulation |
| DFPL | Jan., 1972- | Circulation |
| MFHS | Jan., 1973- | Circulation |

| | | |
|---|---|---|
| MGHS | Jan., 1964- | Circulation |
| BAHS | Current Issues Only | Circulation |
| CPPL | Current Issues Only | Circulation |
| OPL | Current Issues Only | Circulation |
| DHS | Current Issues Only | Circulation |
| LAHS | Current Issues Only | Circulation |
| SPPL | Jan., 1970- | Circulation |
| RPL | [Jan., 1970-] | Circulation |
| CFL | Jan., 1971- | Circulation |
| MHPL | Jan., 1971- | Circulation |
| RVHS | Jan., 1960- Dec., 1968 | Circulation |
| OM | Current Issues Only | Circulation |
| DFHS | July, 1974- | Circulation |
| NFPL | Current Issues Only | Circulation |
| VPL | Jan., 1964- | Circulation |
| SCPL | Jan., 1971- | Circulation |
| WHS | Jan., 1969- | Circulation |
| BFL | Jan., 1975- | Circulation |
| VHS | Jan., 1971- | Circulation |
| MMHS | Jan., 1970- | Circulation |
| TML | Jan., 1969- | Circulation |
| MCL | Jan., 1971- | Circulation |
| SPHS | Jan., 1971- | Circulation |
| BHS | [July, 1971-] | Circulation |
| SAPH | Current Issues Only | Circulation |
| BML | Current Issues Only | Circulation |
| R&L | Jan., 1884- Dec., 1970 | Circulation |

Ladies' Home Journal and Practical Housekeeper. Philadelphia, PA

see Ladies' Home Journal. New York, NY

535 The Ladies' Journal/Fu Nu Tsa Chih. 1915-1920?//. Monthly. Last issue 162 pages, last volume 1844 pages, size 15 x 24. Line drawings, photographs, some in color, commercial advertising. Published in Shanghai, China. Subject focus: rights, health, science, women's movement. In Chinese (100%).

| Mem | v.2, n.10-v.6, n.6; Oct., 1916- June, 1920 | AP/L155 |

536 Ladies' Literary Cabinet. 1819-1822//? Weekly. OCLC 1755439. LC 07-21215. Last issue 8 pages, last volume 112 pages, size 21 x 27. Self-indexed (1820-1821). Available on microfilm: UnM. Published by Woodworth and Heustis, New York, NY. Editor: Samuel Woodworth, Apr. 17, 1819-Aug. 5, 1820. Subject focus: literature, poetry, home economics, biographies, fashion, music. Other holding institutions: [Indiana Union List of Serials, Indianapolis, IN] (ILS), [University of Minnesota Union List, Minneapolis, MN] (MUL), NcWsW (EWF), OKentU (KSU), PPiU (PIT).

| Hist | v.1, n.1-v.6, n.14; Apr. 17, 1819- Aug. 10, 1822 | AP83/LA15 |

| | v.1, n.1-v.7, n.1; Apr. 17, 1819- Dec. 21, 1822 | Microforms |

537 Ladies' Literary Museum; or, Weekly Repository. 1817-1818//. Weekly. Last issue 8 pages, last volume 236 pages. Line drawings, commercial advertising. Available on microfilm: UnM. Published in Philadelphia, PA. Editor: H.C. Lewis. Subject focus: fiction, poetry.

| Hist | v.1, n.1-v.2, n.25; ?, 1817- July 13, 1818 | Microforms |

538 The Ladies' Magazine. 1819-?//. Weekly. Last issue 8 pages, size 12 x 22. Line drawings, commercial advertising. Published by Russell and Edes, Savannah, GA. Subject focus: education, science, history, fiction, poetry.

| Hist | v.1, n.1-26; Feb. 13-Aug. 7, 1819 | AP83/LA1 |

539 The Ladies' Magazine. 1823-1824//? Monthly. OCLC 755146, 1641104. Last issue 32 pages, last volume 384 pages. Commercial advertising. Available on microfilm: UnM. Published in Providence, RI. Subject focus: Christianity, poetry. Other holding institution: OWoC (WOO).

| Hist | v.1, n.1-12; Mar., 1823- June, 1824 | Microforms |

540 The Ladies' Magazine and Literary Gazette. 1828-1833//? Monthly. OCLC 1480225, 4691349. LC 16-16947, mic59-7460. Last issue 48 pages, last volume 576 pages, size 21 x 27. Line drawings, some in color. Self-indexed (1830, 1832-1833). Published in Boston, MA. Editor: Sarah Josepha Hale. Subject focus: fiction, poetry, music. Other holding institutions: ArU (AFU), InU (IUL), [University of Minnesota Union List, Minneapolis, MN] (MUL), NPV (VXW), NcWsW (EWF), OKentU (KSU), [Pittsburgh Regional Library Center-Union List, Pittsburgh, PA] (QPR), TxDN (INT), ViNO (VOD), WMUW (GZN).

| Hist | v.1, n.9-v.2, n.1 3,5,7,9, v.3, n.1-12, v.5, n.1- v.6, n.12; Nov. 1, 1828, Jan., Mar., May, July, Sep., 1829, Jan.-Dec., 1830, Jan., 1832- Dec., 1833 | AP83/LA2 |

541 The Ladies' Miscellany. 1828-1831//? Weekly. OCLC 1586629. LC 18-1143. Last issue 4 pages, last volume 208 pages. Available on microfilm: ResP. Published in Salem, MA. Subject focus: poetry, biographies, fiction, obituaries, marriage announcements. Other holding institutions: [Indiana Union List of Serials, Indianapolis, IN] (ILS), [University of Minnesota Union List, Minneapolis, MN] (MUL), NN (NYP), PPiU (PIT).

| Mem | v.1, n.1-v.2, n.52; Nov. 7, 1828- Mar. 3, 1831 | Microforms |

542 The Ladies' Monthly Museum; or, Polite Repository of Amusement and Instruction. 1798-1832//. Monthly. OCLC 3876605. LC ca07-3598. Last issue 56 pages, last volume 356 pages, size 11 x 18. Line drawings. Self-indexed (1798-1827). Available on microfilm: UnM. Published by Verner & Hood, London, England. Subject focus: fashion, poetry, fiction, biographies. Other holding institutions: OCl (CLE), OO (OBE), TMurS (TXM), TxEU (TXU), ViW (VWM).

## Women's Periodicals and Newspapers

    Mem        July, 1798-        AP/L1559/3
                    Dec., 1827

543 The Ladies' Museum. 1800-1820//? Weekly. OCLC 3810259, 1644300. LC c56-4623. Last issue 4 pages. Available on microfilm: UnM (1800). Published in Philadelphia, PA. Editor: Isaac Ralston. Subject focus: fiction, poetry. Other holding institutions: [University of Minnesota Union List, Minneapolis, MN] (MUL), NcWsW (EWF), OAkU (AKR), OKentU (KSU), OYU (YNG), PPiU (PIT).

    Hist       v.1, n.1-14;      Microforms
                 Feb. 25-
                 June 7, 1800

544 The Ladies' Museum. 1825-1826//? Weekly. OCLC 1645373. Last issue 4 pages, last volume 92 pages. Line drawings. Self-indexed (1825). Available on microfilm: UnM (1825). Published in Providence, RI. Editor: Eaton W. Maxcy. Subject focus: fiction, poetry. Other holding institutions: AzU (AZU), [University of Minnesota Union List, Minneapolis, MN] (MUL), NcWsW (EWF), OKentU (KSU), PPiU (PIT).

    Hist       v.1, n.1-23;      Microforms
                 July 16 -
                 Dec. 31, 1825

545 The Ladies' Museum. 1829-?//. Monthly. OCLC 1755442. Last issue 56 pages, last volume 356 pages, size 13 x 21. Available on microfilm: UnM. Published in London, England. Subject focus: history, poetry, fiction. Other holding institutions: AzTeS (AZS), [University of Minnesota Union List, Minneapolis, MN] (MUL), OAkU (AKR), PCLS (REC), [Pittsburgh Regional Library Center-Union List, Pittsburgh, PA] (QPR), PPiU (PIT).

    Mem        Jan.-Dec., 1829     AP/L1559/4

Ladies National Magazine.   Philadelphia, PA

    see The New Peterson Magazine.
    Philadelphia, PA

546 The Ladies' Pearl. 1840-1843//? Monthly. OCLC 5182226, 1755457, 5182111, 5182037. Last issue 24 pages, last volume 156 pages, size 13 x 22. Line drawings. Self-indexed (1840-1842). Available on microfilm: UnM (1840-1843). Title varies: The Ladies' Pearl, and Literary Gleaner, June, 1840-May, 1841. Published by E. A. Rice and Co., Lowell, MA. Editor: Daniel Wise, June, 1840-May, 1841. Subject focus: poetry, music, art, fiction. Other holding institutions: [University of Minnesota Union List, Minneapolis, MN] (MUL), [New York State Union List, Albany, NY] (NYS), NOneoU (ZBM), NcWsW (EWF), OC1 (CLE), OKentU (KSU).

    Mem       v.1, n.1-12,       Y/95L15
               v.2, n.7-v.3, n.5?;
               June, 1840-
               May, 1841,
               Jan.-Dec., 1842

The Ladies' Pearl, and Literary Gleaner.
    Lowell, MA

    see The Ladies' Pearl.  Lowell, MA

547 Ladies' Port Folio. 1820//. Weekly. OCLC 1755447. Last issue 8 pages, last volume 192 pages. Self-indexed (1820). Available on microfilm: UnM. Published in Boston, MA. Subject focus: fiction, poetry, theater reviews. Other holding institutions: [University of Minnesota Union List, Minneapolis, MN] (MUL), NSbSU (UWM), NcWsW (EWF), OKentU (KSU), PPiU (PIT).

    Hist      v.1, n.1-25;      Microforms
             Jan. 1-
             June 17, 1820

            v.1, n.1-28;      Microforms
             Jan. 1-
             July 8, 1820

The Ladies' Repository.  Boston, MA

    see The Ladies' Repository Religious and
    Literary Magazine for the Home
    Circle.  Boston, MA

548 The Ladies' Repository. 1841-1876//? Monthly. OCLC 1755449. LC 04-28468. Last issue 92 pages, last volume 570 pages, size 15 x 24. Line drawings, commercial advertising. Self-indexed. Available on microfilm: UnM. Title varies: as The Ladies' Repository and Gatherings of the West, Jan., 1841-Dec., 1848. Published in Cincinnati, OH. Editors: Rev. L.L. Hamline, Jan., 1841-Dec., 1843; Rev. E. Thompson, Jan., 1844-Dec., 1845; Rev. B.F. Cefft, Jan., 1846-Dec., 1852; Rev. D.W. Clark, Jan., 1853-Dec., 1863; Rev. I.W. Wiley, Jan., 1864-Dec., 1872; Rev. E. Wentworth, Jan., 1873-June, 1876; Rev. Daniel Curry, June-Dec., 1876. Subject focus: fiction, poetry, Christianity, art. Other holding institutions: AU (ALM), AShC (ASH), ArLUA (AKU), ArU (AFU), FJ (JPL), GA (GAP), ICL (IAL), IGK (IBK), [Indiana Union List of Serials, Indianapolis, IN] (ILS), MBU (BOS), MCR-S (Schlesinger Library on the History of Women in America, Radcliffe College, Cambridge MA), MiMtpT (EZC), [University of Minnesota Union List, Minneapolis MN] (MUL), NII (XIM), NOneoU (ZBM), NR (YQR), NSbSU (YSM), OAkU (AKR), OC1 (CLE), OC1W (CWR), OKentU (KSU), OYU (YNG), PAnL (LVC), PNc

(QNC), PNwC (WFN), PPi (CPL), [Pittsburgh Regional Library Center - Union List, Pittsburgh PA] (QPR), [Emory and Henry College, Emory, VA] (VEH), WM (GZD), WMUW (GZN).

| | | |
|---|---|---|
| Hist | v.1, n.1-<br>v.36, n.6;<br>Jan., 1841-<br>Dec., 1876 | Microforms |
| Mem | v.17, n.1-12;<br>Jan.-Dec., 1857 | AY11/L35 |

The Ladies Repository and Gatherings of the West. Cincinnati, OH

see The Ladies Repository. Cincinnati, OH

549 The Ladies Repository and Literary Magazine for the Home Circle. 1832-1877//? Monthly. OCLC 1755448. Last issue 76 pages, last volume 476 pages, size 23 x 15 (varies). Line drawings. Self-indexed. Published in Boston, MA. Title varies: as Universalist and Ladies' Repository, June 7, 1834-May, 1839; as The Ladies' Repository, July, 1844-June, 1854. Frequency varies: semi-monthly, June 7, 1834-May, 1835. Editors: Daniel D. Smith, June 7, 1834-May, 1836; Henry Bacon, June, 1838-June, 1854. Subject focus: fiction, poetry, music. Other holding institutions: MCR-S (Schlesinger Library on the History of Women in America, Radcliffe College, Cambridge, MA), [University of Minnesota Union List, Minneapolis, MN] (MUL), NR (YQR), OKentU (KSU), OY (YMM).

| | | |
|---|---|---|
| Hist | v.3, n.1-v.4, n.12,<br>v.7, n.1-v.8, n.12,<br>v.13-v.17, v.22,<br>v.37, n.7-v.50,<br>n.6;<br>June 7, 1834-<br>May, 1836,<br>June, 1838-<br>May, 1839,<br>July, 1844-<br>June, 1849,<br>July, 1853-<br>June, 1854,<br>Jan., 1867-<br>Dec., 1873 | AP83/LA4 |

550 The Ladies' Visiter. 1819-1820//. Monthly. OCLC 1587401. Last issue 14 pages. Line drawings. Available on microfilm: UnM. Published in Marietta, PA. Subject focus: fiction, poetry. Other holding institutions: [University of Minnesota Union List, Minneapolis, MN] (MUL), NSbSU (YSM), NcWsW (EWF), OKentU (KSU), PPiU (PIT).

| | | |
|---|---|---|
| Hist | v.1, n.1-2,11,13;<br>May 27-June 21,<br>1819, Feb. 28,<br>Apr. 18, 1820 | Microforms |

Ladies' Visitor. Boston, MA

see Ladies' Afternoon Visitor. Boston, MA

551 The Ladies' Wreath. 1846-1862//? Monthly. OCLC 1755451. Last issue 26 pages, size 24 x 15. Line drawings, some in color, commercial advertising. Indexed: by publisher (1846). Available on microfilm: UnM (1846-1859). Published in New York, NY. Editors: Mrs. S.T. Martyn, May, 1846-Nov., 1850; Helen Irving, Feb.-Oct., 1852. Subject focus: literature, poetry, art. Other holding institution:[University of Minnesota Union List, Minneapolis, MN] (MUL), OClW (CWR), OKentU (KSU), [Pittsburgh Regional Library Center-Union List, Pittsburgh, PA] (QPR), PSrS (SRS), TxDW (IWU), TxLT (ILU).

| | | |
|---|---|---|
| Hist | v.1, n.1-12, v.3,<br>n.4,6-7,9-12,<br>v.4, n.2-3,6-12,<br>v.5, n.2-5,7,<br>v.6, n.10-v.7, n.6;<br>May, 1846-<br>Apr., 1847,<br>Aug., Oct.-<br>Nov., 1848, Jan.-<br>Apr., June-July,<br>Oct., 1849-Apr.,<br>June-Aug., Nov., 1850,<br>Feb.-Oct., 1852 | AP83/LA11 |

552 The Lady's Amaranth. 1839-1841//? Semi-monthly. Last issue 16 pages, last volume 316 pages, size 15 x 23. Line drawings. Self-indexed. Published in Philadelphia, PA. Editor: Joseph Torr. Subject focus: poetry, history, fiction, biographies.

| | | |
|---|---|---|
| Mem | v.1, n.1-v.3, n.8;<br>Jan. 5, 1839-<br>?, 1841 | Y/95/L2 |

The Lady's Book. Philadelphia, PA

see Godey's Magazine. Philadelphia, PA

553 The Lady's Friend. 1864-1873//. Monthly. OCLC 2716229. LC 45-51812. Last issue 56 pages, size 17 x 26. Line drawings. Published by Deacon and Peterson, Philadelphia, PA. Editor: Sarah Webb Peterson. Subject focus: fiction, poetry, art, crafts, fashion, music. Other holding institutions: DSI (SMI), ILfC (IAK), InU (IUL), MCR-S (Schlesinger Library on the History of Women in America, Radcliffe

College, Cambridge, MA), MdFreH (HCF), MeB (BBH), NCorniCC (ZDG), NdU (UND), NmLcU (IRU), OCU (CIN), OCl (CLE), OYesA (ANC), PIm (IMM), PPiU (PIT).

Hist v.8, n.1-12; AP/2/L253
Jan.-Dec., 1871

554 The Lady's Magazine and Musical Repository. 1801-1802//? Monthly. Last issue 72 pages, last volume 398 pages. Line drawings. Available on microfilm: UnM. Published in New York, NY. Subject focus: fiction, poetry, music.

Hist v.1, n.1-v.3, n.6; Microforms
Jan., 1801-
June 1, 1802

555 The Lady's Magazine; and Repository of Entertaining Knowledge. 1792-1793//? OCLC 1623890. LC 07-21214. Last issue 56 pages, last volume 304 pages, size 13 x 22. Line drawings. Self-indexed. Available on microfilm: UnM (1792-1793). Published by W. Gibbons, Philadelphia, PA. Subject focus: fiction, letters, poetry, marriage announcements, obituaries. Other holding institutions: [University of Minnesota Union List, Minneapolis, MN] (MUL), NFQC (XQM), NOneoU (ZBM), OKentU (KSU), PCarlD (DKC).

Hist v.1, n.1-6?; AP83/LA6
June-Nov., 1792

  v.1, n.1-v.2, n.5?; Microforms
June, 1792-?, 1793

556 The Lady's Magazine, or Entertaining Companion for the Fair Sex. 1770-1811//? Monthly. Last issue 94 pages, last volume 630 pages, size 12 x 21. Line drawings. Self-indexed. Published in London, England. Subject focus: history, poetry, biographies, health.

Mem Aug., 1770- AP/L1558
Dec., 1811

557 The Lady's Magazine, or Polite Companion for the Fair Sex. 1759-1766//? Monthly. Last issue 48 pages, last volume 288 pages. Line drawings. Published in London, England. Editor: Mrs. Stanhope. Subject focus: history, education, biographies, religion, literary criticism, theater, poetry.

Mem Jan.-Dec., 1761 Microforms

  Jan.-Dec., 1766 AP45/LA13

558 The Lady's Miscellany; or The Weekly Visitor. 1802-1812//? Weekly. OCLC 1755456, 3810473. LC 56-53057, mic56-4621. Last issue 16 pages, last volume 416 pages. Line drawings, commercial advertising. Self-indexed (1802, 1804-1808, 1810). Available on microfilm: UnM. Published by Ming and Young, New York, NY. Title varies: as The Weekly Visitor or Ladies' Miscellany, Oct. 9, 1802-Oct. 25, 1806; as The Ladys' Weekly Miscellany, Nov. 1, 1806-May 5, 1810. Subject focus: fiction, poetry, music, obituaries, marriage announcements. Other holding institutions: [University of Minnesota Union List, Minneapolis, MN] (MUL), MoU (MUU), NSbSU (YSM), OAkU (AKR), OKentU (KSU), OYU (YNG), PSt (UPM), [AMIGOS Union List of Serials, Dallas, TX] (IUC), TxDW (IWU).

Hist v.1, n.1-v.15, Microforms
n.26;
Oct. 9, 1802-
Oct. 17, 1812

Mem v.1, n.1-v.15, Microforms
n.26;
Oct. 9, 1802-
Oct. 17, 1812

559 The Lady's Monitor. 1801-1802//? Weekly. OCLC 1589377, 3810408. LC mic56-4620. Last issue 8 pages. Available on microfilm: UnM. Published by The Lady's Monitor, New York, NY. Subject focus: fiction, poetry. Other holding institutions: [University of Minnesota Union List, Minneapolis, MN] (MUL), NcWsW (EWF), OAkU (AKR), OYU (YNG), [AMIGOS Union List of Serials, Dallas, TX] (IUC), WMUW (GZN).

Hist v.1, n.1-41; Microforms
Aug. 8, 1801-
May 29, 1802

560 The Lady's Poetical Magazine, or Beauties of British Poetry. 1781-1782//? OCLC 1771529. Last volume 444 pages. Line drawings. Available on microfilm: ResP. Published by James Harrison and Co., London, England. Subject focus: poetry. Other holding institutions: CtY (YUS), [University of Minnesota Union List, Minneapolis, MN] (MUL), MdU-BC (MUB), Tx DW (IWU).

Mem v.1-4; Microforms
1781-1782

561 Lady's Realm. 1896-1913//? Monthly. Last issue 102 pages, last volume 604 pages. Line drawings, photographs. Self-indexed (1896-1913). Available on microfilm: ResP. Published by Hutchinson and Co., London, England. Subject focus: fiction, poetry. Other holding institution: IC (CGP).

| | Mem | v.1, n.1-<br>v.34, n.204;<br>Nov., 1896-<br>Oct., 1913 | Microforms | | | v.1, n.8;<br>Aug., 1973 | Her. 2 UP, R7 |

The Lady's Weekly Miscellany. New York, NY

    see The Lady's Miscellany; or the Weekly Visitor. New York, NY

562 Laguna Beach Chapter - The N.O.W.sletter. 1973-1974?// Monthly. Last issue 4 pages. Line drawings. Available on microfilm: Herstory. Published by the Laguna Beach Chapter, National Organization for Women, Laguna Beach, CA. Title varies: as N.O.W. Newsletter, Mar.-June, 1973. Place of publication varies: Newport Beach, CA, Mar.-June, 1973. Editor: Lynne Smith. Subject focus: children, child care, rights, lobbying, feminism.

| | Hist | v.2, n.3-6;<br>Mar.-June, 1973 | Microforms<br>Her. 2, R 10 |
| | | v.2, n.7-v.3, n.6;<br>July, 1973-<br>June, 1974 | Her. 2 UP, R7 |

Lake Worth N.O.W. Lake Worth, FL

    see The Liberator. Lake Worth, FL

563 Lancaster Women's Liberation. 1971-1974//? Monthly? Last issue 8 pages. Line drawings. Available on microfilm: Herstory. Published by Lancaster Women's Center, Lancaster, PA. Frequency varies: semi-monthly, Sep., 1971-June 17, 1973. Subject focus: consciousness raising, employment, health, education, family, pro-abortion, media, day care, feminism, lobbying.

| | Hist | v.1, n.1-v.2, n.19;<br>Sep., 1971-<br>June 17, 1973 | Her. 2, R 6 |
| | | v.2, n.20-v.3, n.8;<br>July, 1973-<br>June, 1974 | Her. 2 UP, R4 |

564 Las Vegas N.O.W. 1973-1974//? Last issue 6 pages. Line drawings. Available on microfilm: Herstory. Published by Las Vegas Chapter, National Organization for Women, Las Vegas, NV. Subject focus: Equal Rights Amendment, politics, consciousness raising, film reviews, feminism.

| | Hist | v.1, n.5-6;<br>Apr.-May, 1973 | Microforms<br>Her. 2, R 10 |

565 Lavender Vision. 1971//? Unknown. OCLC 2263450, 5210728. Line drawings, photographs. Available on microfilm: Herstory. Published by the Media Center, Cambridge, MA. Subject focus: lesbians, poetry, rights.

| | Hist | v.1, n.1-2;<br>?, May, 1971 | Microforms<br>Her. 1, R 2 |

566 Lavender Woman. 1971-1974//? Irregular. Last issue 16 pages. Line drawings, photographs, commercial advertising. Available on microfilm: Herstory. Published by Lavender Women Collective, Committee of the Gay Women's Caucus, Chicago, IL. Subject focus: lesbians, poetry, satire, art, lobbying.

| | Hist | v.1, n.1-v.2, n.4;<br>Nov., 1971-<br>June, 1973 | Microforms<br>Her. 2, R 6 |
| | | v.2, n.5-v.3, n.4;<br>Aug., 1973-<br>June, 1974 | Her. 2 UP, R4 |

League of Academic Women. Berkeley, CA

    see League of Associated Women. Berkeley, CA

567 League of Associated Women. 1972-1974//? Irregular. Last issue 1 page. Line drawings. Available on microfilm: Herstory. Published by League of Associated Women, Center for Continuing Education for Women, University of California, Berkeley, CA. Title varies: League of Academic Women, Jan. 18, 1972-June, 1973. Subject focus: continuing education, media, professionals, lobbying.

| | Hist | Jan. 18, 1972-<br>June, 1973 | Microforms<br>Her. 2, R6 |
| | | Feb. 14, 1974 | Her. 2 UP, R4 |

League Bulletin. New York, NY

    see Bulletin. New York, NY

League Bulletin. Madison, WI

    see League of Women Voters of Dane County Bulletin. Madison, WI

568 League of Women Voters of Dane County Bulletin. 1949? Monthly, except summer. Judie

Keinmaier, editor, League of Women Voters of Dane County Bulletin, 738 E. Dayton Street, Madison, WI 53703. (608) 255-5636. Last issue 14 pages, size 22 x 28. Available on microfilm: WHi (1969-). Published by League of Women Voters of Dane County, Inc., Madison, WI. Title varies: as League Bulletin, May-June, 1969. Previous editors: Mrs. James Walter, May, 1969-Oct., 1970; Mrs. Jerry McAdow, Nov., 1970-Apr., 1972; Judy Olson, June, 1972-Apr., 1973; Megan Thompson, May-Aug./Sep., 1973; Eleanor Barschall, Dec., 1973-May, 1974; Martha Vetter, June, 1974-Apr., 1975; Linda Lewis and Sharon Malec, May, 1976-Apr., 1978; Linda Lewis, May, 1978. Subject focus: lobbying, law.

| Hist | May, 1969- | Microforms |

569 The Legion Auxiliary Star. 1925-1933?//. Monthly. Last issue 6 pages, size 22 x 28. Line drawings, photographs. Published by the Department of Nebraska American Legion Auxiliary, Mar. 5-Aug. 13, 1925. Editors: Mrs. C.E. McGlasson and Mrs. H.R. Ball, Mar.15-July 2, 1925; Mrs. H.R. Ball, Aug. 13, 1925-Oct. 7, 1926; Mrs. Irene Froid-Fleming, Nov. 11, 1926-Feb., 1933. Subject focus: clubs.

| Hist | v.1, n.1-v.9, n.2; Mar. 5, 1925-Feb., 1933 | F836/7L49 (Cutter) |

Legislative Bulletin. Hartford, CT

    see The Woman Voters' Bulletin. Hartford, CT

Legislative Bulletin. Washington, DC

    see WILPF Legislative Bulletin. Washington, DC

Legislative Bulletin of the Connecticut League of Women Voters. Hartford, CT

    see The Woman Voters' Bulletin. Hartford, CT

570 Legislative Newsletter. 1963-1964?//. Irregular. Last issue 3 pages. Available on microfilm: WHi. Published by the National Information Clearing Office, Women Strike for Peace, Washington, DC. Subject focus: lobbying, peace movement.

| Hist | v.1, n.1-3; Dec. 17, 1963-Mar. 3, 1964 | Microforms |

571 Lehigh Valley N.O.W. 1973-1974//? Monthly. Last issue 2 pages. Available on microfilm: Herstory. Published by Lehigh Valley Chapter National Organization for Women, Bethlehem, PA. Subject focus: employment, health, feminism, Equal Rights Amendment, lobbying.

| Hist | Mar.-June, 1973 | Microforms Her. 2, R10 |
| | July-Sep., 1973 | Her. CUP, R7 |

572 Lesbian Connection. 1975. 8 times a year. $4 for individuals, $13 for institutions. Lesbian Connection, P.O. Box 811, East Lansing, MI 48823. (517) 371-5257. Last issue 26 pages, last volume 168 pages, size 22 x 28. Line drawings, commercial advertising. Indexed: available from publisher. Published by the Ambitious Amazons, East Lansing, MI. Subject focus: lesbians.

| Wom St | v.2, n.3-July, 1976- | Reading Room |

573 The Lesbian Feminist. 1973//? Irregular. Last volume 18 pages. Line drawings. Available on microfilm: Herstory. Published by Lesbian-Feminist Liberation, New York, NY. Subject focus: lesbians, poetry, feminism, art.

| Hist | v.1, n.1-2; Aug. 25-Oct., 1973 | Microforms Her. 3, R 2 |

574 The Lesbian Letter. 1970-1971//? Monthly. OCLC 4891176. LC sc80-332. Last issue 2 pages. Line drawings. Available on microfilm: Herstory. Published by Daughters of Bilitis, New York, NY. Title varies: as Newsletter. Daughters of Bilitis/New York, Oct., 1970-Jan.1971. Editors: Alma, Oct., 1970; Eileen Web, Feb.-May, 1971. Subject focus: lesbians, poetry.

| Hist | Oct., 1970-May, 1971 | Microforms Her. 1, Add. |
| | Feb.-Dec., 1970 | Her. 1, R 14 |

575 Lesbians Fight Back. 1972//? Irregular. Last issue 10 pages. Line drawings. Available on microfilm: Herstory. Published by Philadelphia Radical Lesbians Women's Center, Philadelphia, PA. Subject focus: lesbians, poetry, radical feminism.

| Hist | v.1, n.1-3; July-Sep./Oct., 1972 | Microforms Her. 2, R 7 |

576 The Lesbian Tide. 1971-1978//. Bi-monthly. OCLC 2263486, 3137543, 4560173. Last issue 40 pages, last volume 215 pages, size 22 x 28. Line drawings, photographs, commercial advertising. Available on microfilm: Herstory (1971-1974). Published by the Daughters of Bilitis/Tide Collective, Los Angeles, CA.

## Women's Periodicals and Newspapers

Title varies: as The Tide, June-July, 1974. Frequency varies: monthly, Aug., 1971-Nov., 1974. Editor: Jeanne Cordova. Subject focus: lesbians, poetry, sports. Other holding institutions: CLobS (CLO), CLU (CLU), CU-UC (UCU), [University of Minnesota Union List, Minneapolis, MN] (MUL), [New York State Union List, Albany, NY] (NYS), NGenoU (YGM), PPiU (PIT).

| | | |
|---|---|---|
| Hist | Aug.-Sep., 1971 | Microforms Her. 1, R 14 |
| | Oct., 1971-May/June, 1973 | Her. 1 UP, R 6 |
| | v.2, n.12-v.3, n.11; July, 1973-June, 1974 | Her. CUP, R 7 |
| RBR | v.2, n.5-v.7, n.5; Dec., 1972-Mar./Apr., 1978 | Circulation |

577 <u>Lesbian Voices.</u> 1975-1977//. Quarterly. Last issue 60 pages, last volume 188 pages, size 17 x 22. Line drawings, photographs, commercial advertising. Published by Ms. Atlas Press, San Jose, CA. Editor: R. Nichols. Subject focus: lesbians, gay rights, fiction, poetry, art.

| | | |
|---|---|---|
| Coll | v.2, n.1-v.3, n.1; Winter, 1975/1976-Winter, 1976/1977 | Women's Reading Area |

578 <u>Letters.</u> 1974-1977//. Quarterly. Last issue 68 pages, last volume 130 pages, size 14 x 22. Line drawings, photographs. Published by Letters, New York, NY. Editor: Carole Bevoso. Subject focus: poetry, fiction, letters, art.

| | | |
|---|---|---|
| RBR | v.1, n.1-v.2, n.3; Summer, 1974-Spring?, 1977 | Circulation |

<u>The Liberated Grapevine.</u> Hempstead, NY

see <u>Newsletter of the Women's Liberation Center of Nassau County,</u> Hempstead, NY

579 <u>Liberated Space For the Women of the Haight.</u> 1973-1974//? Irregular. Last issue 12 pages. Line drawings. Available on microfilm: Herstory. Published by Liberated Space For the Women of the Haight, San Francisco, CA. Subject focus: poetry, sexuality, fiction, satire, art.

| | | |
|---|---|---|
| Hist | n.3-4; Feb.-May, 1973 | Microforms Her. 2, R 7 |
| | v.5-7; July-Nov., 1973 | Her. 2 UP, R4 |

<u>The Liberator.</u> Albuquerque, NM

see <u>NOW Newsletter.</u> Albuquerque, NM

580 <u>The Liberator.</u> 1973//? Monthly. Last issue 2 pages. Line drawings. Available on microfilm: Herstory. Published by the Northern Palm Beach/Lake Worth Chapter, National Organization for Women, Lake Worth, FL. Title varies: as Lake Worth N.O.W., Mar.-May, 1973. Subject focus: lobbying, Equal Rights Amendment, feminism.

| | | |
|---|---|---|
| Hist | Mar.-May, 1973; | Microforms Her. 2, R 10 |
| | July-Oct., 1973; | Her. 2 UP, R4 |

581 <u>Libera.</u> 1972-1975//? Quarterly. Last issue 60 pages, size 21 x 28. Line drawings, photographs, commercial advertising. Available on microfilm: UnM. Published by Libera, University of California, Berkeley, CA. Subject focus: poetry, fiction, pro-abortion, lesbians, art.

| | | |
|---|---|---|
| Hist | n.1-4; Winter, 1972-Spring, 1973 | Microforms Her. 2, R 7 |
| RBR | n.1-6; Winter, 1972-Spring, 1975 | Circulation |

582 <u>The Liberator.</u> 1972-1973//. Bi-monthly. Last issue 12 pages. Line drawings, photographs, commercial advertising. Published by Fort Worth Chapter, National Organization for Women, Fort Worth, TX. Editor: Martha Lindsey. Subject focus: pregnancy, religion, poetry, rape, feminism, lobbying, Equal Rights Amendment.

| | | |
|---|---|---|
| Hist | n.1-7; Aug., 1972-May, 1973 | Microforms Her. 2, R 7 |
| | n.8; July/Aug., 1973 | Her. 2 UP, R4 |

583 <u>Life and Labor.</u> 1911-1921//? Monthly. OCLC 1755895, 4240904. LC 12-85. Last issue 34 pages, last volume 260 pages, size 16 x 25. Line drawings, photographs. Self-indexed (1911-1912, 1915-1916, 1920). Available on microfilm: GrP. Published by The National Women's Trade Union League of America, Chicago, IL. Editors: Alice Henry, Feb., 1911-Dec., 1912; Alice Henry and S.M. Franklin, Jan.-July, 1915; S.M Franklin, Aug., 1915-

Jan., 1916; Amy Walker Field, Feb.-Nov., 1916; Mrs. Raymond Robins, Dec., 1916-Dec., 1921. Subject focus: labor unions, workers, education. Other holding institutions: AJacT (AJB), CSt (Stanford University), [Indiana Union List of Serials, Indianapolis, IN], (ILS), InU (IUL), MCR-S (Schlesinger Library on the History of Women in America, Radcliffe College, Cambridge, MA), MeB (BBH), [University of Minnesota Union List, Minneapolis, MN] (MUL), NPV (VXW), NSbSU (YSM), NmLcU (IRU), OCU (CIN).

| | | |
|---|---|---|
| Hist | v.1, n.1-v.2, n.12; v.5, n.1-v.11, n.10; Jan., 1911- Dec., 1912, Jan., 1915- Oct., 1921 | HD/6050/C48 |

584  Life & Labor Bulletin. 1922-1950?//. Irregular. Last issue 3 pages, size 31 x 23. Available on microfilm: WHi (1933-1950). Published by The National Women's Trade Union League of America, Washington, DC. Place of publication varies: Chicago, IL, Aug., 1922-May, 1930. Frequency varies: monthly, Aug., 1922-Feb., 1932. Subject focus: labor unions, workers. Other holding institution: MCR-S (Schlesinger Library on the History of Women in America, Radcliffe College, Cambridge, MA).

| | | |
|---|---|---|
| Hist | v.1, n.1-v.10, n.2; Aug., 1922- Feb., 1932 | HD/6050/"L5 |
| | n.1-113 (n.s.); Apr., 1933- June, 1950 | Microforms |

Life and Light for Heathen Women.
Boston, MA

see Life and Light for Woman.
Boston, MA

585  Life and Light for Woman. 1869-1922//. Monthly. OCLC 2254592. LC 40-23876. Last issue 62 pages, last volume 482 pages, size 13 x 20 (varies). Line drawings, photographs. Self-indexed (1871-1874; 1879). Published by Women's Board of Missions, Boston, MA. Title varies: as Life and Light for Heathen Women, Mar., 1869-Dec., 1872. Frequency varies: quarterly, Mar., 1869-Dec., 1872. Editors: Abbie B. Child, Jan., 1876-Jan., 1893; Mrs. C.M Lamson, Jan.-Dec., 1906; Alice M. Kyle, Jan., 1913-Dec., 1922. Other holding institutions: [University of Minnesota Union List, Minneapolis, MN] (MUL), NUtMY (ZTM), TxDW (IWU). Subject focus: Christianity, poetry.

| | | |
|---|---|---|
| Hist | v.1-v.52, n.12; Mar., 1869- Dec., 1922 | BV/2612/L5 |

586  Lilith. 1972//? Unknown. Last issue 50 pages. Line drawings. Available on microfilm: Herstory. Published in Fresno, CA. Subject focus: poetry, art, literary criticism.

| | | |
|---|---|---|
| Hist | v.1, n.2; June, 1972 | Microforms Her. 2, R 7 |

587  Lilith. 1976. Quarterly. $8 for individuals, $12 for institutions. Susan Weidman Schneider, editor, Lilith, 250 W. 57th Street, Suite 1328, New York, NY. ISSN 0146-2334. OCLC 2694720. LC sc77-511. Last issue 50 pages, size 21 x 28. Line drawings, photographs, some in color, commercial advertising. Published by Lilith Publications, Inc., New York, NY. Subject focus: rights, sexism in Judaism, health, fiction, poetry, interviews, film reviews. Other holding institutions: CLU (CLU), CSt (Stanford University), CtY (YUS), MBTI (BTI), MH-AH (BHA), [University of Minnesota Union List, Minneapolis, MN](MUL), [New York State Union List, Albany, NY] (NYS), OCH (HUC), OU (OSU), PPiU (PIT).

| | | |
|---|---|---|
| Hist | v.1, n.3- Spring/ Summer, 1977- | Circulation |
| Wom St | v.1, n.4- Fall/ Winter, 1977/1978- | Reading Room |

588  Lilith. 1968-1969//. Irregular. OCLC 2263575, 5396624. Last issue 48 pages. Line drawings, photographs. Available on microfilm: Herstory. Published by Women's Majority Union (The Order of the Lead Balloon), Seattle, WA. Subject focus: lesbians, career development, poetry, gay rights.

| | | |
|---|---|---|
| Hist | Fall, 1968, Spring, 1969 | Microforms Her. 1, R 8 |

589  Lilith's Rib. 1973-1974//. Irregular. OCLC 4089520, 2353925. Last issue 6 pages. Line drawings. Available on microfilm: Herstory. Published by the North American Jewish Feminists Organization, Chicago, IL. Subject focus: Jews, feminism.

| | | |
|---|---|---|
| Hist | n.2-3; Nov., 1973- June, 1974 | Microforms Her. 3, R 2 |

590  The Lily. 1849-1894?//. Semi-monthly. OCLC 1587802, 2805747, 2448303. LC 27-14809. Last issue 8 pages, last volume 158 pages. Line drawings, commercial advertising. Available on microfilm: GrP (1849-1850). Published in Richmond, IN. Place of publication varies: Seneca Falls, NY, Jan.1, 1849-July 15, 1853; Mount Vernon, OH, Jan. 2 -Dec. 15, 1854. Frequency varies: monthly, Jan., 1849-1852.

Editor: Amelia Bloomer. Subject focus: temperance, fiction, poetry, law. Other holding institutions: CSt (Stanford University), ICL (IAL), MeB (BBH), [University of Minnesota Union List, Minneapolis, MN] (MUL), MnStpeG (MNG), NCaS (XLM), NGenoU (YGM), NOsU (YOM), PCalS (CSC), [Pittsburgh Regional Library Center-Union List, Pittsburgh, PA] (QPR), PNo (MNL), PPiU (PIT), TMurS (TXM), ViNO (VOD), WMUW (GZN).

| | | |
|---|---|---|
| Hist | v.1, n.1-v.5, n.6,14, v.6, n.1-v.8, n.19, 22-24; Jan. 1, 1849-Mar. 15, 1853, Jan. 2, 1854-Oct. 1, Nov. 15-Dec. 15, 1856 | Microforms |

591 Lincoln NOWsletter. 1972-1974//? Monthly. Last issue 4 pages. Available on microfilm: Herstory. Published by Lincoln Chapter, National Organization for Women, Lincoln, NB. Subject focus: child care, health, feminism, Equal Rights Amendment, lobbying.

| | | |
|---|---|---|
| Hist | Aug., 1972-June, 1973 | Microforms Her. 2, R 10 |
| | July 1, 1973-June 14, 1974 | Her. 2 UP, R 7 |

592 The Link. 1970-1973//? Monthly. Last issue 10 pages. Line drawings, photographs, commercial advertising. Available on microfilm: Herstory. Published by Equal Rights Alliance/The Sisterhood, Chicago, IL. Title varies: as Alliance News, Mar.-June, 1970; Alliance Link, Oct., 1970-Apr., 1972. Subject focus: feminism, lobbying, Equal Rights Amendment, sexism, pro-abortion.

| | | |
|---|---|---|
| Hist | Mar., 1970-Mar., 1973 | Microforms Her. 2 UP, R 4 |

The Lobbyist. Los Angeles, CA

    see Action for Children. Los Angeles, CA

593 The Longest Revolution. 1977. Bi-monthly. $6 for individuals, $12 for institutions. Carol Rowell and Lisa Cobbs, editors, The Longest Revolution, 908 'F' Street, San Diego, CA. ISSN 0146-9967. OCLC 3060736. LC sc77-295. Last issue 16 pages, last volume 100 pages, size 44 x 29. Line drawings, photographs, commercial advertising. Published by The Collective of the Center for Women's Studies and Services, San Diego, CA. Previous editors: Lisa Cobbs, Feb., 1977-Apr./May, 1979; Carol Rowell, June-Aug., 1979. Subject focus: rights, pro-abortion, film reviews, arts, lobbying.

| | | |
|---|---|---|
| Hist | v.1, n.3-Feb., 1977- | Circulation |

594 Long-Time-Coming. 1973-1974//? Irregular. ISSN 0382-5868. OCLC 2627647. LC cn76-32020. Last issue 34 pages. Line drawings. Available on microfilm: Herstory. Published by Long-Time-Coming, Montreal, Quebec, Canada. Editor: Jackie Manthorne. Subject focus: lesbians, poetry, fiction.

| | | |
|---|---|---|
| Hist | v.1, n.1-5,9; July, 1973-Jan.,May/June, 1974 | Microforms Her. 3, R 2 |

595 The Los Angeles Garment Worker. 1917-1918//? Monthly. Last issue 12 pages, size 17 x 26. Line drawings. Published by Garment Worker's Local No. 125, Los Angeles, CA. Subject focus: Chicanas, labor unions, garment industry. In Spanish (50%).

| | | |
|---|---|---|
| Hist | May, 1918 | Pam 74-3399 |

596 Love/Woman. 1970-1971//? Quarterly. OCLC 3363251. Last issue 28 pages, last volume 108 pages, size 22 x 28. Published by Love/Woman, Milwaukee, WI. Editor: Michael J. Phillips. Subject focus: love, poetry. Other holding institution: [University of Minnesota Union List, Minneapolis, MN] (MUL).

| | | |
|---|---|---|
| RBR | v.1, n.1-4; Fall, 1970-Summer, 1971 | Circulation |

597 Luna: A Literary Publication. 1975. Irregular. $5.50 for individuals and institutions. Barbara Giles, editor, Luna: A Literary Publication, 101 Edgevale Road, Kew, Victoria, 3101 Australia. OCLC 3363342. Last issue 40 pages, last volume 112 pages, size 15 x 21. Line drawings, photographs. Published by Luna Collective, Victoria, Australia. Subject focus: poetry, fiction, art.

| | | |
|---|---|---|
| RBR | v.1, n.1-1975- | Circulation |

598 Lutheran Woman's Work. 1908-1960//. Monthly. OCLC 1588446. Last issue 48 pages, size 18 x 24. Line drawings, photographs. Published by the Women's Missionary Society of the United Lutheran Church in America, Philadelphia, PA. Editors: Mrs. W.F. Morehead, Miss Jane Gilbert, Miss Nona M. Diehl. Subject focus: Lutheran Church, Christianity. Other holding institutions: [Indiana Union List of Serials, Indianapolis, IN] (ILS), KLindB (KFB), [University of Minnesota Union List, Minneapolis, MN] (MUL).

| | | | |
|---|---|---|---|
| Hist | v.31, n.9; Sep., 1938 | DKLV/LU (Cutter) | |

**Lysistrada.** Fairchild, CA

see **N.O.W. Press.** Fairchild, CA

599 **Lysistrata.** 1978? Monthly. Lysistrata, 325 W. Gorham Street, Madison, WI 53703. Last issue 2 pages, size 22 x 28. Line drawings. Subject focus: restaurants, business, cooperatives.

| | | |
|---|---|---|
| Hist | Aug./Sep., 1978- | Circulation |

**Lysistrata.** Slippery Rock, PA

see **The Hand.** Slippery Rock, PA

600 **MCN the American Journal of Maternal Child Nursing.** 1976. Bi-monthly. $15 for individuals and institutions. Barbara E. Bishop, editor, MCN the American Journal of Maternal Child Nursing, 555 West 57th Street, New York, NY 10019. (212) 582-8820. ISSN 0361-929X. OCLC 2134192. LC 76-644834. Last issue 72 pages, last volume 400 pages, size 22 x 27. Line drawings, photographs, some in color, commercial advertising. Self-indexed by volume. Subject focus: child care, health, pregnancy. Other holding institutions: AAP (AAA), AJacT (AJB), ArU (AFU), AzFU (AZN), AzTeS (AZS), AzYAW (AZY), CChiS (CCH), CoDU (DVP), COU-DA (COA), [St. Joseph College, Wittanford, CT] (STJ), DCU (DCU), DLC (DLC), DLC (NSD), DNLM (NLM), DeU (DLM), FBoU (FGM), FJUNF (FNP), GASU (GSU), GU (GUA), IDeKN (JNA), IJMac (ICI), InHamP (IPC), InLP (IPL), InU (IUL), KHayF (KFH), KPT (KFP), KSteC (KKQ), KyRE (KEU), KyU (KUK), LHS (LSH), MBNU (NED), MBU (BOS), MBSi (SCL), MdBJ-W (JHW), MiDW (EYW), MiEM (EEM), MiLC (EEL), MiYEM (EYE), MnManS (MNM), [University of Minnesota Union List, Minneapolis, MN] (MUL), MoSMa (MVC), NDFM (VZE), NNR (ZXC), NNU (ZYU), NOneoU (VZH), NSbSU-H (CZB), NSyU (SYB), [Central New York Library Resources Council, Syracuse, NY] (SRR), NUtSU (YTM), NbKS (KRS), NbU (LDL), NcGU (NGU), NjlincB (BCC), OAkU (AKR), OAU (OUN), OBgU (BGU), OC1W-H (CHS), OCoR (RHC), OKentU (KSU), OMtvN (MZN), OSteC (STU), OTMC (MCL), OYU (YNG), OkAdE (ECO), OkTOR (OKO), OrU-M (OHS), PCW (UWC), PPiU (PIT), [Pittsburgh Regional Library Center-Union List, Pittsburgh, PA] (QPR), PPJ (TVJ), PSt (UPM), TCU (TUC), TNTU (TUN), [AMIGOS Union List of Serials, Dallas, TX] (IUC), TxDW (IWU), TxDaB (IDA), TxNacS (TXK), TxU (IXA), ViNO (VOD), ViRCU (VRC), WKenU (GZP).

| | | |
|---|---|---|
| MATC | v.1, n.2- Mar./Apr., 1976- | Cora Hardy Library |

601 **M.L.A. Commission Newsletter.** 1971//? Last issue 6 pages. Line drawings. Published by the Modern Language Association of America, Commission on the Status of Women in the Profession, New York, NY/Middletown, CT. Available on microfilm: Herstory. Subject focus: lobbying, language. Other holding institution: PPiU (PIT).

| | | |
|---|---|---|
| Hist | Apr., June, 1971 | Microforms Her. 1, R16 |

602 **Madame.** 1903-1906//? Monthly. Last issue 32 pages, last volume 192 pages. Line drawings, commercial advertising. Available on microfilm: ResP. Published by The National Council of Women, Indianapolis, IN. Place of publication varies: Springfield, OH, Oct. 10, 1903-Mar., 1904. Subject focus: poetry, education, fiction, fashion, music. Other holding institution: NN (NYP).

| | | |
|---|---|---|
| Mem | v.1, n.1-v.5, n.6; Oct. 10, 1903- Mar., 1906 | Microforms |

603 **Mademoiselle.** 1935. Monthly. $10 for individuals and institutions. Edith Raymond Locke, editor, Mademoiselle, 350 Madison Avenue, New York, NY 10017. Business address: P.O. Box 5204, Boulder, CO 80323. ISSN 0024-9394. OCLC 1715227, 6263240. LC 41-20669. Last issue 188 pages, size 21 x 28. Line drawings, photographs, some in color, commercial advertising. Indexed in: Readers Guide, (1953-). Available on microfilm: UnM; McP (1960-). Published by Condé Nast Publications, Inc., New York, NY. Previous editor: Betsy Tabbot Blackwell, May, 1962-June, 1971. Subject focus: fashion, beauty care, health, food, interior decorating, fiction, film reviews. Other holding institutions: AU (ALM), ArAO (AKO), ArCCA (AKC), ArU (AFU), AzFU (AZN), AzTeS (AZS), AzU (AZU), CSt (Stanford University), CChiS (CCH), CLavC (CLV), CLU (CLU), [Pepperdine University, Malibu, CA] (CPE), CoDU (DVP), DLC (DLC), FMFIU (FXG), GA (GAP), GASU (GSU), IPB (IBA), [Indiana Union List of Serials, Indianapolis, IN] (ILS), InIU (IUP), KPT (KFP), KSteC (KKQ), KWiU (KSW), KyU (KUK), MA (AMH), MBSi (SCL), MWelC (WEL), MWP (WPG), MiAdC (EEA), MiDU (EYU), MiDW (EYW), MiEM (EEM), MiGrC (EXC), MiLC (EEL), MiMtpT (EZC), [University of Minnesota Union List, Minneapolis, MN] (MUL), MnStjos (MNF), MnStpeG (MNG), N (NYG), NAIULS (SUL), [New York State Union List, Albany, NY] (NYS), NBP (VZQ), [Western New York Library Resources Council, Buffalo, NY] (VZX), NCorniCC (ZDG), NCortU (YCM), NFQC (XQM), NIC (COO), NII (XIM), NNR (ZXC), NONEOH ( ZH), NOneoU (ZBM), NR (YQR), NSufR (VVR), NSyU (SYB), NbKS (KRS), NbU (LDL), NcRS (NRC), NdU (UND), NjLincB (BCC), NmLcU (IRU), NmLvH (NMH), O (OHI), OAkU (AKR), OBgU (BGU), OC1 (CLE), OC1U (CSU), OKentU (KSU), OLanU (OUL),

112

OkT (TUL), PClvU (URS), PCoR (ROB), PIm (IMM), [Pittsburgh Regional Library Center-Union List, Pittsburgh, PA] (QPR), PNwC (WFN), PPD (DXU), ScRhW (SWW), TMurS (TXM), TxBelM (MHB), TxDN (INT), TxDW (IWU), TxE (TXP), [AMIGOS Union List of Serials, Dallas, TX] (IUC), TxHU-D (THD), TxLT (ILU), TxNacS (TXK), TxShA (IAU), ViRCU (VRC), VtMiM (MDY), WFon (WIF), WGrU (GZW), [Arrowhead Library System, Janesville Public Library, Janesville WI] (WIJ), WMenU (GZS), WMUW (GZN), WM (GZD).

| | | |
|---|---|---|
| MPL | v.55, n.1- May, 1962- | Literature and Social Sciences Section |
| DFHS | Sep., 1974- | Circulation |
| CFL | Current Issues Only | Circulation |
| OPL | Current Issues Only | Circulation |
| EHS | Current Issues Only | Circulation |
| MATC | Current Issues Only | Cora Hardy Library |
| DHS | Current Issues Only | Circulation |
| BAHS | Current Issues Only | Circulation |
| SAPH | Current Issues Only | Circulation |
| BML | Current Issues Only | Circulation |
| MHHS | Jan., 1972- | Circulation |
| MIPL | Jan., 1975- | Circulation |
| MMHS | Jan., 1970- | Circulation |
| MGHS | May, 1959- | Circulation |
| DFPL | Jan., 1971- | Circulation |
| VHS | Jan., 1970- | Circulation |
| TML | Jan., 1966- | Circulation |
| VPL | Jan., 1971- | Circulation |
| DFHS | Sep., 1974- | Circulation |
| MHPL | Jan., 1971- | Circulation |
| WHS | Feb., 1970- | Circulation |
| PPL | Jan., 1971- | Circulation |
| RPL | Jan., 1971- | Circulation |
| MFHS | Jan., 1972- | Circulation |
| SPHS | Feb., 1972- | Circulation |
| UWBA | Jan., 1969- | Circulation |

604 Madison Women's Union Newsletter. 1975-1977//. Irregular. OCLC 4687235. Last issue 2 pages. Line drawings. Available on microfilm: WHi. Published by the Madison Women's Union, Madison, WI. Subject focus: socialist feminism, labor unions, lobbying.

| | | |
|---|---|---|
| Hist | v.1, n.1, v.2, n.3,5-v.3, n.2; Nov. 29, 1975, May, July, 1976- Mar., 1977 | Microforms |
| Wom St | v.2, n.3-v.3, n.1; July, 1976- Feb., 1977 | Reading Room |

605 Madison YWCA Newsletter. 1980. Irregular. Gratis to individuals and institutions. Last issue 4 pages, size 22 x 28. Line drawings. Published by Madison YWCA, 101 East Mifflin, Madison, WI. Subject focus: sports, clubs.

| | | |
|---|---|---|
| Hist | June, 1980- | Circulation |

606 Magazine of the Daughters of the Revolution. 1893-1896?//. Quarterly. Last issue 42 pages, last volume 202 pages, size 24 x 16. Line drawings, commercial advertising. Self-indexed (1891-1896). Published by the Daughters of the Revolution, New York, NY. Subject focus: history, genealogy, clubs.

| | | |
|---|---|---|
| Hist | v.1, n.1-v.4, n.4; Jan., 1893-Nov., 1896 | E/202.6/A18 |

607 The Mahogany Tree. 1892//. Last issue 12 pages, last volume 174 pages. Line drawings, commercial advertising. Available on microfilm: ResP. Published by The Mahogany Tree, Boston, MA. Editor: Mildred Aldrich. Subject focus: fiction, poetry. Other holding institutions: MB (Boston Public Library), MCR-S (Schlesinger Library on the History of Women in America, Radcliffe College, Cambridge, MA), MH (HLS).

| | | |
|---|---|---|
| Mem | v.1, n.1-v.2, n.14; Jan. 2- Dec. 10, 1892 | Microforms |

The Maiden Voyage. Cambridge, MA

see Focus. Cambridge, MA

608  **Maine Freewoman's Herald.** 1973-1978//. Irregular. Last issue 16 pages, size 42 x 29. Line drawings, photographs, commercial advertising. Available on microfilm: WHi (1975-1978), Herstory (1974). Published by Maine Freewoman's Herald, Portland, ME. Title varies: as Maine Women's Newsletter, Apr./May, 1974. Subject focus: rights, lesbians, workers, poetry, lobbying, Equal Rights Amendment, racism, art.

    Hist    v.3, n.1-v.4, n.10; Summer, 1975- Summer, 1978    Microforms

            v.2, n.1-2 Apr./May- June/July, 1974    Microforms Her. 3 R 2

**Maine Women's Newsletter.** Brunswick, ME

    see **Maine Freewomen's Herald.** Brunswick, ME

609  **Mainely N.O.W.** 1973//? Monthly. Last issue 8 pages. Line drawings, photographs. Available on microfilm: Herstory. Published by Maine Chapter, National Organization for Women, Portland, ME. Editors: Nancy Cushman Dibner and Anne Hazelwood-Brady. Subject focus: feminism, lobbying, Equal Rights Amendment.

    Hist    v.1, n.1-4; Aug.-Nov., 1973    Microforms Her. 3, R 3

610  **Majority Report.** 1971. Bi-weekly. $7.50 for individuals, $20.00 for institutions. Majority Report, 74 Grove Street, New York, NY 10014. (212) 691-4950. ISSN 0145-5745. OCLC 1953572. LC sc77-728. Last issue 8 pages, last volume 212 pages, size 29 x 43. Line drawings, photographs, commercial advertising. Available on microfilm: WHi (1973-1977). Published by Women's Strike Coalition, New York, NY. Frequency varies: monthly, July, 1973-Apr., 1974. Subject focus: rights, law, health, child rearing, sports, labor unions, feminism, theatre reviews. Other holding institutions: CLU (CLU), [New York Central Library Resources Council, Syracuse, NY] (SRR), OU (OSU), PPiU (PIT).

    Hist    v.3, n.3- July, 1973-    Microforms

    Coll    Current Issues Only    Women's Reading Area

611  **Majority Report.** 1971-1974//? Monthly. OCLC 5316331. Last issue 20 pages, last volume 250 pages. Line drawings, photographs, commercial advertising. Published by FOCAS (Feminist Organization for Communication, Action and Service), New York, NY. Available on microfilm: Herstory. Subject focus: satire, prostitution, child care, employment, feminism, Equal Rights Amendment, lobbying, health. Other holding institution: MCR-S (Schlesinger Library on the History of Women in America, Radcliffe College, Cambridge, MA).

    Hist    v.1, n.1-4; May 10- Aug. 26, 1971    Microforms Her. 1, R16

            v.1, n.5-v.3, n.2; Oct., 1971- June, 1973    Her. 1 UP, R6

            v.3, n.3-v.4, n.5; July, 1973- Apr., 1974    Her. CUP, R 2-3

612  **Management Memo.** 1980. Bi-monthly. $12 for individuals and institutions. Management Memo, 317 W. Johnson Street, Madison, WI 53703. (608) 257-7888. Last issue 2 pages, size 22 x 36. Line drawings, commercial advertising. Available on microfilm: WHi. Published by Women in Self-Employment, Madison, WI. Subject focus: business, self-employment, financial management, taxation.

    Hist    v.1, n.3,5- May, Sep., 1980-    Circulation

613  **Man Vrouw Maatschappij (MUM).** 1971-1974//? Irregular. Last issue 24 pages. Line drawings, photographs. Available on microfilm: Herstory. Published in Amsterdam, Holland. Subject focus: feminism. In Dutch (100%).

    Hist    Oct., 1971- June, 1973;    Microforms Her. 2, R 16

            Sep., 1973- May, 1974;    Her. 2UP, R4

614  **The Mantle.** 1945. Tri-annual. Juli Hoier, editor, The Mantle, Eau Claire, WI. Last issue 8 pages, last volume 36 pages, size 14 x 22. Line drawings, photographs. Published by Catholic Junior League of Wisconsin, Eau Claire, WI. Title varies: as Catholic Junior Leagues of Wisconsin, Sep.-Dec., 1945. Place of publication varies: Fond du Lac, WI, Sep., 1945-May, 1946; Beloit, WI, Sep., 1946-June, 1948; Janesville, WI, Sep., 1948-June, 1950; Kenosha, WI, Sep., 1950-June, 1952; Racine, WI, Sep., 1952-May, 1954; Manitowoc, WI, Sep./Oct., 1954-May, 1956; Kenosha, WI, Oct., 1956-June, 1958; Racine, WI, Oct., 1958-June, 1960; Manitowoc, WI, Oct., 1960-June, 1962; Kenosha, WI, Oct., 1962-June, 1964; Eau Claire, WI, Oct., 1964-June, 1966; Racine, WI, Oct., 1966-June, 1968; Janesville, WI, Oct., 1968-June, 1970; Tri-City, WI, Nov., 1970-June, 1972; Kenosha, WI, Oct.,

1972-June, 1974; Racine, WI, Oct., 1974-June, 1976; Manitowoc, WI, Dec., 1976-May, 1978. Previous editors: Rosemary McNulty, Sep., 1945-May, 1946; Frances Bartella, Dec., 1947-June, 1948; Kay Joyce, Apr., 1949-June, 1950; V. Rachel Milhaupt, Sep., 1950-May, 1951; Alice A. Hughes, Sep., 1951-June, 1952; Dorothy Fannin, Sep., 1952-May, 1954; Mary Lou Schuette, Sep./Oct., 1954-Mar., 1955; Corrine Beizel, Oct., 1955-May, 1956; Ruth Lacki, Oct., 1956-June, 1958; Marie Krescanko, Oct., 1958-June, 1960; Nancy Rutherford, Oct., 1960-June, 1962; Marlene Pierce, Oct., 1962-June, 1963; Barbara Fonk, Oct., 1963-June, 1964; Mary Armstrong, Oct., 1964-June, 1966; June Lemke, Oct., 1966-June, 1968; Janet Edwards, Oct., 1968-June, 1970; Rita Wauters, Nov., 1970-June, 1972; Pam Gavigan, Oct., 1974-June, 1976; Helen Cechantek, Dec., 1976-May, 1978. Subject focus: Catholic Church, clubs.

| | | |
|---|---|---|
| Hist | v.1, n.1-<br>Sep., 1945- | F9026/C36/<br>W8113/M<br>(Cutter) |

615 Mariémou. 1968-1976//? Irregular. ISSN 0047-5920. OCLC 5183134. LC 72-626369. Last issue 18 pages, size 21 x 27. Line drawings, photographs. Published by Mouvement National des Femmes, Nouakchott, Mauritania. Editor: Aissata Kane. Subject focus: rights. In French (50%), in Arabic (50%).

| | | |
|---|---|---|
| Mem | n.2,5-10,12-14;<br>Apr./May/<br>June, 1968;<br>July/Aug., 1971-<br>?, 1974,<br>Mar., 1975-<br>Mar., 1976 | AP/M333 |

Marin Women's News Journal. San Rafael, CA

    see The Women's News Journal. San Rafael, CA

Marin NOW. San Rafael, CA

    see NOW Newsletter. San Rafael, CA

616 Martha Matters. 1977-1978//. Irregular. Last issue 6 pages, size 22 x 28. Published by Martha Movement, Arlington, VA. Subject focus: volunteerism, housewives.

| | | |
|---|---|---|
| Wom Ed<br>Res | [v.2, n.3-v.3,<br>n.1];<br>[Mar., 1977-<br>Winter, 1978] | Circulation |

617 Maryland Suffrage News. 1912-1916//? Last issue 8 pages, size 27 x 35. Photographs, commercial advertising. Published by Just Government League of Maryland, Baltimore, MD. Subject focus: pro-suffrage. Other holding institution: MCR-S (Schlesinger Library on the History of Women in America, Radcliffe College, Cambridge, MA).

| | | |
|---|---|---|
| Hist | v.5, n.25;<br>Sep. 16, 1916 | KWZ/+MA<br>(Cutter) |

Mary Wollstonecraft Journal. New Brunswick, NJ

    see Women & Literature. New Brunswick, NJ

Mary Wollstonecraft Newsletter. New Brunswick, NJ

    see Women & Literature. New Brunswick, NJ

618 The Masonic Miscellany and Ladies' Literary Magazine. 1821-1823//. Monthly. Last issue 40 pages, last volume 480 pages. Self-indexed (1821). Available on microfilm: UnM. Published in Lexington, KY. Subject focus: freemasonry, poetry, fiction.

| | | |
|---|---|---|
| Hist | v.1, n.1-v.2,<br>n.12;<br>July, 1821-<br>June, 1823 | Microforms |

619 Matrices. 1977. Bobby Lacy, editor, Matrices, Department of English, Andrews Hall 202, University of Nebraska, Lincoln, NB 68588. Last issue 10 pages, size 22 x 35. Line drawings. Subject focus: lesbians.

| | | |
|---|---|---|
| Wom St | v.1, n.1/2-<br>Fall/Winter,<br>1977/1978 | Reading Room |

620 Matrix. 1970-1973//? Unknown. OCLC 2263924. Last issue 48 pages. Line drawings, photographs. Available on microfilm: Herstory. Published by Charmian, Los Angeles, CA. Subject focus: poetry, art, literature. Other holding institutions: [University of Minnesota Union List, Minneapolis, MN] (MUL), PPiU (PIT), WMUW (GZN).

| | | |
|---|---|---|
| Hist | v.1, v.2;<br>Spring, 1970, 1971 | Microforms<br>Her. 1, R 8 |
| | v.3;<br>1973 | Her. 1 UP, R6 |

*Women's Periodicals and Newspapers*

621 <u>Matrix</u>. 1916. Quarterly. $6 for individuals and institutions. Karen Kothman Allen, editor, Matrix, P.O. Box 9561, Austin, TX 78766. (512) 345-8922. ISSN 0025-598X. OCLC 3422035. LC sn78-4999. Last issue 32 pages, last volume 128 pages. Line drawings, photographs. Published by Women in Communications, Inc., Austin, TX. Previous editors: Lucille Taylor-Pierlot, Fall, 1972-Spring, 1975; Ernestine Wheelock, Summer, 1975-Fall, 1978. Subject focus: media, journalism, professionals, career development. Other holding institutions: DLC (DLC), FJUNF (FNP), IPB (IBA), IU (UIU), MBE (ECL), MiMtpT (EZC), NOneoU (ZBM), NSyU (SYB), OAkU (AKR), OkT (TUL), TxArU (IUA), [AMIGOS Union List of Serials, Dallas, TX] (IUC), TxDW (IWU), WyU (WYU).

| | | |
|---|---|---|
| JR | v.58, n.1-<br>Fall, 1972- | Reading Room |

622 <u>McCalls</u>. 1876. Monthly. $9.95 for individuals and institutions. Robert Stein, editor, McCalls, 230 Park Avenue, New York, NY 10017. Business address: Box 10293, Des Moines, IA 50336. ISSN 0024-8908, 0197-1255. OCLC 4840517, 1586376, 4410903, 5947724, 5462346, 4171150. LC sc79-5631, sn78-5890. Last issue 196 pages, last volume 2352 pages, size 21 x 27. Line drawings, photographs, some in color, commercial advertising. Indexed: Readers Guide (1952-). Available on microfilm: McP (1960-), UnM (1894-). Previous editors: Otis Lee Wiese, Oct., 1957-Feb., 1959; Herbert R. Mayes, Mar., 1959-Feb., 1962; John Mack Carter, Mar., 1962-Feb., 1965. Subject focus: fashion, beauty care, interior decorating, entertaining, food, fiction. Other holding institutions: AU (ALM), ArAR (AKO), AzFU (AZN), AzLeS (AZS), AzU (AZU), CLobS (CLO), CLU (CLU), CU-UC (UCU), [Pepperdine University, Malibu, CA] (CPE), CSt (Stanford University), CoDU (DVP), WeharU (HRM), FJUNF (FNP), GStG (GPM), IaHi (IOQ), IDeKN (JNA), IMgO (IAP), IPB (IBA), [Indiana Union List of Serials, Indianapolis, IN] (ILS), KHayF (KFH), KlindB (KFB), KSteC (KKQ), KyU (KUK), DNAL (AGL), MCR-S (Schlesinger Library on the History of Women in America, Radcliffe College, Cambridge, MA), MiLC (EEL), MiMtpT (EZC), [University of Minnesota Union List, Minneapolis, MN] (MUL), MnU (MNU), MoWgT/MoWgW (ELW), N (NYG), [New York State Union List, Albany, NY] (NYS), [Western New York Library Resources Council, Buffalo, NY] (VZX), NCortU (YCM), NGenoU (YGM), NIC (COC), NNR (ZXC), NR (YQR), NOneoU (ZBM), NSyU (SYB), NbKS (KRS), NbU (LDL), NcD (NDD), NcDurC (NCX), NcRS (NRC), NcWfSB (NVS), NdU (UND), NhMSA (SAC), NjLincB (BCC), NmLcU (IRU), NmLvH (NMH), O (OHI), OAk (APL), OAkU (AKR), OAU (OUN), [Raymond Walters General and Techinal College Library, Blue Ash, OH] (ORW), OCedC (CDC), OCl (CLE), OClU (CSU), OKentU (KSU), OMC (MRC), OTU (TOL), OY (YMM), OkTOR (OKO), OkT (TUL), PAnL (LVC), PCLS (REC), PCoR (ROB), PIm (IMM), PPiAC (AIC), PPi (CPL), [Pittsburgh Regional Library Center-Union List, Pittsburgh, PA] (QPR), ScRhW (SWW), TCollsM (TMS), TMurS (TXM), TxAbH (TXS), TxBelM (MHB), TxCM (TXA), [AMIGOS Union List of Serials, Dallas, TX] (IUC), TxDN (INT), TxDW (IWU), TxDaB (IDA), TxLT (ILU), ViBlbv (VPI), [Emory and Henry College, Emory, VA] (VEH), ViRU (VRU), [Arrowhead Library System, Janesville Public Library, Janesville, WI] (WIJ), WM (GZD), WMUW (GZN).

| | | |
|---|---|---|
| Agric | v.85, n.1-<br>Oct., 1957- | Periodicals Section |
| MPL | v.87, n.1-<br>Jan., 1959- | Literature and Social Sciences Section |
| MATC | Current Issues Only | Cora Hardy Library |
| MHHS | Jan., 1972- | Circulation |
| MIPL | Jan., 1973- | Circulation |
| EHS | Jan., 1970- | Circulation |
| MOPL | Jan., 1975- | Circulation |
| DEPL | Jan., 1971- | Circulation |
| TML | Jan., 1963- | Circulation |
| MGHS | Oct., 1960- | Circulation |
| BHS | Sep., 1974- | Circulation |
| SAPH | Current Issues Only | Circulation |
| MCL | Jan., 1971- | Circulation |
| SPPL | Jan., 1970- | Circulation |
| RPL | Jan., 1970- | Circulation |
| CFL | Jan., 1975- | Circulation |
| MFHS | Jan., 1974- | Circulation |
| VPL | Jan., 1971- | Circulation |
| CPPL | Current Issues Only | Circulation |
| MHPL | Sep., 1971- | Circulation |
| DHS | Current Issues Only | Circulation |
| SCPL | Jan., 1970- | Circulation |
| WHS | June, 1968- | Circulation |
| BFL | Jan., 1975- | Circulation |

| | | | | | | |
|---|---|---|---|---|---|---|
| VHS | Jan., 1970- | Circulation | | Hist | v.1, n.1-4;<br>June 15, 1972-<br>May 1, 1973; | Microforms<br>Her. 2, R 8 |
| MMHS | Jan., 1970- | Circulation | | | v.1, n.5-v.2, n.6;<br>July, 1973-<br>June, 1974; | Her. 2 UP, R4 |
| DFHS | Sep., 1974- | Circulation | | | | |
| OPL | Current Issues Only | Circulation | | | v.3, n.7-<br>July 1, 1975- | Circulation |
| OM | Current Issues Only | Circulation | | JR | v.2, n.6-<br>June 1, 1974- | Circulation |
| MAPL | Current Issues Only | Circulation | | Coll | Current Issues Only | Women's Reading Room |
| BML | Current Issues Only | Circulation | | Wom St | v.5, n.4-<br>Apr., 1977- | Reading Room |
| SPHS | Jan., 1971- | Circulation | | U.W. Ext | v.1, n.6-<br>June, 1972- | Circulation |
| | | | | Wom Ed Res | v.1, n.6-<br>June, 1972- | Circulation |

623 <u>McCall's Needlework and Crafts</u>. 1968. Bi-monthly. $9.95 for individuals and institutions. Rosemary McMurtry, editor, McCall's Needlework and Crafts, 825 7th Avenue, New York, NY 10019. Last issue 184 pages, last volume 1120 pages. Line drawings, photographs, some in color, commercial advertising. Published by A.B.C. Needlework and Crafts, New York, NY. Previous editor: Nania Comstock, Spring, 1970-Fall/Winter, 1972/1973. Subject focus: arts, crafts, needlework, sewing.

| | | |
|---|---|---|
| SPHS | Spring, 1970- | Circulation |

624 <u>Media Report to Women</u>. 1972. Monthly. $15 for individuals, $20 for institutions. Dr. Donna Allen, editor, Media Report to Women, 3306 Ross Place N.W., Washington, DC 20008. (212) 363-0712. ISSN 0145-9651, 0197-3401, 0197-1204. OCLC 2360896, 3758746, 5952870. LC sc77-865, 80-640490. Last issue 12 pages, last volume 168 pages, size 22 x 28. Indexed: Media Report to Women Index/Directory (1972-1976; 1979), REF COLL PN /4784/W7/M4. Available on microfilm: Herstory (1972-1974). Published by Women's Institute for Freedom of the Press, Washington, DC. Frequency varies: quarterly, June 15, 1972-Nov., 1973; monthly, Jan.-June, 1974. Subject focus: rights, media, professionals. Other holding institutions: AzTeS (AZS), CSt (Stanford University), CU-S (CUS), COFS (COF), CoGrU (COV), DLC (DLC), FTaSU (FDA), IC (CGP), IDeKN (JNA), IPB (IBA), IRivgT (IAW), LNX (LNX), MAH (HAM), MBE (ECL), MNS (SNN), MnStcIs (MST), NBronSL (VVS), NGcA (VJA), Nc (NCS), NcGrE (ERE), NcU (NOC), NhD (DRB), OTU (TOL), OkS (OKS), PPT (TEU), PU (PAU), TxLT (ILU), WaU (WAU), WLacU (GZU), WMA (GZA), WMUW (GZN), [University of Wisconsin-Stevens Point, Stevens Point, WI] (WIS), WyU (WYU).

625 <u>Media Women's Monthly</u>. 1969//? Monthly. OCLC 2269641. Last issue 6 pages. Line drawings. Available on microfilm: Herstory. Published by Media Women, New York, NY. Subject focus: pro-abortion, day care, media, radicalism, lobbying, Equal Rights Amendment.

| | | |
|---|---|---|
| Hist | v.1, n.1-2;<br>Oct. 28-<br>Nov. 28, 1969 | Microforms<br>Her. 1, R 16 |

<u>Medical Woman's Journal</u>.   Cincinnati, OH; Washington, DC

   see <u>Pan-American Medical Woman's Journal</u>. Washington, DC

626 <u>Mejane</u>. 1971-1974//? Irregular. OCLC 2264006. Last issue 20 pages. Line drawings, photographs, commercial advertising. Available on microfilm: Herstory. Published in Sydney, Australia. Subject focus: child care, poetry, employment, rights, sexism, feminism, pro-abortion.

| | | |
|---|---|---|
| Hist | n.1-4;<br>Mar.-Sep., 1971 | Microforms<br>Her. 1, R 2 |
| | n.5-10;<br>Nov., 1971-<br>Mar., 1973 | Her. 1 UP, R6 |
| | v.2, n.1-2;<br>July, 1973-<br>Apr., 1974 | Her. CUP, R3 |

627 <u>Memo</u>. 1962-1969//? Irregular. Last issue 28 pages, last volume 196 pages. Line drawings, photographs. Available on microfilm: Herstory (1964-1969), WHi. Published by the National Information Clearinghouse, Women Strike for Peace, Washington, DC. Title varies: as National Information Memo, Dec. 29, 1962-July 2, 1964. Editor: Barbara Bick. Subject focus: peace movement, lobbying.

| Hist | v.1, n.19-v.6, n.11? Dec. 29, 1962- Fall, 1969 | Microforms |
| --- | --- | --- |
|  | v.3, n.1-v.6, n.11? July 20, 1964- Fall, 1969 | Microforms Her. 1, R 9 |

628 <u>Memo</u>. 1970-1973//. Quarterly. Last issue 36 pages, last volume 134 pages, size 17 x 27. Line drawings, photographs, commercial advertising. Available on microfilm: Herstory (1970-1971). Published by Women Strike for Peace, New York, NY. Editor: Amy Swemdlow. Subject focus: peace movement, lobbying.

| Hist | v.1, n.2-v.3, n.2; Summer, 1970- Spring, 1973 | JX/1901/M4 |
| --- | --- | --- |
|  | v.1, n.1-v.2, n.1; Apr., 1970 Fall, 1971 | Microforms Her. 1, R 9 |

629 <u>The Messenger</u>. 1932-1947//? Irregular. Last issue 32 pages, size 15 x 23. Published by National Society Colonial Dames of America, Richmond, VA. Editors: Mrs. Egbert Jones, Mrs. Craig Barron, Mrs. Henry McAllister, Mar., 1940; Mrs. Egbert Jones, Mrs. Henry McAllister, Mrs. James Osgood Wynn, Mar., 1942. Subject focus: history, clubs.

| Hist | Apr., Nov., 1932, June, 1933, May, 1934, Mar., June, 1935, Jan., June, 1936, Mar., 1938, Mar., 1940, Mar., 1942, Oct., 1947 | E/186.4/A06 |
| --- | --- | --- |

630 <u>Michigan University Center for Continuing Education of Women Newsletter</u>. 1968. Semi-annual. Dorothy McGuigan, editor, Michigan University Center for Continuing Education of Women Newsletter, University of Michigan, 330 Thompson Street, Ann Arbor, MI 48109. Last issue 8 pages, last volume 20 pages, size 22 x 28. Line drawings, photographs. Subject focus: research, women's studies, minorities, family, career development, stereotypes, continuing education.

| Mem | v.5, n.2- Fall, 1973- | Periodicals Room |
| --- | --- | --- |

631 <u>Michigan Women</u>. 1977. Irregular. Michigan Women, 815 Washington Square Building, Lansing, MI 48933. Last issue 4 pages, size 22 x 28. Photographs. Published by Michigan Women's Commission, Lansing, MI. Subject focus: rights, workers, health, lobbying.

| Hist | v.1, n.1- Jan., 1977- | Circulation |
| --- | --- | --- |
| Wom Ed Res | v.1, n. 1- Jan., 1977- | Circulation |

632 <u>Middlesex County N.O.W. Newsletter</u>. 1973-1974//? Monthly. Last issue 7 pages. Line drawings. Available on microfilm: Herstory. Published by Middlesex County Chapter, National Organization for Women, Iselin, NJ. Editor: Phyllis Holzschlag and Dee Kenna. Subject focus: feminism, Equal Rights Amendment, employment, education.

| Hist | v.4, n.10-18; Oct., 1973- June, 1974 | Microforms Her. 3, R 3 |
| --- | --- | --- |

633 <u>Midwest Peace and Freedom</u>. 1973. Irregular. Midwest Peace and Freedom, 1213 Race Street, Philadelphia, PA 19107. Subject focus: human rights, peace movement, radicalism.

| Hist | Summer, 1980- | Circulation |
| --- | --- | --- |

634 <u>Midwest Sociologists for Women in Society, Newsletter</u>. 1975-1978//. Irregular. Last issue 12 pages, size 22 x 28. Line drawings. Published by Midwest Sociologists for Women in Society, Chicago, IL. Place of publication varies: Stevens Point, WI, May-Oct., 1975. Editors: Kim Scheppele and Eleanor Miller German. Subject focus: sociologists, research.

| Mem | May?, 1975- Jan., 1978 | Periodicals Room |
| --- | --- | --- |

635 <u>Midwest Women's Legal Group Newsletter</u>. 1972//? Unknown. Last issue 3 pages. Available on microfilm: Herstory. Published by Midwest Women's Legal Group, Chicago, IL. Subject focus: law, sexism, legal services, Equal Rights Amendment.

| Hist | June 1, 1972 | Microforms Her. 2, R 8 |
| --- | --- | --- |

636 The Milwaukee Journal (Charity Edition). 1895//. Last issue 56 pages, size 49 x 60. Line drawings, commercial advertising. Published by The Milwaukee Journal Co., Milwaukee, WI. Editors: Louise Cunningham Bowles, Mary Antisdel Marner, Caroline Sanderson Berry and Ida May Jackson. Subject focus: rights, children, music, drama, utopianism, home economics, newspapers.

| Hist | Feb. 22, 1895 | Circulation |

Milwaukee Section Bulletin, National Council of Jewish Women. Milwaukee, WI

see Bulletin, Milwaukee Section. NCJW. Milwaukee, WI

637 Milwaukee Women's Political Caucus. 1980. Irregular. Gratis to individuals and institutions. Last issue 6 pages, size 22 x 35. Published by Wisconsin Women's Political Caucus, Milwaukee Chapter, 4759 North Berkeley, Milwaukee, WI 53211. Subject focus: lobbying, Equal Rights Amendment.

| Hist | Oct., 1980- | Circulation |

638 The Minerviad. 1822-?//. Semi-monthly. Last issue 8 pages. Available on microfilm: UnM (1822). Published in Boston, MA. Editor: John R. Parker. Subject focus: fiction, poetry.

| Hist | v.1, n.1-13; Mar. 30- Sep. 7, 1822 | Microforms |

639 Miss Black U.S.A. Magazine. 1975-1976//? Quarterly. Last issue 28 pages, size 20 x 27. Line drawings, photographs, some in color, commercial advertising. Published by Youth Together, Inc., Phoenix, AZ. Editor: Major Davis. Subject focus: beauty pageants, Afro-Americans.

| Hist | v.1, n.1-2; Dec., 1975- Apr., 1976 | Circulation |

640 Missionary Magazine (of the Woman's Missionary Society of the African-Methodist-Episcopal Church). 1951. 9 times a year. $5 for individuals and institutions. Hattie Bryant Witt Greene, editor, Missionary Magazine, 1023 North 5th Street, Birmingham, AL 35204. Last issue 24 pages, size 28 x 22. Line drawings, photographs. Published by Women's Missionary Society A.M.E. Church. Subject focus: Afro-Americans, Christianity.

| Hist | v.26, n.5,8, v.27, n.9, v.28, n.6- Jan., May/June, 1977, May/June, 1978, Mar., 1979- | Circulation |

641 Mlle. New York. 1895-1899?//. Bi-weekly. OCLC 5908329. Last issue 16 pages, last volume 104 pages. Line drawings, commercial advertising. Published by the Blumenberg Press, New York, NY. Editor: Vance Thompson. Subject focus: fiction, poetry, literary criticism, art.

| Mem | v.1, n.1-10; v.2, n.1-3; Aug., 1895- Apr., 1896, Nov./Dec., 1898 | Microforms |

642 Modern Bride. 1950. Bi-monthly. $12 for individuals and institutions. Robert W. Houseman, editor, Modern Bride, One Park Avenue, New York, NY 10016. Business address: P.O. Box 2778, Boulder, CO 80323. ISSN 0026-7546. OCLC 1758443. LC sn78-1591. Last issue 260 pages, size 22 x 27. Line drawings, photographs, some in color, commercial advertising. Indexed: Access Index (1975-). Available on microfilm: McP (1977-); UnM (1971-). Published by Tiff-Davis Publishing Company, New York, NY. Subject focus: fashion, weddings, beauty care, travel, interior decorating. Other holding institutions: DLC (DLC), InLP (IPL), [University of Minnesota Union List, Minneapolis, MN] (MUL), [Western New York Library Resources Council, Buffalo, NY] (VZX), NcRS (NRC), OkT (TUL), [Pittsburgh Regional Library Center-Union List, Pittsburgh, PA] (QPR), ScRhW (SWW), TxAU (TXG), WM (GZD).

| MPL | Current Issues Only | Young Adults Area |
| SPPL | Feb/Mar., 1978- | Circulation |

Modern Housekeeping. Boston, MA

see Everyday Housekeeping. Boston, MA

643 Momma; The Newspaper/Magazine for Single Mothers. 1972-1974//? Monthly. OCLC 1775463. Last issue 28 pages, size 29 x 45. Line drawings, photographs, commercial advertising. Available on microfilm: Herstory. Published in Venice, CA. Subject focus: children, child care, career development, sexuality, welfare, biographies, single mothers, family planning, affirmative action. Other holding institutions: DLC (NSD), DeU (DLM), [University of Minnesota Union List, Minneapolis, MN] (MUL), NFQC (XQM), NSbSU (YSM), OKentU (KSU), PPiU (PIT), WMUW (GZN), MCR-S (Schlesinger Library

on the History of Women in America, Radcliffe College, Cambridge, MA).

| Hist | v.1, n.1-6; Dec., 1972-June, 1973 | Microforms Her. 2, R 8 |
| --- | --- | --- |
|  | v.1, n.7-v.2, n.1; July, Oct., 1973-Spring, 1974 | Her. 2 UP, R 5 |
|  | v.1, n.4,6; Mar., June, 1973 | Pam 76-1274 |
| MPL | v.2, n.1-3; Spring-Mar., 1974 | Literature and Social Sciences Section |

644 Momma-The Organization for Single Mothers. 1972//? Monthly. Last issue 4 pages. Line drawings. Available on microfilm: Herstory. Published in Venice, CA. Title varies: as Single Mothers Newsletter, Mar.-Apr., 1972. Subject focus: child care, single mothers, welfare.

| Hist | v.1, n.1-6; Mar.-Aug., 1972 | Microforms Her. 2, R 8 |
| --- | --- | --- |

645 Monmouth County Chapter Newsletter. 1972-1974//? Monthly. Last issue 8 pages. Line drawings, photographs, commercial advertising. Available on microfilm: Herstory. Published by Monmouth County Chapter, National Organization for Women, Red Bank, NJ. Editors: Doris Kulman, Sep., 1972-June, 1973; Doris Kulman and Veda Mathis Drummond, July-Dec., 1973; Elsalyn Drucker and Diane Yarosz, Jan.-June, 1974. Subject focus: education, media, feminism, lobbying, Equal Rights Amendment.

| Hist | Sep., 1972-June, 1973 | Microforms Her. 2, R 11 |
| --- | --- | --- |
|  | July, 1973-June, 1974 | Her. 2 UP, R 7 |

646 Monterey Peninsula N.O.W. 1973-1974//? Monthly. Last issue 5 pages. Line drawings. Available on microfilm: Herstory. Published by Monterey Peninsula Chapter National Organization for Women, Monterey, CA. Editors: Jinks Hoover, Aug.-Nov., 1973; Nancy Nelson, Dec., 1973-Mar., 1974. Subject focus: feminism, lobbying.

| Hist | Apr.-June, 1973 | Microforms Her. 2, R 11 |
| --- | --- | --- |
|  | July, 1973-Mar., 1974 | Her. 2 UP, R7 |

647 Monthly Bulletin of the National League for Woman's Service. 1917-1919//? Monthly. Last issue 4 pages, size 22 x 28. Line drawings, photographs. Published by National League for Woman's Service, New York, NY. Subject focus: war work.

| Hist | v.1, n.1-v.2, n.6/7 Oct. 15, 1917-May/June, 1919 | F836/8N26B (Cutter) |
| --- | --- | --- |

648 The Monthly D.O.B.'R. 1974//? Monthly. Last issue 4 pages. Line drawings. Available on microfilm: Herstory. Published by Daughters of Bilitis/Women for Action, Dallas, TX. Subject focus: lesbians, poetry, lobbying.

| Hist | v.1, n.1-4; Mar.-June, 1974 | Microforms Her. 3, R 1 |
| --- | --- | --- |

649 The Monthly Extract: An Irregular Periodical. 1972-1974//. Bi-monthly. OCLC 1962353. Last issue 12 pages. Line drawings. Available on microfilm: Herstory. Published by New Moon Publications, Stamford, CT. Subject focus: gynecology, self-help, sexism in medicine.

| Hist | v.1, n.1-v.2, n.2; Aug./Sep., 1972-May/June, 1973 | Microforms Her. 2, R 8 |
| --- | --- | --- |
|  | v.2, n.3-v.3, n.2; Sep./Oct., 1973-May/June, 1974 | Her. 2 UP, R5 |

650 Montreal Women's Liberation Newsletter. 1970//? OCLC 2264387. Last issue 22 pages. Line drawings. Available on microfilm: Herstory. Published by Montreal Women's Liberation, Montreal, Quebec, Canada. Subject focus: feminism, poetry, pro-abortion, birth control, self-defense, art.

| Hist | n.2; June, 1970 | Microforms Her. 1, R 16 |
| --- | --- | --- |

651 Moonshadow. 1973-1974//? Irregular. Last issue 8 pages. Line drawings, photographs. Available on microfilm: Herstory. Published by Transexual Action Organization (TAO), Miami Beach, FL. Editor: Angela K. Douglas. Subject focus: transsexuals, transvestites, sex change surgery, sexism.

| Hist | Aug., 1973, Jan./Feb., 1974 | Microforms Her. 3, R 2 |
| --- | --- | --- |

Mother. Stanford, CA

    see Proud Woman. Stanford, CA

652 **The Mother.** 1939-1953//? Quarterly. Last issue 20 pages, last volume 82 pages, size 17 x 25. Line drawings, photographs, commercial advertising. Published by the American Committee on Maternal Welfare, Inc., Chicago, IL. Subject focus: health, pregnancy, child care.

| Agric | v.8, n.1-v.14, n.3; Oct., 1946- Summer, 1953 | Periodicals Section |
|---|---|---|

653 **Moteru Dirva.** 1917. Bi-monthly. $3 for individuals and institutions. Mrs. Dali Murray, editor, Moteru Dirva, 3005 North 124th Street, Brookfield, WI 53005. Last issue 48 pages, size 18 x 25. Line drawings, photographs. Published by the American-Lithuanian Roman Catholic Women's Alliance, Brookfield, WI. Subject focus: Catholic Church, Lithuanian-Americans. In Lithuanian (50%).

| Hist | v.44, n.1- Jan., 1960- | Microforms |
|---|---|---|

654 **The Mother at Home and Household Magazine.** 1869//. Monthly. OCLC 6525142. Last issue 38 pages, last volume 380 pages. Self-indexed. Available on microfilm: ResP. Published by Hosford and Sons, New York, NY. Editor: Mrs. Henry Ward Beecher. Subject focus: home economics, housewives. Other holding institutions: MCR-S (Schlesinger Library on the History of Women in America, Radcliffe College, Cambridge, MA), NjR (NJR), ViBlbv (VPI), TxDW (IWU).

| Mem | v.1, n.1-12; Jan.-Dec., 1869 | Microforms |
|---|---|---|

655 **Mother Jones Gazette.** 1973//. Last issue 10 pages. Line drawings. Available on microfilm: Herstory. Published by the Knoxville Lesbian Collective, Knoxville, TN. Subject focus: lesbians, self-help, poetry, minorities.

| Hist | v.1, n.1; Jan., 1973 | Microforms Her. 2, R 8 |
|---|---|---|

656 **Mother Lode.** 1971-1973//. Irregular. OCLC 2264424. Last issue 8 pages, size 29 x 45. Line drawings. Available on microfilm: Herstory. Published by Women in San Francisco Women's Liberation, San Francisco, CA. Subject focus: feminism, mothers, children, poetry. Other holding institution: PPiU (PIT).

| Hist | n.1-3; Jan., 1971- Summer, 1971 | Microforms Her. 1, R 2 |
|---|---|---|
| | n.4-6; Spring, 1972- Spring, 1973 | Her. 1 UP, R7 |
| | n.1-5; Jan., 1971- Summer, 1972 | Pam 74-1160 |
| Mem | n.1-6; Spring, 1972- Spring, 1973 | +AP/+M9182/L821 |

657 **Mothers for Fair Child Support.** 1972//? Unknown. Last issue 4 pages. Available on microfilm: Herstory. Published by Mothers for Fair Child Support, National Chapter, Forestville, NY. Subject focus: child care, child support, mothers.

| Hist | Nov., 1972 | Microforms Her. 2, R 8 |
|---|---|---|

658 **The Mothers Magazine.** 1833-1873//? Monthly. OCLC 1642075, 3453814. LC 41-187, ca09-1176. Last issue 60 pages, last volume 384 pages, size 21 x 14. Line drawings. Self-indexed (1833-1850). Available on microfilm: KTO (1833-1850). Published by the Mothers Magazine, New York, NY. Editors: Mrs. A.G. Whittelsey, Jan., 1833-1841; Elizabeth Sewell and Myron Finch, Jan.-Dec., 1850. Subject focus: child rearing, family, mothers, fiction, poetry. Other holding institutions: IRA (ICY), MiKW (EXW), [University of Minnesota Union List, Minneapolis, MN] (MUL), NRU (RRR), OAkU (AKR), OC1W (CWR) OY (YMM).

| Agric | [v.1, n.1-v.18, n.12]; [Jan., 1833- Dec., 1850] | Periodicals Section |
|---|---|---|
| Mem | v.10, n.1-v.16, n.10; Jan., 1842- Oct., 1848 | AP/M9183/M191 |

659 **The Motor.** 1886. Bi-monthly. $1 for individuals and institutions. Dorothy M. Smith, editor, The Motor, Rt. 2, Box 51, Baraboo, WI 53913. (608) 356-4354. Last issue 4 pages, last volume 48 pages, size 38 x 29. Line drawings, photographs. Available on microfilm: WHi (1886-1892, 1903-1905, 1915-1961). Published by the Women's Christian Temperance Union of Wisconsin. Title varies: as Our State Work, May 1, 1886-Aug., 1888; WCTU State Work, Sep., 1888-June, 1892. Place of publication varies: Madison, WI, May 1, 1886-Oct., 1908; Milwaukee, WI, Nov., 1908-Nov., 1910; Evansville, WI, Dec., 1910-Oct., 1912; Poynette, WI, Jan., 1915-Apr., 1925; Waupaca, WI, May, 1925-Sep., 1941; Milwaukee, WI, Oct., 1941-Sep., 1946; Chetek, WI, Nov./Dec., 1946-

Nov./Dec., 1960; Rice Lake, WI, Jan., 1961-
Aug., 1962; Madison, WI, Sep.-Nov./Dec., 1962;
Stoughton, WI, Jan., 1963-Sep., 1967; Ripon,
WI, Oct., 1967-Mar., 1972; Chippewa Falls, WI,
Apr., 1972-Dec., 1976. Frequency varies:
monthly, May 1, 1886-Apr., 1890; semi-monthly,
May 1,-Dec. 15, 1890; monthly, Jan., 1891-
Dec., 1976. Previous editors: Mary Eaton,
Emma C. Bascom and Helen Olin, May 1, 1886-
July, 1887; Emma J. Curtis, Ellen W. Lamb,
Helen R. Olin, Aug.-Nov., 1888; Emma J. Curtis
and Ellen W. Lamb, Dec., 1888-June 1, 1890;
Emma J. Curtis and Amy Kellogg Morse, July 1,
1890-June, 1891; Maria F. Hanchett, July,
1891-Oct., 1980; Mrs. W.A. Lawson, Nov., 1908-
Nov., 1909; Mrs. M.E.B. Thompson, Dec., 1910-
Oct., 1916; Mrs. Eva C. Lewis, Nov., 1916-
Dec., 1922; Miss Julia Hutchinson, Jan., 1923-
Oct., 1941; Miss Susie Neff, Nov., 1941-Oct.,
1946; Mrs. Alice Nerlien, Nov./Dec., 1946-
Oct., 1960; Mrs. R.L. Cornwell, Nov./Dec.,
1960-Sep., 1967; Mrs. George Smokey, Oct.,
1967-Mar., 1972; Ruth Rheingans, Apr., 1972-
Dec., 1976. Subject focus: Christianity,
temperance.

| Hist | v.1, n.1-v.6, n.7, v.16, n.7-v.18, n.6, v.26, n.7-v.82, n.4; May 1, 1886- Dec., 1892, Jan., 1903- Dec., 1905, Jan., 1915- Nov./Dec., 1961 | Microforms |
| --- | --- | --- |
| | v.1, n.1- May 1, 1886- | F902/8W87/M (Cutter) |

660 <u>Mountain Moving</u>. 1976. Quarterly. $3 for in-
dividuals and institutions. Mountain Moving,
619 Emerson Street, Evanston, IL 60201. (312)
492-3146. OCLC 5039543. Last issue 32 pages,
size 20 x 27. Line drawings, photographs,
commercial advertising. Published by Women's
Center at Northwestern University, Evanston,
IL. Subject focus: rights, pro-abortion,
health, interviews, film reviews, Equal Rights
Amendment, arts. Other holding institution:
[University of Minnesota Union List, Minneapolis, MN] (MUL).

| Hist | v.1, n.1- Mar. 3, 1976- | Circulation |
| --- | --- | --- |

661 <u>Mountain Moving Day</u>. 1971-1972//. Irregular.
Last issue 12 pages. Line drawings, photographs, commercial advertising. Available
on microfilm: Herstory. Published by Mountain
Moving Day, Inc., Carbondale, IL. Subject
focus: radicalism, health, consciousness-
raising, poetry, art, sexism.

| Hist | v.1, n.1-3; Nov. 20, 1971- Mar., 1972 | Microforms Her. 2, R 8 |
| --- | --- | --- |

662 <u>Moving</u>. 1974//? Irregular. Last issue 10
pages. Line drawings. Available on microfilm:
Herstory. Published by Roanoke Valley Chapter,
National Organization for Women, Salem, VA.
Subject focus: day care, feminism, lobbying,
law, Equal Rights Amendment.

| Hist | v.1-5; Jan.-Summer, 1974 | Microforms Her. 3, R 3 |
| --- | --- | --- |

663 <u>Moving Out</u>. 1971. Semi-annual. $4.50 for in-
dividuals. Margaret Kaminski and Gloria Dyc,
editors, Moving Out, 4866 Third, Wayne State
University, Detroit, MI 48202. OCLC 3428883,
5157262. Last issue 90 pages, last volume 104
pages, size 22 x 28. Line drawings, photographs. Available on microfilm: Herstory
(1971-1974). Published by Wayne Women's Liberation, Wayne State University, Detroit, MI.
Subject focus: fiction, poetry, literature,
feminists, lesbians, music, art, sexuality,
feminism. Other holding institutions: CSt
(Stanford University), CLU (CLU), GU (GUA),
MiDU (EYU), MiEM (EEM), NbU (LDL), OU (OSU),
PPiU (PIT), RPB (RBN), WMUW (GZN).

| Hist | v.1, n.1-2; Mar.-?, 1971 | Microforms Her. 1, R 9 |
| --- | --- | --- |
| | v.2, n.1-2, v.3, n.1-2; 1972-1973 | Her. 1 UP, R7 |
| | v.4, n.1; Winter?, 1974 | Her. CUP, R 3 |
| RBR | v.1, n.2- Fall/Winter, 1971- | Circulation |

664 <u>Ms</u>. 1972. Monthly. $10 for individuals and
institutions. Gloria Steinem, editor, Ms.,
370 Lexington Avenue, New York, NY 10017.
(212) 725-2666. Business address: 123 Garden
Street, Marion, OH 43302. ISSN 0047-8318.
OCLC 1285775, 5046704, 1758803, 4286295.
LC 72-624579. Last issue 102 pages, last
volume 1312 pages, size 21 x 28. Line drawings, photographs, some in color, commercial
advertising. Indexed in: Reader's Guide
(1974-); Women's Studies Abstracts, Abstracts
of Popular Culture, Wallace Memorial Library
(1972-1974), Rochester Institute of Technology. Available on microfilm: McP. Published
by Ms. Magazine Corp., New York, NY. Subject
focus: rights, politics, health, feminism,
fiction, poetry, art, film reviews. Other
holding institutions: ABAU (ABC), [Alabama
Public Library Service, Montgomery, AL]
(ASL), AU (ALM), ArRuA (AKP), ArU (AFU), AzFU
(AZN), AzTeS (AZS), AzU (AZU), CLU (CLU),

[Pepperdine University, Malibu, CA] (CPE), COU-DA (COA), CSt (Stanford University), CU-S (CUS), [Saint Joseph College, West Hartford, CT] (STJ), CtW (WLU), CtY (YUS), [Congressional Research Service, Washington, DC] (CRS), DFT (FTC), SHU (DHU), DI (UDI), DJ (DOJ), DME/DAS (OLA), DeU (DLM), FBoU (FGM), FJUNF (FNP), FMFIU (FXG), FPeU (FWA), GASU (GSU), GU (GUA), ICRC (IAR), ICSX (ICS), IGK (IBK), IPB (IBA), IU (UIU), IaDuU (IOV), IaAS (IWA), IaDmG (IWG), [Indiana Union List of Serials, Indianapolis, IN] (ILS), InU (IUL), KLindB (KFB), KSteC (KKQ), KyU (KUK), LHS (LSH), LNU (LNU), MCR-S (Schlesinger Library on the History of Women in America, Radcliffe College, Cambridge, MA), MA (AMH), MBNU (NED), MBU (BOS), MMeT (TFW), MNS (SNN), MWelC (WFL), MWP (WPG), MdBJ (JHE), [Frostburg State College Library, Frostburg, MD] (MFS), MdStm (MDS), Me (MEA), MeB (BBH), MiAdC (EEA), MiEM (EEM), MiGrC (EXC), MiLC (EEL), MiMtpT (EZC), [University of Minnesota Union List, Minneapolis, MN] (MUL), MnStcls (MST), MnStpeG (MNG), N (NYG), [New York State Union List, Albany, NY] (NYS), NA1f (YAH), NBu (VHB), [Western New York Library Resources Council, Buffalo, NY] (VZX), NCH (YHM), NCorniCC (ZDG), NCortU (YCM), NDFM (VZE), NFQC (XQM), NGenoU (YGM), NIC (COO), NNR (ZXC), NNepaSU (ZLM), NONEOH (VZH), NOneoU (ZBM), NOsU (YOM), NPV (VXW), NPurMC (VYE), NR (YQR), NRU (RRR), NSbSU (YSM), NSbSU-H (VZB), NSufR (VVR), NSyU (SYB), NWM (YWM), NbKS (KRS), NbU (LDL), NcRS (NRC), NhD (DRB), NhMSA (SAC), NhP1S (PSM), NjLincB (BCC), NmLcU (IRU), NmLvH (NMH), NmU (IQU), O (OHI), OAU (OUN), OAk (APL), OAkU (AKR), [Raymond Walters General and Technical College Library, Blue Ash, OH] (ORW), OC1U (CSU), OC1W (CWR), OKentU (KSU), OLanU (OUL), OMC (MRC), OO (OBE), OTMC (MCL), OTU (TOL), OTU-L (UTL), OU (OSU), OY (YMM), OYU (YNG), OkEG (OKG), OkEP (OKZ), OkT (TUL), PBL (LYU), PB1bM (MGC), PBm (BMC), PCW (UWC), PC1vU (URS), PCoR (ROB), PHC (HVC), PNwC (WFN), PPD (DXU), [Pittsburgh Regional Library Center-Union List, Pittsburgh, PA] (QPR), PSC (PSC), PSt (UPC), PU (PAU), ScRhW (SWW), TMurS (TXM), TNJ (TJC), TNTU (TUN), TxAbH (TXS), TxArU (IUA), TxBe1M (MHB), TxCM (TXA), TxDN (INT), TxDW (IWU), TxDaU (IVD), TxLT (ILU), TxNacS (TXK), TxShA (IAU), Vi (VIC), [Emory & Henry College, Emory, VA] (VEH), ViRCU (VRC), ViRU (VRU), ViU (VA@), WM (GZD), WMUW (GZN), WaU (WAU), WeharU (HRM).

| | | |
|---|---|---|
| Hist | v.1, n.1-9; July-Dec., 1972 | Microforms Her. 2 R8-9 |
| | v.2, n.1-12; July, 1973 June, 1974 | Her. 2 UP, R 5 |
| | v.1, n.1- July, 1972 | HQ/1101/M55 |
| Mem | v.1, n.1- July, 1972- | AP/M94 |
| Coll | v.1, n.1- July, 1972- | APA/M875 |
| Agric | Current Issues Only | Periodicals Section |
| MPL | v.1, n.3- Sep., 1972- | Circulation |
| EC | v.7, n.10- Oct., 1979- | Periodicals Section |
| Wom St | v.2, n.10- Oct., 1973- | Reading Room |
| UW Ext | v.2, n.11- Nov., 1973- | Circulation |
| MATC | v.2, n.1- Jan., 1973- | Cora Hardy Library |
| | v.3, n.1- Jan., 1974- | Technical College |
| MIPL | v.2, n.1- Jan., 1973- | Circulation |
| WAPL | v.3, n.9- Sep., 1974- | Circulation |
| JR | v.3, n.1- Jan., 1974- | Circulation |
| MMHS | v.1, n.1- July, 1972- | Circulation |
| UWBA | v.1, n.1- July, 1972- | Circulation |
| SAPH | Current Issues Only | Circulation |
| MGHS | v.3, n.12- Dec., 1974- | Circulation |
| LAHS | Current Issues Only | Circulation |
| SPPL | v.4, n.1- Jan., 1975- | Circulation |
| SPHS | v.3, n.9- Sep., 1974- | Circulation |
| BEL | Current Issues Only | Circulation |
| CFL | Current Issues Only | Circulation |
| VPL | v.2, n.1- Jan., 1973- | Circulation |

| | | |
|---|---|---|
| SCPL | v.4, n.10-<br>Oct., 1975- | Circulation |
| WHS | v.2, n.9-<br>Sep., 1973- | Circulation |
| EHS | Current Issues<br>Only | Circulation |
| MOPL | v.3, n.7-<br>July, 1974- | Circulation |
| RPL | v.1, n.1-<br>July, 1972- | Circulation |
| BAHS | v.3, n.9-<br>Sep., 1974- | Circulation |
| DFHS | v.3, n.6-<br>June, 1974- | Circulation |
| BML | Current Issues<br>Only | Circulation |
| R&L | v.2, n.12-<br>Dec., 1973- | Circulation |

665 Ms. Archivist. 1973//? Unknown. Last issue 12 pages. Available on microfilm: Herstory. Published by the Society of American Archivists, Women's Caucus, Columbus, OH. Subject focus: archivists, rights, professionals. Other holding institution: MCR-S (Schlesinger Library on the History of Women in America, Radcliffe College, Cambridge, MA).

| | | |
|---|---|---|
| Hist | v.1, n.1;<br>Summer, 1973 | Microforms<br>Her. 2, R 9 |
| | v.1, n.2;<br>Fall, 1973 | Her. 2 UP, R 6 |

666 Ms. On Scene, Inter-Studio Feminist Alliance Newsletter. 1973-1974//? Quarterly. Last issue 5 pages. Line drawings. Published by Interstudio Feminist Alliance, Hollywood, CA. Subject focus: media, employment, feminism, sexism in media.

| | | |
|---|---|---|
| Hist | v.1, n.1;<br>Spring, 1973 | Microforms<br>Her. 2, R 6 |
| | v.1, n.3-v.2, n.3;<br>Fall, 1973-<br>Summer, 1974 | Her. 2 UP, R3 |

La Mujer.   Albuquerque, NM

    see NOW Newsletter.   Albuquerque, NM

667 The Muliebrity Majority. 1972-1974//? Irregular. Last issue 10 pages. Line drawings, commercial advertising. Available on microfilm: Herstory. Title varies: as Rockford Chapter Newsletter, Dec., 1972-Mar., 1973. Published by the Rockford Chapter, National Organization for Women, Rockford, IL. Editors: Victoria Hammond, Dec., 1972-Mar., 1973; Victoria Hammond and Dixie Klemm, May-Nov., 1973; Dixie Klemm, Dec., 1973-June, 1974. Subject focus: art, pro-abortion, lobbying, feminism, health, ecology.

| | | |
|---|---|---|
| Hist | v.1, n.1-4;<br>Dec., 1972-<br>June, 1973 | Microforms<br>Her. 2, R 11 |
| | v.1, n.8-v.2, n.6;<br>Aug., 1973-<br>June, 1974 | Her. 2 UP, R8 |

668 Multiple Vision: Changes, Alternatives and New Directions. 1980. Monthly. $5 for individuals and institutions. Ruth Summer, editor, Multiple Vision: Changes, Alternatives and New Directions, P.O. Box 5809, Kansas City, MO 64111. Last issue 16 pages, size 44 x 29. Line drawings, photographs, commercial advertising. Available on microfilm: WHi. Published by Multiple Vision, Inc., Kansas City, MO. Subject focus: feminism.

| | | |
|---|---|---|
| Hist | v.1, n.10-<br>Oct. 1, 1980- | Circulation |

669 Muthah. 1970?//? Unknown. OCLC 1939289. Last issue 64 pages. Available on microfilm: Herstory. Published by Sacramento Women's Liberation, Sacramento, CA. Subject focus: anthropology, history, pro-abortion, law, poetry, mental health.

| | | |
|---|---|---|
| Hist | 1970? | Microforms<br>Her. 1, R 9 |

670 NAC Memo. 1980. Irregular. NAC Memo, Suite 306, 40 St. Clair Avenue East, Toronto, Ontario, Canada, M4R 1M9. (416) 922-3246. Last issue 16 pages, size 36 x 22. Line drawings, photographs. Available on microfilm: WHi. Published by National Action Committee on the Status of Women/Le Comite National d'Action sur le statut de la femme, East Toronto, Ontario, Canada. Subject focus: law, lobbying, rights, politics. In French (30%).

| | | |
|---|---|---|
| Hist | Oct., 1980- | Circulation |

671 N.A.R.A.L. News. 1969//? Unknown. OCLC 2264530. Last issue 6 pages. Line drawings. Available on microfilm: Herstory. Published by the National Association for Repeal of Abortion Laws, New York, NY. Subject focus: pro-abortion, family planning, lobbying.

| | | |
|---|---|---|
| Hist | v.1, n.1;<br>Summer, 1969 | Microforms<br>Her. 1, R 16 |

672  NCAWE News-National Council of Administrative Women in Education. 1951?-1974//? Irregular. OCLC 3419774. Last issue 6 pages. Line drawings, photographs. Available on microfilm: Herstory. Published by the National Education Association, Washington, DC. Subject focus: education, media, lobbying, professionals, politics.

| Hist | v.17, n.1-v.21, n.1; ?, 1968-Sep., 1972 | Microforms Her. 2, R 9 |
|---|---|---|
| | v.21, n.2-5; Nov., 1973- May, 1974 | Her. 2 UP, R 6 |

673  N.C.H.E. News. 1970-1973//? Monthly. OCLC 2264750. Last issue 4 pages, last volume 72 pages. Line drawings. Available on microfilm: Herstory. Published by the National Committee on Household Employment, Washington, DC. Subject focus: employment, sexism, domestic workers, lobbying, equal pay for equal work.

| Hist | v.1, n.1-v.2, n.9; Nov., 1970- Sep., 1971 | Microforms Her. 1, R 16 |
|---|---|---|
| | v.2, n.10-v.4, n.6/7; Oct., 1971- June/July, 1972 | Her. 1 UP, R 7 |
| | v.4, n.8-9/10; Aug.-Sep./Oct., 1973 | Her. CUP, R 3 |

674  NCJW Journal. 1940. 5 times a year. $2 for individuals and institutions. Harriet Rose, editor, NCJW Journal, 15 East 26th Street, New York, NY 10010. ISSN 0148-2106. OCLC 1565310, 1590637. LC sn78-4699, 37-20762. Last issue 16 pages, last volume 60 pages, size 22 x 28. Line drawings, photographs. Published by the National Council of Jewish Women, New York, NY. Title varies: as The Council Woman, Mar./Apr., 1940-Oct./Dec., 1977. Frequency varies: quarterly, Mar./Apr., 1940-Mar./Apr., 1941; bi-monthly, Mar., 1942-May/June, 1944; monthly, Summer-Nov., 1944; 6 times a year, Mar., 1956-Nov., 1967; quarterly, Winter, 1968-Feb., 1972. Previous editors: Viola Paradise, Mar./Apr., 1940-Mar./Apr., 1941; Bernice Solomen Graziani, Mar., 1956-Mar., 1967; Barbara Roth, June, 1967-Winter, 1968; Nancy Volberg, Spring, 1968-Spring, 1969; Ruth Altman, Fall, 1969-Dec., 1977. Subject focus: family, social service, clubs, Jews, Israel, politics. Other holding institutions: [Indiana Union List of Serials, Indianapolis, IN] (ILS), [University of Minnesota Union List, Minneapolis, MN] (MUL), OkT (TUL).

| Hist | v.1, n.1-v.5, n.7-v.18, n.1- Mar./Apr., 1940- Nov., 1944, Mar., 1956- | E/184/J5/C74 |
|---|---|---|
| MPL | Current Issues Only | Literature and Social Science Section |

675  N.E./Bucks N.O.W. Newsletter. 1972-1973//? Monthly. Last issue 7 pages. Line drawings. Available on microfilm: Herstory. Published by the Northeast Bucks Chapter-National Organization for Women, Penndel, PA. Place of publication varies: Levittown, PA, Dec., 1972-June, 1973. Subject focus: Equal Rights Amendment, health, feminism, politics, lobbying, counseling, image.

| Hist | Dec., 1972- June, 1973 | Microforms Her. 2, R 11 |
|---|---|---|
| | July-Sep., 1973 | Her. 2 UP, R7 |

NFRW Focus '68. Washington, DC

see Focus. Washington, DC

676  NFRW: National Federation of Republican Women. 1976-1977//. Irregular. OCLC 4731569. Last issue 13 pages, last volume 35 pages. Available on microfilm: WHi. Published by the National Federation of Republican Women, Washington, DC. Subject focus: politics, Republican Party, clubs, political parties.

| Hist | v.1, n.1-v.2, n.4; Apr., 1976- Dec., 1977 | Microforms |
|---|---|---|

677  NIC Women Newsletter. 1975//. Bi-monthly? Last issue 10 pages, size 22 x 28. Published by the National Interim Committee for a Mass Party of the People, New York, NY. Subject focus: socialism, politics.

| Hist | June/July, 1975 | Pam 76-1736 |
|---|---|---|

N.J. W.E.A.L. Newsletter. Old Bridge, NJ

see N.J. W.E.A.L.er. Old Bridge, NJ

678  N.J. W.E.A.L.er. 1971-1974//? Irregular. Last issue 14 pages. Line drawings, photographs. Available on microfilm: Herstory. Published by The Women's Equity Action League-New Jersey, Old Bridge, NJ. Title varies: as W.E.A.L.-Women's Equity Action League, Nov., 1971-May, 1973; as N.J. W.E.A.L. Newsletter, Oct.-Nov., 1973. Editors: Mariagnes Lattimer,

Nov., 1971-Nov., 1972; Doris A. Schwartz, Feb., 1973-Jan./Mar., 1974. Subject focus: rights, lobbying, health.

| Hist | v.1, n.1-v.2, n.2; Nov., 1971- May, 1973 | Microforms Her. 2, R 19 |
| --- | --- | --- |
| | v.2, n.3-v.3, n.1; Oct., 1973- Jan./Mar., 1974 | Her. 2 UP, R12 |

679 <u>NLIS Newsletter-National Lesbian Information Service</u>. 1972//? Last issue 8 pages. Line drawings. Available on microfilm: Herstory. Published by the National Lesbian Information Service, San Francisco, CA. Subject focus: employment, rights, lobbying, lesbians, gay rights, politics.

| Hist | v.1, n.1; May, 1972 | Microforms Her. 2, R 9 |
| --- | --- | --- |

680 <u>NOW!</u> 1969-1978//? Monthly. OCLC 5331805, 2265290. Last issue 8 pages, size 22 x 28. Line drawings, commercial advertising. Published by National Organization for Women, Los Angeles Chapter, Los Angeles, CA. Available on microfilm: Herstory. Title varies: as N.O.W. News, Nov., 1971-Dec., 1973. Subject focus: rights, pro-abortion, feminism, Equal Rights Amendment, lobbying, health. Other holding institutions: CLU (CLU), PPiU (PIT).

| Wom Ed Res | [Nov., 1971- Dec., 1978] | Circulation |
| --- | --- | --- |

N.O.W.  Falls Church, VA

    see <u>North Virginia N.O.W.</u>
    Alexandria, VA

681 <u>N.O.W.</u> 1969-1974//? Monthly. OCLC 2264701. Last issue 8 pages, last volume 170 pages. Line drawings. Available on microfilm: Herstory. Published by the Berkeley Chapter, National Organization for Women, Berkeley, CA. Title varies: as N.O.W. Newsletter, Dec. 5, 1969-Sep., 1971. Subject focus: pro-abortion, child care, education, employment, sexism, feminism, lobbying, Equal Rights Amendment, rights, welfare, art, health, literature.

| Hist | v.1, n.1-v.2, n.9; Dec. 5, 1969- Sep., 1971 | Microforms Her. 1, R 17 |
| --- | --- | --- |

| | v.2, n.10-v.4, n.3; Oct., 1971- Mar., 1973 | Her. 1 UP, R7 |
| --- | --- | --- |
| | v.4, n.4-6; Apr.-June, 1973 | Her. 1 UP, R8 |
| | v.4, n.7-v.5, n.6; July, 1973- June, 1974 | Her. CUP, R4 |

682 <u>N.O.W.</u>! 1969-1974//? Monthly. OCLC 5331805. Last issue 8 pages, last volume 72 pages. Line drawings, photographs, commercial advertising. Available on microfilm: Herstory. Published by Southern California Chapter/Los Angeles Chapter National Organization for Women, Los Angeles, CA. Editors: Lenore Youngman, Apr., 1969-Apr., 1972; Margaret Hoggan, May, 1972-June, 1974. Subject focus: pro-abortion, child care, education, employment, media, feminism, Equal Rights Amendment, lobbying, rights, law.

| Hist | v.1, n.1-v.3, n.7; Apr., 1969- Aug., 1971 | Microforms Her. 1, R 18 |
| --- | --- | --- |
| | Oct., 1971- June, 1973 | Her. 1 UP, R9 |
| | July, 1973- June, 1974 | Her. CUP, R11 |

683 <u>N.O.W.</u> 1971//. Monthly. OCLC 2265286. Last issue 2 pages. Line drawings. Available on microfilm: Herstory. Published by the Dade County Chapter, National Organization for Women, Coconut Grove, FL. Subject focus: education, sexism, feminism, lobbying, Equal Rights Amendment, rights, child care, pro-abortion, legislation.

| Hist | Jan., Apr., Aug., 1971 | Microforms Her. 1, R 17 |
| --- | --- | --- |

684 <u>N.O.W. Acts.</u> 1968-1973//? Irregular. OCLC 2265287. Last issue 24 pages, last volume 52 pages, size 22 x 28. Line drawings. Available on microfilm: Herstory (1968-1971). Published by the National Organization for Women, Malibu, CA. Place of publication varies: Los Angeles, CA, Winter, 1970-Fall, 1971. Editors: Toni (Virginia) Carabillo, Winter, 1970-Fall, 1971; June Bundy Csida, 1972-Feb. 19, 1973. Subject focus: rights, feminism, lobbying, Equal Rights Amendment. Other holding instituions: [University of Minnesota Union List, Minneapolis, MN] (MUL), NR (YQR),

PPiU (PIT).

| | | |
|---|---|---|
| Hist | v.1, n.1, v.3, n.1-4, v.4, n.1-2; Fall, 1968, Winter/Spring, 1969 Winter-Dec., 1970, Spring-Summer, 1971 | Microforms Her. 1, R 17 |
| | v.3, n.1-v.6, n.1; Winter, 1970- Feb. 16/30, 1973 | HQ/1101/N2 |
| Wom Ed Res | [v.1, n.1-v.6, n.1]; [Fall, 1968- Feb. 16/30, 1973] | Circulation |

685 N.O.W.-Bakersfield. 1972-1974//? Monthly. Last issue 8 pages. Line drawings. Available on microfilm: Herstory. Published by the Bakersfield Chapter, National Organization for Women, Bakersfield, CA. Subject focus: employment, politics, feminism, Equal Rights Amendment, lobbying, rights.

| | | |
|---|---|---|
| Hist | v.1, n.3-v.2, n.6; Mar., 1972- June, 1973 | Microforms Her. 2, R 9 |
| | July, 1973- June, 1974 | Her. 2 UP, R 6 |

NOW Capital Alert. Sacramento, CA

   see Capitol Alert. Sacramento, CA

686 N.O.W.-Durham Chapter. 1973-1974//? Irregular. Last issue 1 pages. Line drawings. Available on microfilm: Herstory. Published by Durham Chapter, National Organization for Women, Durham, NC. Subject focus: feminism, Equal Rights Amendment, lobbying, rights.

| | | |
|---|---|---|
| Hist | Nov., 1973- June, 1974 | Microforms Her. 3, R 3 |

The N.O.W. Forum. Rochester, NY

   see The Forum. Rochester, NY

687 N.O.W.-Green Bay. 1972//? Irregular. Last issue 8 pages. Line drawings. Available on microfilm: Herstory. Published by the Green Bay Chapter, National Organization for Women, Green Bay, WI. Subject focus: feminism, Equal Rights Amendment, lobbying, rights.

| | | |
|---|---|---|
| Hist | June-Dec., 1972 | Microforms Her. 2, R10 |

688 N.O.W. Hear This.... 1971-1974//? Irregular. OCLC 2265289. Last issue 8 pages. Line drawings. Available on microfilm: Herstory (1971-1974). Published by the Portland Chapter, National Organization for Women, Portland, OR. Subject focus: child care, media, employment, politics, feminism, Equal Rights Amendment, lobbying, rights.

| | | |
|---|---|---|
| Hist | v.1, n.1-2; Apr. 14- Oct. 20, 1971 | Microforms Her. 1, R 19 |
| | v.1, n.2-v.3, n.4; Oct., 1971; May/June, 1973 | Her. 1 UP, R11 |
| | v.3, n.8-v.4, n.6; Aug., 1973- June, 1974 | Her. CUP, R5 |

689 N.O.W. Hear This!!. 1969-1970//? Monthly. OCLC 2265288. Last issue 12 pages. Line drawings. Available on microfilm: Herstory. Published by National Organization for Women, Greater Pittsburgh Chapter, Pittsburgh, PA. Title varies: as Women ARE People, June-Oct., 1969. Subject focus: feminism, Equal Rights Amendment, lobbying, rights, media, students, child care, pro-abortion.

| | | |
|---|---|---|
| Hist | v.1, n.1-v.2, n.6; June, 1969- June, 1970 | Microforms Her. 1, R19 |
| | v.2, n.6-9; June-Sep., 1970 | Pam 71-2708 |

690 N.O.W. Hear This. 1972-1974//? Irregular. Last issue 4 pages. Line drawings. Available on microfilm: Herstory. Published by Dallas County Chapter, National Organization for Women, Dallas, TX. Editors: Kathy Drake, Oct., 1972-June, 1973; Carol Holgren, July/Aug., 1973-June, 1974. Subject focus: rape, pro-abortion, politics, feminism, Equal Rights Amendment, lobbying, rights.

| | | |
|---|---|---|
| Hist | Oct., 1972- June, 1974 | Microforms Her. 3 R2-3 |

691 <u>N.O.W. in Annapolis</u>. 1974//? Weekly. Last issue 7 pages. Line drawings. Published by National Organization for Women, Annapolis Legislative Information Office of Maryland, Annapolis, MD. Subject focus: feminism, Equal Rights Amendment, lobbying, rights.

| Hist | v.1, n.1-15; Jan. 7- May 23, 1974 | Microforms Her. 3, R 2 |

692 <u>N.O.W. is the Time</u>. 1974//? Monthly. Last issue 3 pages. Line drawings. Available on microfilm: Herstory. Published by the Tri-State Chapter, National Organization for Women, Evansville, IN. Subject focus: rape, pro-abortion, education, feminism, Equal Rights Amendment, lobbying, rights.

| Hist | Apr.-June, 1974 | Microforms Her. 3, R 2 |

693 <u>N.O.W. is the Time</u>. 1973-1974//? Monthly. Last issue 6 pages. Line drawings. Available on microfilm: Herstory. Published by Thurston County Chapter, National Organization for Women, Olympia, WA. Subject focus: politics, child care, feminism, Equal Rights Amendment, lobbying, rights.

| Hist | v.1, n.1-3; Apr.-June, 1973 | Microforms Her. 2, R 12 |
| | v.1, n.4-v.2, n.6; July, 1973- June, 1974 | Her. 2 UP, R 8 |

<u>N.O.W. Knows</u>. Indianapolis, IN

see <u>IndiaNOWpolis Woman</u>. Indianapolis, IN

694 <u>N.O.W. Long Beach</u>. 1973-1974//? Monthly. Last issue 4 pages. Line drawings. Available on microfilm: Herstory. Published by the Long Beach Chapter, National Organization for Women, Long Beach, CA. Editor: Flo Pickett. Subject focus: child care, poverty, employment, education, feminism, Equal Rights Amendment, lobbying, rights.

| Hist | Aug., 1973- June, 1974 | Microforms Her. 3, R 3 |

695 <u>N.O.W. National F.C.C. Task Force</u>. 1972//? Unknown. Last issue 4 pages. Available on microfilm: Herstory (1972). Published by the National Organization for Women, National Federal Communication Commission Task Force, Chicago, IL. Subject focus: media, feminism, Equal Rights Amendment, lobbying, rights.

| Hist | Nov. 17, 1972 | Microforms Her. 2, R 11 |

696 <u>N.O.W. News</u>. 1970-1974//? Irregular. Last issue 6 pages. Line drawings, photographs, commercial advertising. Available on microfilm: Herstory. Published by the San Fernando Valley Chapter, National Organization for Women, Canoga Park, CA. Title varies: as N.O.W.sletter, May, 1970-Dec., 1972. Place of publication varies: Sherman Oaks, CA, May, 1970-June, 1973. Editors: Troyce Henry, May, 1970-June, 1973; Evelyn Retamal, July, 1973-Mar., 1974; Charlotte Ellis, May-June, 1974. Subject focus: education, feminism, Equal Rights Amendment, rights, lobbying.

| Hist | v.1, n.1-3,6; Mar.-July, Oct., 1970 | Microforms Her. 1, R 19 |
| | v.3, n.1-2, v.4, n.2-3; Nov.-Dec., 1972, May-June, 1973 | Her. 1 UP, R11 |
| | v.4, n.4-v.5, n.6; July, 1973- June, 1974 | Her. CUP, R5 |

697 <u>N.O.W. News</u>. 1970-1974//? Monthly. OCLC 2265303. Last issue 8 pages, last volume 132 pages. Line drawings. Available on microfilm: Herstory. Published by Sacramento Area Chapter, National Organization for Women, Sacramento, CA. Title varies: as The N.O.W. View, Oct., 1970-Apr., 1971; Sacramento N.O.W. Newsletter, Nov., 1971-Jan., 1974. Editors: Joyce Mason, July-Aug., 1973; Ruth Ordas, Sep., 1973-Jan., 1974; Pamela Graham, Mar.-June, 1974. Subject focus: politics, employment, marriage, family, feminism, Equal Rights Amendment, lobbying, rights.

| Hist | n.1-5; Oct., 1970- Apr., 1971 | Microforms Her. 1, R 19 |
| | v.1, n.3-v.2, n.3; Nov., 1971- June, 1973 | Her. 1 UP, R11 |
| | v.2, n.4-15?; July, 1973- June, 1974 | Her. CUP, R5 |

<u>N.O.W. News</u>. Fullerton, CA

see <u>Action N.O.W.</u> Santa Ana, CA

698 <u>N.O.W. News</u>. 1973-1974//? Irregular. Last issue 8 pages. Line drawings, commercial advertising. Available on microfilm: Herstory. Published by the National Organization for

Women, San Jose Chapter, San Jose, CA. Editor: Betty Turner. Subject focus: child care, politics, minority women, feminism, Equal Rights Amendment, lobbying, rights.

    Hist     v.2, n.1,3,5;    Microforms
               Nov., 1973-     Her. 3, R 3
               Jan., May, 1974

699 N.O.W. News. 1972. Monthly. Last issue 8 pages. Line drawings. Available on microfilm: Herstory. Published by Twin Cities Chapter, National Organization for Women, Minneapolis, MN. Editor: Miriam Butwin. Subject focus: employment, feminism, Equal Rights Amendment, lobbying, rights.

    Hist     July-Aug., 1972    Microforms
                                    Her. 2, R 12

NOW News. Phoenix, AZ

    see Phoenix Chapter Newsletter. Phoenix, AZ

700 N.O.W. News. 1972-1974//? Irregular. Last issue 8 pages. Line drawings. Available on microfilm: Herstory. Published by the Passaic County Chapter, National Organization for Women, Passaic, NJ. Title varies: as Chapter News, Oct., 1972-Jan., 1973. Place of publication varies: Clifton, NJ, Oct., 1972-Jan., 1973; Wayne, NJ, Feb.-June, 1973. Subject focus: religion, pro-abortion, education, feminism, Equal Rights Amendment, lobbying, rights.

    Hist     v.1, n.12-v.2,    Microforms
               n.5;              Her. 2, R 11
               Oct., 1972--
               June, 1973

               [v.2, n.6-v.3,    Her. 2 UP, R 8
               n.6];
               [Sep., 1973-
               June, 1974]

701 N.O.W. News. 1974//? Monthly. Last issue 3 pages. Line drawings. Available on microfilm: Herstory. Published by Northern Chautauqua County Chapter, National Organization for Women, Fredonia, NY. Subject focus: feminism, Equal Rights Amendment, lobbying, rights.

    Hist     v.4, n.2-3;     Microforms
               Feb.-Mar., 1974   Her. 3, R 3

702 The N.O.W. News. 1969-1974//? Irregular. OCLC 2265294. Last issue 6 pages. Line drawings. Available on microfilm: Herstory. Published by the New York State Chapter, National Organization for Women, Syracuse, NY. Title varies: as N.O.W. News and Notes, Nov., 1969-Oct., 1971. Place of publication varies: Skaneateles, NY, Nov., 1969-Oct., 1971. Editor: Gwen Kwik, Nov., 1969-Feb., 1973?; Dierdre Viera, Mar.-June, 1973. Subject focus: pro-abortion, child care, employment, religion, politics, education, feminism, Equal Rights Amendment, lobbying, rights, sexism in education.

    Hist     Nov., 1969-     Microforms
               Oct., 1971      Her. 1, R 19

               Nov., 1971-     Her. 1 UP, R8
               June, 1973

               July, 1973-     Her. CUP, R3
               June 3, 1974

703 N.O.W. News. 1972-1974//? Monthly. Last issue 4 pages. Line drawings. Available on microfilm: Herstory. Published by the Cincinnati Chapter, National Organization for Women, Cincinnati, OH. Title varies: as Cincinnati Chapter Newsletter, June, 1972-June, 1973. Subject focus: education, employment, feminism, Equal Rights Amendment, lobbying, rights.

    Hist     June, 1972-     Microforms
               June, 1973      Her. 2, R 9

               July, 1973-     Her. 2 UP, R6
               Feb., 1974

N.O.W. News. Los Angeles, CA

    see NOW! Los Angeles, CA

NOW News and Notes. Skaneateles, NY

    see The NOW News. Syracuse, NY

NOW Newsletter. Berkeley, CA

    see NOW. Berkeley, CA

NOW Newsletter. Los Angeles, CA

    see NOW! Los Angeles, CA

N.O.W. Newsletter. Newport Beach, CA

    see Laguna Beach Chapter - The N.O.W.s-letter. Laguna Beach, CA

N.O.W. Newsletter. Indianapolis, IN

    see IndiaNOWpolis Woman. Indianapolis, IN

N.O.W. Newsletter. St. Louis, MO

    see "... & Nothing Less". St. Louis, MO

N.O.W. Newsletter. Fairfield, OH

    see Up to N.O.W.  Fairfield, OH

704  N.O.W. Newsletter. 1973-1974//? Irregular. Last issue 6 pages. Line drawings. Available on microfilm: Herstory. Published by Fresno Chapter, National Organization for Women, Fresno, CA. Subject focus: politics, feminism, Equal Rights Amendment, lobbying, rights.

| Hist | Feb.-May, 1973 | Microforms Her. 2, R 10 |
|---|---|---|
|  | July, 1973-June, 1974 | Her. 2 UP, R 6 |

705  N.O.W. Newsletter. 1970-1974//? Irregular. OCLC 2263847. Last issue 1 page. Line drawings, photographs. Available on microfilm: Herstory. Published by the Marin County Chapter, National Organization for Women, San Rafael, CA. Title varies: as Marin N.O.W., May, 1970-June, 1971. Subject focus: feminism, Equal Rights Amendment, lobbying, rights, sexism.

| Hist | May, 1970, July-Oct., 1971 | Microforms Her. 1, R 18 |
|---|---|---|
|  | Aug., Dec., 1970, Jan.-June, 1971 | Her. 1, Add. |
|  | Nov., 1971-June, 1973 | Her. 1 UP, R9 |
|  | July, 1973-June, 1974 | Her. CUP, R 4 |

706  N.O.W. Newsletter. 1971-1974//? Monthly. Last issue 4 pages. Line drawings. Available on microfilm: Herstory. Published by the Santa Barbara Chapter, National Organization for Women, Santa Barbara, CA. Editors: Barbara Silver, Dec., 1971-Dec., 1972; Cynthia Larson, Jan.-Dec., 1973; Terri Arnold, Jan.-Feb., 1974; Tara Brown, Mar.-June, 1974. Subject focus: sexism, feminism, Equal Rights Amendment, lobbying, rights.

| Hist | v.1, n.1-v.2 n.16; Dec., 1971-May, 1973 | Microforms Her. 2, R 12 |
|---|---|---|
|  | v.2, n.10 [n.s] - v.3, n.6; Oct., 1973-June, 1974 | Her. 2 UP, R8 |

707  The N.O.W. Newsletter. 1971-1974//? Monthly. OCLC 2265296. Last issue 8 pages. Line drawings, photographs, commercial advertising. Available on microfilm: Herstory. Published by the Denver Chapter, National Organization for Women, Denver, CO. Subject focus: education, child care, pro-abortion, feminism, Equal Rights Amendment, lobbying, rights.

| Hist | Jan.-Sep., 1971 | Microforms Her. 1, R17 |
|---|---|---|
|  | Oct., 1971-June, 1973 | Her. 1UP, R 8-9 |
|  | July, 1973-June, 1974 | Her. CUP, R3 |

708  N.O.W. Newsletter. 1973-1974//? Irregular. Last issue 8 pages. Line drawings. Available on microfilm: Herstory. Published by: Peoria Chapter, National Organization for Women, Peoria, IL. Subject focus: feminism, Equal Rights Amendment, lobbying, rights.

| Hist | v.1, n.2-8; Nov., 1973-June, 1974 | Microforms Her. 3, R 3 |
|---|---|---|

709  N.O.W. Newsletter. 1970-1971//? Irregular. OCLC 2265297. Last issue 2 pages. Line drawings. Available on microfilm: Herstory. Published by: Muncie Chapter, National Organization for Women, Muncie, IN. Subject focus: employment, pro-abortion, politics, feminism, Equal Rights Amendment, lobbying, rights.

| Hist | [Apr. 15, 1970-June 9, 1971] | Microforms Her. 1, R 18 |
|---|---|---|

710  N.O.W. Newsletter. 1971-1974//? Monthly. Last issue 4 pages. Line drawings. Available on microfilm: Herstory. Published by Union County Chapter, National Organization for Women, Mountainside, NJ. Place of publication varies: Westfield, NJ, Apr., 1971-June, 1973. Subject focus: child care, pro-abortion, politics, feminism, Equal Rights Amendment, lobbying, rights, education.

| Hist | Apr., 1971-June, 1973 | Microforms Her. 2, R 12 |
|---|---|---|
|  | Summer, 1973-June, 1974 | Her. 2 UP, R8 |

711  N.O.W. Newsletter. 1969-1974//? Monthly. OCLC 2265298. Last issue 8 pages. Line drawings, commercial advertising. Available on microfilm: Herstory. Published by the Central New Jersey Chapter, National Organization for Women, Princeton, NJ. Subject focus: feminism, Equal Rights Amendment, lobbying, rights, child care, family, sexism, pro-abortion, employment, self-defense.

| Hist | May, 1969-Sep., 1971 | Microforms Her. 1, R 18 |
|---|---|---|

Oct., 1971–      Her. 1 UP, R 8
June, 1973

July/Aug., 1973–   Her. CUP, R 3
June, 1974

712 <u>N.O.W. Newsletter</u>. Monthly. 1970-1974//? OCLC 2269304. Last issue 10 pages. Line drawings, photographs. Available on microfilm: Herstory. Published by the New Mexico Chapter, National Organization for Women, Albuquerque, NM. Title varies: as The Revolution, Feb.-Mar., 1970; The Liberator, Apr., 1970; The Free Enquirer, May, 1970; Woodhull & Claflin's Weekly, June-Aug., 1970; La Mujer, Sep., 1970; La Voz De La Mujer, Oct., 1970-Nov., 1971. Editors: Kay F. Reinartz and Rob Stitig, Fe.-Apr., 1970; Kay F. Reinartz, May, 1970-Apr., 1971; Fran Hogan, May-Nov., 1971; Marcy Levine, Oct., 1972; Chris Soule, Judy Husa and Merrillee Dolan, Nov., 1972-May, 1973; Chris Soule and Merrillee Dolan, Sep., 1973-June, 1974. Subject focus: feminism, Equal Rights Amendment, lobbying, rights, politics, media, poetry, family, children, child care. Other holding institution: MCR-S (Schlesinger Library on the History of Women in America, Radcliffe College, Cambridge, MA).

Hist   v.1, n.2-v.2, n.8;   Microforms
       Feb., 1970–            Her. 1, R 19
       Aug., 1971

       v.2, n.9;              Her. 1, Add.
       July, 1970

       v.3, n.1-v.4, n.5;    Her. 1 UP, R 7
       Nov., 1971–
       May, 1973

       v.4, n.6-v.5, n.5;    Her. CUP, R 3
       Sep., 1973–
       June, 1974

713 <u>N.O.W. Newsletter</u>. 1973-1974//? Monthly. Last issue 4 pages. Line drawings, commercial advertising. Available on microfilm: Herstory. Published by Staten Island Chapter, National Organization for Women, Staten Island, NY. Subject focus: feminism, Equal Rights Amendment, lobbying, rights, politics, pro-abortion.

Hist   v.2, n.4,6;           Microforms
       Apr., June, 1973       Her. 2, R 12

       v.2, n.7-v.3, n.6;    Her. 2 UP, R 8
       July, 1973–
       June, 1974

714 <u>N.O.W. North</u>. 1971-1974//? Monthly. Last issue 10 pages. Line drawings. Available on microfilm: Herstory. Published by the North Suburban Chapter, National Organization for Women, Northbrook, IL. Title varies: as N.O.W.sletter, July-Sep., 1973. Place of publication varies: Skokie, IL, Nov., 1971-June, 1973. Subject focus: feminism, Equal Rights Amendment, lobbying, rights, politics, image.

Hist   v.1, n.1-v.2, n.6;    Microforms
       Nov., 1971–            Her. 2, R 11
       June, 1973

       v.2, n.7-v.3, n.6;    Her. 2 UP, R7
       July, 1973–
       June, 1974

715 <u>N.O.W. Notes</u>. 1969-1973//? Monthly? OCLC 2265299, 4962520. Last issue 8 pages. Line drawings. Available on microfilm: Herstory. Published by National Organization for Women, Atlanta Chapter, Atlanta, GA. Subject focus: feminism, Equal Rights Amendment, lobbying, rights, child care, employment, pro-abortion, politics, education, sexism.

Hist   v.1, n.1-v.3, n.3;    Microforms
       June, 1969–            Her. 1, R17
       Oct., 1971

       v.4, n.1-v.5, n.4;    Her. 1 UP, R 7
       Dec., 1971–
       May, 1973

       v.5, n.5,7–            Her. CUP, R3
       v.6, n.2;
       June/July,
       Sep.-Nov., 1973

716 <u>N.O.W. Notes</u>. 1973-1974//? Monthly. Last issue 12 pages. Line drawings. Available on microfilm: Herstory. Published by Erie County Suburban Chapter, National Organization for Women, Hiler, NY. Subject focus: rape, education, feminism, Equal Rights Amendment, lobbying, rights.

Hist   v.1, n.1-8;            Microforms
       Nov., 1973–            Her. 3, R 3
       June, 1974

717 <u>N.O.W. Notes</u>. 1972//? Irregular. Last issue 1 page. Available on microfilm: Herstory. Published by Tacoma Chapter, National Organization for Women, Tacoma, WA. Subject focus: feminism, Equal Rights Amendment, lobbying, rights.

Hist   v.1, n.1-4;            Microforms
       July-Nov., 1972        Her. 2, R 12

718 <u>N.O.W.-Now</u>. 1971-1974//? Monthly. Last issue 8 pages. Line drawings, photographs. Available on microfilm: Herstory. Published by Northern New Jersey Chapter, National Organization for Women, Ho-Ho-Kus, NJ. Title varies: as Newsletter, Oct.-Dec., 1971. Frequency varies: monthly, Oct., 1971-Aug., 1973;

irregular, Nov., 1973-Mar., 1974. Editors: Ruth Etzi, Oct., 1971-Feb., 1972; Valerie Woodworth, Mar., 1972. Subject focus: child care, politics, education, employment, feminism, Equal Rights Amendment, lobbying, rights.

| Hist | v.2, n.4-<br>v.3, n.12;<br>Oct., 1971-<br>June, 1973 | Microforms<br>Her. 1 UP, R10 |
|---|---|---|
|  | July, 1973-<br>Mar., 1974 | Her. CUP, R 4 |

N.O.W. or Never. Paris, France

    see P.O.W. Paris, France

719 N.O.W....or Never. 1972-1974//? Monthly. Last issue 4 pages. Line drawings. Available on microfilm: Herstory. Published by N.O.W....or Never, Southwest Cook County Chapter, National Organization for Women, Worth, IL. Title varies: as Southwest Cook County Chapter, N.O.W. Newsletter. Editor: Brucetta Alford, Nov., 1972-Feb., 1974. Subject focus: pro-abortion, feminism, Equal Rights Amendment, lobbying, rights.

| Hist | v.1, n.1-6;<br>Nov., 1972-<br>June, 1973 | Microforms<br>Her. 2, R 12 |
|---|---|---|
|  | v.1, n.8-v.2, n.2;<br>July, 1973-<br>Feb., 1974 | Her. 2 UP, R8 |

720 N.O.W.-Palo Alto Chapter. 1972-1974//? Irregular. Last issue 10 pages. Line drawings. Available on microfilm: Herstory. Published by the Palo Alto Chapter, National Organization for Women, Palo Alto, CA. Subject focus: consumerism, feminism, Equal Rights Amendment, lobbying, rights.

| Hist | Sep., 1972-<br>May, June, 1973 | Microforms<br>Her. 2, R 11 |
|---|---|---|
|  | July, 1973-<br>June, 1974 | Her. 2 UP, R7 |

721 N.O.W. Pamona Valley Chapter Newsletter. 1970-1974//? Irregular. OCLC 2265300. Last issue 4 pages. Line drawings. Available on microfilm: Herstory. Published by the Pamona Valley Chapter, National Organization for Women, Claremont, CA. Title varies: as Newsletter, July 24, 1970-Mar. 16, 1971. Editor: Jeane Shapiro, Sep./Oct., 1973-Summer, 1974. Subject focus: pro-abortion, feminism, Equal Rights Amendment, lobbying, rights, self-defense.

| Hist | July 24-<br>Sep., 1970-<br>Jan. 23-Mar. 16,<br>1971 | Microforms<br>Her. 1, R 19 |
|---|---|---|
|  | Sep., 1972-<br>June/July, 1973 | Her. 1, R 11 |
|  | Sep./Oct., 1973-<br>Summer, 1974 | Her. CUP, R 5 |

722 N.O.W. Peninsula Women's Coalition. 1973//? Monthly. Last issue 1 page. Line drawings. Available on microfilm: Herstory. Published by the Peninsula Women's Coalition-Chapter, National Organization for Women, Palos Verdes Estates/Rolling Hills Estates, CA. Editor: Elizabeth Stone. Subject focus: feminism, Equal Rights Amendment, lobbying, rights.

| Hist | v.2, n.5-6;<br>May-June, 1973 | Microforms<br>Her. 2, R 11 |
|---|---|---|

NOW Press. Shreveport, LA

    see Press on NOW. Shreveport, LA

723 N.O.W. Press. 1973-1974//? Irregular. Last issue 6 pages. Line drawings. Available on microfilm: Herstory. Published by the Solano County Chapter, National Organization for Women, Fairchild, CA. Title varies: as Lysistrada, May, 1973. Subject focus: self-defense, consciousness raising, feminism, Equal Rights Amendment, lobbying, rights.

| Hist | n.1;<br>May, 1973 | Microforms<br>Her. 2, R 12 |
|---|---|---|
|  | July, 1973-<br>Apr., 1974 | Her. 2 UP, R8 |

724 N.O.W. Regional News West. 1971//? Unknown. OCLC 2265301. Last issue 6 pages. Line drawings. Available on microfilm: Herstory. Published by National Organization for Women, Western Region, Costa Mesa, CA. Editors: Shirley Barnard and Joy Conners. Subject focus: feminism, Equal Rights Amendment, lobbying, rights, welfare, pro-abortion, self-defense.

| Hist | ?, 1971 | Microforms<br>Her. 1, R 17 |
|---|---|---|

725 N.O.W. San Diego County Chapter News. 1971-1974//? Monthly. OCLC 2265302. Last issue 4 pages. Line drawings, commercial advertising. Available on microfilm: Herstory. Published by San Diego County Chapter, National Organization for Women, San Diego, CA. Editors: Joan Casale Watkins, July 15, 1973-Apr., 1974; Joan T. Casale, May-June, 1974. Sub-

ject focus: employment, education, politics, religion, child care, professionals, pro-abortion, reproduction, feminism, Equal Rights Amendment, lobbying, rights.

| Hist | v.2, n.2-10; Feb.-Oct., 1971 | Microforms |
| --- | --- | --- |
| | v.2, n.11- v.4, n.6; Nov., 1971- June, 1973 | Her. 1 UP, R11 |
| | v.4, n.7- v.5, n.3; July 15, 1973- June, 1974 | Her. CUP, R 5 |

726 <u>N.O.W.-San Gabriel Valley Chapter</u>. 1973-1974//? Irregular. Last issue 4 pages. Line drawings. Available on microfilm: Herstory. Published by National Organization for Women, San Gabriel Valley Chapter, La Crescenta, CA. Editor: Etta Lee Flaherty. Subject focus: feminism, Equal Rights Amendment, lobbying, rights, employment, politics, rape, self-defense.

| Hist | v.2, n.11- v.3, n.6/7; Nov., 1973- May/June, 1974 | Microforms Her. 3, R 3 |
| --- | --- | --- |

<u>N.O.W.sletter</u>. Sherman Oaks, CA

   see <u>N.O.W. News</u>. Canoga Park, CA


<u>N.O.W.sletter</u>. Northbrook, IL

   see <u>N.O.W. North</u>. Northbrook, IL


727 <u>The N.O.W.sletter</u>. 1973-1974//? Monthly. Last issue 8 pages. Line drawings. Available on microfilm: Herstory. Published by Southern Prince George's County Chapter, National Organization for Women, Temple Hills, MD. Editors: Dolly Packard, Nov., 1973-Jan., 1974; Marj Chingan, Feb.-June, 1974. Subject focus: feminism, Equal Rights Amendment, lobbying, rights, child care, pro-abortion, education, housing, employment.

| Hist | v.2, n.11- v.3, n.6; Dec., 1973- June, 1974 | Microforms Her. 3, R 3 |
| --- | --- | --- |

728 <u>N.O.W.sletter</u>. 1971//? Monthly. Last issue 6 pages. Line drawings. Available on microfilm: Herstory. Published by Seattle-King County Chapter, National Organization for Women, Seattle, WA. Title varies: as A Voice N.O.W., Jan. 10-May 17, 1971. Editor: Linda Miller. Subject focus: feminism, Equal Rights Amendment, lobbying, rights, pro-abortion, employment, child care, legislation, education.

| Hist | v.1, n.2-7; Jan. 10-July, 1971 | Microforms Her. 1, R 20 |
| --- | --- | --- |

729 <u>N.O.W. Springfield</u>. 1973-1974//? Monthly. Last issue 3 pages. Line drawings. Available on microfilm: Herstory. Published by the Springfield Chapter, National Organization for Women, Springfield, IL. Editor: Linda Miller. Subject focus: feminism, Equal Rights Amendment, lobbying, rights, employment, politics.

| Hist | Oct., 1973- June, 1974 | Microforms Her. 3, R 3 |
| --- | --- | --- |

730 <u>N.O.W. Task Force:Marriage, Divorce, and Family Relations</u>. 1972-1973//? Last issue 4 pages. Line drawings. Available on microfilm: Herstory. Published by the National Organization for Women, Task Force on Marriage, Divorce, and Family Relations, Greenwich, CT. Editor: Betty Berry. Subject focus: marriage, divorce, family relations, feminism, Equal Rights Amendment, lobbying, rights.

| Hist | v.2, n.1; May 25, 1973 | Microforms Her. 2, R 11 |
| --- | --- | --- |

<u>The NOW View</u>. Sacramento, CA

   see <u>N.O.W. News</u>. Sacramento, CA


<u>N.O.W. Virginia Beach Chapter</u>. Virginia Beach, VA

   see <u>Right N.O.W</u>. Virginia Beach, VA


<u>N.O.W. What</u>? Thousand Oaks, CA

   see <u>Conejo Valley Chapter Newsletter</u>. Thousand Oaks, CA


731 <u>N.O.W. What</u>. 1972//? Unknown. Last issue 4 pages. Available on microfilm: Herstory. Published by the Princeton Chapter, National Organization for Women, Princeton, NJ. Sub-

ject focus: feminism, Equal Rights Amendment, lobbying, rights.

Hist    n.3;    Microforms
June, 1972    Her. 2, R 11

732    N.O.W. Women & Arts Task Force Newsletter. 1974//? Irregular. Last issue 12 pages. Line drawings. Available on microfilm: Herstory. Published by the National Organization for Women, Task Force on Women and the Arts, Rowayton, CT. Editor: Ann Roche. Subject focus: media, feminism, Equal Rights Amendment, lobbying, rights.

Hist    Jan., Spring,    Microforms
1974    Her. 3, R 3

733    N.O.W. York Times (Supplement to the New York Times). 1970-1971//? OCLC 2265304. Last issue 4 pages. Line drawings, photographs. Available on microfilm: Herstory. Published by New York City National Organization for Women, New York, NY. Editor: Nancy Borman. Subject focus: satire, humor, feminism, Equal Rights Amendment, lobbying, rights.

Hist    v.1, n.1,    Microforms
v.2, n.1;    Her. 1, R 2
Aug. 27, 1970,
Aug. 26, 1971

734    N.O.W. York Woman. (Supplement to the Manhattan Tribune). 1970-1971//? Irregular. OCLC 2265305. Last issue 4 pages. Line drawings, photographs. Available on microfilm: Herstory. Published by the New York City National Organization for Women, New York, NY. Editors: Donna Loercher and Mary Phillips. Subject focus: politics, feminism, Equal Rights Amendment, lobbying, rights.

Hist    May 2, Aug. 3,    Microforms
1970, May,    Her. 1, R 2
June,
July, 1971
Aug., 1971    Her. 1 Add.

735    The N.O.W. York Woman. 1971-1974//? Monthly. Last issue 16 pages. Line drawings, photographs, commercial advertising. Available on microfilm: Herstory. Published by National Organization for Women, New York City Chapter, New York, NY. Subject focus: pro-abortion, employment, education, feminism, Equal Rights Amendment, lobbying, rights.

Hist    Dec., 1971-    Microforms
June, 1973    Her. 1 UP, R10

v.2, n.1-12;    Her. CUP, R 4
July, 1973-
June, 1974

736    NTFP NEWS. 1979//. Unknown. Last issue 8 pages, size 45 x 29. Line drawings, photographs. Published by the National Task Force on Prostitution, San Francisco, CA. Editor: Pricilla Alexander. Subject focus: decriminalization of prostitution, prostitution.

Hist    v.1, n.1;    Circulation
Sep./Oct., 1979

737    NUC Women's Caucus. 1971//? Weekly. Last issue 17 pages, size 22 x 28. Published by John Brown Women's Caucus, Providence, RI. Subject focus: women's studies.

Hist    n. 7-8;    Pam 72-2671
Apr. 1-7, 1971

738    NUC Women's Caucus Newsletter. 1966-1970//? Irregular. OCLC 2265313. Last issue 18 pages. Line drawings, photographs. Available on microfilm: Herstory (1968-1970). Published by the Women's Caucus of the New University Conference Chicago, IL. Subject focus: poetry, sex education, sociology, media, collectives, education, politics, teaching.

Hist    v.3, n.1-10;    Microforms
Sep., 1968-    Her. 1, R 16
June 14, 1970

739    NWPC Newsletter. 1971. Irregular. $15 for individuals and institutions. Sharon Flynn, editor, NWPC Newsletter, 1921 Pennsylvania Avenue, NW, Washington, DC 20006. (202) 785-2911. OCLC 2365445. Last issue 4 pages, last volume 80 pages, size 22 x 28. Photographs. Published by National Women's Political Caucus, Washington, DC. Title varies: as W74 Win With Women, Jan./Feb.-Nov./Dec., 1974. Subject focus: politics, Equal Rights Amendment. Other holding institutions: MiEM (EEM), [University of Minnesota Union List, Minneapolis, MN] (MUL), WaU (WAU).

Hist    v.1, n.1-    Circulation
Dec. 10, 1971-

Wom Ed    v.1, n.1-    Circulation
Res    [Fall, 1977];
Dec. 10, 1971-
Fall, 1977

740    NYRF Newsletter. 1972-1974//? Monthly. Last issue 6 pages, size 36 x 22. Line drawings. Available on microfilm: Herstory. Published by the New York Radical Feminist, New York, NY. Editor: Judie Pasternak. Subject focus:

rights, rape, lesbians, prostitution, media, film reviews, satire, child care, radical feminism, sexism.

| Hist | v.2, n.9, v.3, n.2-5; Aug./Sep., 1972, Feb.-May, 1973 | Microforms Her. 2 R 13 |
|---|---|---|
|  | v.3, n.9-v.4, n.6; Sep., 1973-June, 1974 | Her. 2 UP, R 9 |
|  | v.3, n.9; Sep., 1973 | Pam 74-3312 |

741 N.Y. WSP Peaceletter. 1962-1974//? Irregular. OCLC 2265016. Last issue 4 pages. Line drawings, photographs. Available on microfilm: Herstory. Published by Women Strike for Peace/New York Women Strike for Peace, New York, NY. Title varies: as WSP Newsletter, Summer, 1962-July, 1967; WSP--New York Newsletter, Sep., 1967-Aug. 7, 1968. Subject focus: politics, prisons, peace movement, lobbying, draft.

| Hist | Summer, 1962-Sep., 1971 | Microforms Her. 1, R 23 |
|---|---|---|
|  | v.4, n.7-v.5, n.5; July, 1973-June/July, 1974 | Her. CUP, R 8 |

742 Napa Valley Women's Center Newsletter. 1973-1974//? Monthly. Last issue 7 pages. Line drawings. Available on microfilm: Herstory. Published by Napa Valley Women's Center, Napa Valley, CA. Subject focus: poetry, Chicanas, rights. In Spanish (10%).

| Hist | v.1, n.1-3; Apr.-June, 1973 | Microforms Her. 2, R 9 |
|---|---|---|
|  | July, 1973-May, 1974 | Her. 2 UP, R6 |

743 Nassau Herald's Sisterhood Week. 1971//? Weekly. Last issue 4 pages. Line drawings, photographs. Available on microfilm: Herstory. Published by Nassau Herald, Far Rockaway, NY. Editor: Nancy Borman. Subject focus: education, professionals, health, sexism in advertising, rights, self-help.

| Hist | v.1, n.1-11; Sep.-Dec. 16, 1971 | Microforms Her. 2, R 9 |
|---|---|---|

744 National Abortion Rights Action League Newsletter. 1969. Monthly. $5 for individuals and institutions. Rebecca Saady Bingham, editor, National Abortion Rights Action League Newsletter, 825 15th Street, N.W., Washington, DC 20005. Last issue 12 pages, size 22 x 28. Line drawings, photographs. Subject focus: pro-abortion, lobbying.

| Coll | Current Issues Only | Women's Reading Area |
|---|---|---|
| Wom Ed Res | v.11, n.4-May/June, 1979- | Circulation |

745 National Ad Hoc Committee for ERA. 1970//? Irregular. OCLC 2264580. Last issue 4 pages. Available on microfilm: Herstory. Published by National Ad Hoc Committee for ERA, Falls Church, VA. Subject focus: lobbying, Equal Rights Amendment.

| Hist | July 1-Nov. 30, 1970 | Microforms Her. 1, R 16 |
|---|---|---|

The National Altrusan. Shreveport, LA; Phoenix, AZ; Lincoln, NB

see International Altrusan. Chicago, IL

746 National Association for Women Deans, Administrators and Counselors. 1938. Quarterly. $12 for individuals and institutions. Dr. Patricia Rueckel, editor, National Association for Women Deans, Administrators and Counselors, 1625 I Street N.W., Suite 624-A, Washington, DC 20006. ISSN 0094-3460. OCLC 6134903, 6126013, 2394781, 6134841, 1794158. LC 74-644948. Last issue 48 pages, size 17 x 25. Indexed by: Education Index (1940-1973), Current Index to Journals in Education; Women Studies Abstracts. Available on microfilm: Herstory (1973), UnM (1938-1973). Published by the National Association for Women Deans, Administrators and Counselors. Previous editors: Ruth Strang, June, 1938-June, 1960; Kate Hevner Mueller, Oct., 1960-Fall, 1969; Bette J. Soldwedel, Winter, 1970-Summer, 1972; Dr. Margaret C. Berry, Fall, 1972-Summer, 1977. Subject focus: students, rights, educators, professionals. Other holding institutions: AU (ALM), ArU (AFU), AzFU (AZN), CLU (CLU), CLobS (CLO), COU-DA (COA), DLC (DLC), DeU (DLM), FBoU (FGM), FJUNF (FNP), FPeU (FWA), GASU (GSU), GCarrWG (CWC), GFoF (GFV), IC (CGP), ICL (IAL), [Indiana Union List of Serials, Indianapolis, IN] (ILS), InND (IND), KyLoU (KLG), MBNU (NED), MH-Ed (HMG), MWelC (WEL), MiEM (EEM), MiGrC (EXC), MiMtpT (EZC), [University of Minnesota Union List, Minneapolis, MN] (MUL), [New York State Union List, Albany, NY] (NYS), NBrockU (XBM), NCortU (YCM), NFQC (XQM), NGcCC (VVX), NIC (COO), N (NYG), NRU (RRR), NSbSU (YSM), NSyU (SYB), NUtSU (YTM), NcD (NDD), NcRS (NRC), NbU (LDL), OAkU (AKR), OBgU (BGU), OC1W (CWR), OKentU (KSU), OU (OSU), OYU (YNG), OkTU (OKT), OkU (OKU), PIm (IMM), PPD (DXU), PPiU (PIT), [Pittsburgh Regional Library Center-Union List, Pittsburgh, PA] (QPR), PU (PAU), RPB (RBN),

ScRhW (SWW), ScU (SUC), TMurS (TXM), TNJ (TJC), TxCM (TXA), [AMIGOS Union List of Serials, Dallas, TX] (IUC), TxDN (INT), TxDW (IWU), TxSmS (TXI), ViBlbv (VPI), WM (GZD), WMUW (GZN).

| | | |
|---|---|---|
| Hist | v.37, n.1; Fall, 1973 | Microforms Her. 3, R 2 |
| Mem | v.1, n.1- June, 1938- | AP/N283/A869/J |
| R&L | v.32, n.1- Spring, 1968- | Circulation |

747 National Business Woman. 1917. 9 times a year. $8.50 for individuals and institutions. Louise G. Wheeler, editor, National Business Woman, 2012 Massachusetts Avenue, N.W., Washington, DC 20036. ISSN 0027-8831. OCLC 1681024, 2262204, 4731580. LC 29-9228rev. Last issue 30 pages, last volume 300 pages. Line drawings, photographs, some in color. Published by the National Federation of Business and Professional Women's Clubs. Title varies: as The Independent Woman, Jan., 1926-Oct., 1956. Place of publication varies: New York, NY, Jan., 1926-May, 1956. Frequency varies: monthly, Jan., 1926-Dec., 1961; 11 times a year, Jan., 1962-Dec., 1975; 10 times a year, Jan./Feb., 1976-July/Aug., 1979. Previous editors: Alice Waller, Jan., 1926-Sep., 1927; Helen Havener, Feb., 1928-Dec., 1931; Winifred Willson, Feb., 1932-Apr., 1943; Frances Maule, June, 1943-Oct., 1955; Faye Marley, Nov., 1955-Aug., 1956; Bonnie C. Kowall, Sep., 1956-Dec., 1957; Lucy R. Baggett, Mar., 1958-Dec., 1970; Lola S. Tilden, Jan./Feb., 1971-Aug., 1976. Subject focus: rights, clubs, business, professionals. Other holding institutions: ArU (AFU), AzFU (AZN), AzTeS (AZS), DeU (DLM), CChiS (CCH), GA (GAP), IPB (IBA), InLP (IPL), KHayF (KFH), KLindB (KFB), LHS (LSH), MCR-S (Schlesinger Library on the History of Women in America, Radcliffe College, Cambridge, MA), MiMtpT (EZC), [University of Minnesota Union List, Minneapolis, MN] (MUL), NbU (LDL), NhP1S (PSM), [New York State Union List, Albany, NY] (NYS), NBu (VHB), [Western New York Library Resources Council, Buffalo, NY] (VZX), NIC (COO), N (NYG), NR (YQR), NSyU (SYB), OAkU (AKR), O (OHI), OO (OBE), OTU (TOL), OU (OSU), OY (YMM), OkT (TUL), PAnL (LVC), PCoR (ROB), PE1C (ELZ), PPi (CPL), [Pittsburgh Regional Library Center-Union List, Pittsburgh, PA] (QPR), PPiU (PIT), PPD (DXU), ScRhW (SWW), TNJ (TJC), TxAbH (TXS), TxBelM (MHB), TxCM (TXA), [AMIGOS Union List of Serials, Dallas, TX] (IUC), TxDN (INT), TxDW (IWU), TxLT (ILU), WaU (WAU), WM (GZD).

| | | |
|---|---|---|
| Mem | [v.10, n.1-v.24, n.4] v.24, n.6- [Jan., 1926- Apr., 1945] June, 1945- | AP/N273/B99 |
| MPL | v.48, n.1- Jan., 1964- | Business and Science Section |
| R&L | Jan., 1940- Dec., 1959 | Circulation |

748 The National Bulletin. 1891-1896//? Monthly. Last issue 4 pages, size 15 x 22. Published by The Women's Tribune, Washington, DC. Subject focus: pro-woman suffrage.

| | | |
|---|---|---|
| Hist | v.1, n.5-6,10, v.2, n.3,6,8, v.3, n.4-6; Feb.-Mar., 1891; Apr., June, Aug., 1894; Aug., 1895-Feb., 1896 | Pam 76-1786 |
| | v.1, n.5-7; Feb.-Apr., 1891 | KWZ/NA (Cutter) |

749 The National Citizen and Ballot Box. 1876-1881//? Monthly. OCLC 2255813, 1963936. LC 05-1526. Last issue 4 pages, last volume 24 pages. Line drawings, commercial advertising. Available on microfilm: CrP. Title varies: as The Ballot Box, Apr., 1876-Apr., 1878. Place of publication varies: Toledo, OH, Apr., 1876-Apr., 1878. Published by the Toledo Woman Suffrage Association, Syracuse, NY. Editors: Sarah R.L. Williams, Apr., 1876-Apr., 1878; Matilda Joslyn Gage, May, 1878. Subject focus: pro-suffrage. Other holding institutions: CSt (Stanford University), [University of Minnesota Union List, Minneapolis, MN] (MUL), MeB (BBH), NCaS (XLM), NhD (DRB), OKentU (KSU), TMurS (TXM).

| | | |
|---|---|---|
| Hist | v.1, n.1-v.6, n.6; Apr., 1876- Oct., 1881 | Microforms |

750 National Communications Network for the Elimination of Violence Against Women. 1977-1978//. Bi-monthly? Last issue 32 pages. Line drawings. Published by the National Communications Network for the Elimination of Violence Against Women, Cambridge, MA. Subject focus: rape, self-defense.

| | | |
|---|---|---|
| Hist | v.1, n.4-v.1, n.4 (sic); Dec., 1977- Feb., 1978 | Circulation |

National Council of Jewish Women Bulletin, Milwaukee Section, Milwaukee, WI

    see Bulletin, Milwaukee Section. NCJW, Milwaukee WI

National Council of Jewish Women, Milwaukee Section Bulletin. Milwaukee, WI

see Bulletin, Milwaukee Section. NCJW. Milwaukee, WI

751 National Council of Jewish Women Newsletter. 1933-1937//. Irregular. Last issue 78 pages, last volume 117 pages, size 22 x 28. Line drawings. Published by the National Council of Jewish Women, New York, NY. Subject focus: education, immigration, peace movement, social service, Jews.

| Hist | v.1, n.1-v.4, n.2; Jan., 1933- Spring, 1937 | F8399JE/+8N27 (Cutter) |

752 The National Council of Women of the United States Bulletin. 1966? Bi-monthly. $10 for individuals and institutions. Business address: 777 United Nations Plaza, New York, NY 10017. (212) 697-1278. Last issue 8 pages, size 21 x 27. Line drawings, photographs. Published by the National Council of Women of the United States, New York, NY. Subject focus: clubs, United Nations.

| Hist | v.27, n.9- Aug., 1980- | Circulation |

753 National Defense Bulletin. 1933-1938//. Irregular. Last issue 8 pages, last volume 44 pages, size 17 x 25. Line drawings. Published by the National Society of the Daughters of the Revolution, New York, NY. Editors: Margaret P. Coblentz, Oct./Nov., 1933-Apr./May, 1936; Lucy C. McDaniel, Oct./Nov., 1936-Mar./Apr., 1938. Subject focus: national security, politics, defense policy, immigration.

| Hist | v.1, n.1-v.5, n.4; Oct./Nov., 1933- Apr./May, 1938 | VA/23/A1/N3 |

National Information Memo. Washington, DC

see Memo. Washington, DC

754 The National League for Women's Service Weekly Bulletin. 1919?//. Weekly. Last issue 1 page, size 31 x 41. Published by the National League for Women's Service, New York, NY. Subject focus: social service, volunteers, war work.

| Hist | v.1, n.19, 21; Oct. 23, Nov. 6, 1919 | F836/+8NA (Cutter) |

755 National Magazine; or Lady's Emporium. 1830-1831//. Monthly. OCLC 1774017. Last issue 82 pages, last volume 240 pages. Available on microfilm: UnM, McA. Published in Baltimore, MD. Editor: Mary Barney. Subject focus: education, fiction, poetry. Other holding institutions: OKentU (KSU), [University of Minnesota Union List, Minneapolis, MN] (MUL), NcGU (NGU).

| Hist | v.1, n.1-v.2, n.3; Nov., 1830- July, 1831 | Circulation |

756 National N.O.W. Times. 1968. Monthly. $6 for students, members, $20 for individuals, $25 institutions. Toni Carabillo and Judith Meuli, editors, National N.O.W. Times, 1126 Hi-Point Street, Los Angeles, CA 90035. Business address: The National Organization for Women, Inc., 425 13th Street, NW, Suite 1048, Washington, DC. (202) 347-2279. ISSN 0149-4740. OCLC 6895953, 3494944, 2319299, 6895893. Last issue 16 pages, size 43 x 29. Line drawings, photographs, commercial advertising. Available on microfilm: WHi (1979-); microfiche: McP. Published by the National Organization for Women, Inc., Los Angeles, CA. Subject focus: politics, feminism, Equal Rights Amendment, lobbying, rights. Other holding institutions: CLU (CLU), CU-UC (UCU), COU-DA (COA), [Bureau of the Census, Washington, DC] (CBU), HU (HUH), IaDmG (IWG), ICMR (IBF), InU (IUL), MiEM (EEM), [University of Minnesota Union List, Minneapolis, MN] (MUL), NBrockU (XBM), NBronSL (VVS), [Western New York Library Resources Council, Buffalo, NY] (VZX), NR (YQR), OY (YMM), PBL (LYU), [AMIGOS Union List of Serials, Dallas, TX] (IUC), TxDW (IWU), WM (GZD).

| Hist | v.12, n.5- May, 1979- | Circulation |
| MPL | v.11, n.1- Dec., 1978/ Jan., 1979- | Literature and Social Science Section |
| Wom Ed Res | v.11, n.3- Mar., 1979- | Circulation |

757 The National News. 1927. Bi-monthly. $1 for individuals and institutions. Kitty Moore, editor, The National News, National Headquarters, 777 N. Meridian Street, Indianapolis, IN 46204. (317) 635-8411, ext. 200. Business address: Circulation Department, 2457 E. Washington Street, Indianapolis, IN 46201. Last issue 22 pages, last volume 282 pages, size 22 x 28. Line drawings, photographs, commercial advertising. Published by the American Legion Auxiliary, Indianapolis, IN. Title varies: The American Legion Auxiliary Bulletin, Jan.-Dec., 1935; National

News of the American Legion Auxiliary, Jan., 1936-Nov./Dec., 1974. Frequency varies: monthly, Jan., 1935-May, 1971. Previous editors: Mr. Lee J. Furran, Mar.-Aug., 1966; Mrs. Kathryn Steeg Arnold, Sep., 1966-May/June, 1972; Margaret R. Thompson, July/Aug., 1972-Nov./Dec., 1974. Subject focus: veterans, volunteers, clubs.

Hist    v.9, n.1-v.18, n.12;    D/570/A14/A3
v.25, n.1-v.43, n.7,
v.46, n.1-
Jan., 1935-
Dec., 1944,
Jan., 1951-
Nov./Dec., 1974,
Jan./Feb., 1977-

v.19, n.1-v.24,    Microforms
n.12;
Jan., 1945-
Dec., 1950

National News of the American Legion Auxiliary. Indianapolis, IN

see The National News. Indianapolis, IN

758 National Notes. 1971//? Unknown. Last issue 4 pages. Line drawings. Available on microfilm: Herstory. Published by the Intercollegiate Association of Women Students (IAWS), Columbus, OH. Subject focus: students, education.

Hist    Oct., 1971    Microforms
Her. 1, R 15

759 National Organization for Women-Ann Arbor. 1974//? Unknown. Last issue 6 pages. Line drawings. Available on microfilm: Herstory. Published by the Ann Arbor Chapter, National Organization for Women, Ann Arbor, MI. Editor: Barbara Fahmie. Subject focus: feminism, Equal Rights Amendment, lobbying, rights, health, poetry.

Hist    May, 1974    Microforms
Her. 3, R 2

760 National Organization for Women; National Task Force-Marriage, Divorce, and Family Relations Newsletter. 1973-1974//? Irregular. Last issue 6 pages. Line drawings. Available on microfilm: Herstory. Published by the National Organization for Women; National Task Force-Marriage, Divorce, and Family Relations, New York, NY. Editor: Betty Berry. Subject focus: marriage, divorce, family, Social Security, feminism, Equal Rights Amendment, rights, lobbying.

Hist    v.2, n.2-v.3, n.1;    Microforms
Aug., 1973-    Her. 2 UP, R8
Spring, 1974

761 National Publicity Committee Bulletin. 1933-1934//? Last issue 16 pages, size 27 x 42. Photographs. Published by National Society of the Daughters of the American Revolution, Washington, DC. Subject focus: history, education, citizenship, clubs.

Hist    Oct., 1933,    Pam 76-3744
Apr., Oct., 1934

762 National Society of United States Daughters of 1812 Bulletin. 1924?//. Unknown. Last issue 4 pages, size 16 x 26. Published by the National Society, United States Daughters of 1812, New York, NY. Subject focus: history, clubs, genealogy.

Hist    n.17;    EF/.8N27/NY
June, 1924    (Cutter)

763 National Society United States Daughters of 1812 News-letter. 1907. Tri-annual. Mrs. Charles G. Holle, editor, National Society United States Daughters of 1812 News-letter, 1461 Rhode Island Avenue, NW, Washington, DC 20005. Business address: 2540 Massachusetts Avenue, NW, Washington, DC 20005. (202) 462-4680. Last issue 87 pages, size 14 x 22. Photographs. Published by the National Society United States Daughters of 1812, Washington, DC. Place of publication varies: New York, NY, Feb. 8, 1907-Mar., 1927; Narberth, PA, June, 1927-June, 1931. Frequency varies: irregular, Feb. 8, 1907-Mar., 1919; tri-annual, June, 1919-June, 1927; quarterly, Oct., 1931-Mar., 1970. Previous editors: Mrs. Percy Young Schelly, July, 1940-Mar., 1943; Mrs. Lloyd DeWitt Smith, July, 1943-Oct., 1945; Mrs. Lucius W. McConnell, July, 1946-Dec., 1948; Mrs. Fredrick B. Ingram, July, 1948-Dec., 1951; Mrs. Fredric G. Bauer, July, 1952-Mar., 1955; Mrs. Herbert T. Windsor, July, 1955-Mar., 1958; Mrs. Vel Stephens, July, 1958-Mar., 1961; Mrs. Charles W. Crankshaw, July, 1961-Mar., 1964; Mrs. Henry P. Boggs, July, 1964-Mar., 1965; Mrs. Edward J. Owens, July, 1965-Mar., 1967; Mrs. Cecil T. Hays, July, 1967-Mar., 1970; Mrs. Ira J. Dietrich, July, 1970-Feb., 1973; Mrs. Enos A. Horst, July, 1973-Feb., 1976; Mrs. Earl L. Whitaker, July, 1976-? Subject focus: genealogy, clubs, history.

Hist    v.1, n.3-    E/351.6/A3
Feb. 8, 1907-

764 National Suffrage News. 1915-1917//? Monthly. OCLC 2395192. Last issue 20 pages, last

volume 80 pages. Line drawings, photographs. Available on microfilm: ResP (1916-1917). Published by the National American Woman Suffrage Association, New York, NY. Editor: Rose Young. Title varies: Headquarters Newsletter, Jan. 15, 1916-Jan., 1917. Subject focus:pro-suffrage. Other holding institutions: [Indiana Union List of Serials, Indianapolis, IN] (ILS), InU (IUL), [University of Minnesota Union List, Minneapolis, MN] (MUL), NR (YQR), OY (YMM), ScU (SUC), WM (GZD).

| Mem | v.2, n.1-v.3, n.4; Jan. 15, 1916- May, 1917 | Microforms |

765 The National Voter. 1951. Quarterly. $2 for individuals and institutions. Madelyn Bonsignore, editor: 1730 M Street, NW, Washington, DC 20036. (202) 296-1770. ISSN 0028-0372. OCLC 1604351. LC 66-93750, sn78-5555. Last issue 30 pages, last volume 120 pages, size 22 x 14. Line drawings, photographs. Published by the League of Women Voters of the United States, Washington, DC. Frequency varies: irregular, May 15, 1951-Jan., 1971; bi-monthly, Mar./Apr., 1971-Sep./Oct., 1972; 5 times a year, Nov./Dec., 1972-Jan./Feb., 1974. Previous editors: Ada Barnett Stough, May 15 -Nov. 1, 1951; Mrs. Alexander Guyol, Jan. 1, 1952-Aug. 31, 1954; Dorothy Felker Girton, Sep. 15, 1954-Mar., 1966; Mary Ellen Sayre, Apr.-Sep., 1966; Margaret O'Brien, Oct., 1966-Feb., 1967; Mary Youry, Apr., 1967-Aug./Sep., 1969. Subject focus: politics, lobbying. Other holding institutions: CLobS (CLO), CLU (CLU), CSdS (CDS), [Congressional Research Service, Washington, DC] (CRS), DLC (DLC), FMFIU (FXG), [Indiana Union List of Serials, Indianapolis, IN] (ILS), MCR-S (Schlesinger Library on the History of Women in America, Radcliffe College, Cambridge, MA), MMeT (TFW), MiMtpT (EZC), [University of Minnesota Union List, Minneapolis, MN] (MUL), [New York State Union List, Albany, NY] (NYS), [Western New York Library Resources Council, Buffalo, NY] (VZX), NFQC (XQM), N (NYG), NR (YQR), OKentU (KSU), [AMIGOS Union List of Serials, Dallas, TX] (IUC), WaU (WAU), WM (GZD).

| Hist | v.1, n.1- May 15, 1951- | E/740/N36 |

| R&L | v.12, n.8-v.27, n.2; Jan., 1963- Summer, 1977 | Circulation |

| MPL | Sep., 1971- Feb., 1973, Summer, 1974 | Literature and Social Science Section |

766 National Women's Political Caucus. 1971-1974//? Irregular. Last issue 3 pages. Line drawings. Available on microfilm: Herstory. Published by National Women's Political Caucus-Alameda County-Northern California, Berkeley, CA. Subject focus: politics, Equal Rights Amendment.

| Hist | July 11, 1971- June 17, 1973 | Microforms Her. 2, R 12 |
| | July 3, 1973- June, 1974 | Her. 2 UP, R8 |

767 National Women's Political Caucus. 1971-1974//? Irregular. Last issue 8 pages. Line drawings, photographs. Available on microfilm: Herstory. Published by the National Women's Political Caucus, National Headquarters, Washington, DC. Subject focus: politics, lobbying, Equal Rights Amendment, minorities.

| Hist | v.1, n.1-v.3, n.3; July 10, 1971- June, 1973 | Microforms Her. 2, R 13 |
| | v.2, n.5-v.3, n.4; July, 1973- May, 1974 | Her. 2 UP, R9 |

768 National Women's Political Caucus Newsletter. 1972//? Last issue 3 pages. Line drawings. Published by San Diego Chapter, National Women's Political Caucus, San Diego/La Jolla, CA. Subject focus: politics, lobbying.

| Hist | n.2; Apr. 6, 1972 | Microforms Her. 2, R 12 |

769 National Women's Political Caucus of Contra Costa County. 1974//? Last issue 2 pages. Line drawings. Available on microfilm: Herstory. Published by the National Women's Political Caucus of Contra Costa County, Walnut Creek, CA. Subject focus: politics, lobbying, rights.

| Hist | May, 1974 | Microforms Her. 3, R 3 |

770 National Women's Political Caucus-Orange County Chapter. 1973-1974//? Irregular. Last issue 2 pages. Line drawings. Available on microfilm: Herstory. Published in Irvine, CA. Editor: Vivian Hall. Subject focus: politics, rape, lobbying.

| Hist | v.1, n.1-3, v.2, n.1; Aug.-Oct., 1973, June, 1974 | Microforms Her. 3, R 3 |

771 National Women's Political Caucus-Southern California Section. 1971-1974//? Last issue 2 pages, last volume 14 pages. Line drawings. Available on microfilm: Herstory. Published by Los Angeles Metropolitan/Southern California Section, National Women's Political Caucus Los Angeles, CA. Subject focus: politics, lobbying, fund raising, Equal Rights Amendment.

    Hist        v.1, n.1-v.2, n.4;    Microforms
                Dec., 1971-          Her. 2, R 13
                June, 1973

                July, 1973-          Her. 2 UP, R 9
                June, 1974

772 Native Sisterhood. 1969-1976//. Irregular. ISSN 0703-9190. OCLC 3951264. LC cn78-30179. Last issue 22 pages, size 22 x 28. Line drawings. Published by Canadian Native Sisterhood Organization of Penitentiary Women, Kingston, Ontario, Canada. Editors: Elaine Antone, 1974; Violet Boucher, Feb., 1976. Subject focus: rights, fiction, prisoners, Native Americans, poetry. Other holding institutions: CaOONL (NLC), [University of Minnesota Union List, Minneapolis, MN] (MUL).

    Mem      ?, 1974-        Periodicals
           Feb., 1976     Room

Navy Wifeline. Washington, DC

    see Wifeline. Alexandria, VA

773 Network. 1978. Monthly. $7 for individuals and institutions. Network, 383 S. 6th East, Salt Lake City, UT 84102. (801) 532-6095. Last issue 20 pages, size 29 x 40. Line drawings, photographs, commercial advertising. Subject focus: finances, poetry, art, workers, biographies.

    Wom Ed    v.1, n.1,3,6,    Circulation
    Res        v.2, n.3-
            Apr., June,
            Sep., 1978,
            June, 1979-

774 Nevermind. 1973//. Quarterly. Last issue 38 pages, size 22 x 28. Line drawings. Published by the Nevermind Press, Sacramento, CA. Subject focus: poetry, art.

    RBR      v.1, n.1;      Circulation
          ?, 1973

775 New American Movement, Women's Newsletter on Socialist Feminism. 1973?//? Unknown. Last issue 12 pages. Line drawings. Available on microfilm: Herstory. Published by Charlotte Perkins Gilman Chapter of the New American Movement on Socialist Feminism, Durham, NC. Subject focus: socialist feminism.

    Hist      n.3;          Microforms
          June, 1973     Her. 2, R 13

776 New Books on Women and Feminism. 1979. Gratis for individuals and institutions. Linda Parker, editor, New Books on Women and Feminism, 728 State Street, Madison, WI 53706. (608) 263-5754. Last issue 96 pages, size 28 x 23. Available on microfilm: WHi. Published by the Women's Studies Librarian-at-Large, University of Wisconsin System, 112A Memorial Library, Madison, WI 53706. Subject focus: feminism, women's studies.

    Hist      n.1-          Circulation
          June, 1979-

777 The New Broom (A Legislative Newsletter for Massachusetts Women). 1970-1971//? Monthly. OCLC 2264826. Last issue 4 pages. Line drawings. Available on microfilm: Herstory. Published in Boston, MA. Subject focus: employment, politics, commissions on women, law, birth control, Equal Rights Amendment, pro-abortion, divorce. Other holding institution: MCR-S (Schlesinger Library on the History of Women in America, Radcliffe College, Cambridge, MA).

    Hist      v.1, n.1-11;    Microforms
          Oct., 1970-     Her. 1, R 16
          Sep., 1971

          v.1, n.12-13;   Her. 1 UP, R12
          Oct.-Nov., 1971

778 New Carolina Woman. 1970-1971//? Irregular. OCLC 2264829. Last issue 8 pages. Line drawings, photographs. Available on microfilm: Herstory. Published by the Women of Knightdale, Knightdale/Fayetteville, NC. Subject focus: welfare, poetry, law, consumerism, Equal Rights Amendment. Other holding institution: MCR-S (Schlesinger Library on the History of Women in America, Radcliffe College, Cambridge, MA).

    Hist      v.1, n.1-4;    Microforms
          Nov., 1970-     Her. 1, R 2
          Summer, 1971

779 The New Century for Woman. 1876//. Weekly. LC 9-13397. Last issue 8 pages, last volume 212 pages, size 42 x 30. Line drawings, commercial advertising. Self-indexed. Available on microfilm: ResP, McA. Published by the Women's Centennial Committee, Philadelphia, PA. Subject focus: employment, workers, Philadelphia Centennial Exhibition, poetry. Other holding institution: CtY (YUS).

|      |              |                |
|------|--------------|----------------|
| Hist | n.1-27;      | KWZ/"7NS32     |
|      | May 13-      | (Cutter)       |
|      | Nov. 11, 1876|                |
|      |              |                |
| Mem  | n.1-27;      | Microforms     |
|      | May 13-      |                |
|      | Nov. 11, 1876|                |

780 New Directions for Women. 1972. Quarterly. $4 for individuals, $7 for institutions. Paula Kassell, editor, New Directions for Women, 223 Old Hook Road, Westwood, NJ 07675. (201) 666-4677. ISSN 0160-1075. OCLC 3617120, 2366684. LC sn80-52. Last issue 24 pages, last volume 96 pages. Line drawings, photographs, commercial advertising. Available on microfilm: UnM (1973-), McP, Herstory (1973-1974). Published by New Directions, Inc., Westwood, NJ. Title varies: as New Directions for Women in New Jersey, Winter, 1975. Place of publication varies: Dover, NJ, Winter, 1975-Winter, 1976/1977. Previous editors: Paula S. Kassell, Jan., 1972-Spring, 1973; Paula S. Kassell and Janet Earley Manning, Summer, 1973-Winter, 1974; Vera Goodman, Spring, 1974. Subject focus: rights, health, workers, lobbying, child care, poetry, employment, law. Other holding institutions: CSt (Stanford University), INS (IAI), IU (UIU), InU (IUL), KMK (KKS), Ku-L (KFL), MBSi (SCL), [University of Minnesota Union List, Minneapolis, MN] (MUL), MoUst (UMS), NA1U (NAM), NNR (ZXC), NBronSL (VVS), NCH (YHM), NSchU (ZWU), NTRS (ZRS), OU (OSU), PHC (HVC), [AMIGOS Union List of Serials, Dallas, TX] (IUC), TxDW (IWU), VtU (VTU), WaU (WAU), WMUW (GZN), WyU (WYU).

|       |                      |                |
|-------|----------------------|----------------|
| Hist  | v.1, n.1-v.2, n.2;   | Microforms     |
|       | Jan., 1972-          | Her. 2, R 13   |
|       | Spring, 1973         |                |
|       |                      |                |
|       | v.2, n.3-v.3, n.2;   | Her. 2UP, R 9  |
|       | Summer, 1973-        |                |
|       | Spring, 1974         |                |
|       |                      |                |
|       | v.4-                 | Microforms     |
|       | Winter, 1975-        |                |
|       |                      |                |
| Coll  | Current Issues       | Women's        |
|       | Only                 | Reading Area   |
|       |                      |                |
| Wom St| v.7, n.1-            | Reading Room   |
|       | Spring, 1978-        |                |
|       |                      |                |
| Wom Ed| v.7, n.3-            | Circulation    |
| Res   | Autumn, 1978-        |                |

781 New Directions for Women in Delaware. 1973-1974//? Irregular. Last issue 12 pages. Line drawings. photographs, commercial advertising. Available on microfilm: Herstory. Published in Newark, DE. Editor: Gloria Stuber. Subject focus: politics, education, sports, health, children, lobbying, Equal Rights Amendment.

|      |                     |              |
|------|---------------------|--------------|
| Hist | v.1, n.1-v.2, n.1;  | Microforms   |
|      | Summer, 1973-       | Her. 3, R 3  |
|      | Summer, 1974        |              |

New Directions for Women in New Jersey. Dover, NJ

see New Directions for Women. Westwood, NJ

The New England Kitchen Magazine. Boston, MA

see Everyday Housekeeping. Boston, MA

782 New England Offering, and Mill Girls' Magazine. 1848-1850?//. Monthly. OCLC 1759777, 2848370, 2934437. LC cau07-5444. Last issue 24 pages, last volume 278 pages, size 21 x 14. Line drawings. Published by T.W. Harris, Greenwood Reprint Corporation, Westport, CT. Editor: Harriet Farley. Subject focus: fiction, poetry. Other holding institutions: CtY (YUS), NGenoU (YGM), [Indiana Union List of Serials, Indianapolis, IN] (ILS), KU (KKU), [University of Minnesota Union List, Minneapolis, MN] (MUL), MnStcls (MST), NNU (ZYU), NPV (VXW), PPiD (DUQ), [Pittsburgh Regional Library Center-Union List, Pittsburgh, PA] (QPR), PPiU (PIT), PSrS (STS).

|      |                   |               |
|------|-------------------|---------------|
| Hist | v.1, n.1-v.8, n.3;| HQ/1101/N45   |
|      | Apr., 1848-       |               |
|      | Mar., 1850        |               |

783 The New Era. 1885//?. Monthly. OCLC 1695668. Last issue 32 pages, last volume 384 pages, size 18 x 26. Line drawings, commercial advertising. Published in Chicago, IL. Editor: Elizabeth Boynton Harbert. Subject focus: fiction, poetry, suffrage, biographies. Other holding institutions: MCR-S (Schlesinger Library on the History of Women in America, Radcliffe College, Cambridge, MA), [University of Minnesota Union List, Minneapolis, MN] (MUL).

|      |                |            |
|------|----------------|------------|
| Hist | v.1, n.1-12;   | KWZ/N52    |
|      | Jan.-Dec., 1885| (Cutter)   |

784 The New Feminist. 1968-1971//? Irregular. OCLC 2264849. Last issue 12 pages. Line drawings, photographs. Available on microfilm: Herstory. Published by National Organization for Women, New York City Chapter, New York, NY. Editor: Rita Mae Brown. Subject focus: pro-abortion, education, family, child care, lobbying, feminism, Equal Rights Amendment, rights.

|      |                   |              |
|------|-------------------|--------------|
| Hist | v.2, n.7-8;       | Microforms   |
|      | Summer-Fall, 1969 | Her. 1, R19  |

785 The New Feminist. 1969-1973//? Quarterly. OCLC 2264848. Last issue 24 pages. Line drawings. Available on microfilm: Herstory, McL. Published by The New Feminists, Toronto, Ontario, Canada. Subject focus: rights, feminism, consciousness raising, sexism, poetry, media, education, politics, self-defense. Other holding institution: PPiU (PIT).

| | | |
|---|---|---|
| Hist | v.1, n.1,3,5-8, v.2, n.1-3; Nov. 17, 1969, Jan., Mar.-May, 1970, Jan.-July, 1971 | Microforms Her. 1, R 16 |
| | v.2, n.4-v.4, n.1; Oct., 1971- Mar., 1973 | Her. 1 UP, R12 |
| | v.1, n.8-v.4, n.1; Oct., 1970- Mar., 1973 | Pam 74-468 |
| | [Nov., 1969- May, 1971] | Her. 1, Add. |

786 The New Freewoman. 1913?//. Semi-monthly. Last issue 20 pages, size 22 x 32. Commercial advertising. Available on microfilm: British Library (1913-1919). Published in Oxford, England. Subject focus: poetry, philosophy, theatre reviews, fiction, art.

| | | |
|---|---|---|
| RBR | v.1, n.1-13; June 15- Dec. 15, 1913 | Circulation |

The New Lady's Magazine, or Polite and Entertaining Monthly for the Fair Sex. London, England

    see The New Lady's Magazine, or, Polite, Useful, and Entertaining Monthly for the Fair Sex. London, England

The New Lady's Magazine, or, Polite, Entertaining, and Fashionable Monthly for the Fair Sex. London, England

    see The New Lady's Magazine, or, Polite, Useful, and Entertaining Monthly for the Fair Sex. London, England.

787 The New Lady's Magazine, or Polite, Useful, and Entertaining Monthly for the Fair Sex. 1786-1795//. Monthly. Last issue 16 pages, last volume 192 pages. Line drawings. Self-indexed. Available on microfilm: ResP. Published by Alexander Hogg, London, England. Title varies: as The New Lady's Magazine, or, Polite and Entertaining Monthly for the Fair Sex, Feb.-Dec., 1786; as The New Lady's Magazine, or, Polite, Entertaining, and Fashionable Monthly for the Fair Sex, Jan., 1787-Feb., 1790; as The New Lady's Magazine, or, Polite, Useful, Entertaining, and Fashionable Monthly for the Fair Sex, Mar., 1790-Nov., 1791; The New Lady's Magazine, or, Polite, Useful, and Entertaining Companion for the Fair Sex, Dec., 1791-Dec., 1792. Editor: Rev. Mr. Charles Stanhope. Subject focus: poetry, biographies, music, cooking, fashion. In French (5%). Other holding institution: CtY (YUS).

| | | |
|---|---|---|
| Mem | Feb., 1786- Dec., 1795 | Microforms |

The New Lady's Magazine, or, Polite, Useful, Entertaining, and Fashionable Monthly for the Fair Sex. London, England

    see The New Lady's Magazine, or, Polite, Useful, and Entertaining Monthly for the Fair Sex. London, England

The New Lady's Magazine, or, Polite, Useful, and Entertaining Companion for the Fair Sex. London, England

    see The New Lady's Magazine, or, Polite, Useful, and Entertaining Monthly for the Fair Sex. London, England

788 The New Peterson Magazine. 1842-1898//. Monthly. OCLC 4260481, 4260509, 4260493, 2253974, 2254007, 2254002, 4260501. Last issue 102 pages, last volume 568 pages, size 15 x 24. Line drawings, photographs, some in color, commercial advertising. Self-indexed (1847-1848, 1852-1854, 1857-1880, 1883, 1885, 1887-1892). Available on microfilm: UnM (1842-1897). Published by Penfield Publishing Co., Philadelphia, PA. Title varies: as Ladies National Magazine, Jan., 1847-Dec., 1848; Peterson's Magazine, Jan., 1853-Nov., 1892. Editor: Mrs. Ann S. Stephens, Jan., 1847-May, 1855. Subject focus: fiction, poetry, fashion, arts, crafts. Other holding institutions: AU (ALM), ArU (AFU), AzTeS (AZS), CtHT (TYC), [Indiana Union List of Serials, Indianapolis, IN] (ILS), LU (LUU), [University of Minnesota Union List, Minneapolis, MN] (MUL), NA1f (YAH), NR (YQR), NSbSU (YSM), NVP (VXW), NbCrD (NBD), NcCU (NKM), OC1 (CLE), OC1W (CWR), OKentU (KSU), PAnL (LVC), [AMIGOS Union List of Serials, Dallas, TX] (IUC), WaU (WAU), WM (GZD), WMUW (GZN).

| | | |
|---|---|---|
| Hist | v.11, n.1-v.14, n.6, v.23, n.1-v.24, n.6, v.27, n.5, v.31, n.1-v.78, n.6, v.83, n.1-v.84, n.6, v.87, n.1-v.88, n.6, v.91, n.1-v.102, n.6; | AP83/PE46 |

Jan., 1847-Dec., 1848,
Jan., 1853-Dec., 1854,
May, 1855, Jan., 1857-
Dec., 1880, Jan.-Dec., 1883,
Jan.-Dec., 1885,
Jan., 1887-Dec., 1892

789 The New Voter. 1910-1911//? Monthly. Last issue 10 pages, last volume 90 pages. Line drawings, commercial advertising. Available on microfilm: ResP. Published by The Equal Suffrage League, Baltimore, MD. Frequency varies: semi-monthly, Nov. 15, 1910-Feb. 15, 1911. Editor: Anne M. Wagner. Subject focus: pro-suffrage, politics. Other holding institution: MCR-S (Schlesinger Library on the History of Women in America, Radcliffe College, Cambridge, MA).

| Mem | v.1, n.1-10; Nov. 15, 1910- May 1, 1911 | Microforms |

790 New Woman. 1971. Bi-monthly. $11 for individuals and institutions. Margaret Harold Whitehead, editor, New Woman, 314 Royal Poinciana Way, Palm Beach, FL 33480. Business address: P.O. Drawer 189, Palm Beach, FL 33480. ISSN 0028-6974. OCLC 5854140, 2251312. LC 75-25971. Last issue 112 pages, last volume 1344 pages, size 21 x 28. Line drawings, photographs, some in color, commercial advertising. Available on microfilm: UnM. Published by New Woman, Inc., Palm Beach, FL. Subject focus: beauty care, health, food, workers. Other holding institutions: CtY (YUS), DLC (DLC), FJUNF (FNP), GASU (GSU), [Indiana Union List of Serials, Indianapolis, IN] (ILS), KSteC (KKQ), KYBB (KBE), LLafS (LWA), MCR-S (Schlesinger Library on the History of Women in America, Radcliffe College, Cambridge, MA), MBU (BOS), MnDuU (MND), [University of Minnesota Union List, Minneapolis, MN] (MUL), NCorniCC (ZDG), NOneoU (ZBM), NcD (NDD), NbU (LDL), NjLincB (BCC), NjParB (BER), OAkU (AKR), OMC (MRC), [Pittsburgh Regional Library Center-Union List, Pittsburgh, PA] (QPR), PPiU (PIT), TxAU (TXG), [AMIGOS Union List of Serials, Dallas, TX] (IUC), TxDN (INT), TxDW (IWU).

| MPL | v.8, n.2- Mar./Apr., 1978- | Literature and Social Science Section |

791 New Womankind. 1973//? Irregular. Last issue 6 pages. Line drawings. Available on microfilm: Herstory. Published in Louisville, KY. Subject focus: pro-abortion, politics, rights.

| Hist | v.1, n.4-5; Oct.-Dec., 1973 | Microforms Her. 3, R 4 |

792 New Women's Times. 1975. Monthly. $15 for individuals, $30 for institutions. New Women's Times, 804 Meigs Street, Rochester, NY 14620. ISSN 0161-164X. OCLC 3885912. LC sc79-4421, sn78-5963. Last issue 12 pages, last volume 144 pages, size 29 x 44. Line drawings, photographs, commercial advertising. Published by New Women's Times, Inc., Rochester. NY 14620. Frequency varies: bi-weekly, Oct., 1978-Aug., 1980. Subject focus: rights, politics, employment, health. Other holding institutions: IU (UIU), NEE (VXE), NOneoU (ZBM), NR (YQR), OU (OSU), WU (GZM).

| Hist | v.1, n.1- Jan., 1975- | Circulation |
| Coll | Current Issues Only | Women's Reading Area |

793 New York State N.O.W. 1974//? Monthly. Last issue 16 pages. Line drawings. Available on microfilm: Herstory. Published by New York State Chapter, National Organization for Women, Fredonia, NY. Editor: Joanne Schweik. Subject focus: feminism, Equal Rights Amendment, lobbying, rights.

| Hist | v.1, n.1; June, 1974 | Microforms Her. 3, R 3 |

New York Weekly Museum. New York, NY

see The New York Weekly Museum, or Polite Repository of Amusement and Instruction. New York, NY

794 The New York Weekly Museum, or Polite Repository of Amusement and Instruction. 1788?-1817//. Weekly. Last issue 8 pages, last volume 408 pages, size 12 x 21. Self-indexed, 1812-1816. Available on microfilm: UnM (1788-1817). Published in New York, NY. Title varies: The Weekly Museum, July 7, 1792-Aug. 10, 1805; New York Weekly Museum, Aug. 17, 1805. Subject focus: poetry, fiction, obituaries, marriage announcements.

| Hist | [v.5, n.217- v.3[n.s.] n.26] [July 7, 1792- Apr. 27, 1816] | AP/2/"L22/ Rare Book Collection |

795 New Yorkers for Abortion Law Repeal Newsletter. 1970-1973//? Irregular. OCLC 1343301. Last issue 12 pages. Line drawings. Available on microfilm: Herstory. Published by New Yorkers for Abortion Law Repeal, New York, NY. Subject focus: pro-abortion, law, politics, media.

| Hist | v.2, n.2; Feb., 1970 | Microforms Her. 1, R 17 |

*Women's Periodicals and Newspapers*

        Mar., 1972-     Her. 1 UP, R12
        Apr., 1973

796  <u>Newfoundland Status of Women Council Newspaper</u>. 1974. Irregular. $5 for individuals, $10 for institutions. Newfoundland Status of Women Council Newsletter, P.O. Box 6072, St. Johns, Newfoundland, A1C 5X8. (709) 753-0220. Last issue 16 pages, last volume 120 pages, size 22 x 28. Line drawings. Published by Newfoundland Status of Women Council, St. Johns, Newfoundland. Subject focus: rights, politics, labor unions, poetry, law, workers.

    Hist     v.1, n.1-     HQ/1459/N4/N43
             Jan./Feb., 1974-

797  <u>News</u>. 1972//? Unknown. Last issue 4 pages, size 22 x 28. Published by the Women's Liberation Center, Philadelphia, PA. Subject focus: feminism.

    Hist     Jan., 1972     Pam 74-3407

    <u>News and Notes from the Feminist Press</u>.
        Old Westbury, NY

        see <u>Women's Studies Newsletter</u>.
        Old Westbury, NY

    <u>News and Opinions of Women</u>.  San Francisco, CA

        see <u>Woman N.O.W.</u>  San Francisco, CA

798  <u>News and Views</u>. 1971-1973//. Monthly. Last issue 2 pages. Line drawings. Available on microfilm: Herstory. Published by the Willamette Valley Chapter, National Organization for Women, Salem, OR. Subject focus: feminism, Equal Rights Amendment, lobbying, rights, employment, affirmative action.

    Hist     v.1, n.1-6;     Microforms
             Dec., 1971-     Her. 2, R 12
             May, 1972

799  <u>News and Views from Federally Employed Women</u>. 1969. Bi-monthly. $8 for individuals and institutions. Tracy Cook, editor, News and Views from Federally Employed Women, National Press Building, No. 481, Washington, DC 20045. (202) 638-4404. ISSN 0162-2471, 0047-3477. OCLC 4143917, 2326157. LC sn78-238, sn78-4946. Last issue 16 pages, last volume 72 pages, size 22 x 28. Line drawings, photographs, commercial advertising. Available on microfilm: McP (1969-1976), Herstory (1969-1974). Published by Federally Employed Women, Inc., Washington, DC. Title varies: as F.E.W.'S News and Views, June, 1969-June/July, 1979. Frequency varies: irregular, June, 1969-June, 1974. Previous editors: Barbara Boardman, Jan., 1970-Apr., 1971; B. Tennant, Feb., 1972-Jan., 1973; Anne Stommel and Dorothy Williams, May-Dec., 1973; Daisy B. Fields, Apr.-Aug., 1974; Julie Kisielewski, Oct., 1974-June, 1975; Daisy B. Fields, Aug./Sep., 1975-Dec., 1977/Jan., 1978; Julie A. Corvalho and Mary Fuller, Feb./Mar., 1978-June/July, 1979. Subject focus: Equal Rights Amendment, lobbying, employment, government workers, professionals. Other holding institution: DME/DAS (OLA).

    Hist     v.1, n.2-     Circulation
             June, 1969-

             v.1, n.2, v.2,    Microforms
             n.2-v.3, n.4;    Her. 1, Add
             June, 1969,
             Jan., 1970-
             Aug., 1971

             Aug., 1970     Her. 1, R 14

             v.4, n.1-v.5, n.4;  Her. 1 UP, R4
             Nov., 1971-
             May, 1973

             v.6, n.1-v.7, n.3;  Her. CUP, R2
             Aug., 1973-
             June, 1974

    Wom Ed   v.2, n.1-v.10,   Circulation
    Res      n.2;
             Oct., 1969-
             Oct./Nov., 1976

800  <u>News Bulletin</u>. 1953-1974?//. Irregular. ISSN 0538-2912. OCLC 2302002. Last issue 42 pages, size 22 x 28. Line drawings, photographs. Published by the Inter-American Commission of Women, Washington, DC. Subject focus: Latin America, rights. Other holding institutions: AzU (AZU), DeU (DLM), [Indiana Union List of Serials, Indianapolis, IN] (ILS), MWelC (WEL), [New York State Union List, Albany, NY] (NYS), NIC (COO).

    Mem     n.18-31;     HQ/1239/I474
            July/Dec., 1961-
            Sep., 1974

801  <u>News Bulletin</u>. 1922?-1926?//. Unknown. Last issue 4 pages, size 22 x 28. Line drawings, photographs. Published by Woman's Board of Missions of the Interior, Chicago, IL. Subject focus: missions.

    Hist     [Jan., 1922-    DS/WO
             Sep., 1926]     (Cutter)

802  <u>News Bulletin</u>. 1923-1924//? Irregular. Last issue 2 pages, size 22 x 33. Published by the American Legion Auxiliary Department of Wyoming, Rawlins, WY. Title varies: as

Bulletin, ?, 1923-Dec., 1923. Subject focus: clubs.

    Hist    ?, 1923-    F836/8A51A/WY
            Apr. 5, 1924    (Cutter)

803 News for N.O.W. 1973-1974//? Irregular. Last issue 4 pages. Line drawings. Available on microfilm: Herstory. Published by the Orlando Chapter, National Organization for Women, Orlando, FL. Editor: Joyce Chumbley. Subject focus: rape, consciousness raising, law, feminism, Equal Rights Amendment, lobbying, rights.

    Hist    Nov. 27, 1973,    Microforms
            Jan. 26, 1974    Her. 3, R 3

News from EVE. Union, NJ

    see The EVE News. Union, NJ

804 News From FEPC. 1971-1974//? Irregular. Last issue 4 pages. Photographs. Available on microfilm: Herstory. Published by the Fair Employment Practice Commission, Dept. of Industrial Relations, Division of Fair Employment Practices, San Francisco, CA. Title varies: as FEPC News, Apr./May, 1971-June/July, 1973. Subject focus: employment, affirmative action, law, sexism in employment.

    Hist    n.42-47;    Microforms
            Apr./May, 1971-    Her. 2, R 4
            June/July, 1973

            July 6, 1973-    Her. 2 UP, R 3
            May 8, 1974

805 News From the National Organization for Women. 1972//? Last issue 2 pages. Available on microfilm: Herstory. Published by Fullerton Chapter, National Organization for Women, Fullerton, CA. Subject focus: feminism, Equal Rights Amendment, lobbying, rights.

    Hist    Mar. 30, 1972    Microforms
                             Her. 2, R 10

806 News From the Woman's Institute. 1974//? Last issue 3 pages. Line drawings. Available on microfilm: Herstory. Published by Bergen Community College, Division of Community Services, Paramus, NJ. Subject focus: art, education.

    Hist    v.1, n.1-2;    Microforms
            ?, 1974    Her. 3, R 5

News Letter. Northampton, MA

    see D.A.R. News Letter. Northampton, MA

807 News Letter. 1926?//. Monthly. Last issue 6 pages, size 22 x 28. Published by the American Legion Auxiliary, Department of Pennsylvania, Philadelphia, PA. Subject focus: clubs.

    Hist    Feb.-Mar., 1926    F836/+8A51A/PA
                                (Cutter)

808 The News Sheet-Notes From the Committee to Promote Women's Studies. 1974//? Unknown. OCLC 2367921. Last issue 4 pages. Line drawings. Available on microfilm: Herstory. Published by National Organization for Women, Committee to Promote Women's Studies, Cherry Hill, NJ. Editors: Elaine Heffernan and Sarah Slavin Schramm. Subject focus: women's studies, education.

    Hist    n.1;    Microforms
            Apr., 1974    Her. 3, R 2

809 Newsette, The Private Weekly Letter for Women. 1959//? Weekly. Last issue 4 pages, size 22 x 28. Line drawings. Published by Newsette Publishing Company, Washington, DC. Subject focus: economics, investments.

    Hist    Feb. 10, 1959    Pam 76-4287

810 Newsheet for the Conference of Indochinese and North American Women, Vancouver, British Columbia, Canada. 1971//? Unknown. OCLC 2265093. Last issue 2 pages. Available on microfilm: Herstory. Published by the Conference of Indochinese and North American Women, Vancouver, British Columbia, Canada. Editor, Marie Cardiasmenos. Subject focus: sexism, racism.

    Hist    July, 1971    Microforms
                          Her. 1, R 16

Newsletter. Phoenix, AZ

    see Phoenix Chapter Newsletter. Phoenix, AZ

811 Newsletter. 1970//? Unknown. OCLC 2267438. Last issue 1 page. Available on microfilm: Herstory. Published by San Francisco Bay Area Women in Technical Trades, Berkeley, CA. Subject focus: employment, labor unions, workers.

    Hist    May 23, 1970    Microforms
                           Her. 1, R 20

Newsletter. Claremont, CA

    see N.O.W. Panoma Valley Chapter Newsletter. Claremont, CA

Newsletter. Corte Madera, CA

    see Women's International League for Peace and Freedom, Marin Branch. Corte Madera, CA

812 Newsletter. 1966//? Unknown. OCLC 2269621. Last issue 1 page. Available on microfilm: Herstory. Published by the Women's International League for Peace and Freedom, Livermore Branch, Livermore, CA. Subject focus: peace movement.

    Hist    Nov., 1966    Microforms Her. 1, R 22

813 Newsletter. 1969//? Unknown. OCLC 2269629. Last issue 2 pages. Available on microfilm: Herstory. Published by Women's International League for Peace and Freedom, San Mateo Branch, Millbrae, CA. Subject focus: peace movement.

    Hist    Oct., 1969    Microforms Her. 1, R 22

814 Newsletter. 1967-1970//? Irregular. OCLC 2269627. Last issue 3 pages. Line drawings. Available on microfilm: Herstory. Published by Women's International League for Peace and Freedom, Northern California Branch, Monterey, CA. Subject focus: peace movement, rights.

    Hist    June 19, 1967-    Microforms Jan. 30, 1970    Her. 1, R 22

815 Newsletter. 1969//? Unknown. OCLC 2269628. Last issue 2 pages. Available on microfilm: Herstory. Published by the Women's International League for Peace and Freedom, San Gabriel Valley Branch, Monterey Park, CA. Editor: Mrs. Maurice Saiger. Subject focus: peace movement.

    Hist    June, 1969    Microforms Her. 1, R 22

Newsletter. Palo Alto, CA

    see Women's International League for Peace and Freedom, Palo Alto Branch. Palo Alto, CA

816 Newsletter. 1971//? Unknown. OCLC 2269616. Last issue 1 page. Line drawings, photographs. Available on microfilm: Herstory. Published by Women's Ad-Hoc Abortion Coalition, San Francisco, CA. Subject focus: pro-abortion, law, lobbying.

    Hist    June 8, 28, 1971    Microforms Her. 1, R 22

Newsletter. San Mateo, CA

    see San Mateo County N.O.W. News. Burlingame, CA

Newsletter. San Pedro, CA

    see Harbor - South Bay Chapter Newsletter. San Pedro, CA

817 Newsletter. 1970//? Unknown. OCLC 2269625. Last issue 3 pages. Line drawings. Available on microfilm: Herstory. Published by the Women's International League for Peace and Freedom, Monterey Peninsula Branch, Seaside, CA. Editor: Jocelyn Tyler. Subject focus: peace movement.

    Hist    Nov. 24, 1970    Microforms Her. 1, R 22

818 Newsletter. 1971//? Unknown. OCLC 2268928. Last issue 16 pages. Line drawings, photographs. Available on microfilm: Herstory. Published by the United Women's Contingent, Washington, DC. Subject focus: peace movement, rights.

    Hist    n.2;    Microforms Apr. 2-24, 1971    Her. 1, R 22

819 Newsletter. 1971//? Unknown. OCLC 2264703. Last issue 4 pages. Available on microfilm: Herstory. Published by National Organization for Women, Des Moines Chapter, Des Moines, IA. Subject focus: feminism, Equal Rights Amendment, lobbying, rights.

    Hist    Sep., 1971    Microforms Her. 1, R 18

820 Newsletter. 1971-1973//? Irregular. OCLC 2264708. Last issue 3 pages. Line drawings. Available on microfilm: Herstory. Published by the Wichita Chapter National Organization for Women, Wichita, KS. Subject focus: education, politics, rape, feminism, Equal Rights Amendment, lobbying, rights, employment.

    Hist    Sep. 20, 1971    Microforms Her. 1, R 20

            Oct. 1, 1971-    Her. 1 UP, R12 Summer, 1973

## Women's Periodicals and Newspapers

        Sep., 1973        Her. CUP, R 6

821 Newsletter. 1970-1974//? Irregular. Monthly. OCLC 2260562. Last issue 16 pages. Line drawings. Available on microfilm: Herstory. Published by the Eastern Massachusetts Chapter, National Organization for Women, Boston, MA. Subject focus: pro-abortion, education, employment, media, film reviews, consciousness raising.

| Hist | Apr., June, Sep., 1970 | Microforms Her. 1, Add |
|---|---|---|
|  | v.2, n.1-9; Jan.-Sep., 1971 | Her. 1, R 18 |
|  | v.2, n.9-v.4, n.6; Oct., 1971-June, 1973 | Her. 1 UP, R 8 |
|  | July, 1973-June 1, 1974 | Her. CUP, R 4 |

822 Newsletter. 1970//? Unknown. OCLC 2269626. Last issue 4 pages. Available on microfilm: Herstory. Published by the Women's International League for Peace and Freedom, New England Regional Conference, Boston, MA. Subject focus: peace movement, politics, rights.

| Hist | Nov. 11, 1970 | Microforms Her. 1, R 22 |
|---|---|---|

Newsletter. Martha's Vineyard, MA

    see Image of Women Task Force. Martha's Vineyard, MA

Newsletter. Ho-Ho-Kus, NJ

    see N.O.W.-NOW. Ho-Ho-Kus, NJ

823 Newsletter. 1970-1971//? Irregular. OCLC 2265209. Last issue 12 pages. Available on microfilm: Herstory. Published by the Northern New Jersey Chapter, National Organization for Women, Westwood, NJ. Title varies: as Northern New Jersey Chapter, N.O.W., Sep., 1970-June, 1971. Editor: Ruth Rozett. Subject focus: children, media, feminism, Equal Rights Amendment, lobbying, rights, child care, education, self-defense, pro-abortion.

| Hist | v.1, n.3-13, v.2, n.3; Sep., 1970-June, Sep., 1971 | Microforms Her. 1, Add |
|---|---|---|
|  | v.1, n.11-13; Apr.-June, 1971 | Her. 1, R 19 |

Newsletter. Brooklyn, NY

    see Brooklyn N.O.W. News. Brooklyn, NY

824 Newsletter. 1969-1974//? Monthly. OCLC 2263682. Last issue 12 pages. Line drawings, photographs. Available on microfilm: Herstory. Published by the Long Island/Nassau Chapter, National Organization for Women, Great Neck, NY. Frequency varies: irregular, Dec. 4, 1969-Oct./Nov., 1971. Subject focus: pro-abortion, education, employment, media, law, sexism.

| Hist | Dec. 4, 1969-Sep./Oct., 1971 | Microforms Her. 1, R 18 |
|---|---|---|
|  | Oct./Nov., 1971-May, 1973 | Her. 1 UP, R 9 |
|  | Oct., 1973-May, 1974 | Her. CUP, R 4 |

The Newsletter. New York, NY

    see City Wide Women's Liberation Newsletter. New York, NY

Newsletter. New York, NY

    see Women's Center Newsletter. New York, NY

825 Newsletter. 1971//? Unknown. OCLC 2264706. Last issue 1 page. Available on microfilm: Herstory. Published by the Salem Chapter, National Organization for Women, Salem, OR. Subject focus: feminism, Equal Rights Amendment, lobbying, rights, media, politics.

| Hist | June 3, 1971 | Microforms Her. 1, R 19 |
|---|---|---|

826 Newsletter. 1968//? Unknown. OCLC 2269611. Last issue 5 pages. Line drawings. Available on microfilm: Herstory. Published by the Philadelphia Branch, Women Strike for Peace, Philadelphia, PA. Subject focus: songs, peace movement.

| Hist | ?, 1968 | Microforms Her. 1, R 23 |
|---|---|---|

827 Newsletter. 1971//? Irregular. OCLC 2264704. Last issue 8 pages. Available on microfilm: Herstory. Published by the Fort Worth Chapter, National Organization for Women, Fort Worth, TX. Editor: Kathi Miller. Subject focus: welfare, pro-abortion, poverty, feminism, Equal Rights Amendment, lobbying, rights, sexism.

*Women's Periodicals and Newspapers*

| Hist | May, July, 1971 | Microforms Her. 1, R 18 |
|---|---|---|

Newsletter. Falls Church, VA

    see North Virginia N.O.W. Alexandria, VA

828 Newsletter by the New Getting On Women's Collective. 1971//? Unknown. OCLC 2265097. Last issue 6 pages. Line drawings. Available on microfilm: Herstory. Published by the Getting On Women's Collective, East Lansing, MI. Subject focus: poetry, rights.

| Hist | Jan. 11, 1971 | Microforms Her. 1, R 15 |
|---|---|---|

829 Newsletter. Center for Continuing Education of Women. 1971-1974//? Quarterly. OCLC 2259068. Last issue 6 pages. Line drawings, photographs. Available on microfilm: Herstory. Published by the University of Michigan, Ann Arbor, Ann Arbor, MI. Editor: Dorothy McGuigan. Subject focus: education, commissions on women, continuing education.

| Hist | Fall, 1971 | Microforms Her. 1, R 14 |
|---|---|---|
| | Fall, 1972, Winter, 1973 | Her. 1 UP, R12 |
| | Fall, 1973, Summer, 1974 | Her. CUP, R6 |

Newsletter. Daughters of Bilitis/New York. New York, NY

    see The Lesbian Letter. New York, NY

830 Newsletter for, by, and About Woman. 1973//? Monthly. Last issue 4 pages. Line drawings. Available on microfilm: Herstory. Published by the Women's Center, Southeastern Massachusetts University, North Dartmouth, MA. Subject focus: health, pro-abortion.

| Hist | n.1-4; Feb.-May, 1973 | Microforms Her. 2, R 13 |
|---|---|---|
| | v.2, n.1-3; Sep?-Nov?, 1973 | Her. 2 UP, R13 |

Newsletter - Human Rights for Women. Washington, DC

    see HRW Newsletter. Washington, DC

831 Newsletter. National Council of Jewish Women. 1933-1937?//. Irregular. Last issue 78 pages, size 22 x 28. Line drawings. Published by the National Council of Jewish Women, New York, NY. Subject focus: Judaism, Jews, lobbying, education, immigration, peace movement, social service, social legislation.

| Hist | [Jan., 1933- Spring, 1937] | F8299JE/+8N27 (Cutter) |
|---|---|---|

832 Newsletter of the Society for Women in Philosophy. 1972//? Unknown. Last issue 16 pages. Available on microfilm: Herstory. Published by The Society for Women in Philosophy, Macomb, IL. Subject focus: philosophy, professionals, employment.

| Hist | n.1; Jan., 1972 | Microforms Her. 2, R 15 |
|---|---|---|

833 Newsletter of the Women's Caucus for Political Science. 1970-1972//? Quarterly. OCLC 2265100. Last issue 17 pages. Line drawings. Available on microfilm: Herstory. Published by the Women's Caucus for Political Science, Gainsville, FL. Editor: Carol Barner Barry. Subject focus: political science, politics, professionals, education, biographies, sexism, lobbying.

| Hist | v.1, n.1-5; Winter, 1970- Summer, 1971 | Microforms Her. 1, R 22 |
|---|---|---|
| | Fall, 1971- Winter, 1972 | Her. 1 UP, R18 |

834 Newsletter of the Women's Liberation Center of Nassau County. 1972-1974//? Monthly. Last issue 10 pages. Line drawings, commercial advertising. Available on microfilm: Herstory. Published by the Women's Liberation Center, Nassau County, Hempstead, NY. Title varies: as Women's Center Newsletter, Mar.-Dec., 1972; as Women's Liberation Center of Nassau County Newsletter, Jan.-Apr., 1973; as The Liberated Grapevine, May, 1973-Apr., 1974. Editor: Marianna Meyer. Subject focus: literature, poetry, consciousness-raising, art, sports.

| Hist | n.1-15; Mar., 1972- June, 1973 | Microforms Her. 2, R 7 |
|---|---|---|
| | v.3, n.1-v.4, n.6; July/Aug.- June, 1974 | Her. 2 UP, R9 |

835 Newsletter-Philadelphia Women's Center. 1972//? Unknown. Last issue 4 pages. Available on microfilm: Herstory. Published by the Philadelphia Women's Center, Philadelphia, PA. Subject focus: employment, housing, media.

## Women's Periodicals and Newspapers

<table>
<tr><td>Hist</td><td>Mar., 1972</td><td>Microforms<br>Her. 2, R 13</td></tr>
</table>

836 <u>Newsletter-Research Committee on Sex Roles in Society</u>. 1973-1974//? Irregular. Last issue 4 pages. Available on microfilm: Herstory. Published by the International Sociological Association Research Committee on Sex Roles in Society, Boulder, CO. Subject focus: sex roles, research.

<table>
<tr><td>Hist</td><td>n.1-2;<br>Feb.-<br>June, 1973</td><td>Microforms<br>Her. 2, R 14</td></tr>
<tr><td></td><td>n.3-4;<br>Sep. 4, 1973-<br>June 26, 1974</td><td>Her. 2 UP, R10</td></tr>
</table>

<u>Newsletter-Society of Women Engineers</u>. Seattle, WA

see <u>U.S. Woman Engineer</u>. Seattle, WA

837 <u>Newsletter-Women's International League for Peace and Freedom, Paterson-Wayne, New Jersey Branch</u>. 1973-1974//? Irregular. Last issue 2 pages. Line drawings. Available on microfilm: Herstory. Published by The Women's International League for Peace and Freedom, Paterson, NJ. Subject focus: peace movement, lobbying, international relations, militarism.

<table>
<tr><td>Hist</td><td>Jan. 8, 1973-<br>May 21, 1974</td><td>Microforms<br>Her. 3, R 5</td></tr>
</table>

838 <u>Newsletter (Women's Studies Research Center)</u>. 1979. Quarterly. Dr. Suzanne Pingree, editor, Newsletter (Women's Studies Research Center), 209 North Brooks Street, Madison, WI 53706. (608) 263-4703. Last issue 8 pages, last volume 36 pages, size 28 x 23. Line drawings, photographs. Available on microfilm: WHi. Published by the Women's Studies Research Center, University of Wisconsin. Subject focus: women's studies, motherhood, educators, scholars, students.

<table>
<tr><td>Hist</td><td>v.1, n.1-<br>Sep., 1979-</td><td>Circulation</td></tr>
</table>

839 <u>9 to 5 News</u>. 1971. Bi-monthly. $3 to $5 for individuals and institutions. Jacqueline Clermont and Lucie Ferranti, editors, 9 to 5 News, 140 Clarendon Street, Boston, MA 02116. (617) 536-6003. Last issue 4 pages, size 29 x 43. Line drawings, photographs, commercial advertising. Available on microfilm: Herstory, (1971-1974). Published by 9 to 5, Organization for Woman Office Workers, Boston, MA. Title varies: as 9 to 5: Newsletter for Boston Area Office Workers, Dec., 1971/Jan., 1972-Summer, 1973. Subject focus: office workers, employment, sexism in employment.

<table>
<tr><td>Hist</td><td>v.1, n.1-4;<br>Dec., 1971/<br>Jan., 1972-<br>Summer, 1973</td><td>Microforms<br>Her. 2, R 13</td></tr>
<tr><td></td><td>v.1, n.5-v.2, n.3;<br>Oct./Nov., 1973-<br>Apr./May, 1974</td><td>Her. 2 UP, R9</td></tr>
<tr><td></td><td>v.9, n.5-<br>Oct./Nov., 1980-</td><td>Circulation</td></tr>
</table>

<u>9 to 5: Newsletter for Boston Area Office Workers</u>. Boston, MA

see <u>9 to 5 News</u>. Boston, MA

840 <u>No More Cages: A Bi-Monthly Women's Prison Newsletter</u>. 1979. Bi-monthly. $6 for individuals and institutions. No More Cages: A Bi-monthly Women's Prison Newsletter, P.O. Box 90, Brooklyn, NY 11215. Last issue 34 pages, size 28 x 23. Line drawings, photographs. Available on microfilm: WHi (1980-). Published by Women Free Women in Prison, Brooklyn, NY. Place of publication varies: West Nyack, NY, May, 1979-Apr., 1980. Subject focus: Native Americans, behavior modification, lesbians, Afro-Americans.

<table>
<tr><td>Hist</td><td>v.1, n.6-<br>Feb./Apr., 1980-</td><td>Circulation</td></tr>
</table>

841 <u>No More Fun and Games; A Journal of Female Liberation</u>. 1968-1971//? Irregular. OCLC 2265148. Last issue 192 pages, size 16 x 23. Line drawings, photographs. Available on microfilm: Herstory. Published by Cell 16/ Female Liberation, Boston/Cambridge, MA. Place of publication varies: Somerville, MA, Dec., 1969-Apr., 1970. Subject focus: rights, politics, poetry, fiction, child care, revolution. Other holding institutions: MCR-S (Schlesinger Library on the History of Women in America, Radcliffe College, Cambridge, MA), PPiU (PIT), NSbSU (YSM).

<table>
<tr><td>Hist</td><td>n.2-5;<br>Feb., 1969-<br>July, 1971</td><td>Microforms<br>Her. 1, R 10</td></tr>
<tr><td></td><td>n.6;<br>May, 1973</td><td>Her. 1 UP, R12</td></tr>
<tr><td></td><td>n.1-5;<br>Oct., 1968-<br>July, 1971</td><td>Pam 71-1986</td></tr>
<tr><td>Mem</td><td>n.1-4;<br>Oct., 1968-?1971</td><td>AP/J83/F329</td></tr>
</table>

842 Norfolk N.O.W. Newsletter. 1974//? Monthly. Last issue 12 pages. Line drawings. Available on microfilm: Herstory. Published by Norfolk Chapter, National Organization for Women, Norfolk, VA. Editor: Donna Redmond. Subject focus: feminism, Equal Rights Amendment, lobbying, rights.

| Hist | Apr.-June, 1974 | Microforms Her. 3, R 3 |

843 The North Carolina Booklet. 1901-1926//. Monthly. OCLC 1695434. LC 05-32199rev. Last issue 44 pages, last volume 112 pages. Line drawings, photographs. Self-indexed. Published by North Carolina Society, Daughters of the American Revolution, Raleigh, NC. Frequency varies: monthly, May, 1901-Apr., 1905; quarterly, July, 1905-Oct., 1926. Editors: Miss Martha Helen Haywood and Mrs. Hubert Haywood, 1901-1902; Mary Hilliard Hinton and Mrs. E.E. Moffitt, May, 1903-Apr., 1910; Mary Hilliard Hinton, July, 1910-Apr., 1916; Mary Hilliard Hinton and Mrs. E.E. Moffitt, Apr., 1916-Oct., 1926. Subject focus: history, genealogy, heraldry. Other holding institutions: [Indiana Union List of Serials, Indianapolis, IN] (ILS), [University of Minnesota Union List, Minneapolis, MN] (MUL).

| Hist | v.1, n.1-v.23, n. 4; May, 1901- Oct., 1926 | F/251/N86 |

844 North Dakota Women's Liberation Newsletter. 1971//? Quarterly. OCLC 2265201. Last issue 25 pages. Line drawings. Available on microfilm: Herstory. Published by North Dakota Women's Liberation, Minot, ND. Subject focus: poetry, pro-abortion, birth control, health, feminism, unwed mothers.

| Hist | Spring-Fall, 1971 | Microforms Her. 1, R 17 |

845 North Virginia N.O.W. 1970-1974//? Monthly. OCLC 2265214. Last issue 12 pages. Line drawings. Available on microfilm: Herstory. Published by the Northern Virginia Chapter, National Organization for Women, Alexandria, VA. Title varies: as Newsletter, Apr., 1970-Sep., 1971; as N.O.W., Oct., 1971-Mar., 1973. Place of publication varies: Falls Church, VA, Apr., 1970-June, 1973. Frequency varies: weekly, May 1-21, 1970. Subject focus: employment, sexism, politics, education, poverty, pro-abortion, media.

| Hist | Apr., 1970- Sep. 17, 1971 | Microforms Her. 1, R 20 |
| | v.2, n.1-v.3, n.6; Oct., 1971- June, 1973 | Her. 1 UP, R10 |
| | v.3, n.7-8, v.4, n.5-6; Aug.-Sep., 1973, May-June, 1974 | Her. CUP, R 4 |

846 Northern California N.O.W. Newsletter. 1967//? Unknown. Last issue 3 pages. Line drawings. Available on microfilm: Herstory. Published by Northern California Regional National Organization for Women, San Francisco, CA. Subject focus: media, feminism, Equal Rights Amendment, lobbying, rights.

| Hist | n.5; Apr., 1967 | Microforms Her. 2, R 11 |

Northern New Jersey Chapter, N.O.W. Westwood, NJ

see Newsletter. Westwood, NJ

The Northern Woman. Thunder Bay, Ontario

see Northern Woman Journal. Thunder Bay, Ontario

847 Northern Woman Journal. 1975. Bi-monthly. $5 for individuals, $9 for institutions. Northern Woman Journal, 316 Bay Street, Thunder Bay, Ontario, Canada. Last issue 20 pages, size 40 x 29. Line drawings, photographs, commercial advertising. Title varies: as The Northern Woman, ?, 1975. Subject focus: rights, law, health, child rearing, poetry.

| Hist | v.2, n.3- ?, 1975- | Microforms |
| RBR | v.5, n.2- Feb., 1978- | Circulation |

848 Nosotras: Boletin Bilingue. 1974//? Monthly. Last issue 14 pages. Available on microfilm: Herstory. Published by the Do Grupo Latino-Americano de Mujeres en Paris, Paris, France. Subject focus: sexuality, film reviews, birth control, Latinas, career development. In Spanish (50%), in Portuguese (50%).

| Hist | v.1, n.2-6; Feb.-June, 1974 | Microforms Her. 3, R 4 |

849 Not for Women Only. 1974-1979//. Irregular. OCLC 4691900. Last issue 58 pages, size 26 x 20. Line drawings, photographs. Published by the Defense Fuel Supply Center, Federal Women's Program Committee, Alexandria, VA. Editor: Patti A. Boose. Subject focus: workers, rights, women's studies, child care, biographies. Other holding institutions: DGPO (GPO), KEmt (KKR), [Central New York Library Resources Council, Syracuse, NY] (SRR),

[Polk State School and Hospital, Polk, PA] (PHO).

| Hist | n.8-9; Feb./Aug., 1977-May, 1978 | Circulation |

850 Notes. 1969-1971//? Annual. Last issue 142 pages, size 22 x 28. Line drawings, photographs. Available on microfilm: Herstory, McP. Published by New York Women, New York, NY. Subtitle varies: as Notes from the First Year; from the Second Year; from the Third Year. Editors: Shulamith Firestone, 1970; Shulamith Firestone and Anne Koedt, 1971. Subject focus: rights, politics, history, art.

| Hist | n.1-3; 1969-1971 | Microforms Her. 1, R 10 |
| | n.1-3; 1969-1971 | Pam 72-1532, 72-1533, 72-1534 |
| Mem | n.3; ?, 1971 | HQ/1426/N66 (Cutter) |

851 Notes to Sisters in Social Work. 1971-1972//? Last issue 6 pages. Line drawings. Available on microfilm: Herstory. Published in Urbana, IL. Subject focus: social work, women's studies, minorities, professionals, politics, child care, health.

| Hist | ?, 1971-Fall, 1972 | Microforms Her. 2, R 13 |

Le Nouveau Femina. Paris, France

see Femina Illustration. Paris, France

852 NOWLETTER. 1971-1973//? Monthly. OCLC 2264700. Last issue 4 pages, last volume 154 pages. Line drawings. Available on microfilm: Herstory. Published by the National Organization for Women, Baton Rouge Chapter, Baton Rouge, LA. Subject focus: feminism, Equal Rights Amendment, lobbying, rights, child care, media, politics, fiction, sexism.

| Hist | v.1, n.1-6; Mar.-Sep., 1971 | Microforms Her. 1, R 17 |
| | v.1, n.7-v.2, n.6; Oct., 1971-June, 1973 | Her. 1 UP, R7 |
| | v.2, n.7-10; July-Dec., 1973 | Her. CUP, R 3 |

853 Nueva Acción Feminina. 1968-1972//? Irregular. OCLC 2265321. Last issue 8 pages. Line drawings, photographs. Available on microfilm: Herstory. Published in Montevideo, Uruguay. Editor: Q.F. Ana Maria Redondo. Subject focus: employment. In Spanish (100%). Other holding institutions: [University of Minnesota Union List, Minneapolis, MN] (MUL), PPiU (PIT).

| Hist | v.1, n.1-v.3, n. 15; July 15, 1968-Aug. 15, 1971 | Microforms Her. 1, R 2 |
| | June 12, 1969 | Her. 1, Add |
| | v.4, n.16-17; Jan.-Apr., 1972 | Her. 1 UP, R12 |

854 The Nurturing Family. 1976//? Irregular. Last issue 8 pages. Line drawings. Published by United States Department of Agriculture, Cooperative Extension Programs, University of Wisconsin Extension, Madison, WI. Subject focus: family, marriage, single parents, education.

| U.W. Ext. | v.1, n.1-2; Jan.-June, 1976 | Circulation |

855 Nylaende Tidsskrift for Kvindernes Sak. 1887-1927?//. Monthly. OCLC 1760956. Last issue 16 pages, last volume 400 pages, size 15 x 23. Line drawings, photographs, commercial advertising. Available on microfilm: McA. Published in Christiania, Norway. Editor: Gina Krog. Subject focus: rights, suffrage, biographies, law, Christianity. In Norwegian (100%). Other holding institutions: [University of Minnesota Union List, Minneapolis, MN] (MUL).

| Mem | [v.1, n.1-v.20, n.21]; [Jan. 1, 1887-Nov. 1, 1906] | AP/N995 |

856 O.C.W.E.-Oregon Council for Women's Equality. 1971-1973//? Quarterly. Last issue 4 pages. Line drawings. Available on microfilm: Herstory. Published by the Oregon Council for Women's Equality, Portland, OR. Subject focus: lobbying, rights, employment, child care, education.

| Hist | v.1, n.5, v.2, n.1-v.3, n.1; Oct. 15, 1971, Jan. 15, 1972-Mar. 28, 1973 | Microforms Her. 1 UP, R13 |
| | v.3, n.2-3; Sep.-Nov., 1973 | Her. CUP, R 6 |

857 <u>O.M.A. (Organizacao Da Muhler de Angola)</u>. 1970//? Unknown. OCLC 2265468. Last issue 16 pages. Line drawings, photographs. Available on microfilm: Herstory. Published in Dar Es Salaam, Tanzania. Subject focus: poetry, revolution.

| Hist | n.4; July 10, 1970 | Microforms Her. 1, R 10 |

858 <u>O.S.U. Women Liberation Newsletter</u>. 1971//? Irregular. OCLC 2265572. Last issue 5 pages. Available on microfilm: Herstory. Published by Ohio State University Women's Liberation, Columbus, OH. Subject focus: students, lobbying, education, children, politics, pro-abortion.

| Hist | Jan. 21-May, 1971 | Microforms Her. 1, R 20 |

859 <u>O.W.L. Newsletter</u>. 1973//? Irregular. Last issue 3 pages. Available on microfilm: Herstory. Published by Oakland Women's Liberation, Oakland, CA. Subject focus: health.

| Hist | Jan.8-Mar.18, 1973 | Microforms Her. 2, R 13 |

860 <u>The OAKES Newsletter</u>. 1970-1974//? Monthly. Last issue 4 pages, last volume 40 pages. Line drawings. Available on microfilm: Herstory. Published by Helen Oakes/Acorn Educational Press, In., Philadelphia, PA. Editor: Helen Oakes. Subject focus: education, public schools, teachers, continuing education, school integration, sex roles, personal finance.

| Hist | v.1, n.1-v.4, n.10; Apr., 1970- June, 1973 | Microforms Her. 2, R 13 |
| | v.5, n.1-10; Sep., 1973- June, 1974 | Her. 2 UP, R 9 |

861 <u>Off Our Backs</u>. 1970. 11 times a year. $7 for individuals, $20 for institutions. Off Our Backs, 1724 20th St. NW, Washington, DC 20009. (202) 234-8072. ISSN 0030-0071. OCLC 1038241, 5729287. LC sn78-1596. Last issue 32 pages, last volume 300 pages, size 29 x 41. Line drawings, photographs, commercial advertising. Indexed in: Alternative Press Index; Publishers Index (1970-1974); Women's Studies Abstracts, New Periodical Index. Available on microfilm: Herstory (1970-1974). Published by Off Our Backs, Inc., Washington, DC. Frequency varies: monthly, Feb. 27-Apr. 25, 1970; bi-weekly, May 16-Dec. 31, 1970; every three weeks, Jan. 21-May 27, 1971; monthly, June 24, 1971-June, 1977. Subject focus: labor unions, health, gay rights, prisons, film reviews, poetry. Other holding institutions: AzFU (AZN), CLobS (CLO), COU-DA (COA), GEU (EMU), IaDmD-L (IWD), [Indiana Union List of Serials, Indianapolis, IN] (ILS), MCR-S (Schlesinger Library on the History of Women in America, Radcliffe College, Cambridge, MA), MBU (BOS), MiEM (EEM), MiMtpT (EZC), MnStpeG (MNG), NCH (YHM), NCortU (YCM), NFQC (XQM), NPV (VXW), NsbSU (YSM), NhD (DRB), NmU (IQU), OAkU (AKR), OAU (OUN), OKentU (KSU), OU (OSU), PBL (LYU), PNwC (WFN), PPiU (PIT), [Pittsburgh Regional Library Center-Union List, Pittsburgh, PA] (QPR), [AMIGOS Union List of Serials, Dallas, TX] (IUC), WU (GZM), WeharU (HRM).

| Hist | v.1, n.1-v.2,n.1; Feb. 27, 1970- Sep., 1971 | Microforms Her. 1, R 3 |
| | v.2, n.2-v.3,n.8; Oct., 1971- May, 1973 | Her. 1 UP, R 12-13 |
| | v.3, n.9-v.4,n.7; July/Aug., 1973- June, 1974 | Her. CUP, R 6 |
| | v.1, n.1- Feb. 27, 1970- | Microforms |
| Coll | Current Issues Only | Women's Reading Room |
| Wom St | v.6, n.1- Jan., 1975- | Reading Room |
| Mem | Current Issues Only | Periodicals Room |
| MPL | v.4, n.7- July/Aug., 1973- | Literature and Social Sciences Section |

<u>Official Bulletin of Wisconsin Federation of Business and Professional Woman's Clubs</u>. Merrill, WI

see <u>The Wisconsin Business Woman</u>. Merrill, WI

862 <u>Ohio-Kentucky News</u>. 1965?. Quarterly. Barbara Janis, editor, Ohio-Kentucky News, 3233 Euclid Avenue, Cleveland, OH 44115. Last issue 4 pages, size 43 x 28. Line drawings, photographs. Published by Ohio-Kentucky Region International Ladies' Garment Workers' Union, Cleveland, OH. Previous editor: Ann Metcalfe, Jan./Feb./Mar., 1971-Nov./Dec., 1972. Subject focus: labor unions, garment industry.

| Hist | v.7, n.1,v.8,n.4, v.11, n.1- Jan./Feb./Mar., 1971, Nov./Dec., 1972, Mar., 1976- | Circulation |

863 Ohio Report: News from the Women's Services Division of the Ohio Bureau of Employment Services. 1972. Bi-monthly. Sherry S. Bell, editor, Ohio Report: News from the Women's Services Division of the Ohio Bureau of Employment Services, 145 South Front Street, Columbus, OH 43216. (614) 466-4496. OCLC 5993485, 4339880. Last issue 4 pages, last volume 24 pages, size 28 x 23. Photographs. Available on microfilm: WHi (1979-); Herstory (1972-1974). Published by Women's Services Division, Ohio Bureau of Employment Services, Columbus, OH. Title varies: as Women's Division News, 1969-1971; as Ohio Women, Spring, 1972-Oct., 1974. Previous editor: Laura A. Farrington, July, 1976-July, 1979. Subject focus: rights, employment, unemployment, Social Security. Other holding institutions: OClCo (CXP), [Ohio Legislative Service Commission, Columbus, OH] (OLG), OKentU (KSU), OY (YMM).

| Hist | v.1, n.1-v.2,n.2; Spring, 1972- June, 1973 | Microforms Her. 2, R 13 |
|---|---|---|
| | v.2, n.3-v.3,n.2; Oct., 1973-?, 1974 | Her. 2UP, R 9 |
| | v.5, n.1- June, 1979- | Circulation |

864 The Ohio Sew Biz. 1978. Irregular. Barbara Janis, editor, The Ohio Sew Biz, 3233 Euclid Avenue, Cleveland, OH 44115. Last issue 6 pages, last volume 8 pages, size 43 x 28. Line drawings, photographs. Published by the International Ladies' Garment Workers Union, Cleveland, OH. Subject focus: labor unions, garment industry.

| Hist | v.1, n.1- Nov., 1978- | Circulation |
|---|---|---|

Ohio Woman. Columbus, OH

   see Ohio Report: News from the Women's Services Division of the Ohio Bureau of Employment Services. Columbus, OH

865 The Ohio Woman Voter. 1922?//. Monthly. Last issue 16 pages, size 17 x 26. Photographs, commercial advertising. Published by The Ohio League of Women Voters, Columbus, OH. Editor: Olga Anna Jones. Subject focus: judicial reform, politics.

| Hist | v.1, n.4; Oct., 1922 | KWZ/OH (Cutter) |
|---|---|---|

866 Ombudswoman. 1973//? Last issue 5 pages. Line drawings. Available on microfilm: Herstory. Published by the College of Law, University of Arizona, Tucson, AZ. Subject focus: law, education, career development, students.

| Hist | v.1, n.1; Dec., 1973 | Microforms Her. 3, R 4 |
|---|---|---|

867 On Campus With Women. 1971. Irregular. Bernice Sandler, editor, On Campus With Women, 1818 R Street NW, Washington, DC 20009. OCLC 2376679, 3075159. Last issue 26 pages, size 22 x 28. Line drawings. Available on microfilm: Herstory (1971-1974), UnM. Published by Project on the Status and Education of Women-Association of American Colleges. Title varies: as Association of American Colleges Project on the Status and Education of Women, Nov., 1971-June, 1972. Subject focus: education, lobbying, minorities, sexism in education, affirmative action, career development, employment, sports, Title IX, international news, minority women. Other holding institutions: CLU (CLU), COU-DA (COA), [Indiana Union List of Serials, Indianapolis, IN] (ILS), MBTI (BTI), MH-AH (BHA), MH-Ed (HMG), [University of Minnesota Union List, Minneapolis, MN] (MUL), OSteC (STU), PBL (LYU), TxCM (TXA).

| Hist | n.1-6; Nov., 1971- May, 1973 | Microforms Her. 2, R 1 |
|---|---|---|
| | n.7-9; Dec., 1973- June, 1974 | Her. 2 UP, R1 |
| Coll | Current Issues Only | Women's Reading Area |
| Wom St | n.18- Oct., 1977- | Reading Room |
| Wom Ed Res | n.1- Nov., 1971- | Circulation |
| IMC | n.12- Nov., 1975- | Periodicals Section |

868 On Our Way. 1973-1974//? Monthly. Last issue 9 pages. Line drawings. Available on microfilm: Herstory. Published by Waterbury Area Woman's Center, Inc., Waterbury, CT. Editor: Pauline Tanguay. Subject focus: child care, self-defense, poetry, health, media, politics.

| Hist | July, 1973- May, 1974 | Microforms Her. 3, R 4 |
|---|---|---|

869 On Our Way. 1971-1974//? Irregular. OCLC 2376742. Last issue 4 pages. Line drawings. Available on microfilm: Herstory. Published by Women's Center Office, Cambridge, MA. Title varies: as The Women's Center Newsletter, Apr.-Sep./Oct., 1973. Subject focus: peace movement, workers, radicalism, image,

poetry, art, politics.

| | | |
|---|---|---|
| Hist | v.1, n.1-v.3,n.6;<br>Oct. 29, 1971-<br>June, 1973 | Microforms<br>Her. 2, R 18 |
| | v.3, n.7-9;<br>July/Aug., 1973-<br>June, 1974 | Her. 2 UP, R9 |

870 <u>On Our Way</u>. 1973-1974//? Monthly? Last issue 16 pages. Line drawings, size 22 x 28. Published in Edmonton, Alberta, Canada. Subject focus: rights, mental health, film reviews.

| | | |
|---|---|---|
| Mem | v.2, n.1;<br>Feb., 1974? | AP/057/093 |

871 <u>On the Way</u>. 1971-1974//. Monthly. OCLC 2265474. Last issue 20 pages. Line drawings, photographs, commercial advertising. Available on microfilm: Herstory. Published by Anchorage Women's Liberation, Anchorage, AK. Subject focus: family planning, law, welfare, child care, education, sexism, students, self-defense.

| | | |
|---|---|---|
| Hist | Jan.-Sep., 1971 | Microforms<br>Her. 1, R 20 |
| | v.2, n.1-v.3, n.5;<br>Jan., 1972-<br>June, 1973 | Her. 1 UP, R13 |
| | v.3, n.6-12;<br>Oct., 1973-<br>Apr., 1974 | Her. CUP, R 6 |

872 <u>One-to-One - A Lesbian/Feminist Journal of Communication</u>. 1973?//. Unknown. Last issue 24 pages. Line drawings. Available on microfilm: Herstory. Published in New York, NY. Subject focus: lesbians, literature, feminism, media.

| | | |
|---|---|---|
| Hist | v.1, n.1;<br>Winter, 1973 | Microforms<br>Her. 2, R 13 |

873 <u>Onna: Newsletter from Women in Japan</u>. 1972?//. Unknown. Last issue 10 pages. Line drawings. Available on microfilm: Herstory. Published in Tokyo, Japan. Subject focus: satire, sexism, prostitution, workers, education.

| | | |
|---|---|---|
| Hist | n.1-2;<br>?, 1972 | Microforms<br>Her. 2, R 13 |

874 <u>The Opening</u>. 1971?//. Unknown. OCLC 2265495. Last issue 46 pages. Line drawings. Available on microfilm: Herstory. Published by The Know Inc., Pittsburgh, PA. Subject focus: poetry, self-defense, venereal disease, biographies.

| | | |
|---|---|---|
| Hist | v.1, n.1;<br>Aug., 1971 | Microforms<br>Her. 1, R 10 |

875 <u>The Operatives' Magazine</u>. 1841-1842//? Monthly. OCLC 1761328. Last issue 18 pages, last volume 192 pages. Line drawings. Available on microfilm: ResP. Published by the Operatives Magazine/An Association of Females, Lowell, MA. Subject focus: literature, fiction, poetry. Other holding institutions: CtY (YUS), [University of Minnesota Union List, Minneapolis, MN] (MUL), OO (OBE).

| | | |
|---|---|---|
| Mem | n.1-12;<br>Apr., 1841-<br>Mar., 1842 | Microforms |

<u>Orange County Chapter N.O.W. Newsletter</u>. Fullerton, CA

see <u>Action N.O.W.</u>  Santa Ana, CA

876 <u>Orange County Women's Coalition</u>. 1971//? Irregular. OCLC 2265511. Last issue 18 pages. Line drawings. Available on microfilm: Herstory. Published by the Women's Center, Costa Mesa, CA. Subject focus: media, politics, lesbians, poetry, self-defense, birth control, pro-abortion. Other holding institution: PPiU (PIT).

| | | |
|---|---|---|
| Hist | May-July, 1971 | Microforms<br>Her. 1, R20 |

877 <u>The Other Woman</u>. 1972-1974?//. Irregular. ISSN 0315-8306. OCLC 2097707. LC cn76-300164. Last issue 20 pages. Line drawings, photographs. Available on microfilm: Herstory. Published in Toronto/Willowdale, Ontario, Canada. Subject focus: poetry, radicalism, politics, prostitution, pro-abortion, lesbians, sexism in education, health.

| | | |
|---|---|---|
| Hist | v.1, n.1-2,4;<br>May-Sep., 1972,<br>Mar., 1973 | Microforms<br>Her. 2, R 13 |
| | v.1, n.6-v.2,n.5;<br>July/Aug., 1973-<br>June, 1974 | Her. 2 UP, R9 |

878 <u>Our Aim</u>. 1966? Irregular. Our Aim, 100 East 17th Street, New York, NY 10001. OCLC 5958223. Last issue 8 pages, size 32 x 23. Line drawings, photographs. Published by International Ladies' Garment Workers Union, Local 91, New York, NY. Subject focus: labor unions, garment industry. In Spanish (50%). Other holding institution: NIC (COO).

| | | |
|---|---|---|
| Hist | v.14, n.2-<br>Mar., 1979- | Circulation |

*Issues in Health Care of Women* 2, nos. 3–4 (May–August 1980).
©by Hemisphere Publishing Corporation.

**Journal of the National Association for Women Deans, Administrators, & Counselors**

Winter 1981     Volume 44, No. 2

*Journal of the National Association for Women Deans, Administrators, & Counselors* 44, no. 2 (Winter 1981). ©1980, The National Association for Women Deans, Administrators, and Counselors.

*Kinesis*, July 1980.

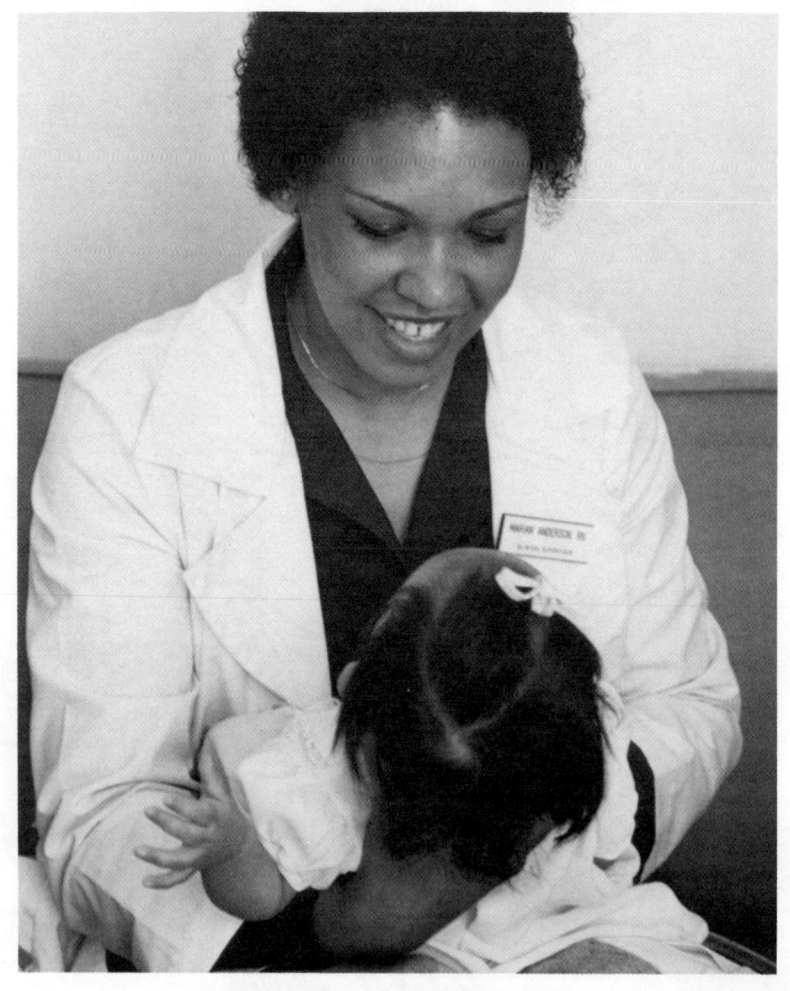

# MCN
## THE AMERICAN JOURNAL OF MATERNAL CHILD NURSING

**SEPTEMBER/OCTOBER 1981**

**A CHILD DROWNS: A NURSING PERSPECTIVE**
**THE MOTHER'S POSTPARTAL GRIEF WORK**
**DIFFERENTIATING CHILDHOOD DERMATOLOGIC CONDITIONS**

MCN, *The American Journal of Maternal Child Nursing,* September –October 1981.

*Ms.* 8, no. 7 (January 1980).

*National News* 50, no. 4 (July–August 1981).

# NATIONAL NOW TIMES

Vol. XIII, No. 6 — 10    Official Journal of the National Organization for Women (NOW)    June, 1980

## Over 90,000 March In Chicago

by Sandy Roth

Over 90,000 supporters of the Equal Rights Amendment converged on Chicago's Grant Park on May 10 for what was called the largest march in Chicago's history and the largest gathering in support of the ERA ever in the state of Illinois.

Marchers came from every state of the union and represented over 300 organizations and delegations.

The massive event, which had been conceived and coordinated by NOW, drew to Chicago the largest group of ERA supporters assembled since the July 9, 1978 National ERA March for Ratification and Extension held in Washington, DC. That event had also been coordinated by NOW.

"We could not have been more pleased with the turnout," said Jane Wells-Schooley, NOW's Vice President Action who was the overall coordinatory of the event. "NOW members from all over the country helped to mobilize supporters from their areas. Illinois NOW and Chicago NOW did a spectacular job in mobilizing ERA supporters from their state."

Also key to the organizing effort as well as to the turnout was the work of the American Association of University Women and organized labor.

"AAUW volunteer activists were an important contingent of the march organizing team," noted Wells-Schooley, "and helped to bring over 1,000 AAUW members to Chicago."

Labor participation in the march was tremendous as exemplified by large delegations from UAW, Steelworkers, Coalition of Labor Union Women, Teamsters and other delegations too numerous to mention.

The march, which took place along the shores of beautiful Lake Michigan, brought together the thousands, most of whom were dressed in traditional suffragist white, for a processional-style march reminiscent of the early 1900 suffragist marches and was patterned after the 1977 Alice Paul March and the 1978 National ERA March in Washington. The throngs of supporters were organized into delegations, by organization and geographical designation, and the stately purple, white and gold delegation banners unfurled in the Chicago lakeside breezes.

### More Than Expected

Marchers began arriving by bus as early as 6:15 a.m. from all parts of the country. Although organizers had expected about four hundred busses to arrive, the actual count ran well over 550. "We had a color and number system to accommodate 400 buses and we just ran out of numbers," said Alice Cohan, Chief Bus Marshall, "I knew we had a winner when we had to start making up numbers on 'ERA YES' stickers so that people could find their bus after the rally."

In addition to thousands who rode on buses from all parts of the country,

### News Flash

On May 14, the Ninth Circuit Court of Appeals granted NOW's motion for a stay of proceedings pending the appeal of NOW's request to be allowed to intervene as a party in the Idaho/Washington State case challenging the extension. The appeal was granted by Circuit Judges Alarcon and Nelson.

many as long as 24 hours, the ranks were swelled by those who came in on chartered planes, vans, private cars, trains, and public transportation from the Chicago area. "We had a scare when we heard a rumor that there might be a local transportation strike on Friday night," said Maureen Rogman, Logistics Coordinator for the March and Great Lakes Regional Director. "All we knew was that we had 2,000 people coming in from Dupage and we had to get them in. Fortunately, our alternate plan was never needed. Everybody made it."

Chartered airplanes from Michigan, Virginia, Washington, DC, and as far away as California brought thousands. For those participants, the trip was almost as much fun as the March itself. "The flight from California was a real energizer," said CA State Coordinator Karen Peters. "The San Fernando Marching Band was on the plane along with lots of other Californians. We even had non-NOW members join before the trip was over. It was great fun for all."

Supporters dug down deep and held fundraisers to pay the costs of bringing the thousands to the Windy City. Many NOW chapters joined forces with local AAUW, NWPC and League chapters as well as trade union locals not only to raise the money for their buses but to recruit supporters for the trip. Many supporters who were unable to make the trip pledged $36 (for Illinois—the 36th State) or more to fund those who could make the trek. "We knew that extra effort was being

*Please turn to Pg. 3, Col. 1*

Muriel Fox, NOW LDEF president, carries the ERA flag at the head of the march. NOW members from Illinois carry the banner.

Photo Credit: Doug Roth

**ERA Countdown**
June 1, 1980
to
June 30, 1982
759 Days

# network

**THE MONTHLY FOR UTAH'S WORKING WOMEN**

January 1980

bulk rate
u.s. postage
paid
permit no. 3008
salt lake city, utah

349 south 6th east
salt lake city, utah

# WOMEN ENTREPRENEURS

en·tre·pre·neur: *n.* *A person who organizes, operates, and assumes the risk for business ventures.*

*Network*, January 1980.

*New Directions for Women* 8, no. 5 (Winter 1979–80).

*Off Our Backs* 10, no. 3 (March 1980).

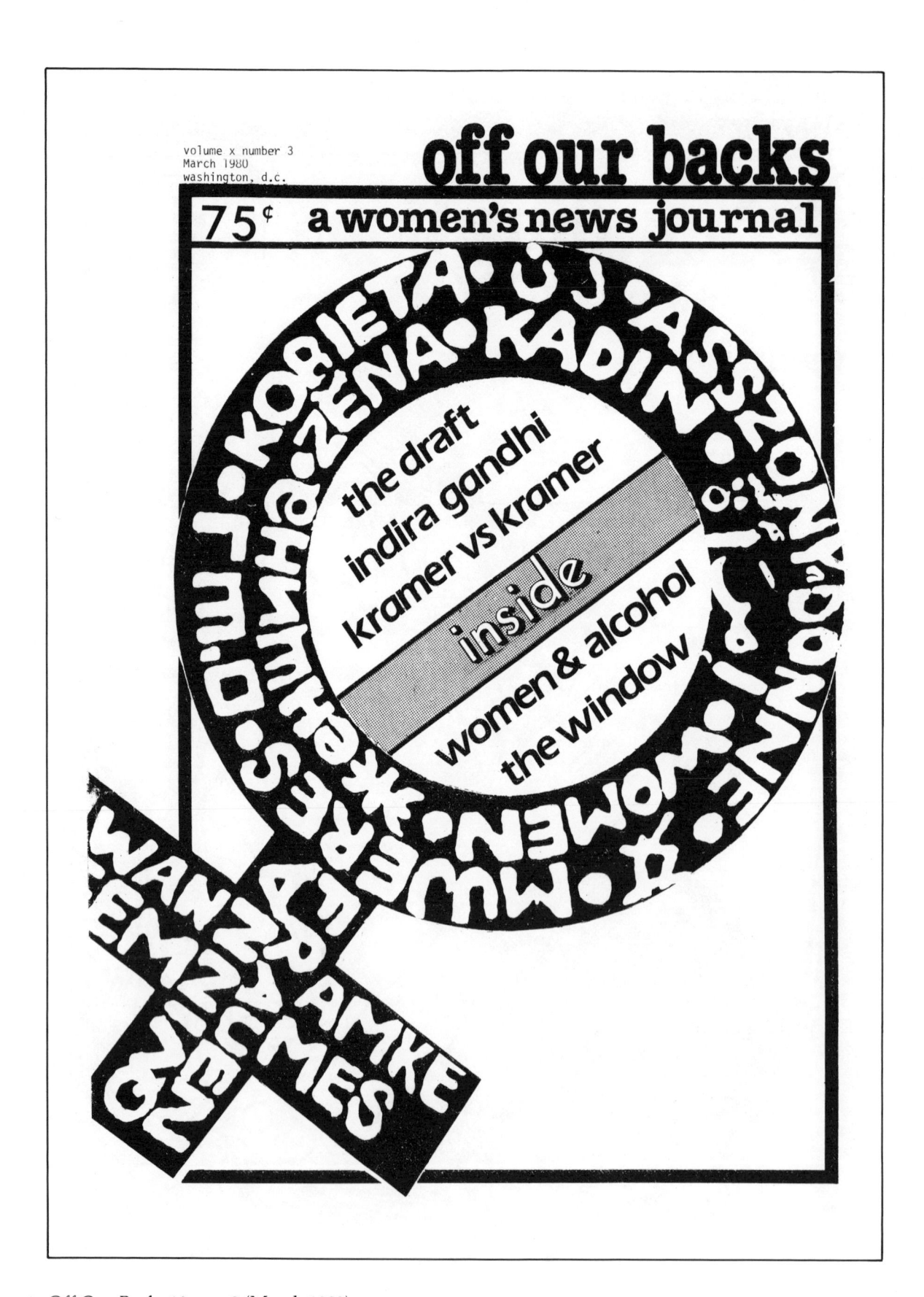

*Pan Pipes*, Winter 1980.

Middle East IV  Namibia's Independence Struggle  1980 Index
National Health Care  Constitutional Referendum (page 23)

# PEACE & FREEDOM

a publication of the U.S. Section of the Women's International League for Peace & Freedom

Elizabeth Raynham

VOL. 40, NO. 9
ISSN 0015-9093
50¢

DECEMBER 1980

*Peace & Freedom* 40, no. 9 (December 1980).

# The Phyllis Schlafly Report

VOL. 15, NO. 4, SECTION 2     BOX 618, ALTON, ILLINOIS 62002     NOVEMBER, 1981

## How ERA Would Change Federal Laws

Proponents of the Equal Rights Amendment often argue, "We need ERA because 800 Federal laws discriminate on account of sex." This report examines those 800 laws and how ERA would change them. It reveals how our nation would be dramatically changed if ERA ever became part of the U.S. Constitution.

The source of the "800 laws" argument is a 230-page book entitled *Sex Bias in the U.S. Code: A Report of the U.S. Commission on Civil Rights* published in April 1977. The U.S. Commission on Civil Rights is a Federal agency established by Congress to investigate and study discrimination and make reports to Congress.

*Sex Bias in the U.S. Code* was actually written by Ruth Bader Ginsburg and Brenda Feigen-Fasteau (who were paid with tax funds under Contract No. CR3AK010). Ginsburg is one of the two most widely quoted pro-ERA lawyers. Her name appears as one of the feminist lawyers in most of the gender cases that have reached the Supreme Court in the last decade. At the time *Sex Bias* was written, she was a professor of law at Columbia Law School and used the assistance of 15 Columbia Law School students. In 1980, President Jimmy Carter appointed Ginsburg to the second highest court in our country, the U.S. Court of Appeals for the District of Columbia. Feigen-Fasteau was a director of the Women's Rights Project for the American Civil Liberties Union, and has appeared in TV network and other debates on ERA with Phyllis Schlafly.

Thus, *Sex Bias in the U.S. Code* is a good index to what ERA would do. It was written by the two top ERA activist female lawyers, it was published by the U.S. Commission on Civil Rights, and it was funded by the Federal Government during the Carter Administration.

*Sex Bias in the U.S. Code* was written and published in order to identify all the Federal laws that discriminate against women, and to recommend the specific changes demanded by the women's lib movement in order to eliminate "sex bias" and to conform to "the equality principle" of ERA. (p. 10) *Sex Bias in the U.S. Code* makes it clear that, if ERA were ever added to the Constitution, ERA would accomplish *all* these changes in one stroke. *Sex Bias in the U.S. Code* also makes it clear that ERA activists are trying to accomplish the same results by changing Federal statutes. The ERAers are constantly pressuring the President and Congress to eliminate all the laws that discriminate on account of sex.

*Sex Bias in the U.S. Code* is, therefore, a handbook to prove what the ERA will do and what the ERAers want. The book proves that the legal consequences of ERA and the social and political goals of the ERAers are radical, irrational, and unacceptable to Americans. *Sex Bias* convicts the ERAers out of their own mouths. In the view of the authors, *all* the proposed changes listed in *Sex Bias* are needed in order to achieve "the equality principle" of ERA.

An old adage warns, "Would that mine enemy had written a book." Well, the top ERA lawyers wrote one, and they've provided a powerful weapon against ERA. Here is a summary of the changes demanded by the book *Sex Bias in the U.S. Code*. All quotations below are directly from the book and are identified by page numbers.

### ERA Changes in Employment

The box below shows what changes ERA will bring in employment.

[ ]

That's right, NOTHING! *Sex Bias in the U.S. Code* proves that ERA will do absolutely nothing in employment! *Sex Bias in the U.S. Code* explodes all the phony arguments made by the ERAers about the job discrimination and "59¢."

*Sex Bias* tries to claim that two Federal laws discriminate on sex in employment — and both claims are completely false. *Sex Bias* falsely claims that there is a "sex-age differential in 41 U.S.C. #35 setting a minimum age of 16 for boys and 18 for girls employed by public contractors." (p. 217) The fact is that the age was equalized for boys and girls in 1968. *Sex Bias* falsely claims that women are prohibited from working in coal mines. (p. 217) The fact is that more than 3,000 women are coal miners today.

### ERA Changes in the Military

**1. Women must be drafted when men are drafted.**

"Supporters of the equal rights principle firmly reject draft or combat exemption for women, as Congress did when it refused to qualify the Equal Rights Amendment by incorporating any military service exemption. The equal rights principle implies that women must be subject to the draft if men are, that military assignments must be made on the basis of individual capacity rather than sex." (p. 218)

"Equal rights and responsibilities for men and women implies that women must be subject to draft registration if men are. Congressional debate on the Equal Rights Amendment points clearly to an understanding of this effect on the Amendment." (p. 202)

*Phyllis Schlafly Report* 15, no. 4, sec. 2 (November 1981).

*Plainswoman* 5, no. 1 (September 1981).

*Response* 13, no. 7 (July–August 1981).

*Primipara* 7, no. 1 (Spring–Summer 1981).

*Secretary*, December–January 1981.

879 Our Boston. 1926?//. Monthly. Last issue 36 pages, size 17 x 24. Line drawings, photographs, commercial advertising. Published by The Women's Municipal League of Boston, Boston, MA. Editor: Catherine E. Russell. Subject focus: history, volunteers. Other holding institution: MCR-S (Schlesinger LIbrary on the History of Women in America, Radcliffe College, Cambridge, MA).

| Hist | v.1, n.5; Apr., 1926 | JW/8BO (Cutter) |

880 Our Country Newsletter. 1973?//. Unknown. Last issue 3 pages. Line drawings. Available on microfilm: Herstory. Published in San Francisco, CA. Subject focus: social change, rights.

| Hist | v.1, n.1; Aug., 1973 | Microforms Her. 3, R 4 |

881 Our Newsletter. 1974?//. Monthly? Last issue 5 pages. Line drawings. Available on microfilm: Herstory. Published by Vancouver Women's Health Collective, Vancouver, British Columbia, Canada. Title varies: as Vancouver Women's Health Collective Newsletter, ?Jan?, 1974. Subject focus: health, self-help, sexuality, birth control, nursing.

| Hist | v.1, n.1-5; ?Jan?-May, 1974 | Microforms Her. 3, R 4 |

882 Our Sisters, Ourselves. 1971-1972?//. Irregular. Last issue 48 pages. Line drawings, photographs. Available on microfilm: Herstory. Published by Foothill College, Palo Alto, CA. Subject focus: health, poetry, Lamaze technique, education, film reviews, politics, media.

| Hist | Nov., 1971, Winter-Spring, 1972 | Microforms Her. 2, R 13 |

Our State Work. Madison, WI

see The Motor. Baraboo, WI

883 Outcry. 1977. Bi-monthly. $5 for individuals and institutions. Outcry, 1228 W. Mitchell Street, Milwaukee, WI 53204. Last issue 6 pages, size 22 x 28. Line drawings, commercial advertising. Published by Task Force on Battered Women and Sojourner Truth House, Inc., Milwaukee, WI. Frequency varies: monthly, Feb.-Dec., 1977. Subject focus: battered women, pornography.

| Wom Ed Res | v.1, n.1- Feb., 1977- | Circulation |

884 PEER Perspective. 1975. Tri-annual. Robin Gordon, editor, PEER Perspective, 1029 Vermont Avenue, NW, Suite 800, Washington, DC 20005. (202) 332-7337. OCLC 2377813. Last issue 4 pages, last volume 12 pages, size 22 x 28. Line drawings, photographs. Published by Project on Equal Education Rights, National Organization for Women, Legal Defense and Education Fund, Washington, DC. Subject focus: rights, education. Other holding institutions: MH-Ed (NMG), [University of Minnesota Union List, Minneapolis, MN] (MUL), [AMIGOS Union List of Serials, Dallas, TX] (IUC), TxDW (IWU), TxU (TXQ).

| IMC | v.3, n.2- July, 1977- | Periodicals Section |
| Wom Ed Res | v.1, n.2- Apr., 1975- | Circulation |

885 P.E.O. Record. 1889?-1967//. Monthly. Last issue 32 pages, last volume 400 pages, size 20 x 28. Line drawings, photographs. Published by the Protect Each Other Sisterhood, Des Moines, IA. Place of publication varies: Mount Morris, IL, Jan., 1923-Oct., 1931; Mendota, IL, Nov., 1931-Dec., 1961. Editors: Winona Evans Reeves, Jan., 1923-Sep., 1949; Edith Markham Wallace, Oct., 1949-Dec., 1961; Alvena Mattes, Jan., 1962-Feb., 1966. Subject focus: education, peace movement, clubs.

| Hist | v.36, n.1-v.79, n.12; Jan., 1923-Dec., 1967 | KW/8PI/R (Cutter) |

886 PM. 1970-1971//? Irregular. OCLC 3393769. Last issue 8 pages. Line drawings, commercial advertising, size 21 x 29. Published by the Florida Free Press, Tallahassee, FL. Subject focus: bibliographies. Other holding institution: [University of Minnesota Union List, Minneapolis, MN] (MUL).

| Hist | n.2-3; Aug., 1970-Apr., 1971 | Pam 72-890 |

887 P.O.W. 1973-1974//? Monthly. Last issue 6 pages. Line drawings, commercial advertising. Available on microfilm: Herstory. Published by International Chapter-National Organization for Women/Paris Organization of Women, Paris, France. Title varies: N.O.W. or Never, Mar.-Oct., 1973. Subject focus: art, feminism, Equal Rights Amendment, lobbying, pro-abortion, rights, health.

| Hist | v.1, n.2-5; Mar.-June, 1973 | Microforms Her. 2, R 11 |
| | v.2, n.1-5; Oct., 1973-Feb., 1974 | Her. 2 UP, R 8 |

888 PWC Newsletter. 1973?//. Unknown. Last issue 6 pages. Line drawings. Available on microfilm: Herstory. Published by Professional Women's Caucus, New York, NY. Subject focus: professionals, employment.

| Hist | May, 1973 | Microforms Her. 2, R 14 |

889 PWR Newsletter. 1973?//. Irregular. Last issue 4 pages. Line drawings. Available on microfilm: Herstory. Published by Pennsylvanians for Women Rights, Lancaster, PA. Subject focus: child care, rights, employment, education.

| Hist | v.1, n.1-2; Mar.-May, 1973 | Microforms Her. 2, R 13 |
| | v.1, n.3-4; Sep.-Dec., 1973 | Her. 2 UP, R9 |

890 Page One. 1973?//. Unknown. Last issue 4 pages. Available on microfilm: Herstory. Published in Atlanta, GA. Editors: Martha Gaines and Darlene Roth-White. Subject focus: employment, lobbying.

| Hist | v.1, n.1; June, 1973 | Microforms Her. 2, R 13 |
| | v.1, n.2; July, 1973 | Her. 2 UP, R 9 |

891 Paid My Dues. 1974. Quarterly. $8 for individuals, $12 for institutions. Karen Corti and Kathryn Gohl, editors, Paid My Dues, P.O. Box 6517, Chicago, IL 60680. (312) 929-5592. ISSN 0097-8035. OCLC 1799171. LC 75-642126. Last issue 40 pages, last volume 172 pages. Line drawings, photographs, commercial advertising. Self-indexed. Available on microfilm: Herstory (1974). Published by Calliope Publishing Inc., Chicago, IL. Place of publication varies: Milwaukee, WI, Apr., 1974-Mar., 1976. Previous editors: Toni L. Armstrong, Karen Carti, Judy Erickson, Kathryn Judd, Nov?, 1978-Mar., 1979; Kathryn Gohl, Karen Corti, Toni Armstrong, Mar.-Dec., 1979. Subject focus: music, touring, interviews. Other holding institutions: CtY (YUS), DLC (DLC), MNS (SNN), [University of Minnesota Union List, Minneapolis, MN] (MUL), NBu (VHB), OU (OSU), PPiU (PIT).

| Hist | v.1, n.1-2; Apr.-May, 1974 | Microforms Her. 3, R4 |
| Music | v.1, n.1- Apr., 1974- | Circulation |
| Coll | Current Issues Only | Women's Reading Area |

| MPL | v.2, n.4- Winter, 1978- | Art Section |

892 Palmerston North Women's Liberation in Unison. 1973//. Bi-monthly. Last issue 6 pages. Line drawings. Available on microfilm: Herstory. Published by Palmerston North Women's Liberation, Palmerston North, New Zealand. Subject focus: politics, pro-abortion, child care.

| Hist | Mar./Apr.- May/June, 1973 | Microforms Her. 2, R 13 |
| | July/Aug.- Sep./Oct., 1973 | Her. 2 UP, R9 |

893 Pan Pipes of Sigma Alpha Iota. 1908. Quarterly. $6 for individuals and institutions. Margaret W. Maxwell, editor, Pan Pipes of Sigma Alpha Iota, 4119 Rollins Avenue, Des Moines, IA 50312. ISSN 0031-0611. OCLC 1715274, 2449420. LC 51-25772, sn78-5219. Last issue 40 pages, last volume 222 pages, size 17 x 25. Line drawings, photographs. Published by Sigma Alpha Iota, Menasha, WI. Previous editors: Edna Rait Hutton, Nov., 1963-May, 1973; Ethel M. Bullard, Nov., 1973-May, 1979. Subject focus: clubs. Other holding institutions: AzTeS (AZS), DCU (DCU), DHU (DHU), FTaSU (FDA), MiEM (EEM), MiMtpT (EZC), [University of Minnesota Union List, Minneapolis, MN] (MUL), NSbSU (YSM), NbU (LDL), OAU (OUN), OU (OSU), OkU (OKU), (Pittsburgh Regional Library Center, Pittsburgh, PA] (QPR), PPiC (PMC), PPiD (DUQ), TNJ (TJC), TU (TKN), [AMIGOS Union List of Serials, Dallas, TX] (IUC), TxDN (INT), WaU (WAU).

| Music | v.64, n.1-v.68, n.4; Nov., 1971- May, 1976 | ML/1/P21 |
| MPL | v.56, n.1- Nov., 1963- | Art and Music Section |

894 Pan-American Medical Woman's Journal. 1893-1952//. Bi-monthly. ISSN 0096-6819. OCLC 1604548, 2265659. Last issue 24 pages, last volume 288 pages, size 17 x 26. Line drawings, photographs, some in color, commercial advertising. Available on microfilm: UnM. Published by the Pan-American Women's Alliance, Washington, DC. Title varies: as Medical Woman's Journal, Jan., 1942-Nov./Dec., 1951. Place of publication varies: Cincinnati, OH, Jan., 1942-Dec., 1950. Editor: Elizabeth Mason-Hohl. Subject focus: medicine, health care, doctors. Other holding institutions: DLC (NSD), [University of Minnesota Union List, Minneapolis, MN] (MUL), OC1W-H (CHS), OrU-M (OHS), PPiU (PIT).

## Women's Periodicals and Newspapers

      CHS        v.49, n.1-        Q/7M46443
                v.59, n.7;
                Jan., 1942-
                July, 1952

895  The Pan-Pacific Union. 1928//? Monthly. Last issue 4 pages. Size 17 x 25. Published in Honolulu, HI. Subject focus: Pacific area, law, health.

      Hist      Sep., 1928      Pam 72-1045

896  Pandora. 1970. Monthly. $6 for individuals and institutions. Pandora, P.O. Box 5094, Seattle, WA 98105. (206) 525-7479. ISSN 0031-0719. OCLC 226584. LC sc77-1414. Last issue 16 pages, size 39 x 29. Line drawings, photographs, commercial advertising. Available on microfilm: UnM (1972-1973), WHi, Herstory. Frequency varies: bi-weekly, Oct. 18, 1970-Mar. 19, 1974. Subject focus: rights, labor unions, politics. Other holding institutions: [University of Minnesota Union List, Minneapolis, MN] (MUL), NFQC (XQM), NSbSU (YSM), PPiU (PIT), MCR-S (Schlesinger Library on the History of Women in America, Radcliffe College, Cambridge, MA).

      Hist      v.1, n.1-26;      Microforms
                Oct., 1970-       Her. 1, R 20
                Oct. 5, 1971

                v.2, n.1-v.3,     Her. 1 UP, R13
                n. 19;
                Oct. 19, 1971-
                June 26, 1973

                v.3, n.20-v.4,    Her. CUP, R 6
                n. 12;
                July 10, 1973-
                June, 1974

                v.1, n.1-        Microforms
                Oct. 18, 1970-

897  Pandora, a Quarterly for Women. 1962//? Quarterly. Last issue 30 pages. Line drawings. Published by Pandora, Inc., Los Angeles, CA. Editors: Ruth Angress and Anne Wigger. Subject focus: family, psychology, fiction, poetry.

      Hist      v.1, n.1-2;       Pam 79-1734
                Spring-
                Summer, 1962

898  Pandora's Box. 1970//? Irregular. OCLC 2265685. Last issue 10 pages. Line drawings. Available on microfilm: Herstory. Published by Women's Union-Women's Liberation San Diego State College, San Diego, CA. Subject focus: education, lobbying, pro-abortion, rights, students, birth control, child care.

Other holding institutions: MCR-S (Schlesinger Library on the History of Women in America, Radcliffe College, Cambridge, MA), [University of Minnesota Union List, Minneapolis, MN] (MUL).

      Hist      v.1, n.1-3,5;     Microforms
                Mar.-June,       Her. 1, R 20
                Nov., 1970

                v.1, n.4;         Her. 1, Add
                Aug., 1970

899  Panorama Preview. 1971//? Unknown. Last issue 12 pages. Line drawings, photographs. Available on microfilm: Herstory. Published in New York, NY. Subject focus: health, alcoholism, drug abuse.

      Hist      v.3, n.3;         Microforms
                ?, 1971          Her. 2, R 13

900  The Paraclete. 1974//? Last issue 8 pages. Line drawings. Available on microfilm: Herstory. Published in San Francisco, CA. Subject focus: religion, poetry, art, feminism.

      Hist      v.1, n.1;         Microforms
                Mar. 8, 1974     Her. 3, R 4

901  Partisans. 1970//? Irregular. OCLC 2265740. Last issue 254 pages. Line drawings, photographs. Available on microfilm: Herstory. Published by Red Action Administration, Paris, France. Subject focus: politics, radicalism, stereotypes, children, economics. In French (100%).

      Hist      n.54-55;         Microforms
                July-Oct., 1970  Her. 1, R 10

902  The Patriot. 1938-1975//. Semi-annual. Last issue 12 pages, last volume 24 pages, size 16 x 25. Published by National Society, Daughters of the Revolution, New York, NY. Frequency varies: quarterly, Oct., 1938-Jan., 1949; tri-annual, Nov., 1949-June, 1974. Editors: Mary Agnes Miller, Jan., 1939-Apr., 1943; Mrs. Albert J. Sigel, Feb.-June, 1944; Mrs. Anthony Conrad Eiser, Nov., 1944-June, 1946; Mary Agnes Miller, Nov., 1946-May, 1950; Mabel L. Smiley, Nov., 1950-Feb., 1961; Mrs. Robert A. Reiter, Spring/Summer, 1961-June, 1971; Mrs. Herbert Block, Nov., 1971-Nov., 1975. Subject focus: history, clubs, lobbying.

      Hist      v.1,n.1,v.38,n.2;  E/202.6/A3
                Oct., 1938-
                Nov., 1975

903  Peace & Freedom. 1941. Irregular. $4 for individuals and institutions. Barbara

Armentrout, editor, Peace & Freedom, 1213 Race Street, Philadelphia, PA 19107. (215) 503-7110. ISSN 0015-9093. OCLC 2265762, 2255123. Last issue 24 pages, last volume 192 pages, size 22 x 28. Line drawings, photographs. Available on microfilm: Herstory (1971-1974), WHi (1941-1973). Published by Women's International League for Peace and Freedom (W.I.L.P.F.), Philadelphia, PA. Title varies: as Four Lights, Mar., 1966-Jan., 1970. Previous editors: Celia Daldy, Mar., 1966-Mar., 1967; Martha Molarsky, Apr.-July, 1967; Elizabeth Weideman, Oct., 1967-July, 1969; Gladys P. Thomas, Oct.-Nov., 1969; Angela Hoffmann, Dec., 1969-July, 1970; Eloise Henkel, Oct., 1970; Pat McKeown, Nov., 1970-Feb., 1971; Naomi Marcus, June, 1971-July, 1975; Barbara Benton Rafter, Sep., 1975-June, 1976. Subject focus: rights, affirmative action, education, international relations, lobbying, peace movement, Equal Rights Amendment, politics. Other holding institutions: [Indiana Union List of Serials, Indianapolis, IN] (ILS), MCR-S (Schlesinger Library on the History of Women in America, Radcliffe College, Cambridge, MA), MNS (SNN), [University of Minnesota Union List, Minneapolis, MN] (MUL), PPiU (PIT).

| | | |
|---|---|---|
| Hist | [v.27,n.2-v.33, n.6]; [Feb., 1966-June, 1971] | Microforms Her. 1, R 22 |
| | v.33,n.8-v.34,n.4; Nov., 1973-May, 1974 | Her. 3, R 5 |
| | v.26,n.3- Mar., 1966- | Microforms |
| Wom Ed Res | [v.36,n.9-v.38,n.1] [Nov./Dec., 1976-Jan./Feb., 1978] | Circulation |

904 Peace Times. 1971//? Unknown. OCLC 2265764. Last issue 4 pages. Line drawings, photographs. Available on microfilm: Herstory. Published by the Women's International League for Peace and Freedom, San Jose Peace Center, San Jose, CA. Subject focus: lobbying, peace movement.

| | | |
|---|---|---|
| Hist | Apr., 1971 | Microforms Her.1, R 22 |

Pedestal. Vancouver, British Columbia, Canada

see Women Can. Vancouver, British Columbia, Canada

905 Penn Women's News. 1973-1974//? Monthly. Last issue 14 pages. Line drawings. Available on microfilm: Herstory. Published by the Women's Center, University of Pennsylvania, Philadelphia, PA. Subject focus: education, students, counseling, child care, poetry, humor.

| | | |
|---|---|---|
| Hist | v.2, n.1-6; Oct., 1973-Apr., 1974 | Microforms Her. 3, R 4 |

906 People's and Howitt's Journal. 1846-1851//? Monthly. OCLC 2449561. Last issue 72 pages, last volume 364 pages. Line drawings. Available on microfilm: ResP, UnM. Published by The People's Journal, London, England. Title varies: as The People's Journal, Jan., 1846-June, 1848; as The People's Journal with which is incorporated Howitt's Journal, July-Dec., 1848. Editor: John Saunders. Subject focus: fiction, poetry, biographies. Other holding institutions: CtY (YUS), [University of Minnesota Union List, Minneapolis, MN] (MUL), [Pittsburgh Regional Library Center, Union List, Pittsburgh, PA] (QPR), PPi (CPL), PPiU (PIT).

| | | |
|---|---|---|
| Mem | Jan., 1846-June, 1851 | Microforms |

The People's Journal. London, England

see People's and Howitt's Journal. London, England

The People's Journal with which is incorporated Howitt's Journal. London, England

see People's and Howitt's Journal. London, England

Peterson's Magazine. Philadelphia, PA

see The New Peterson Magazine. Philadelphia, PA

907 Petit Courrier des Dames. 1821-1868//. 6 times a month. Last issue 12 pages, last volume 108 pages. Line drawings. Available on microfilm: ResP. Published in Paris, France. Subject focus: fashion, theater. In French (100%). Other holding institutions: DLC (DLC), IaAS (IWA), MU (AUM), NBuG (BHB), NN (NYP), [Columbia University, New York, NY] (NNC), NjR (NJR), WM (GZD).

| | | |
|---|---|---|
| Mem | v.14,n.2-v.89,n.?; Jan. 10, 1828-Aug. 29, 1868 | Microforms |

908 The Pharos, A Collection of Periodical Essays. 1786-1787//? Bi-weekly. Last issue 10 pages, last volume 296 pages. Available on micro-

film: ResP. Published in London, England. Subject focus: fiction, poetry. Other holding institution: CtY (YUS).

| | | |
|---|---|---|
| Mem | v.1, n.1-v.2, n.50; Nov. 7, 1786- Apr. 28, 1787 | Microforms |

909 Philadelphia N.O.W., Newsletter. 1970-1974?//. Monthly. OCLC 2266067. Last issue 12 pages. Line drawings. Available on microfilm: Herstory. Published by the Philadelphia Chapter, National Organization for Women, Philadelphia, PA. Subject focus: lobbying, Equal Rights Amendment, feminism, rights, media, politics, employment, marriage, health, pro-abortion.

| | | |
|---|---|---|
| Hist | Sep., 1970- Sep., 1971 | Microforms Her. 1, R 19 |
| | Oct., 1971- June, 1973 | Her. 1 UP, R11 |
| | July, 1973- June, 1974 | Her. CUP, R 5 |

The Philadelphia Repository and Weekly Repository. Philadelphia, PA

see The Repository and Ladies' Weekly Museum. Philadelphia, PA

910 The Philadelphia Women's Political Caucus Newsletter. 1972-1973?//. Monthly. Last issue 9 pages. Line drawings, photographs, commercial advertising. Available on microfilm: Herstory. Published by The Philadelphia Women's Political Caucus, Philadelphia, PA. Subject focus: politics, pro-abortion, rape, sexism, lobbying, Equal Rights Amendment.

| | | |
|---|---|---|
| Hist | v.1, n.1-v.2,n.5; Jan. 25, 1972- May, 1973 | Microforms Her. 2, R 12 |

The Philanthropist. New York, NY

see Vigilance. New York, NY

911 Phoenix Chapter Newsletter. 1970-1974//? Irregular. OCLC 2264705. Last issue 6 pages. Available on microfilm: Herstory. Published by: Phoenix Chapter, National Organization for Women, Phoenix, AZ. Title varies: as Newsletter, July, 1970-Oct., 1972; N.O.W. News, Jan.-Feb., 1973. Editors: Edythe Jensen, Oct., 1970-June, 1973; Susan Hedstrom, July, 1973-June/July, 1974. Subject focus: child care, feminism, Equal Rights Amendment, lobbying, rights.

| | | |
|---|---|---|
| Hist | July, 1971 | Microforms Her. 1, R 19 |
| | Oct., 1970 | Her. 1, Add |
| | Oct., 1971- June, 1973 | Her. 1 UP, R11 |
| | July, 1973- June/July, 1974 | Her. CUP, R 5 |

912 The Phyllis Schlafly Report. 1967? Monthly. $5 for individuals and institutions. Phyllis Schlafly, editor, The Phyllis Schlafly Report, Box 618, Alton, IL 62002. ISSN 0556-0152. OCLC 4105633. LC sn78-5180. Last issue 10 pages, last volume 94 pages, size 22 x 28. Subject focus: Equal Rights Amendment, lobbying, new right, politics.

| | | |
|---|---|---|
| Hist | v.5, n.10- Jan., 1972- | Circulation |
| MPL | Current Issues Only | Literature and Social Science Section |

Pi Lambda Theta Journal. Menasha, WI

see Educational Horizons. Bloomington, IN

913 Pioneer Woman. 1926. 7 times a year. $5 for individuals and institutions. David C. Gross and Judith A. Sokoloff, editors, Pioneer Woman, 200 Madison Avenue, New York, NY 10016. ISSN 0032-0021. OCLC 4108155. LC sn78-519. Last issue 32 pages, size 28 x 22. Line drawings, photographs, commercial advertising. Available on microfilm: Herstory, OCAJ (1960). Published by Women's Labor Zionist Organization of America, New York, NY. Previous editor: Ruth Levine, Sep., 1973. Subject focus: art, Jews, Zionism, labor Zionism, politics, biographies, Judaism. In Hebrew (15%). Other holding institutions: MdBJ (JHE), OCH (HUC), OkOk (OKE), OkU (OKU).

| | | |
|---|---|---|
| Hist | v.18, n.6; Sep., 1973 | Microforms Her. 3, R 4 |
| | v.23, n.1, v.24, n.4, v.25, n.1- Jan./Feb., 1978, Sep., 1979, Dec., 1979/Jan., 1980- | Circulation |

914 Pittsburgh Women's Center. 1972?//. Last issue 1 page. Available on microfilm: Herstory. Published in Pittsburgh, PA. Subject focus: feminism.

Hist    Apr., 1972    Microforms
Her. 2, R 13

915 Plainswoman. 1977. Bi-monthly. $6 for individuals and institutions. Jean Butenhoff Vivian, editor, Plainswoman, P.O. Box 8027, Grand Forks, ND 58202. ISSN 0148-902X. OCLC 3400725. LC sc78-247. Last issue 16 pages, last volume 88 pages, size 28 x 22. Line drawings, photographs. Published by Plainswoman, Inc., Grand Forks, ND. Frequency varies: monthly, Oct., 1977-Aug., 1979. Subject focus: rights, health, aging, art, lobbying, poetry, biographies. Other holding institutions: [University of Minnesota Union List, Minneapolis, MN] (MUL), NdU (UND), OU (OSU).

Hist    v.1, n.1-    Circulation
Oct., 1977-

916 Planned Parenthood-World Population Washington Memo. 1973?//. Last issue 2 pages. Line drawings. Available on microfilm: Herstory. Published by Planned Parenthood, Washington, DC. Subject focus: lobbying, Medicaid, pro-abortion.

Hist    Dec. 13, 1973    Microforms
Her. 3, R 4

917 The Planner. 1969-1970?//. Irregular. OCLC 1762459. Last issue 6 pages. Line drawings, photographs. Available on microfilm: Herstory. Published by the Minnesota Planning and Counseling Center for Women, Office of Student Affairs, University of Minnesota, Minneapolis, MN. Subject focus: education, students, child care, counseling, career development, rights, Equal Rights Amendment. Other holding institutions: MnHi (MHS), [University of Minnesota Union List, Minneapolis, MN] (MUL).

Hist    v.1,n.1,3,    Microforms
v.2, n.1-2;    Her. 1, R 20
Oct., Aug., 1969,
Oct., Dec., 1970

918 Plexus. 1974. Monthly. $5 for individuals, $10 for institutions. Chris Orr, editor, Plexus, 2600 Dwight Way, Berkeley, CA 94704. (415) 841-2476. Last issue 20 pages, last volume 192 pages, size 45 x 29. Line drawings, photographs, commercial advertising. Available on microfilm: Herstory (1974). Published by Feminist Publishing Alliance, Inc., Berkeley, CA. Previous editors: Chris Orr, Oct., 1977-Jan., 1978; Nancy Williamson, Feb.-Sep., 1978. Subject focus: rights, gay rights, politics, poetry, fiction, film reviews, media, art.

Hist    n.1;    Microforms
Mar. 15-31, 1974    Her. 3, R 4

v.4, n.1-    Circulation
Mar., 1977-

919 Political Caucus of Wichita Women. 1973-1974?//. Irregular. Last issue 4 pages. Line drawings. Available on microfilm: Herstory. Published by National Political Women's Caucus, Wichita, KS. Subject focus: politics, affirmative action, child care, sexism.

Hist    Feb. 12, Apr. 13,    Microforms
1973    Her. 2, R 13

July, 1973-    Her. 2 UP, R9
Apr., 1974

920 Political Equality Series. 1896-1905//? Monthly. Last issue 4 pages, size 8 x 15. Published by National American Woman Suffrage Association, Warren, OH. Place of publication varies: Philadelphia, PA, Dec., 1896-Feb., 1897. Subject focus: pro-suffrage.

Hist    v.1, n.9-11;    KWZ/PO
[n.s.]    (Cutter)
v.1, n.2,4;
Dec., 1896-
Feb., 1897,
Nov., 1904, Jan., 1905

921 Polka. A Polish Women's Magazine. 1935. Quarterly. $2 for individuals and institutions. Polka, A Polish Woman's Magazine, 1004 Pittston Avenue, Scranton, PA 18505. ISSN 0032-3594. OCLC 1762589. LC sn78-5752. Last issue 24 pages, last volume 96 pages, size 19 x 28. Line drawings, photographs, commercial advertising. Published by The United Societies of the Polish Women of Adoration of the Most Blessed Sacrament, Scranton, PA. Subject focus: clubs, Polish-Americans, Catholic Church. In Polish (50%). Other holding institution: [University of Minnesota Union List, Minneapolis, MN] (MUL).

Hist    v.43, n.3-    Circulation
July/Aug.,
Sep., 1977-

922 Portcullis. 1973?//. Unknown. Last issue 24 pages. Line drawings, photographs, commercial advertising. Available on microfilm: Herstory. Published by The Portcullis Family, Los Angeles, CA. Subject focus: lesbians, lifestyles, astrology, self-defense, poetry, health.

Hist    v.1, n.1;    Microforms
Jan., 1973    Her. 2, R 13

923 Power of Women. 1974?//. Unknown. Last issue 16 pages. Line drawings, photographs. Available on microfilm: Herstory. Published in London, England. Subject focus: politics, consumerism, fiction, employment, wages.

| Hist | v.1, n.1; Mar./Apr., 1974 | Microforms Her. 3, R 4 |

924 Le Premier. 1970-1972//. Bi-monthly. Last issue 40 pages, size 22 x 28. Line drawings. Published by Louisiana Correctional Institution for Women, Saint Gabriel, LA. Editors: Dawn Webb, Jan./Feb., 1970; Carolyn Deville, Aug., 1970-June, 1971; Kathy Fountain, Oct., 1971-Winter, 1972. Subject focus: prisoners, vocational rehabilitation, poetry, fiction, art.

| Crim Just | [Jan./Feb., 1970-Winter, 1972] | Circulation |

925 Press on N.O.W. 1973-1974?//. Monthly. Last issue 5 pages. Line drawings. Available on microfilm: Herstory. Published by Shreveport Caddo-Bossier Chapter, National Organization for Women, Shreveport, LA. Title varies: as N.O.W. Press, Mar.-Apr., 1973. Editors: Jeanie Hill and Ellen Page. Subject focus: feminism, Equal Rights Amendment, lobbying, rights, politics, poetry.

| Hist | v.1, n.4-7; Mar.-June, 1973; | Microforms Her. 2, R 9 |
| | v.1, n.7-v.2,n.7; June, 1973-June/July, 1974 | Her. 2 UP, R 6 |

926 Primapara. 1974. Semi-annual. $3 for individuals and institutions. Diane Nichols, editor, Primapara, P.O. Box 371, Oconto, WI 54153. Last issue 48 pages, last volume 96 pages, size 14 x 21. Line drawings. Subject focus: poetry.

| RBR | (Founders' Issue), v.1, n.1- Oct., 1974, May, 1975- | Circulation |
| MPL | (Founders' Issue), v.1, n.1- Oct., 1974, May, 1975, | Literature and Social Science Section |

927 Prime Time. 1971-1977//. Bi-monthly. OCLC 2380326, 5370990. Last issue 24 pages, last volume 186 pages. Line drawings, photographs, commercial advertising. Available on microfilm: Herstory (1971-1974), WHi (1974-1977). Published by Prime Time, Inc., New York, NY. Place of publication varies: Piermont, NY, July, 1973-June, 1974. Frequency varies: monthly, Jan., 1974-Jan., 1976. Editor: Marjory Collins. Subject focus: senior women, aging, health, ecology, agism, sexuality, art, self-help. Other holding institution: MCR-S (Schlesinger Library on the History of Women in America, Radcliffe College, Cambridge, MA).

| Hist | v.1, n.1-13; Sep., 1971-June, 1973 | Microforms Her. 2, R 9 |
| | v.1, n.14-v.2, n.5; July, 1973-June, 1974 | Her. 2 UP, R 9 |
| | v.2, n.4-v.5,n.8 May, 1974-June/July, 1977 | Microforms |
| Soc Work | v.2, n.1-v.5,n.8; Jan., 1974-June/July, 1977 | Circulation |
| Wom St | v.5, n.7-8; Apr./May-June/July, 1977 | Reading Room |
| Wom Ed Res | v.2, n.5-v.5,n.8; May, 1974-June/July, 1977 | Circulation |

928 Pro Se: National Law Women's Newsletter. 1971-1977?//. Irregular. ISSN 0093-8858. OCLC 1792675. LC 74-642388. Last issue 11 pages, last volume 44 pages, size 22 x 28. Line drawings. Available on microfilm: Herstory (1971-1974). Published by Pro Se Collective, Boston, MA. Place of publication varies: Washington, DC, Dec., 1971, Feb., 1972. Subject focus: law, education, lobbying, rights, students, lawyers. Other holding institutions: DGU-L (GUL), DLC (DLC), [University of Minnesota Union List, Minneapolis, MN] (MUL), NIC (COO), OkU (OKL), PPiU (PIT).

| Hist | v.1, n.1-v.2,n.1; Dec., 1971-Sep., 1972 | Microforms Her. 2, R 14 |
| | v.3, n.1,3; Sep./Oct., 1973, Jan./Feb., 1974 | Her. 2UP, R 9 |
| Law | v.1, n.1-v.5,n.1; Dec., 1971-Apr./May, 1977 | Circulation |

929 Profile. 1978. Monthly. Phyllis A. Bermington, editor, Profile, 416 1/2 Third Street, Suite 2, Wausau, WI 54401. (715) 842-7051, 842-5663. Last issue 4 pages, size 22 x 18. Available on microfilm: WHi (1980). Title varies: as The Spokeswoman, Feb.-Mar., 1978. Published by The Women's Community, Inc., Wausau, WI.

Subject focus: displaced homemakers, motherhood, workers.

| | | |
|---|---|---|
| Hist | v.3, n.7-<br>July, 1980- | Circulation |
| Wom Ed<br>Res | v.1, n.2-<br>Feb., 1978- | Circulation |

930   Progress. 1901-1910//? Monthly. Last issue 4 pages, last volume 26 pages. Available on microfilm: ResP. Published by National American Woman Suffragists Association, New York, NY. Subject focus: pro-suffrage. Other holding institution: MCR-S (Schlesinger Library on the History of Women in America, Radcliffe College, Cambridge, MA).

| | | |
|---|---|---|
| Mem | v.1, n.1-v.10,<br>n.6;<br>Oct., 1901-<br>June, 1910 | Microforms |

The Progressive Woman.   Girard, KS;
    Chicago, IL

see The Coming Nation.   Chicago, IL

931   Progressive Woman. 1971-1972?//. Semi-monthly. ISSN 0033-0833. OCLC 1775403. LC 77-616584. Last issue 34 pages, last volume 386 pages. Line drawings, photographs, commercial advertising. Available on microfilm: Herstory. Published by Corson Publishing, Inc., Middlebury, IN. Frequency varies: monthly, July, 1971-Mar., 1972. Editor: Rosalie P. Corson. Subject focus: health, ESP, art, biographies, economics, travel, business, politics, professionals. Other holding institutions: [Indiana Union List of Serials, Indianapolis, IN] (ILS), [University of Minnesota Union List, Minneapolis, MN] (MUL), NSbSU (YSM), PPiCC (HHC), [Pittsburgh Regional Library Center-Union List, Pittsburgh, PA] (QPR).

| | | |
|---|---|---|
| Hist | v.1, n.1-3;<br>July-Sep., 1971 | Microforms<br>Her. 1, R 10 |
| | v.1, n.4-v.2,<br>n.15;<br>Oct., 1971-<br>Dec., 1972 | Her. 1 UP, R14 |

932   Protect Abortion Rights. 1979. Irregular. Gratis for individuals and institutions. Protect Abortion Rights, P.O. Box 9711, Madison, WI. (608) 238-2338. Last issue 8 pages, size 22 x 28. Line drawings, photographs. Subject focus: pro-abortion.

| | | |
|---|---|---|
| Hist | Mar., 1979- | Circulation |

933   Proud Woman. 1971-1972?//. OCLC 2264422. Last issue 12 pages. Line drawings, photographs, commercial advertising. Available on microfilm: Herstory. Published by Mother Publications, Stanford, CA. Title varies: as Mother, June-Dec., 1971. Editor: R.G. Parker. Subject focus: lesbians, poetry, rights. Other holding institution: MCR-S (Schlesinger Library on the History of Women in America, Radcliffe College, Cambridge, MA).

| | | |
|---|---|---|
| Hist | v.1, n.1-3;<br>June-Aug., 1971 | Microforms<br>Her. 1, R 2 |
| | v.1, n.5-v.2,n.1;<br>Oct., 1971-<br>Apr., 1972 | Her. 1 UP, R14 |

934   Psychology of Women Quarterly. 1976. Quarterly. $40 for individuals and institutions. Gloria Babladelis, editor, Psychology of Women Quarterly, Dept. of Psychology, California State University, Hayward, CA 95454. Business address: 72 5th Ave., New York, NY 10011. ISSN 0361-6843. OCLC 2529664. LC 76-12952, sc76-790. Last issue 146 pages, last volume 320 pages, size 15 x 23. Line drawings. Indexed in: Psychological Abstracts, Human Resources Abstracts, Sociological Abstracts, Social Sciences Citation Index, Current Contents/Social and Behavioral Science, (CIJE), Chicorel Abstracts to Reading and Learning Disabilities, Child Development Abstracts and Bibliography, Development and Welfare, Human Sexuality Update, Marriage and Family Review. Published by Human Sciences Press, New York NY. Subject focus: psychology, research. Other holding institutions: ABAU (ABC), AU (ALM), ArU (AFU), AzTeS (AZS), AzU (AZU), CSt (Stanford University), CChiS (CCH), CLSU (CSL), CLU (CLU), CLamB (CBC), CLobS (CLO), CU-Riv (CRU), CoDU (DVP), CtNIC (CTL), CtW (WLU), CtY (YUS), DGC-K (GOG), DHU (DHU), DLC (DLC), DeU (DLM), FJUNF (FNP), FMFIU (FXG,FXN), FTaSU (FDA), FU (FUG), GASU (GSU), GEU (EMU), GU (GUA), GVaS (GYG), IaCfT (NIU), ICI (IAH), INS (IAI), IPB (IBA), IU (UIU), KyLoH (KLG), KyU (KUK), LNT (LRU), MBTI (BTI), MBU (BOS), MH (HUL), MNS (SNN), [University of Minnesota Union List, Minneapolis, MN] (MUL), MNtcA (BAN), MShM (MTH), MWH (HCD), MWelC (WFL), MdBJ (JHE), MdStm (MDS), MiDU (EYU), MiEM (EEM), MiMtpT (EZC), MoU (MUU), MoUst (UMS), NA1U (NAM), [New York State Union List, Albany, NY] (NYS), NBC (VDB), NBM (VVD), NBrockU (XBM), NCH (YHM), NDFM (VZE), NGenoU (YGM), NIC (COO), NNCH-G (ZGM), NNU (ZYU), NOneoU (ZBM), NOsU (YOM), NPV (VXW), NSbSU (YSM), NSbSU-H (VZB), NSyU (SYB), NbKS (KRS), NbU (LDL), NcCU (NKM), NcU (NOC), NcWsW (EWF), NhD (DRB), NmLcU (IRU), NmU (IQU), OAkU (AKR), OCU (CIN), ODaWU (WSU), OMC (MRC), OTU (TOL), OkS (OKS), OkU (OKU), PBbS (PBB), PCW (UWC), PNwC (WFN), PPiU (PIT), PSC (PSC), PU (PAU), RPB (RBN), TCU (TUC), TMurS (TXM), TNJ (TJC), TxCM (TXA), [AMIGOS Union List Of Serials, Dallas, TX]

(IUC), TxDW (IWU), TxDN (INT), TxHU (TXH), ViNO (VOD), ViRCU (VRC), ViRU (VRU), ViW (VWM), VtU (VTU), WaU (WAU), WMUW (GZN), WeharU (HRM), Wu-M (CZH).

| Mem | v.1, n.1-<br>Fall, 1976- | AP/P974/031 |
| Wom St | v.1, n.1-<br>Fall, 1976- | Reading Room |
| CHS | v.1, n.1-<br>Fall, 1976- | Periodicals Section |

935 Purple Rage. 1972?//. Unknown. Last issue 14 pages. Line drawings, commercial advertising. Available on microfilm: Herstory. Published in New York, NY. Subject focus: lesbians, politics, radicalism, food, poetry.

| Hist | Mar., 1972? | Microforms Her. 2, R 14 |

936 Purple Star: Journal of Radicalesbians. 1970?//. Unknown. OCLC 2266664. Last issue 24 pages. Line drawings. Available on microfilm: Herstory. Published by Women's Liberation of Ann Arbor, Ann Arbor, MI. Subject focus: art, poetry, lesbians, politics, radicalism.

| Hist | v.1, n.1;<br>Spring, 1970 | Microforms Her. 1, R 10 |

937 Quad Cities Chapter N.O.W. 1972-1974?//. Monthly. Last issue 4 pages. Line drawings. Available on microfilm: Herstory. Published by Quad Cities Chapter, National Organization for Women, Moline, IL. Subject focus: feminism, Equal Rights Amendment, lobbying, rights, consciousness raising, poetry.

| Hist | July, 1972-<br>June, 1973 | Microforms Her. 2, R 11 |
| | July, 1973-<br>June, 1974 | Her. 2 UP, R8 |

938 Quaderni Di Lotta Feminista. 1972-1973?//. Last issue 142 pages. Available on microfilm: Herstory. Published in Padova, Italy. Subject focus: rights, employment. In Italian (100%).

| Hist | n.1;<br>Dec., 1972 | Microforms Her. 2, R 14 |
| | n.2-4?;<br>?, 1973 | Her. 2 UP, R4 |

939 Quebecoises Deboutte. 1972-1974//? Monthly. Last issue 20 pages, size 22 x 28. Line drawings, photographs. Available on microfilm: Herstory. Published by Le Centre des Femmes, Montreal, Quebec, Canada. Subject focus: rights, politics, French-Canadians, poetry, family planning. In French (100%).

| Hist | v.1, n.1-6;<br>Nov., 1972-<br>Mar., 1973 | Pam 74-3923 |
| | v.1, n.1;<br>Nov., 1972 | Microforms Her. 2, R 14 |
| | v.1, n.7-9;<br>July/Aug., 1973-<br>Mar., 1974 | Her. 2UP, R 9 |

940 Quest: A Feminist Quarterly. 1974. Quarterly. $9 for individuals, $25 for institutions. Quest: A Feminist Quarterly, Inc., P.O. Box 8843, Washington, DC 20003. Business address: 2000 P Street NW, Washington, DC 20036. ISSN 0098-955X. OCLC 2242837. LC 75-646061. Last issue 96 pages, last volume 400 pages, size 15 x 22. Line drawings, photographs, commercial advertising. Indexed in: Abstracts of Popular Culture; Women Studies Abstracts. Previous editor: Beverly Fisher, Fall, 1974-Summer, 1978. Subject focus: feminism, politics. Other holding institutions: AU (ALM), AzU (AZU), CSt (Stanford University), CLSU (CSU), CLobS (CLO), COU-DA (COA), CtW (WLU), CtY (YUS), DLC (DLC), DeU (DLM), FMFIU (FXG), FU (FUG), GASU (GSU), GU (GUA), IU (UIU), InND (IND), InU (IUL), KMK (KKS), KyU (KUK), LNU (LNU), MAH (HAM), MBTI (BTI), MBU (BOS), MCE (BPS), MH-AH (BHA), MWe1C (WFL), [University of Minnesota Union List, Minneapolis, MN] (MUL), MnStpeG (MNG), NA1U (NAM), [New York State Union List, Albany, NY] (NYS), NIC (COO), NR (YQR), NcCU (NKM), NhD (DRB), NmLcU (IRU), OCU (CIN), OU (OSU), OYU (YNG), PBL (LYU), PPiU (PIT), [University of Wisconsin-Stevens Point, Stevens Point, WI] (WIS).

| Hist | v.1, n.2-<br>Fall, 1974- | HQ/1101/Q4 |
| Coll | Current Issues Only | Women's Reading Area |
| Wom St | v.1, n.1-<br>Summer, 1974- | Reading Room |
| Mem | v.1, n.1-<br>Summer, 1974- | AP/Q518/W |

941 The RC Communicator. 1978. Irregular. Karlyn Ellard and Susan Thomas, editors, The RC Communicator, Resource Center for Women's Programs, Room 103B, Sandels Building, Florida State University, Tallahassee, FL 32306. Last issue 4 pages, size 22 x 28. Subject focus: employment re-entry, workers.

| Wom St | v.1, n.7-<br>Sep., 1978- | Reading Room |

942 RCC News. 1980. Bi-monthly. RCC News, P.O. Box 1312, Madison, WI 53701. (608) 251-7273. Last issue 8 pages, size 28 x 23. Line drawings. Available on microfilm: WHi. Published by Madison Rape Crisis Center, Madison, WI. Subject focus: rape, incest, child sexual abuse, Dane County Project on Rape, family violence.

    Hist    v.1, n.2-    Circulation
             July, 1980-

Racine Convenience. Racine, WI

    see Convenience Magazine. Racine, WI

943 Raising Cain. 1971-1974?//. Irregular. Last issue 12 pages. Line drawings, commercial advertising. Available on microfilm: Herstory. Published by Washington Area Women's Center, Washington, DC. Title varies: as Women's Liberation Bulletin, Nov./Dec., 1971-Dec., 1972; Washington Area Women's Center Bulletin, Jan., 1973-Feb., 1974. Subject focus: lobbying, health, pro-abortion.

    Hist    Nov./Dec., 1971-    Microforms
             June, 1973    Her. 2, R 16

             July, 1973-    Her. 2 UP,
             May, 1974    R 9-10

944 Rapport. 1973-1974//? Irregular. Last issue 2 pages. Line drawings. Available on microfilm: Herstory. Published by The Women's Liberation Center, Evanston, IL. Subject focus: rape, literature, health, consciousness raising, pro-abortion, Equal Rights Amendment, sexism.

    Hist    n.9-22;    Microforms
             Aug., 1973-    Her. 3, R 4
             June 13, 1974

945 Rat. 1968-1971//? OCLC 2269631. Last issue 16 pages. Line drawings, photographs. Available on microfilm: Herstory (1970-1971), WHi. Published by Women's LibeRATion, New York, NY. Subject focus: politics, radicalism, lesbians, gay rights, rights, poetry, sexism. Other holding institutions: AU (ALM), MCR-S (Schlesinger Library on the History of Women in America, Radcliffe College, Cambridge, MA), [University of Minnesota Union List, Minneapolis, MN] (MUL), NFQC (XQM), OKentU (KSU), PPiU (PIT).

    Hist    Jan. 26, 1970-    Microforms
             Aug. 2, 1971    Her. 1, R 3

             Apr. 5, 1968-    Microforms
             Aug. 2, 1971

946 La Razon Mestiza. 1974?//. Unknown. OCLC 2381261. Last issue 6 pages. Line drawings, photographs. Available on microfilm: Herstory. Published by Concilio Mujeres, San Francisco, CA. Subject focus: education, employment, arts, Chicanas.

    Hist    n.1;    Microforms
             Mar., 1974    Her. 3, R 4

947 Reach Out. 1971-1972?//. Irregular. OCLC 2266772. Last issue 5 pages. Line drawings. Available on microfilm: Herstory. Published by The New Detroit Daughters of Bilitis, Detroit/Dearborn, MI. Subject focus: poetry, gay rights, pro-abortion, education, lesbians.

    Hist    v.1, n.1-4;    Microforms
             May-Sep., 1971    Her. 1, R 14

             v.1, n.5-6;    Her. 1UP, R 2
             Dec., 1971-
             Mar., 1972

948 Real Women. 1971//? Irregular. OCLC 2266781. Last issue 7 pages. Line drawings. Available on microfilm: Herstory. Published by Saint Louis Women's Liberation, St. Louis, MO. Subject focus: housing, child care, education, law, prison reform.

    Hist    Apr.-Summer, 1971    Microforms
                                  Her. 1, R 20

949 Red Star. 1970-1971//? Irregular. OCLC 2266810. Last issue 8 pages. Line drawings, photographs. Available on microfilm: Herstory. Published by Red Women's Detachment, New York, NY. Subject focus: politics, radicalism, welfare, family, monogamy, prostitution, revolution.

    Hist    n.1-5;    Microforms
             Mar., 1970-    Her. 1, R 20
             Mar., 1971

950 Redbook. 1903. Monthly. $7.95 for individuals and institutions. Sey Chassler, editor, Redbook, 230 Park Avenue, New York, NY 10017. Business address: Box 5242, Des Moines, IA 50340. (800) 247-5470. ISSN 0034-2106. OCLC 1763595. LC sn78-4277. Last issue 212 pages, last volume 2564 pages, size 21 x 27. Line drawings, photographs, some in color, commercial advertising. Indexed: in Readers' Guide to Periodical Literature (1961-). Available on microfilm: McP (1969-), UnM. Published by The Redbook Publishing Company, New York, NY. Subject focus: interior decoration, beauty care, fiction, fashion, food, crafts. Other holding institutions: [Alabama Public Library Service, Montgomery, AL] (ASL), AU (ALM), ArAO (AKO), ArAT (AKH), ArCCA (AKC), AzFU (AZN), AzTeS (AZS), AzU (AZU), CFS (CFS), CLSU

(CSL), COU-DA (COA), CoDU (DVP), CtS (FEM), FBoU (FGM), FJUNF (FNP), GA (GAP), GAuA (GJG), IPB (IBA), InAndC (INA), InU (IUL), KyRE (KEU), LHS (LSH), MiKW (EXW), MiLC (EEL), MiMtpT (EZC), [New York State Union List, Albany, NY] (NYS), [Western New York Library Resources Council, Buffalo, NY] (VZX), NCorniCC (ZDG), NCortU (YCM), NGcCC (VVX), NIC (COO), NNR (ZXC), NOneoU (ZBM), NR (YQR), [Central New York Library Resources Council, Syracuse, NY] (SRR), NSyU (SYB), NcCU (NKM), NcGU (NGU), NcRS (NRC), NcWfSB (NVS), NdU (UND), NbKS (KRS), NbU (LDL), NjLincB (BCC), NmLcU (IRU), NmLvH (NMH), OCl (CLE), OKentU (KSU), OTU (TOL), OU (OSU), OkLC (OKC), OkT (TUL), PPD (DXU), ScRhW (SWW), TCollsM (TMS), TMurS (TXM), TxAbH (TXS), TxBelM (MHB), TxCM (TXA), TxDW (IWU), [AMIGOS Union List of Serials, Dallas, TX] (IUC), TxLT (ILU), TxNacS (TXK), ViRCU (VRC), [Arrowhead Library System, Janesville Public Library, Janesville, WI] (GZD), MCR-S (Schlesinger Library on the History of Women in America, Radcliffe College, Cambridge, MA).

| | | |
|---|---|---|
| MPL | v.135, n.11-<br>Nov., 1962- | Literature and Social Science Section |
| MATC | v.147, n.10-<br>Oct., 1974- | Cora Hardy Library |
| MHHS | v.145, n.1-<br>Jan., 1972- | Circulation |
| MIPL | v.148, n.1-<br>Jan., 1975- | Circulation |
| EHS | v.147, n.1-<br>Jan., 1974- | Circulation |
| DFPL | v.146, n.1-<br>Jan., 1973- | Circulation |
| MFHS | v.146, n.1-<br>Jan., 1973- | Circulation |
| BEL | Current Issues Only | Circulation |
| SAPH | Current Issues Only | Circulation |
| MCL | v.145, n.1-<br>Jan., 1972- | Circulation |
| SCPL | v.143, n.2-<br>Feb., 1970- | Circulation |
| LAHS | Current Issues Only | Circulation |
| VHS | v.142, n.1-<br>Jan., 1969- | Circulation |
| CFL | v.148, n.1-<br>Jan., 1975- | Circulation |
| MGHS | v.138, n.11-<br>Nov., 1967- | Circulation |
| OM | Current Issues Only | Circulation |
| OPL | Current Issues Only | Circulation |
| SPHS | v.144, n.2-<br>Feb., 1971- | Circulation |
| WHS | v.143, n.7-<br>July, 1970- | Circulation |
| BFL | Current Issues Only | Circulation |
| RPL | [v.143, n.1-]<br>[Jan., 1970-] | Circulation |
| DFHS | v.147, n.8-<br>Aug., 1974- | Circulation |
| VPL | v.140, n.1-<br>Jan., 1967- | Circulation |
| BHS | [v.148, n.1-]<br>[Jan., 1975-] | Circulation |
| BML | Current Issues Only | Circulation |

951 <u>Reflector</u>. 1969. Irregular. Barbara Schleret and Pat Capistrant, editors, Reflector, Minnesota Correctional Institute for Women, Box 7, Shakopee, MN 55379. Last issue 33 pages, size 22 x 28. Line drawings. Previous editors: Sandy Oppegard, Winter, 1970-Spring, 1972; Samantha Maria Xanthes, Spring/Summer-Fall, 1975; Peggy Schern and Mary Berseth, Nov., 1977; Peggy Schern, Mar., 1978. Subject focus: poetry, fiction, health, religion, art, prisoners.

| | | |
|---|---|---|
| Crim Just | Winter, 1969- | Circulation |

952 <u>Refractory Girl</u>. 1973-1978//. Irregular. OCLC 4304441. Last issue 48 pages, size 21 x 27. Line drawings, photographs, commercial advertising. Available on microfilm: Herstory (1973-1974). Published by Women's Study Group/Every Woman Press, Chippendale, New South Wales, Australia. Place of publication varies: Sydney, Australia, Summer, 1973-Summer, 1974. Subject focus: rights, education, child care, children's literature, history, research, poetry. Other holding institutions: CLU (CLU), CtY (YUS), [University of Minnesota Union List, Minneapolis, MN] (MUL).

| | | |
|---|---|---|
| Hist | n.1-3;<br>Summer-Winter,<br>1973 | Microforms<br>Her. 3, R 14 |

| | n.4-5;<br>Spring-<br>Summer, 1974 | Her. 2 UP, R10 |
|---|---|---|
| Coll | n.12-16;<br>Sep., 1976-<br>May, 1978 | Women's<br>Reading Area |

953 Remember Our Fire. 1969//? Unknown. OCLC 2266845. Last issue 16 pages. Line drawings. Available on microfilm: Herstory. Published by Shameless Hussy Press, Berkeley, CA. Subject focus: poetry.

| Hist | n.1-3;<br>?, 1969 | Microforms<br>Her. 1, R 11 |
|---|---|---|

The Remonstrance. Boston, MA

    see The Remonstrance Against Woman's Suffrage. Boston, MA

954 The Remonstrance Against Woman Suffrage. 1890-1920//. Quarterly. ISSN 0092-3966. OCLC 1788506, 2450108, 4378928, 4379207. LC 73-646033. Last issue 8 pages, last volume 32 pages, size 29 x 21. Line drawings, photographs. Available on microfilm: ResP, RPB. Published by the Massachusetts Association Opposed to the Further Extension of Suffrage to Women, Boston, MA, 1890-Apr., 1915; by the Women's Anti-Suffrage Association of Massachusetts, Boston, MA, July, 1915-Oct., 1920. Title varies: as The Remonstrance, 1890-Oct., 1913. Frequency varies: annual, 1890-1906. Subject focus: anti-suffrage. Other holding institutions: DLC (DLC), [Indiana Union List of Serials, Indianapolis, IN] (ILS) NN (NYP), NPV (VXW), NcGU (NGU), PPi (CPL), [Pittsburgh Regional Library Center Union List, Pittsburgh, PA] (QPR).

| Hist | 1900-Oct., 1920 | KWZ/M41/R<br>(Cutter) |
|---|---|---|
| Mem | 1890-Oct., 1920 | Microforms |

955 The Reply. 1913-1915?//. Monthly. OCLC 5744722. LC 21-6730. Last issue 28 pages, last volume 308 pages. Line drawings, photographs, commercial advertising. Available on microfilm: ResP, McA, DLC. Published by Mac-A-Nan Press, New Canaan, CT. Editor: Helen S. Harman-Brown. Subject focus: anti-suffrage. Other holding institutions: CSt (Stanford University), MH (HLS), NCH (YCM).

| Hist | v.1, n.1-v.2,<br>n.10;<br>May 13, 1913-<br>May, 1915 | Microforms |
|---|---|---|

| Mem | v.1, n.1-v.2,<br>n. 10;<br>May 13, 1913-<br>May, 1915 | Microforms |
|---|---|---|

956 The Repository and Ladies Weekly Museum. 1800-1806//? Weekly. OCLC 1763732, 3938344. LC mic56-4625. Last issue 8 pages, last volume 128 pages. Self-indexed (1800-1804). Available on microfilm: UnM. Published by David Hogan, Philadelphia, PA. Title varies: as The Philadelphia Repository and Weekly Repository, Nov. 15, 1800-June 29, 1805. Editors: David Hogan, Nov. 15, 1800-Dec. 24, 1803; John W. Scott, Jan 7-Dec. 29, 1804; Thomas Irwin, Jan. 5-June 29, 1805; Solomon Slender (pseud.), Dec. 14, 1805-Mar. 15, 1806. Subject focus: fiction, poetry, music. Other holding institutions: AzTeS (AZS), [University of Minnesota Union List, Minneapolis, MN] (MUL), NSbSU (YSM), NcWsW (EWF), OKentU (KSU), OYU (YNG), PPiU (PIT).

| Hist | v.1, n.1-v.6,<br>n. 13;<br>Nov. 15, 1800-<br>Mar. 15, 1806 | Microforms |
|---|---|---|

957 The Republican Clubwoman. 1961-1967//. Monthly. Last issue 4 pages, last volume 34 pages, size 22 x 28. Line drawings, photographs. Published by The National Federation of Republican Women, Washington, DC. Editor: Elizabeth Fielding, Feb., 1964-Dec., 1967. Subject focus: Republican Party, clubs, politics, political parties.

| Hist | v.1, n.1-v.7,n.9;<br>Mar., 1961-<br>Dec., 1967 | JK/2351/R43 |
|---|---|---|

958 Research in Progress. 1971-1973//? Irregular. OCLC 2321946. Last issue 6 pages. Available on microfilm: Herstory. Published by Women's Caucus For the Modern Languages, (Modern Language Association), West Lafayette, IN. Subject focus: linguistics, research, education. Other holding institutions: [University of Minnesota Union List, Minneapolis, MN] (MUL), NFQC (XQM), NbU (LDL), NhD (DRB), WMUW (GZN).

| Hist | v.1, n.2-4, v.2,<br>n.1-3;<br>Fall, 1971-<br>Spring, 1972,<br>Sep., 1972-<br>Mar., 1973 | Microforms<br>Her. 1 UP, R 7 |
|---|---|---|

959 Research in Progress. 1971//? Unknown. OCLC 2266904. Last issue 6 pages. Available on microfilm: Herstory. Published by Women's Caucus for the Modern Languages, Slippery Rock, PA. Subject focus: linguistics.

| | | | |
|---|---|---|---|
| Hist | v.1, n.1;<br>Summer, 1971 | Microforms<br>Her. 1, R 16 | |
| | v.1, n.2? | Her. 1 UP, R 6 | |

960 Research in Progress-Women's Caucus for the Modern Languages. 1973-1974//? Irregular. Last issue 8 pages. Available on microfilm: Herstory. Published by Women's Caucus for the Modern Languages, University of Pittsburgh, Pittsburgh, PA. Subject focus: research, education, linguistics.

| | | | |
|---|---|---|---|
| Hist | v.3, n.1-4;<br>Sep., 1973-<br>Mar./June, 1974 | Microforms<br>Her. CUP, R 3 | |

961 Resources for Feminist Research/Documentation Sur la Recherche Feministe. 1973. Quarterly. $15 for individuals, $25 for institutions. Margrit Eichler, Jennifer Newton, Marylee Stephenson, and Carol Zavitz, editors, Resources for Feminist Research/Documentation Sur la Recherche Feministe, Department of Sociology, Ontario Institute for Studies in Education, 252 Bloor Street West, Toronto, Ontario, Canada M5S 1V6. ISSN 0707-8412. OCLC 5585549. LC cn79-31946. Last issue 82 pages, last volume 498 pages, size 22 x 28. Line drawings, commercial advertising. Indexed in: American Humanities Index, America: History and Life, Historical Abstracts, Canadian Education Index, Women Studies Abstracts, Sociological Abstracts. Subject focus: research, sex roles, women's studies. Other holding institutions: AzTeS (AZS), CaOONL (NLC), HU (HUH), InLP (IPL), NBronSL (VVS), WMUW (GZN), WaU (WAU).

| | | |
|---|---|---|
| Mem | v.6,n.1-<br>Mar., 1978- | Periodicals<br>Section |

962 Response. 1969. 11 issues per year. $4 for individuals and institutions. Carol Marie Herb, editor, Response, Room 1323, 475 Riverside Drive, New York, NY 10027. Business address: 7820 Reading Road, Cincinnati, OH 45237. Last issue 50 pages, size 21 x 28. Line drawings, photographs. Subject focus: missions, rights, Christianity.

| | | |
|---|---|---|
| Hist | v.1, n.1-<br>Jan., 1969- | BX/8201/R46 |
| SPPL | v.7, n.5-<br>May, 1975- | Circulation |
| CFL | Current Issues<br>Only | Circulation |

963 Response to Violence and Sexual Abuse in the Family. 1976. Irregular. Pilar Saavedra-Vela and Karen Crest, editors, Response to Violence and Sexual Abuse in the Family, 2000 P Street NW, Suite 508, Washington, DC 20036.

(202) 872-1770. OCLC 5079311. Last issue 8 pages, last volume 63 pages, size 22 x 28. Published by the Center for Women Policy Studies, Washington, DC. Previous editors: P.J. Marschner, Dec., 1976-June/Aug., 1978; Pilar Saavedra-Vela, Oct., 1978-Apr., 1979; Pilar Saavedra-Vela, Anne Miller, and Penny Watts, May/June-July, 1979; Pilar Saavedra-Vela and Denise Boles, Aug., 1979. Subject focus: lobbying, family violence. Other holdinf institutions: [Congressional Research Service, Washington, DC] (CRS), NcDL (NDL).

| | | |
|---|---|---|
| Crim Just | v.1, n.1-<br>Oct., 1976- | Circulation |
| Soc Work | v.1, n.9-<br>July/Aug., 1978- | Circulation |
| Coll | Current Issues<br>Only | Women's<br>Reading Area |
| Wom Ed | v.1, n.4-<br>Apr./June, 1977- | Circulation |

964 The Restless Eagle. 1971//? Unknown. OCLC 2266929. Last issue 2 pages. Available on microfilm: Herstory. Published by The Isla Vista Women's Center, Goleta, CA. Subject focus: child care.

| | | |
|---|---|---|
| Hist | July, 1971 | Microforms<br>Her. 1, R 20 |

965 Revista de la Associacion Feminina de Camagüey. 1921-1926//. Monthly. Last issue 30 pages, last volume 210 pages. Line drawings, photographs, commercial advertising. Available on microfilm: ResP. Published by Associacion Feminina de Camagüey, Camagüey, Cuba. Editor: Isabel Esperanza Betancourt. Subject focus: poetry, fiction. In Spanish (100%). Other holding institution: NN (NYP).

| | | |
|---|---|---|
| Mem | n.25-67;<br>Jan., 1923-<br>July, 1926 | Microforms |

The Revolution. Albuquerque, NM

see N.O.W. Newsletter. Albuquerque, NM

966 The Revolution. 1868-1872//. Weekly. OCLC 1963797, 2606949, 2759932, 1644047. LC 10-660. Last issue 16 pages, last volume 416 pages, size 21 x 30. Line drawings, commercial advertising. Available on microfilm: GrP (1868-1871), UnM. Published by The Revolution, New York, NY. Editors: Elizabeth Cady Stanton and Parker Pillsbury, Jan. 8, 1868-July 1, 1869; Elizabeth Cady Stanton, July 8, 1869-May 26, 1870; Laura Curtis Bullard, June 2, 1870-Oct. 12, 1871. Subject focus: rights, pro-suffrage, employment, poetry, literary criticism. Other

holding institutions: CSt (Stanford University), CLobS (CLO), CPT (CIT), FTaSU (FDA), GASU (GSU), ICL (IAL), MdFreH (HCF), MCR-S (Schlesinger Library on the History of Women in America, Radcliffe College, Cambridge, MA), MeB (BBH), [University of Minnesota Union List, Minneapolis, MN] (MUL), MnStpeG (MNG), NhD (DRB), NCaS (XLM), NFredU (XFM), NSyU (SYB), OAkU (AKR), OKentU (KSU), PPi (CPL), PPiU (PIT), [Pittsburgh Regional Library Center Union List, Pittsburgh, PA] (QPR), ViNO (VOD).

| Hist | v.1, n.1?-v.6, n.26; Jan. 8, 1868-Dec. 29, 1870 | KWZ/"R454 (Cutter) |
| --- | --- | --- |
|  | v.1, n.2-v.8, n.15; Jan. 15, 1868-Oct. 12, 1871 | Microforms |

967   Revolution Within the Revolution. 1972//? Unknown. Last issue 22 pages. Line drawings. Available on microfilm: Herstory. Published by Women's Caucus of Action Latin America, Cambridge, MA. Subject focus: revolution, radicalism, politics, birth control, poetry, Latinas.

| Hist | v.1, n.3; Mar., 1972 | Microforms Her. 2, R 14 |
| --- | --- | --- |

968   Revue de Morale Sociale. 1899-1903//. Quarterly. Last issue 142 pages, last volume 508 pages. Line drawings, commercial advertising. Available on microfilm: ResP, McA. Published by V. Giard and E. Briere, Geneva, Switzerland. Editors: Louis Bridel, Mar., 1899-June, 1900; Alfred de Meuron, Sep., 1900-Dec., 1903. Subject focus: law, economics, sex roles, education. In French (100%). Other holding institution: CtY (YUS).

| Mem | Mar., 1899-Dec., 1903 | Microforms |
| --- | --- | --- |

969   La Revue Féministe. 1895-1897//. Monthly. Last issue 64 pages, last volume 968 pages. Available on microfilm: McA, ResP. Published by La Revue Féministe, Paris, France. Editor: Clotilde Dissard. Frequency varies: semi-monthly, Oct., 1895-Dec., 1896. Subject focus: suffrage, intellectuals. In French (100%).

| Mem | v.1, n.1-v.3, n.4; Oct., 1895-Apr., 1897 | Microforms |
| --- | --- | --- |

970   Rhode Island Chapter of N.O.W. Newsletter. 1972-1974//? Monthly. Last issue 7 pages. Line drawings, commercial advertising. Available on microfilm: Herstory. Published by Rhode Island Chapter, National Organization for Women, Providence, RI. Subject focus: consciousness raising, feminism, Equal Rights Amendment, lobbying, rights, politics.

| Hist | July, 1972-June, 1973 | Microforms Her. 2, R 11 |
| --- | --- | --- |
|  | July, 1973-June, 1974 | Her. 2 UP, R 8 |

971   Right N.O.W. 1972-1974//? Monthly. Last issue 8 pages, last volume 80 pages. Line drawings. Available on microfilm: Herstory. Published by Columbus Chapter, National Organization for Women, Columbus, OH. Subject focus: feminism, lobbying, Equal Rights Amendment, rights, media, politics, child care.

| Hist | v.1, n.1-v.2, n.6; Jan., 1972-June, 1973 | Microforms Her. 2, R9-10 |
| --- | --- | --- |
|  | v.2, n.7-v.3, n7; July, 1973-June, 1974 | Her. 2 UP, R 6 |

972   Right N.O.W! 1973-1974//? Irregular. Last issue 3 pages. Line drawings. Available on microfilm: Herstory. Published by Right N.O.W./Virginia Beach Chapter, National Organization for Women, Virginia Beach, VA. Title varies: as N.O.W., Virginia Beach Chapter, June, 1973. Subject focus: feminism, Equal Rights Amendment, lobbying, rights.

| Hist | June, 1973 | Microforms Her. 2, R 12 |
| --- | --- | --- |
|  | July, 1973-Feb., 1974 | Her. 2 UP, R 8 |

973   The Rock. 1972//? Unknown. Last issue 14 pages. Line drawings. Available on microfilm: Herstory. Published by Women's Reformatory, Rockwell City, IA. Subject focus: prisoners, poetry, drug abuse.

| Hist | Oct., 1972 | Microforms Her. 2, R 14 |
| --- | --- | --- |

Rockford Chapter Newsletter. Rockford, IL

    see The Muliebrity Majority.
    Rockford, IL

974   Room: A Women's Literary Journal. 1976-1977//. Semi-annual. Last issue 72 pages, last volume 136 pages, size 14 x 22. Line drawings, photographs. Published by Room: A Women's Literary Journal, San Francisco, CA. Editors: Kathy Barr and Gail Newman. Subject focus: poetry, fiction, art.

| | | | |
|---|---|---|---|
| RBR | v.1, n.1-2,3; ?, 1976-1977 | Circulation | |

975 Room of One's Own. 1975. Quarterly. $8.50 for individuals, $10 for institutions. Room of One's Own, P.O. Box 46160 Station G, Vancouver, British Columbia, Canada V6R 4G5. ISSN 0316-1609. OCLC 2248303. LC cn75-33152. Last issue 90 pages, last volume 334 pages, size 13 x 20. Line drawings, photographs, commercial advertising. Available on microfilm: MML. Published by the Growing Room Collective, Vancouver, British Columbia, Canada. Subject focus: poetry, arts, fiction. Other holding institutions: CSt (Stanford University), CLU (CLU), CaOONL (NLC), CtY (YUS), IU (UIU), [University of Minnesota Union List, Minneapolis, MN] (MUL), NTRS (ZRS), OkU (OKU), WMUW (GZN).

| | | | |
|---|---|---|---|
| RBR | v.1, n.1- Spring, 1975- | Circulation | |

976 Room of Our Own. 1973-1974//? Irregular. Last issue 7 pages. Line drawings. Available on microfilm: Herstory. Published by The Women's Studies Library, Baltimore, MD. Subject focus: libraries, art, reading.

| | | | |
|---|---|---|---|
| Hist | v.1, n.1-2; Sep. 4, 1973- Summer, 1974 | Microforms Her. 3, R 4 | |

977 Rutgers Women's Caucus Newsletter. 1973//? Monthly. Last issue 3 pages. Available on microfilm: Herstory. Published by Rutgers University Women's Caucus, New Brunswick, NJ. Editor: Rita Getty. Subject focus: continuing education, higher education.

| | | | |
|---|---|---|---|
| Hist | v.2, n.1-3; Feb.-Apr., 1973 | Microforms Her. 2, R 14 | |
| | v.3, n.1-2; Sep. 30-Nov. 16, 1973 | Her. 2 UP, R10 | |

978 SAA Women's Caucus Newsletter. 1975. Irregular. Irene Cortinovis and Anne Kenney, editors: SAA Women's Caucus Newsletter, MSU Libraries, Memphis, TN 38152. Last issue 3 pages, size 22 x 28. Published by The Society of American Archivists, Memphis, TN. Title varies: as Women's Caucus Newsletter, Dec., 1975. Previous editors: Nancy Kaufer, Eleanor McKay, Christine Rongone, and Susan Davis Sharlin, Dec., 1975-Apr., 1976; Eleanor McKay, Nancy Kaufer, and Christine Rongone, Feb., 1977; Eleanor McKay, Aug., 1977; Irene Cortinovis and Linda Henry, Jan.-Aug., 1978; Irene Cortinovis, Nov., 1978; Irene Cortinovis and Anne Kenney, Aug., 1979. Subject focus: professionals, archivists.

| | | | |
|---|---|---|---|
| Hist | v.1, n.1- Dec., 1975- | Circulation | |

979 SANEnews. 1978. Irregular. Mark Masselli, editor, SANEnews, Box 1076, Middletown, CT 06457. Last issue 8 pages, size 22 x 28. Photographs. Published by The Community Health Center, Middletown, CT. Subject focus: battered women, family violence, lobbying, shelter.

| | | | |
|---|---|---|---|
| Soc Work | v.1, n.5- Jan., 1979- | Circulation | |
| Wom Ed Res | v.1, n.2- Mar., 1978- | Circulation | |

980 SF Women for Peace Newsletter. 1967-1974//? Irregular. OCLC 2267646. Last issue 6 pages. Line drawings, photographs. Available on microfilm: Herstory. Published by San Francisco Branch, Women Strike for Peace, San Francisco, CA. Subject focus: peace movement, nuclear weapons, politics, rights, racism.

| | | | |
|---|---|---|---|
| Hist | June, 1967- Oct., 1971 | Microforms Her. 1, R 23 | |
| | Nov., 1971- June/July, 1973 | Her. 1 UP, R14 | |
| | Aug., 1973- Feb., 1974 | Her. CUP, R 8 | |

SFWR News. New York, NY

see SFWR Stewardesses for Women's Rights. New York, NY

981 SFWR Stewardesses for Women's Rights. 1973-1976//. Irregular. OCLC 5006380. Last issue 12 pages. Line drawings, photographs. Available on microfilm: WHi, Herstory (1973-1974). Published by Stewardesses for Women's Rights, New York, NY. Title varies: as Stewardesses for Women's Rights, Dec., 1973; SFWR News, Nov./Dec., 1974. Subject focus: rights, airline industry, lobbying, flight attendants, occupational health and safety.

| | | | |
|---|---|---|---|
| Hist | v.1, n.7, v.2, n.6-v.4, n.3; Dec., 1973, June, 1974- Mar./Apr., 1976 | Microforms | |
| | v.1, n.1-2; Feb.15-May, 1973 | Her. 2, R16 | |
| | v.1, n.3-v.2, n.6; July, 1973- June, 1974 | Her. 2UP, R11 | |

982 S.O.S.-Speak Out Sisters. 1971-1972//? Last issue 4 pages. Line drawings. Available on microfilm: Herstory. Published by Speak Out Sisters, Temple University, Philadelphia, PA. Title varies: as TWL Newsletter, Oct. 22, 1971 [Temple Women's Liberation]. Subject focus: women's studies, pro-abortion, education.

| Hist | v.1, n.1,v.2,n.2; Oct. 22, 1971, Mar. 8, 1972 | Microforms Her. 2, R 16 |

983 S.O.S./Stephanie's Office Service. 1969//? Unknown. OCLC 2268142. Last issue 2 pages. Available on microfilm: Herstory. Published by Stephanie Hartman, Syracuse, NY. Subject focus: feminism.

| Hist | Dec. 10, 1969 | Microforms Her. 1, R 21 |

984 SWS Newsletter. 1971. Quarterly. $9 for individuals, $15 for institutions. Janet Hunt, editor, SWS Newsletter, Department of Sociology, University of Maryland, College Park, MD 20742. OCLC 2267858. Last issue 12 pages, last volume 68 pages, size 22 x 28. Line drawings, photographs. Published by Sociologists for Women in Society, College Park, MD. Available on microfilm: Herstory (1971-1974). Title varies: as Women's Caucus Newsletter, Oct., 1970. Place of publication varies: San Francisco, CA, May, 1971-Nov., 1972; Ithaca, NY, Winter-Autumn, 1973; Cambridge, MA, Winter, 1974-Dec., 1975; Brooklyn, NY, Mar., 1976; Boston, MA, May, 1976; Tampa, FL, Oct., 1976-Mar., 1977; Washington, DC, Oct., 1977-July, 1978. Previous editor: Arlene Daniels, May, 1971-Nov., 1972. Subject focus: professionals, research, rights, teaching, sociologists, higher education, sociology. Other holding institution: PPiU (PIT).

| Mem | v.1, n.1- May, 1971- | AP/S6784/F692 |
| Hist | v.1, n.1-3; Mar.-Aug., 1971 | Microforms Her. 1, R 21 |
|  | v.1, n.4-v.3, n.3; Oct./Nov., 1971- Summer, 1973 | Her. 1 UP, R15 |
|  | v.3, n.4-v.4, n.3; Autumn, 1973- Spring, 1974 | Her. CUP, R 7 |

985 Sabot. 1972//? Unknown. OCLC 2267367. Last issue 26 pages. Line drawings, photographs, commercial advertising. Available on microfilm: Herstory. Published by Sabot, Seattle, WA. Subject focus: health, child care, humor, prostitution, radicalism, politics, poetry, lesbians, satire.

| Hist | Mar?, 1972? | Microforms Her. 2, R 14 |

Sacramento N.O.W. Newsletter. Sacramento, CA

see N.O.W. News. Sacramento, CA

986 Sacramento Women for Peace Newsletter. 1970//? OCLC 2267370. Unknown. Last issue 6 pages. Available on microfilm: Herstory. Published by Sacramento Branch, Women Strike for Peace, Sacramento, CA. Subject focus: WSP, bail bonds, peace movement, nuclear weapons, politics.

| Hist | July, 1970 | Microforms Her. 1, R 23 |

987 Sacramento Women's Center and Bookstore Newsletter. 1973-1974//? Monthly. Last issue 3 pages. Line drawings. Available on microfilm: Herstory. Published by Sacramento Women's Center and Bookstore, Sacramento, CA. Subject focus: education, media, welfare, child care, employment, bookstores.

| Hist | v.1, n.1-v.2,n.6; July, 1973- June, 1974 | Microforms Her. 3, R 4 |

988 Saint Joan's Alliance Newsletter. 1970-1974//? Irregular. OCLC 2267389. Last issue 12 pages, photographs. Available on microfilm: Herstory. Published by Saint Joan's Alliance, Milwaukee, WI. Editor: C. Virginia Finn, Aug., 1970-Mar., 1974. Subject focus: rights, Equal Rights Amendment, education, poetry, Catholic Church.

| Hist | Aug., 1970 | Microforms Her. 1, R 20 |
|  | Mar., Apr., July, 1971 | Her. 1, Add |
|  | Jan., 1972- June, 1973 | Her. 1 UP, R14 |
|  | Aug., 1973- Mar., 1974 | Her. CUP, R 6 |

989 St. Johns County N.O.W. 1972-1973//? Irregular. Last issue 2 pages. Line drawings. Available on microfilm: Herstory. Published by St. Johns County Chapter, National Organization for Women, St. Augustine, FL. Subject focus: feminism, Equal Rights Amendment, lobbying, rights, child care, pro-abortion.

| | Hist | v.1, n.1-v.2,n.2;<br>June, 1972-<br>Feb., 1973 | Microforms<br>Her. 2, R 11 |
|---|---|---|---|

St. Louis N.O.W.  St. Louis, MO

    see "... & Nothing Less".  St. Louis, MO

990   St. Louis Organization for Women's Rights. 1972-1973//? Monthly. Last issue 4 pages. Line drawings, photographs. Available on microfilm: Herstory. Published by St. Louis Organization for Women's Rights, St. Louis, MO. Editors: Sarah Wernick Lockeretz, Sep., 1972-Jan., 1973; Willie Lockeretz, Feb.-Mar., 1973. Subject focus: image, credit, health, pro-abortion, Equal Rights Amendment, sexism in education.

| | Hist | v.1, n.1-5;<br>Sep., 1972-<br>Mar., 1973 | Microforms<br>Her. 2, R 14 |
|---|---|---|---|

991   San Fernando Valley Women's Political Caucus Newsletter. 1972-1974//? Irregular. Last issue 6 pages. Line drawings, photographs. Available on microfilm: Herstory. Published by San Fernando Valley Women's Political Caucus, North Hollywood, CA. Subject focus: politics, lobbying, Equal Rights Amendment, welfare, pro-abortion.

| | Hist | May 18, 1972-<br>June 29, 1973 | Microforms<br>Her. 2, R 12 |
|---|---|---|---|
| | | July 27, 1973-<br>May 23, 1974 | Her. 2 UP, R9 |

992   San Francisco Branch Women's International League for Peace and Freedom. 1967-1974. Irregular. OCLC 2269623. Last issue 8 pages. Available on microfilm: Herstory. Published by Women's International League for Peace and Freedom, San Francisco Branch, San Francisco, CA. Title varies: as Bulletin, Dec., 1967-May, 1971. Subject focus: politics, peace movement, lobbying. Other holding institution: [University of Minnesota Union List, Minneapolis, MN] (MUL).

| | Hist | Dec., 1967-<br>May, 1971 | Microforms<br>Her. 1, R 22 |
|---|---|---|---|
| | | Nov., 1971-<br>June, 1973 | Her. 1 UP, R18 |
| | | Aug./Sep., 1973-<br>June, 1974 | Her. CUP, R 8 |

San Francisco N.O.W. Newsletter.  San Francisco, CA

    see Woman N.O.W.  San Francisco, CA

993   San Francisco Women's Center. 1972-1974//? Unknown. Last issue 1 page. Line drawings. Available on microfilm: Herstory. Published by San Francisco Women's Center, San Francisco, CA. Subject focus: sexuality.

| | Hist | Undated(1972?) | Microforms<br>Her. 2, R 14 |
|---|---|---|---|
| | | Apr., 1974 | Her. 2 UP, R10 |

994   San Francisco Women's Newsletter. 1970-1973//? Monthly. OCLC 2269639. Last issue 18 pages. Line drawings, photographs. Available on microfilm: Herstory. Published by San Francisco Women's Liberation, San Francisco, CA. Title varies: as Women's Liberation Newsletter, May 20, 1970-June, 1973. Subject focus: child care, pro-abortion, poetry, art.

| | Hist | May 20, 1970-<br>July 12, 1971 | Microforms<br>Her. 1, R 21 |
|---|---|---|---|
| | | Nov., 1971-<br>June, 1973 | Her. 1 UP, R18 |
| | | Aug., 1973 | Her. CUP, R 6 |

995   San Joaquin N.O.W. 1971-1974//? Bi-monthly. Last issue 14 pages. Available on microfilm: Herstory. Published by San Joaquin Chapter, National Organization for Women, Stockton, CA. Frequency varies: monthly, Nov., 1971-Mar., 1973. Editor: Carol Benson. Subject focus: child care, politics, feminism, Equal Rights Amendment, lobbying, rights.

| | Hist | v.1, n.1-v.2,n.8;<br>Nov., 1971-<br>July/Aug., 1973 | Microforms<br>Her. 2, R 11 |
|---|---|---|---|
| | | v.2, n.9-v.3,n.4;<br>Aug., 1973-<br>Apr./May, 1974 | Her. 2 UP, R 8 |

996   San Mateo County N.O.W. News. 1971-1974//? Irregular. OCLC 2264707. Last issue 1 page. Line drawings. Available on microfilm: Herstory. Published by San Mateo County Chapter, National Organization for Women, Burlingame, CA. Title varies: as Newsletter, July 22, 1971-May/June, 1973. Place of publication varies: San Mateo, CA, July 22, 1970?-Sep., 1971. Editors: Barbara Miller, July 22, 1971-May/June, 1973; Nancy Fritz, July, 1973-June, 1974. Subject focus: feminism, Equal Rights Amendment, lobbying, rights, pro-abortion. Other holding institutions: [University of Minnesota Union List, Minneapolis, MN] (MUL).

| | Hist | v.1,n.1-2,4<br>?, July 22,<br>Sep., 1971 | Microforms<br>Her. 1, R 20 |
|---|---|---|---|

|  |  |  |
|---|---|---|
| | Oct., 1971–<br>May/June, 1973 | Her. 1 UP, R11 |
| | July, 1973–<br>June, 1974 | Her. CUP, R 5 |

997 Santa Clara County Women's Political Caucus. 1973-1974//? Irregular. Last issue 2 pages. Available on microfilm: Herstory. Published by Santa Clara County Women's Political Caucus, San Jose, CA. Subject focus: lobbying, politics.

| Hist | Mar. 17,-?-<br>May 17, 1973 | Microforms<br>Her. 2, R 13 |
|---|---|---|
| | July, 1973–<br>May, 1974 | Her. 2 UP, R9 |

The Santa Cruz Women's Center Newsletter. Santa Cruz, CA

see Definitely Biased. Santa Cruz, CA

998 Santa Fe Women's Community Magazine. 1974//? Unknown. Last issue 16 pages. Line drawings. Available on microfilm: Herstory. Published by Santa Fe Women's Community, Santa Fe, NM. Subject focus: art, lesbians, poetry, politics, children.

| Hist | v.1, n.2;<br>Undated(?1974?) | Microforms<br>Her. 3, R 4 |
|---|---|---|

999 Sapphire. 1973//? Unknown. Last issue 42 pages. Line drawings. Available on microfilm: Herstory. Published by Sapphire, San Francisco, CA. Subject focus: satire, humor, film reviews, literature.

| Hist | v.1, n.1;<br>Feb.-Mar., 1973 | Microforms<br>Her. 2, R 14 |
|---|---|---|

1000 Sappho. 1971? Monthly. $11.70 for individuals and institutions. Jacqueline Forster, editor, Sappho, 20 Dorset Square, London, England NW1 6QB, 01-724-3636. Last issue 16 pages, last volume 408 pages, size 22 x 28. Line drawings, commercial advertising. Available on microfilm: Herstory (1971?-1974). Published by Sappho Publication, Ltd., London, England. Frequency varies: irregular, 1971?-May?, 1973. Subject focus: lesbians, poetry, astrology, satire, sexuality, media, film reviews.

| Hist | v.1, n.1-v.2,n.2;<br>1971?-May, 1973 | Microforms<br>Her. 2, R 14 |
|---|---|---|
| | v.2, n.3-v.3,n.2;<br>July, 1973–<br>May, 1974 | Her. 2 UP, R10 |

| Mem | v.2, n.1–<br>Apr., 1973– | AP/S2413/L |
|---|---|---|

1001 Saskatoon Women's Liberation Newsletter. 1974//? Irregular. OCLC 2174165. Last issue 18 pages. Line drawings. Available on microfilm: Herstory. Published by Saskatoon Women's Centre, Saskatoon, Saskatchewan, Canada. Subject focus: child care, poetry, lesbians, health, politics, lobbying. Other holding institution: CaOONL (NLC).

| Hist | Feb.-Mar.,<br>June, 1974 | Microforms<br>Her. 3, R 4 |
|---|---|---|

1002 Say it N.O.W. 1971//? Unknown. Last issue 1 page. Available on microfilm: Herstory. Published by San Antonio Chapter, National Organization for Women, San Antonio, TX. Subject focus: feminism, Equal Rights Amendment, lobbying, rights.

| Hist | v.1, n.1;<br>Feb., 1971 | Microforms<br>Her. 2, R 11 |
|---|---|---|

1003 Scarlet Letter. 1971-1972//. Irregular. OCLC 2267506. Last issue 8 pages, last volume 108 pages, size 22 x 28. Line drawings, photographs. Available on microfilm: McP, Herstory. Published by The Scarlet Letter Collective, Madison, WI. Subject focus: rights, politics, poetry, art, lesbians.

| Hist | v.1, n.1-7;<br>May, 1971–<br>Summer, 1972 | HQ/1101/"S3 |
|---|---|---|
| | v.1, n.1-3;<br>May-Sep., 1971 | Microforms<br>Her. 1, R20 |
| | v.1, n.4-5;<br>Oct., 1971–<br>Jan., 1972 | Her. 1 UP, R11 |
| MPL | v.1, n.4-8;<br>Sep., 1971–<br>Oct., 1972 | Literature and<br>Social<br>Science<br>Section |

1004 Seattle Women Act for Peace. 1964-1974//? Irregular. Last issue 3 pages. Line drawings, photographs. Available on microfilm: Herstory. Published by Seattle Women Act for Peace, Seattle, WA. Subject focus: politics, rights, peace movement, lobbying, nuclear weapons.

| Hist | Mar., 1964–<br>May/June, 1973 | Microforms<br>Her. 2, R14-15 |
|---|---|---|
| | July, 1973–<br>June, 1974 | Her. 2 UP, R10 |

1005 Second Coming. 1970-1971//? Irregular. OCLC 2267577. Last issue 16 pages. Line drawings, photographs. Available on microfilm: Herstory. Published by Austin Women's Liberation Movement, Austin, TX. Subject focus: poetry, law. Other holding institution: [University of Minnesota Union List, Minneapolis, MN] (MUL).

| Hist | v.1, n.1-10;<br>Dec. 1, 1970-<br>Aug. 30, 1971 | Microforms<br>Her. 1, R 4 |
|---|---|---|
|  | v.1, n.11-12;<br>Oct.-Nov., 1971 | Her. 1 UP, R14 |

1006 The Second Page. 1970-1975//. Irregular. OCLC 2383560. Last issue 4 pages, last volume 80 pages. Line drawings, photographs. Available on microfilm: Herstory, (1970-1973), WHi. Published by Second Page, San Francisco, CA. Title varies: as Women's Page, Sep. 15, 1970-Nov., 1971. Subject focus: rights, politics, humor, workers, child care, employment, satire. Other holding institution: [University of Minnesota Union List, Minneapolis, MN] (MUL).

| Hist | v.1, n.1-v.3,n.1;<br>Oct., 1970-<br>Feb., 1975 | Microforms |
|---|---|---|
|  | v.1, n.1-5;<br>Sep. 15, 1970-<br>Apr./May, 1971 | Her. 1, R 4 |
|  | v.1, n.6-v.2,n.1;<br>Nov., 1971-<br>Summer, 1973 | Her. 1 UP, R14 |
|  | v.2, n.2;<br>Nov./Dec., 1973 | Her. CUP, R 6 |

1007 The 2nd Revolution: Newsletter of the Women's Studies Program, San Diego State. 1970?-1971//? Irregular. OCLC 2267578. Last issue 12 pages, size 18 x 22. Line drawings. Available on microfilm: Herstory. Published by Women's Studies Program, San Diego State College, San Diego, CA. Subject focus: women's studies, peace movement, child care, politics, racism, higher education, poetry, pro-abortion, music.

| Hist | Dec. 7, 1970-<br>May 24, 1971 | Microforms<br>Her. 1, R 21 |
|---|---|---|
|  | Apr?-May 24, 1971 | Pam 74-3398 |

1008 The Second Wave: A Magazine of the New Feminism. 1971. Quarterly. $8 for individuals, $16 for institutions. Second Wave, Box 344, Cambridge A, Cambridge, MA 02139. ISSN 0048-9980. OCLC 2267579, 2978740, 3920269. LC 76-25749. Last issue 52 pages, last volume 204 pages, size 28 x 28. Line drawings, photographs, commercial advertising. Indexed: in Alternative Press Index. Available on microfilm: Herstory (1971-1974). Published by Female Liberation/Second Wave, Inc., Cambridge, MA. Subject focus: politics, motherhood, fiction, art, radical feminism, poetry. Other holding institutions: CLU (CLU), FBoU (FGM), FTS (FHM), M (MAS), MBNU (NED), MBU (BOS), MiMtpT (EZC), [University of Minnesota Union List, Minneapolis, MN] (MUL), NCH (YHM), [Central New York Library Resources Council, Syracuse, NY] (SRR), NbU (LDL), NhD (DRB), PPiU (PIT), WaU (WAU).

| RBR | v.1, n.1-<br>Spring, 1971- | Circulation |
|---|---|---|
| Hist | v.1, n.1-v.4,n.1;<br>Spring, 1971-<br>Summer, 1975 | HQ/1101/S43 |
|  | v.1, n.1-2;<br>Spring-<br>Summer, 1971 | Microforms<br>Her. 1, R11 |
|  | v.1, n.3-v.2,n.4;<br>Fall, 1971-<br>Fall, 1973 | Her. 1 UP,<br>R 14-15 |
|  | v.3, n.1-2;<br>Spring-<br>Summer, 1974 | Her. CUP, R 6 |

1009 The Secretary. 1941. 10 times a year. $7 for individuals and institutions. Shirley S. Englund, editor, The Secretary, National Secretaries Association, 2440 Pershing Road, Suite G-10, Kansas City, MO. ISSN 0037-0622. OCLC 1765338. LC 49-7. Last issue 34 pages, size 21 x 27. Line drawings, photographs, commercial advertising. Title varies: as Today's Secretary, Jan., 1961-June, 1966. Subject focus: secretaries. Other holding institutions: ArU (AFU), AzFU (AZN), AzTeS (AZS), COU-DA (COA), [Congressional Research Service, Washington, DC] (CRS), DBS (NBS), DFT (FTC), DI (UDI), DME/DAS (OLA), FMFIU (FXG), KHayF (KFH), KyU (DUD), MiLC (EEL), MiMtpT (EZC), [University of Minnesota Union List, Minneapolis, MN] (MUL), MoUst (UMS), [Western New York Library Resources Council, Buffalo, NY] (VZX), NR (YQR), NcElcE (NPE), NhPlS (PSM), O (OHI), OAkU (AKR), OCC (OCC), OKentU (KSU), OYU (YNG), PCoR (ROB), PPiC (PMC), [Pittsburgh Regional Library Center Union List, Pittsburgh, PA] (QPR), TCollsM (TMS), TMurS (TXM), TNTU (TUN), [AMIGOS Union List of Serials, Dallas, TX (IUC), TxDN (INT), TxDW (IWU), TxLT (ILU), ViRCU (VRC), WM (GZD).

| MPL | Jan., 1961- | Business and<br>Social<br>Sciences<br>Section |
|---|---|---|

190

1010 <u>Seventeen</u>. 1942. Monthly. $9.95 for individuals and institutions. Midge Turk Richardson, editor, Seventeen, 850 Third Avenue, New York, NY 10022. Business address: Seventeen Magazine, Radnor, PA 19088. ISSN 0037-301X. OCLC 1643827, 4042983, 5077587. LC sn78-80. Last issue 146 pages, last volume 1780 pages, size 20 x 28. Line drawings, photographs, some in color, commercial advertising. Indexed: in Readers' Guide to Periodical Literature (1961-). Available on microfilm: UnM (1944-). Previous editors: Emil A. Haupt, Jan., 1966-Dec., 1970; H.F. Lenfest, Jan., 1971-Mar., 1973; Rubye Graham, Mar., 1974-Oct., 1975. Subject focus: teen-agers, fashion, beauty care, food, fiction. Other holding institutions: ArAT (AKH), AzFU (AZN), AzTeS (AZS), CChiS (CCH), CLU (CLU), CoDU (DVP), CtY (YUS), CAuA (GJG), IDeKN (JNA), InIU (IUP), [Indiana Union List of Serials, Indianapolis, IN] (ILS), InU (IUL), KSteC (KKQ), KyRE (KEU), LHS (LSH), LMN (LNE), LU (LUU), MiLC (EEL), [University of Minnesota Union List, Minneapolis, MN] (MUL), MoS (SVP), [Western New York Library Resources Council, Buffalo, NY] (VZX), NCorniCC (ZDG), NOneoU (ZBM), NR (YQR), [Central New York Library Resources Council, Syracuse, NY (SRR), NbKS (KRS), NcRS (NRC), O (OHI), OAkU (AKR), OCl (CLE), OY (YMM), OkT (TUL), PPD (DXU), PPi (CPL), PPiAC (AIC), [Pittsburgh Regional Library Center Union List, Pittsburgh, PA] (QPR), ScCleU (SEA), ScRhW (SWW), TxBelM (MHB), TxCM (TXA), TxDN (INT), TxDW (IWU), [AMIGOS Union List of Serials, Dallas, TX] (IUC), TxLT (ILU), TxNacS (TXK), [Emory & Henry College, Emory, VA] (VEH), [Arrowhead Library System, Janesville Public Library, Janesville, WI] (WIJ), WM (GZD), WMUW (GZN).

| | | | | | |
|---|---|---|---|---|---|
| MPL | v.25, n.1-<br>Jan., 1966- | Literature and Social Science Section | BAHS | Current Issues Only | Circulation |
| MATC | v.29, n.1-<br>Jan., 1970- | Cora Hardy Library | CPPL | Current Issues Only | Circulation |
| MHHS | v.30, n.1-<br>Jan., 1971- | Circulation | BML | Current Issues Only | Circulation |
| MIPL | v.32, n.1-<br>Jan., 1973- | Circulation | LAHS | Current Issues Only | Circulation |
| BFL | v.34, n.1-<br>Jan., 1975- | Circulation | EHS | v.29, n.1-<br>Jan., 1970- | Circulation |
| VHS | v.27, n.1-<br>Jan., 1968- | Circulation | MOPL | v.34, n.8-<br>Aug., 1975- | Circulation |
| MMHS | v.29, n.1-<br>Jan., 1970- | Circulation | DFPL | v.30, n.1-<br>Jan., 1971- | Circulation |
| DFHS | v.33, n.6-<br>June, 1974- | Circulation | TML | v.27, n.1-<br>Jan., 1968- | Circulation |
| VPL | v.28, n.1-<br>Jan., 1969- | Circulation | SPHS | v.24, n.1-<br>Jan., 1965- | Circulation |
| | | | OM | Current Issues Only | Circulation |
| | | | SAPH | Current Issues Only | Circulation |
| | | | MGHS | v.22, n.1-<br>Jan., 1963- | Circulation |
| | | | SCPL | v.31, n.1-<br>Jan., 1972- | Circulation |
| | | | WHS | v.28, n.1-<br>Jan., 1969- | Circulation |
| | | | PPL | v.30, n.1-<br>Jan., 1971- | Circulation |
| | | | SPPL | v.30, n.1-<br>Jan., 1971- | Circulation |
| | | | RPL | [v.29, n.1-]<br>[Jan., 1970-] | Circulation |
| | | | CFL | v.34, n.1-<br>Jan., 1975- | Circulation |
| | | | MFHS | v.33, n.1-<br>Jan., 1974- | Circulation |
| | | | BEL | Current Issues Only | Circulation |
| | | | BHS | [v.30, n.7-]<br>[July, 1971-] | Circulation |
| | | | OPL | Current Issues Only | Circulation |
| | | | DHS | Current Issues Only | Circulation |

XVII Century Newsletter. Bastrop, LA

see Seventeenth Century Review. Washington, DC

1011 Seventeenth Century Review. 1958. Tri-annual. $3 for individuals and institutions. Mrs. Thomas Burchett, editor, 1300 New Hampshire Avenue NW, Washington, DC 20036. Last issue 64 pages, last volume 132 pages, size 16 x 22. Line drawings, photographs. Published by the National Society of Colonial Dames XVII Century. Title varies: as XVII Century Newsletter, Dec., 1958-Mar., 1960. Place of publication varies: Bastrop, LA, Dec., 1958-Oct., 1960; Gary, IN, Fall, 1961-June, 1963; Ashland, KY, Nov., 1963. Frequency varies: irregular, Dec., 1958-Oct., 1960. Previous editors: Mrs. Allen Turpin, Dec., 1958-Oct., 1960; Mrs. Joseph Janowski, Fall, 1961-June, 1963. Subject focus: history, genealogy.

| Hist | v.1, n.1-v.4, n.4, v.5, n.1- Dec., 1958-Fall, 1961, Feb., 1963 | E/186.99/"C55/ S4 |

1012 Sewing Circle. 1977?-1979//. Unknown. Last issue 8 pages, size 22 x 28. Photographs. Published by Western Pennsylvania District Council Local 424-445, International Ladies' Garment Workers Union, Johnstown, PA. Editor: Tom Matthews. Subject focus: labor unions, AFL-CIO, Garment industry.

| Hist | Nov?, 1977, Apr., 1979 | Circulation |

1013 Sex Discrimination in Education. 1975-1976//. Irregular. Last issue 12 pages. Line drawings. Published in Ann Arbor, MI. Subject focus: non-sexist teaching materials, sexism in education.

| Wom Ed Res | v.1, n.1/2- v.2, n.1/2; Oct./Dec., 1975- Oct./Dec., 1976 | Circulation |

1014 Sex Roles: A Journal of Research. 1975. Monthly. $35 for individuals, $98 for institutions. Phyllis Katz, editor, Sex Roles: A Journal of Research, Institute for Research on Social Problems, 711 Walnut St., Boulder, CO 80302. ISSN 0360-0025. OCLC 2243426, 5730123, 1712778, 2253925. LC 75-646987. Last issue 347 pages, size 21 x 23. Line drawings. Indexed in: Abstracts on Criminology and Penology, Child Development Abstracts and Bibliography, Contemporary Sociology, Current Contents, Excerpta Medica, Family Planning Perspectives, Human Sexuality Update, Psychological Abstracts, Referativnyi Zhurnal, Sage Family Studies Abstracts, Social Sciences Citation Index, Sociological Abstracts, The Psychological Reader's Guide, The SIECUS Report, and Zeitschrift fuer Kinder und Jugendpsychiatrie. Available on microfilm: UnM (1979-). Published by the Plenum Publishing Co., New York, NY. Subject focus: divorce, sexism in education, rape, sex roles, professionals. Other holding institutions: AU (ALM), AzFU (AZN), AzTeS (AZS), CChiS (CCH), CLS (CLA), CLU (CLU), CLamB (CBC), CLobS (CLO), COU-DA (COA), CoDU (DVP), CtY (YUS), WeharU (HRM), DCU (DCU), DHU (DHU), DLC (DLC), DeU (DLM), FU (FUG), FBoU (FGM), FJUNF (FNP), FPeU (FWA), FTaSU (FDA), GASU (GSU), GAT (GAT), GEU (EMU), IaCfT (NIU), ICI (IAH), ICL (IAL), ICharE (IAD), IDeKN (JNA), IPB (IBA), InU (IUL), InND (IND), InIU (IUP), KHayF (KFH), KyLoU (KLG), KyRE (KEU), KyU (KUK), MBU (BOS), MBNU (NED), MH (HUL), MH-Ed (HMG), MMeT (TFW), MNS (SNN), MWelC (WEL), DNLM (NLM), MdStm (MDS), MiDW (EYW), MiEM (EEM), MiHolH (EXH), MiMtpT (EZC), MiYEM (EYE), [University of Minnesota Union List, Minneapolis, MN] (MUL), MoU (MUU), MoOW (WTU), MsU (MUM), NcGU (NGU), NcRS (NRC), NbOB (BTC), NhD (DRB), NmLcU (IRU), NmU (IQU), [New York State Union List, Albany, NY] (NYS), NBC (VDB), NCH (YHM), NCaS (XLM), NCortU (YCM), NFQC (XQM), NGenoU (YGM), NHemH (ZIH), NIC (COO), NNR (ZXC), NNCU-G (ZGM), NNepaSU (ZLM), NPV (VXW), NPurU (ZPM), NRU (RRR), NSbSU (YSM), NSbSU-H (VZB), NSchU (ZWU), NSyU (SYB), [Central New York Library Resources Council, Syracuse, NY] (SRR), NWM (YWM), OAkU (AKR), OAU (OUN), OKentU (KSU), OMC (MRC), OO (OBE), OTU (TOL), OkS (OKS), PU (PAU), PCW (UWC), PLF (LFM), PPiU (PIT), PPSJ (SJD), RPB (RBN), ScCleU (SEA), TMurS (TXM), TNJ (TJC), TNTU (TUN), [AMIGOS Union List of Serials, Dallas, TX] (IUC), TxCM (TXA), TxDN (INT), TxDW (IWU), TxU (IXA), TxNacS (TXK), ViNO (VOD), ViRU (VRU), ViRCU (VRC), ViW (VWM), VtU (VTU), WaU (WAU), WKenU (GZP), WMenU (GZS), WMUW (GZN), WPlaU (GZV), Wu-M (GZH), [University of Wisconsin-Stevens Point, Stevens Point, WI] (WIS).

| Mem | v.1, n.1- Mar., 1975- | Periodicals Section |
| Soc Work | Current Issues Only | Circulation |

1015 Shakti. 1973//? Irregular. Last issue 8 pages. Line drawings. Available on microfilm: Herstory. Published by Northern Prince George's County Chapter, National Organization for Women, Greenbelt, MD. Editor: Barbara Hardisty. Subject focus: feminism, Equal Rights Amendment, lobbying, rights, pro-abortion.

| Hist | v.1, n.3-4; July-Sep., 1973 | Microforms Her. 3, R 3 |

1016 Shameless Hussy Review. 1972-1978//? Quarterly. OCLC 3450942. Last issue 58 pages, size 18 x 24. Line drawings. Published by the Shameless Hussy Press, Berkeley, CA. Frequency varies: annual, 1972-1976. Subject focus: art, fiction, poetry. Other holding institutions: [University of Minnesota Union List, Minneapolis, MN] (MUL), NA1U (NAM), PPT (TEU), PPiU (PIT), TxCM (TXA).

RBR    v1, n.4-v.2, n.1;    Circulation
       1976-Spring?, 1978

1017 Shenabe Quai. 1979? Irregular. Shenabe Quai, North American Indian Women's Council on Chemical Dependency, Route 2, Box 8, Turtle Lake, WI 54889. Last issue 8 pages, size 28 x 22. Line drawings, photographs. Subject focus: alcoholism, drug abuse, Native Americans.

Hist    Feb., 1979-            Circulation

1018 Sheryns Nifty Newsletter. 1970//? Irregular. OCLC 2267660. Available on microfilm: Herstory. Published by Sheryn Kallowaay, Berkeley, CA. Editor: Sheryn Kallowaay. Subject focus: workers, sexuality, fertility.

Hist    v.1, n.1-2;           Microforms
        May/June-             Her. 1, R 21
        June 16, 1970

1019 Shrew. 1971//? Unknown. OCLC 2267674. Last issue 24 pages. Line drawings. Available on microfilm: Herstory. Published by Women's Liberation, Brisbane, Queensland, Australia. Subject focus: poetry, sex education, employment, rights, migrants, labor unions, sexuality.

Hist    v.1, n.3;             Microforms
        May, 1971             Her. 1, R 21

1020 Shrew. 1969-1973//? Irregular. OCLC 2267675. Last issue 14 pages. Line drawings, photographs. Available on microfilm: Herstory. Published by Women's Liberation Workshop of Bedfordshire, London, England. Subject focus: birth control, pro-abortion, child care, poetry, third world, employment.

Hist    Nov., 1969-           Microforms
        June, 1971            Her. 1, R 11

        Feb.-Sep., 1971       Her. 1 Add.

        v.3, n.9-v.4, n.4;    Her. 1 UP, R15
        Dec., 1971-?1972

        v.5, n.3-4;           Her. CUP, R 6
        Aug./Sep.-
        Oct., 1973

1021 The Sibyl; A review of the tastes, errors, and Fashions of society. 1856-1864//. Monthly. Last issue 8 pages, last volume 1248 pages, size 22 x 31. Line drawings, commercial advertising. Available on microfilm: WHi. Frequency varies: semi-monthly, July, 1856-Aug., 1862. Published in Middletown, NY. Editor: Lydia Sayer Hasbrouck. Subject focus: rights, health, clothes, poetry. Other holding institution: MCR-S (Schlesinger Library on the History of Women in America, Radcliffe College, Cambridge, MA).

Hist    v.1, n.1-v.8, n.12;   KW83/7S564
        July 1, 1856-         (Cutter)
        June, 1864

        v.1, n.1-v.8, n.12;   Microforms
        July 1, 1856-
        June, 1864

1022 Sibyl-Child. 1975. Quarterly. $16 for individuals and institutions. Candyce Homnick Stapen, editor, Sibyl-Child, P.O. Box 1773, Hyattsville, MD 20788. Business address: 12618 Billington Rd., Silver Spring, MD 20904. ISSN 0161-715X. OCLC 2568590, 3114227. LC 78-643577, sc78-971. Last issue 72 pages, last volume 124 pages, size 14 x 21. Line drawings, photographs. Published by Sibyl-Child Press, Inc., Hyattsville, MD. Subject focus: poetry, fiction, art, photography. Other holding institutions: CCC (HDC), CtY (YUS), DGW (DGW), DLC (DLC), IU (UIU), KMK (KMS), [University of Minnesota Union List, Minneapolis, MN] (MUL), NIC (COO), [New York State Union List, Albany, NY] (NYS), NTRS (ZRS), OU (OSU), PPiU (PIT).

RBR     v.1, n.1-            Circulation
        Winter, 1975-

1023 Signs: A Journal of Women in Culture and Society. 1975. Quarterly. $18 for individuals, $15 for students, $30 for institutions. Catherine Stimpson, editor, Signs: A Journal of Women in Culture and Society, Barnard Hall, Barnard College, New York, NY 10027. Business address, 5801 Ellis Avenue, Chicago, IL 60637. ISSN 0097-9740. OCLC 1362618. LC 75-649469. Last issue 228 pages, size 15 x 23. Line drawings, commercial advertising. Indexed in: America: History and Life, Current Contents: Social and Behavioral Sciences, Modern Language Abstracts, Psychological Abstracts, Social Sciences Citation Index, Sociological Abstracts, Women Studies Abstracts. Available on microfilm: UnM. Subject focus: research. Other holding institutions: AAP (AAA), AU (ALM), ArAT (AKH), ArCCA (AKC), ArStC (ASU), ArU (AFU), AzFU (AZN), AzTeS (AZS), CSt (Stanford University), CLU (CLU), CLobS (CLO), CSdS (CDS), CU-S (CUS), COLH (COL), COU-DA (COA), CtHT (TYC), CtW (WLU), CtY (YUS), DAL (ARL), DAU (FAU), DCU (DCU), DHU (DHU), DLC (NSD/DLC), DSI

(SMI), [Congressional Research Service, Washington, DC] (GRS), FBoU (FGM), FJUNF (FNP, FMFIU (FXG/FXN), FSpE (FEC), FTS (FHM), FTaSU (FDA), FU (FUG), FU-L (FUB), GASU (GSU), GAuA (GJG), T (SPI), ICI (IAH), ICL (IAL), ICRC (IAR), ICSX (ICS), IDeKN (JNA), IGK (IBK), ILS (ICG), IMgO (IAP), IaDL (IOH), IaDuU (IOV), IaLG (IOF), InND (IND), InU (TUL), InValU (IVU), KHayF (KFH), KPT (KFP), KSteC (KKQ), KyU (KUK), MBNU (NED), MBTI (BTI), MBU (BOS), MCE (BPS), MH (HUL), MH-AH (BHA), MMeT (TFW), MNS (SNN), MNodS (SMU), MSohG (BCT), MWA (AQM), MWC (CKM), MWelC (WFL), MdBJ (JHE), MdStM (MDS), MiDU (EYU), MiLC (EEL), MiMtpT (EZC), [University of Minnesota Union List, Minneapolis, MN] (MUL), MnSST (MNT), MoKU (UMK), MoSMa (MVC), N (NYG), [New York State Union List, Albany, NY] (NYS), NBC (VDB), NBu (VHB), [Western New York Library Resources Council, Buffalo, NY] (VZX), NCH (YHM), NCaS (XLM), NCorniCC (ZDG), NCortU (YCM), NDFM (VZE), NEE (VXE), NFQC (XQM), NGcCC (VVX), NGenoU (YGM), NIC (COO), NNepaSU (ZLM), NOneoU (ZBM), NOsU (YOM), NPV (VXW), NR (YQR), NRU (RRR), NSbSU (YSM), NSbSU-H (VZB), NSufR (VVR), NSyU (SYB), [Central New York Library Resources Council, Syracuse, NY] (SRR), NUtC (VVV), NbKS (KRS), NbOB (BTC), NbU (LDL), Nc (NCS), NcGU (NGU), NcRS (NRC), NcWfSB (NVS), NhD (DRB), NjBLC (BLO), NjJStP (STP), NjLincB (BCC), NmLcU (IRU), O (OHI), OAkU (AKR), OAU (OUN), [Raymond Walters General and Technical College Library, Blue Ash, OH] (ORW), OC1W (CWR), ODaWU (WSU), OKentU (KSU), OTU (TOL), OU (OSU), OYU (YNG), Ok (OKD), OkTOR (OKO), OrSaW (OWS), PBL (LYU), PB1bM (MGC), PBm (BMC), PCW (UWC), PEL (LAF), PE1C (ELZ), PHC (HVC), PIm (IMM), INWC (WFN), PPT (TEU), PPiPT (PKT), PPiU (PIT), PSC (PSC), PU (PAU), ScGF (SFU), ScRhW (SWW), TCU (TUC), TMSC (TWS), TMurS (TXM), TNJ (TJC), TNTU (TUN), TSewU (TWU), TxArU (IUA), TxCM (TXA), TxDN (INT), [AMIGOS Union List of Serials, Dallas, TX] (IUC), TxHU (TXH), TxLT (ILU), TxNacS (TXK), TxShA (IAU), UM (UUC), [Emory & Henry College, Emory, VA] (VEH), ViFreM (VMW), ViNO (VOD), ViRCU (VRC), ViRU (VRU), WaU (WAU), WKenU (TZP), WMUW (GZN), WeharU (HRM), WM (GZD).

| | | |
|---|---|---|
| Mem | v.1, n.1- Autumn, 1975- | AP/S5787/C |
| Coll | Current Issues Only | Women's Reading Area |
| Wom St | v.1, n.2- Winter, 1975- | Reading Room |
| Soc Work | v.1, n.1-v.2, n.4; Autumn, 1975- Summer, 1977 | Circulation |
| Law | v.1, n.1- Autumn, 1975- | Periodicals Section |
| EC | v.1, n.1- Autumn, 1975- | Periodicals Section |

1024  Simplicity Fashion Magazine. 1970? Quarterly. $6 for individuals and institutions. Simplicity Fashion Magazine, 200 Madison Avenue, New York, NY 10016. Last issue 96 pages, last volume 384 pages. Line drawings, photographs, some in color, commercial advertising. Published by Simplicity Pattern Co., Inc., New York, NY. Subject focus: sewing, fashion, arts, crafts.

| | | |
|---|---|---|
| DHS | Current Issues Only | Circulation |

1025  Sing Heavenly Muse. 1978. Semi-annual. $4 for individuals, $6 for institutions. Sue Ann Martinson, editor, Sing Heavenly Muse, P.O. Box 14027, Minneapolis, MN 55414. Last issue 68 pages, size 17 x 21. Line drawings. Subject focus: poetry, fiction, art.

| | | |
|---|---|---|
| RBR | n.1- Spring, 1978- | Circulation |

Single Mothers Newsletter.  Venice, CA

see Momma-the Organization for Single Mothers.  Venice, CA

1026  Sinister Wisdom. 1976. Quarterly. $9 for individuals, $12 for institutions. Harriet Desmoines and Catherine Nicholson, editors, Sinister Wisdom, 3136 R St., Lincoln, NB 68503. Last issue 104 pages, size 15 x 23. Line drawings, photographs. Place of publication varies: Charlotte, NC, July, 1976-Winter, 1978. Frequency varies: tri-annual, July, 1976-Winter, 1978. Subject focus: lesbians, poetry, fiction, photography, art.

| | | |
|---|---|---|
| RBR | n.1- July, 1976- | Circulation |
| Wom St | n.2- Fall, 1976- | Reading Room |

1027  Siren: A Journal of Anarcho-Feminism. 1971-1973//? Unknown. Last issue 16 pages. Line drawings. Available on microfilm: Herstory. Published by Anarcho-Feminists, Chicago, IL. Subject focus: welfare, radical feminism, poetry, politics.

| | | |
|---|---|---|
| Hist | v.1, n.1-2; ?-Apr., 1971 | Microforms Her. 1, R 21 |
| | v.1, n.3-n.8; Feb., 1972- Mar., 1973? | Her. 1 UP, R15 |

|  |  |  |
|---|---|---|
| | v.1, n.9-10;<br>?,-Sep., 1973 | Her. CUP, R 6 |

1028 Sister. 1970-1975//. Monthly. OCLC 2030047, 2263383, 2353987. Last issue 16 pages, last volume 196 pages. Line drawings, photographs, commercial advertising. Available on microfilm: WHi (1973-1975), Herstory (1970-1974). Published by The Women's Center, Venice, CA. Title varies: as L.A. Women's Liberation Newsletter, July, 1970-Mar., 1972; as L.A. Women's Center Newsletter, Apr.-Dec., 1972. Place of publication varies: Los Angeles, CA, July, 1970-June, 1973. Subject focus: rights, politics, health, communications, pro-abortion, education, ecology, self-defense, pregnancy, rape, poetry, film reviews. Other holding institutions: CLU (CLU), [University of Minnesota Union List, Minneapolis, MN] (MUL), PPiU (PIT), WMUW (GZN).

| Hist | v.4,n.6-v.6,n.6;<br>Aug., 1973-<br>Dec., 1975 | Microforms |
|---|---|---|
| | v.1,n.1-v.2,n.1;<br>July, 1970-<br>Aug., 1971 | Her. 1, R 16 |
| | v.2, n.2;<br>Sep., 1971 | Her. Add. |
| | v.2,n.3-v.4,n.4;<br>Oct., 1971-<br>June, 1973 | Her. 1 UP, R15 |
| | v.4,n.5-13;<br>July, 1973-<br>Mar., 1974 | Her. CUP, R 6 |

1029 Sister. 1973-1979//. Monthly. Last issue 24 pages, last volume 172 pages, size 29 x 22. Line drawings, photographs, commercial advertising. Published in New Haven, CT. Subject focus: rights, health, law, theatre, art, film reviews.

| Hist | v.1,n.3-v.8,n.1;<br>Jan., 1974-<br>Jan./Feb., 1979 | Circulation |
|---|---|---|

1030 Sister Courage. 1975-1978//. Irregular. OCLC 5027178. Last issue 16 pages, last volume 56 pages. Line drawings, photographs, commercial advertising. Available on microfilm: WHi. Published by Sister Courage, Inc., Allston, MA. Subject focus: rights, affirmative action, gay rights, health, child rearing, theatre, art, music, fiction.

| Hist | v.1,n.1-v.3,n.3;<br>Oct., 1975-<br>May, 1978 | Microforms |
|---|---|---|

1031 Sister News. 1972-1974//? Irregular. Last issue 10 pages. Line drawings, photographs. Available on microfilm: Herstory. Published by Women's Center, University of Connecticut, Storrs, CT. Title varies: as Free Women's Collective Newsletter, Apr. 3-Oct. 18, 1972; as Women's Center Newsletter, Dec. 1, 1972-Apr. 16, 1973. Subject focus: arts, crafts, politics, poetry, pro-abortion, sexism.

| Hist | v.1,n.1-v.2,n.3;<br>Apr. 3, 1972-<br>Apr./May, 1973 | Microforms<br>Her. 2, R 15 |
|---|---|---|
| | v.2,n.4-v.3,n.1;<br>Aug. 1, 1973-<br>Apr./May, 1974 | Her. 2 UP, R10 |

1032 Sister Switchboard. 1973-1974//? Monthly. Last issue 2 pages. Line drawings. Available on microfilm: Herstory (1974). Published by The Women's Union, Denver, CO. Subject focus: consciousness raising, poetry.

| Hist | Nov. 10, 1973-<br>Jan. 15, 1974 | Microforms<br>Her. 3, R 4 |
|---|---|---|

1033 Sisterhood. 1971//? Unknown. OCLC 2267707. Last issue 34 pages. Line drawings. Available on microfilm: Herstory. Published by Gay Women's Liberation Front, New York, NY. Subject focus: poetry, lesbians.

| Hist | v.1;<br>?, 1971 | Microforms<br>Her. 1, R 11 |
|---|---|---|

1034 Sisterlife. 1972-1974//? Irregular. Last issue 32 pages. Line drawings. Available on microfilm: Herstory. Published by Feminists for Life, Columbus, OH. Title varies: Feminists for Life, ?, 1972-July, 1973. Subject focus: pro-abortion, poetry, rape, politics, consumerism, lobbying.

| Hist | v.1,n.1-v.2,n.1;<br>?, 1972-June, 1973 | Microforms<br>Her. 2, R 5 |
|---|---|---|
| | July, 1973,<br>Jan., 1974 | Her. 2 UP, R10 |

1035 Sisters. 1970//? Unknown. OCLC 2267709. Last issue 54 pages. Line drawings. Available on microfilm: Herstory. Published by Tallahassee Women's Liberation, Tallahassee, FL. Subject focus: poetry, economics, literature, politics, Haiku.

| Hist | July, 1970 | Microforms<br>Her. 1, R 11 |
|---|---|---|

1036 Sisters: By and For Gay Women. 1970-1974//? Irregular. ISSN 0049-0644. OCLC 2267708. Last issue 34 pages, last volume 68 pages, size

14 x 22. Line drawings, photographs, commercial advertising. Available on microfilm: Herstory. Published by Daughters of Bilitis, San Francisco, CA. Subject focus: lesbians, poetry, art. Other holding institution: [University of Minnesota Union List, Minneapolis, MN] (MUL).

| Hist | v.1,n.1-v.2,n.9;<br>July 19, 1970-<br>Sep., 1971 | Microforms<br>Her. 1, R 14 |
|---|---|---|
|  | Oct., 1971- | Her. 1 UP, R 3 |
|  | Aug., 1973-<br>May, 1974 | Her. CUP, R1-2 |
| RBR | v.3,n.1-v.6,n.2;<br>Jan., 1972-<br>Mar?, 1974 | Circulation |

1037 Sisters in Poverty. 1970-1972//? Irregular. OCLC 2267710. Last issue 6 pages. Line drawings. Available on microfilm: Herstory. Published by New Mexico Chapter, National Organization for Women, Task Force on Women in Poverty, Albuquerque, NM. Subject focus: poverty, welfare, feminism, Equal Rights Amendment, lobbying, rights, law.

| Hist | v.1,n.1-3;<br>June, 1970-<br>July, 1971 | Microforms<br>Her. 1, R 19 |
|---|---|---|
|  | v.3, n.1;<br>June, 1972 | Her. 1 UP, R 7 |

1038 Sisters in Solidarity. 1971-1972//? Monthly. OCLC 2267711. Last issue 8 pages. Line drawings. Available on microfilm: Herstory. Published by Women's Liberation, Denver, CO. Subject focus: pro-abortion, theatre, poetry.

| Hist | Feb. 27, 1972 | Microforms<br>Her. 1, R 21 |
|---|---|---|
|  | Nov., 1971-<br>Oct., 1972 | Her. 1 UP, R15 |

1039 Sisters in Struggle. 1972//? Unknown. Last issue 6 pages. Line drawings. Available on microfilm: Herstory. Published by Merritt College Women's Collective, Oakland, CA. Subject focus: politics, lobbying, higher education, students.

| Hist | Nov., 1972 | Microforms<br>Her. 2, R 15 |
|---|---|---|

1040 Sisters Stand. 1971//? Unknown. Last issue 10 pages. Line drawings. Available on microfilm: Herstory. Published by Sisters Stand, University of Utah, Salt Lake City, UT. Subject focus: poetry, health, welfare.

| Hist | v.1, n.1;<br>Dec., 1971 | Microforms<br>Her. 2, R 15 |
|---|---|---|

1041 Sisters Today. 1929. Monthly, except July and August. $7 for individuals and institutions. Sister Mary Anthony Wagner, editor, Sisters Today, St. Benedict's Convent, St. Joseph, MN 56374. Business address: St. John's Abbey, Collegeville, MN. ISSN 0037-590X. OCLC 1714387. LC sn78-871. Last issue 62 pages, last volume 748 pages. Line drawings, photographs, commercial advertising. Self-indexed at end of each volume; indexed in Catholic Periodical Index. Previous editor: Father Daniel Durken, OSB, Jan., 1970-July, 1979. Subject focus: Cahtolic Church, poetry, convents. Other holding institutions: FTaSU (FDA), [Indiana Union List of Serials, Indianapolis, IN] (ILS), KSteC (KKQ), MBTI (BTI), MnHi (MHS), [University of Minnesota Union List, Minneapolis, MN] (MUL), NhMSA (SAC), [LaRoche College, Pittsburgh, PA] (PLR), [AMIGOS Union List of Serials, Dallas, TX] (IUC), TxDaU (IVD).

| EC | v.41, n.5-<br>Jan., 1970- | Circulation |
|---|---|---|

1042 Sisters Unite. 1970//? Unknown. OCLC 2267712. Last issue 5 pages. Line drawings. Available on microfilm: Herstory. Published by University of Houston Women's Liberation Front, Houston, TX. Subject focus: pro-abortion, child care.

| Hist | v.1, n.1;<br>Dec., 1970 | Microforms<br>Her. 1, R 21 |
|---|---|---|

1043 Skilled Jobs for Women, Inc. Newsletter. 1977//. Monthly. Last issue 2 pages, size 22 x 28. Line drawings. Published by Skilled Jobs for Women, Inc., Madison, WI. Subject focus: employment.

| Wom Ed<br>Res | n.1;<br>July 15, 1977 | Circulation |
|---|---|---|

1044 Skirting the Capitol with Marian Ash. 1967-1974//? Irregular. OCLC 2267719, 2384270. Last issue 6 pages, last volume 100 pages. Available on microfilm: Herstory. Published by Marian Ash, Sacramento, CA. Editor: Marian Ash. Subject focus: law, lobbying. Other holding institutions: MCR-S (Schlesinger Library on the History of Women in America, Radcliffe College, Cambridge, MA), [University of Minnesota Union List, Minneapolis, MN] (MUL).

| Hist | v.1,n.1-v.3,<br>n.25;<br>July 24, 1967-<br>June 30, 1969 | Microforms |
|---|---|---|

*Women's Periodicals and Newspapers*

        v.1, n.1-v.5,     Her. 1, R 21
        n.18;
        July 24, 1967-
        Sep. 7, 1971

        Dec., 1969-         Her. Add.
        Sep., 1970

        v.5, n.19-v.7,    Her. 1 UP, R15
        n.7;
        Oct. 15, 1971-
        June 18, 1973

        v.7, n.8-v.8, n.5;   Her. CUP, R 7
        Aug. 6, 1973-
        May 27, 1974

1045  The Skylark (Voice of N.O.W.). 1971//? Irregular. OCLC 2267722. Last issue 2 pages. Line drawings. Available on microfilm: Herstory. Published by Monterey Chapter, National Organization for Women, Monterey, CA. Subject focus: feminism, Equal Rights Amendment, lobbying, rights, poetry.

    Hist      Mar.-May, 1971     Microforms
                                           Her. 1, R 18

1046  Smogbelly. 1973//? Monthly. Last issue 8 pages. Line drawings. Available on microfilm: Herstory. Published by The Riverside Women's Center, Riverside, CA. Subject focus: poetry, pro-abortion, rape.

    Hist      v.1, n.1-5;      Microforms
             July-Nov., 1973    Her. 3, R 4

1047  The Social Mirror. 1893-1895//? Unknown. Last issue 22 pages, size 31 x 24. Line drawings, commercial advertising. Published in Milwaukee, WI. Subject focus: fashion, fiction.

    Hist      v.3, n.1;       Pam 74-6199
             Aug., 1895

1048  Socialist International Women. Bulletin. 1979. Bi-monthly. Vera Matthias, editor, Socialist International Women, Bulletin, 88a St. Johns Wood High Street, London NW8 7SJ England. Telephone 01-586-1101. Last issue 12 pages, last volume 68 pages, size 22 x 27. Line drawings, photographs. Subject focus: socialism, international relations, third world.

    Mem     v.1, n.1-      AP/1616/C888/B
            Jan./Feb., 1979-

    The Socialist Woman.   Chicago, IL; Girard, KS

       see The Coming Nation.  Chicago, IL

1049  Socialist Woman. 1971-1974//? Irregular. OCLC 2267782. Last issue 16 pages. Line drawings, photographs. Available on microfilm: Herstory. Published by Socialist Woman Groups/International Marxist Groups, London, England. Subject focus: labor unions, politics, lobbying, socialism.

    Hist     Mar./Apr.,      Microforms
           July/Aug., 1971   Her. 1, R 11

           Oct./Nov., 1971-  Her. 1 UP, R15
           Summer, 1972

           July/Aug., 1973,  Her. CUP, R 7
           Spring, 1974

1050  Socialist Woman. 1969-1971//? Bi-monthly. OCLC 2267783. Last issue 10 pages, last volume 58 pages. Line drawings, photographs. Available on microfilm: Herstory. Published by Nottingham Socialist Women's Committee, Nottingham, England. Subject focus: labor unions, politics, socialism, workers.

    Hist    v.1, n.3-v.3, n.1;  Microforms
          May/June, 1969-  Her. 1, R 11
          Jan./Feb., 1971

1051  Society for Humane Abortion Newsletter. 1966-1971//? Irregular. OCLC 2267834. Last issue 8 pages. Line drawings. Available on microfilm: Herstory. Published by Society for Humane Abortion, San Francisco, CA. Subject focus: pro-abortion, sex education, lobbying, birth control.

    Hist    [v.2, n.2-v.7,   Microforms
          n.2];            Her. 1, R 21
          [Apr./May, 1966-
          Summer, 1971]

          v.7, n.3;      Her. 1 UP, R15
          Winter, 1971

1052  Society for the Study of Social Problems. 1972-1973//? Unknown. Last issue 4 pages. Line drawings. Available on microfilm: Herstory. Published by University of California, San Diego, CA. Editors: Lenore Weitzman and Rose Somerville. Subject focus: family, image.

    Hist     n.1;         Microforms
          Winter, 1972-1973  Her. 2, R 15

1053  Sojourner. 1975. Monthly. $8 for individuals, $16 for institutions. Allison A. Platt, editor, Sojourner, 143 Albany Street, Cambridge, MA 02139. (617) 661-3567. ISSN 0191-8699. OCLC 4656277. LC sn79-2799. Last issue 32 pages, size 29 x 44. Line drawings, photographs, commercial advertising. Subject focus: rights, biographies, fiction, film reviews. Other holding institutions: MShM (MTH), [New York State Union List, Albany, NY] (NYS), NIC (COO).

| Coll | Current Issues Only | Women's Reading Area |
|---|---|---|
| Wom Ed Res | v.4, n.9- May, 1979- | Circulation |

1054 Sojourner. 1975. 9 times a year. Phyllis Watts Lafontaine, editor, Sojourner, Office of Women's Studies, 134 Derby Hall, 154 N. Oval Mall, Columbus, OH 43210. OCLC 6439627. Last issue 8 pages, last volume 74 pages, size 22 x 28. Line drawings, photographs. Published by Office of Women's Studies, Ohio State University. Subject focus: research, women's studies, higher education, professionals, employment. Other holding institution: OU (OSU).

| Wom St | v.2, n.4- Jan., 1976- | Reading Room |
|---|---|---|

1055 Solana. 1976-1978//? Unknown. Last issue 43 pages, last volume 93 pages, size 18 x 21. Line drawings, photographs. Published by Androgyny Press, Saint Louis, MO. Editor: Terri Anderson. Subject focus: fiction, poetry, art, photography.

| RBR | v.1,n.1-v.2,n.?; May, 1976- Spring, 1978 | Circulation |
|---|---|---|

1056 Somerset County Chapter N.O.W. Newsletter. 1974//? Monthly. Last issue 8 pages. Line drawings. Available on microfilm: Herstory. Published by Somerset County Chapter, National Organization for Women, Martinsville, NJ. Subject focus: feminism, Equal Rights Amendment, rights, lobbying, politics.

| Hist | May-June, 1974 | Microforms Her. 3, R 3 |
|---|---|---|

1057 So's Your Old Lady. 1973//? Irregular. OCLC 1779955. Last issue 42 pages. Line drawings, photographs. Available on microfilm: Herstory. Published by Lesbian Resource Center, Minneapolis, MN. Subject focus: lesbians, poetry, fiction. Other holding institution: [University of Minnesota Union List, Minneapolis, MN] (MUL).

| Hist | n.1-2; Feb.-June, 1973 | Microforms Her. 2, R 15 |
|---|---|---|
|  | n.3-4; July/Aug.- Nov./Dec., 1973 | Her. 2 UP, R10 |

1058 Soundings. 1942. Irregular. Gratis to individuals and institutions. Sylvia Stanley and Rose Downey, editors, Soundings, 2500 North Mayfair Road, P.O. Box 26395, Milwaukee, WI 53226. (414) 476-1050. Last issue 4 pages, last volume 28 pages. Line drawings, photographs. Published by the Girl Scouts of Milwaukee Area, Inc., Milwaukee, WI. Previous editors: Helen Rothfus, June, 1966; Teddi A. Grant, Oct., 1967-Feb./Mar., 1968; Mary Ann Budnik, Oct., 1968-Mar., 1969; Gretchen Wenzel, May, 1969-May, 1973; Margaret Stacey, Nov., 1973-Aug./Sep., 1975; Margaret Stacey and Karen Gleason, Dec., 1975-Aug./Sep., 1976; Margaret Stacey, Oct., 1976; Margaret Stacey and Susan Apker, Nov./Dec., 1976; Susan Apker, Jan., 1977-May/June, 1980; Sylvia Stanley, Sep., 1980. Subject focus: Girl Scouts.

| Hist | v.1,n.1- Jan., 1942- | F902M6/8G52 (Cutter) |
|---|---|---|

1059 The Source: A Feminist Newsletter. 1973-1974//? Monthly. Last issue 8 pages. Line drawings, photographs. Available on microfilm: Herstory. Published by The Women's Caucus of Bucks County Community College, Newtown, PA. Subject focus: feminism, politics, sexism in education.

| Hist | n.1-2; May-June, 1973 | Microforms Her. 2, R 15 |
|---|---|---|
|  | n.3-14; July, 1973- June, 1974 | Her. 2 UP, R10 |

1060 Sourceline. 1975. Irregular. $3 for individuals and institutions. Sourceline, Alaska Women's Resource Center, 204 East 5th Avenue, Suite 224, Anchorage, AK 99501. (907) 276-0528. Last issue 16 pages, last volume 80 pages, size 43 x 29. Line drawings, photographs, commercial advertising. Subject focus: rights, lesbians, gay rights, labor unions, health, poetry, biographies, lobbying.

| Hist | v.1, n.6, v.3, n.1-2, 5- Dec., 1975, Jan.-Mar., Aug., 1977- | Circulation |
|---|---|---|

1061 Southeastern Connecticut N.O.W. News/Notes. 1973//? Monthly. Last issue 3 pages. Line drawings. Available on microfilm: Herstory. Published by Southeastern Connecticut Chapter, National Organization for Women, Stonington, CT. Editor: Mary Walker. Subject focus: non-sexist children's materials, education, lobbying.

| Hist | Feb.-June, 1973 | Microforms Her. 2, R 12 |
|---|---|---|

*Women's Periodicals and Newspapers*

        July 26, 1973      Her. 2 UP, R 8

1062 <u>Southern Women's Magazine</u>. 1904-1905//? Monthly. Last issue 66 pages, last volume 792 pages. Line drawings, photographs, commercial advertising. Available on microfilm: ResP. Editors: Marie Goodwin Stewart and Charlotte Stewart. Published in Atlanta, GA. Subject focus: beauty care, humor, fashion, fiction, poetry, children. Other holding institution: DLC (DLC).

  Mem      v.1,n.1-v.4,n.1;    Microforms
           Feb., 1904-
           Aug., 1905

<u>Southwest Cook County Chapter N.O.W. News-letter</u>. Worth, IL

  see <u>N.O.W....or Never</u>. Worth, IL

1063 <u>Soviet Woman</u>. 1945. Monthly. Valentina Fedotova, editor, Soviet Woman, 22 Kuznetzky Most, Moscow K-31 USSR. ISSN 0038-5913. OCLC 1606325, 2267989. LC 52-38741. Last issue 40 pages, last volume 480 pages, size 26 x 34. Line drawings, photographs, some in color. Available on microfilm: Herstory (1970-1971). Published by the Soviet Women's Committee and the Central Council of Trade Unions of the USSR. Frequency varies: bi-monthly, Nov./Dec., 1945-Nov./Dec., 1953. Previous editors: Zincuda Gagarina, Nov./Dec., 1945-Sep./Oct., 1946; Maria Ovsyannikova, Jan./Feb., 1948-Jan., 1969. Subject focus: politics, literature, art. Other holding institutions: CLSU (CSL), CSU (CSU), GASU (GSU), GVaS (GYG), [Indiana Union List of Serials, Indianapolis, IN] (ILS), InU (IUL), MiEM (EEM), MiMtpT (EZC), [University of Minnesota Union List, Minneapolis, MN] (MUL), N (NYG), [New York State Union List, Albany, NY] (NYS), [Western New York Library Resources Council, Buffalo, NY] (VZX), NIC (COO), NNepaSU (ZLM), [Central New York Library Resources Council, Syracuse, NY] (SRR), NSyU (SYB), OC1 (CLE), OC1U (CSU), OkEP (OKZ), OkTOR (OKO), PPiU (PIT), ScRhW (SWW), ScU (SUC), [AMIGOS Union List of Serials, Dallas, TX] (IUC), WMUW (GZN).

  Hist     Sep., 1970-     Microforms
          Sep., 1971;     Her. 1, R 11

  Mem     Nov./Dec., 1945-  AP/S732/W872

1064 <u>The Sow's Ear</u>. 1977. Tri-annual. $4.50 for individuals and institutions. Edith Loyd, editor, The Sow's Ear, P.O. Box 1653, Pittsburg, CA 94565. OCLC 4141173. Last issue 28 pages, last volume 95 pages, size 14 x 22. Line drawings. Published by the Blue Collar Press, Pittsburg, CA. Subject focus: poetry, art. Other holding institution: [University of Minnesota Union List, Minneapolis, MN] (MUL).

  RBR      v.1, n.1-       Circulation
           Summer, 1977-

1065 <u>The Spare Rib</u>. 1970-1974//? Irregular. OCLC 2268012, 2269603. Last issue 12 pages. Line drawings. Available on microfilm: Herstory. Published by Women Mobilized for Change, Chicago, IL. Title varies: as Women Mobilized for Change, ?, 1970. Subject focus: rights, poetry, politics, peace movement. Other holding institutions: [University of Minnesota Union List, Minneapolis, MN] (MUL).

  Hist    ?, 1970         Microforms
                            Her. 1, R 12

        May 24-Sep., 1971  Her. 1, R 21

        Oct., 1971-      Her. 1 UP, R15
        June, 1973

        Mar., 1974      Her. CUP, R 7

1066 <u>Spare Rib</u>. 1972. Monthly. $27.50 for individuals, $37 for institutions. Spare Rib, 114 George Street, Berkhamstead, Hertfordshire, England HP4 2EJ. ISSN 0306-7971. OCLC 5237209. Last issue 48 pages, size 22 x 30. Line drawings, photographs, commercial advertising. Published by Spare Ribs Ltd., London, England. Place of publication varies: London, England, 1972-? Previous editors: Marsha Rowe and Rosie Boycott, 1972-? Subject focus: politics, labor unions, history, employment, media, fiction, film reviews, television reviews.

  Hist    n.3-12;         Microforms
        Sep., 1972-     Her. 2, R 15
        June, 1973

        n.14-28;        Her. 2 UP,
        Aug., 1973-?,   R 10-11
        1974

  Coll    Current Issues   Women's
        Only              Reading Area

1067 <u>Spazm: Sofia Perouskaya and Andrei Zhelyabou, Memorial Coeducational Society for People's Freedom through Women's Liberation</u>. 1969//? OCLC 2268014. Last issue 36 pages. Line drawings, photographs. Available on microfilm: Herstory. Published by the Women's History Research Center, Berkeley, CA. Subject focus: media, literature, radicalism, peace movement, politics.

  Hist    Apr. 25 -      Microforms
        Dec. 18, 1969   Her. 1, R 21

<u>Speakout</u>. Boston, MA

  see <u>Speakout News Views</u>. Boston, MA

1068 <u>Speakout</u>. 1972-1973//? Monthly. Last issue 22 pages. Line drawings, commercial advertising. Available on microfilm:

Herstory. Published in Albany, NY. Frequency varies: irregular, Jan.-July/Aug., 1972. Subject focus: lobbying, Equal Rights Amendment, politics, pro-abortion, poetry, employment.

| Hist | Jan., 1972-<br>June, 1973 | Microforms<br>Her. 2,<br>R 15-16 |
|---|---|---|
|  | July, 1973-<br>June, 1974 | Her. 2 UP, R11 |

1069 Speakout News Views. 1970-1974//? Irregular. OCLC 2258584. Last issue 4 pages. Line drawings, photographs. Available on microfilm: Herstory. Published by The Unitarian Universalist Women's Federation, Boston, MA. Title varies: as The Bridge, Mar., 1970-Sep./Oct., 1972; as Speakout, Nov., 1972-June 15, 1973. Editor: Mary Lou Thompson. Subject focus: Unitarian Universalist Association, politics, rights.

| Hist | Mar., 1970-<br>Feb., 1971 | Microforms<br>Her. 1, R 5 |
|---|---|---|
|  | Sep./Oct., 1971-<br>June 15, 1973 | Her. 1 UP, R15 |
|  | Mar., 1974 | Her. CUP, R 7 |

1070 Special Bulletin. 1940-1944//? Irregular. Last issue 29 pages, size 14 x 23. Line drawings. Published by the U.S. Dept. of Labor, Women's Bureau, Washington, DC. Subject focus: labor unions, war work, workers.

| Hist | n.1-20;<br>?, 1940-June, 1944 | △/L13./10: |
|---|---|---|

1071 Spectre. 1971-1972//. Bi-monthly? Last issue 16 pages, size 40 x 29. Line drawings, photographs. Available on microfilm: Herstory. Published by Spectre Collective, Ann Arbor, MI. Subject focus: lesbians, rights.

| Hist | n.4-6;<br>Sep/Oct., 1971-<br>Jan./Feb., 1972 | Pam 71-3387 |
|---|---|---|
|  | n.1-4;<br>Mar./Apr.-<br>Sep./Oct., 1971 | Microforms<br>Her. 1, R 4 |
|  | n.5-6;<br>Nov./Dec., 1971-<br>Jan./Feb., 1972 | Her. 1 UP, R15 |

1072 The Speculator. 1974//? Irregular. Last issue 5 pages. Line drawings. Available on microfilm: Herstory. Published by Women's Health Center, Honolulu, HI. Editor: Nancy Moser. Subject focus: health, politics, rape.

| Hist | n.2-4;<br>Jan.-May, 1974 | Microforms<br>Her. 3, R 4 |
|---|---|---|

1073 The Spinners. 1934-1935//? Bi-monthly. Last issue 28 pages, size 15 x 23. Published in New York, NY. Editors: Eugenia T. Finn, Virginia Keating Orton, and Antoinette Scudder. Subject focus: poetry.

| RBR | v.2, n.2;<br>May/June, 1935 | Circulation |
|---|---|---|

1074 Spinning Off: A Monthly Newsletter of Women's Culture Published at the Women's Building. 1979. Monthly. $7.50 for individuals and institutions. Cheri Gaulke, editor, Spinning Off, Women's Building, 1727 North Spring Street, Los Angeles, CA 90012. (213) 221-6161. Last issue 4 pages, size 43 x 29. Line drawings, photographs, commercial advertising. Available on microfilm: WHi. Published by Women's Community, Inc., Los Angeles, CA. Subject focus: arts, literature.

| Hist | May, 1979,<br>Mar., 1980- | Circulation |
|---|---|---|

1075 The Spokeswoman. 1970. Monthly. $16 for individuals, $27 for institutions. Karen Wellisch, editor, The Spokeswoman, 53 West Jackson, Suite 525, Chicago, IL. 60604. (312) 663-5060. ISSN 0038-7738. OCLC 1766357, 5071945, 5914383. LC sn78-609, sc79-3832. Last issue 18 pages, last volume 200 pages. Line drawings, photographs. Available on microfilm: UnM (1970 -1978). Subject focus: education, employment, pro-abortion, health, politics, lobbying, Equal Rights Amendment. Other holding institutions: AU (ALM), AzTeS (AZS), CSt (Stanford University), CLobS (CLO), CSdS (CDS), CStbW (CWS), CU-UC (UCU), COLH (COL), COU-DA (COA), CtNlc (CTL), CtW (WLU), CtY (YUS), [Congressional Research Service, Washington, DC] (CRS), FJUNF (FNP), MFMIU (FXG), IRA (ICY), [Indiana Union List of Serials, Indianapolis, IN] (ILS), InU (IUL), KMK (KKS), KWiU (KSW), MBNU (NED), MCR-S (Schlesinger Library on the History of Women in America, Radcliffe College, Cambridge, MA), MBTI (BTI), MBU (BOS), MH-AH (BHA), MWelC (WFL), MdBJ (JHE), DME/DAS (OLA), MiMtpT (EZC), [University of Minnesota Union List, Minneapolis, MN] (MUL), MnStjos (MNF), McRS (NRC), NbKS (KRS), NhD (DRB), NmU-L (NML), N (NYG), [New York State Union List, Albany, NY] (NYS), NCH (YHM), NPQC (XQM), NHemH (ZIH), NIC (COO), NOneoU (ZBM), NPV (VXW), NRU (RRR), NSbSU (YSM), NSufR (VVR), [Central New York Library Resources Council, Syracuse, NY] (SRR), OAkU (AKR), PBL (LYU), PBm (BMC), PPD (DXU), PPiC (PMC), PPiU (PIT), [Pittsburgh Regional Library Center-Union List, Pittsburgh, PA] (QPR), PSC (PSC), ScRhW (SWW), [AMIGOS Union List of Serials, Dallas, TX] (IUC), VtU (VTU), WaU

(WAU), WMUW (GZN).

| Hist | v.1, n.1-v.2,n.3;<br>June 5, 1970-<br>Sep. 1, 1971 | Microforms<br>Her. 1 R 21 |
|---|---|---|
| | v.2, n.4-v.3,n.12;<br>Oct., 1971-<br>June, 1973 | Her. 1 UP,<br>R 15-16 |
| | v.4, n.1-12;<br>July 15, 1973-<br>June 15, 1974 | Her. CUP, R 7 |
| | v.2, n.5, v.4,n.1-<br>v.5, n.1;<br>Sep. 15, 1971,<br>July 15, 1973-<br>July 15, 1974 | Pam 79-1741 |
| | v.6,n.1-v.9,n.9;<br>July 15, 1976-<br>Dec., 1979 | Microforms |
| Coll | Current Issues<br>Only | Women's<br>Reading Area |
| Wom St | v.8, n.10-<br>Apr. 15, 1978- | Reading Room |
| Mem | v.1, n.1-<br>June 5, 1970- | AP/S76195 |
| MATC | v.5, n.6-<br>May, 1975- | Cora Hardy<br>Library |
| MMRL | Current Issues<br>Only | Circulation |

The Spokeswoman. Wausau, WI

see Profile. Wausau, WI

1076 Spokeswoman For Abortion Law Repeal. 1972//? Unknown. ISSN 0700-8279. OCLC 3423253. LC cn77-318297. Last issue 8 pages. Line drawings, photographs. Available on microfilm: Herstory. Published by Canadian Women's Coalition to Repeal Abortion Laws, Toronto, Ontario, Canada. Subject focus: pro-abortion, law, politics. Other holding institutions: CaOONL (NLC), [University of Minnesota Union List, Minneapolis, MN] (MUL).

| Hist | v.1, n.1;<br>Apr., 1972 | Microforms<br>Her. 2, R 16 |
|---|---|---|

1077 Sportswoman. 1973-1978//? 10 times a year. Last issue 68 pages, size 22 x 27. Line drawings, photographs, some in color, commercial advertising. Available on microfilm: McP (1975-1978); UnM. Published by Amazon Publications, Inc., Palatine, IL. Place of publication varies: Lafayette, CA, Oct., 1976-Jan., 1977. Editors: Sally Ride, Oct.- Nov., 1976; Lorraine Rorke, Jan., 1977; Mary Kathleen Taylor, Oct./Nov., 1977. Subject focus: sports.

| IMC | v.4,n.4-5,<br>v.5, n.1,8;<br>Oct.-Nov.,1976,<br>Jan., Oct./Nov., 1977 | Periodicals<br>Section |
|---|---|---|
| Coll | v.4, n.4-v.5,<br>n.1, 8;<br>Oct., 1976-<br>Jan., Oct./Nov.,<br>1977 | Women's<br>Reading Area |

1078 The Sportswoman. 1973-1974//? Quarterly. Last issue 30 pages. Line drawings, photographs, commercial advertising. Available on microfilm: Herstory. Published by Jensen-Fane Publications, Long Beach, CA. Editor: Marlene Jensen. Subject focus: sports, biographies.

| Hist | v.1, n.1-2;<br>Spring-<br>Summer, 1973 | Microforms<br>Her. 2, R 16 |
|---|---|---|
| | v.1, n.3-v.2,n.6;<br>July, 1973-<br>June, 1974 | Her. 2 UP,R 11 |

1079 Spreading the News. 1923//? Unknown. Last issue 4 pages, size 18 x 30. Published by Sixth Region of the National League of Women Voters, Hastings, NB. Editor: Mrs. Charles H. Dietrich. Subject focus: health.

| Hist | v.1, n.4;<br>Feb. 9, 1923 | KWZ/NA<br>(Cutter) |
|---|---|---|

The Standard Delineator of Fashions, Fancy Work, and Millinery. New York, NY

see The Designer and the Woman's Magazine. New York, NY

Standard Designer. New York, NY

see The Designer and the Woman's Magazine. New York, NY

1080 Stardust. 1940. Monthly. Bart Lanier Stafford III, editor, Stardust, 1212 Lake Shore Drive, Suite 10-A, Chicago, IL 60610. Last issue 68 pages, last volume 470 pages, size 21 x 28. Line drawings, photographs, commercial advertising. Published by Stardust Magazine Agency, Inc., Chicago, IL. Place of publication varies: Milwaukee, WI, Jan./Feb., 1941-Dec., 1973. Previous editors: Emilye Loignon, Jan./Feb., 1943-Dec., 1973. Subject focus: clubs.

| | | | | | |
|---|---|---|---|---|---|
| Hist | v.4, n.1/2-3/4, 9/10- Jan./Feb.-Mar./Apr., Sep./Oct., 1943- | HS/853.7/W5/S8 | | v.1,n.1-v.6,n.3; Summer, 1973- Summer, 1980 | Circulation |

The State Church Woman. San Diego, CA

   see Church Women United, State News. Whittier, CA

The State U.C.W. News. Riverside, CA

   see Church Women United, State News. Whittier, CA

State United Church Women United News. Riverside, CA; Whittier, CA

   see Church Women United, State News. Whittier, CA

1081 The Stateswoman: Current Issues of Women's Equality. 1979. $10 for students and some retirees, $20 for individuals and institutions. Marian Thompson, editor, The Stateswoman: Current Issues of Women's Equality, P.O. Box 7354, Madison, WI 53707. (608) 255-9809. Business address: 625 West Washington Avenue, Madison, WI 53703. Last issue 8 pages, size 43 x 29. Line drawings. Available on microfilm: WHi (1979). Published by Wisconsin Feminist Project Fund, Inc., Madison, WI. Subject focus: rights, politics, family violence, feminism, law reform, welfare, pro-abortion.

| | | |
|---|---|---|
| Hist | v.1, n.1- Sep., 1979- | Circulation |
| Coll | Current Issues Only | Women's Reading Area |
| MPL | v.1, n.1- Sep., 1979- | Literature and Social Science Section |

1082 Status of Women News. 1973-1980//. Quarterly. ISSN 0381-9418. OCLC 2227734. LC cn76-300903. Last issue 56 pages, last volume 232 pages, size 21 x 28. Line drawings, photographs. Available on microfilm: Herstory (1973-1974). Published by the National Action Committee on the Status of Women, Toronto, Ontario, Canada. Subject focus: rights, politics, career development, retirement, biographies, lobbying, film reviews. In French (50%). Other holding institutions: CaOONL (NLC), WMUW (GZN).

| | | |
|---|---|---|
| Hist | v.1, n.1-2; Summer, 1973- Winter, 1974 | Microforms Her. 3 R 4 |

1083 Statutes of Liberty. 1970//? Unknown. OCLC 2268136. Last issue 14 pages. Line drawings, photographs. Available on microfilm: Herstory. Published by Women of Rochester, Rochester, NY. Subject focus: child care, poetry, Black Panthers.

| | | |
|---|---|---|
| Hist | v.1, n.2; Oct., 1970 | Microforms Her. 1, R 11 |

Stewardesses for Women's Rights. New York, NY

   see SFWR Stewardesses for Women's Rights. New York, NY

Stony Brook N.O.W. Newsletter. Stony Brook, NY

   see Suffolk N.O.W. Stony Brook, NY

1084 Street Paper. 1971//? Unknown. Last issue 20 pages. Line drawings, photographs, commercial advertising. Available on microfilm: Herstory. Published in Salt Lake City, UT. Subject focus: pro-abortion, politics, radicalism, sexism, peace movement.

| | | |
|---|---|---|
| Hist | v.1, n.3; Mar.5-23, 1971 | Microforms Her. 2, R 16 |

1085 Stri-Dharma. 1918?-1936//? Irregular. Last issue 40 pages, last volume 212 pages, size 18 x 25. Line drawings, photographs, commercial advertising. Published by Women's Indian Association, Madras, India. Editors: Shirimati Malati Patwardhan, May, 1929-Nov., 1930; Muthulakshoni Reddi, Nov., 1931-July/Aug., 1936. Subject focus: pro-suffrage, education. rights, law. In Hindi (15%), in Tamil (15%), in Telugu (15%).

| | | |
|---|---|---|
| Mem | [v.7, n. 7-v.19, n.6]; [May, 1929- July/Aug., 1936] | AP/S916 |

1086 Struggle. 1971-1972//? Unknown. Last issue 4 pages. Available on microfilm: Herstory. Published by Sibylline House, Edmonton, Alberta, Canada. Subject focus: politics, radicalism, gay rights, poetry, consciousness raising, lesbians.

| | | |
|---|---|---|
| Hist | v.1, n.1-3; ?, 1971-1972 | Microforms Her. 2, R 16 |

1087 Suffolk N.O.W. 1972-1974//? Irregular. Last issue 2 pages. Line drawings. Available on microfilm: Herstory. Published by Suffolk County Chapter, National Organization for Women, Stony Brook, NY. Title varies: as Stony Brook N.O.W. Newsletter, Summer, 1972-June, 1973. Subject focus: politics, feminism, Equal Rights Amendment, lobbying, rights, child care.

| Hist | Summer, 1972-<br>June, 1973 | Microforms<br>Her. 2, R 12 |
|---|---|---|
|  | Mar.-May, 1974 | Her. 2 UP, R8 |

1088 Suffragist. 1913-1921//. Monthly. OCLC 1585922. LC 16-25411. Last issue 28 pages. Line drawings, photographs, commercial advertising. Available on microfilm: DLC. Frequency varies: weekly, Nov. 15, 1913-Sep. 20, 1919. Published by Congressional Union for Woman Suffrage, Washington, DC. Editors: Rheta C. Dorr, Nov. 15, 1913-May 30, 1914; Lucy Burns, May 13-Dec. 30, 1916; Vivian Pierce, Jan. 24, 1917-Sep. 21, 1918; Clara Wold, Sep. 28-Dec. 28, 1918; Sue S. White, May 24-Sep. 20, 1919; Florence B. Boeckel, Feb., 1920-Jan./Feb., 1921. Subject focus: rights, employment, politics, pro-abortion. Other holding institutions: CSt (Stanford University), [University of Minnesota Union List, Minneapolis, MN] (MUL), OAkU (AKR), OKentU (KSU), WM (GZD), MCR-S (Schlesinger Library on the History of Women in America, Radcliffe College, Cambridge, MA).

| Hist | v.1,n.1-v.9,n.1;<br>Nov. 15, 1913-<br>Jan./Feb., 1921 | Microforms |
|---|---|---|
|  | [v.2, n.11-v.4, n.51], v.8,n.1-v.9, n.1<br>[Mar. 14, 1914-Dec. 16, 1916]<br>Feb., 1920-Jan./Feb., 1921 | KWZ/+S94<br>(Cutter) |

1089 Sunbury. 1974//? Tri-annual. Last issue 78 pages. Available on microfilm: Herstory. Published in New York, NY. Editor: Virginia Scott. Subject focus: poetry.

| Hist | v.1, n.1;<br>Apr., 1974 | Microforms<br>Her. 3, R 4 |
|---|---|---|

1090 Sunnyvale-Southbay N.O.W. Newsletter. 1970-1974//? Irregular. OCLC 2267904. Last issue 6 pages. Line drawings. Available on microfilm: Herstory. Published by South Bay Chapter, National Organization for Women, Sunny Vale, CA. Editors: Enid Davis, Sep., 1970-June/July, 1973; Sandra Smith, July/Aug., 1973-June, 1974. Subject focus: media, pro-abortion, sexism, children, politics.

| Hist | Sep., 1970-<br>Sep., 1971 | Microforms<br>Her. 1, R 20 |
|---|---|---|
|  | Oct., 1971-<br>June/July, 1973 | Her. 1 UP, R12 |
|  | July/Aug., 1973-<br>June, 1974 | Her. CUP, R 5 |

1091 Surfacing. 1974//? Unknown. Last issue 8 pages. Line drawings, commercial advertising. Available on microfilm: Herstory. Published by the Woman's Centre, Victoria, British Columbia, Canada. Subject focus: health, politics.

| Hist | v.1, n.2;<br>Apr., 1974 | Microforms<br>Her. 3, R 4 |
|---|---|---|

1092 Susan Saxe Defense Committee Newsletter. 1976-1977//. Irregular. OCLC 5072196. Last issue 12 pages. Line drawings, photographs. Available on microfilm: WHi. Published by Susan Saxe Defense Committee, West Somerville, MA. Subject focus: Susan Saxe, lesbians, feminism.

| Hist | n.1-5;<br>Jan?, 1976-<br>Feb., 1977 | Microforms |
|---|---|---|

1093 Switchbored. 1969//? Unknown. OCLC 2268293. Last issue 10 pages. Line drawings. Available on microfilm: Herstory. Published by Women Incensed at Telephone Company Harassment, New York, NY. Subject focus: poetry, telephone industry workers, American Telephone and Telegraph.

| Hist | Aug., 1969 | Microforms<br>Her. 1, R 21 |
|---|---|---|

1094 Sydney Women's Liberation Newsletter. 1970-1974//? Irregular. OCLC 2269640. Last issue 8 pages. Line drawings, photographs. Available on microfilm: Herstory. Published by Sydney Women's Liberation, Sydney, New South Wales, Australia. Subject focus: pro-abortion, poetry, law, sexism, lobbying.

| Hist | July, 1970-<br>June, 1971 | Microforms<br>Her. 1, R 23 |
|---|---|---|
|  | Sep., 1971 | Her. Add. |
|  | Nov., 1971 | Her. 1 UP, R16 |
|  | Oct., 1973-<br>Mar., 1974 | Her. CUP, R 7 |

1095 TABS. 1978. Quarterly. $8.50 for individuals, $17 for institutions. Lucy Picco Simpson, editor, TABS, 744 Carroll Street, Brooklyn, NY

11215. (212) 788-3478. ISSN 0160-371X. OCLC 3672124. LC sc78-906. Last issue 16 pages, last volume 64 pages, size 22 x 28. Line drawings, photographs. Subject focus: rights, education, biographies. Other holding institution: FTS (FHM).

| IMC | v.1, n.2- Winter, 1978- | Periodicals Section |

TWL Newsletter. Philadelphia, PA

    see S.O.S.-Speak Out Sister. Philadelphia, PA

Task Force on the Status of Women in Education. San Francisco, CA

    see AERA * Women's Caucus Newsletter. San Francisco, CA

1096 The Tattler. 1969-1972//. Irregular. Last issue 14 pages, size 22 x 28. Line drawings. Published by Iowa Training School for Girls, Mitchellville, IA. Subject focus: poetry, prisoners, art.

| Crim Just | Nov., 1969- Dec., 1972 | Circulation |

1097 Tell-A-Woman. 1972-1974//? Monthly. Last issue 6 pages. Line drawings, commercial adveritising. Available on microfilm: Herstory. Published by Women's Liberation Center, Media Workshop, Philadelphia, PA. Subject focus: media, rights, pro-abortion, arts, crafts, employment, film making, poetry.

| Hist | v.1, n.1-v.2,n.4; Feb., 1972- Apr., 1973 | Microforms Her. 2, R 16 |
| | v.2,n.8-v.3, n.6; Aug., 1973-June, 1974 | Her. 2UP, R 11 |

1098 The Temperance Educational Quarterly. 1910-1917//? Quarterly. Last issue 34 pages, last volume 68 pages. Line drawings. Available on microfilm: ResP. Published by the Bureau of Scientific Temperance Investigation and Department of Scientific Temperance Instruction of the World's and National Women's Christian Temperance Union, Milwaukee, WI. Subject focus: temperance. IU (UIU).

| Mem | v.1,n.1-v.8,n.2; Jan., 1910- Apr., 1917 | Microforms |

1099 The Texan Woman. 1973//? Unknown. Last issue 32 pages. Line drawings, photographs, commercial advertising. Available on microfilm: Herstory. Published in Austin, TX. Subject focus: sexism in education, employment, poetry, biographies, fiction, record reviews.

| Hist | May-Aug., 1973 | Microforms Her. 3, R 4 |

Texas W.E.A.L. Newsletter. Dallas, TX

    see W.E.A.L. Texas Newsletter. Dallas, TX

1100 Texas Women's Political Caucus Newsletter. 1973//? Monthly. Last issue 6 pages. Line drawings, commercial advertising. Available on microfilm: Herstory. Published by National Women's Political Caucus, Texas Chapter, Austin, TX. Subject focus: lobbying, education, Latinas, politics, communication.

| Hist | v.1,n.1-2; Oct.-Nov., 1973 | Microforms Her. 3, R 3 |

Themis. Los Angeles, CA

    see Thesmophoria. Oakland, CA

1101 Thesmophoria. 1979. 8 times a year. $5 for individuals and institutions. Thesmophoria, 2927 Harrison Street, Oakland, CA 94611. Last issue 6 pages, last volume 36 pages, size 21 x 22. Line drawings, commercial advertising. Available on microfilm: WHi. Published by Susan B. Anthony Coven No. 1, Covenant of the Goddess, Oakland, CA. Title varies: as Themis, 1979-1980. Place of publication varies: Los Angeles, CA, 1979-1980. Subject focus: witches, religion.

| Hist | v.1, n.1- Midsummer, 1979- | Circulation |

1102 13th Moon. 1973. Semi-annual. $6 for individuals, $12 for institutions. Ellen Marie Bissert, editor, 13th Moon, Box 3, Drawer F, Inwood Station, New York, NY 10034. ISSN 0094-3320. OCLC 2587697. LC 76-647817. Last issue 120 pages, last volume 224 pages, size 15 x 23. Line drawings, photographs. Indexed in: Abstracts of Popular Culture, Index of American Periodical Verse. Published by 13th Moon, Inc., New York, NY. Subject focus: art, poetry, fiction. Other holding institutions: AzTeS (AZS), COFS (COF), CtY (YUS), DLC (DLC), FU (FUG), GFoF (GFV), IaCfT (HIU), LU (LUU), [University of Minnesota Union List, Minneapolis, MN] (MUL), [New York State Union List, Albany, NY] (NYS), NA1U (NAM), NIC (COO), [Central New York Library Resources Council, Syracuse, NY] (SRR), NTRS (ZRS), NcCU (NKM), NcD (NDD), NcGU (HGU), NbU (LDL), NhD (DRB), OU (OSU), TxU (IXA).

| RBR | v.1,n.1- Spring/Summer, 1973- | Circulation |

1103 Through the Door. 1978. Quarterly. Through

the Door, 11 North Third Avenue, Sturgeon Bay, WI 54235. Last issue 8 pages, size 22 x 28. Published by the Women's Employment Project, Sturgeon Bay, WI. Subject focus: employment, lobbying.

| Wom Ed Res | n.1, 3; Sep., 1978, Mar., 1979- | Circulation |

1104 Through the Looking Glass. 1971//? Irregular. OCLC 2268542. Line drawings, photographs. Available on microfilm: Herstory. Published by The Women's Center, Philadelphia, PA. Subject focus: rights, politics, poetry.

| Hist | v.1, n.1-2; Feb.-Apr., 1971 | Microforms Her. 1, R 4 |

1105 Through the Looking Glass: A Women's & Childrens Newsletter. 1975. Bi-monthly. Free to prisoners and poor people, $7 for individuals, $12 for institutions. Through the Looking Glass, P.O. Box 22061, Seattle, WA 98122. Business address: Gay Community Social Services, P.O. Box 2228, Seattle, WA 98122. Last issue 56 pages, size 28 x 22. Line drawings, photographs, commercial advertising. Available on microfilm: WHi (1980). Subject focus: racism, prisoners, criminal justice system, Afro-Americans, Native Americans, Puerto Ricans, child advocacy, biographies.

| Hist | v.1,n.1,v.5,n.7- May, 1976, Sep./Oct., 1980- | Circulation |

The Tide. Los Angeles, CA

    see The Lesbian Tide. Los Angeles, CA

1106 The Tiny Triangle. 1923-1927//? Irregular. Last issue 8 pages, size 16 x 17. Photographs. Published by Young Women's Christian Association, Madison, WI. Subject focus: clubs.

| Hist | v.1,n.1-3,v.2, n.1-3,v.3,n.1, v.5, n.1; Oct., 1923-Apr., Oct., 1924- May, 1925, Jan., 1926, Jan., 1927 | F/902/MI/840 (Cutter) |

1107 Tippecanoe N.O.W. News. 1973-1974//? Monthly. Last issue 5 pages. Line drawings. Available on microfilm: Herstory. Published by Tippecanoe Chapter, National Organization for Women, West Lafayette, IN. Subject focus: pro-abortion, rape, child care, feminism, Equal Rights Amendment, lobbying, rights.

| Hist | Dec., 1973- June, 1974 | Microforms Her. 3, R 3 |

1108 Title VIII Report. 1970//. Bi-weekly. OCLC 2268586. Last issue 6 pages, size 22 x 28. Line drawings, photographs. Available on microfilm: Herstory. Published by Professional and Technical Programs, Inc., New York, NY. Editor: Barbara Jordan Moore. Subject focus: sexism in employment, professionals, Equal Rights Amendment, business.

| Hist | v.1, n.1-8; June 15- Sep. 21, 1970 | Microforms Her. 1, R 21 |
| | v.1, n.9-10; Oct.-Nov?. 1970 | Her. Add. |
| Wom Ed Res | v.1, n.3-8; July 13- Sep. 21, 1970 | Circulation |

1109 To, For, By & About Women. 1971//? Irregular. OCLC 2268590. Last issue 3 pages. Line drawings. Available on microfilm: Herstory. Published by Charlotte Women's Center, Charlotte, NC. Subject focus: peace movement, rights, poetry, Vietnamese.

| Hist | v.2, n.7-8; Apr. 26- June 25, 1971 | Microforms Her. 1, R 21 |

1110 Toads. 1975//. Unknonw. OCLC 1597226. Last issue 12 pages, size 29 x 41. Line drawings, photographs, commercial advertising. Published by United Sisters, Tampa, FL. Subject focus: rights, legal aid, fiction, law, poetry. Other holding institution: PPiU (PIT).

| Hist | v.1, n.1; June, 1975 | Pam 75-980 |

Today's Secretary. Kansas City, MO

    see The Secretary. Kansas City, MO

1111 Today's Secretary. 1899. Monthly. $6.75 for individuals, $5.95 for institutions. Nhora Cortes-Comerer, editor, Today's Secretary, 1221 Avenue of the Americas, New York, NY 10020. Business address: 2211 Fordem Avenue, Madison, WI 53704. ISSN 0040-8565. OCLC 1639100. LC 50-52904. Last issue 32 pages, size 22 x 28. Line drawings, photographs, some in color, commercial advertising. Available on microfilm: UnM, McP. Subject focus: secretaries, fashion, business education. Other holding institutions: [Alabama Public Library Service, Montgomery, AL] (ASL), AU (ALM), ArAO (AKO), ArU (AFU), AzFU (AZN), AzTeS (AZS), DLC (DLC), DeU (DLM), FBoU (FGM), FJF (FJK), FJUNF (FNP), UPB (IBA), InU (IUL), KSteC (KKQ), KyU (KUK), LLcM (LHA), MiLC (EEL), [University of Minnesota

Union List, Minneapolis, MN] (MUL), NAlfC (YDM), NCorniCC (ZDG), NSbSU (YSM), [Central New York Library Resources Council, Syracuse, NY] (SRR), NbKS (KRS), NbU (LDL), NcEUcE (NPE), NjLincB (NCC), OAU (OUN), OAkU (AKR), [Raymond Walters Deneral and Technical College Library, Blue Ash, OH] (ORW), OCedC (CDC), OKentU (KSU), OTU (TOL), OYU (YNG), OkTOR (OKO), PCoR (ROB), PNwC (WFN), PPiAC (AIC), PPiC (PMC), PPiD (DUQ), [Pittsburgh Regional Library Center Union List, Pittsburgh, PA] (QPR), ScRhW (SWW), TCollsM (TMS), TMurS (TXM), TxAbH (TXS), TxBelM (MHB), TxDN (INT), TxDW (IWU), [AMIGOS Union List of Serials, Dallas, TX] (IUC), TxDaB (IDA), TxLT (ILU), ViRCU (VRC), WM (GZD), WMaPI-RL (GZR), WeharU (HRM).

    MATC    v.72, n.5-    Cora Hardy
               Feb., 1970-    Library

1112 Together. 1973//? Irregular. Last issue 4 pages. Line drawings, photographs. Available on microfilm: Herstory. Published by Women's Resource Center, UCLA, Los Angeles, CA. Editor: Karen Zimmerman. Subject focus: women's studies, education, students, politics, child care.

    Hist    v.1, n.1-v.2,n.1;    Microforms
           Jan.-Apr., 1973    Her. 2, R 16

1113 Together. 1973-1974//? 8 times a year. OCLC 4041796. Last issue 12 pages. Line drawings, photographs, commercial advertising. Available on microfilm: Herstory. Published by Associated Students of UCLA Communications Board, Los Angeles, CA. Editor: Karen Zimmerman. Subject focus: health, fiction, students, sports, education, humor. Other holding institution: [University of Minnesota Union List, Minneapolis, MN] (MUL).

    Hist    v.1, n.1-6;    Microforms
           Oct. 15, 1973-    Her. 2 UP, R11
           May 20, 1974

1114 Toilet: A Weekly Collection of Literary Pieces Principally Designed for the Amusement of the Ladies. 1801//. Weekly. OCLC 1587717, 4014973. LC mic56-4596. Last issue 6 pages. Available on microfilm: UnM. Published in Charlestown, SC. Subject focus: fiction, poetry, humor. Other holding institutions: AzTeS (AZS), [University of Minnesota Union List, Minneapolis, MN] (MUL), NcWsW (EWF), NSbSU (YSM), OAkU (AKR), OKentU (KSU), OYU (YNG), PPiU (PIT), [AMIGOS Union List of Serials, Dallas, TX] (IUC), WMUW (GZN).

    Hist    v.1, n.1-8;    Microforms
           Jan. 17-
           Feb. 28, 1801

1115 Tooth and Nail. 1969-1970//. Irregular. Last issue 22 pages, size 22 x 28. Line drawings. Available on microfilm: Herstory. Published by Bay Area Women's Liberation, Berkeley, CA. Subject focus: rights, politics. Other holding institution: MCR-S (Schlesinger Library on the History of Women in America, Radcliffe College, Cambridge, MA).

    Hist    v.1, n.1-4;    Microforms
           Aug. 15, 1969-    Her. 1, R 11
           Jan., 1970

           v.1, n.2-4;    Pam 71-706
           Oct., 1969-
           Jan., 1970

1116 The Torch. 1972-1974//? Monthly. Last issue 3 pages. Line drawings. Available on microfilm: Herstory. Published by DuPage Chapter, National Organization for Women, Glen Ellyn, IL. Subject focus: politics, education.

    Hist    v.1, n.8-v.2,n.6;    Microforms
           Aug., 1972-    Her. 2, R 10
           June, 1973

           v.2, n.7-v.3,n.6;    Her. 2 UP, R6
           July, 1973-
           June, 1974

1117 Le Torchon Brule. 1972//? Unknown. OCLC 2268625. Last issue 24 pages. Line drawings, photographs. Available on microfilm: Herstory. Published by French Women's Liberation, Paris, France. Subject focus: feminism, birth control, pro-abortion. In French (100%).

    Hist    n.1-2?    Microforms
           ?, 1972    Her. 1, R 4

           n.3-7?    Her. 1 UP, R16
           ?, 1972

1118 Toronto Women's Liberation Movement Newsletter. 1971//? Unknown. OCLC 2268627. Last issue 26 pages. Line drawings. Available on microfilm: Herstory. Published by Toronto Women's Liberation, Toronto, Ontario, Canada. Subject focus: education, pro-abortion, politics, health, poetry, Vietnamese.

    Hist    Mar., 1971    Microforms
                            Her. 1, R 21

1119 Touchstone: Wisconsin Women in the Arts Newsletter. 1972. Unknown. Estella Lauter and Karen H. Winzenz, editors, Touchstone, Room 728 Lowell Hall, 610 Langdon Street, Madison, WI 53706. Last issue 12 pages, size 22 x 28. Line drawings. Subject focus: arts, lobbying.

|  | Coll | Current Issues Only | Women's Reading Area |
|--|--|--|--|

1120 Town & Country. 1846. Monthly. $18 for individuals and institutions. Frank Zachary, editor, Town & Country, 717 Fifth Avenue, New York, NY. Business address: P.O. Box 10082, Des Moines, IA 50340. ISSN 0040-9952. OCLC 1680936, 5878257. LC sn78-1125, sn80-11182. Last issue 268 pages, size 23 x 28. Line drawings, photographs, some in color, commercial advertising. Indexed in: Access Index (1975-). Available on microfilm: UnM. Subject focus: celebrities, socialites, fashion, health, beauty care, interior decoration, travel. Other holding institutions: ArAT (AKH), AzTeS (AZS), DeU (DLM), MiEM (EEM), [University of Minnesota Union List, Minneapolis, MN] (MUL), [Western New York Library Resources Council, Buffalo, NY] (VZX), NIC (COO), NR (YQR), NSbSU (YSM), [Central New York Library Resources Council, Syracuse, NY] (SRR), NcD (NDD), NcGA (NQA), OCl (CLE), OKentU (KSU), OkT (TUL), PCLS (REC), [Pittsburgh Regional Library Center, Union List, Pittsburgh, PA] (QPR), TxCM (TXA), [AMIGOS Union List of Serials, Dallas, TX] (IUC), WMUW (GZN).

| MPL | v.133, n.4985-<br>Jan., 1979- | Literature and Social Science Section |
|--|--|--|

1121 Traffic Jam. 1971//? OCLC 2268654. Unknown. Last issue 2 pages. Line drawings. Available on microfilm: Herstory. Published by Women at A.T. & T., Seattle, WA. Subject focus: American Telephone and Telegraph, telephone industry workers, lobbying, sexism in employment, employment.

| Hist | n.1-2;<br>Feb. 1-22, 1971 | Microforms<br>Her. 1, R 21 |
|--|--|--|

1122 Trans Sister. 1967-1971//? 6 times a year. OCLC 2268659. Last issue 8 pages, last volume 48 pages. Line drawings. Available on microfilm: Herstory. Published by National Catholic Center for Interracial Justice, Dekalb/Chicago, IL. Subject focus: Catholic Church, nuns, priests, education.

| Hist | v.1, n.1-v.4,n.5;<br>Nov., 1967-<br>May, 1971 | Microforms<br>Her. 1, R 21 |
|--|--|--|

Transit Home Companion. Madison, WI

   see Women's Transit Home Companion. Madison, WI

1123 Trenton N.O.W. 1973-1974//? Irregular. Last issue 7 pages. Line drawings. Available on microfilm: Herstory. Published by Trenton Chapter, National Organization for Women, Trenton, NJ. Title varies: as And N.O.W..., Trenton, Nov., 1973. Subject focus: feminism, Equal Rights Amendment, lobbying, rights, pro-abortion.

| Hist | n.1-3;<br>Oct., Nov.,<br>Dec., 1973/<br>Jan., 1974 | Microforms<br>Her. 3, R 3 |
|--|--|--|

1124 Trial. 1970//? Unknown. OCLC 2268707. Last issue 4 pages. Line drawings, photographs. Available on microfilm: Herstory. Published by Total Repeal of Illinois Abortion Laws, Chicago, IL. Subject focus: pro-abortion, lobbying.

| Hist | Oct. 29, 1970 | Microforms<br>Her. 1, R 21 |
|--|--|--|

1125 Triple Jeopardy. 1971-1975//. Irregular. OCLC 2268724. Last issue 18 pages. Line drawings, photographs. Available on microfilm: WHi (1974-1975), Herstory (1971-1974). Published by Third World Women's Alliance, New York, NY. Editor: Frances M. Beal. Subject focus: racism, imperialism, sexism, Third World, health, radicalism, politics, international relations. In Spanish (10-100%).

| Hist | v.1, n.1;<br>Sep./Oct., 1971 | Microforms<br>Her. 1, R 4 |
|--|--|--|
|  | v.1,n.2,v.2,<br>n.3-4;<br>Nov., 1971;<br>Mar./Apr.-<br>June/July, 1973 | Her. UP, R 16 |
|  | v.3,n.1-3/4;<br>Sep./Oct., 1973-<br>Mar./Apr., 1974 | Her. CUP, R 7 |
|  | v.3,n.4-v.4,n.2;<br>Mar./Apr., 1974-<br>Summer, 1975 | Microforms |

1126 A True Republic. 1891-1904//? Monthly. Last issue 24 pages, last volume 288 pages. Line drawings, commercial advertising. Available on microfilm: ResP. Published in Cleveland, OH. Editor: Mrs. Sarah M. Perkins. Subject focus: pro-suffrage, temperance.

| Mem | v.1,n.1-v.14,<br>n.12;<br>July, 1891-<br>Dec., 1904 | Microforms |
|--|--|--|

1127 Tucson N.O.W. 1972-1974//? Monthly. Last issue 2 pages. Line drawings. Available on microfilm: Herstory. Published by Tucson Chapter, National Organization for Women, Tucson, AZ. Editor: Alison Dawson. Subject focus: feminism, Equal Rights Amendment, lobbying, rights, sexism, pro-abortion, politics.

| Hist | v.1, n.11-<br>v.2, n.6;<br>Nov., 1972-<br>June, 1973 | Microforms<br>Her. 2, R 12 |
|---|---|---|
| | v.2, n.7-v.3, n.6;<br>July, 1973-<br>June, 1974 | Her. 2 UP, R 8 |

1128 Turn of the Screwed. 1970-1971//? Irregular. OCLC 2268785. Last issue 12 pages. Line drawings. Available on microfilm: Herstory. Published by Dallas Area Women's Liberation, Dallas, TX. Subject focus: children, rights, periodical reviews, sexism.

| Hist | v.1, n.5-6,8;<br>Nov. 30, 1970-<br>Jan. 31,<br>June 18, 1971 | Microforms<br>Her. 1, R 22 |
|---|---|---|

1129 Twin Cities Woman. 1977-1979//. Monthly. ISSN 0192-4907. OCLC 3472881, 5460286. LC sn79-6875. Last issue 32 pages, last volume 332 pages. Line drawings, photographs, commercial advertising. Available on microfilm: WHi. Published by Twin Cities Woman, Inc., Minneapolis, MN. Editors: Victoria Sprague, Apr., 1977-Oct., 1978; Marcia Appel, Nov., 1978-May, 1979. Subject focus: fashion, food, arts. Other holding institution: [University of Minnesota Union List, Minneapolis, MN] (MUL).

| Hist | v.1, n.1-v.3,n.5;<br>Apr., 1977-<br>May, 1979 | Microforms |
|---|---|---|

1130 Twin Cities Women's Union. 1973-1974//? Irregular. Last issue 4 pages. Line drawings. Available on microfilm: Herstory. Published in Minneapolis, MN. Subject focus: child care, pro-abortion, lobbying.

| Hist | Mar. 15-<br>Apr. 3, 1973 | Microforms<br>Her. 2, R 16 |
|---|---|---|
| | Aug., 1973-<br>June, 1974 | Her. 2 UP, R11 |

1131 Tyolaisnainen. 1930-1935//? Weekly. Last issue 12 pages, last volume 624 pages. Line drawings, photographs, commercial advertising. Place of publication varies: Superior, WI, Oct. 8, 1930-June 30, 1931. Published by Finnish Federation, Inc., New York, NY. Subject focus: career development, workers. In Finnish (100%).

| Hist | v.1, n.1-v.2,<br>n.47;<br>Oct. 8, 1930-<br>Nov. 25, 1931 | HQ/1101/"T9 |
|---|---|---|
| | v.4, n.10-v.6,<br>n.52;<br>Mar. 8, 1933-<br>Dec. 26, 1935 | Microforms |

1132 U.A.W. Women's Department Special Bulletin. 1965-1969//? Irregular. Last issue 12 pages. Line drawings, photographs. Available on microfilm: Herstory. Published by United Auto Workers, Women's Department, Detroit, MI. Subject focus: equal pay for equal work, employment, rights, labor unions, auto industry workers, sexism in employment, lobbying, child care.

| Hist | June, 1965-<br>Jan., 1969 | Microforms<br>Her. 2, R 16 |
|---|---|---|

1133 U.N.S.W. Women's Liberation. 1971//? Unknown. Last issue 3 pages. Available on microfilm: Herstory. Published by University of New South Wales Women's Liberation, Glebe, Australia. Subject focus: education, family, health.

| Hist | Mar., 1971 | Microforms<br>Her. 2, R 16 |
|---|---|---|

1134 U.S. Woman Engineer. 1954. 5 times a year. $12 for individuals and institutions. Barbara Krohn, editor, U.S. Woman Engineer, 835 Securities Building, Seattle, WA 98101. (206) 622-3538. Business address: Room 305, 345 E. 47th Street, New York, NY 10017. (212) 644-7500. ISSN 0272-7838, 0038-0067. OCLC 6380740, 2268289. LC 80-648264. Last issue 36 pages. Line drawings, photographs, some in color, commercial advertising. Available on microfilm: Herstory (1972-1974). Published by United Engineering Center, Society of Woman Engineers, New York, NY. Title varies: as Newsletter-Society of Woman Engineers, ?, 1954-Jan./Feb., 1970. Previous editor: Terry Smith, Sep., 1972-May, 1974. Subject focus: engineers, professionals, biographies. Other holding institutions: DACE (AED), DLC (DLC), NdU (UND).

| Hist | v.19, n.1-5;<br>Sep., 1972-<br>May, 1973 | Microforms<br>Her. 2, R 15 |
|---|---|---|
| | v.20, n.1-5;<br>Sep., 1973-<br>May, 1974 | Her. 2 UP, R10 |

US/United Sisters. Tampa, FL

    see United Sisters Magazine. Tampa, FL

1135 U.U.W.F. Newsletter. 1971//? Unknown. OCLC 2269120. Last issue 8 pages. Line drawings, photographs. Available on microfilm: Herstory. Published by Unitarian Universalist Women's Federation, Boston, MA. Subject focus: Unitarian Universalist Association, Equal Rights Amendment, human rights, child care, bibliographies.

| Hist | Mar., May, 1971 | Microforms Her. 1, R22 |

1136 U.W.A. News. 1970//? Irregular. OCLC 2269121. Last issue 2 pages. Line drawings. Available on microfilm: Herstory. Published by University Women's Association, University of Chicago, Chicago, IL. Subject focus: higher education, counseling, education.

| Hist | v.1, n.1-2; Jan.-Mar., 1970 | Microforms Her. 1, R 22 |

The Udder Side. New York, NY

    see Cowrie. New York, NY

1137 De Uitbuiting Van De Vrouw. 1971//? OCLC 2268815. Last issue 44 pages. Line drawings. Available on microfilm: Herstory. Published by Een Dolle Mina Publikatie, Antwerp, Belgium. Subject focus: workers, rights. In Dutch (100%).

| Hist | ?, 1971 | Microforms Her. 1, R 6 |

1138 The Una. A Paper Devoted to the Elevation of Women. 1853-1855//? Monthly. OCLC 2255518. LC ca09-1456. Last issue 16 pages, last volume 160 pages. Line drawings, commercial advertising. Available on microfilm: McA. Published in Boston, MA. Place of publication varies: Providence, RI, Feb. 1853-Dec., 1854. Editors: Paulina Wright Davis, Feb. 1, 1853-Dec., 1854; Paulina Wright Davis and Caroline Wells Healy Dael, Jan.-Oct. 15, 1855. Subject focus: rights, poetry, art. Other holding institutions: [University of Minnesota Union List, Minneapolis, MN] (MUL), CSt (Stanford University), TMurS (TXM).

| Hist | v.1, n.1-v.3, n.10; Feb. 1, 1853-Oct. 15, 1855 | Microforms |

1139 The Underground Woman. 1970//? Irregular. OCLC 2268832. Last issue 9 pages. Line drawings. Available on microfilm: Herstory. Published by St. Louis Women's Liberation, St. Louis, MO. Subject focus: politics, sexuality, education, child care, sexism.

| Hist | v.1, n.1-4,6 Apr. 1-May 1, July, 1970 | Microforms Her. 1, R 22 |

1140 The Union Maid. 1975//? Monthly. Last issue 4 pages, size 22 x 28. Line drawings. Published by Madison-Janesville CLUW (Coalition of Labor Union Women), Madison, WI. Editor: Carol Birr. Subject focus: affirmative action, politics, labor unions, lobbying, workers.

| Hist | v.1, n.1-2; July-Aug., 1975 | Pam 76-2435 |

The Union Signal and the World's White Ribbon. Chicago, IL

    see The Union Signal. Evanston, IL

1141 The Union Signal. 1875? Monthly. $4.50 for individuals and institutions. Mrs. Herman Stanley, editor, the Union Signal, 1730 Chicago Avenue, Evanston, IL 60201. ISSN 0041-7033. OCLC 1767985. LC sn78-1786. Last issue 16 pages, size 29 x 23. Line drawings, photographs, commercial advertising. Self-indexed (1927-). Available on microfilm: WHi (1897-1913); OHi (1883-1933). Title varies: as The Union Signal and the World's White Ribbon, Jan. 5, 1893-May 21, 1903. Place of publication varies: Chicago, IL, Jan. 4, 1883-May 21, 1903. Frequency varies: weekly, Jan. 4, 1883-Apr. 3, 1954; bi-weekly, Apr. 17, 1954-Feb. 22, 1969. Previous editors: Mary B. Willard, Jan. 4, 1883-Dec. 31, 1885; Mary Allen West, Jan. 6, 1887-Dec. 27, 1888; Frances E. Willard and Mary Allen West, Jan. 5-19, 1893; Frances E. Willard, Jan. 26, 1893-Nov. 24, 1898; Lillian M. N. Stevens, Dec. 15, 1898-July 16, 1914; Julia F. Deane, July 23-Dec. 24, 1914; Anna A. Gordon, Jan. 1, 1915-Sep. 25, 1926; Ella A. Boole, Oct. 16, 1926-Oct. 28, 1933; Ida B. Wise Smith, Nov. 4, 1933-Oct. 28, 1944; D. Leigh Colvin, Nov. 4, 1944-Oct. 24, 1953; Mrs. Glenn G. Hays, Nov. 7, 1953-Oct. 24, 1959; Mrs. Fred J. Tooze, Nov. 14, 1959-Oct., 1974. Subject focus: prohibition, Christianity, fiction, poetry. Other holding institutions: AzTeS (AZS), CLU (CLU) I (SPI), IaHi (IOQ), IaLG (IOF), [Indiana Union List of Serials, Indianapolis, IN] (ILS), KLindB (KFB), KSteC (KKQ), MCR-S (Schlesinger Library on the History of Women in America, Radcliffe College, Cambridge, MA), [University of Minnesota Union List, Minneapolis, MN] (MUL), PCLS (REC), PNwC (WFN), [Pittsburgh Regional Library Center-Union List, Pittsburgh, PA] (QPR), ScU (SUC), TCollsM (TMS).

| | | |
|---|---|---|
| Hist | v.9, n.1-v.11, n.52, v.13,n.1-v.14, n.52, v.19, n.1-v.21, n.50; v.40, n.1-<br>Jan. 4, 1883-<br>Dec. 31, 1885;<br>Jan. 6, 1887-<br>Dec. 27, 1888;<br>Jan. 5, 1893-<br>Dec. 26, 1895;<br>Jan. 1, 1914- | HV/5285/U5 |
| | v.23, n.1-v.39, n.46;<br>Jan. 7, 1897-<br>Nov. 13, 1913 | Microforms |

Union W.A.G.E. Newsletter. Berkeley, CA

 see Union W.A.G.E. San Francisco, CA

1142 Union W.A.G.E. 1971. Bi-monthly. $4 for individuals, $10 for institutions. Pam Allen, editor, Union W.A.G.E.. P.O. Box 40904, San Francisco, CA 94140. Business address: 37-A 29th Street, San Francisco, CA 94110. (415) 282-6777. ISSN 0300-6336. OCLC 1498005, 2268871, 3940023, 3940110. Last issue 16 pages, size 29 x 45. Line drawings, photographs. Indexed: in Women Studies Abstracts, Available on microfilm: UnM, Herstory (1971-1974). Published by Union Women's Alliance to Gain Equality, Berkeley, CA. Title varies: as Union WAGE Newsletter, June-Dec., 1971. Place of publication varies: Berkeley, CA, June, 1971-July/Aug., 1975. Frequency varies: irregular, June-Dec., 1971. Previous editors: Gretchen Mackler, Jan./Feb.-Sep./Oct., 1972. Subject focus: rights, employment, lobbying, labor unions, workers. Other holding institutions: CtY (YUS), DLC (NSD), NmU-L (NML), OU (OSU), WaU (WAU), [AMIGOS Union List of Serials, Dallas, TX] (IUC).

| | | |
|---|---|---|
| Hist | v.1,n.1-4;<br>May-Aug., 1971 | Microforms<br>Her. 1, R 22 |
| | v.1,n.6-v.2, n.17;<br>Oct., 1971-<br>May/June, 1973 | Her. 1 UP, R16 |
| | v.2, n.18-23;<br>July/Aug., 1973-<br>May/June, 1974 | Her. CUP, R 7 |
| | v.1, n.2, 6-<br>June, Oct., 1971- | Circulation |
| Coll | Current Issues Only | Women's Reading Area |

1143 United Daughters of the Confederacy Magazine. 1938. Monthly. $3 for individuals and institutions. Mrs. W. Zack Huggins, editor, United Daughters of the Confederacy Magazine, 328 North Blvd., Richmond, VA 23220. OCLC 1768006. Last issue 30 pages, last volume 312 pages, size 22 x 29. Photographs, commercial advertising. Previous editors: Lucy C. Smith, Feb., 1967-Mar., 1969; Elizabeth H.W. Smith, Apr., 1969-Jan., 1973; Mrs. Archie C. Watson, Feb., 1973-Dec., 1974; Mrs. Eldon M. Jett, Jan., 1975-Jan., 1977; Mrs. Henry D. Ferris, Feb., 1977-Dec., 1978. Subject focus: clubs, genealogy, history. Other holding institutions: AU (ALM), FBoU (FGM), FMIFIU (FGX), IGK (IBK), [University of Minnesota Union List, Minneapolis, MN] (MUL), [New York State Union List, Albany, NY] (NYS), NIC (COO), OkT (TUL), [AMIGOS Union List of Serials, Dallas, TX] (IUC).

| | | |
|---|---|---|
| Hist | v.30, n.2-<br>Feb., 1967- | E/483.5/A19 |

1144 United Sisters Magazine. 1973-1975. Irregular. Last issue 30 pages, last volume 226 pages, size 20 x 27. Line drawings, photographs, commercial advertising. Available on microfilm: Herstory (1973-1974). Published by the Women's Center, Tampa, FL. Title varies: as US/United Sisters, Mar., 1973-Jan., 1974. Frequency varies: monthly, Mar., 1973-Jan., 1974. Editors: Ginger Daire-Reber, Apr., 1973-Jan., 1974; Ginger Daire-Reber and Ramey Fair, Feb., 1974-Aug?, 1975. Subject focus: radical feminism, lesbians, pro-abortion, health, poetry, art.

| | | |
|---|---|---|
| Hist | v.1, n.1-11, v.2, n.3;<br>Mar., 1973-<br>Jan., 1974,<br>Aug?, 1975 | HO/1101/U5 |
| | v.1, n.1-4;<br>Mar.-June, 1973 | Microforms<br>Her. 2, R 16 |
| | v.1, n.5-11;<br>Aug., 1973-<br>Jan., 1974 | Her. 2 UP, R11 |

Universalist and Ladies Repository. Boston, MA

 see The Ladies' Repository Religious and Literary Magazine for the Home Circle. Boston, MA

1145 University of Michigan Papers in Women's Studies. 1974-1978//. Irregular. OCLC 1781972, 5094974, 5777686. Last issue 112 pages, last volume 562 pages, size 21 x 28. Line drawings. Indexed: in Women's Studies Abstracts. Published by University of Michigan, Ann Arbor, MI. Subject focus: women's studies, research. Other holding institutions: AU (ALM), ArU (AFU), AzTeS (AZS), AzU (AZU), CArcHT (CHU), CSt (Stanford University), CLobS (CLO), CLSU (CSL), CLU (CLU), CSfST (CSF), CtY (YUS), FOFT (FTU), FU (FUG), GEU (EMU), CU (CUA), InU (IUL), KMK (KKS), KyU (KUK), MBNU (NED), MH (HLS), MH (HUL), MWelC (WEL), MiEM (EEM), MiU (EYM), [University of Minnesota Union List, Minneapolis, MN] (MUL), MoU (MUU), [New York State Union List, Albany, NY] (NYS), NBrockU (XBM), NBronSL (VVS), NIC (COO), NPV (VXW), NbU (LDL), NjR (NJR), NmU (IQU), OO (OBE), OU (OSU), PBL (LYU), PPiU (PIT), [AMIGOS Union List of Serials, Dallas, TX] (IUC), TxDW (IWU), TxLT (ILU), ViW (VWM), WMA (GZA).

| Coll | v.1, n.1-v.5, n.1?; Feb., 1974-May, 1978 | Women's Reading Area |
| Wom St | v.1, n.1-v.5, n.1?; Feb., 1974-May, 1978 | Reading Room |

1146 <u>University Women</u>. 1974. Irregular. Dr. Marion Swoboda, editor, University Women, 1802 Van Hise Hall, Madison, WI 53706. (608) 262-6404. Last issue 8 pages, size 22 x 28. Published by Central Administration, University of Wisconsin System, Madison, WI. Subject focus: workers, higher education.

| Coll | Current Issues Only | Women's Reading Area |
| IMC | Current Issues Only | Periodical Section |
| Wom St | v.2, n.9- Sep. 25, 1975- | Reading Room |
| UW Ext | v.1, n.1- Jan. 23, 1974- | Circulation |
| Wom Ed Res | v.1, n.3- Mar. 28, 1974- | Circulation |
| UWBA | v.1, n.5- May, 1974- | Circulation |

1147 <u>Up From the Basement</u>. 1973-1974//? Irregular. Last issue 12 pages. Line drawings. Available on microfilm: Herstory. Published by Women's Center, San Jose, CA. Subject focus: racism, poetry, children, education, birth control, lobbying.

| Hist | v.2, n.12-v.3, n.5; Aug., 1973-May/June, 1974 | Microforms Her. 3, R 4 |

1148 <u>Up From Under</u>. 1971-1978//. Irregular. ISSN 0042-0670. OCLC 1768827, 1489919. LC 78-23557. Last issue 66 pages, last volume 314 pages, size 19 x 28. Line drawings, photographs. Indexed: in Alternative Press Index. Available on microfilm: Herstory (1971-1973), UnM. Published in New York, NY. Subject focus: rights, health, poetry, workers, fiction. Other holding institutions: ArU (AFU), DeU (DLM), FBoU (FGM), InIU (IUP), InU (IUL), LNU (LNU), MCR-S (Schlesinger Library on the History of Women in America, Radcliffe College, Cambridge, MA), [University of Minnesota Union List, Minneapolis, MN] (MUL), NcWfSB (NVS), NhD (DRB), OAU (OUN), PPiU (PIT), TxLT (ILU), WaU (WAU).

| Hist | v.1, n.1-3; May/June, 1971-Jan./Feb., 1972 | Microforms Her. 1, R 11 |
| | v.1, n.4; Winter, 1971-1972 | Her. 1UP, R16 |
| | v.1, n.5; Summer?, 1973 | Her. CUP, R 7 |
| | v.1, n.1-5; May/June, 1971-Summer?, 1973 | HQ/1101/U6 |
| MPL | v.1, n.1-5; May/June, 1971-Summer?, 1973 | Literature and Social Science Section |

1149 <u>Up to N.O.W.</u> 1973-1974//? Irregular. Last issue 8 pages. Line drawings. Available on microfilm: Herstory. Published by Butler County Chapter National Organization for Women, Fairfield, OH. Title varies: as N.O.W. Newsletter, Dec., 1973. Editors: Sandra Bray and Janice Bennett. Subject focus: feminism, Equal Rights Amendment, lobbying, rights, politics, art, self-help.

| Hist | v.1, n.1-5; Dec., 1973-May, 1974 | Microforms Her. 3, R 2 |

1150 <u>Upstream</u>. 1977-1980//. Monthly. ISSN 0700-9992. OCLC 3279461. LC cn77-31525. Last issue 20 pages, size 42 x 29. Line drawings, photographs, commercial advertising. Published by Feminist Publications of Ottawa, Ottawa, Ontario, Canada. Subject focus: rights, sports, feminism, history, arts, health. Other holding institution: CaOONL (NLC). In French (0-5%).

| Hist | v.2, n.3-v.4, n.5; Apr., 1978-July, 1980 | Microforms |

<u>Uppity Woman</u>. San Francisco, CA

see <u>Woman N.O.W.</u> San Francisco, CA

1151 VOW News Letter. 1961//? Monthly. Last issue 8 pages, size 22 x 14. Published by Voice of Women, U.S.A., Cleveland, OH. Editor: Jessie Tucker. Subject focus: peace movement.

| Hist | v.1, n.1-2; Nov., 15-Dec. 15, 1961 | Pam 76-1406 |

1152 The Valley Women's Center. 1974//? Irregular. Last issue 6 pages. Line drawings. Available on microfilm: Herstory. Published by The Valley Women's Center, Northampton, MA. Subject focus: child care, health.

| Hist | Apr./May-June, 1974? | Microforms Her. 3, R 4 |

Vancouver's Women's Health Collective Newsletter. Vancouver, British Columbia, Canada

see Our Newsletter. Vancouver, British Columbia, Canada

1153 Vassar Newsletter. 1971//? Unknown. OCLC 2269134. Last issue 4 pages. Line drawings. Available on microfilm: Herstory. Published by San Francisco Vassar Club, San Francisco, CA. Editor: Jane Murphy. Subject focus: clubs, biographies.

| Hist | June 15, Sep. 15, 1971 | Microforms Her. 1, R 22 |

1154 Velvet Fist. 1970-1972//? Irregular. ISSN 0315-8292. OCLC 5248368, 2269148. LC cn77-318142. Last issue 8 pages. Line drawings, photographs. Available on microfilm: Herstory. Published by Velvet Fist/Toronto Women's Liberation, Toronto, Ontario, Canada. Subject focus: pro-abortion, child care, lobbying, poetry, workers. Other holding institution: CaOONL (NLC).

| Hist | v.1, n.1-7; Sep., 1970-Aug., 1971 | Microforms Her. 1, R 4 |
| | v.1,n.8-v.2,n.4; Oct., 1971-?, 1972 | Her. 1 UP, R16 |

1155 Velvet Glove. 1971-1972//? Bi-monthly? OCLC 2269149. Last issue 24 pages. Line drawings, photographs, commercial advertising. Available on microfilm: Herstory, McP. Published by Velvet Glove Press, Livermore, CA. Editor: Ellen Kerrigan Smith. Subject focus: poetry, sexism, ecology. Other holding institutions: [University of Minnesota Union List, Minneapolis, MN] (MUL), PPiU (PIT).

| Hist | n.1-4; Jan./Feb.-Sep./Oct., 1971 | Microforms Her. 1, R 11 |
| | n.5-7; Dec., 1971/Jan.-June/July, 1972 | Her. 1 UP, R16 |
| RBR | n.6; Feb./Mar., 1972 | Circulation |

1156 Ventura N.O.W. Chapter. 1973-1974//? Irregular. Last issue 4 pages. Line drawings. Available on microfilm: Herstory. Published by Ventura Chapter, National Organization for Women, Ventura, CA. Subject focus: feminism, Equal Rights Amendment, lobbying, rights.

| Hist | Feb.-June, 1973 | Microforms Her. 2, R 12 |
| | July, 1974 | Her. 2 UP, R8 |

1157 La Vie Heureuse. 1902-1914//? Monthly. Last issue 24 pages, last volume 402 pages. Line drawings, photographs. Available on microfilm: ACRPP. Published in Paris, France. Subject focus: recreation, fiction, arts, fashion, music. In French (100%).

| Mem | Oct., 1902-July, 1914 | Microforms |

1158 Vigilance. 1886-1914//? Monthly. Last issue 32 pages, last volume 432 pages. OCLC 1717016. Available on microfilm: ResP. Published by the American Vigilance Association, New York, NY. Title varies: as The Philanthropist, Jan., 1886-Oct., 1909. Subject focus: anti-vice groups. Other holding institutions: NN (NYP), OC1W (CWR), [AMIGOS Union List of Serials, Dallas, TX] (IWU).

| Mem | v.1, n.1-v.27, n.1; Jan., 1886-Jan., 1914 | Microforms |

1159 The Vocal Majority. 1968-1974//? Irregular. ISSN 0148-4230. OCLC 2269273. LC 77-643140. Last issue 20 pages. Line drawings, photographs. Available on microfilm: Herstory. Published by Washington, DC Chapter National Organization for Women, Washington, DC. Title varies: as The Activist, Feb., 1968. Editors: Alice Frandsen, Dec., 1970-?; Nancy Trenchard, ?-Sep., 1973; Violet Malinski, Jan.-Apr., 1974. Subject focus: media, law, education, child care, children's literature, professionals, art, employment, pro-abortion, sexism, lobbying, politics, health. Other holding institution: DLC (DLC), [University of Minnesota Union List, Minneapolis, MN] (MUL).

| | | |
|---|---|---|
| Hist | Feb., 1968, May/June, 1970 | Microforms Her. Add. |
| | v.1,n.1-v.2,n.9 Dec., 1970- Sep., 1971 | Her. 1, R 20 |
| | v.2, n.10- v.4, n.6; Oct., 1971- June, 1973 | Her. 1 UP, R12 |
| | v.4,n.7-v.5,n.6; July, 1973- May, 1974 | Her. CUP, R 5-6 |

1160 <u>Vocational Center for Women</u>. 1971-1973//? Last issue 3 pages. Line drawings, photographs. Available on microfilm: Herstory, (1973). Published by Nassau County Department of General Services, Carle Place, NY. Subject focus: education, vocational guidance, Equal Rights Amendment.

| | | |
|---|---|---|
| Hist | v.3, n.1; May 22, 1973 | Microforms Her. 2, R16 |

1161 <u>Vogue</u>. 1892. Monthly. $15 for individuals and institutions. Grace Mirabella, editor, Vogue, 350 Madison Avenue, New York, NY 10017. Business address: Box 5201, Boulder, CO. ISSN 0042-8000. OCLC 1769261, 5429855, 5248372, 6046266. LC 08-36997. Last issue 408 pages, size 21 x 28. Line drawings, photographs, some in color, commercial advertising. Available on microfilm: UnM, McP (1960-), KtO (1892-1906). Frequency varies: weekly, Dec., 1892-Feb., 1910; semi-monthly, Feb., 1910-Dec., 1942; 20 times a year, Jan., 1946-Dec., 1972. Previous editors: Edna Woolman Chase, Jan. 1, 1936-Dec., 1951; Jessica Davis, Jan., 1952-Dec., 1962; Diana Vreeland, Jan., 1963-June, 1971. Subject focus: fashion, beauty care, health, travel, art, film reviews, interviews. Other holding institutions: AU (ALM), ArAO (AK), ArL (AKD), ArU (AU), AzFU (AZN), AzTeS (AZS), AzU (AZU), CSt (Stanford University), CLU (CLU), CtS (FEM), CtW (WLU), CtY (YUS), DLC (DLC), DeU (DLM), FJUNF (FNP), FMFIU (FXG), FPeU (FWA), IPB (IBA), [Indiana Union List of Serials, Indianapolis, IN] (ILS), InU (IUL), KLindB (KFB), KSteC (KKQ), MBE (ECL), MBU (BOS), MWP (WPG), MWelC (WEL), MiAdC (EEA), MiEM (EEM), MiMtpT (EZC), [University of Minnesota Union List, Minneapolis, MN] (MUL), MnStjos (MNF), [New York State Union List, Albant, NY] (NYS), [Western New York Library Resources Council, Buffalo, NY] (VZX), NCH (YHM), NCorniCC (ZDG), NFQC (XQM), NGenoU (YGM), NIC (COO), NOneoU (ZBM), NPV (VXW), NR (YQR), NSbSU (YSM), NSyU (SYB), [Central New York Library Resources Council, Syracuse, NY] (SRR), NcDurC (NCX), NcEUce (NPE), NcGU (NGU), NcRS (NRC), NcU (NOC), NdU (UND), NbKS (KRS), NbU (LDL), NmLcU (IRU), NmLvH (NMH), NmU (IQU), O (OHI), OAkU (AKR), OC1 (CLE), OC1W (CWR), OKentU (KSU), OTU (TOL), OY (YMM), OYU (YNG), OkT (TUL), PCoR (ROB), PIm (IMM), PNwC (WFN), PPD (DXU), PPi (CPL), PPiAC (AIC), PPiC (PMC), PPiU (PIT), [Pittsburgh Regional Library Resources Council Union List, Pittsburgh, PA] (QPR), ScRhW (SWW), ScU (SUC), TMurS (TXM), TxAbH (TXS), TxBeIM (MHB), TxCM (TXA), TxDN (INT), TxDW (IWU), [AMIGOS Union List of Serials, Dallas, TX] (IUC), TxLT (ILU), TxU (IXA), ViBlbV (VPI), [Emory & Henry College, Emory, VA] (VEH), ViRCU (VRC), VtMiM (MDY), WM (GZD).

| | | |
|---|---|---|
| Agric | [v.1,n.1-v.86, n.24]; [Dec. 17, 1892- Dec. 15, 1935] | Microforms |
| | [v.87, n.1-v.115, n.4]; [Jan., 1936- Mar. 1, 1950] | Periodicals Section |
| MPL | v.118, n.7- July, 1953- | Literature and Social Science Section |
| MATC | v.135, n.1- Jan., 1970- | Cora Hardy Library |
| LAHS | Current Issues Only | Circulation |
| MMHS | v.136, n.4- Apr., 1971- | Circulation |
| TML | Current Issues Only | Circulation |
| SPHS | v.136, n.1- Jan., 1971- | Circulation |
| WHS | v.138, n.1- Jan., 1973- | Circulation |
| SPPL | v.136, n.1- Jan., 1971- | Circulation |
| UWBA | v.133, n.1- Jan., 1968- | Circulation |
| SCPL | v.135, n.3- Mar., 1970- | Circulation |
| MCHS | v.133, n.1- Jan., 1968- | Circulation |
| MIPL | v.138, n.1- Jan., 1973- | Circulation |
| RPL | [v.137, n.1-] [Jan., 1972-] | Circulation |
| CFL | v.140, n.1- Jan., 1975- | Circulation |

| | | | | | |
|---|---|---|---|---|---|
| DFHS | v.139, n.7-<br>July, 1974- | Circulation | | v.9, n.1-v.10,<br>n.2;<br>Mar., 1972-<br>Apr., 1973 | Her. 1 UP, R16 |
| VPL | v.139, n.1-<br>Jan., 1974- | Circulation | | v.10, n.3-v.11,<br>n.2;<br>July, 1973-<br>Apr., 1974 | Her. CUP, R 7 |

1162  The Voice of the American Agri-Woman. 1975. Irregular. $5 for individuals and institutions. Sharon Steffens, editor, The Voice of the American Agri-Woman, Route 1, Dubois, IL 62831. Last issue 4 pages, size 29 x 43. Line drawings, photographs. Subject focus: agriculture, farmers, ranchers, rights.

| | | |
|---|---|---|
| Wom Ed<br>Res | v.3, n.2-<br>Mar./Apr., 1977- | Circulation |

A Voice N.O.W.  Seattle, WA

    see N.O.W.sletter.  Seattle, WA

1163  Voice of the Women's Liberation Movement. 1968-1969//. Irregular. OCLC 2269286. Last issue 24 pages. Line drawings, photographs. Available on microfilm: Herstory. Published by Chicago Women's Liberation Movement, Chicago, IL. Subject focus: rights, politics, pro-abortion, film reviews, peace movement.

| | | |
|---|---|---|
| Hist | v.1, n.1-7;<br>Mar., 1968-<br>Mar?, 1969 | Microforms<br>Her. 1, R 22 |
| | v.1, n.1, 5-7;<br>Mar., 1968,<br>Jan.-Mar?, 1969 | Pam 69-966 |

1164  Voice of Women. 1970//? Unknown. OCLC 2269287. Last issue 2 pages. Line drawings. Available on microfilm: Herstory. Published by Voice of Women of New England, Newtonville, MA. Subject focus: peace movement.

| | | |
|---|---|---|
| Hist | July 13, 1970 | Microforms<br>Her. 1, R 22 |

1165  Voice of Women-La Voix Des Femmes. 1960?-1974//? Quarterly. ISSN 0382-0866, 0382-0874. OCLC 2218092, 2218043. LC cn76-300320, cn76-300318. Last issue 8 pages. Line drawings, photographs. Available on microfilm: Herstory. Published in New York, NY. Subject focus: nuclear weapons, international relations, research, children, peace movement, minorities, pro-abortion, ecology, politics, education. In French (10-20%). Other holding institutions: CaOONL (NLC), [University of Minnesota Union List, Minneapolis, MN] (MUL), NSbSU (YSM).

| | | |
|---|---|---|
| Hist | [1960-June, 1971] | Microforms<br>Her. 1, R 22 |

La Voz de la Mujer.  Albuquerque, NM

    see NOW Newsletter.  Albuquerque, NM

W74 Win With Women.  Washington, DC

    see NWPC Newsletter.  Washington, DC

1166  WAM/Women's Action Movement Newsletter. 1969-1972//. Irregular. Last issue 3 pages, size 22 x 28. Published by Women's Action Movement, Madison, WI. Subject focus: politics, pro-abortion, poetry, birth control.

| | | |
|---|---|---|
| Hist | Nov., 1970, Feb. 8-20, Mar. 19, Oct.-Nov., 1971, Jan., May, Oct., 1972 | Pam 73-1606 |
| RBR | July, 1971-<br>Jan., 1972 | Circulation |
| MPL | July, 1971-<br>Jan., 1972 | Literature and Social Science Section |

1167  WAND (Women's Association News Digest). 1954-1979//. Quarterly. Last issue 20 pages, last volume 124 pages, size 22 x 14. Line drawings, photographs, some in color. Published by Women's Association, Church of God (Seventh-Day), Westminster, CO. Editors: Emogene Coulter, Spring/Summer, 1977; Donna Griffin, Fall, 1977-Fall, 1979. Subject focus: Christianity, motherhood, child rearing, poetry.

| | | |
|---|---|---|
| Hist | v.24, n.1-v.26, n.2;<br>Spring/Summer, 1977-Fall, 1979 | Circulation |

1168  WAVAW. 1977. Irregular. Gratis to individuals and institutions. WAVAW, 1727 North Spring Street, Los Angeles, CA 90012. (212) 223-8771. Last issue 8 pages, size 28 x 22. Line drawings, photographs. Available on microfilm: WHi. Published by Women Against Violence Against Women, Pacific Coast Media Center, Los Angeles, CA. Subject focus: pornography, battered women, rape prevention, media.

| | | |
|---|---|---|
| Hist | n.1–<br>May, 1977– | Circulation |

1169 **WCML-Midwest Newsletter.** 1973//? Irregular. Last issue 6 pages. Line drawings. Available on microfilm: Herstory. Published by Women's Caucus for Modern Languages-Midwest Modern Language Association, Whitewater, WI. Subject focus: education, media, linguistics.

| | | |
|---|---|---|
| Hist | Oct.–Dec. 10, 1973 | Microforms<br>Her. 3, R 5 |

**WCTU State Work.** Madison, WI

see **The Motor.** Baraboo, WI

1170 **W.E.A.L.-National Committee Reports Newsletter.** 1972//. Unknown. Last issue 4 pages. Available on microfilm: Herstory. Published by Women's Equity Action League, State College, PA. Subject focus: rights, lobbying.

| | | |
|---|---|---|
| Hist | Apr. 15, 1972 | Microforms<br>Her. 2, R19 |

1171 **WEAL National Newsletter.** 1973//? Monthly? Last issue 8 pages, size 18 x 22. Published by Women's Equity League, Washington, DC. Subject focus: rights, lobbying. Other holding institution: CSt (Stanford University).

| | | |
|---|---|---|
| Hist | n.1;<br>May, 1973 | Pam 76-4394 |

1172 **W.E.A.L. Texas Newsletter.** 1972-1974//? Monthly. Last issue 8 pages. Line drawings. Available on microfilm: Herstory. Published by Women's Equity Action League, Texas, Dallas, TX. Editor: Kay Bieberdorf, Dec., 1972-June, 1973. Subject focus: lobbying, rights, Equal Rights Amendment.

| | | |
|---|---|---|
| Hist | Mar., 1972–<br>June, 1973 | Microforms<br>Her. 2, R 19 |
| | July, 1973–<br>June, 1974 | Her. 2 UP, R13 |

1173 **WEAL Washington Report.** 1971. Bi-monthly. $10 for individuals and institutions. Pat Reuss and Sarah Jane Knoy, editors, WEAL Washington Report, 805 15th Street NW, No. 822, Washington, DC 20005. OCLC 2269387. Last issue 14 pages, last volume 26 pages, size 22 x 28. Line drawings. Available on microfilm: Herstory (1971-1974). Published by Women's Equity Action League. Frequency varies: irregular, 1971-Oct. 29, 1973. Previous editors: Ellen Sudow, Carol T. Foreman, and Margaret Fahs, Dec. 1, 1972; Ellen Sudow and Carol T. Foreman, Jan. 7, 1973-Nov., Dec., 1974; Leslie Gladstone, Sep., 1975-Dec., 1978. Subject focus: rights, lobbying.

| | | |
|---|---|---|
| Hist | n.1;<br>?, 1971 | Microforms<br>Her. 1, R 22 |
| | v.2, n.2-13;<br>Oct., 1971–<br>June, 1973 | Her. 1 UP, R 18 |
| | v.2, n.14-v.3,<br>n.4;<br>Sep. 26, 1973–<br>June 14, 1974 | Her. CUP, R8 |
| | n.1–<br>?, 1971– | Circulation |
| Coll | Current Issues<br>Only | Women's<br>Reading Area |
| Wom Ed<br>Res | v.4, n.3; v.5,<br>n.6-v.6, n.6;<br>June, 1975;<br>Dec., 1976–<br>Dec., 1977 | Circulation |

**W.E.A.L. – Women's Equity Action League.** Old Bridge, NJ

see **N.J. W.E.A.L.er.** Old Bridge, NJ

1174 **WEECN Network News & Notes.** 1977-1979//. Quarterly. Size 22 x 28. Published by Women's Education Equity Communications Network. Frequency varies: irregular, Dec., 1977-Sep., 1978. Editors: Rita M. Costick, Dec., 1977-Sep., 1978; Valerie Wheat, Winter, 1978-Summer, 1979; Rick Grasso, Fall, 1979. Subject focus: women's studies, higher education, sexism in education, lobbying.

| | | |
|---|---|---|
| Wom Ed<br>Res | Dec., 1977–<br>Fall, 1979 | Circulation |

1175 **WHOM Newsletter.** 1973. Bi-monthly. $3 for individuals and institutions. Sally Rubinstein and Deborah Stultz, editors, WHOM Newsletter, Minnesota Historical Society, 690 Cedar Street, St. Paul, MN 55101. Business address: Box 80021, Como Station, St. Paul, MN 55108. OCLC 2395120. Last issue 5 pages, last volume 40 pages, size 22 x 28. Available on microfilm: Herstory (1973-1974). Published by Women Historians of the Midwest. Previous editors: Dorothy Perry Kidder and Patricia C. Harpole, Jan. 25-July, 1973; Dorothy Perry Kidder, Oct., 1973-Feb., 1973; Rhoda Gilman, May, 1974-Nov., 1977; Sally Rubinstein, Jan.-Dec., 1978. Subject focus: women's studies, historians, employment, fellowships.

| | | | |
|---|---|---|---|
| Hist | v.1, n.1-2; Jan. 25-Mar., 1973 | Microforms Her. 2, R 17 | |
| | v.1, n.3-v.2, n.2; July, 1973-Mar., 1974 | Her. 2 UP, R12 | |
| | v.1, n.1- Jan. 25, 1973- | Circulation | |

1176 <u>W.I.A. Newsletter-Women in the Arts</u>. 1973-1974//? Monthly. OCLC 3718231. Last issue 4 pages. Line drawings. Available on microfilm: Herstory. Published by Women in the Arts, New York, NY. Subject focus: art. Other holding institutions: [University of Minnesota Union List, Minneapolis, MN] (MUL), [New York State Union List, Albany, NY] (NYS).

| Hist | v.1, n.1; June, 1973 | Microforms Her. 2, R 18 |
|---|---|---|
| | v.1, n.2-11; July, 1973-June, 1974 | Her. 2 UP, R12 |

1177 <u>WIC Status Report</u>. 1978. Monthly. Gratis to individuals and institutions. Diane Heintzelman, editor, WIC Status Report, Room 10, Statehouse, Columbus, OH 43215. (614) 466-5880, (800) 282-3040. OCLC 4402720. Last issue 2 pages, last volume 24 pages, size 36 x 22. Published by State of Ohio Women's Information Center, Legislative Reference Bureau. Subject focus: lobbying. Other holding institutions: OClCo (CXP), OKentU (KSU).

| Hist | v.1, n.1- Jan., 1978- | Circulation |
|---|---|---|

1178 <u>WICCE</u>. 1973//? Last issue 16 pages. Line drawings, photographs, commercial advertising. Available on microfilm: Herstory. Published by WICCE, Philadelphia, PA. Subject focus: lesbians, poetry.

| Hist | v.1, n.1; Fall, 1973 | Microforms Her. 3, R 4 |
|---|---|---|

1179 <u>W.I.D. Notes</u>. 1980. Monthly. Jane Knowles, editor, W.I.D. Notes, 310 King Hall, University of Wisconsin, Madison, WI 53706. (608) 262-3657. Published by MUCIA-Midwest University Consortium for International Activities, Inc. Place of publication varies with each issue: Minneapolis, MN; Champaign-Urbana, IL; East Lansing, MI; Bloomington, IN, 1980-Mar., 1981. Subject focus: cooperatives, agriculture.

| U.W. Co-op | Current Issues Only | Circulation |
|---|---|---|

1180 <u>WILPF Legislative Bulletin</u>. 1967. Irregular. $8 for individuals and institutions. Legislative Office, U.S. Section, Women's International League for Peace and Freedom, 120 Maryland Avenue NE, Washington, DC 20002. (202) 546-8644. Last issue 8 pages, size 22 x 28. Line drawings, some in color. Available on microfilm: WHi. Title varies: as Action Memo, Apr. 10, Sep. 25, 1967; Action Bulletin, Aug. 24, 1967, Jan. 26, 1968-Aug. 1, 1969; Legislative Bulletin, Oct. 20, 1969-Dec. 22, 1971. Subject focus: lobbying, politics.

| Hist | v.1, n.1?- Apr. 10, 1967- | Microforms |
|---|---|---|

1181 <u>WIN News</u>. 1975. Quarterly. Fran P. Hosken, editor, WIN News, Lexington, MA. ISSN 0145-7985. OCLC 2694733. LC 77-641756. Last issue 90 pages, last volume 328 pages, size 18 x 29. Line drawings. Indexed in Women Studies Abstracts. Subject focus: health, violence, history, science, media. Other holding institutions: CoDU (DVP), DLC (DLC), [Congressional Research Service, Washington, DC] (CRS), FU (FUG), GU (GUA), InU (IUL), MBTI (BTI), MH-AH (BHA), MWalB (MBB), MiEM (EEM), [University of Minnesota Union List, Minneapolis, MN] (MUL), MnU (MNU), NA1U (NAM), NBronSL (VVS), NCH (YHM), NPV (VXW), NcCU (NKM), OU (OSU), PBm (BMC), ViBlbv (VPI), CSt (Stanford University).

| Mem | v.1, n1- Jan., 1975- | AP/W8725/I 516 |
|---|---|---|
| Wom St | v.3, n.1-4; Winter-Fall, 1977 | Reading Room |

1182 <u>W.I.N.-Women's International Network</u>. 1973//? Last issue 12 pages. Line drawings. Available on microfilm: Herstory. Published by Women's International Network, Lexington, MA. Editor; Fran P. Hosken. Subject focus: communications, media.

| Hist | n.1; Summer, 1973 | Microforms Her. 2, R19 |
|---|---|---|

1183 <u>W.I.S. Club Newsletter</u>. 1975-1977//. Irregular. Last issue 6 pages, size 22 x 28. Photographs. Published by Women Intercollegiate Sports Club, Madison, WI. Subject focus: sports, clubs.

| Wom Ed Res | v.2, n.1-2; Oct., 1976-Jan., 1977 | Circulation |
|---|---|---|

1184 <u>WISE</u>. 1971//? Unknown. OCLC 2269573. Last issue 9 pages. Line drawings. Available on microfilm: Herstory. Published by Women for the Inclusion of Sexual Expression, New York, NY. Subject focus: sexuality, pro-abortion,

*Women's Periodicals and Newspapers*

FOCAS: Feminists Organization for Commission, Action, and Service, birth control.

| Hist | Summer, 1971 | Microforms Her. 1, R 22 |

1185 <u>WM-Jacksonville Women's Movement</u>. 1970-1974//? Monthly. Last issue 4 pages. Line drawings. Available on microfilm: Herstory. Published by Jacksonville Chapter, National Organization for Women, Jacksonville, FL. Title varies: as Call to Action, Jan., 1971-Nov., 1972. Subject focus: feminism, Equal Rights Amendment, lobbying, rights, politics.

| Hist | v.1,n.2-v.2,n.7; Jan., 1971- June 9, 1973 | Microforms Her. 2, R 10 |
| | v.2,n.8-v.3,n.6; July, 1973- June, 1974 | Her. 2 UP, R 6-7 |

1186 <u>WOAR Newsletter</u>. 1973-1976//? Irregular. Last issue 11 pages, size 22 x 28. Line drawings. Available on microfilm: Herstory. (1973-1974). Published by Women Organized Against Rape, Philadelphia, PA. Subject focus: rape prevention, lobbying, self-defense, counseling.

| Hist | v.1, n.1-3; ?, 1973- Apr., 1974 | Microforms Her. 3, R 5 |
| Crim Just | Nov., 1975- Aug., 1976 | Circulation |

1187 <u>WOARpath</u>. 1977. Semi-annual. Lynne Moncrief, editor, WOARpath, 1220 Sansom Street, Philadelphia, PA 19107. Published by Women Organized Against Rape. Last issue 19 pages, size 22 x 28. Line drawings, photographs. Subject focus: rape prevention, education, self-defense, counseling, lobbying.

| Crim Just | Summer, 1978- | Circulation |

1188 <u>WONAAC</u>. 1971-1973//. Irregular. OCLC 2269648. Last issue 4 pages. Line drawings, photographs. Available on microfilm: WHi, Herstory. Published by Women's National Abortion Action Coalition, New York, NY. Title varies: as Women's National Abortion Coalition, June 4-July 7, 1971; as WONAAC Newsletter, Sep. 16, 1971-Dec., 1972. Place of publication varies: Washington, DC, Sep. 16-Oct. 21, 1971. Subject focus: pro-abortion, rights, lobbying.

| Hist | June 4- Sep. 16, 1971 | Microforms Her. 1, R 23 |
| | Oct., 1971- Summer, 1973 | Her. 1 UP, R18 |
| | Sep. 16, 1971- Summer, 1973 | Microforms |

<u>WONAAC Newsletter</u>. Washington, DC; New York, NY

see <u>WONAAC</u>. New York, NY

<u>WSP--New York Newsletter</u>. New York, NY

see <u>N.Y. WSP Newsletter</u>. New York, NY

<u>WSP Newsletter</u>. New York, NY

see <u>N.Y. WSP Peaceletter</u>. New York, NY

1189 <u>WSP at the United Nations</u>. 1963//? Unknown. OCLC 2269610. Last issue 6 pages. Line drawings. Available on microfilm: Herstory. Published by Women Strike for Peace at the United Nations, New York, NY. Subject focus: peace movement, United Nations, international relations.

| Hist | June, Oct., 1963 | Microforms Her. 1, R 23 |

<u>WTA Newsletter</u>. Madison, WI

see <u>Women's Transit Home Companion</u>. Madison, WI

1190 <u>WWD</u>. 1910. Daily. $50 for individuals. WWD, 7 East 12th Street, New York, NY 10003. (212) 741-4000. ISSN 0149-5380. OCLC 3504983, 5584178, 1781845, 1639543. LC 77-641341. Last issue 48 pages, size 28 x 38. Line drawings, photographs, commercial advertising. Available on microfilm: KtO (1910-1941), Fairchild Publications (1911-). Published by Fairchild Publications, New York, NY 10003. Subject focus: fashion, garment industry. Other holding institutions: AU (ALM), ArU (AFU), AzTeS (AZS), AzU (AZU), [California State University, Dominguez Hills, Carson, CA] (CDH), CChiS (CCH), [Pepperdine University, Malibu, CA] (CPE), CSUuP (CPS), WeharU (HRM), COU-DA (COA), DeU (DLM), [Congressional Research Service, Washington, DC] (CRS), DFT (FTC), DHU (DHU), DLC (DLC), FBoU (FGM), FJUNF (FNP), GASU (GSU), GEU (EMU), IaCfT (NIU), IaDmD (IOD), ICI (IAH), INS (IAI), IU (UIU), [Indiana Union List of Serials, Indianapolis, IN] (ILS), InIU (IUP), InU-M (IUM), InU (IUL), KPT (KFP), KyRE (KEU), LNX (LNX), LU-L (LUL), LU (LUU), MBNU (NED), MBU (BOS), MBSi (SCL), MChB (BXM), MH (HUL), MMeT (TFW), MWMU (WQM), [Frostburg State College Library, Frostburg, MD] (MFS), MiAdC (EEA), MiDW

(EYW), MiEM (EEM), MiGrC (EXC), MiLC (EEL), MiMtpT (EZC), [University of Minnesota Union List, Minneapolis, MN] (MUL), MNQ (MNQ), MnStjos (MNF), MnSU (MNP), MsU (MUM), [New York State Union List, Albany, NY] (NYS), NBu (VHB), [Western New York Library Resources Council, Buffalo, NY] (VZX), NCorniCC (ZDG), NCortU (YCM), NEE (VXE), NFQC (XQM), NGcCC (VVX), NIC (COO), N (NYG), NNR (ZXC), NNepaSU (ZLM), NOneoU (ZBM), NPurU (ZPM), NR (YQR), NSbSU-H (VZB), NSchU (ZWU), NSufR (VVR), NSyU (SYB), [Central New York Library Resources Council, Syracuse, NY] (SRR), NcRS (NRC), NbOB (BTC), NbU (LDL), NjLincB (BCC), NjNCM (NJN), OAkU (AKR), OAU (OUN), OBgU (BGU), [Raymond Walters General and Technical College Library, Blue Ash, OH] (ORW), OC1W-H (CHS), OC1U (CSU), [State Library of Ohio Catalog Center, Columbus, OH] (SLC), ODaWU-H (WMN), OKentU (KSU), O (OHI), OTMC (MCL), OU (OSU), OYU (YNG), OrSaW (OWS), OrU-M (OHS), PBm (BMC), PCoR (ROB), PIm (IMM), PManM (MAN), PPD (DXU), PPiU (PIT), PPiU-L (PLA), [Pittsburgh Regional Library Center-Union List, Pittsburgh, PA] (QPR), PSt (UPM), ScCleU (SEA), ScRhW (SWW), TCU (TUC), TMurS (TXM), TNJ (TJC), TxBelM (MHB), [School of Aerospace Medicine, Brooks AFB, TX] (TBM), TxAu (TXG), TxCM (TXA), TxDN (INT), [AMIGOS Union List of Serials, Dallas, TX] (IUC), TxNacS (TXK), [AMIGOS Bibliographic Council, Richardson, TX] (IIC), TxShA (IAU), TxSmS (TXI), ViBlbv (VPI), ViNO (VOD), ViRCU (VRC), WaU (WAU), WGrU (GZW), [Arrowhead Library System, Janesville Public Library, Janesville, WI] (WIJ), WMenU (GZS), WMUW (GZN).

| Agric | Current Issues Only | Periodicals Section |
| --- | --- | --- |
| MATC | Current Issues Only | Cora Hardy Library |
| MPL | Jan., 1970- | Literature and Social Science Section |

War Work Bulletin. New York, NY

   see Blue Triangle News. New York, NY

Washington Area Women's Center Bulletin. Washington, DC

   see Raising Cain. Washington, DC

1191 The Washington County Woman. 1974//? Irregular. Last issue 10 pages. Line drawings. Available on microfilm: Herstory. Published by Washington County Chapter National Organization for Women, Hagerstown, MD. Subject focus: feminism, Equal Rights Amendment, lobbying, rights, education, marriage, politics, employment, sports.

| Hist | Mar.-May/June, 1974 | Microforms Her. 3, R 3 |
| --- | --- | --- |

1192 The Washington Equal Times. 1978. $15 for institutions. The Washington Equal Times, P.O. Box 2389, Washington, DC 20013. Last issue 22 pages, size 28 x 22. Line drawings, photographs, commercial advertising. Available on microfilm: WHi (1979-). Published by National Organization for Women, Washington Metro Area Chapters, Washington, DC 20013. Subject focus: feminism, Equal Rights Amendment, lobbying, rights, affirmative action.

| Hist | v.2,n.4,v.3,n.2- Apr., 1979, Feb., 1980- | Circulation |
| --- | --- | --- |

1193 Washington Newsletter. 1949-1971//. Irregular. OCLC 2269353. Last issue 8 pages. Line drawings. Available on microfilm: WHi (1949-1970), Herstory (1967-1971). Published by the Women's International League for Peace and Freedom, Washnington, DC. Subject focus: legislation, lobbying, rights, international relations, peace movement.

| Hist | [Oct. 1, 1967-Feb. 2, 1971] | Microforms Her. 1, R 22 |
| --- | --- | --- |
| | Feb. 23, 1949-Jan., 1970 | Microforms |

1194 Washington Newsletter. 1950-1961//? Monthly. Last issue 8 pages, last volume 42 pages, size 22 x 28. Line drawings, photographs. Published by the National Federation of Republican Women, Washington, DC. Subject focus: Republican Party, politics, political parties.

| Hist | v.8, n.6-v.12, n.1; Oct., 1957-Jan., 1961 | JU83R/N265/W (Cutter) |
| --- | --- | --- |

1195 Washington Newsletter for Women. 1970//? Irregular. ISSN 0043-7506. OCLC 2269354. LC sc77-860. Last issue 4 pages, size 22 x 28. Line drawings. Available on microfilm: Herstory. Published by Barrer and Associates, Washington, DC. Editors: Lois E. Buge, May-June, 1970; Angela M. Schruber, July-Dec., 1970. Subject focus: rights, politics, pro-abortion, Equal Rights Amendment, lobbying. Other holding institutions: GU (GUA), MnStpeG (MNG), [University of Minnesota Union List, Minneapolis, MN] (MUL).

| Hist | v.1, n.3; July, 1970 | Microforms Her. Add. |
| --- | --- | --- |
| | v.1, n.4-5; Aug.1-11, 1970 | Her. 1, R 22 |

|  |  |  |
|---|---|---|
|  | v.1, n.2-21;<br>May-Dec. 31, 1970 | Pam 72-1691 |
| Wom Ed<br>Res | v.1, n.1-5;<br>Mar.-Aug., 1970 | Circulation |

1196 Washington State Women's Political Caucus. 1973//? Last issue 8 pages. Line drawings. Available on microfilm: Herstory. Published in Tacoma, WA. Editor: Marjorie Wilkerson. Subject focus: politics, lobbying.

|  |  |  |
|---|---|---|
| Hist | v.1,n.1?-v.2, n.1;<br>July-?Nov., 1973? | Microforms<br>Her. 3, R 4 |

1197 Washington Women's Representative. 1976. Bi-weekly. $25 for individuals, $37 for institutions. Nina Hegstedt, editor, Washington Women's Representative, 854 National Press Building, Washington, DC 20045. ISSN 0164-890X. OCLC 4051367. LC sn79-4665. Last issue 8 pages, last volume 168 pages, size 22 x 28. Line drawings. Title varies: as Women's Washington Representative, Sep. 24, 1976-Aug. 12, 1978; Women's Washington Report, Sep. 12, 1977-Jan. 12, 1978. Frequency varies: monthly, Sep. 24, 1976-Jan. 12, 1978. Previous editor: Susan Tenenbaum, Sep. 24, 1976-Jan. 12, 1978. Subject focus: health, employment, credit, law. Other holding institutions: CSdS (CDS), DI (UDI), [Bureau of the Census, Washington, DC] (CBU), [Congressional Research Service, Washington, DC] (CRS), LNT (LRU), NcRS (NRC), NmU-L (NML), MA1U (NAM), NSbSU (YSM), TxU (TXQ).

|  |  |  |
|---|---|---|
| Law | v.1, n.10-<br>Sep. 24, 1976- | Circulation |

1198 Waukesha FreeWoman. 1975-1977//. Monthly. OCLC 5574369. Last issue 12 pages. Line drawings. Available on microfilm: WHi. Published by Waukesha Chapter, National Organization for Women, Waukesha, WI. Editors: Chris Roerden, Apr. 4, 1975-Sep., 1976; Amy Mountcastle, Oct., 1976; Gerry Pas, Aug., 1977. Subject focus: feminism, Equal Rights Amendment, lobbying, rights.

|  |  |  |
|---|---|---|
| Hist | n.1-27;<br>Apr. 4, 1975-<br>Aug., 1977 | Microforms |
| Wom Ed<br>Res | n.5-27;<br>Sep. 5, 1975-<br>Aug., 1977 | Circulation |

1199 The Way We See It. 1970//? Unknown. OCLC 2269384. Last issue 18 pages. Line drawings, photographs. Available on microfilm: Herstory. Published by Springfield Women's Liberation, Springfield, MA. Subject focus: poetry, education, welfare, married women.

|  |  |  |
|---|---|---|
| Hist | n.1;<br>Aug. 26, 1970 | Microforms<br>Her. 1, R 11 |

1200 Weekly Magazine and Ladies' Miscellany. 1816-1824//? Weekly. OCLC 1536887, 1536888, 3392144, 1639710. LC 37-13767, mic56-4513. Last issue 4 pages, last volume 159 pages. Line drawings. Self-indexed (1816-1818). Available on microfilm: UnM (1816-1819, 1824). Published in Boston, MA. Title varies: as Boston Weekly Magazine, Oct. 12, 1816-May 8, 1819. Subject focus: fiction, poetry. AzTeS (AZD), DeU (DLM), InLP (IPL), [University of Minnesota Union List, Minneapolis, MN] (MUL), NCortU (YCM), NGcA (VJA), NOneoU (ZBM), NcWsW (EWF), OC1W (CWR), OKentU (KSU), OYU (YNG), PPiPP (PTP), PPiU (PIT), [Pittsburgh Regional Library Center-Union List, Pittsburgh, PA] (QPR), TMurS (TXM), [AMIGOS Union List of Serials, Dallas, TX] (IUC), WMUW (GZN).

|  |  |  |
|---|---|---|
| Hist | v.1, n.1-v.3, n.26, [n.s.]<br>v.1, n.1-40;<br>Oct. 12, 1816-<br>May 8, 1819,<br>Mar. 20-<br>Dec. 18, 1824 | Microforms |

The Weekly Museum. New York, NY

    see The New York Weekly Museum, or Polite Repository of Amusement and Instruction. New York, NY

The Weekly Visitor or Ladies' Miscellany. New York, NY

    see The Lady's Miscellany; or the Weekly Visitor. New York, NY

1201 West Coast Association of Women Historians Newsletter. 1970-1974//? Irregular. Last issue 12 pages. Line drawings. Available on microfilm: Herstory. Published by West Coast Association of Women Historians, Sacramento, CA. Editors: S. Joan Moon and Gretchen Schwenn, Dec., 1973-May, 1974. Subject focus: education, history, historians.

|  |  |  |
|---|---|---|
| Hist | v.1, n.1-v.4,n.1;<br>Oct., 1970-<br>May, 1973 | Microforms<br>Her. 2, R 16 |
|  | v.4, n.2-v.5, n.1;<br>Dec., 1973-<br>May, 1974 | Her. 2 UP, R12 |

1202 West-East Bag (W.E.B.). 1972-1973//? Unknown. OCLC 2269458. Last issue 8 pages. Line drawings. Available on microfilm: Herstory. Published by International Liaison Network of

Women Artists, Los Angeles, CA/New York, NY. Subject focus: art, artists, education.

| Hist | ?, 1972 | Microforms Her. 1, R 22 |
|---|---|---|
|  | June, 1972 | Her. 1 UP, R16 |
|  | Sep., 1973 | Her. CUP, R 7 |

1203 Western Canadian Women's News Service. 1974-1976//? Monthly? OCLC 5576345. Last issue 24 pages. Line drawings. Available on microfilm: Herstory (1974), WHi. Published by Western Canadian Women's News Service, Vancouver, British Columbia, Canada. Subject focus: rights, politics, lobbying.

| Hist | June 10, 1974 | Microforms Her. 3, R 4 |
|---|---|---|
|  | [June 10, 1974-Mar., 1976] | Microforms |

Western Connecticut NOW Newsletter. Stratford, CT

see How's NOW. Bridgeport, CT

1204 The Western Ladies Casket. 1824//? Weekly? OCLC 1643173. Last issue 18 pages. Line drawings. Available on microfilm: UnM. Published in Connersville, IN. Subject focus: science, fiction. Other holding institutions: FGULS (FUL), [University of Minnesota Union List, Minneapolis, MN] (MUL), NcWsW (EWF), OKentU (KSU), PPiU (PIT), [AMIGOS Union List of Serials, Dallas, TX] (IUC).

| Hist | v.1, n.5; Feb. 1, 1824 | Microforms |
|---|---|---|

1205 Western Region N.O.W. 1973//? Irregular. Last issue 6 pages. Line drawings. Available on microfilm: Herstory. Published by Western Region Chapter, National Organization for Women, Seattle, WA. Subject focus: feminism, Equal Rights Amendment, lobbying, rights, politics.

| Hist | Jan., Apr., 1973; | Microforms Her. 2, R 12 |
|---|---|---|

1206 We've Only Just Begun. 1974//? Monthly. Last issue 4 pages. Line drawings. Available on microfilm: Herstory. Published by Schoolcraft/Livonia Chapter, National Organization for Women, Farmington, MI. Subject focus: feminism, Equal Rights Amendment, lobbying, rights, education.

| Hist | v.1, n.2-3; Jan.-Feb., 1974 | Microforms Her. 3, R 3 |
|---|---|---|

1207 What NOW. 1970. Monthly. $5 for individuals and institutions. Anne Covert, editor, What NOW, P.O. Box 174, Milwaukee, WI 53201. OCLC 2269507. Last issue 12 pages, last volume 114 pages, size 18 x 22. Line drawings, commercial advertising. Available on microfilm: Herstory (1971-1974). Published by the National Organization for Women, Milwaukee Chapter. Previous editors: Ellen Giuseppi, Sep., 1972-Se., 1973; Susan Luecke, Oct., 1973-Mar., 1975; D'Ann Prior, Apr., 1975-July, 1976. Subject focus: feminism, Equal Rights Amendment, lobbying, rights, pro-abortion, politics. Other holding institutions: [University of Minnesota Union List, Minneapolis, MN] (MUL), WM (GZD).

| Hist | v.1, n.1-11; Nov., 1970-Sep., 1971 | Microforms Her. 1, R 18 |
|---|---|---|
|  | v.2, n.2-v.3, n.8; Dec., 1971-June, 1973 | Her. 1 UP, R 9-10 |
|  | v.2, n.9-v.4, n.8; July, 1973-June, 1974 | Her. CUP, R 4 |
|  | v.2, n.1-Sep., 1972 | Circulation |
| Wom Ed Res | v.8, n.1-Jan., 1978- | Circulation |

1208 What She Wants. 1973. Monthly. $6 for individuals, $10 for institutions. What She Wants, P.O. Box 18465, Cleveland Heights, OH 44118. OCLC 4008089. Last issue 16 pages, last volume 192 pages, size 37 x 29. Line drawings, photographs, commercial advertising. Available on microfilm: Herstory (1973-1974). Subject focus: workers, rights, labor unions, health, pro-abortion, poetry. Other holding institutions: OKentU (KSU), OU (OSU).

| Hist | v.1, n.1-2; May-June, 1973 | Microforms Her. 2, R 16 |
|---|---|---|
|  | v.1, n.3-v.2, n.2; July, 1973-June, 1974 | Her. 2 UP, R12 |
|  | [v.1, n.1-v.5, n.6], n.8-[May, 1973-Jan.,] Mar., 1978- | Circulation |

1209 Which Way/Witch Way. 1979. Monthly. $12 for individuals ($15.60 in Canada), $19.50 for institutions. Janice Scot Reeder, editor, Which Way/Witch Way, Rt. 1, Box 601C, Pompano Beach, FL 33067. (305) 421-4636, 428-9713. Last issue 20 pages, last volume 182 pages, size 28 x 22. Line drawings, commercial advertising. Published by Craeftgemont Witancoveyne, Inc., Pompano Beach, FL. Subject focus: witches, neo-paganism.

| Hist | v.1, n.1-12; Sep., 1979-Aug., 1980 | Circulation |

1210 Whirlwind. 1974//? Bi-monthly. Last issue 20 pages. Line drawings. Available on microfilm: Herstory. Published by Whirlwind, Chicago, IL. Subject focus: poetry, fiction, art.

| Hist | v.1, n.1; ?, 1974 | Microforms Her. 3, R 4 |

1211 White House News on Women. 1979. Irregular. Sarah Weddington, editor, White House News on Women, The White House, Washington, DC 20500. Last issue 8 pages, size 22 x 28. Line drawings, photographs. Published by the Interdepartmental Task Force on Women. Subject focus: politics, social legislation.

| Wom Ed Res | v.2, n.2- July?, 1979- | Circulation |

1212 Whole Woman. 1972-1974//. Irregular. OCLC 5588840. Last issue 8 pages. Line drawings, photographs, commercial advertising. Available on microfilm: Herstory, WHi. Published in Madison, WI. Subject focus: rights, politics, women's studies, students, art, lesbians, poetry, film reviews.

| Hist | v.1, n.1-6; Oct. 23, 1972-June, 1973 | Microforms Her. 2, R 16 |
| | v.1, n.8-v.2, n.3; Sep. 24, 1973-May, 1974 | Her. 2 UP, R12 |
| | v.1, n.1-v.2, n.4; Oct. 23, 1972-Oct., 1974 | Microforms |
| MPL | v.1, n.1-v.2, n.1; Oct. 23, 1972-Mar., 1974 | Literature and Social Science Section |

1213 The Whole Woman Catalog. 1971//? Unknown. Last issue 48 pages. Line drawings. Available on microfilm: Herstory. Published by The Whole Woman Catalog, Portsmouth, NH. Subject focus: self-help, rights.

| Hist | v.1; Fall, 1971 | Microforms Her. 2, R 16 |

1214 Why Not N.O.W. 1974//? Irregular. Last issue 8 pages. Line drawings. Available on microfilm: Herstory. Published by Tri-Cities Chapter, National Organization for Women, Richland, WA. Subject focus: feminism, Equal Rights Amendment, lobbying, rights, politics, consciousness raising.

| Hist | v.1, n.2,5?; Feb., May, June, 1974 | Microforms Her. 3, R 3 |

1215 Wifeline. 1974. Quarterly. Jeanne A. Dumene, editor, Wifeline, Department of the Navy, Print Media Division, Hoffman Number 2, 200 Stovell Street, Alexandria, VA 22332. OCLC 4507937. Last issue 16 pages, size 20 x 26. Line drawings, photographs. Title varies: as Navy Wifeline, Winter, 1974-Spring, 1975. Place of publication varies: Washington, DC, Winter, 1974-Spring, 1978. Previous editors: Mrs. Michael J. Brennan, Winter, 1974-Spring, 1975; Ginny Siegfried, Summer-Fall, 1978. Subject focus: Navy wives, military families, child care. Other holding institutions: IU (UIU), OKentU (KSU), Ok (OKD), P (PHA), TxLT (ILU), [U.S. Government Printing Office - Serials, Alexandria, VA] (GPA).

| Hist | Winter, 1974, Spring, 1975, Summer, 1978- | D△201/25: |

1216 Wildcat Woman. 1973//? Last issue 4 pages. Line drawings, photographs. Available on microfilm: Herstory. Published by Wildcat Woman, Baltimore, MD. Subject focus: labor unions, workers, Diplomat Tie Company.

| Hist | ?, 1973 | Microforms Her. 3, R 4 |

1217 Wildflowers. 1970-1971//? Irregular. OCLC 2269547. Last issue 24 pages. Line drawings, photographs. Available on microfilm: Herstory. Published in Isla Vista, CA. Subject focus: poetry, music, child care, self-defense, revolution.

| Hist | v.1, n.1-3; Nov., 1970-Spring, 1971 | Microforms Her. 1, R 4 |

Winning Spirit. Washington, DC

see Challenge. Washington, DC

Wisconsin Auxiliary Newsletter. Green Bay, WI

see Wisconsin Hospital Association Auxiliaries. Milwaukee, WI

1218 The Wisconsin Business Woman. 1927. Quarterly. $.75 for individuals and institutions. Sharon Thatcher, editor, The Wisconsin Business

Woman, 407 1/2 Scott Street, Merrill, WI 54492. ISSN 0508-9921. OCLC 5389974. LC sn79-7588. Last issue 8 pages, last volume 48 pages, size 22 x 28. Line drawings, photographs. Available on microfilm: WHi (1927-1958). Published by the Wisconsin Federation of Business and Professional Women's Clubs, Inc. Title varies: as Official Bulletin of Wisconsin Federation of Business and Professional Women's Clubs, Oct., 1927-May, 1928. Place of publication varies: Racine, WI, Oct., 1928-Apr., 1934; Sheboygan, WI, Nov., 1935-May, 1938; Kaukauna, WI, Dec., 1938-May, 1939; Madison, WI, Mar., 1940-Apr., 1941; Menasha, WI, Nov., 1941-Apr., 1942; Stevens Point, WI, Apr., 1944-June, 1946; New London, WI, Oct., 1946; Milwaukee, WI, May, 1950; Green Bay, WI, Summer-Fall, 1950; Two Rivers, WI, July, 1954-May, 1956; Lake Mills, WI, Sep., 1956-Aug., 1975; La Crosse, WI, Oct., 1975-Apr., 1979. Previous editors: Estelle J. Glass, Oct., 1928-Apr., 1934; Marion Koch, Nov., 1935-May, 1938; Genevieve De Brue Anderson, Dec., 1938-May, 1939; Margaret Snyder, Mar., 1940-Apr., 1941; Edna Robertson, Nov., 1941-Apr., 1942; Marie Swallow, Apr., 1944-June, 1946; Martha Loss, Oct., 1946-Sep., 1949; Agnes Foster, Jan., 1950; Elizabeth R. Pratt, May, 1950; Martha Ann Hollenbeck, Summer, 1950; Marge Miley, July, 1954-Spring, 1961; Edith Zipse, Summer, 1961-Apr., 1963; Marjorie Miley, July, 1963-Apr., 1969; Margaret Jane Park, Aug., 1969-Apr., 1971; Marjorie Miley, July, 1971-Apr., 1974; Eileen M. Kramer, Aug., 1974-Apr., 1979. Subject focus: clubs, business. Other holding institution: WM (GZD).

| | | |
|---|---|---|
| Hist | [Spring, 1927-Dec., 1958] | Microforms |
| | May, 1958- | HD/6050/W5 |
| MPL | June, 1972- | Business and Science Section |

1219 The Wisconsin Citizen. 1887-1919//. Monthly. Last issue 4 pages, size 28 x 44. Line drawings. Available on microfilm: WHi (1887-1917). Published by Wisconsin Woman Suffrage Association, Waukesha, WI. Place of publication varies: Racine, WI, Aug., 1887-Oct., 1894; Brodhead, WI, Nov., 1894-Sep., 1898; Evansville, WI, Oct., 1898-May, 1899; Brodhead, WI, June, 1899-May, 1914. Editors: Mrs. M.P. Dingee, Aug., 1887-Oct., 1894; Helen H. Charleton, Nov., 1894-Sep., 1898; Marilla Andrews, Oct., 1898-May, 1899; Helen H. Charleton, June, 1899-Nov., 1906; Lena V. Newman, Dec., 1906-May, 1914; Mrs. Henry M. Youmans, June, 1914, Jan., 1917. Subject focus: pro-suffrage, rights, politics. Other holding institution: MCR-S (Schlesinger Library on the History of Women in America, Radcliffe College, Cambridge, MA).

| | | |
|---|---|---|
| Hist | v.1, n.1-v.30, n.1; Aug., 1887-Jan., 1917 | Microforms |
| | v.8, n.1-v.12, n.11; v.13, n.1-v.30, n.1; Nov., 1894-Sep., 1898; June/July, 1899-Jan., 1917 | F902/"8W873/W (Cutter) |

1220 The Wisconsin Clubwoman. 1917. Quarterly. $1 for individuals and institutions. Mrs. George N. Mueller, editor, The Wisconsin Clubwoman, 25 W. Main Street, Suite 506, Madison, WI 53703. Last issue 6 pages, last volume 30 pages, size 22 x 28. Line drawings, photographs. Published by Wisconsin Federation of Women's Clubs. Place of publication varies: Menasha, WI, Dec., 1917-Sep., 1918; DePere, WI, Mar., 1919-Nov./Dec., 1936; Waukesha, WI, Jan., 1937-June, 1939; Milwaukee, WI, Oct., 1939-July/Aug., 1941; Stevens Point, WI, Sep./Oct., 1950-Oct./Nov., 1975; Milwaukee, WI, Jan./Feb., 1976. Frequency varies: bi-monthly, Dec., 1917-Jan./Feb., 1960; five times a year, Mar./Apr./May, 1960-Jan./Feb., 1976; bi-monthly, Mar./Apr., 1976-Jan./Feb./Mar., 1978. Previous editors: Mrs. Paul L. Halline, Apr., 1918-Jan., 1937; Mrs. H.L. Horning and A.F. Potts, Mar., 1937-Jan., 1939; Jennie Schrage, Mar.-June, 1939; Mrs. Herbert V. Kohler, Oct., 1939-July/Aug., 1941; Jennie Schrage, Sep./Oct., 1941-May/June, 1948; Mrs. W.C. Cartwright, Sep./Oct., 1948-May/June, 1951; Mrs. D.W. Heck, July/Aug., 1951-July/Aug., 1952; Mrs. L.A. Leadbetter, Sep./Oct., 1952-July/Aug., 1956; Mrs. Raymond Rightsell, Sep./Oct., 1956-Mar./Apr./May, 1961; Mrs. Otis Mehlberg, Sep./Oct., 1961-Apr./May, 1964; Mrs. Gene Harrison, Summer, 1964-Summer, 1970; Mrs. Byron Musken, Sep., 1970-Feb., 1972; Shirley Vance, May, 1973-Mar./Apr., 1976. Subject focus: clubs.

| | | |
|---|---|---|
| Hist | v.1, n.1-Dec., 1917- | HQ/1905/W5 |
| R&L | v.1, n.1-v.33, n.2; v.35, n.2-Dec., 1917-Mar., 1950, Mar., 1952- | Circulation |

1221 Wisconsin Hospital Association Auxiliaries. 1960-1973//? Monthly. Last issue 5 pages, last volume 42 pages. Line drawings. Available on microfilm: WHi. Published in Milwaukee, WI. Title varies: as The Auxiliary Newsletter, Oct., 1960-Apr., 1962; as Wisconsin Auxiliary Newsletter, May, 1962-Oct., 1966. Place of publication varies: Manitowoc, WI, Oct., 1960-May, 1962; Green Bay, WI, Apr., 1962-Oct., 1966; Manitowoc, WI, Mar., 1966-Dec., 1968; Watertown, WI, Jan., 1969-Dec., 1970;

Milwaukee, WI, Jan., 1971-Jan., 1973. Editors: Mrs. Edwin Hilbert, Jan., 1969-Dec., 1970; Mrs. Saul Padik, Jan., 1971-Jan., 1973. Subject focus: hospital volunteers.

| Hist | v.1, n.1-v.73, n.1; Oct., 1960-Jan., 1973 | Microforms |
|---|---|---|

1222 <u>Wisconsin N.O.W. Newsletter</u>. 1976-1977//. Irregular. Last issue 6 pages, size 22 x 28. Line drawings. Published by National Organization for Women, Manitowoc, WI. Subject focus: feminism, Equal Rights Amendment, lobbying, rights.

| Wom Ed | May 25, 1976-Apr. 13, 1977 | Circulation |
|---|---|---|

1223 <u>Wisconsin News Letter</u>. 1937-1939//? Irregular. Last issue 4 pages. Available on microfilm: WHi. Published by the Wisconsin Daughters of the American Revolution, Neenah, WI. Editor: Mrs. Helen K. Stuart. Subject focus: clubs.

| Hist | n.1-19; May, 1937-May, 1939 | Microforms |
|---|---|---|

1224 <u>Wisconsin Tribal Women's News. Najinakwe</u>. 1974-1976//. Irregular. Last issue 8 pages, size 22 x 28. Line drawings. Published in Madison, WI. Subject focus: Native Americans, rights, biographies.

| Wom Ed Res | v.1, n.1-v.3,n.1; Aug., 1974-Nov., 1976 | Circulation |
|---|---|---|

1225 <u>Wisconsin Women for Agriculture Newsletter</u>. 1974. Irregular. $5 for individuals and institutions. Audrey Sickinger, editor, Wisconsin Women for Agriculture, Rt. 1, Cato, WI 54206. (414) 775-4257. Last issue 8 pages, last volume 76 pages, size 22 x 28. Line drawings, photographs. Published by Wisconsin Agri-Women. Place of publication varies: Valders, WI, Jan?, 1974-Sep?, 1976; Kewaunee, WI, ?, 1977-?, 1980. Previous editors: Irene Berge, Jan?, 1974-Sep., 1976; Nancy ?. 1977-?, 1980. Subject focus: agriculture, farmers, farm life, cooperatives.

| Wom Ed Res | v.2, n.1-July, 1976- | Circulation |
|---|---|---|
| U.W. Co-op | Current Issues Only | Circulation |

1226 <u>Wisconsin Women in the Arts Newsletter</u>. 1976? Irregular. Wisconsin Women in the Arts Newsletter, Room 728 Lowell Hall, 610 Langdon Street, Madison, WI 53706. Size 22 x 28. Line drawings, photographs, commercial advertising. Previous editor: Kathy Greathouse, Jan., 1977. Subject focus: arts, art reviews, poetry.

| Wom St | June, 1976-Jan., 1977 | Reading Room |
|---|---|---|
| Wom Ed Res | Mar., 1977- | Circulation |

1227 <u>Wisconsin Women Library Workers Newsletter</u>. 1976. Irregular. $6 for individuals, students $2.50, $10 for institutions. Lynne Martin Erikson and Kathryn Leide, editors, Wisconsin Women Library Workers Newsletter, P.O. Box 1004, Oshkosh, WI 54902. OCLC 4126944. Last issue 10 pages, last volume 50 pages, size 22 x 28. Line drawings. Place of publication varies: West Bend, WI, Sep?, 1976. Previous editors: Patti Geidel, Mar.-Dec., 1977; Rhonda Gandel, Kathleen Weibel, and Susan Griffith, Feb., 1978; Mary Alice Seemeyer, Apr., 1978; Judy Reynolds, Aug., 1978. Subject focus: libraries. Other holding institution: WMUW (GZN).

| Lib Sch | v.1, n.1-Sep?, 1976- | Circulation |
|---|---|---|
| Wom Ed Res | v.1, n.1-4; Sep?, 1976-June, 1977 | Circulation |

1228 <u>Wisconsin Women Newsletter</u>. 1970. Irregular. Marian Thompson, editor, Wisconsin Women Newsletter, 428 Lowell Hall, 610 Langdon Street, Madison, WI 53706. OCLC 2269569, 3937445. Last issue 25 pages, last volume 66 pages, size 22 x 28. Line drawings. Available on microfilm: Herstory (1970-1974). Published by the Center for Women and Family Living Education, University Extension, University of Wisconsin-Madison. Title varies: as Women's Education Newsletter, Mar.-Oct., 1970. Subject focus: law, lobbying, workers. Other holding institutions: [University of Minnesota Union List, Minneapolis, MN] (MUL), PPiU (PIT), WM (GZD).

| Hist | v.1,n.1-4; Mar., 1970-Aug., 1971 | Microforms Her. 1, R 22 |
|---|---|---|
| | v.2,n.1-v.3,n.1; Feb., 1972-Jan., 1973 | Her. 1 UP, R16 |
| | v.3,n.2-v.4,n.1; Aug., 1973-May, 1974 | Her. CUP R 7 |
| Mem | v.1,n.1-Mar., 1970- | AP/W8725/E264 |

*Women's Periodicals and Newspapers*

| | | |
|---|---|---|
| Coll | Current Issues Only | Women's Reading Area |
| MPL | v.3, n.2; June, 1972 | Literature and Social Science Section |
| UW Ext | v.1, n.3; Feb., 1971 | Circulation |
| Wom Ed Res | v.8, n.3- Dec., 1978- | Circulation |

1229 <u>Wisconsin Women's Political Caucus</u>. 1972. Irregular. Pat Muller, editor, Wisconsin Women's Political Caucus, P.O. Box 2233, Madison, WI 53701. Last issue 8 pages, size 22 x 28. Published by Wisconsin Women's Political Caucus. Previous editor: Jane Lepeska, June, 1975-Jan., 1978. Subject focus: rights, lobbying, affirmative action.

| | | |
|---|---|---|
| Hist | v.3, n.1, n.5- June, 1975, Feb., 1976- | Circulation |
| MPL | v.3, n.5- Feb., 1976- | Literature and Social Science Section |
| Wom Ed Res | v.1, n.1- Dec., 1972- | Circulation |

1230 <u>Wisconsin Women's Political Caucus/Dane County Newsletter</u>. 1973. Virginia Zwickey, editor, 602 Pine Street, Madison, WI 53715. (608) 257-9703. Business address: P.O. Box 2233, Madison, WI 53701. Last issue 4 pages, size 28 x 22. Line drawings, photographs. Available on microfilm: WHi. Published by Wisconsin Women's Political Caucus, Dane County Chapter. Title varies: as Dane County Women's Political Caucus, Oct., 1975. Previous editor: Andrea (Dede) Graff, Feb./Mar., 1976. Subject focus: politics.

| | | |
|---|---|---|
| Hist | Summer, 1973- | Circulation |

1231 <u>La Wisp</u>. 1967. Monthly. $3 for individuals and institutions. Mary Clarke, editor, La Wisp, 5539 West Pico Boulevard, Los Angeles, CA 90019. OCLC 2263382, 5588802. Last issue 6 pages. Line drawings, photographs. Available on microfilm: WHi (1968-), Herstory (1967-1974). Published by Southern California Women Strike for Peace. Previous editors: Mary Clarke and Lisa Strada, Sep.-Nov., 1968; Mary Clarke and Varda Ullman, Dec., 1968-Jan., 1970; Mary Clarke, Kathleen McNamara, and Varda Ullman, Feb.-Apr., 1970; Mary Clarke and Varda Ullman, May, 1970-May,11972; Mary Clarke, Kitty Howe, and Varda Ullman, June-Aug., 1972; Mary Clarke, and Roz Levine, Apr.-Nov., 1973. Subject focus: peace movement, anti-nuclear movement, Jeanette Rankin Brigade. Other holding institution: [University of Minnesota Union List, Minneapolis, MN] (MUL).

| | | |
|---|---|---|
| Hist | Oct., 1967- Sep., 1971 | Microforms Her. 1, R 23 |
| | Oct., 1971- June, 1973 | Her. 1 UP, R17 |
| | July, 1973- June, 1974 | Her. CUP, R 8 |
| | Sep., 1968- | Microforms |

1232 <u>Wochenblatt fuer's Schoene Geschlecht</u>.1779//? Semi-weekly. OCLC 1643003. LC 68-108984. Last issue 6 pages, last volume 550 pages. Published in Leipzig, Germany. 1966 reprint edition by Mueller and Kiepenhauer, Ha$_n$au, Germany. Subject focus: fiction, poetry, biographies, art, artists. In German (100%). Other holding institutions: [University of Minnesota Union List, Minneapolis, MN] (MUL), OBgU (BGU).

| | | |
|---|---|---|
| Mem | May-Dec. 29, 1779 | AP/W838/S371 |

1233 <u>Woman</u>. 1887-1888//? Monthly. Last issue 122 pages, last volume 1464 pages. Line drawings, commercial advertising. Self-indexed. Available on microfilm: ResP. Published by The Woman Publishing Co., New York, NY. Subject focus: fiction, biographies, history. Other holding institution: NN (NYP).

| | | |
|---|---|---|
| Mem | v.1, n1-v.2,n.1; Nov., 1887- June, 1888 | Microforms |

1234 <u>Woman</u>. 1973//? Irregular. Last issue 12 pages. Line drawings. Available on microfilm: Herstory. Published by Campus Women's Forum, University of California, Berkeley, CA. Subject focus: education, affirmative action, professionals, career development, higher education.

| | | |
|---|---|---|
| Hist | n.1-3; Jan.-Mar./ Apr., 1973 | Microforms Her. 2, R 16 |

1235 <u>Woman</u>. 1972//? Unknown. Last issue 7 pages. Available on microfilm: Herstory. Published by Davis Women's Forum, University of California, Davis, CA. Subject focus: health, rights, pro-abortion.

| | | |
|---|---|---|
| Hist | v.2, n.3; May/June, 1972 | Microforms Her. 2, R 16 |

1236  Woman. 1973//? Monthly. Last issue 16 pages. Line drawings, photographs, commercial advertising. Published by Woman, Los Angeles, CA. Editor: Susanne Smolka. Subject focus: health, pro-abortion, art, politics.

| Hist | Feb.-Mar., 1973 | Microforms Her. 2, R 15 |

1237  Woman. 1973//? Monthly. Last issue 18 pages. Line drawings, photographs, commercial advertising. Available on microfilm: Herstory. Published by Community Women's Newspaper/Woman, Kalamazoo, MI. Subject focus: health, pro-abortion, child care, poetry, self-help, childbirth.

| Hist | v.1, n.1-4; Feb. 15-June, 1973 | Microforms Her. 2, R 16 |
| | v.1, n.5; July, 1973 | Her. 2 UP, R12 |

1238  The Woman Activist. 1971-1974//. Monthly. ISSN 0049-7770. OCLC 2269537. LC sn78-1834. Last issue 16 pages, last volume 120 pages, size 22 x 28. Line drawings. Published in Falls Church, VA. Editor: Flora Crater. Subject focus: law, lobbying, Equal Rights Amendment, politics. Other holding institutions: [Congressional Research Service, Washington, DC] (CRS), [University of Minnesota Union List, Minneapolis, MN] (MUL), NcRS (NRC), OU (OSU), PPiU (PIT), ScRhW (SWW).

| Hist | v.1, n.1-10; Jan. 14-Sep. 15, 1971 | Microforms Her. 1, R 22 |
| | v.1, n.11-v.3, n.6; Oct., 1971-June, 1973 | Her. 1 UP, R16 |
| | v.3, n.7-v.4, n.6; July, 1973-June, 1974 | Her. CUP, R 8 |
| Wom Ed Res | v.2, n.9-v.4, n.1; Sep., 1972-Jan., 1974 | Circulation |

1239  Woman and Revolution. 1972-1974//? Irregular. OCLC 2269598. Last issue 24 pages. Line drawings, photographs, commercial advertising. Available on microfilm: Herstory. Published by The Spartacist League, New York, NY. Subject focus: radicalism, employment, revolution.

| Hist | v.3; 1972 | Microforms Her. 1 UP, R17 |
| | n.4,6; Fall, 1973, Summer, 1974 | Her. CUP, R 7-8 |

1240  The Woman Athletic. 1916?-1930//? Monthly. Last issue 48 pages, size 33 x 25. Line drawings, photographs, commercial advertising. Published by Illinois Women's Athletic Club, Chicago, IL. Editors: Bernice Challenger Bost, Oct., 1926-Nov., 1927; Alice Louise Fretter, Dec., 1927; Marjorie Savage Caudle, Jan., 1928; Edna J. Asmus, Feb., 1928-Jan., 1929; Alice McKinstry, Feb., 1929; Beth Goock, Mar., 1929-Jan., 1930. Subject focus: sports, health, art, clubs, theater reviews.

| Hist | v.11, n.10-12, v.12, n.1-v.14, n.3,9-v.15, n.1; Oct.-Dec., 1926, Jan., 1927-Mar., Oct., 1929-Jan., 1930 | F896C/+7W87 (Cutter) |

1241  Woman Becoming. 1972-1974//. Irregular. OCLC 2144017. Last issue 80 pages, size 17 x 22. Line drawings. Available on microfilm: Herstory. Published in Pittsburgh, PA. Subject focus: poetry, rights, fiction. Other holding institution: CtY (YUS).

| Hist | v.1, n.1; Dec., 1972 | Microforms Her. 2, R 17 |
| | v.1,n.2,v.2,n.1; July, 1973, Feb., 1974 | Her. 2 UP, R12 |
| Mem | v.1,n.2,v.2,n.1; July, 1973, Feb., 1974 | AP/W8679/B398 |

1242  The Woman Bowler. 1936. Monthly, bi-monthly in summer. $3 for individuals and institutions. Chris Igler, editor, Woman Bowler, 5301 South 76th Street, Greendale, WI. (414) 421-9000. ISSN 0043-7255. OCLC 2252120. LC sn78-6103. Last issue 46 pages, last volume 494 pages, size 21 x 28. Line drawings, photographs, commercial advertising. Published by Women's International Bowling Congress. Place of publication varies: Columbus, OH, Sep., 1972. Previous editor: Helen Latham, Sep., 1972-Dec., 1978. Subject focus: bowling, sports. Other holding institutions: [University of Minnesota Union List, Minneapolis, MN] (MUL), TxDN (INT), TxDW (IWU), [AMIGOS Union List of Serials, Dallas, TX] (IUC), TxNacS (TXK), ViRCU (VRC).

| Hist | v.36, n.8-Sep., 1972- | Circulation |

The Woman Citizen. New York, NY

   see The Woman's Journal. New York, NY

1243 The Woman Constitutionalist. 1964. Irregular. $3 for individuals and institutions. Mary D. Cain, editor, The Woman Constitutionist, 310 West Robb Street, P.O. Box 220, Summit, MS 39666. ISSN 0043-728X. OCLC 1775456. LC sn78-1835. Last issue 8 pages, last volume 96 pages, size 29 x 39. Line drawings, photographs. Available on microfilm: UnM, WHi (1967-), Herstory (1970-1971). Published by Women for Constitutional Government. Subject focus: politics, lobbying, Equal Rights Amendment. Other holding institutions: CLobS (CLO), MiEM (EEM).

| | | |
|---|---|---|
| Hist | v.6, n.12-v.7, n.7; Aug. 8, 1970- Mar. 13, 1971 | Microforms Her. 2, R 17 |
| | v.4, n.4- Dec. 2, 1967- | Microforms |

1244 Woman N.O.W. 1969-1974//? Monthly. OCLC 2261333. Last issue 4 pages. Line drawings, photographs. Available on microfilm: Herstory. Published by National Organization for Women, San Francisco Chapter, San Francisco, CA. Title varies: as News and Opinions of Women, Feb., 1969-June, 1971; Free Woman, July, 1971; Uppity Woman, Aug.-Sep., 1971; Free Woman, Oct., 1971; San Francisco N.O.W. Newsletter, Nov., 1971-Oct., 1972. Subject focus: marriage, family, media, pro-abortion, rape, lobbying, feminism, Equal Rights Amendment, rights, politics. Other holding institution: PPiU (PIT).

| | | |
|---|---|---|
| Hist | Feb., 1969- Sep., 1971 | Microforms Her. 1, R 20 |
| | June, Sep., 1969, Feb., Oct., 1971 | Her. Add. |
| | Oct., 1971- June, 1973 | Her. 1 UP, R11 |
| | July, 1973- June, 1974 | Her. CUP, R 5 |

1245 The Woman Patriot. 1918-1932//. Monthly. OCLC 2704396. LC 21-12430. Last issue 8 pages, last volume 96 pages, size 23 x 30. Line drawings, photographs. Available on microfilm: ResP (1918-1931); GW (1919-1932); McA. Published by the Woman Patriot Corporation, Washington, DC. Frequency varies: weekly, Apr.,27, 1918-Apr. 16, 1921; semi-monthly, May 1, 1921-Jan. 15, 1931. Editor: Minnie Bronson, Apr. 27, 1918-Apr. 24, 1920. Subject focus: patriotism, politics, socialism, anti-suffrage, feminism. Other holding institutions: InU (IUL), MNS (SNN), MdFreH (HCF), MeB (BBH), CSt (Stanford University), MCR-S (Schlesinger Library on the History of Women in America, Radcliffe College, Cambridge, MA), [University of Minnesota Union List, Minneapolis, MN] (MUL), NmLcU (IRU), OCU (CIN), PP (PLF), PPiU (PIT), N (NYG), TxDW (IWU).

| | | |
|---|---|---|
| Hist | v.1, n.1-v.8, n.24; Apr. 27, 1918- Dec. 15, 1924 | KWZ/"W85 (Cutter) |
| | [v.9, n.1-v.15, n.8]; [Jan. 15, 1925- Aug., 1931] | KWZ/+W85 (Cutter) |
| Mem | [v.1, n.1-v.15, n.11]; [Apr. 27, 1918- Nov., 1931] | Microforms |

The Woman Physician. Paterson, NJ

   see Journal of the American Medical Women's Association. New York, NY

1246 The Woman Rebel. 1914//. Monthly. OCLC 3796831, 4245724. LC 76-641825. Last issue 8 pages, last volume 56 pages. Available on microfilm: GwP, WHi. Published in New York, NY. Editor: Margaret H. Sanger. Subject focus: rights, labor unions, workers, birth control, pro-abortion, class consciousness, career development. Archives of Social History reprint, 1976. Other holding institutions: AzU (AZU), CArcHT (CHU), CCC (HDC), [California State University, Hayward, CA] (CSH), COU-DA (COA), CSt (Stanford University), CTurS (CTU), CtY (YUS), DLC (DLC), IU (UIU), InU (IUL), KMK (KKS), MCM (MYG), MH (HUL), [University of Minnesota Union List, Minneapolis, MN] (MUL), MdFreH (HCF), MeB (BBH), MiDW (EYW), NGcA (VJA), NcGU (NGU), OAkU (AKR), OCU (CIN), OO (OBE), TxShA (IAU).

| | | |
|---|---|---|
| Hist | v.1, n.1-7; Mar., Sep./Oct., 1914 | Microforms |

1247 Woman Suffrage Leaflet. 1888-1904//? Bi-monthly. OCLC 4544939. Last issue 4 pages, size 14 x 25. Published by the American Woman Suffrage Association, Boston, MA. Frequency varies: bi-weekly, Sep. 15, 1888-May 1, 1890. Subject focus: pro-suffrage. Other holding institution: PBm (BMC).

| | | |
|---|---|---|
| Hist | [v.1, n.4-v.11, n.5]; [Sep. 15, 1888- Sep., 1904] | KWZ/WO (Cutter) |

Woman Talk. Honolulu, HI

    see Continuing Currents. Honolulu, HI

Woman Voter and the Newsletter. New York, NY

    see The Woman Voter. New York, NY

1248   The Woman Voter. 1910-1917//. Monthly. OCLC 2152675, 2395192. Last issue 28 pages, last volume 140 pages. Line drawings, photographs, commercial advertising. Available on microfilm: GwP. Published by the Woman Suffrage Party, New York, NY. Title varies: as Woman Voter and the Newsletter, Feb.-Dec., 1913. Editors: Minnie J. Reynolds, Mar.-May, 1911; Mary R. Beard, Sep., 1911-Apr., 1912; Florence Woolston, May, 1912-May, 1917. Subject focus: pro-suffrage, labor unions, lobbying, workers, poetry. Other holding institutions: CSt (Stanford University), IaSIB (IOE), IGreviC (IAG), IElgJ (IFH), MeB (BBH), OKentU (KSU), PPiU (PIT), IMurS (TXM), TSewU (TWU), TxAbC (TXC), ViAlTh (VTS), ViNO (VOD), WvBeC (WVB).

| | | |
|---|---|---|
| Hist | v.1,n.1-v.8,n.5;<br>Feb., 1910-<br>May, 1917 | Microforms |
| | v.2,n.9,v.5,n.3,5,<br>v.6,n.4,6;<br>Oct., 1911,<br>Mar., May, 1914,<br>Apr., June, 1915 | KWZ/WO<br>(Cutter) |

1249   The Woman Voters' Bulletin. 1921-1939//. Bi-weekly. Last issue 4 pages, last volume 60 pages. Available on microfilm: ResP. Published by the Connecticut League of Women Voters, Hartford, CT. Title varies: as Legislative Bulletin of the Connecticut League of Women Voters, Feb. 14-May 27, 1921; as Legislative Bulletin, June, 1921. Frequency varies: weekly, Feb. 14-May 27, 1921; quarterly, June-Oct., 1921; monthly, Nov., 1921-Jan., 1923; weekly, Feb. 3-June 9, 1924; monthly, July, 1924-Jan., 1925; weekly, Feb. 6-June 15, 1925; bi-monthly, July-Aug., 1925; monthly, Sep., 1925-Feb., 1927; weekly, Feb. 4, 1927-Apr. 22, 1927; monthly, May-June, 1927; bi-monthly, July-Aug., 1927; monthly, Sep., 1927-Jan., 1929; weekly, Feb. 1-May 10, 1929; bi-monthly, July-Aug., 1929; monthly, Sep., 1929-Mar., 1931; weekly, Mar. 5-Apr. 21, 1931; semi-monthly, May 1-June 1, 1931; monthly, Aug., 1931-Jan., 1933; weekly, Feb. 1-Apr. 10, 1933; bi-weekly, Apr. 24-June 5, 1933; monthly, Sep., 1933-Jan., 1935; bi-weekly, Feb. 8, 1935-May 3, 1935; monthly, June, 1935-Dec., 1936; bi-weekly, Jan. 18-Sep. 28, 1937; monthly, Oct., 1937-Jan., 1939. Editors: Mrs. William H. Deming and Ruth McIntire Dadourian, Feb. 14-June, 1921; Ruth McIntire Dadourian, Oct., 1921-June 9, 1923; Marjory Cheney, July, 1923-Sep., 1924; Julia Margaret Hicks, Oct., 1924-June, 1926; Beatrice H. Marsh, July-Aug., 1926-May 10, 1929; Grace P. Asserson, June 1, 1929-Nov., 1934; Mrs. Landon T. Raymond, Dec., 1934-Oct., 1936; Mrs. Edward Pousland, Nov., 1936-Sep. 28, 1937; Mrs. Henry S. Beers, Oct., 1937-Feb. 10, 1939; Mrs. G. Gardiner Russell, Feb. 24-Sep. 27, 1939. Subject focus: politics. Other holding institutions: Ct (CZL), TxDW (IWU).

| | | |
|---|---|---|
| Mem | v.1,n.1-v.19,<br>n.15;<br>Feb. 14, 1921-<br>Sep. 27, 1939 | Microforms |

1250   The Woman Worker. 1921-1942//. Bi-monthly. OCLC 1770063. Last issue 16 pages, last volume 96 pages, size 16 x 25. Self-indexed (1938-1941). Published by the United States Department of Labor, Women's Bureau, Washington, DC. Subject focus: labor unions, war work, minimum wage. Other holding institutions: [University of Minnesota Union List, Minneapolis, MN] (MUL), PPiU (PIT).

| | | |
|---|---|---|
| Hist | v.18, n.1-<br>v.22, n.3;<br>Jan., 1938-<br>May, 1942 | ∆/L13./8:/<br>18-22 |

1251   Woman Worker. 1970//? Unknown. Last issue 12 pages. Line drawings. Available on microfilm: Herstory. Published in Los Angeles, CA. Subject focus: employment, equal pay for equal work, workers, child care.

| | | |
|---|---|---|
| Hist | May, 1970 | Microforms<br>Her. 2, R 17 |

1252   Womanhood. 1898-1907//? Monthly. Last issue 52 pages, last volume 398 pages. Line drawings, photographs, commercial advertising. Each volume self-indexed. Available on microfilm: ResP, McA. Published in London, England. Editor: Ada S. Ballin. Subject focus: literature, science, art, health, beauty care, pro-suffrage. Other holding institution: NN (NYP).

| | | |
|---|---|---|
| Mem | v.3, n.13-<br>v.17, n.103<br>Dec., 1899-<br>June, 1907 | Microforms |

1253   Womankind. 1971-1973//. Monthly. Last issue 15 pages, last volume 204 pages. Line drawings, photographs. Available on microfilm: Herstory, WHi. Published by Chicago Women's Liberation Union, Chicago, IL. Subject focus: rights, Equal Rights Amendment, economics, politics, child rearing, health, poetry.

| | | |
|---|---|---|
| Hist | v.1,n.1-v.2,n.5;<br>Sep., 1971-<br>Jan., 1973 | Microforms |
| | v.1, n.1;<br>Sep., 1971 | Her. 1, R 4 |
| | v.1,n.2-3,<br>v.2, n.5;<br>Oct.-Nov., 1971,<br>Jan., 1973 | Her. 1 UP, R16 |
| | v.3, n.1;<br>Sep., 1973 | Her. CUP, R 7 |

1254 <u>Womankind.</u> 1971//? Irregular. OCLC 2269594. Last issue 18 pages. Line drawings, photographs, commercial advertising. Available on microfilm: Herstory. Published by Women of Detroit, Detroit, MI. Subject focus: rights, welfare, motherhood, poetry, health, food, law.

| | | |
|---|---|---|
| Hist | v.1, n.1-2;<br>May/June-Sep.,<br>1971 | Microforms<br>Her. 1, R 4 |
| | v.1, n.3-4;<br>Oct.-Nov., 1971 | Her. 1 UP, R16 |

1255 <u>Womankind.</u> 1977. Bi-monthly. $4 for individuals, $15 for institutions. Judith LaFourest, editor, Womankind, P.O. Box 16306, Indianapolis, IN 46216. (317) 299-2276. Last issut 12 pages, last volume 52 pages, size 45 x 29. Line drawings, photographs, commercial advertising. Frequency varies: irregular, 1977-1978. Subject focus: rights, politics, women's studies, film reviews, poetry, fiction.

| | | |
|---|---|---|
| Hist | v.1, n.1-<br>?, 1977- | Circulation |

1256 <u>Womankind.</u> 1970-1971//? Irregular. Last issue 28 pages, size 22 x 28. Line drawings, photographs. Available on microfilm: Herstory. Published by the Women's Newspaper Collective, Louisville, KY. Subject focus: rights, welfare, motherhood, poetry.

| | | |
|---|---|---|
| Hist | v.1, n.1-7;<br>Dec., 1970-<br>July, 1971 | Microforms<br>Her. 1, R 4 |
| | v.1, n.5, 7-8;<br>Apr. 20, July-<br>Nov., 1971 | Pam 75-3071 |

1257 <u>Womanpower.</u> 1971-1979//? ISSN 0300-6594. OCLC 1359713. LC sc77-1127. Last issue 8 pages. Line drawings. Available on microfilm: Herstory (1971-1974). Published by Betsy Hogan Associates, Brookline, MA. Subject focus: labor law, lobbying, employment, education, professionals, affirmative action. Other holding institutions: CSdS (CDS), DHU (DHU), FMFIU (FXG), IDeKN (HNA), [University of Minnesota Union List, Minneapolis, MN] (MUL), OYU (YNG).

| | | |
|---|---|---|
| Hist | v.1, n.1;<br>Oct., 1971 | Microforms<br>Her. 1, R 22 |
| | v.1,n.1-v.3,n.6;<br>Oct., 1971-<br>June, 1973 | Her. 1 UP,R16 |
| | v.3,n.7-v.4,n.6;<br>July, 1973-<br>June, 1974 | Her. CUP, R7 |

<u>Womanspace.</u>  Los Angeles, CA

    see <u>Womanspace Journal.</u>  Los Angeles, CA

1258 <u>The Woman's Bulletin.</u> 1912-1913//? Monthly. Last issue 36 pages, size 16 x 24. Line drawings, photographs, commercial advertising. Available on microfilm: ResP. Published by The Woman's Bulletin Company, Los Angeles, CA. Editor: Harriet H. Barry. Subject focus: pro-suffrage, politics, volunteers, child rearing. Other holding institution: NN (NYP).

| | | |
|---|---|---|
| Hist | v.1,n.1,v.2,n.7;<br>June, 1912,<br>Dec., 1913 | KWZ/WO<br>(Cutter) |
| Mem | v.1,n.1,7,9-12;<br>June, 1912,<br>Jan., Mar.-June, 1913 | Microforms |

1259 <u>Woman's City Club Bulletin.</u> 1916-1918//? Last issue 22 pages, size 17 x 24. Line drawings, commercial advertising. Published by Woman's City Club of Cincinnati, Cincinnati, OH. Editors: Mrs. Alfred Friedlander, Mrs. W.E. Stillwell, Mrs. F.J. Hooker. Subject focus: volunteers, clubs.

| | | |
|---|---|---|
| Hist | v.3, n.1;<br>Aug., 1918 | JW/.8CI<br>(Cutter) |

1260 <u>The Woman's Column.</u> 1888?-1950?// Bi-weekly. OCLC 2704324. LC 60-57861. Last issue 4 pages, size 27 x 33. Line drawings, photographs. Available on microfilm: GwP (1892-1904). Published in Boston, MA. Frequency varies: weekly, Nov. 14, 1891-Dec. 25, 1897. Editor: Alice Stone Blackwell. Subject focus: pro-suffrage, career development, professionals. Other holding institutions: AU (ALM), CSt (Stanford University), CCC (HDC), CtY (YUS), InU (IUL), MNS (SNN), MeB (BBH), MCR-S (Schlesinger Library on the History of Women in America, Radcliffe College, Cambridge, MA), [University of Minnesota Union List, Minneapolis, MN] (MUL), NmLcU (IRU), NPV (VXM), OCU (CIN),

PPiU (PIT).

| | | |
|---|---|---|
| Hist | [v.4, n.46-v.17, n.8]; [Nov. 14, 1891- Apr. 16, 1904] | Microforms |
| | [v.4, n.46-v.17, n.8]; [Nov. 14, 1891- Apr. 16, 1904] | Room 225 |

1261 The Woman's Council Magazine. 1894-1896//? Monthly. Last issue 16 pages, last volume 192 pages, size 20 x 27. Commercial advertising. Published in Minneapolis, MN. Editor: Mrs. J.M. Parker. Subject focus: clubs, history, philanthropy, art, literary criticism.

| | | |
|---|---|---|
| Hist | v.1, n.1-v.2,n.5; Sep., 1894- Feb., 1896 | KW/7W87 (Cutter) |

1262 Woman's Day. 1937. 15 times a year. $16.50 for individuals and institutions. Geraldine Rhodes, editor, Woman's Day, 1 Fawcett Place, Greenwich, CT 06830. Business address: 1515 Broadway, New York, NY 10036. ISSN 0043-7336. OCLC 1770065, 6148543. LC sn78-4300. Last issue 166 pages, last volume 1992 pages, size 21 x 28. Line drawings, photographs, some in color, commercial advertising. Indexed: in Access Index (1975-). Available on microfilm: McP (1973-), UnM (1973-). Frequency varies: monthly, Jan., 1971-Oct., 1976. Subject focus: health, medicine, fashion, beauty care, crafts, interior decoration, food. Other holding institutions: DeU (DLM), GAuA (GJG), IMgO (IAP), [Indiana Union List of Serials, Indianapolis, IN] (ILS), InLP (IPL), MiEM (EEM), MCR-S (Sclesinger Library on the History of Women in America, Radcliffe College, Cambridge, MA), [University of Minnesota Union List of Serials, Minneapolis, MN] (MUL), [Western New York Library Resources Council, Buffalo, NY] (VZX), NCortU (YCM), NR (YQR), [Central New York Library Resources Council, Syracuse, NY] (SRR), OC1 (CLE), OY (YMM), OkT (TUL), [Pittsburgh Regional Library Center-Union List, Pittsburgh, PA] (QPR), TxAbH (TXS), TxDW (IWU), [AMIGOS Union List of Serials, Dallas, TX] (IUC), WM (GZD).

| | | |
|---|---|---|
| Agric | v.34, n.1- Jan., 1971- | Periodicals Section |
| MPL | v.9,n.1-v.30, n.7, v.35, n.1- Jan., 1945- July, 1967, Jan., 1972- | Business and Science Section |
| VPL | v.39, n.1- Jan., 1976- | Circulation |
| LAHS | Current Issues Only | Circulation |
| BEL | Current Issues Only | Circulation |
| BML | Current Issues Only | Circulation |
| WHS | v.34, n.9- Sep., 1971- | Circulation |
| EHS | Current Issues Only | Circulation |
| OM | Current Issues Only | Circulation |
| MCL | v.38, n.1- Jan., 1975- | Circulation |
| MIPL | v.37, n.1- Jan., 1974- | Circulation |
| WAPL | v.36, n.1- Jan., 1973- | Circulation |
| TML | v.23, n.1- Jan., 1960- | Circulation |
| SPHS | Current Issues Only | Circulation |

The Woman's Dreadnought. London, England

see The Worker's Dreadnought. London, England

1263 The Woman's Exponent. 1872-1914//. Monthly. Last issue 7 pages, last volume 104 pages. Commercial advertising. Available on microfilm: ResP. Published by the Church of Jesus Christ of Latter-Day Saints, Salt Lake City, UT. Frequency varies: semi-monthly, Feb. 7, 1873-May 15, 1896. Editor: Louise L. Greene, Feb. 7 -June 25, 1873; Lula Greene Richards, July 1, 1873-Nov. 15, 1875; Lula Greene Richards and Emmeline B. Wells, Dec. 1, 1875-July 15, 1877; Emmeline B. Wells, Aug. 1, 1877-Feb., 1914. Subject focus: Mormonism, pro-suffrage, fiction. Other holding institution: MCR-S (Sclesinger Library on the History of Women in America, Radcliffe College, Cambridge, MA).

| | | |
|---|---|---|
| Mem | v.1, n.17-v.41, n.14; Feb. 7, 1873- Feb., 1914 | Microforms |

1264 Woman's Herald of Industry & Social Science Cooperator. 1881-1884//? Monthly. Last issue

8 pages, last volume 80 pages. Line drawings, commercial advertising. Available on microfilm: ResP. Published in San Francisco, CA. Editor: Marietta L. Stow. Subject focus: radical feminism, health, food, temperance, recreation. Other holding institution: NN (NYP).

| Mem | v.1, n.1-v.3, n.10; Sep., 1881- Oct., 1884 | Microforms |

1265 Woman's Home Companion. 1873-1957//? Monthly. OCLC 1643036, 4403747, 6529113. LC 57-27197. Last issue 112 pages, last volume 1476 pages, size 25 x 34. Line drawings, photographs, some in color, commercial advertising. Indexed in: Readers' Guide to Periodical Literature (1904-1957). Available on microfilm: UnM (1873-1910). Published by The Crowell-Collier Publishing Company, Springfield, OH. Editors: Gertrude B. Lane, Jan., 1934-Jan., 1941; Willa Roberts, Feb., 1941-May, 1943; William A.H. Birnie, June, 1943-Jan., 1953; Woodrow Wierig, Feb., 1953-Aug., 1956; Theodore Strauss, Sep-Dec., 1956. Subject focus: food, fashion, homemakers, child rearing, crafts, fiction. Other holding institutions: AzTeS (AZS), DSI (SMI), InU (IUL), [University of Minnesota Union List, Minneapolis, MN] (MUL), NR (YQR), [Central New York Library Resources Council, Syracuse, NY] (SRR), OAk (APL), OCl (CLE), OClW (CWR), OO (OBE), OY (YMM), OkT (TUL), PPi (CPL), PPiD (DUQ), [Pittsburgh Regional Library Center-Union List, Pittsburgh, PA] (QPR), ScU (SUC), TMurS (TXM), TxBelM (MHB), TxCM (TXA), [AMIGOS Union List of Serials, Dallas, TX] (IUC), TxDW (IWU), TxLT (ILU), WM (GZD).

| Agric | [v.47, n.1-v.83, n.12]; [Jan., 1920- Dec., 1956] | Periodicals Section |
| MPL | v.75,n.2-v.84,n.1; Feb., 1948- Jan., 1957 | Literature and Social Science Section |
| Hist | v.25, n.12-v.26, n.11, [v.28, n.2-v.36, n.1]; Dec., 1898- Nov., 1899, [Feb., 1901- Jan., 1909] | Circulation |

1266 Woman's Home Missions. 1920-1940//. Monthly (bi-monthly in summer). Last issue 32 pages, last volume 352 pages, size 19 x 27. Line drawings, photographs. Published by Women's Home Missionary Society of the Methodist Episcopal Church, Cincinnati, OH. Frequency varies: monthly, Jan., 1920-Dec., 1933. Editors: Mrs. Levi Gilbert, Jan., 1920-July, 1932; Bertha M. Stephenson, Aug.-Sep., 1932; Ruth Esther Wheaton, Oct., 1932-July/Aug., 1940. Subject focus: Christianity, missions.

| Hist | v.37, n.1-v.57, n.7; Jan., 1920- July/Aug., 1940 | DS/7W7 (Cutter) |

1267 Woman's Journal. 1870-1917//. Weekly. OCLC 1642811, 4521519, 4547049. Last issue 6 pages, last volume 126 pages. Line drawings, photographs, commercial advertising. Self-indexed, (1874-1877, 1879-1888, 1890-1896, 1898-1904, 1906-1907, 1910-1914, 1916). Available on microfilm: WHi, UnM, ResP. Published by The National Woman Suffrage Association, Worcester, MA. Title varies: as Woman's Journal and Suffrage News, Oct. 19, 1912-Dec. 30, 1916. Place of publication varies: Boston, MA and Chicago, IL, Jan. 8-Dec. 31, 1870; Boston, MA, Chicago, IL, and St. Louis, MO, Jan. 7, 1871-Dec. 25, 1875; Boston, MA, Jan. 1, 1876-Apr. 7, 1917. Editors: Mary A. Livermore, Jan. 8, 1870-Dec. 30, 1871; Julia Ward Howe, Lucy Stone, Henry B. Blackwell, T.W. Higgenson, and Mary Livermore, Jan. 6, 1872-Dec. 27, 1879; Lucy Stone, Jan. 3, 1880-Feb. 3, 1883; Lucy Stone, Henry B. Blackwell, and Alice Stone Blackwell, Feb. 10, 1883-Oct. 21, 1893; Henry B. Blackwell and Alice Stone Blackwell, Oct. 28, 1893-Sep. 11, 1909; Alice Stone Blackwell, Sep. 18, 1909-May 26, 1917. Subject focus: pro-suffrage, rights. Other holding institutions: MCR-S (Schlesinger Library on the History of Women in America, Radcliffe College, Cambridge, MA), MiEM (EEM), [University of Minnesota Union List, Minneapolis, MN] (MUL), NBronSL (VVS), OClW (CWR), PPi (CPL), [Pittsburgh Regional Library Center-Union List, Pittsburgh, PA] (QPR), ScU (SUC), WM (GZD).

| Hist | v.1, n.1-v.48, n.21; Jan. 8, 1870- May 26, 1917 | Microforms |
|  | v.2, n.1-v.48, n.21; Jan. 7, 1871- May 26, 1917 | Circulation |
| Mem | v.1, n.1-v.48, n.21; Jan. 8, 1870- May 26, 1917 | Microforms |

1268 The Woman's Journal. 1917-1931//. Monthly. OCLC 2395192. LC 18-15984. Last issue 24 pages, last volume 252 pages. Line drawings, photographs, commercial advertising. Self-indexed: (1917, 1920-1924, 1926-1930); Readers Guide to Periodical Literature, (1924-1931). Available on microfilm: WHi, McA, UnM, ResP. Published by The Woman

Citizen Corp., New York, NY. Title varies: as The Woman Citizen, June 2, 1917-Dec., 1927. Frequency varies: weekly, June 2, 1917-Apr. 9, 1921; bi-weekly, Apr. 23, 1921-June 27, 1925. Editors: Rose Young, June 2, 1917-Apr. 9, 1921; Virginia Roderick, Apr. 23, 1921-June, 1931. Subject focus: pro-suffrage, rights, career development. Other holding institutions: [Indiana Union List of Serials, Indianapolis, IN] (ILS), InU (IUL), MCR-S (Schlesinger Library on the History of Women in America, Radcliffe College, Cambridge, MA), [University of Minnesota Union List, Minneapolis, MN] (MUL), NR (YQR), OY (YMM), ScU (SUC), WM (GZD).

| | | |
|---|---|---|
| Hist | v.1, n.1-v.16, n.6; June 2, 1917-June, 1931 | Microforms |
| Mem | v.1, n.1-v.16, n.6; June 2, 1917-June, 1931 | Microforms |

1269 Woman's Journal. 1971-1972//? Quarterly. OCLC 2269590. Last issue 40 pages, last volume 138 pages. Line drawings. Available on microfilm: Herstory. Published by The Valley Women's Center, Northampton, MA. Subject focus: poetry, fiction, literature.

| | | |
|---|---|---|
| Hist | v.1, n.1; Mar., 1971 | Microforms Her. 1, R 11 |
| | v.1, n.2-v.2, n.1; Fall, 1971-Aug., 1972 | Her. 1 UP, R17 |

Woman's Journal and Suffrage News. Worchester, MA

see Woman's Journal. Worchester, MA

1270 Woman's Label League Journal. 1903-1922//? Monthly. Last issue 16 pages, last volume 192 pages, size 16 x 25. Line drawings. Published by Woman's International Union Label League and Traders Union Auxiliary, Chicago, IL. Editor: Anna Fitzgerald. Subject focus: labor unions, child labor, workers, rights.

| | | |
|---|---|---|
| Hist | v.14, n.1-v.20, n.11; Jan., 1916-Nov. 20, 1922 | HFLA/8W84/J (Cutter) |

1271 The Woman's Leader. 1909-1933//. Monthly. OCLC 2451651, 5896207. Last issue 14 pages, last volume 72 pages. Line drawings, commercial advertising. Available on microfilm: ResP. Published by The Women's Movement for Reform, Manchester, England. Title varies: as The Common Cause, Apr. 15, 1909-Jan. 30, 1920; The Woman's Leader and the Common Cause, Feb. 6, 1920-Apr., 1932. Frequency varies: weekly, Apr. 15, 1909-Oct. 2, 1931. Subject focus: pro-suffrage, clubs. Other holding institutions: NN (NYP), PPi (CPL), [Pittsburgh Regional Library Center-Union List, Pittsburgh, PA] (QPR), TxDW (IWU), ViBlbv (VPI).

| | | |
|---|---|---|
| Mem | v.1, n.1-v.25, n.5; Apr. 15, 1909-Mar., 1933 | Microforms |

The Woman's Leader and the Common Cause. Manchester, England

see The Woman's Leader. Manchester, England

1272 The Woman's Magazine. 1894-1910//? Monthly. Last issue 44 pages. Line drawings, photographs, commercial advertising. Available on microfilm: ResP. Published by The Lewis Publishing Co., St. Louis, MO. Editor: E.G. Lewis. Subject focus: fiction, fashion, gardening, homemakers, farm life. Other holding institution: DLC (DLC).

| | | |
|---|---|---|
| Mem | v.8, n.1-[Apr., 1910]; Dec., 1902-Apr., 1910 | Microforms |

1273 Woman's Missionary Advocate. 1880-1910//? Last issue 44 pages, last volume 288 pages. Photographs, commercial advertising. Available on microfilm: ResP. Published by The Board of Missions of the Methodist Episcopal Church, Nashville, TN. Editor: Mrs. Frank N. Butler. Subject focus: missions, Christianity, poetry. Other holding institution: CtY (YUS).

| | | |
|---|---|---|
| Mem | v.1, n.1-v.31, n.6; July, 1880-Dec., 1910 | Microforms |

1274 Woman's Missionary Friend. 1869-1940//. Monthly. OCLC 1696894, 1587075. Last issue 36 pages, last volume 418 pages, size 16 x 24. Line drawings, photographs. Available on microfilm: ResP. Published by The Woman's Foreign Missionary Society, Boston, MA. Title varies: as The Heathen Woman's Friend, May, 1869-Dec., 1895. Editors: Mrs. William F. Warren, May, 1869-Mar., 1893; Mary Warren Ayars, Apr.-Oct., 1893; Louise Manning Hodgkins, Nov., 1893-Dec., 1905; Elizabeth C. Northrup, Jan., 1906-Dec., 1918; Effie A. Merrill, Jan., 1919-Nov., 1930. Subject focus: Christianity, missions. Other holding institutions: CtY-D (YU#), [University of Minnesota Union List, Minneapolis, MN] (MUL), TxDW (IWU).

| | | |
|---|---|---|
| Hist | v.7, n.12-v.63, n.1; June, 1876- Nov., 1930 | DS/+7HA (Cutter) |
| Mem | v.1,n.1-v.36, n.12; May, 1869- Dec., 1904 | Microforms |

1275 Woman's Outlook. 1919-1926//? Bi-weekly. Last issue 32 pages, last volume 384 pages. Line drawings, commercial advertising. Available on microfilm: ResP. Published in Glasgow, Scotland. Frequency varies: monthly, Nov., 1919-June, 1924. Subject focus: fashion, health, workers, gardening, biographies, poetry. Other holding institution: NN (NYP).

| | | |
|---|---|---|
| Mem | v.1,n.1-v.7,n.103; Nov., 1919- Apr. 10, 1926 | Microforms |

1276 A Woman's Place-Newsletter. 1973//? Last issue 6 pages. Line drawings. Available on microfilm: Herstory. Published in Montreal, Quebec, Canada. Subject focus: arts, crafts.

| | | |
|---|---|---|
| Hist | ?, Aug.-Sep?, 1973 | Microforms Her. 3, R 4 |

1277 The Woman's Press. 1907-1931//? Monthly. OCLC 2269591. Last issue 62 pages, last volume 520 pages, size 30 x 23. Line drawings, photographs, commercial advertising. Published by The National Board of Young Women's Christian Associations, New York, NY. Title varies: as The Association Monthly, Feb., 1910-Jan., 1922. Editors: Mary Louise Allen, Feb.-Nov., 1910; Rhoda E. McCulloch, Sep., 1918-Aug., 1931. Subject focus: politics, religion, economics, education, fiction, poetry. Other holding institution: PPiU (PIT).

| | | |
|---|---|---|
| Hist | v.4, n.1, 4-5, 7, 9-10,v.12,n.9-11, v.13,n.1-v.15,n.8, v.16,n.1,v.25,n.8; Feb., May-June, Aug., Oct.-Nov., 1910, Sep.-Nov., 1918, Jan., 1919-Aug., 1921, Jan., 1922, Aug., 1931 | DU83/+Y76A (Cutter) |

The Woman's Protest. New York, NY

see The Woman's Protest Against Woman Suffrage. New York, NY

1278 The Woman's Protest against Woman Suffrage. 1912-1918//? Monthly. Last issue 18 pages, last volume 144 pages. Available on microfilm: ResP. Published by the National Association Opposed to Woman Suffrage, New York, NY. Title varies: as The Woman's Protest, May, 1912-Dec., 1913. Subject focus: anti-suffrage. Other holding institutions: CSt (Stanford University), NN (NYP).

| | | |
|---|---|---|
| Mem | v.1,n.1-v.11,n.8; May, 1912- Feb., 1918 | Microforms |

1279 Woman's Review of Political Research. 1939//? Monthly. Last issue 96 pages, size 26 x 17. Line drawings, photographs, commercial advertising. Published by Women's Review of Political Research, Inc., Chicago, IL. Editor: Vivian Bennet. Subject focus: lobbying, politics.

| | | |
|---|---|---|
| Hist | v.1, n.1, v.2, n.2-4; ?, Apr.- Sep./Oct., 1939 | KWZ/.W88 (Cutter) |

1280 The Woman's Standard. 1886-1911//? Monthly. Last issue 4 pages, last volume 44 pages. Available on microfilm: ResP. Published by Iowa Woman Suffrage Association, Waterloo, IA. Place of publication varies: Des Moines, IA, Sep., 1886-Feb., 1897; Sutherland, IA, Mar., 1897-Mar., 1899. Editors: Mary J. Coggeshall, Sep., 1886-Aug., 1888; Martha J. Callahan, Sep., 1888; Evelyn M. Russell, Oct., 1888-Aug., 1890; Evelyn M. Russell, Lizzie B. Read, and Carrie Lane Chapman, Sep., 1890-Dec., 1890; Lizzie B. Read and Carrie Lane Chapman, Jan., 1891-Dec., 1892; Katherine M. Pierce, Jan., 1893-Feb., 1897; Roma W. Woods, Mar., 1897-Mar., 1899; Sarah Ware Whitney, Apr.-Aug., 1899; Sarah Ware Whitney and J.O. Stevenson, Sep., 1899-Mar., 1909; J.O. Stevenson, Apr., 1909-Oct., 1910; Mary J. Coggeshall, Feb.-Mar., 1911. Subject focus: pro-suffrage. Other holding institution: CLSU (CSL).

| | | |
|---|---|---|
| Mem | v.1,n.1-v.23, n.11 [n.s.]; Sep., 1886- Mar., 1911 | Microforms |

1281 The Woman's Tribune. 1883-1909//? Bi-weekly. LC 32-24141. Last issue 4 pages, last volume 60 pages, size 30 x 43. Line drawings, commercial advertising. Available on microfilm: DLC, ResP. Published by National American Woman Suffrage Association, Portland, OR. Place of publication varies: Beatrice, NB, Nov. 1, 1883-Nov. 16, 1889; Washington, DC and Beatrice, NE, Dec. 7, 1889-Dec. 31, 1892; Washington, DC, Jan. 7, 1893-Aug. 20, 1904; Portland, OR and Washington, DC, Oct. 29,

*Sisters Today* 53, no. 1 (August–September 1981). ©1981 by *Sisters Today*, Order of St. Benedict, Inc.

## Socialist International WOMEN BULLETIN

Number 2/81

**Contents:**

Working group reports
11th Conference, Madrid
9-10 November 1980

Peace — not just an issue for women
Alva Myrdal

**Editor**
Irmtraut Leirer

**Design**
Quivica Graphics

**Setting**
Pauline George Processing

**Published by**
Socialist International Women
88a St Johns Wood High Street,
London NW8 7SJ, England.
Telephone 01-586 1101
Telex 261735

# Women and peace

'We socialist women note that the arms race cannot be understood unless we analyse the persistence of different types of imperialism in international relations. This situation is present in different fields: military, economic and even in cultural and social relations.

'The maintenance of military supremacy leads certain countries into a senseless arms race which endangers the survival of the world. The existence of stockpiles of nuclear and conventional arms in the hands of certain countries makes it impossible for mankind to live together in terms of obtaining peace.'

This introduction of our resolution in Madrid forms the basis of this Bulletin. The working group reports deal with ways and means of how to achieve a more peaceful world.

Alva Myrdal's article tries to explain why women, but not women alone, should engage themselves in the struggle for peace. It was first published in "Morgon Bris" the journal of our Swedish comrades. It is directed to the Swedish situation, but it also contains many arguments which we as socialist women as a whole should discuss. The article itself has found a wide debate in the latest issue of Morgon Bris, which came out in January of this year.

*Socialist International Women Bulletin*, no. 2 (July–August 1981).

*13th Moon* 5, nos. 1–2 (1977).

*Union Signal* 107, no. 5 (May 1981).

*United Daughters of the Confederacy Magazine* 44, no. 7 (July 1981).

October 1980

# U.S.Woman Engineer®

Magazine of the Society of Women Engineers

*U.S. Woman Engineer* (the magazine of the Society of Women Engineers) 27, no. 1 (October 1980). ©1980 by the Society of Women Engineers.

# WOARPATH

APRIL, 1981 — A Semiannual Newsletter to Supporting Members — Vol. 7, No. 4

## Update: Fighting Rape

*by Berit Lakey*

On my desk sits a simple crystal cube. It bears the inscription, "LDA Award 1980." The crystal is a symbol, a sign that WOAR has "arrived." At its annual fundraising ball last December, The Philadelphia Bar Foundation presented the Louis D. Apothaker Award to Women Organized Against Rape in recognition of WOAR's "contribution to the pursuit of justice in Philadelphia." The $1,500 check that accompanied the Tiffany crystal was much needed and appreciated, but it was the recognition by the legal community that pleased us the most. This recognition will be useful as WOAR continues to advocate for the needs of the victims in the legal system.

Another milestone in WOAR's advocacy work was reached in January, 1981, when Mayor Green announced that the new Sex Crimes Unit in the Police Department was ready to start its work. Mayor Green pledged the formation of this Unit during his campaign as a result of WOAR's lobbying efforts. At the press conference both the Mayor and the Police Commissioner gave WOAR credit for its role in the initiation and in the training of the Unit members. With the Sex Crimes Unit in place, all investigations of sexual assault cases will now be conducted by male/female teams, all of whom have had special training in dealing with the circumstances surrounding these crimes. WOAR is hoping that the Unit will improve the investigation process by having greater awareness of the victims' needs.

When the Pennsylvania Sentencing Commission held hearings in Philadelphia last Fall, Lynn Marks, WOAR's Legal Coordinator, testified in favor of stricter minimum sentences. In our letter explaining our position we recognized that stiffer sentences of rapists will not in themselves be more than a partial solution to the problem of rape. Stiffer sentences will keep dangerous offenders off the street longer, and will also signify to victims that the community recognizes the severity of the crime done to them. Stiffer sentences will *not* rehabilitate the offenders. The time must come soon when the issue of offender rehabilitation is taken seriously in Pennsylvania. Currently, practically nothing is being done.

A minor, but significant, legal action on our part was to join in a suit filed by Women's Law Project and others to stop the Pennsylvania Department of Welfare from cutting off Medicaid abortions. WOAR's particular interest is the fate of girls and women who get pregnant after rape or incestuous abuse. Department of Public Welfare (DPW) regulations demanded that rape be reported to the authorities within 72 hours after the crime was committed, and that incest be reported 72 hours after the pregnancy was diagnosed. In addition to the additional pressures this puts on low-income victims at a time of crisis, the regulations were also terribly

continued next page

*WOARpath* 7, no. 4 (April 1981). ©1981 by Women Organized Against Rape.

*Woman Pioneer* 24, no. 2 (March–April 1979).

**FOR SMART INFLATION-FIGHTERS!**
**75 Ways to Stretch Money**

**BONUS! Pull-Out Super Heroes Super Healthy Cookbook**

JULY 14, 1981

# Woman's Day

69¢

**ALSO!**
- Blueberry Treats
- BARGAIN Barbecues
- 30 Summer Salads
- EXCLUSIVE "Joy of Cooking" Favorites!

plus
- COOKTIPS for the Disaster-Prone
- & Money-Saving Menus
- & our Silver Spoon Winner!

**Decorate with Charming Country Accents**

**Pennywise Fashions in Our Piggybank Boutique**

**Cool & Pretty Hairdos Including Lady Diana's**

**Home-Cooling $$-Savers**

Easy Peach-Melba Shortcake

Contents Page 11

*Woman's Day* 44, no. 9 (July 14, 1981).

# WOMEN & EMPLOYMENT

THE NEWSLETTER OF **NWEE**, NATIONAL WOMEN'S EMPLOYMENT & EDUCATION, INC.

## "To Change Things, We've Got to Take the Initiative Ourselves," Says Texas' First Lady.

*Mrs. William P. Clements, Jr.*

NWEE supporter Rita Clements, wife of Texas governor William Clements, has taken a key role in the overhaul of welfare in the state through her participation in the NWEE Texas Advisory Council on Employment, Training and Welfare Reform. A firm believer in grass-roots level changes, Mrs. Clements will provide leadership in the efforts of the Texas Council, a committee designed to study the problems and opportunities in Texas of low income and women on A.F.D.C. welfare as they seek employment and skills training.

Commenting on what she has already practiced in working to form the Advisory Council, First Lady Clements commented, "If we are going to change things, we've got to take the initiative ourselves."

Outlining the objectives of this new program, part of the ongoing Texas efforts of the National Women's Employment and Education, Inc. (NWEE), Mrs. Clements said, "We've got to look within ourselves and within our communities for the answers, instead of looking to Washington or Austin."

The four major objectives of the Advisory Council's initial program are:
- Work with private sector employers and low-income women, especially those supported by A.F.D.C. Welfare, child support or displaced homemakers, in various Texas communities to lay the groundwork for future implementation of the NWEE Model Program.
- Analysis and evaluation of data from San Antonio, Dallas and El Paso, cities currently served by NWEE.
- Analysis and evaluation of such federally funded welfare programs as CETA, WIN and AFDC and comparatives with NWEE and its private-sector orientation. This effort is designed to examine effective and cost-efficient methods of improving the quality of life of low-income women.
- Development of a community education program aimed at reaching and motivating low-income women and their prospective private sector employers.

*Continued page 2*

## Barbara Bush Observes NWEE Work First Hand

Barbara Bush, wife of Vice President George Bush, got a personal look at the NWEE Model Program in San Antonio. Spending a day of sessions with NWEE Founder and President Lupe Anguiano and staff, Mrs. Bush visited a classroom where she spoke with program participants. Pledging her support to NWEE's struggle to reform the welfare system, Mrs. Bush provided encouragement and inspiration to staff and enrollees alike.

| Special thanks to the following 1981 supporters: | |
|---|---|
| Atlantic Richfield Foundation | $25,000 |
| Exxon | 5,000 |
| Equitable Life Assurance | 5,000 |
| Anonymous Donor | 10,000 |

*Women & Employment* 3, no. 1 (1981).

# Women Artists News

Volume 6 / Number 5      November 1980      $1.50

**Managing the Business of Art**

**Profile of Marcy Pesner**

**Reviews of Exhibitions in New York**

ISSN 0149 7081

*Women Artists News* 6, no. 5 (November 1980). ©*Women Artists News*. Reprinted with permission.

*Women at Work*, no. 2 (Summer 1980). ©1980 by International Labor Organization.

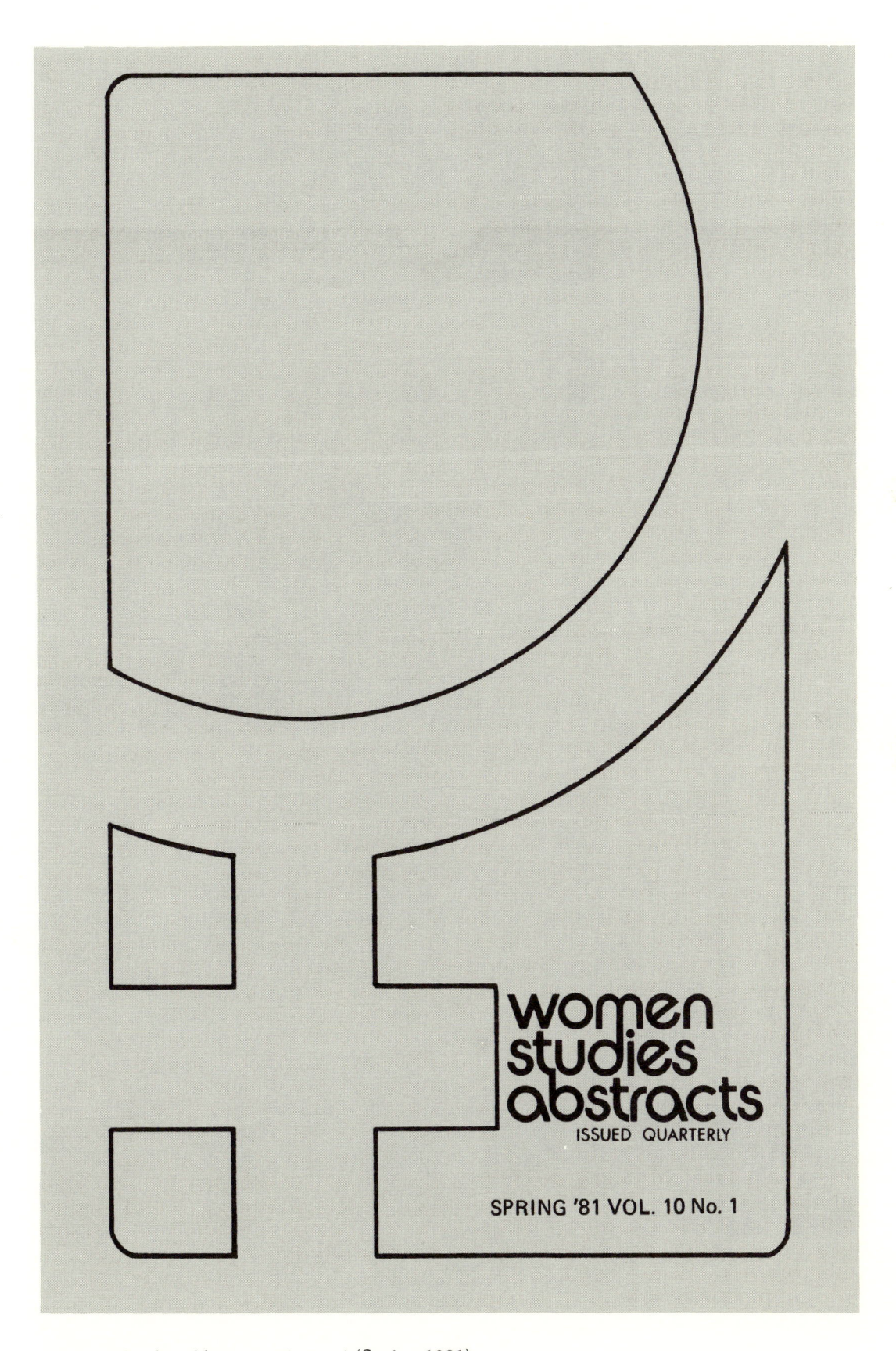

*Women Studies Abstracts* 10, no. 1 (Spring 1981).

# Women's Studies Quarterly

Fall 1981 — Volume IX, Number 3 — $3.50

Formerly *Women's Studies Newsletter*

A Publication of The Feminist Press and The National Women's Studies Association

## IN THIS ISSUE

- 2  Editorial: Controversy, Crisis, and Commitment within NWSA
- 3  Readers' Speakout
- 43 Newsbriefs — *Marian S. Robinson*

*Gerda Lerner* — See Newsbriefs, p. 43.
*Joan Hoff Wilson*

## SPECIAL FEATURES

- 23 Berkshire Conference on the History of Women
   Keynote Address: Politics and Professionalism—Women Historians in the 1980s — *Joan W. Scott*
- 33 American Historical Association Guidelines on Hiring Women Historians in Academia — *Committee on Women Historians, AHA*

*Historians at Vassar, see p. 23.*

## THE 1981 NWSA CONVENTION

- 4  Keynote Address: Disobedience Is What NWSA Is Potentially About — *Adrienne Rich*
- 7  Keynote Address: The Uses of Anger — *Audre Lorde*

### CONSCIOUSNESS-RAISING SESSIONS

- 13 An Overview — *Yolanda T. Moses and Peg Strobel*
- 13 One Facilitator's View — *Gayle Lauradunn*
- 14 An "Experienced" Group — *Pamella Farley*
- 15 For Jewish Women — *Annette Kolodny*
- 16 An Asian-American Woman's View — *Alice Chai*

*Third World Caucus at NWSA — See p. 16.*

### IMPRESSIONS OF THE NWSA CONVENTION

- 16 What About "The Rest of Us?" — *Leila Ahmed*
- 17 An Asian-American Perspective — *Krishna Lahiri*
- 17 NWSA As Metaphor for the United States — *Dearbhal NiCharthaigh*
- 18 Remarks on Two Literary Sessions — *Jo Gillikin*
- 18 Birth and Coming of Age — *Virginia Cyrus*
- 19 Community Education — *Betsy Brinson*
- 20 In Storrs, Connecticut, Without a Pass — *Rita M. Kissen*
- 21 Visual Arts — *Estella Lauter*

## NWSA NEWS AND VIEWS

- 35 NWSA Launches $100 Fund!
- 35 From the Steering Committee
- 36 Resolutions and Recommendations Presented to the NWSA Delegate Assembly · June 3, 1981
- 37 Report from the NWSA Task Force on the Defense of Women's Studies Personnel
- 38 Women's Studies Program Administrators Form Caucus — *Barbara Hillyer Davis*
- 39 We Salute Mariam K. Chamberlain
- 42 NWSA Calendar

---

*Women's Studies Quarterly* 9, no. 3 (Fall 1981). ©1981 by The Feminist Press.

*Wonder Woman*, no. 283 (September 1981). Wonder Woman is a registered trademark of DC Comics Inc. and is used with permission. Illustration ©1981 by DC Comics Inc.

# ZARJA THE DAWN

URADNO GLASILO SLOVENSKE ŽENSKE ZVEZE — OFFICIAL PUBLICATION SLOVENIAN WOMEN'S UNION

NUMBER 9     SEPTEMBER, 1981     VOLUME 53

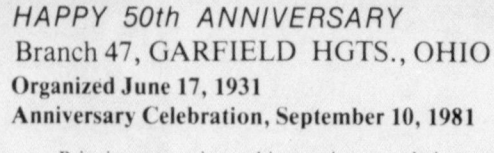

### HAPPY 50th ANNIVERSARY
Branch 47, GARFIELD HGTS., OHIO

**Organized June 17, 1931**
**Anniversary Celebration, September 10, 1981**

Bringing memories and interesting speculation on the occasion that prompted this wonderful picture, we present the officers and members of Br. 47 as they were in 1931. In the front row we can identify the following: beginning second from left, Jennie Pugelj, Recording Secretary, Antonia Dolinar, Treasurer, Mary C. Bates, Vice-President, Louise Zidanic, President, Rev. John J. Oman, Spiritual Advisor, Founder, Marie Prisland, Helen Tomazic, Secretary and Organizer, Ida Brozic, Frances Bricel and Valentina Bizjak, Auditors. They are before the Slovenian National Home in Newburgh.

The branch won first place in the membership campaign that year with Mrs. Tomazic herself enrolling 104 members in less than one month.

*Zarja/The Dawn* 53, no. 9 (September 1981).

1904-May 26, 1906. Frequency varies: monthly, Nov. 1, 1883-Nov., 1887; weekly, Dec. 10, 1887-Apr. 18, 1896; bi-weekly, May 2, 1896-Nov. 30, 1901; weekly, Dec. 14, 1901-Apr. 9, 1904. Editor: Clara Bewick Colby. Subject focus: rights, politics, pro-suffrage. Other holding institutions: DLC (DLC), MCR-S Schlesinger Library on the History of Women in America, Radcliffe College, Cambridge, MA).

| | | |
|---|---|---|
| Hist | v.1,n.2-v.25,n.15; Nov., 1883-Dec. 12, 1908 | JK/1880/W7 |
| Mem | v.1, n.2-v.25,n.21; Nov., 1883-Mar. 6, 1909 | Microforms |

1282 <u>Woman's Voice</u>. 1970//? Unknown. Last issue 19 pages. Available on microfilm: Herstory. Published by Women's Committee-Socialist Workers Party, Boston, MA. Subject focus: socialism, biographies.

| | | |
|---|---|---|
| Hist | v.1, n.1; Jan., 1970 | Microforms Her. 2, R 17 |

1283 <u>The Woman's Voice and Public School Champion</u>. 1890-1907//? Monthly. Last issue 4 pages, last volume 12 pages. Line drawings, commercial advertising. Available on microfilm: ResP. Published by Woman's Publishing Company, Boston, MA. Frequency varies: weekly, Jan. 9, 1890-May 15, 1897. Editor: Eliza Trask Hill. Subject focus: public schools, homemakers. Other holding institution: MB (Boston Public Library).

| | | |
|---|---|---|
| Mem | v.1, n.1-v.17,n.3; Jan. 9, 1890-Apr., 1907 | Microforms |

1284 <u>Woman's Way</u>. 1973-1974//? Irregular. Last issue 10 pages. Line drawings. Available on microfilm: Herstory. Published in San Anselmo, CA. Subject focus: employment, health.

| | | |
|---|---|---|
| Hist | May/June, 1973 | Microforms Her. 2, R 17 |
| | Dec., 1973-Apr., 1974? | Her. 2 UP, R12 |

1285 <u>Woman's Welfare</u>. 1902-1905//. Quarterly. Last issue 62 pages, last volume 134 pages, size 18 x 23. Line drawings, photographs, commercial advertising. Available on microfilm: ResP. Published by the National Cash Register, Dayton, OH. Title varies: as The Century Club Advance, Jan./Mar., 1903. Editors: Maude Kendall, Jan./Mar., 1903-Apr., 1905; Annie Marion MacLean, Nov., 1905. Subject focus: working women, working conditions, career development, workers. Other holding institution: CtY (YUS).

| | | |
|---|---|---|
| Hist | v.1,n.2,v.2,n.1, 3-4, v.2,n.1,3; Jan./Mar., 1903, Mar., 1904, Oct., 1904-Jan., Apr., Nov., 1905 | HFSPW83/ .7W842 (Cutter) |
| | v.1, n.3; Apr./June, 1903 | KWX/WO (Cutter) |
| Mem | v.1, n.4-v.3,n.3; Oct., 1903-Nov., 1905 | Microforms |

1286 <u>Woman's Work</u>. 1886-1924//. Monthly. OCLC 1590828, 1716919. Last issue 24 pages, last volume 290 pages, size 24 x 16. Line drawings, photographs. Self-indexed (1886-1921). Available on microfilm: McA. Published by The Woman's Board of Foreign Missions of the Presbyterian Church U.S.A., New York, NY. Title varies: as Woman's Work for Woman and Our Mission Field, Dec., 1885-June, 1890; Woman's Work for Woman, July, 1890-Dec., 1904. Subject focus: Christianity, missions, social services. Other holding institutions: [Indiana Union List of Serials, Indianapolis, IN] (ILS), MiMtpT (EZC), [University of Minnesota Union List, Minneapolis, MN] (MUL), PPi (CPL), [Pittsburgh Regional Library Center-Union List, Pittsburgh, PA] (QPR).

| | | |
|---|---|---|
| Hist | v.1,n.1-v.34,n.12; Dec., 1885-Dec., 1921 | DS/.7W8 (Cutter) |
| | v.1, n1-v.39,n.3; Dec., 1885-Mar., 1924 | Microforms |

Woman's Work for Woman. New York, NY

see <u>Woman's Work</u>. New York, NY

1287 <u>Woman's Work for Woman</u>. 1875-1885//. Monthly. Last issue 36 pages, last volume 400 pages, size 24 x 16. Line drawings, photographs. Self-indexed (1875-1885). Published by Woman's Foreign Missionary Society of the Presbyterian Church, Philadelphia, PA. Editors: Miss J.C. Thompson, Mar., 1875-June, 1883; Mary Lombard, July, 1883-Sep., 1885. Subject focus: Christianity, missions, social services.

| | | |
|---|---|---|
| Hist | v.5,n.1-v.15, n.11; Mar., 1875-Nov., 1885 | DS/7W8 (Cutter) |

Woman's Work for Woman and Our Mission Field. New York, NY

see Woman's Work. New York, NY

1288 Woman's Work in Heathen Lands. 1883-1890//? Irregular. Last issue 32 pages. Available on microfilm: ResP. Published by J. Menzies & Co., Edinburgh, Scotland. Editors: J. Parlane and R. Parlane. Subject focus: Free Church of Scotland, missions. Other holding institution: CtY (YUS).

| Mem | n.1-35; Apr., 1883- Oct., 1890 | Microforms |

1289 The Woman's World. 1888-1890//? Monthly. Last issue 48 pages, last volume 664 pages. OCLC 1770069, 5341672. Available on microfilm: ResP. Published by Cassell & Co., Ltd. London, England. Editor: Oscar Fingall O'Flahertie Wills Wilde. Subject focus: biographies, history, fiction, poetry, fashion. Other holding institutions: AzTeS (AZS), CtY (YUS), FGULS (GUL), [Indiana Union List of Serials, Indianapolis, IN] (ILS), InU (IUL), MiMtpT (EZC), [University of Minnesota Union List, Minneapolis, MN] (MUL), MnSCC (MNE), NNepaSU (ZLM), [Central New York Library Resources Council, Syracuse, NY (SRR), OAkU (AKR), PPi (CPL), [Pittsburgh Regional Library Center, Union List, Pittsburgh, PA] (QPR), ScRhW (SWW), TxDW (IWU).

| Mem | v.1,n.1-v.3, n.[12]; Jan., 1888- Dec., 1890 | Microforms |

1290 Woman's World. 1958-1971//? Quarterly. OCLC 1590057. LC sar63-890. Last issue 64 pages, last volume 450 pages, size 21 x 28. Line drawings, photographs, some in color, commercial advertising. Published in Karachi, Pakistan. Frequency varies: bi-monthly, Jan./Feb.-Nov./Dec., 1967; irregular, Jan., 1968-Dec., 1970. Editor: Mujeeb M. Akram. Subject focus: fashion, beauty care, health, recreation, fiction. Other holding institution: [University of Minnesota Union List, Minneapolis, MN] (MUL).

| Mem | v.10, n.1/2- v.14, n.1; Jan./Feb., 1967- Jan?, 1971 | AP/W869/W927 |

1291 Woman's World. 1971-1972//? Irregular. OCLC 2269592. Last issue 24 pages. Line drawings, photographs. Available on microfilm: Herstory. Published in New York, NY. Subject focus: employment, politics, pro-abortion, law, ecology.

| Hist | v.1,n.1-2; Apr. 15-July/Aug., 1971 | Microforms Her. 1, R 4 |
| | v.1,n.3-v.2,n.1; Nov./Dec., 1971- July/Sep., 1972 | Her. 1 UP,R17 |

1292 Womansmith. 1975-1977//? Quarterly. Last issue 48 pages, size 17 x 21. Line drawings, photographs. Published in Massapequa, NY. Subject focus: poetry, art, photography.

| RBR | v.1, n.1; Fall, 1975 | Circulation |

1293 Womanspace Journal. 1973//. Bi-monthly. Last issue 40 pages, size 21 x 28. Line drawings, photographs, commercial advertising. Available on microfilm: Herstory. Published by Womanspace-West Coast Art Center, Los Angeles, CA. Title varies: as Womanspace, Feb./Mar., 1973. Editor: Ruth Iskin. Subject focus: rights, arts.

| Hist | v.1, n.1-3; Feb./Mar.- Summer, 1973 | Microforms Her. 2, R 17 |
| Mem | v.1, n.1-3; Feb./Mar.- Summer, 1973 | AP/W868/J82 |

Womb at the Top. Rockville, MD

see From N.O.W. On. Rockville, MD

1294 Women. 1970//? Irregular. OCLC 2269597. Last issue 6 pages. Line drawings. Available on microfilm: Herstory. Published by Philadelphia Area Women's Liberation Movement, Philadelphia, PA. Subject focus: pro-abortion, politics, child care, peace movement, consciousness raising.

| Hist | v.1, n.1-8?; Mar. 30-Dec., 1970 | Microforms Her. 1, R 22 |

1295 Women: A Berkshire Women's Liberation Newsletter. 1972-1974//? Irregular. Last issue 21 pages. Line drawings. Available on microfilm: Herstory. Published by Berkshire Women's Liberation, Lenox, MA. Subject focus: rights, lobbying.

| Hist | v.1, n.1, v.2, n.2, v.3,n.3; Feb. 28, 1972, Apr. 21, May 31, 1973 | Microforms Her. 2, R 17 |

|  |  |  |
|---|---|---|
|  | v.2, n.4-v.3, n.4;<br>July 10, 1973-<br>June/July, 1974 | Her. 2 UP, R12 |

1296  Women: A Journal of Liberation. 1969. Quarterly. $6 for individuals, $15 for institutions. Women: A Journal of Liberation, 3028 Greenmount Avenue, Baltimore, MD 21218. (301) 235-5245. ISSN 0043-7433. OCLC 1696334. LC 73-13942. Last issue 66 pages, last volume 184 pages, size 22 x 28. Line drawings, photographs. Indexed in: Alternative Press Index; Women Studies Abstracts. Available on microfilm: McP (1969-1971), Herstory (1971-1974), UnM (1971-1974). Frequency varies: 5 times a year, Fall, 1969-Winter, 1969-1970. Subject focus: rights, politics, child rearing, history, fiction, poetry, art. Other holding institutions: ArU (AFU), AzFU (AZN), AzTeS (AZS), CSt (Stanford University), CLU (CLU), CU-S (CUS), CtW (WLU), DLC (DLC,NSD), FBoU (FGM), FJUNF (FNP), [Indiana Union List of Serials, Indianapolis, IN] (ILS), InU (IUL), KSteC (KKQ), KyU (KUK), MBNU (NED), MCR-S (Schlesinger Library on the History of Women in America, Radcliffe College, Cambridge, MA), MBTI (BTI), MBU (BOS), MH-AH (BHA), MNtcA (BAN), MWelC (WEL), MdBJ (JHE), MiEM (EEM), MwGrC (EXC), MiMtpT (EZC), [University of Minnesota Union List, Minneapolis, MN] (MUL), NcRS (NRC), NcWfSB (NVS), NbU (LDL), NmLcU (IRU), [SUNY OCLC, Albany, NY] (TQW), [New York State Union List, Albany, NY] (NYS), [Western New York Library Resources Council, Buffalo, NY] (VZX), NCH (YHM), NFQC (XQM), NGcCC (VVX), NIC (COO), NNR (ZXC), NOneoU (ZBM), NPV (VXW), NPurMC (VYE), NR (YQR), NRU (RRR), NSufR (VVR), [Central New York Library Resources Council, Syracuse, NY] (SRR), OKentU (KSU), OO (OBE), OYU (YNG), PBL (LYU), PBm (BMC), PNwC (WFN), PPD (DXU), PPiU (PIT), [Pittsburgh Regional Library Center-Union List, Pittsburgh, PA] (QPR), TxCM (TXA), [AMIGOS Union List of Serials, Dallas, TX] (IUC), TxShA (IAU), VtMiM (MDY).

|  |  |  |
|---|---|---|
| Hist | v.1,n.1-v.2,n.3;<br>Fall, 1969-<br>Spring, 1971 | Microforms<br>Her. 1 R 12 |
|  | v.2,n.4-v.3,n.3;<br>Fall, 1971-<br>Summer, 1972 | Her. 1 UP, R12 |
|  | June 20, 1974 | Her. CUP, R 7 |
|  | v.1, n.1-<br>Fall, 1969- | HQ/1101/W35 |
| Coll | Current Issues<br>Only | Women's<br>Reading Area |
| Wom Ed<br>Res | v.1,n.3,v.3,n.3-4;<br>Summer, 1970,<br>Summer, 1972-<br>Fall?, 1974 | Circulation |

|  |  |  |
|---|---|---|
| Wom St | v.2, n.1,4-<br>Fall, 1970,<br>Spring, 1971 | Reading Room |
| Mem | v.1, n.1-<br>Fall, 1969- | AP/W8693 |
| MPL | v.2, n.1-<br>Fall, 1970- | Literature<br>and Social<br>Sciences<br>Section |

1297  Women Against Violence in Pornography & Media Newspage. 1977. Monthly. Women against Violence in Pornography & Media Newspage, P.O. Box 14614, San Francisco, CA. (415) 552-2709. Last issue 4 pages, size 22 x 28. Line drawings, photographs. Subject focus: pornography, violence.

|  |  |  |
|---|---|---|
| Wom Ed<br>Res | v.3, n.3-<br>Apr., 1979- | Circulation |

1298  Women and Art. 1971//? Unknown. Last issue 20 pages. Line drawings, photographs, commercial advertising. Available on microfilm: Herstory. Published in New York, NY. Subject focus: art, students, museums, art criticism.

|  |  |  |
|---|---|---|
| Hist | Winter, 1971 | Microforms<br>Her. 2, R 17 |

1299  Women and Employment. 1978. Irregular. Lupe Anguiano, editor, Women and Employment, P.O. Box 9385, San Antonio, TX 78204. Last issue 8 pages, size 22 x 28. Photographs. Published by National Women's Employment and Education Inc. Subject focus: employment, poor people.

|  |  |  |
|---|---|---|
| Wom Ed<br>Res | v.1, n.1-<br>July/Aug., 1978- | Circulation |

1300  Women & Film. 1972-1975//? Tri-annual. OCLC 1770070. Last issue 128 pages, size 20 x 27. Line drawings, photographs. Available on microfilm: Herstory (1972-1973). Published by Persistence of Vision, Inc., Berkeley, CA. Editors: Siew-Hwa Beh and Sawnie Sayler. Subject focus: film reviews, filmmaking. Other holding institutions: (CLSU (CSL), InU (IUL), MBU (BOS), [University of Minnesota Union List, Minneapolis, MN] (MUL), NFQC (XQM), NSbSU (YSM), NcU (NOC), OAU (OUN).

|  |  |  |
|---|---|---|
| Hist | v.1, n.1-4;<br>Spring, 1972-?,<br>1973 | Microforms<br>Her. 2, R 17 |
| Mem | v.1,n.1-v.2,n.7;<br>Spring, 1972-<br>Summer, 1975 | AP/W86935/A64 |

|  | Wom St | v.2, n.7;<br>Summer, 1975 | Reading Room |
|---|---|---|---|
|  | WCTR | v.1,n.1-v.2,n.7;<br>Spring, 1972-<br>Summer, 1975 | Circulation |

1301 Women & Health. 1974. Quarterly. $20 for individuals, $36 for institutions. Helen S. Marieskind, editor, Women & Health, c/o The Haworth Press, 149 Fifth Avenue, New York, NY 10010. Last issue 112 pages, last volume 312 pages, size 15 x 23. Commercial advertising. Indexed in: Excerpta Medica; Sociological Abstracts, Hospital Literature Index; Women's Studies Abstracts, Psychological Abstracts. Subject focus: medicine, health.

|  | CHS | v.4, n.1-<br>Spring, 1977- | Periodicals<br>Section |
|---|---|---|---|

1302 Women & Health. 1976. Bi-monthly. Ellie Engler, editor, Women & Health, SUNY/College at Old Westbury, New York, NY 11568. ISSN 0363-0242. OCLC 2447206. LC 76-648355. Last issue 32 pages, size 22 x 28. Published by the Biological Sciences Program, State University of New York, College at Old Westbury, Old Westbury, NY. Previous editor: Helen S. Marieskind, Jan./Feb.-July/Aug., 1977. Subject focus: medicine, health. Other holding institutions: AAP (AAA), ABAU (ABC), CLobS (CLO), CU-Riv (CRU), DCU (DCU), DGW (DGW), DLC (DLC), DSI (SMI), FTS (FHM), GASU (GSU), GEU (EMU), GEU-M (EMM), HU (HUH), InU (IUL), InU-M (IUM), MBNU (NED), MShM (MTH), [University of Minnesota Union List, Minneapolis, MN] (MUL), MoSW (STU), NbOU (NBU), NbU (LDL), [New York State Union List, Albany, NY] (NYS), NBM (VVD), NCortU (YCM), NDFM (VZE), NIC (COO), NNepaSU (ZLM), NSbSU (YSM), NSbSU-H (VZB), OU (OSU), [AMIGOS Union List of Serials, Dallas, TX] (IUC), TxDW (IWU), TxU (IXA), ViNO (VOD), ViRCU (VRC), VtU (VTU).

|  | CHS | v.1, n.1-<br>Jan./Feb., 1976- | Circulation |
|---|---|---|---|
|  | Wom St | v.2, n.1-<br>July/Aug., 1977- | Reading Room |

1303 Women & Health Roundtable. 1977. Irregular. Women & Health Roundtable, 2000 P Street NW, Suite 403, Washington, DC 20036. Last issue 4 pages, size 22 x 28. Published by The Federation of Organizations for Professional Women. Subject focus: lobbying, health.

|  | Wom Ed<br>Res | v.1, n.10-<br>Dec., 1977- | Circulation |
|---|---|---|---|

1304 Women & Language News. 1976. Tri-annual. $3 for individuals and institutions. Women and Language News, Linguistics Department, Stanford University, Stanford, CA 94305. Last issue 24 pages, size 22 x 28. Subject focus: sexism in language, linguistics, research.

|  | Wom St | v.1, n.1-<br>Jan., 1976- | Reading Room |
|---|---|---|---|

1305 Women and Law: Articles Collected by Hofstra Law Women's Organization. 1978. Semi-annual. Women and Law, School of Law, Hofstra University, Hempstead, NY. OCLC 4937998. LC sc79-4480. Last issue 110 pages, size 17 x 26. Subject focus: law, rights, pro-abortion. Other holding institutions: [San Diego County Law Library, San Diego, CA] (CDL), FMU-L (FML), HU (HUH), Ku-L (KFL), LNL-L (LLT), LU-L (LUL), [University of Minnesota Union List, Minneapolis, MN] (MUL), MnU-L (MLL), NIC (COO), NcDL (NDL), NmU-L (NML), Ok (OKD), WU-L (GZL).

|  | Law | Fall-<br>Winter, 1978- | Circulation |
|---|---|---|---|

1306 Women & Literature. 1972. Quarterly. $10 for individuals, $15 for institutions. Janet M. Todd, editor, Women & Literature, Department of English, Douglass College, Rutgers University, New Brunswick, NJ 08903. ISSN 0147-1759. OCLC 2715989. LC sc77-1293, 78-645103. Last issue 54 pages, last volume 118 pages, size 15 x 23. Line drawings, commercial advertising. Indexed in: Abstracts of English Studies; MLA International Bibliography; Women Studies Abstracts. Available on microfilm: UnM (1975-1976); JAI (1973-1978). Title varies: as Mary Wollstonecraft Newsletter, July, 1972-Dec., 1973; as Mary Wollstonecraft Journal, May, 1974. Frequency varies: semi-annual, Spring, 1976-Fall, 1978. Subject focus: literature, writers, literary criticism. Other holding institutions: ABAU (ABC), AU (ALM), AzTeS (AZS), CLU (CLU), COU-DA (COA), CtY (YUS), CSt (Stanford University), DLC (DLC), DeU (DLM), FPeU (FWA), FU (FUG), GAT (GAT), GAuA (GJG), GU (GUA), IU (UIU), InND (IND), InU (IUL), KyU (KUK), LLafS (LWA), LNT (LRU), LNU (LNU), LU (LUU), MCM (MYG), MBNU (NED), MH (HLS,HUL), MWelC (WEL), MdBJ (JHE), MdBt (TSC), MeB (BBH), MiDW (EYW), MiEM (EEM), MiMtpT (EZC), MiYEM (EYE), [University of Minnesota Union List, Minneapolis, MN] (MUL), MnSthos (MNF), MoU (MUU), [New York State Union List, Albany, NY] (NYS), NAlU (NAM), NBrockU (XBM), NCH (YHM), NDFM (VZE), NFQC (XQM), NIC (COO), NNR (ZXC), NPV (VXW), NRU (RRR), NSbSU (YSM), [Central New York Library Resources Council, Syracuse, NY] (SRR), NSyU (SYB), NcWsU (EWF), NdU (UND), NbU (LDL), NhD (DRB), OAkU (AKR), OOxM (MIA), OTU (TOL), OkAdE (ECO), OkS (OKS), OKTU (OKT), PPD (DXU), PU (PAU), ScRhW (SWW), ScU (SUC), TxArU (IUA), TxCM (TXA), [AMIGOS Union List of Serials, Dallas, TX] (IUC), TxDW (IWU), ViBlbv (VPI), ViRCU (VRC), ViRU (VRU), ViW (VWM).

|  | Mem | v.1, n.1-<br>July, 1972- | PN/471/M3 |
|---|---|---|---|

|  | Wom St | v.4, n.1-<br>Spring, 1976- | Reading Room |

1307 <u>Women and Missions.</u> 1924-1946 //. Monthly. OCLC 2451654. Last issue 30 pages, last volume 288 pages, size 17 x 26. Line drawings, photographs. Self-indexed (1924-1944). Published by Woman's Committees of the Boards of Missions of the Presbyterian Church in the U.S.A., New York, NY. Editors: Lucia P. Towne, Nov., 1925-Nov., 1940; Florence Hayes, Mar., 1941-Jan., 1944. Subject focus: Christianity, missions, social services. Other holding institutions: [University of Minnesota Union List, Minneapolis, MN] (MUL), NcU (NOC), PPi (CPL), PPiPT (PKT), [Pittsburgh Regional Library Center-Union List, Pittsburgh, PA] (QPR).

|  | Hist | v.40, n.2-[n.s.]<br>v.20, n.10;<br>May, 1924-<br>Jan., 1944 | DS/7W9<br>(Cutter) |

1308 <u>Women & Politics.</u> 1980. Quarterly. $24 for individuals, $48 for institutions. Sarah Slavin Schramm, editor, Women & Politics, 1265 Birchwood Blvd., Pittsburgh, PA 15206. Business address: 149 5th Avenue, New York, NY 10010. (212) 228-2800. ISSN 0195-7732. OCLC 5661577. LC 80-644752, sn79-8972. Last issue 97 pages, size 21 x 24. Self-indexed. Published by the Haworth Press, Inc., New York, NY. Subject focus: sexism in education, Equal Rights Amendment, politics, sexism. Other holding institutions: AzTeS (AZS), CSdS (CDS), CSUuP (CPS), CsjU (CSJ), DGW (DGW), DLC (DLC), FBoU (FGM), HU (HUH), KyLoU (KLG), MnDuU (MND), NIC (COO), NSbSU (YSM), OOxM (MIA), TxDW (IWU), TxWicM (TMI), ViNO (VOD), WaU (WAU), NChB (BXM).

|  | Mem | v.1, n.1-<br>Spring, 1980- | Periodicals<br>Room |

1309 <u>Women and Revolution.</u> 1971. Tri-annual. $4 for individuals and institutions. Women and Revolution, Spartacist Publishing Co., P.O. Box 1377 G.P.O., New York, NY 10001. (212) 925-2428. OCLC 2269598. Last issue 8 pages. Line drawings, photographs. Available on microfilm: Herstory (1971). Published by Women's Commission of the Spartacist League. Place of publication varies: San Francisco, CA, May/June-Sep./Oct., 1971. Subject focus: radicalism, socialism, rights, child care. Other holding institutions: CLU (CLU), CU-UC (UCU).

|  | Hist | v.1, n.1-2;<br>May/June-<br>Sep./Oct., 1971 | Microforms<br>Her. 1 R 4 |
|  |  | v.1, n.1-<br>May/June, 1971- | Circulation |

1310 <u>Women and Work.</u> 1972. Monthly. Last issue 8 pages, size 22 x 28. Line drawings. Available on microfilm: McA (1975-); Herstory (1973-1974). Published by the United States Department of Labor, Office of Information, Publications and Reports, Washington, DC 20210. Editor: Shelley Nopper. Subject focus: employment, job training, equal pay for equal work, law.

|  | Hist | n.3-6;<br>Mar.-June, 1973 | Microforms<br>Her. 2, R 17 |
|  |  | July, 1973-<br>June, 1974 | Her. 2 UP,R12 |
|  | MPL | Mar., 1974- | Business and<br>Science<br>Section |
|  | Wom Ed<br>Res | Apr., 1973- | Circulation |

1311 <u>Women and the City's Work.</u> 1915-1923//? Weekly. Last issue 34 pages, last volume 170 pages. Line drawings. Available on microfilm: ResP. Published by the Women's Municipal League of the City of New York, New York, NY. Editor: Marian Booth Kelley. Subject focus: New York City, public schools, parks. Other holding institution: IC (UIU).

|  | Mem | v.1, n.1-v.8,<br>n.35;<br>Nov. 8, 1915-<br>May 29, 1923 | Microforms |

1312 <u>Women and Work Newsletter.</u> 1978. Irregular. Women and Work Newsletter, Women's Bureau, Department of Employment and Youth Affairs, 239 Bourke Street, Melbourne 3000, Australia. Last issue 4 pages, size 22 x 28. Subject focus: law, workers, employment.

|  | Soc Work | v.2, n.2-<br>Apr., 1979- | Circulation |

1313 <u>Women are Human.</u> 1972-1974//? Monthly. OCLC 4041859. LC sc80-948. Last issue 4 pages, last volume 146 pages. Line drawings. Self-indexed (at end of each volume). Available on microfilm; Herstory. Published by Maid Library, Ohio State University, Columbus, OH. Subject focus: education, politics. Other holding institutions: GU (GUA), InU (IUL), [University of Minnesota Union List, Minneapolis, MN] (MUL), NBronSL (VVS), OU (OSU).

|  | Hist | v.1, n.1-v.2,<br>n.25;<br>May 26, 1972-<br>June 29, 1973 | Microforms<br>Her. 2, R17 |

v.2,n.26-v.3,            Her. 2 UP,R12
July 6, 1973-
June 21, 1974

Women ARE People. Pittsburgh, PA

   see N.O.W. Hear This! Pittsburgh, PA

1314 Women are Powerful. 1971//? Irregular. OCLC 2269599. Last issue 8 pages. Line drawings. Available on microfilm: Herstory. Published by Riverside Chapter National Organization for Women, Riverside, CA. Subject focus: child care, peace movement, lobbying, Equal Rights Amendment, rights, politics, welfare.

Hist     v.1, n.1-3;     Microforms
          Mar. 22-        Her. 1, R 19
          June 8, 1971

1315 Women Artists Newsletter. 1975. Monthly. $7 for individuals, $10 for institutions. Cindy Lyle, editor, Women Artists Newsletter, P.O. Box 3304, Grand Central Station, New York, NY 10017. ISSN 0149-7081. OCLC 3534670. LC sc78-127. Last issue 14 pages, size 22 x 28. Line drawings, photographs. Subject focus: artists. Other holding institutions: CtY (YUS), DNGA (NGA), FJUNF (FNP), IU (UIU), InIU (IUP), MNS (SNN), MiKW (EKW), [University of Minnesota Union List, Minneapolis, MN] (MUL), MnStpeG (MNG), NA1fC (YDM), NSbSU (YSM), NcU (NOC), NhD (DRB), OAkU (AKR), PPiU (PIT), ViRCU (VRC), WMUW (GZN).

Coll     Current Issues    Women's
         Only             Reading Area

1316 Women as Women as Women. 1971-1974//? Bi-monthly. OCLC 2269637. Last issue 18 pages. Line drawings. Available on microfilm: Herstory. Published by Kansas City Women's Liberation Union, Kansas City, MO. Title varies: as Women's Liberation Union Newsletter, Mar., 1970-Jan./Feb., 1974. Frequency varies: monthly, Mar., 1970-Dec., 1972. Subject focus: pro-abortion, media, collectives, poetry, lobbying, health food, rights, child care, film reviews.

Hist     v.1, n.8-10;    Microforms
          Mar., May, 1971  Her. 1, R 23

          v.2,n.6-v.3,n.3;  Her. 1 UP, R18
          Dec., 1972-
          June/July, 1973

          v.3,n.4-v.4,n.1;  Her. CUP, R 8
          June/July, 1973-
          May/June, 1974

1317 Women at Work. 1973-1974//? Irregular. Last issue 5 pages. Available on microfilm: Her-

story. Published by Women's Bureau-Canada, Department of Labour, Ottawa, Ontario, Canada. Subject focus: rights, workers, lobbying, civil service. In French (100%).

Hist     v.1,n.2-v.2,n.2;  Microforms
          Dec., 1973-     Her. 3, R 5
          Apr., 1974

1318 Women at Work. 1977. Semi-annual. $5.35 for individuals and institutions. Krishna Ahooja-Patel, editor, Women at Work, CH-1211, Geneva 22, Switzerland. OCLC 3722864. LC 78-641944. Last issue 34 pages, last volume 64 pages, size 16 x 24. Published by The Office for Women Workers, International Labor Office. Frequency varies: tri-annual, Mar.-Nov., 1977. Subject focus: labor law, workers, employment, wages. Other holding institutions: CLSU (CSL), CLU (CLU), CLobS (CLO), CSdS (CDS), CtY (YUS), DGW-L (GWL), DL (ULL), DLC (DLC), [Environmental Protection Agency-Headquarters Library, Washington, DC] (EJB), FTaSU (FDA), FU (FUG), GASU (GSU), IU (UIU), InIU (IUP), KMK (KKS), LU (LUU), MCM (MYG), MBNU (NED), MWelC (WEL), MIEM (EEM), MiU (EYM), NBu (VHB), NIC (COO), NSsS (VZS), NSyU (SYB), NbU (LDL), NhD (DRB), OC1W (CWR), OU (OSU), PMb (BMC), OCLS (REC), PSC (PSC), TxHU (TXH), TxU (IXA), UU (UUM).

LTC     v.1,n.1-        Periodicals
          Mar., 1977-     Section

Mem     v.1, n.1-       Periodicals
          Mar., 1977-     Room

1319 Women Can. 1969-1975//? Irregular. ISSN 0016-5476, 1319-1001. OCLC 2242112, 2442111, 2265770. LC cn76-302365, cn75-34720, cn75-34719. Last issue 16 pages. Line drawings, photographs. Available on microfilm: MCL, Herstory (1969-1974), WHi (1974). Published by the Vancouver Women's Caucus, Vancouver, British Columbia, Canada. Title varies: as Pedestal, Winter, 1969-Feb., 1974. Subject focus: rights, child rearing, motherhood, health, poetry, self-help. Other holding institutions: CaOONLY (NLC), MCR-S (Schlesinger Library on the History of Women in America, Radcliffe College, Cambridge, MA), [University of Minnesota Union List, Minneapolis, MN] (MUL), NFQC (XQM), OKentU (KSU), WMUW (GZN).

Hist     v.1,n.1-v.3,n.8;  Microforms
          Fall, 1969-     Her. 1, R 3
          Aug./Sep., 1971

          v.3,n.9-v.5,n.5;  Her. 1 UP,
          Oct., 1971-     R 13-14
          June, 1973

          v.5,n.6,v.6,n.1;  Her. CUP, R 6
          Oct., 1973-
          Jan., 1974

*Women's Periodicals and Newspapers*

|  | v.1,n.2-v.6,n.4;<br>Winter, 1969-<br>May/July, 1974 | Microforms |
|---|---|---|
| Mem | v.6,n.2-v.7,n.2;<br>Feb., 1974-<br>Mar./Apr., 1975 | Microforms |

1320 <u>Women Caucus Newsletter</u>. 1974//? Irregular. Last issue 2 pages. Line drawings. Available on microfilm: Herstory. Published by South New England Conference, United Methodist Church, Wellesley, MA. Subject focus: Christianity, Methodism.

| Hist | v.1, n.1, 3;<br>Oct., 1973,<br>May, 1974 | Microforms<br>Her. 3, R 5 |
|---|---|---|

1321 <u>Women for Change</u>. 1971-1974//? Monthly. Last issue 8 pages, last volume 132 pages. Line drawings, photographs, commercial advertising. Available on microfilm: Herstory. Published by Women For Change Center, Dallas, TX. Frequency varies: monthly, Nov., 1971-May, 1973; semi-monthly, June/July, 1973. Subject focus: counseling, child care, employment, higher education, politics, media.

| Hist | v.1,n.1-v.2,<br>n.8/9;<br>Nov., 1971-<br>June/July, 1973 | Microforms<br>Her. 2, R 17 |
|---|---|---|
|  | v.2, n.10-v.3,n.7;<br>Aug., 1973-<br>June, 1974 | Her. 2 UP, R12 |

1322 <u>Women for Legislative Action Bulletin</u>. 1972-1974//? Monthly. Last issue 12 pages. Line drawings. Available on microfilm: Herstory. Published by Women for Legislative Action, Los Angeles, CA. Editor: Eva Korn. Subject focus: politics, amnesty, peace movement, lobbying.

| Hist | v.1,n.10-v.3,n.6;<br>June, 1972-<br>June, 1973 | Microforms<br>Her. 2, R 17 |
|---|---|---|
|  | v.3,n.7-v.4,n.6;<br>Sep., 1973-<br>June, 1974 | Her. 2 UP, R12 |

<u>Women for Peace Newsletter</u>. Berkeley, CA

see <u>East Bay Women for Peace Newsletter</u>. Berkeley, CA

1323 <u>Women Geoscientists Committee Newsletter</u>. 1974. Semi-annual. Denise D. Pieratti, editor, Women Geoscientists Committee Newsletter, Woodward-Clyde Consultants, P.O. Box 1149, Orange, CA 92668. Business address: American Geological Institute, Women Geoscientists Committee, 5205 Leesburg Pike, Falls Church, VA 22041. Last issue 6 pages, size 22 x 28. Line drawings. Subject focus: geoscientists.

| Geology | n.1-<br>Oct., 1974- | Circulation |
|---|---|---|

1324 <u>Women Hold Up Half the Sky</u>. 1974//? Irregular. Last issue 20 pages. Line drawings. Available on microfilm: Herstory. Published by New People's Center, Yokosuka, Japan. Subject focus: prostitution, child care, poetry, soldiers, Afro-Americans.

| Hist | n.1-3;<br>Feb.?-May, 1974 | Microforms<br>Her. 3, R 5 |
|---|---|---|

1325 <u>Women in Action</u>. 1973-1974//? Monthly. Last issue 6 pages. Line drawings. Available on microfilm: Herstory. Published in Glasgow, Scotland. Subject focus: pro-abortion, employment, sexism, birth control, rights.

| Hist | Oct., 1973-<br>June, 1974 | Microforms<br>Her. 3, R 5 |
|---|---|---|

1326 <u>Women in Action</u>. 1967//? Monthly. Last issue 10 pages, size 18 x 22. Line drawings. Published by Women in Action, New York, NY. Subject focus: rights, radicalism.

| Hist | n.2;<br>Apr., 1967 | Pam 71-905 |
|---|---|---|

1327 <u>Women in Action</u>. 1969-1978//? Bi-monthly. ISSN 0090-2489. OCLC 1770071. LC sn79-9619. Last issue 8 pages, last volume 48 pages, size 22 x 28. Line drawings, photographs. Available on microfilm: Herstory (1971-1974). Published by The U.S. Civil Service Commission, Federal Women's Program, Washington, DC. Subject focus: government workers, civil service. Other holding institutions: COU-DA (COA), CtHT (TYC), DC (DCL), DI (UDI), I (SPI), ICD-L (IBC), ICharE (IAD), IU (UIU), KEmT (KKR), MMiltC (CUM), [University of Minnesota Union List, Minneapolis, MN] (MUL), MoStcL (MOQ), NBu (VHB), NCortU (YCM), NEE (VXE), NGenoU (YGM), NR (YQR), OAkU (AKR), OKentU (KSU), Ok (OKD), OkTU (OKT), OkU (OKL), P (PHA), PPD (DXU), PPiU (PIT), TMurS (TXM), TxLT (ILU), TxShA (IAU), [United States Government Printing Office-Serials, Alexandria, VA] (GPA).

| Hist | v.1,n.9-v.3,n.3;<br>Sep., 1971-<br>Summer, 1973 | Microforms<br>Her. 2, R17 |
|---|---|---|
|  | v.3,n.3-v.4,n.2;<br>Summer, 1973-<br>Spring, 1974 | Her. 2 UP,R12 |

|  |  |  |
|---|---|---|
| Wom Ed Res | [v.1,n.6-v.8,n.6]; [Nov., 1969-Nov./Dec., 1978] | Circulation |

1328 <u>Women in Cell Biology</u>. 1973-1974//? Irregular. Last issue 6 pages. Line drawings. Available on microfilm: Herstory. Published by Department of Biology, OML, Yale University, New Haven, CT. Subject focus: education, employment, research, professionals, career development, biologists, sexism.

|  |  |  |
|---|---|---|
| Hist | v.2,n.1-v.3, n.5/6; Fall, 1973- May/June, 1974 | Microforms Her. 3, R 5 |

1329 <u>Women in City Government United Newsletter</u>. 1970//? Unknown. OCLC 2269601. Last issue 2 pages. Line drawings. Available on microfilm: Herstory. Published by Women in City Government United, New York, NY. Subject focus: employment, rights, sexism in government employment, civil service, government workers.

|  |  |  |
|---|---|---|
| Hist | n.1; Aug. 26, 1970 | Microforms Her. 1, R 22 |

1330 <u>Women in Communications, Inc., National Newsletter</u>. 1968. Monthly. Women in Communications, Inc., P.O. Box 9561, Austin, TX 78766. (512) 345-8922. Last issue 8 pages, last volume 96 pages, size 22 x 28. Line drawings, photographs. Subject focus: education, employment, communications.

|  |  |  |
|---|---|---|
| JR | v.10, n.2- Nov., 1977- | Circulation |

1331 <u>Women in Geography</u>. 1974//? Unknown. Last issue 2 pages. Line drawings. Available on microfilm: Herstory. Published by Department of Geography, H.B.C., Syracuse University, Syracuse, NY. Subject focus: geographers.

|  |  |  |
|---|---|---|
| Hist | v.2, n.1; Mar., 1974 | Microforms Her. 3, R 5 |

1332 <u>Women in German</u>. 1975? Irregular. $7 for individuals and institutions. Women in German, Department of German, 818 Van Hise Hall, University of Wisconsin-Madison, Madison, WI 53706. Last issue 8 pages, size 22 x 28. Line drawings. Subject focus: employment, Germanists, teachers.

|  |  |  |
|---|---|---|
| Wom St | [n.6-16], 19- [Feb. 18, 1976- Nov. 30, 1978], May 5, 1979- | Reading Room |

1333 <u>Women in Libraries</u>. 1971. 5 times a year. $4 for individuals, $6 for institutions. Kay Cassell, editor, 44 Nathaniel Blvd., Delmar, NY 12054. OCLC 3092777. Last issue 8 pages, last volume 40 pages, size 22 x 28. Indexed: by publisher, 1971-1977. Published by ALA/SRRT (American Library Association, Social Responsibilities Roundtable), Task Force on Women. Place of publication varies: Slingerlands, NY, Sep., 1975-June, 1977. Frequency varies: bi-monthly, Jan.-June, 1976. Subject focus: libraries, librarians, women's studies. Other holding institutions: AzU (AZU), CLU (CLU), IU (UIU), In (ISL), InU (IUL), LU (LUU), MiMtpT (EZC), [University of Minnesota Union List, Minneapolis, MN] (MUL), NFQC (XQM), PPD (DXU), TNJ (TJC), WaU (WAU), WM (GZD).

|  |  |  |
|---|---|---|
| Lib Sch | v.5, n.1- Sep., 1975- | Circulation |

1334 <u>Women in Struggle</u>. 1970? Irregular. Women in Struggle, P.O. Box 324, Winneconne, WI 54986. ISSN 0049-7819. OCLC 2269602. Last issue 8 pages, size 22 x 28. Line drawings. Available on microfilm: Herstory (1971-1972). Subject focus: rights, politics, pro-abortion, health, lobbying.

|  |  |  |
|---|---|---|
| Hist | Jan./Feb.- Sep./Oct., 1971 | Microforms Her. 1 R 22 |
|  | Oct., 1971- Nov./Dec., 1972 | Her. 1 UP,R17 |
|  | July/Aug., 1971, July/Aug., 1972- Dec., 1975 | Circulation |
| Wom Ed Res | Sep./Oct., 1974- | Circulation |

1335 <u>Women in the Church</u>. 1972-1973//? Last issue 4 pages. Available on microfilm: Herstory. Published by Synod of Southern California Task Force on Women, United Presbyterian Church in the United States of America, Los Angeles, CA. Editor: Marjorie Dole. Subject focus: Presbyterianism, lobbying.

|  |  |  |
|---|---|---|
| Hist | Oct., 1972, Feb.,June, 1973 | Microforms Her. 2, R 18 |

1336 <u>Women in the World</u>. 1974//? Unknown. Last issue 2 pages. Line drawings. Available on microfilm: Herstory. Published by U.S. Department of State, Bureau of Public Affairs, Washington, DC. Subject focus: social change.

|  |  |  |
|---|---|---|
| Hist | June 14, 1974 | Microforms Her. 3, R 5 |

1337 Women Lawyer's Journal. 1911. Quarterly. Ethel B. Danzig, editor, Women Lawyer's Journal, 1155 East 60th Street, Chicago, IL 60637. ISSN 0043-7468. OCLC 1770072. LC 40-25442, sn78-1599. Last issue 40 pages, last volume 152 pages, size 16 x 23. Photographs. Indexed in: Index to Legal Periodicals (1943-). Available on microfilm: UnM, Herstory (1969). Published by National Association of Women Lawyers. Place of publication varies: Cincinnati, OH, Jan., 1944-Mar., 1947; New York, NY, Spring-Summer, 1947; San Francisco, CA, Fall, 1969. Previous editors: Jean Smith Evans, Dec., 1938-Aug., 1942; Elizabeth F. Reed, Jan.-Dec., 1943; Ernestine Breisch Powell, Jan.-Fall, 1944; Catherine Donovan, Spring-Winter, 1945; Victoria Gilbert, Mar.-Sep., 1946; Katherine K. Makielski, Mar.-Summer, 1947; Dorothy Blender, Fall, 1947-Fall, 1949; Eileen Flynn, Winter-Summer, 1941; Amalia Pasternacki, Fall, 1951-Summer, 1952; Alma Zola Groves, Fall, 1952-Summer, 1954; Josephine M. Pisani, Fall, 1954-Summer, 1955; Mary M. Connelly, Fall, 1955-Spring, 1956; Dorothy Yancy, Fall, 1956; Eva M. Mack, Winter-Summer, 1958; Maria C. Meute, Fall, 1958-Spring, 1960; Nina Miglionico, Fall, 1960-Summer, 1961; Josephine M. Brown, Fall, 1961-Summer, 1963; Mary Louise D. McLeod, Fall, 1963-Spring, 1964; Elizabeth Gurling, Fall, 1964-Summer, 1965; Adele T. Weaver, Fall, 1965-Summer, 1966; Lois G. Forer, Fall, 1966-Summer, 1967; Florence P. Shientag, Fall, 1967-Summer, 1968; Dorothy M. Jones, Fall, 1968-Summer, 1969; Marjorie M. Childs, Winter-Summer, 1970; Phyllis Shampanier, Fall, 1970-Summer, 1971; Mary Jeanne Coyne, Fall, 1971-Summer, 1972; Lee Berger Anderson, Fall, 1972-Summer, 1973; Mary A. Pappas, Fall, 1973-Summer, 1974; Lee Penland, Fall, 1974-Summer, 1976; Helen G. Nasif, Fall, 1976. Subject focus: lawyers, law, lobbying. Other holding institutions: CSt (Stanford University), [Congressional Research Service, Washington, DC] (CRS), FMFIU (FXN), FU-L (FUB), ICD-L (IBC), [Indiana Union List of Serials, Indianapolis, IN] (ILS), LNL-L (LLT), M (MAS), MCR-S (Schlesinger Library on the History of Women in America, Radcliffe College, Cambridge, MA), [University of Minnesota Union List, Minneapolis, MN] (MUL), MoKU (UMK), [Creighton University Law Library, Omaha, NE] (CLL), [New York State Union List, Albany, NY] (NYS), NIC (COO), N (NYG), [Central New York Library Resources Council, Syracuse, NY] (SRR), [University of Akron Law Library, Akron, OH] (AKL), OTU-L (UTL), [Pittsburgh Regional Library Center-Union List, Pittsburgh, PA] (QPR), [AMIGOS Union List of Serials, Dallas, TX] (IUC), WMUW (GZN).

| | | |
|---|---|---|
| Hist | v.55, n.4; (centennial issue) Fall, 1969 | Microforms Her. 2, R 18 |
| Law | v.30- 1944- | Circulation |
| WSLL | v.25, n.1- Dec., 1938- | Circulation |

1338 Women Library Workers. 1976. Bi-monthly. $5 for members, $7 for non-members. Women Library Workers, P.O. Box 9052, Berkeley, CA 94709. OCLC 2864777. Last issue 24 pages, size 18 x 21. Line drawings, photographs. Place of publication varies: San Francisco, CA, Jan., 1976-Dec., 1977. Subject focus: Equal Rights Amendment, libraries, librarians. Other holding institutions: AzU (AZU), CoDU (DVP), COFS (COF), FOFT (FTU), LU (LUU), MiMtpT (EZC), MiU (EYM), [University of Minnesota Union List, Minneapolis, MN] (MUL), MnU (MNU), NbOB (BTC), NA1U (NAM), NFQC (XQM), OCl (CLE), PPiU (PIT), TxDW (IWU), TxU (IXA), WM (GZD).

| | | |
|---|---|---|
| Mem | n.1- Jan., 1976- | Periodicals Room |
| Lib Sch | n.1- Jan., 1976- | Circulation |

Women Mobilized for Change. Chicago, IL

  see The Spare Rib. Chicago, IL

1339 Women NOW! 1971-1972//? Irregular. OCLC 2269604. Last issue 16 pages. Line drawings, photographs. Available on microfilm: Herstory. Published by Nottingham Women's Liberation Group, Nottingham, England. Subject focus: history, rights.

| | | |
|---|---|---|
| Hist | v.1, n.1-2; Mar./Apr.- May/June, 1971 | Microforms Her. 1, R 12 |
| | ?, 1972 | Her. 1 UP, R17 |

1340 Women New York. 1976. Bi-monthly. Annette Samuels, editor, Women New York, Executive Chamber/State of New York, 1350 Avenue of the Americas, New York, NY 10019. OCLC 5060218. LC sc79-4173. Last issue 8 pages, last volume 48 pages, size 22 x 28. Line drawings, photographs. Published by The Women's Division of the State of New York. Previous editor: Jewell Jackson McCabe, Apr./May-Nov./Dec., 1976. Subject focus: lobbying, civil service, government workers. Other holding institutions: IU (UIU), N (NYG), [New York State Union List, Albany, NY] (NYS), NFredU (XFM), NGenoU (YGM).

## Women's Periodicals and Newspapers

| | | |
|---|---|---|
| Wom Ed Res | v.1,n.3-6, v.3, n.1- Apr./May- Nov./Dec., 1976, Mar./Apr., 1978- | Circulation |

**1341** <u>Women of China</u>. 1952-//? Monthly. OCLC 5050439. Last issue 55 pages, size 13 x 20. Line drawings, photographs, some in color. Published by All China Democratic Women's Federation, Peking, China. Subject focus: biographies, workers, marriage,law. Other holding institutions: CLSU (CSL), CLobS (CLO), OSfU (CUF), InU (IUL), KyLoU (KLG).

| | | |
|---|---|---|
| Mem | June, 1953 | AP/W87/1953 |

**1342** <u>Women of Vietnam</u>. 1966-1974//? Quarterly? ISSN 0512-1825. OCLC 2236085. Last issue 32 pages, last volume 140 pages, size 18 x 27. Line drawings, photographs. Available on microfilm: Herstory. Published by Vietnam Women's Union, Hanoi, Vietnam. Subject focus: biographies, peace movement, Vietnam, children, poetry. Some issues in French (100%). Other holding institutions: DHU (DHU), [New York State Union List, Albany, NY] (NYS), NIC (COO).

| | | |
|---|---|---|
| Hist | [1966-1971] | Microforms Her. 1, R 12 |
| | [1971] | Her. Add. |
| | [1972] | Her. 1 UP, R17 |
| | [1974] | Her. CUP, R 8 |
| Mem | [1967-1968] | AP/W8722/031 |

**1343** <u>Women of the Whole World</u>. 1946. Quarterly. $2.50 for individuals and institutions. Krystyna Niedzielska, editor, Women of the Whole World, Women's International Democratic Federation, Unter den Linden 13, 108 Berlin, German Democratic Republic, 2 00 U3 31/2 07 11 17. ISSN 0043-7476. OCLC 1770073. Last issue 56 pages, last volume 280 pages, size 20 x 29. Line drawings, photographs, some in color. Available on microfilm: Herstory (1965-6, 1974). Frequency varies: irregular, Feb., 1951-Nov., 1955; monthly, Jan., 1961-Dec., 1965. Previous editor: Wanda Tycner, Spring?, 1973-Summer, 1977. Subject focus: rights, Third World, peace movement, disarmament, children. Occasional (100%)German or (100%) French editions. Other holding institutions: CLU (CLU), CU-UC (UCU), [Indiana Union List of Serials, Indianapolis, IN] (ILS), MBNU (NED), [University of Minnesota Union List, Minneapolis, MN] (MUL), OAkU (AKR), PPiU (PIT), PSC-P (PSP).

| | | |
|---|---|---|
| Hist | 1965-1966 | Microforms Her. 1, R 12 |
| | 1974 | Her. Add. |
| Mem | [Feb., 1951- Nov., 1955], Jan., 1959- | AP/W872 |
| Wom Ed Res | Spring?, 1963, Spring?, 1968- Spring?, 1972 | Circulation |

**1344** <u>Women on the March</u>. 1957-1977//. Monthly. ISSN 0509-0881. OCLC 1770975. LC 77-924390. Last issue 20 pages, last volume 362 pages, size 22 x 28. Published by The Women's Department of All India Congress Committee, New Delhi, India. Editor: Mukul Banerjee. Subject focus: socialism, politics, rights, education, poetry, children. Other holding institutions: CLU (CLU), [University of Minnesota Union List, Minneapolis, MN] (MUL), [New York State Union List, Albany, NY] (NYS), NIC (COO), WaU (WAU).

| | | |
|---|---|---|
| Mem | v.18,n.1- v.21, n.12; Jan., 1974- Dec., 1977 | AP/W8722/058 |

**1345** <u>Women on Top</u>. 1973//? Unknown. Last issue 3 pages. Line drawings. Available on microfilm: Herstory. Published by Earlham College Women's Center, Richmond, IN. Subject focus: higher education, counseling, students.

| | | |
|---|---|---|
| Hist | Oct. 26, 1973 | Microforms Her. 3, R 5 |

**1346** <u>Women Reaching Women Newsletter</u>. 1979. Carol Marklein, editor, Women Reaching Women Newsletter, 333 West Mifflin Street, Suite 4, Madison, WI 53703. (608) 257-7970. Last issue 8 pages, size 28 x 22. Line drawings. Available on microfilm: WHi (1980-). Published by Wisconsin Association on Alcohol and Other Drug Abuse. Previous editor: Pamela Leindecker, Jan./Feb., 1980. Subject focus: lesbians, alcoholism, drug abuse.

| | | |
|---|---|---|
| Hist | v.2, n.1- Jan./Feb., 1980- | Circulation |

**1347** <u>Women Speaking</u>. 1958. Quarterly. $5 for individuals and institutions. C. Esther Hodge, editor, Women Speaking, 70 Westmount Road, London SE9 1JE England. Telephone 01-850-4621. ISSN 0049-7827. OCLC 2269607. Last issue 24 pages, last volume 96 pages. Line drawings, photographs, commercial advertising. Published by Paxton Press Ltd. Available on microfilm: Herstory (1969-1974). Frequency varies: semi-annual, 1970; tri-annual, 1971. Subject focus: politics, language, health, arts, religion, education. Other holding institutions: MCR-S (Schlesinger Library on the

History of Women in America, Radcliffe College, Cambridge, MA), MWelC (WEL), MiMtpT (EZC), [University of Minnesota Union List, Minneapolis, MN] (MUL), PPiU (PIT), ScRhW (SWW), TxDN (INT), [AMIGOS Union List of Serials, Dallas, TX] (IUC).

| | | |
|---|---|---|
| Hist | v.2, n.17-27; Jan., 1969- July/Sep., 1971 | Microforms Her. 1, R 12 |
| | v.2, n.28-v.3, n.2; Oct./Dec., 1971- Apr./June, 1973 | Her. 1 UP, R17 |
| | v.3, n.3-6; July/Sep., 1973- Apr./June, 1974 | Her. CUP, R 8 |
| Wom Ed Res | [v.3,n.7-v.4,n.7]; 11- [July, 1974- July, 1975], July, 1976- | Circulation |

1348 Women Strike for Peace. 1963-1971//? Irregular. OCLC 2269609. Last issue 3 pages. Line drawings, photographs. Available on microfilm: Herstory. Published by Women Strike for Peace, National Office, Washington, DC. Subject focus: politics, nuclear weapons, peace movement, Vietnam War, disarmament, draft.

| | | |
|---|---|---|
| Hist | Jan., 1963- June 21, 1971 | Microforms Her. 1, R 23 |

1349 Women Strike for Peace. 1970-1973//? Irregular. OCLC 2269608. Last issue 2 pages. Line drawings. Available on microfilm: Herstory. Published by Women Strike for Peace, National Office, New York, NY. Editor: Amy Swerdlow, Spring, 1972-June, 1973. Subject focus: peace movement, disarmament, nuclear weapons, politics.

| | | |
|---|---|---|
| Hist | June 22, 1970- June 21, 1971 | Microforms Her. 1, R 23 |
| | v.2,n.2-v.3,n.6; Spring, 1972- June, 1973 | Her. 1 UP, R17 |

1350 Women Studies Abstracts. 1972. Quarterly. $25 for individuals, $45 for institutions. Sara Stauffer Whaley, editor, Women Studies Abstracts, P.O. Box 1, Rush, NY 14543. (716) 533-1251/1376. ISSN 0049-7835. OCLC 1770074, 4408733. LC 72-623243. Last issue 87 pages, last volume 212 pages, size 23 x 15. Index available from publisher. Available on microfilm: UnM, Herstory (1972-1974). Published by Rush Publishing Co., Inc., Rush, NY. Subject focus: abstracts, education, sex roles, family, employment, religion, sports, health, history, literature, art, media reviews. Other holding institutions: ABAU (ABC), AJacT (AJB), AU (ALM), ArU (AFU), AzFU (AZN), AzTeS (AZS), CLU (CLU), CSS (CSA), CU-S (CUS), CoDI (COI), COLH (COL), COU-DA (COA), CtY (YUS), CSt (Stanford University), [Congressional Research Service, Washington, DC] (CRS), DLC (DLC), DeU (DLM), FBoU (FGM), FJUNF (FNP), FMFIU (FXG), FPeU (FWA), FT (TNH), FTaSU (FDA), GAuA (GJG), GVaS (GYG), IaDmG (IWG), IaDuU (IOV), ICL (IAL), ICNE (IAO), IChamP (IAQ), IDeKN (JNA), ILocL (ICX), IPB (IBA), IPfsG (IAF), IU (UIU), [Indiana Union List of Serials, Indianapolis, IN] (ILS), InND (IND), InTI (ISU), InU (IUL), KSteC (KKQ), KYBB (KBE), KyLoU (KLG), KyMurT (KMS), KyRE (KEU), LGra (LGS), MBNU (NED), MBSi (SCL), MBTI (BTI), MBU (BOS), MCR-S (Schlesinger Library on the History of Women in America, Radcliffe College, Cambridge, MA), MChB (BXM), MH (HUL,HLS), MH-AH (BHA), MH-Ed (HMG), MMeT (TFW), MMiltC (CUM), MNoW (WHE), MNodS (SMU), MWelC (WEL), MdBJ (JHE), MdStm (MDS), MiAC (EZA), MiAllG (EXG), MiEM (EEM), MiGrC (EXC), MiKC (EXK), MiLC (EEL), MiMtpT (EZC), MiRochOU (EYR), [University of Minnesota Union List, Minneapolis, MN] (MUL), MnNC (MNN), MnStjos (MNF), MnStpeG (MNG), MO (MOL), MoCoS (MOV), MoUst (UMS), NcMhC (NCM), NcRS (NRC), NcWfSB (NVS), NbU (LDL), NhD (DRB), NjJStP (STP), NmLcU (IRU), [New York State Union List, Albany, NY] (NYS), N (NYG), [Western New York Library Resources Council, Buffalo, NY] (VZX), NCH (YHM), NCaS (XLM), NCrniCC (ZDG), NCortU (YCM), NFQC (XQM), NGenoU (YGM), NIC (COO), NNC-T (VVT), NNCU-G (ZGM), NNR (ZXC), NNUT (VYN), NNepaSU (ZLM), NOwU (ZOW), NPV (VXW), NR (YQR), NRU (RRR), NSbSU (YSM), NSbSU-H (VZB), NStC (VYS), NSufR (VVR), [Central New York Library Resources Council, Syracuse, NY] (SRR), NSyU (SYB), OAU (OUN), OAkU (AKR), OBgU (BGU), OClW (CWR), OGK (KEN), OGraD (DNU), OKentU (KSU), OO (OBE), OTU (TOL), OU (OSU), OYU (YNG), OYesA (ANC), OkTOR (OKO), OrMcL (OLC), PBL (LYU), PBm (BMC), PBlbM (MGC), PGC (GDC), PLF (LFM), PleB (PBU), PPiU (PIT), [Pittsburgh Regional Library Center-Pittsburgh, PA] (QPR), PNwC (WFN), PPD (DXU), PU (PAU), ScRhW (SWW), SdU (USD), TNJ (TCollsM (TMS), TxCM (TXA), TxDW (IWU), TxSaU (TXJ), TxU (IXA), TxViHU (TXV), [Emory and Henry College, Emory, VA] (VEH), ViNO (VOD), ViRCU (VRC), ViRU (VRU), VtMiM (MDY), WAL (WIB), WKenU (GZP), WMenU (GZS).

| | | |
|---|---|---|
| Hist | v.1,n.1-v.2,n.2; Winter, 1972- Spring, 1973 | Microforms Her. 2, R 18 |
| | v.2,n.3-v.3,n.1; Summer, 1973- Winter, 1974 | Her. 2UP, R13 |
| | v.1,n.1- Winter, 1972- | Z/7962/W65 |

*Women's Periodicals and Newspapers*

|  | Mem | v.1, n.1-<br>Winter, 1972- | Z/7962/W65 |
|---|---|---|---|
|  | Coll | Current Issues<br>Only | Women's<br>Reading Area |
|  | Wom St | v.3,n.4,v.7,n.1-<br>Feb., 1974,<br>Winter, 1978/1979- | Reading Room |
|  | CFD | v.1, n.1-<br>Winter, 1972- | Circulation |

1351 <u>Women Studies Research Center Newsletter</u>. 1979. Quarterly. Dr. Suzanne Pingree, editor, Women Studies Research Center Newsletter, 209 N. Brooks Street, Madison, WI 53706. Last issue 4 pages, size 22 x 28. Line drawings, photographs. Subject focus: research, motherhood.

|  | Coll | Current Issues<br>Only | Women's<br>Reading Area |
|---|---|---|---|
|  | Wom Ed<br>Res | v.1, n.1-<br>Sep., 1979- | Circulation |

1352 <u>Women: To, By, Of, For and About</u>. 1970//? ISSN 0043-7492. OCLC 1789287. LC 73-647090. Last issue 72 pages. Line drawings, photographs, commercial advertising. Available on microfilm: Herstory. Published by New Moon Publication, Inc., Stamford, CT. Subject focus: fiction, sterilization, poetry, food, karate, law. Other holding institution: MCR-S (Schlesinger Library on the History of Women in America, Radcliffe College, Cambridge, MA).

|  | Hist | v.1, n.1;<br>?, 1970 | Microforms<br>Her. 1, R 11 |
|---|---|---|---|

1353 <u>Women Today</u>. 1971. Bi-weekly. $33 for individuals and institutions. Barbara Jordan Moore, editor, Women Today, 621 National Press Building, Room 621, Washington, DC 20045. (202) 628-6999. ISSN 0043-7506. OCLC 1099668, 3095945. LC sc77-860. Last issue 6 pages, last volume 162 pages, size 22 x 28. Line drawings. Available on microfilm: Herstory (1971-1974). Published by Today News Service, Inc., Washington, DC. Subject focus: Equal Rights Amendment, law, lobbying, politics. Other holding institutions: AU (ALM), ArU (AFU), CSt (Stanford University), CLU (CLU), CSdS (CDS), CtY (YUS), DACE (AED), [Congressional Research Service, Washington, DC] (CRS), FJUNF (FNP), FTS (FHM), ICL (IAL), InU (IUL), [Indiana Union List of Serials, Indianapolis, IN] (ILS), MWelC (WEL), DNAL (AGL), MiMtpT (EZC), [University of Minnesota Union List, Minneapolis, MN] (MUL), NcRS (NRC), NbU (LDL), NBu (VHB), NCH (YHM), [Western New York Library Resources Council, Buffalo, NY] (VZX), NGcCC (VVX), NSbSU (YSM), [Central New York Library Resources Council, Syracuse, NY] (SRR), O (OHI), OAU (OUN), OBgU (BGU), OC1U-L (LMC), OKentU (KSU), OU (OSU), PCoR (ROB), PPiU (PIT), [Pittsburgh Regional Library Center Union List, Pittsburgh, PA] (QPR), TxDW (IWU), [AMIGOS Union List of Serials, Dallas, TX] (IUC).

|  | Hist | v.1, n.1-14;<br>Feb. 1-<br>Aug. 14, 1971 | Microforms<br>Her. 1, R 23 |
|---|---|---|---|
|  |  | v.1, n.14-17;<br>Aug. 14-<br>Sep. 20, 1971 | Her. Add. |
|  |  | v.1, n.18-v.3,<br>n.13;<br>Oct. 4, 1971-<br>June 25, 1973 | Her. 1 UP,<br>R 17-18 |
|  |  | v.3,n.14-v.4,<br>n.13;<br>July 9, 1973-<br>June 24, 1974 | Her. CUP, R8 |
|  |  | v.7, n.3-<br>Feb. 7, 1977- | Circulation |
|  | Coll | Current Issues<br>Only | Women's<br>Reading Area |

1354 <u>Women Unite N.O.W.</u> 1971-1974//? OCLC 2259157. Last issue 8 pages. Line drawings. Available on microfilm: Herstory. Published by National Organization for Women, Cleveland Chapter, Cleveland, OH. Title varies: as Channel "C" N.O.W. Newsletter, Jan., 1971-Mar., 1972. Subject focus: education, employment, religion, Equal Rights Amendment, lobbying, rights, politics, pro-abortion, teenagers. Other holding institution: [New York State Union List, Albany, NY] (NYS).

|  | Hist | Jan., Apr.,<br>July, 1971 | Microforms<br>Her. 1, R 17 |
|---|---|---|---|
|  |  | Nov., 1971-<br>June, 1973 | Her. 1 UP,R8 |
|  |  | Aug., 1973-<br>Mar., 1974 | Her. CUP, R 3 |

1355 <u>Women United</u>. 1971-1972//? Irregular. Last issue 2 pages. Line drawings. Available on microfilm: Herstory. Published in Washington, DC. Subject focus: Equal Rights Amendment, lobbying.

|  | Hist | n.1-19;<br>Apr. 4, 1971-<br>Apr. 3, 1972 | Microforms<br>Her. 2, R 18 |
|---|---|---|---|

1356 <u>Women United</u>. 1972-1974//? Irregular. Last issue 8 pages. Line drawings, photographs.

Available on microfilm: Herstory. Published by Women United for Action, New York, NY. Title varies: as Women United for Action, Aug. 21, 1972-Nov. 30, 1973. Subject focus: consumerism, homemakers. In Spanish (40%).

| Hist | v.1, n.1-3;<br>Aug. 21, 1972-<br>June, 1973 | Microforms<br>Her. 2, R 18 |
|---|---|---|
|  | v.1,n.3-v.2,n.5;<br>July 6, 1973-<br>May, 1974 | Her. 2 UP, R13 |

Women United for Action. New York, NY

see Women United. New York, NY

1357 Women United for November 6 Newsletter. 1971//? Unknown. Last issue 1 page. Line drawings. Available on microfilm: Herstory. Published in San Francisco, CA. Subject focus: peace movement.

| Hist | Oct., 1971 | Microforms<br>Her. 2, R 18 |
|---|---|---|

1358 Women West. 1970//? Monthly. OCLC 2269614. Last issue 7 pages. Line drawings, photographs, commercial advertising. Available on microfilm: Herstory. Published in South Pasadena, CA. Editors: Jane Lewis Brandt and Gail Winston Hammond. Subject focus: satire, health, consumerism, poetry, humor.

| Hist | v.1, n.1-2;<br>Nov.-<br>Dec., 1970? | Microforms<br>Her. 1, R 4 |
|---|---|---|

1359 Womenews. 1977. Bi-monthly. Nancy Kymn Harvin, editor, Womenews, 512 Finance Building, Harrisburg, PA 17120. Last issue 4 pages, last volume 24 pages, size 38 x 28. Line drawings, photographs. Published by the Pennsylvania Commission for Women. Previous editors: Judy P. Hansen, May-Oct./Nov., 1977; Janet L. Beals, Jan./Feb.-Mar./Apr., 1978; Sarah S. Forth, May/June-July/Aug., 1978. Subject focus: lobbying, human services.

| Hist | v.1, n.1-<br>May, 1977- | Circulation |
|---|---|---|

1360 Women's Abortion Coalition. 1972-1973//? Irregular. Last issue 3 pages. Line drawings, photographs. Available on microfilm: Herstory. Published by Western Regional Office of Women's National Abortion Action Coalition-WONAAC, San Francisco, CA. Title varies: as Women's Abortion Coalition Newsletter, Jan.-Mar., 1972. Subject focus: pro-abortion, politics, sterilization, birth control, lobbying.

| Hist | Jan., 1972-<br>Jan. 17, 1973 | Microforms<br>Her. 2, R 18 |
|---|---|---|

Women's Abortion Coalition Newsletter. San Francisco, CA

see Women's Abortion Coalition. San Francisco, CA

1361 Women's Advocate. 1973. Irregular. $4 for individuals and institutions. Leslie Mercer, editor, Women's Advocate, Minnesota Women's Center, 306 Walter Library, University of Minnesota, Minneapolis, MN 55455. ISSN 0300-6611. OCLC 1360056, 1713682, 2362013. Last issue 4 pages, last volume 12 pages, size 22 x 28. Previous editor: Betty Anne Burch, Mar., 1977. Subject focus: women's studies, employment. Other holding institution: [University of Minnesota Union List, Minneapolis, MN] (MUL).

| Hist | v.5,n.3,v.6,n.6-<br>Mar., 1977,<br>Sep., 1978- | Circulation |
|---|---|---|
| Wom Ed<br>Res | v.2, n.8-<br>July/Aug., 1974- | Circulation |

1362 Women's Agenda. 1976-1978//? ISSN 0149-0532. OCLC 2878275. LC sc77-1008. Last issue 16 pages, size 21 x 28. Line drawings, photographs. Published by Women's Action Alliance, New York, NY. Editor: Ellen B. Sweet. Subject focus: rights, pro-abortion, law, health. Other holding institutions: CSt (Stanford University), CtY (YUS), MBTI (BTI), MH-AH (BHA), MiMtpT (EZC), [University of Minnesota Union List, Minneapolis, MN] (MUL), NcRS (NRC), [New York State Union List, Albany, NY] (NYS), NIC (COO), NOneoU (ZBM), NPV (VXW), OAkU (AKR), OOxM (MIA), PPT (TEU).

| Wom St | v.2,n.5-v.3,n.3;<br>May, 1977-<br>Apr., 1978 | Reading Room |
|---|---|---|
| Wom Ed<br>Res | v.1,n.4-v.2,n.3;<br>June, 1976-<br>Mar., 1977 | Circulation |

1363 Women's Bureau Bulletin. 1919-1975//? Irregular. ISSN 0083-3606. OCLC 3349364, 1768698. LC 19-7913rev4. Last issue 33 pages, size 15 x 23. Published by the U.S. Department of Labor, Women's Bureau, Washington, DC. Subject focus: workers; each issue has a specific focus. Other holding institutions: ArU (AFU), COU-DA (COA), DHEW (HEW), DLC (DLC), DeU (DLM), ICSU (IAA), MWelC (WEL), DNAL (AGL), MdBJ (JHE), [University of Minnesota Union List, Minneapolis, MN] (MUL), MnSCC (MNE), NhD (DRB), [New York State Union List, Albany, NY] (NYS), NIC (COO), NR (YQR),

ViB1bv (VPI).

Hist     n.60-296;     Δ/L13./3:
         1927-1971

         n.1-297;      Microforms
         1919-1975

1364    Women's Bureau Newsletter. 1976. Quarterly. Myroslava Pidhirnyj, editor, Women's Bureau Newsletter, 400 University Avenue, Toronto, Ontario, Canada. ISSN 0381-4416. OCLC 2588436. LC cn76-82598. Last issue 4 pages. Photographs. Published by Women's Bureau, Ontario Ministry of Labor. Previous editor: Judy Stoffman, Dec., 1976-Apr., 1977. Subject focus: rights, law, economic conditions. Other holding institution: CaOONL (NLC).

Hist     v.1,n.1-v.2,n.1,    Circulation
         v.3,n.1-v.4,n.1,3-
         Mar., 1976-
         Apr., 1977,
         Jan., 1978-
         Feb., Aug., 1979-

1365    Women's Business News. 1979. Bi-monthly. Gratis to individuals and institutions. Mary E. McGraw, editor, Women's Business News, P.O. Box 539, Madison, WI 53705. (608) 233-8480. Last issue 8 pages, size 29 x 46. Line drawings, photographs, commercial advertising. Published by Women's Business News, Madison, WI. Subject focus: business.

Hist     v.1, n.4-     Circulation
         May/June, 1980-

Women's Caucus Newsletter. College Park, MD

     see SWS Newsletter. College Park, MD

Women's Caucus Newsletter. Memphis, TN

     see SAA Women's Caucus Newsletter. Memphis, TN

1366    Women's Caucus-Religious Studies Newsletter. 1972-1973//? Irregular. Last issue 4 pages. Line drawings. Available on microfilm: Herstory. Published by the Graduate Theological Union Women's Caucus, Berkeley, CA. Subject focus: religious education.

Hist     v.1, n.1-2;     Microforms
         Fall, 1972-      Her. 2, R 18
         Mar., 1973

         v.1, n.3/4;     Her. 2 UP, R13
         Fall, 1973

1367    The Women's Center. 1973//? Unknown. Last issue 2 pages. Available on microfilm: Herstory. Published by Young Women's Christian Association of Oahu, Honolulu, HI. Subject focus: Christianity.

Hist     Mar., 1973     Microforms
                           Her. 2, R 18

1368    Women's Center-Baltimore. 1974//? Unknown. Last issue 5 pages. Line drawings, commercial advertising. Available on microfilm: Herstory. Published by Baltimore Women's Center, Baltimore, MD. Subject focus: consciousness raising.

Hist     Apr., 1974?     Microforms
                            Her. 3, R 5

1369    Women's Center Bulletin. 1972//? Irregular. Last issue 1 page. Line drawings. Available on microfilm: Herstory. Published by Women's Center-Tampa, Tampa, FL. Subject focus: education.

Hist     n.2,4;     Microforms
         Sep., Dec., 1972     Her. 2, R 19

Women's Center News. Orange, NJ

     see Focus on Women. Orange, NJ

Women's Center Newsletter. Santa Cruz, CA

     see Definitely Biased. Santa Cruz, CA

Women's Center Newsletter. Storrs, CT

     see Sister News. Storrs, CT

The Women's Center Newsletter. Cambridge, MA

     see On Our Way. Cambridge, MA

Women's Center Newsletter. Hempstead, NY

     see Newsletter of the Women's Liberation Center of Nassau County. Hempstead, NY

1370    Women's Center Newsletter. 1971-1973//? Irregular. Last issue 6 pages. Line drawings. Available on microfilm: Herstory. Published by Women's Center-Stanford, Stanford, CA. Subject focus: politics, health, child care, sexism, education, self-help, pro-abortion.

Hist     Nov., 1971?-     Microforms
         May, 1973        Her. 2, R19

1371 Women's Center Newsletter. 1973-1974//? Irregular. Last issue 3 pages. Line drawings. Available on microfilm: Herstory. Published by Women's Center, University of Idaho, Moscow, ID. Title varies: as Awareness, Jan., 1973. Subject focus: affirmative action, education, students, rights, sexism.

| Hist | v.1, n.1-4; Jan.-May 11, 1973 | Microforms Her. 2, R 18 |
|---|---|---|
| | v.2, n.1-6; Sep. 17, 1973- May 10, 1974 | Her. 2 UP, R13 |

1372 Women's Center Newsletter. 1970-1973//? Irregular. OCLC 2269632. Last issue 6 pages. Line drawings. Available on microfilm: Herstory. Published by Women's Liberation Center of New York, New York, NY. Title varies: as Newsletter, June, 1970-Apr., 1971. Subject focus: pregnancy, pro-abortion, housing. Other holding institution: PPiU (PIT).

| Hist | June, 1970- Apr., 1971 | Microforms Her. 1, R 22 |
|---|---|---|
| | Dec., 1971- Summer, 1973 | Her. 1 UP, R18 |

1373 Women's Center Newsletter. 1972-1974//? Irregular. Last issue 2 pages. Line drawings, commercial advertising. Available on microfilm: Herstory. Published by Women's Center-Poughkeepsie, Poughkeepsie, NY. Subject focus: pro-abortion, art, consciousness raising, child care, divorce, counseling.

| Hist | v.1,n.2-v.2,n.1; June, 1972- June, 1973 | Microforms Her. 2, R 19 |
|---|---|---|
| | v.2, n.2-12; July, 1973- June, 1974 | Her. 2 UP, R 9 |

1374 Women's Circle. 1956. Monthly. $7 for individuals and institutions. Marjorie Pearl, editor, Women's Circle, P.O. Box 428, Seabrook, NH 03874. ISSN 0509-089X. OCLC 5396555. LC sn79-7581. Last issue 64 pages, size 22 x 28. Line drawings, photographs, commercial advertising. Published by the Tower Press, Seabrook, NH. Subject focus: food, arts, crafts, biographies, self-help.

| MHPL | Jan., 1976- Sep., 1980 | Circulation |
|---|---|---|

1375 The Women's Collection Newsletter. 1974. Irregular. The Women's Collection Newsletter, Northwestern University Library, Evanston, IL 60201. OCLC 2255989. Last issue 8 pages, size 22 x 28. Line drawings. Published by the Special Collections Department, Northwestern University. Subject focus: libraries. Other holding institution: [University of Minnesota Union List of Serials, Minneapolis, MN] (MUL).

| Hist | n.1- Apr., 1974- | Circulation |
|---|---|---|
| Lib Sch | n.4- Mar., 1976- | Circulation |
| Wom Ed Res | n.6-7; Mar.-Dec., 1978 | Circulation |

1376 Women's Communication Network. 1974//? Unknown. Last issue 6 pages. Line drawings. Available on microfilm: Herstory. Published by Madison Women's News, Madison, WI. Subject focus: communications.

| Hist | n.1; Apr. 1, 1974 | Microforms Her. 3, R 5 |
|---|---|---|

1377 Women's Community Center Newsletter. 1976? Monthly. $3 for individuals and institutions. Women's Community Center, 3440 State Street, Eau Claire, WI 54701. (715) 834-0628. Last issue 8 pages, size 28 x 22. Line drawings. Available on microfilm: WHi (1980). Published by Women's Community Center, Inc. Subject focus: rights, battered women, women's shelters.

| Hist | June, 1980- | Circulation |
|---|---|---|

Women's Division News. Columbus, OH

    see Ohio Report: News from the Women's Services Division of the Ohio Bureau of Employment Services. Columbus, OH

1378 Women's Education. 1962-1968//. Quarterly. ISSN 0512-1868. OCLC 177075. Last issue 8 pages, last volume 36 pages, size 22 x 28. Published by the American Association of University Women Educational Foundation, Washington, DC. Editors: Mary Tanham, Mar., 1962-Dec., 1963; Dora R. Evers, Dec., 1964-Dec., 1968. Subject focus: education, employment, professionals. Other holding institutions: DeU (DLM), [Indiana Union List of Serials, Indianapolis, IN] (ILS), IPB (IBA), MiMtpT (EZC), [University of Minnesota Union List, Minneapolis, MN] (MUL), OkS (OKS), PPD (DXU), ScU (SUC), ScRhW (SWW), WaU (WAU).

| U.W.Ext | v.1,n.1-v.7,n.3; Mar., 1962- Sep., 1968 | Circulation |
|---|---|---|

| | | | |
|---|---|---|---|
| Wom Ed Res | v.1,n.1-v.7,n.4; Mar., 1962- Dec., 1968 | Circulation | |

Women's Education Newsletter. Madison, WI

　　see Wisconsin Women Newsletter.
　　Madison, WI

1379 Women's Employment Opportunity Program. 1977//. Irregular. Last issue 4 pages, size 22 x 28. Line drawings. Published in Wausau, WI. Editors: Linda Lawrence and Marilyn Sherman, May-June, 1977; Linda Lawrence and Josephine Pierce, Sep. 22-Nov. 10, 1977. Subject focus: employment.

| | | |
|---|---|---|
| Wom Ed Res | [n.8-17] [May-Nov. 10, 1977] | Circulation |

1380 Women's Fact Bulletin. 1943-1945//? Irregular. Last issue 4 pages, size 22 x 28. Photographs. Published by The Australian News and Information Bureau, New York, NY. Subject focus: World War II, war work.

| | | |
|---|---|---|
| Mem | n.1-24; June, 1943- Nov., 1945 | +F0902/+AU72/W (Cutter) |

1381 Women's Forum. 1970//? Monthly? OCLC 2269618. Last issue 7 pages. Line drawings. Available on microfilm: Herstory. Published by Women's Forum, University of California-Davis, Davis, CA. Subject focus: continuing education, pro-abortion, employment, higher education, child care.

| | | |
|---|---|---|
| Hist | v.1, n.3-4; Mar.-Apr., 1970 | Microforms Her. 1, R 22 |

1382 Women's Forum. 1974//? Unknown. Last issue 8 pages. Line drawings, commercial advertising. Available on microfilm: Herstory. Published by Indiana University Student Association-Women's Affairs, Bloomington, IN. Subject focus: art, poetry, literature, rape, pro-abortion, drug abuse, higher education, students.

| | | |
|---|---|---|
| Hist | n.1; Mar., 1974 | Microforms Her. 3, R 5 |

1383 Women's Franchise. 1907-1909//. Last issue 12 pages, last volume 772 pages. Line drawings, commercial advertising. Each volume indexed. Available on microfilm: ResP. Published by The Woman Citizen Publishing Society, London, England. Subject focus: pro-suffrage. Other holding institution: MCR-S (Schlesinger Library on the History of Women in America, Radcliffe College, Cambridge, MA).

| | | |
|---|---|---|
| Mem | v.1,n.1-v.2,n.63; June 27, 1907- Sep. 9, 1909 | Microforms |

1384 Women's Free Express. 1974//? Bi-monthly. Last issue 34 pages. Line drawings, photographs, commercial advertising. Available on microfilm: Herstory. Published in Nashville, TN. Frequency varies: monthly, Mar.-Apr., 1974. Subject focus: film reviews, law, health, politics, poetry, self-help, child care.

| | | |
|---|---|---|
| Hist | v.1, n.1-3 Mar.-June/ July, 1974 | Microforms Her. 3, R 5 |
| | v.1, n.4; Aug./Sep., 1974 | Pam 75-2783 |

1385 Women's Group National Newsletter. 1971-1972//? Irregular. OCLC 2269619. Last issue 2 pages. Line drawings. Available on microfilm: Herstory. Published by the Women's Group, Johannesburg, South Africa. Subject focus: pro-abortion, consciousness raising, birth control.

| | | |
|---|---|---|
| Hist | v.1, n.1-2 ?-Sep., 1971 | Microforms Her. 1, R22 |
| | Nov.-Dec., 1971/ Jan., 1972 | Her. 1 UP,R18 |

1386 The Women's Industrial News. 1897-1919//? Quarterly. Last issue 18 pages, last volume 44 pages. Available on microfilm: ResP. Published by Women's Industrial Journal, London, England. Subject focus: labor unions. Other holding institution: NN (NYP).

| | | |
|---|---|---|
| Mem | v.1,n.1-v.22, n.83; Sep., 1897- Apr., 1919 | Microforms |

1387 Women's Information Center Newsletter. 1972//? Last issue 18 pages. Line drawings, photographs, commercial advertising. Available on microfilm: Herstory. Published by Women's Information Center, Dewitt, NY. Subject focus: crafts, arts, self-help.

| | | |
|---|---|---|
| Hist | v.1, n.1; Oct., 1972 | Microforms Her. 2, R 19 |

1388 Women's Information Network. 1978-1980//. Monthly. Last issue 8 pages, size 29 x 36. Line drawings, photographs, commercial advertising. Published by Women's Network International, Inc., Los Angeles, CA. Editor: Deborah Cipolla. Subject focus: business.

| | | | |
|---|---|---|---|
| Wom Ed Res | v.1,n.10-v.2,n.5 Jan., 1979- Apr., 1980 | Circulation | |

1389 **Women's Information Network Bulletin.** 1972-1973//? Irregular. Last issue 1 page. Line drawings. Available on microfilm: Herstory. Published by Cluster Communication Committee, University of Michigan, Ann Arbor, MI. Subject focus: continuing education, employment, higher education, sexism in education.

| | | | |
|---|---|---|---|
| Hist | v.1,n.1-v.2,n.12; Mar. 13, 1972- Summer, 1973 | Microforms Her. 2, R 19 | |

1390 **Women's Initiatives.** 1980. Quarterly. Lauri Roman Bernfeld, editor, Women's Initiatives, Office of the Governor, State Capitol, Madison, WI 53703. OCLC 6749635. Last issue 12 pages. Line drawings, photographs. Subject focus: lobbying, battered women, history.

| | | | |
|---|---|---|---|
| Hist | v.1, n.1- May, 1980- | Circulation | |

1391 **Women's Interart Center Newsletter.** 1972//? Unknown. Last issue 1 page. Line drawings. Available on microfilm: Herstory. Published by Women's Interart Center, New York, NY. Subject focus: art, artists, dance, therapy.

| | | | |
|---|---|---|---|
| Hist | May?, Summer, Oct., 1972 | Microforms Her. 2, R 19 | |

1392 **Women's International League for Peace and Freedom, Baltimore Branch.** 1969//? Unknown. OCLC 2265062. Last issue 4 pages. Line drawings, photographs. Available on microfilm: Herstory. Published by Women's International League for Peace (W.I.L.P.F.), Baltimore, MD. Subject focus: peace movement.

| | | | |
|---|---|---|---|
| Hist | Mar., 1969 | Microforms Her. 1, R 22 | |

1393 **Women's International League for Peace and Freedom, Berkeley-East Bay Branch.** 1967-1974//? Irregular. OCLC 2258271. Last issue 3 pages. Line drawings. Available on microfilm: Herstory. Published by Women's International League for Peace and Freedom, Berkeley-East Bay Branch (W.I.L.P.F.), Berkeley, CA. Title varies: as Berkeley-East Bay Branch Newsletter, Aug., 1967-May, 1973. Editor: Bernice Harding. Subject focus: peace movement, rights, politics, lobbying.

| | | | |
|---|---|---|---|
| Hist | Aug., 1967- Mar., 1971 | Microforms Her. 1, R 22 | |
| | Nov./Dec., 1972- May, 1973 | Her. 1 UP,R18 | |
| | Oct., 1973- June, 1974 | Her. CUP, R8 | |

1394 **Women's International League for Peace and Freedom, Marin Branch.** 1969-1974//? Irregular. OCLC 2269624. Last issue 4 pages. Line drawings. Available on microfilm: Herstory. Published by Women's International League for Peace and Freedom, Marin County Branch (W.I.L.P.F.), Corte Madera, CA. Title varies: as Newsletter, Oct., 1969-May/June, 1973. Subject focus: peace movement, lobbying.

| | | | |
|---|---|---|---|
| Hist | Oct., 1969- Sep. 30, 1971 | Microforms Her. 1, R 22 | |
| | Nov., 1971- May/June, 1973 | Her. 1 UP,R18 | |
| | Sep., 1973- June, 1974 | Her. CUP, R8 | |

1395 **Women's International League for Peace and Freedom Newsletter.** 1975? Monthly. Marty Jenkins, editor, Women's International League for Peace and Freedom, 2109 Center Avenue, Madison, WI. Last issue 4 pages, size 22 x 28. Subject focus: rights, peace movement.

| | | | |
|---|---|---|---|
| Hist | Apr., 1979- | Circulation | |
| Wom St | Nov./Dec., 1975- | Reading Room | |
| MPL | Current Issues Only | Literature and Social Science Section | |

1396 **Women's International League for Peace and Freedom, Palo Alto Branch.** 1970-1974//? Irregular. OCLC 2269622. Last issue 4 pages. Line drawings. Available on microfilm: Herstory. Published by Women's International League for Peace and Freedom (W.I.L.P.F.), Palo Alto Branch, Palo Alto, CA. Title varies: as Newsletter, Mar., 1970-May/June, 1973. Subject focus: politics, draft, peace movement, lobbying.

| | | | |
|---|---|---|---|
| Hist | Mar., 1970- Aug., 1971; | Microforms Her. 1, R 22 | |
| | Oct./Nov., 1971- May/June, 1973; | Her. 1 UP,R18 | |
| | Sep., 1973- June, 1974; | Her. CUP, R8 | |

1397 **Women's International League for Peace and Freedom, Union County Newsletter.** 1974//? Last issue 2 pages. Line drawings. Available on microfilm: Herstory. Published by Women's International League for Peace and Freedom (W.I.L.P.F.), Fanwood, NJ. Subject focus: peace movement, politics.

| Hist | Apr., 1974 | Microforms Her. 3, R 5 |

1398 The Women's International Quarterly. 1912-1920//? Quarterly. Last issue 128 pages, last volume 512 pages. Available on microfilm: ResP. Published by the World's Young Women's Christian Association, London, England. Subject focus: Christianity. Other holding institution: CtY (YUS).

| Mem | v.1,n.1-v.8,n.4; Oct., 1912- Apr., 1920 | Microforms |

1399 Women's Law Center. 1973-1974//? Irregular. Last issue 4 pages. Line drawings. Available on microfilm: Herstory. Published in New York, NY. Subject focus: law, legal aid.

| Hist | n.1-3; Sep., 1973- May, 1974 | Microforms Her. 3, R 5 |

1400 Women's Law Journal. 1971-1977//? Semi-annual. ISSN 0195-5608. OCLC 2802439. LC 79-644177. Last issue 86 pages, last volume 162 pages, size 22 x 28. Available on microfilm: UnM. Published by the Women's Law Journal, Inc., Los Angeles, CA. Subject focus: law, students, lawyers. Other holding institutions: CSt (Stanford University), DLC (DLC), FTaSU-L (FSL), FU-L (FUB), IaDmD-L (IWD), Ku-L (KFL), LNL-L (LLT), MoKU (UMK), NIC (COO), OC1U-L (LMC), OTU-L (UTL), OkU (OKL), PPiU (PIT), [AMIGOS Union List of Serials, Dallas, TX] (IUC), TxLT-L (TTL), TxU (TXQ), WMUW (GZN).

| Law | v.1, n.1-2; ?. 1976 | Circulation |

Women's Liberation Bulletin. Washington, DC

see Raising Cain. Washington, DC

Women's Liberation Center of Nassau County Newsletter. Hempstead, NY

see Newsletter of the Women's Liberation Center of Nassau County. Hempstead, NY

1401 Women's Liberation News. 1970-1971//? Irregular. OCLC 2269634. Last issue 2 pages. Line drawings. Available on microfilm: Herstory. Published by Rhode Island Women's Liberation Union, Providence, RI. Subject focus: child care, pro-abortion.

| Hist | Aug. 10, 1970- Apr. 9, 1971 | Microforms Her. 1, R23 |

1402 Women's Liberation News. 1970-1971//? Irregular. OCLC 2269635. Last issue 11 pages. Line drawings, photographs. Available on microfilm: Herstory. Published by Vancouver Women's Liberation Alliance, Vancouver, British Columbia, Canada. Subject focus: pro-abortion, education, equal pay for equal work, lobbying, rights.

| Hist | v.1, n.1-3; Oct. 21, 1970- Feb. 10, 1971 | Microforms Her. 1, R 23 |

Women's Liberation Newsletter. San Francisco, CA

see San Francisco Women's Newsletter. San Francisco, CA

1403 Women's Liberation Newsletter. 1969-1970//? Irregular. OCLC 2269636. Last issue 8 pages. Line drawings, photographs. Available on microfilm: Herstory. Published by Women's Liberation, Cambridge, MA. Subject focus: pro-abortion, image, health, politics, radicalism, revolution. Other holding institution: [University of Minnesota Union List, Minneapolis, MN] (MUL).

| Hist | v.1, n.3-6; Oct., 1969- July, 1970 | Microforms Her. 1, R23 |

1404 Women's Liberation Newsletter. 1970//? OCLC 2269638. Last issue 3 pages. Line drawings. Available on microfilm: Herstory. Published by Ottawa Women's Liberation Committee, Ottawa, Ontario, Canada. Editors: Valerie Angus and Carol Buck. Subject focus: birth control, rights, sexism in advertising.

| Hist | v.1, n.1; Jan./Feb., 1970 | Microforms Her. 1, R 23 |

Women's Liberation Union Newsletter. Kansas City, MO

see Women as Women as Women. Kansas City, MO

1405 Women's Liberation Union of Rhode Island. 1972-1974//? Monthly. Last issue 4 pages. Line drawings. Available on microfilm: Herstory. Published by Women's Liberation Union, Providence, RI. Editor: Lesley Doonan. Subject focus: pro-abortion, welfare, lobbying, rights, child care.

| | Hist | Feb., 1972-<br>May, 1973 | Microforms<br>Her. 2, R 19 |

| | | July, 1973-<br>June, 1974 | Her. 2 UP, R13 |

1406 Women's Lobby Quarterly. 1974-1975//. Quarterly. OCLC 4093529. Last issue 16 pages, size 22 x 28. Photographs. Published by Women's Lobby, Inc., Washington, DC. Subject focus: rights, lobbying, biographies. Other holding institution: OU (OSU).

| | Wom Ed<br>Res | Nov., 1974-<br>Apr., 1975 | Circulation |

1407 Women's Media Project. 1973-1974//. Last issue 3 pages. Line drawings. Available on microfilm: Herstory. Published in Memphis, TN. Subject focus: media, television, civil service, film.

| | Hist | July 25,<br>Oct. 23, 1973,<br>Jan. 29, 1974 | Microforms<br>Her. 3, R 5 |

1408 The Women's Municipal League of Boston Bulletin. 1910-1917//? Monthly. Last issue 40 pages, size 15 x 23. Line drawings, photographs. Published by the Women's Municipal League of Boston, Boston, MA. Subject focus: civil service.

| | Hist | v.1, n.1-4<br>Feb.-Mar., 1917 | JW/8BO<br>(Cutter) |

Women's National Abortion Coalition.
New York, NY

see W.O.N.A.A.C. National Newsletter.
New York, NY

1409 Women's News. 1975-1976//. Monthly. Last issue 2 pages, size 22 x 28. Published in Madison, WI. Subject focus: feminism.

| | Wom St | v.1,n.2-v.2,n.2<br>Dec. 11, 1975-<br>Feb. 23, 1976 | Reading Room |

1410 Women's News Exchange! 1972//. Semi-monthly. Last issue 4 pages. Line drawings, commercial advertising. Published by Sally Carter, Boca Raton, FL. Editor: Sally Carter. Subject focus: child care, politics, pro-abortion.

| | Hist | v.1, n.1-4<br>Feb. 15-<br>May 17, 1972 | Microforms<br>Her. 2, R 19 |

1411 The Women's News Journal. 1972-1975//? Monthly. OCLC 5654631, 5654608. Last issue 12 pages, last volume 149 pages. Line drawings, commercial advertising. Available on microfilm: WHi (1973-1975); Herstory (1972-1974). Published by Marin Women's Publishing Co-operative, San Rafael, CA. Title varies: as Marin Women's News Journal, July, 1973-Apr., 1975. Subject focus: rights, health, child rearing, pro-abortion, satire, poetry, self-help, film reviews, lobbying, humor.

| | Hist | v.2,n.2-v.4,n.5;<br>July, 1973-<br>Oct., 1975 | Microforms |

| | | v.1,n.2-v.2,n.1;<br>June, 1972-<br>June, 1973 | Her. 2, R 7 |

| | | v.2,n.2-v.3.n.2;<br>July, 1973-<br>June, 1974 | Her. 2UP, R 4 |

1412 Women's Newsletter. 1971-1974//? Semi-monthly. OCLC 2269642. Last issue 8 pages. Line drawings. Available on microfilm: Herstory. Published by Free University Women's Center, Berkeley/Oakland, CA. Place of publication varies: Berkeley, Aug. 16, 1971-Jan. 29, 1973. Subject focus: education, rape.

| | Hist | Aug. 16-<br>Sep. 30, 1971 | Microforms<br>Her. 1, R 23 |

| | | Oct. 4/11, 1971-<br>June, 1973 | Her. 1UP, R19 |

| | | July 9, 1973-<br>June 25, 1974 | Her. CUP, R8 |

1413 Women's Newspaper. 1971//? Irregular. OCLC 2269643. Last issue 8 pages. Line drawings, photographs. Available on microfilm: Herstory. Published by Women's Newspaper Women, London, England. Subject focus: poetry, birth control, lesbians.

| | Hist | n.1-3;<br>Mar. 6-<br>June 5, 1971 | Microforms<br>Her. 1, R 4 |

1414 Women's Opportunities Center Newsletter. 1971-1974//? Semi-annual. Last issue 4 pages. Line drawings. Available on microfilm: Herstory. Published by Women's Opportunities Center, University of California Extension, Crawford Hall, Irvine, CA. Editors: Linda Algazi, Feb., 1971-Mar., 1973; Gleah Brown, Oct., 1973; Jeanne Golding, Spring, 1974. Subject focus: continuing education, employment, career development, students, professionals.

## Women's Periodicals and Newspapers

| | | |
|---|---|---|
| Hist | Feb., 1971-<br>Mar., 1973 | Microforms<br>Her. 2, R 19 |
| | Oct., 1973-<br>Spring, 1974 | Her. 2 UP, R13 |

Women's Page. San Francisco, CA

   see Second Page. San Francisco, CA

1415 Women's Pages. 1974//? Monthly. Last issue 6 pages. Line drawings. Available on microfilm: Herstory. Published by Women's Center of Richmond, Richmond, VA. Subject focus: Equal Rights Amendment, minorities, labor unions, politics.

| | | |
|---|---|---|
| Hist | v.1,n.2-3, 5;<br>Feb.-Mar.,<br>May, 1974 | Microforms<br>Her. 3, R 5 |

1416 Women's Peace Movement Bulletin; a Monthly Information Exchange For All Women's Peace Groups. 1962-1964//. Monthly. Last issue 12 pages, size 36 x 22. Published by Women Strike for Peace, Urbana, IL. Editor: Rachel Weller. Subject focus: peace movement.

| | | |
|---|---|---|
| Hist | v.2,n.9-v.3,n.6<br>Oct. 20, 1963-<br>June 20, 1964 | JQ/"W89<br>(Cutter) |

1417 The Women's Place Newsletter. 1972-1974//? Irregular. Last issue 8 pages. Line drawings. Available on microfilm: Herstory. Published by The Women's Place, Toronto, Ontario, Canada. Subject focus: self-help, child care, education.

| | | |
|---|---|---|
| Hist | July, 1972-<br>June, 1973 | Microforms<br>Her. 2, R 19 |
| | July, 1973-<br>June, 1974 | Her. 2UP, R13 |

1418 Women's Political Caucus/Milwaukee [Newsletter]. 1980? Unknown. Sue Poetzel, editor, Women's Political Caucus/Milwaukee Newsletter, 4759 North Berkeley, Milwaukee, WI 53211. Last issue 5 pages, size 36 x 22. Line drawings. Available on microfilm: WHi. Published by Milwaukee Women's Political Caucus, Wisconsin Women's Political Caucus. Subject focus: politics, politicians.

| | | |
|---|---|---|
| Hist | Oct., 1980- | Circulation |

1419 Women's Political Times. 1976. 6 times a year. $15 for individuals and institutions. Robbie Snow, editor, Women's Political Times, 1411 K Street NW, Washington, DC. ISSN 0195-1688. OCLC 4041910. LC sn79-7528. Last issue 18 pages, size 29 x 45. Line drawings, photographs, commercial advertising. Published by National Women's Political Caucus. Subject focus: rights, politics. Other holding institutions: InU (IUL), ICMR (IBF), [University of Minnesota Union List, Minneapolis, MN] (MUL).

| | | |
|---|---|---|
| Wom Ed<br>Res | v.1,n.2,v.2,n.1;<br>v.4, n.4-<br>Aug., 1976,<br>Winter, 1977,<br>Aug., 1979- | Circulation |

1420 Women's Press. 1970-1980//? Monthly. OCLC 2269645. Last issue 16 pages, last volume 142 pages, size 29 x 42. Line drawings, photographs. Available on microfilm: Herstory (1970-1974), WHi (1970-1972), UnM (1974). Published in Eugene, OR. Subject focus: rights, health, child rearing, politics, poetry. Other holding institutions: PPiU (PIT), WoU (WAU)

| | | |
|---|---|---|
| Hist | v.1,n.1-v.2,n.3<br>Dec., 1970-<br>May, 1972 | Microforms |
| | v.1,n.1-7;<br>Dec., 1970-<br>Aug., 1971 | Her. 1, R 4 |
| | v.1,n.9-v.3,n.4;<br>Oct., 1971-<br>June, 1973 | Her. 1 UP, R19 |
| | v.3,n.5-v.4,n.3<br>July/Aug., 1973-<br>May, 1974 | Her. CUP, R8 |

1421 Women's Report. 1973-1979//. Bi-monthly. OCLC 1789271. LC 73-647064. Last issue 20 pages, last volume 120 pages, size 21 x 30. Line drawings, photographs. Published by the Women's Lobby and the Fawcett Society, London, England. Subject focus: rights, education, law, socialism, politics, health. Other holding institutions: CLU (CLU), DLC (DLC), ViBlbv (VPI).

| | | |
|---|---|---|
| Coll | v.5,n.4-v.7,n4;<br>May/June, 1977-<br>June/July, 1979 | Women's<br>Reading Area |

1422 Women's Resource Center (Newsletter). 1978. Monthly. Gratis. Women's Resource Center (Newsletter), 2101 Main Street, Stevens Point, WI 54481. (715) 346-4851. Last issue 16 pages, size 28 x 22. Line drawings. Available on microfilm: WHi. Frequency varies: bi-weekly, Apr. 10, 1978-Feb. 14, 1980. Subject focus: self-help, lobbying, education.

| | | |
|---|---|---|
| Hist | v.1,n.1-<br>Apr. 10, 1978- | Circulation |
| Wom Ed Res | v.1,n.10-<br>Aug. 26, 1978- | Circulation |

1423 <u>Women's Rights Newsletter</u>. 1970-1971//? Irregular. OCLC 2269646. Last issue 4 pages. Line drawings. Available on microfilm: Herstory. Published by State Women's Caucus, California Democratic Council, Los Angeles, CA. Editor: Ruth Ehrlich. Subject focus: Democratic Party, lobbying, Equal Rights Amendment, rights, political parties.

| | | |
|---|---|---|
| Hist | May, 1970-<br>June 26, 1971 | Microforms<br>Her. 1, R 23 |
| | Feb., 1970,<br>Mar., 1971 | Her. 1 Add. |

1424 <u>Women's Rights Law Reporter</u>. 1971. Quarterly. $12 for individuals, $24 for institutions. Susan Vercheak, editor, Women's Rights Law Reporter, 15 Washington Street, Newark, NJ. ISSN 0085-8269. OCLC 1795817. LC. 74-647333. Last issue 158 pages, last volume 230 pages, size 22 x 28. Indexed: in Contents Current Legal Periodicals, Women Studies Abstracts, Public Affairs Information Service, Inc., Sociological Abstracts, Alternative Press Index. Line drawings, photographs, commercial advertising. Available on microfilm: UnM (1971-1974), Herstory (1971-1974). Published by Rutgers Law School, Newark, NJ. Place of publication varies: New York, NY, July/Aug., 1971. Frequency varies: bi-monthly, July/Aug., 1971; bi-annual, 1972; semi-annual, Fall/Winter, 1972-1973; Summer, 1973; annual, Winter, 1974-Spring/Summer, 1977. Subject focus: law, poverty, pro-abortion, prisoners, labor unions, birth control, child care, sexism in law, rights. Other holding institutions: AAP (AAA), AzFU (AZN), CLavC (CLV), [California State University, Dominguez Hills, Carson, CA] (CDH), CSt (Stanford University), CSdS (CDS), Ct (CZL), [Congressional Research Service, Washington, DC] (CRS), DGU-L (GUL), DLC (DLC), DUSC (LAW), DeU (DLM), FGULS (FUL), FJUNF (FNP), FU-L (FUB), IaDmG (IWG), IC (CGP), INS (IAI), InIU (IUP), [Indiana Union List of Serials, Indianapolis, IN] (ILS), InU (IUL), LNL-L (LLT), MCR-S (Schlesinger Library on the History of Women in America, Radcliffe College, Cambrigde, MA), MAH (HAM), MWelC (WEL), DME/DAS (OLA), MeLB (BTS), MiEM (EEM), MiKW (EXW), MiMtpT (EZC), MnSH-L (MHL), [University of Minnesota Union List, Minneapolis, MN] (MUL), MoKU (UMK), NhD (DRB), NAILS (YZA), NCH (YHM), NIC (COO), NNR (ZXC), [Central New York Library Resources Council, Syracuse, NY] (SRR), NOsU (YOM), NPV (VXW), NSbSU (YSM), NSufR (VVR), OAU (OUN), [University of Cincinnati, Marx Law Library, Cincinnati, OH] (OML), OC1U-L (LMC), [University of Dayton, Law Library, Dayton, OH] (ODL), OkS (OKS), OkU (OKL), PPiU (PIT), P (PHA), TxCM (TXA), [AMIGOS Union List of Serials, Dallas, TX] (IUC), TxDW (IWU), TxLT-L (TTL), ViRCU (VRC), VtU (VTU).

| | | |
|---|---|---|
| Hist | v.1, n.1;<br>July/Aug., 1971 | Microforms<br>Her. 1, R 12 |
| | v.1, n.2-4;<br>Spring, 1972-<br>Spring, 1973 | Her. 1 UP,<br>R 19-20 |
| Law | v.1, n.1-<br>July/Aug., 1971- | Circulation |
| WSLL | v.1, n.1-<br>July/Aug., 1971- | Circulation |

1425 <u>Women's Sports</u>. 1979. Monthly. $12.50 for individuals and institutions. Margaret Roach, editor, Women's Sports, 314 Town and Country Village, Palo Alto, CA 94301. Business address: P.O. Box 50483, Palo Alto, CA 94303. ISSN 0163-7428. OCLC 4473335. LC sn78-6917. Last issue 60 pages. Line drawings, photographs, some in color, commercial advertising. Published by Women's Sports Publications, Inc. Subject focus: sports, health, fiction. Other holding institutions: ArU (AFU), AzTeS (AZS), [Pepperdine University, Malibu, CA] (CPE), CU-SB (CUT), CoDU (DVP), COU-DA (COA), GU (GUA), GVaS (GYG), HU (HUH), IaLG (IOF), ICharE (IAD), INS (IAI), IU (UIU), KSteC (KKQ), KyRE (KEU), LLafS (LWA), LNU (LNU), Me (MEA), MiAC (EZA), MiAlbC (EXA), MiMtpT (EZC), MiU (EYM), MiYEM (EYE), [University of Minnesota Union List, Minneapolis, MN] (MUL), MnNS (MNO), NBrockU (XBM), NBronSL (VVS), NCortU (YCM), NCH (YHM), NOneoU (ZBM), [Central New York Library Resources Council, Syracuse, NY (SRR), NTRS (ZRS), NcCU (NKM), NdU (UND), [Morris County Free Library, Whippany, NJ] (NWM), OCedC (CDC), OrSaW (OWS), PLF (LFM), [Pittsburgh Regional Library Center-Union List, Pittsburgh, PA] (QPR), PPiU (PIT), TU (TKN), TxBeal (TXR), [AMIGOS Union List of Serials, Dallas, TX] (IUC), TxDW (IWU), TxLT (ILU), TxNacS (TXK), TxShA (IAU), TxNacS (TXK), VtMiM (MDY), [Arrowhead Library System, Janesville Public Library, Janesville, WI] (WIJ), WyU (WYU).

| | | |
|---|---|---|
| IMC | v.1, n.1-<br>Jan., 1979- | Periodicals<br>Section |

1426 <u>Women's Struggle</u>. 1971-1974//? Irregular. OCLC 2269647. Last issue 74 pages. Line drawings. Available on microfilm: Herstory. Published by Women's Liberation National Coordinating Committee, Hemel Hempstead, Hartfordshire, England. Place of publication varies: London, England, 1970-1971. Subject focus: education, pro-abortion, child care, birth control, employment, media.

| | | | |
|---|---|---|---|
| Hist | v.1, n.2-4; ?, 1971 | Microforms Her. 1, R 23 | |
| | v.2,n.1-v.3,n.3; Dec. 30, 1971-Aug., 1972? | Her. 1 UP, R20 | |
| | v.3,n.4-v.4,n.1; Oct. 20, 1973-June 22, 1974 | Her. CUP, R 8 | |

1427 <u>Women's Studies, An Interdisciplinary Journal</u>. 1973. Tri-annual. $29 for individuals, $64.50 for institutions. Wendy Martin, editor, Women's Studies, An Interdisciplinary Journal, Department of English, Queens College, CUNY, Flushing, NY. Business address: 42 William IV Street, London WC2, England. ISSN 0049-7878. OCLC 1791887. LC 74-641303. Last issue 162 pages, last volume 356 pages, size 15 x 22. Line drawings, photographs. Indexed in: Abstracts of Popular Culture, Women Studies Abstracts, self-indexed. Available on microfilm: Gordon & Breach Science Publishers (1972). Published by Gordon & Breach Science Publishers, Limited. Subject focus: women's studies, poetry, political science, art history, psychology, sociology, literature, history, art, law, economics, anthropology, film reviews. Other holding institutions: AU (ALM), ArU (AFU), AzFU (AZN), AzTeS (AZS), CLobS (CLO), CSt (Stanford University), CLU (CLU), COU-DA (COA), CtW (WLU), CtY (YUS), DLC (DLC), DeU (DLM), FBoU (FGM), FMFIU (FXG), FU (FUG), IaDuU (IOV), [Indiana Union List of Serials, Indianapolis, IN] (ILS), (ILS), InND (IND), InU (IUL), InU-M (IUM), KyU (KUK), MBNU (NED), MCR-S (Schlesinger Library on the History of Women in America, Radcliffe College, Cambridge, MA), MBU (BOS), MWA (AQM), MWelC (WEL), MdBJ (JHE), DME/DAS (OLA), MiMtpT (EZC), MiYEM (EYE), [University of Minnesota Union List, Minneapolis, MN] (MUL), MoU (MUU), [New York State Union List, Albany, NY] (NYS), NBC (VDB), NCortU (YCM), NFQC (XQM), NGcCC (VVX), NIC (COO), NNR (ZXC), NOneoU (ZBM), NRU (RRR), NSbSU (YSM), NSufR (VVR), [Central New York Library Resources Council, Syracuse, NY] (SRR), OAkU (AKR), OAU (OUN), PBL (LYU), PBm (BMC), PCoR (ROB), PLF (LFM), [Pittsburgh Regional Library Center-Union List, Pittsburgh, PA] (QPR), PPiU (PIT), PU (PAU), ScRhW (SWW), TxCM (TXA), [AMIGOS Union List of Serials, Dallas, TX] (IUC), TxLT (ILU), ViRCU (VRC), ViRU (VRU), WKenU (GZP), NcGU (NGU), NcRS (NRC), NbKS (KRS), NbU (LDL), NhD (DRB).

| | | | |
|---|---|---|---|
| Hist | v.1,n.1; ?, 1972 | Microforms Her. 2, R 19 | |
| Wom St | v.3, n.1- ?, 1975- | Reading Room | |
| Mem | v.5, n.1- ?, 1977- | Periodicals Room | |

1428 <u>Women's Studies in Indiana</u>. 1975? Women's Studies in Indiana, Memorial Hall East 130, Indiana University, Bloomington, IN 47405. Last issue 10 pages, size 22 x 28. Editor: Marlene Heinemann, Oct./Nov., 1978-Apr./May, 1979. Subject focus: women's studies, research.

| | | |
|---|---|---|
| Wom St | v.4,n.2-3,5, v.5, n.2- Oct./Nov., 1978-Dec./Jan., Apr./May, Nov./Dec., 1979- | Reading Room |

1429 <u>Women's Studies International Quarterly</u>. 1978. Quarterly. $30 for individuals, $61 for institutions. Dale Spender, editor, Women's Studies International Quarterly, Institute of Education, University of London, 20 Bedford Way, London, England. ISSN 0148-0685. OCLC 3712026. LC sn79-5686. Last issue 134 pages, last volume 402 pages, size 18 x 24. Line drawings, commercial advertising. Available on microfilm: Pergamon Press (1978-). Subject focus: research, women's studies. Other holding institutions: AAP (AAA), AzTeS (AZS), CU-Riv (CRU), COFS (COF), CtY (YUS), DGW (DGW), HU (HUH), ICharE (IAD), IGK (IBK), IU (UIU), InU (IUL), KPT (KFP), KWiU (KSW), MH (HUL), [University of Minnesota Union List, Minneapolis, MN] (MUL), MnStpeG (MNG), NCortU (YCM), NSyU (SYB), PBbS (PBB), PPiPT (PKT), ViRCU (VRC), ViU (VA@), WMUW (GZN).

| | | |
|---|---|---|
| Mem | v.1, n.1- Spring?, 1978- | Periodicals Room |

1430 <u>Women's Studies News</u>. 1976. Quarterly? Janice Leone, editor, University of Wisconsin, P.O. Box 413, Milwaukee, WI 53201. Last issue 8 pages, size 22 x 28. Line drawings. Previous editor: Sandra Schroeder, Summer/Winter, 1976. Subject focus: women's studies, research.

| | | |
|---|---|---|
| Wom St | v.1,n.1-2, v.5, n.1- Spring-Summer, 1976, Fall, 1979- | Reading Room |

1431 <u>Women's Studies Quarterly.</u> 1972. Quarterly. $10 for individuals, $15 for institutions. Florence Howe, editor, Women's Studies Quarterly, Box 334 Old Westbury, NY. ISSN 0363-1133. OCLC 1714552. LC sc76-476. Last issue 36 pages, last volume 132 pages, size 22 x 28. Line drawings, photographs, commercial advertising. Available on microfilm: Herstory (1971-1974). Published by the Feminist Press and the National Women's Studies Association. Title varies: as News and Notes from the Feminist Press, Fall, 1971-Summer, 1972. Subject focus: women's studies, higher education, educators, professionals. Other holding institutions: AAP (AAA), AU (ALM), ArU (AFU), AzTeS (AZS), CArcHT (CHU), CLobS (CLO), CLU (CLU), [University of Redlands, Redlands, CA] (CUR), CSdS (CDS), CtY (YUS), FBoU (FGM), FTS (FHM), IaDmG (IWG), ICRC (IAR), IRA (ICY), InIU (IUP), InU (IUL), KMK (KKS), KPT (KFP), KSteC (KKQ), KyU (KUK), LU (LUU), MBTI (BTI), MH (HLS(, MH (HUL), MH-AH (BHA), MWelC (WEL), MiEM (EEM), MiMtpT (EZC), [University of Minnesota Union List, Minneapolis, MN] (MUL), MoU (MUU), NhD (DRB), NbU (LDL), [New York State Union List, Albany, NY] (NYS), NCH (YHM), NGcCC (VVX), NIC (COO), NOneoU (ZBM), NRU (RRR), NSbSU (YSM), [Central New York Library Resources Council, Syracuse, NY] (SRR), OAkU (AKR), OCU (CIN), OO (OBE), OOeM (MIA), OTU (TOL), OU (OSU), OYU (YNG), OkS (OKS), PBm (BMC), PBL (LYU), P (PHA), PSC (PSC), PU (PAU), ScRhW (SWW), TNJ (TJC), [AMIGOS Union List of Serials, Dallas, TX] (IUC), TxDW (IWU), ViRCU (VRC), ViRU (VRU), WMaPI-RL (GZR), WU (GZM).

| | | |
|---|---|---|
| Wom St | v.1, n.1-<br>Fall, 1972- | Reading Room |
| Mem | v.1, n.6-<br>Winter, 1973/1974- | Periodicals Room |
| Wom Ed Res | v.1-<br>Fall, 1972- | Circulation |
| Hist | v.1,n.1-v.2,n.4;<br>Fall, 1971-<br>Summer, 1973 | Microforms<br>Her. 2, R 19 |
| | v.1,n.5-v.2,n.2;<br>Fall, 1973-<br>Spring, 1974 | Her. CUP, R13 |
| MPS | Fall, 1973- | Circulation |

1432 Women's Suffrage Journal. 1870-1890//?Weekly. Last issue 8 pages, last volume 88 pages. Line drawings, commercial advertising. Available on microfilm: ResP. Published by Tribner and Company, London, England. Editor: Lydia Ernestine Becker. Subject focus: pro-suffrage. Other holding institution: DLC (DLC).

| | | |
|---|---|---|
| Mem | v.2,n.16-v.21, n.218<br>June 1, 1871-<br>Aug. 1, 1890 | Microforms |

1433 Women's Track World. 1967. Monthly. $14 for individuals and institutions. S.F. Vincent Reel, editor, Women's Track World, P.O. Box 4092, Riverside, CA 92514. ISSN 0043-7573, 0193-8312. OCLC 3721200, 1815002. LC sn78-1836, sc79-3298. Last issue 48 pages, size 22 x 28. Line drawings, photographs, some in color, commercial advertising. Subject focus: sports. Other holding institutions: AU (ALM), [Pepperdine University, Malibu, CA] (CPE), CArcHT (CHU), CLSU (CSL), CLobS (CLO), CStbW (CWS), CSUuP (CPS), FTaSU (FDA), GVaS (GYG), IDeKN (JNA), InIU (IUP), MnDuU (MND), [University of Minnesota Union List, Minneapolis, MN] (MUL), NCortU (YCM), NII (XIM), NTRS (ZRS), NcRS (NRC), TxCM (TXA), [AMIGOS Union List of Serials, Dallas, TX] (IUC), TxDW (IWU), TxLT (ILU), TxNacS (TXK).

| | | |
|---|---|---|
| Coll | Current Issues Only | Women's Reading Area |

Women's Transit Authority Newsletter.
Madison, WI

see Women's Transit Home Companion.
Madison, WI

1434 Women's Transit Home Companion. 1974. Monthly. Women's Transit Home Companion, 306 North Brooks Street, Madison, WI 53715. (608) 256-3710, 263-1700. Last issue 5 pages, size 22 x 28. Line drawings. Available on microfilm: WHi. Published by the Women's Transit Authority. Title varies: as Women's Transit Authority Newsletter, Mar./Apr., 1974; as WTA Newsletter, Oct., 1974; as Transit Home Companion, May, 1976-Apr., 1978; as In Transit, Aug.-Nov., 1978. Subject focus: rape prevention.

| | | |
|---|---|---|
| Hist | Mar./Apr., 1974- | Circulation |
| Wom St | Mar?, 1976-<br>June/July, 1978 | Reading Room |

1435 The Women's Union Journal. 1876-1890//. Monthly. Last issue 10 pages, last volume 120 pages. Commercial advertising. Available on microfilm: ResP. Published by Women's Protective and Provident League, 36 Lincoln's Innfields, London, England. Subject focus: workers, poetry. Other holding institutions: COU-DA (COA), NN (NYP).

| | | |
|---|---|---|
| Mem | v.8,n.84-<br>v.15, n.179<br>Jan., 1883-<br>Dec. 15, 1890 | Microforms |

1436 Women's Universal Movement, Inc. 1970-1974//? Irregular. Last issue 4 pages. Line drawings. Available on microfilm: Herstory. Published by Women's Universal Movement, Inc., New York, NY. Subject focus: United Nations, international relations.

| | | |
|---|---|---|
| Hist | n.3-8;<br>Dec., 1970-<br>Jan., 1973 | Microforms<br>Her. 2, R 19 |
| | n.9-10;<br>July, 1973-<br>Mar., 1974 | Her. 2UP, R13 |

1437 Women's Voices. 1972-1974//? Irregular. Last issue 32 pages. Line drawings, photographs, commercial advertising. Available on microfilm: Herstory. Published by Women's Voices, State University of New York, Buffalo, NY. Subject focus: politics, education, health, poetry, art.

| | | |
|---|---|---|
| Hist | v.1,n.2-5, v.2, n.3; Sep./Oct., 1972-May/June, 1973, Spring/Summer, 1974 | Microforms Her. 2, R 20 |
| | v.2, n.1,3; Oct./Nov., 1973, Spring/Summer, 1974 | Her. 2 UP,R13 |

Women's Washington Report. Washington, DC

    see Washington's Women's Representative. Washington, DC

Women's Washington Representative. Washington, DC

    see Washington Women's Representative. Washington, DC

Women's Wear Daily. New York, NY

    see WWD. New York, NY

1438 Women's Work and War. 1918-1919//. Monthly. Last issue 4 pages. Available on microfilm: WHi. Published by The National Women's Trade Union League, Chicago, IL. Editor: Anne Forsyth. Subject focus: World War I, labor unions, politics, rights. Other holding institution: MCR-S (Schlesinger Library on the History of Women in America, Radcliffe College, Cambridge, MA).

| | | |
|---|---|---|
| Hist | v.2, n.1,2 Jan.-Feb., 1919 | Microforms |
| | v.1,n.1-v.2,n.3 Feb., 1918-Apr./May, 1919 | F836/+8NA (Cutter) |

1439 WomenSports. 1974-1978//. Monthly. ISSN 0095-0661. OCLC 4443603, 1796160. LC 74-647853. Last issue 72 pages, last volume 784 pages, size 22 x 27. Line drawings, photographs, some in color, commercial advertising. Available on microfilm: UnM (1974-1976). Published by WomenSports Publishing Company, New York, NY. Place of publication varies: San Mateo, CA, Jan., 1975. Editors: Rosalie Muller Wright, Jan./July, 1975; Larry King, Aug., 1975-Dec., 1975; Pamela Van Wagenen, Nov., 1976; LeAnne Schreiber, Dec., 1976-Feb., 1978. Subject focus: sports, biographies. Other holding institutions: ArRuA (AKP), AzTeS (AZS), AzU (AZU), CLobS (CLO), CLO (CCO), CLSU (CSL), CLU (CLU), CU-Riv (CRU), COU-DA (COA), CtY (YUS), DLC (DLC), DeU (DLM), FBoU (FGM), FTaSU (FDA), FU (FUG), IaCfT (NIU), IaLG (IOF), InU (IUL), KLindB (KFB), KMK (KKS), KSteC (KKQ), KyRE (KEU), LNU (LNU), MMiltC (CUM), MiAdC (EEA), MiAlbC (EXA), MiMtpT (EZC), [University of Minnesota Union List, Minneapolis, MN] (MUL), MnStjos (MNF), [New York State Union List, Albany, NY] (NYS), NBrockU (XBM), NBu (VHB), NCortU (YCM), NCH (YHM), NGenoU (YGM), NIC (COO), NNR (ZXC), NOneoU (ZBM), NRU (RRR), [Central New York Library Resources Council, Syracuse, NY] (SRR), NcGU (NGU), NcRS (NRC), NdU (UND), NbU (LDL), NhD (DRB), OAU (OUN), OCanM (MAL), OCl (CLE), OTU (TOL), OU (OSU), OkT (TUL), OrSaW (OWS), [Pittsburgh Regional Library Center-Union List, Pittsburgh, PA] (QPR), PP (PLF), PPiU (PIT), ScRhW (SWW), TCollsM (TMS), TMurS (TXM), TU (TKN), TxAU (TXG), TxCM (TXA), [AMIGOS Union List of Serials, Dallas, TX] (IUC), TxDW (IWU), InLS (ILA), TxNacS (TXK), TxShA (IAU), [Emory and Henry College, Emory, VA] (VEH), WM (GZD).

| | | |
|---|---|---|
| IMC | v.3,n.11-v.5,n.2 Nov., 1976-Feb., 1978 | Periodicals Section |
| Coll | v.4,n.1-v.5,n.2 Jan., 1977-Feb., 1978 | Women's Reading Area |
| Mem | v.2,n.1-12, v.3, n.12 Jan.-Dec., 1975, Dec., 1976 | AP/W8722/S765 |
| MPL | v.1,n.11-v.5,n.2 Nov., 1974-Feb., 1978 | Literature and Social Science Section |
| MATC | July, 1975-Feb., 1978 | Technical Center |
| MMHS | Aug., 1974-Feb., 1978 | Circulation |
| MFHS | Jan., 1975-Feb., 1978 | Circulation |
| MHHS | Jan., 1975-Feb., 1978 | Circulation |
| MIPL | Jan., 1976-Feb., 1978 | Circulation |
| MAHS | Sep., 1975-Feb., 1978 | Circulation |
| SCPL | Aug., 1975-Feb., 1978 | Circulation |

1440 Wonder Woman. 1942. Monthly. $7.95 for individuals and institutions. Joe Orlando, editor, Wonder Woman, 75 Rockefeller Plaza, New York, NY 10019. Business address: 14 Vanderventer Avenue, Port Washington, NY 11050. Last issue 36 pages, last volume 432 pages. Line drawings, some in color, commercial advertising. Published by DC Comics, Inc., New York, NY. Subject focus: comics, fiction.

MPL     Current Issues Only     Young Adults Area

Woodhull & Claflin's Weekly. Albuquerque, NM

see NOW Newsletter. Albuquerque, NM

1441 Woodhull & Claflins Weekly. 1870-1876//. Weekly. Last issue 16 pages, last volume 480 pages. Line drawings, commercial advertising. Available on microfilm: UnM, DLC. Published in New York, NY. Editors: Victoria C. Woodhull and Tennie C.(Tennessee) Claflin. Subject focus: morality, sexuality, free love.

Hist     v.1,n.1-v.12, n.27?; May 14, 1870- June 10, 1876     Microforms

1442 Worcester Women's Press. 1973-1974//? Monthly. Last issue 18 pages. Line drawings. Available on microfilm: Herstory (1974). Published by Worcester Women's Press, The Women's Center, Worcester, MA. Subject focus: aging, pro-abortion, health, politics, crimes against women, sexism, workers.

Hist     n.11-14; Mar.-June, 1974     Microforms Her. 3, R 5

1443 Workers Dreadnought. 1914-1924//. Weekly. OCLC 2558154, 2557084. Last issue 8 pages, last volume 104 pages. Line drawings, photographs, commercial advertising. Available on microfilm: WmP, Uk (British Library). Published by East London Federation of Suffragettes, London, England. Title varies: as The Woman's Dreadnought, Mar. 8, 1914-July 21, 1917. Editor: Sylvia Pankhurst. Subject focus: pro-suffrage, socialism, internationalism, workers, communism. Other holding institutions: AJacT (AJB), CSt (Stanford University), InU (IUL), NcGU (NGU), OKentU (KSU), ViNO (VOD), GASU (GSU), [Indiana Union List of Serials, Indianapolis, IN] (ILS).

Mem     v.1,n.1-v.11, n.13; Mar. 8, 1914- July 14, 1924     Microforms

EC     v.1,n.1-v.4,n.17 Mar. 8, 1914- June 21, 1917     Microforms

1444 The Working Mother. 1971-1973//? OCLC 2269666. Last issue 12 pages. Line drawings, photographs. Available on microfilm: Herstory. Published by The Voice of Mother's and Children's Liberation, Maternal Information Services, Inc., New York, NY. Subject focus: working women, child care, rights, sexism, pro-abortion. Other holding institution: MCR-S (Schlesinger Library on the History of Women in America, Radcliffe College, Cambridge, MA).

Hist     v.1, n.1; Summer, 1971     Microforms Her. 1, R 23

v.1,n.2-v.2,n.1; Fall, 1971- Winter, 1972-1973     Her. 1 UP R20

1445 Working Woman. 1976. Monthly. $12 for individuals and institutions. Kate Rand Lloyd, editor, Working Woman, 1180 Avenue of the Americas, New York, NY 10036. Business address: P.O. Box 10132, Des Moines, IA 50340. ISSN 0145-5761. OCLC 7331931, 5764722, 2761141. LC 77-640037. Last issue 104 pages, last volume 1246 pages, size 21 x 28. Line drawings, photographs, some in color, commercial advertising. Available on microfilm: UnM. Published by Hal Publications, New York, NY. Subject focus: fashion, health, food, consumerism, employment, health, career development, professionals. Other holding institutions: AzTeS (AZS), [Pepperdine University, Malibu,,CA] (CPE), CChiS (CCH), CLSU (CSL), CLU (CLU), CLobS (CLO), COFS (COF), COU-DA (COA), CPom (PFO), CsjU (CSJ), CtY (YUS), WeharU (HRM), [St. Joseph College, West Hartford, CT] (STJ), DAU (EAU), DHU (DHU), DLC (DLC), DME/DAS (OLA), DT (DTL), FU (FUG), GMarS (GAS GVaS (GYG), IC (CGP), ICRC (IAR), ICSX (ICS), IMgO (IAP), INS (IAI), IU (UIU), IaLG (IOF), InTI (ISU), KMK (KKS), [Charles River Associates, Cambridge, MA] (CRA), MBSi (SCL), MNS (SNN), Me (MEA), MiD (EYP), MiDU (EYU), MiU (EYM), MnDuU (MND), [University of Minnesota Union List, Minneapolis, MN] (MUL), MNQ (MNQ), MnStjos (MNF), MoU (MUU), MoUst (UMS), MsU (MUM), [New York State Union List, Albany, NY] (NYS), NBX (VDB), NBu (VHB), NEE (VXE), NIC (COO), NOneoU (ZBM), NOsU (YOM), NR (YQR), NPV (VXW), [Central New York, Library Resources Council, Syracuse, NY] (SRR), NSufR (VVR), NTRS (ZRS), OAU (OUN), OC1W-H (CHS), OCU (CIN), OKentU (KSU), OOcM (MIA), OSteC (STU), OU (OSU), OkAdE (ECO), OkS (OKS), OkShB (OKB), OkTahN (OKN), PPD (DXU), PManM (MAN), [Pittsburgh Regional Library Center-Union List, Pittsburgh, PA] (QPR), PCLS (REC), PCoR (ROB), [AMIGOS Union List of Serials, Dallas, TX] (IUC), TxAu (TXG), TxCM (TXA), TxDa (IGA), TxDN (INT),

TxDW (IWU), TxNacS (TXK), TxSmS (TXI), UOW
(UUO), ViU (VA@), ViBlbv (VPI), WA (WIQ), WaU
(WAU), WFon (WIF), WMUW (GZN), [Arrowhead
Library System, Janesville Public Library,
Janesville, WI] (WIJ).

| MPL | v.3, n.3-<br>Mar., 1978- | Literature and Social Science Section |
|---|---|---|
| MATC | v.2, n.6-<br>June, 1977- | Cora Hardy Library |

1446  The Working Woman. 1887-1891//? Weekly. Last issue 4 pages. Available on microfilm: WHi. Published by Woman's National Industrial League, Washington, DC. Editor: Charlotte Smith. Subject focus: rights, workers, personal finance, politics.

| Hist | v.1, n.23, v.3,<br>n.2,8,10, v.4,n.1-<br>Oct. 15, 1887,<br>Apr. 5, Aug. 17,<br>Oct. 18, 1890,<br>Jan. 5-May 5,<br>July 25, 1891 | Microforms |
|---|---|---|

1447  The Working Woman. 1929-1935//? Monthly. Last issue 4 pages, last volume 170 pages. Line drawings, photographs. Available on microfilm: WHi. Published by the Woman's Department, Central Committee, Communist Party of the U.S.A., New York, NY. Editors: Anna Damin, Dec., 1929; Margaret Cowl, Nov., 1934-Dec., 1935. Subject focus: rights, politics, communism, workers.

| Hist | v.1,n.3-v.6,n.11;<br>Dec., 1929-<br>Dec., 1935 | Microforms |
|---|---|---|

1448  The Working Woman's Journal. 1888-1895//? Monthly. Last issue 8 pages. Line drawings, commercial advertising. Available on microfilm: Herstory. Published by the New Century Guild of Working Women, Philadelphia, PA. Subject focus: poetry, workers.

| Hist | v.8, n.8,10;<br>Oct. 5,<br>Dec. 7, 1895 | Microforms |
|---|---|---|

1449  XX Chromosome Chronicle, A Magazine About Women. 1978-1979//? 8 times a year. OCLC 7012551. Last issue 35 pages, size 26 x 18. Line drawings. Published by Women's Studies Committee, Sangamon State University, Springfield, IL. Subject focus: women's studies, health.

| Hist | v.2, n.8;<br>Summer, 1979 | Pam 80-1598 |
|---|---|---|

YWCA Bulletin War Work Council.  New York, NY

see Blue Triangle News.  New York, NY

1450  Y.W.C.A. in Motion. 1971-1972//? Unknown. Last issue 8 pages. Line drawings, photographs. Available on microfilm: Herstory. Published by Young Women's Christian Association, San Francisco, CA. Subject focus: education, prisoners, Christianity, politics.

| Hist | v.1, n.4;<br>Feb. 15, 1972 | Microforms<br>Her. 2, R 20 |
|---|---|---|

1451  YWCA-News of the Atlanta YWCA. 1973-1974//? Irregular. Last issue 4 pages. Line drawings, photographs. Available on microfilm: Herstory. Published by the Young Women's Christian Association of Greater Atlanta, Atlanta, GA. Subject focus: Christianity.

| Hist | Oct., Fall, 1973,<br>Feb., 1974 | Microforms<br>Her. 3, R 5 |
|---|---|---|

1452  YWCA-Plainfield Organization for Women's Equal Rights. 1972//? Unknown. Last issue 4 pages. Line drawings. Available on microfilm: Herstory. Published by Young Women's Christian Association-Plainfield Organization for Women's Equal Rights, Plainfield, NJ. Subject focus: lobbying, politics, pro-abortion, Christianity.

| Hist | Mar., 1972 | Microforms<br>Her. 2, R 13 |
|---|---|---|

1453  Y.W.C.A. Women's Resource Center. 1973//? Monthly. Last issue 4 pages. Line drawings. Available on microfilm: Herstory. Published by Young Women's Christian Association, Natick, MA. Subject focus: history, education, Christianity.

| Hist | Mar. 28-<br>Apr. 28, 1973 | Microforms<br>Her. 2, R 20 |
|---|---|---|

1454  Yale Break. 1969-1971//? Irregular. OCLC 2269742. Last issue 7 pages. Line drawings. Available on microfilm: Herstory. Published by New Haven Women's Liberation, New Haven, CT. Subject focus: students, higher education, sexism in education, rights, Yale Non-Faculty Action Committee. Other holding institution: [University of Minnesota Union List, Minneapolis, MN] (MUL).

| Hist | Sep., 1969-<br>Jan. 1, 1971 | Microforms<br>Her. 1, R 23 |
|---|---|---|
| | Apr., 1970 | Her. 1 Add. |

1455  The Yellow Ribbon. 1972-1974//? Irregular. Last issue 10 pages. Line drawings. Available on microfilm: Herstory. Published by United Methodist Women's Caucus, Evanston, IL. Subject focus: religion, Methodism, employment, rights, child care. In Spanish (10%).

| Hist | v.1, n.1-6;<br>June, 1972-<br>May, 1973 | Microforms<br>Her. 2, R 20 |
|---|---|---|
|  | v.2, n.1-4;<br>Sep., 1973-<br>Spring, 1974 | Her. 2 UP, R 13 |

1456 Young Miss. 1953. 9 times a year. $9.95 for individuals. Lois Cantwell, editor, Young Miss, 80 New Bridge Road, Bergenfield, NJ 07621. Business address: 685 3rd Avenue, New York, NY 10017. ISSN 0044-0833. OCLC 1770370. LC sn78-164. Last issue 74 pages, last volume 676 pages. Line drawings, photographs. Indexed in: Subject Index to Children's Magazines. Published by Parents Magazine Enterprises, Gruner & Jahr, USA, Inc. Subject focus: celebrities, girls, teenagers, fiction, fashion, music. Other holding institutions: [University of Minnesota Union List, Minneapolis, MN] (MUL), [Western New York Library Resources Council, Buffalo, NY] (VZX), [Central New York Library Resources Council, Syracuse, NY] (SRR), OkT (TUL), TxAu (TXG), [AMIGOS Union List of Serials, Dallas, TX] (IUC), WFon (WIF).

| MPL | v.26, n.257-<br>Jan., 1980- | Children's<br>Area |
|---|---|---|

1457 Your Cue From CCEW. 1967-1973//? Irregular. Last issue 4 pages. Line drawings. Available on microfilm: Herstory. Published by the Council for the Continuing Education of Women-Miami Dade Community College, Miami, FL. Subject focus: continuing education, Equal Rights Amendment, lobbying, career development, employment.

| Hist | Winter, 1967-<br>Spring/Summer, 1973 | Microforms<br>Her. 2, R 20 |
|---|---|---|

1458 Zarja - The Dawn. 1928. 11 times a year. $6 for individuals and institutions. Corinne Leskovar, editor, Zarja-The Dawn, 2035 West Cermak Road, Chicago, IL 60608. (312) 847-6679. Business address: 431 N. Chicago St., Joliet, IL 60432. (815) 727-1926. ISSN 0044-1848. OCLC 1774233. LC sn78-1161. Last issue 48 pages, last volume 328 pages, size 19 x 28. Line drawings, photographs, commercial advertising. Published by Slovenian Women's Union of America. Frequency varies: monthly, Feb., 1950-June, 1970. Previous editor: Albina Novak, Feb., 1950-Dec., 1951. Subject focus: Slovenians. In Slovenian (20%). Other holding institution: [University of Minnesota Union List, Minneapolis, MN] (MUL).

| Hist | [v.22, n.2-v.28,<br>n.12], v.30, n.12-<br>[Feb., 1950-<br>Dec., 1956],<br>Dec., 1958- | AP/58/S55/Z3 |
|---|---|---|

Zeitschrift fuer Frauen-Stimmrecht: Monatschrift fuer die staatsbuergerliche Bildung der Frau. Berlin, Germany

see Zeitschrift fuer Frauen-Stimmrecht: Organ fuer die staatsbuergerliche Bildung. Berlin, Germany

1459 Zeitschrift fuer Frauen-Stimmrecht: Organ fuer die staatsbuergerliche Bildung der Frau. 1907-1918//. Semi-monthly. Last issue 4 pages, last volume 48 pages. Line drawings, commercial advertising. Available on microfilm: McA. Published by W.& S. Loewenthal, Berlin, Germany. Title varies: as Zeitscrift fuer die Frauen-Stimmrecht: Zeitscrift fuer die Politischen Interessen der Frau/Publications Organ des Deutschen Verbandig fuer Frauen-Stimmrecht und seiner Zweigvereine, Jan. 1, 1907-Jan. 15, 1912; Zeitschrift fuer Frauen-Stimmrecht: Monatschrift fuer die staatsbuergerliche Bildung der Frau, Feb. 1, 1912-Jan. 1, 1913. Frequency varies: monthly, Jan., 1907-Jan., 1913. Editors: Anita Augspurg, Jan., 1907-Feb., 1912; Minna Cauer, Apr., 1912-Dec., 1918. Subject focus: pro-suffrage, rights. In German (100%).

| Mem | v.1, n.1-<br>[v.12, n.24]<br>Jan., 1907-<br>Dec., 1918 | Microforms |
|---|---|---|

Zeitschrift fuer die Frauen-Stimmrecht: Zeitschrift fuer die Politischen Interessen der Frau/Publications Organ des Deutschen Verbandig fuer Frauen-Stimmrecht und seiner Zweigvereine. Berlin, Germany

see Zeitschrift fuer Frauen-Stimmrecht: Organ fuer die staatsbuerger Bildung. Berlin, Germany

1460 Zeitschrift Fur Sexualwissenschaft. 1908//? Last volume 736 pages. Available on microfilm: ResP. Published in Leipzig, Germany. Editor: Dr. Magnus Hirschfeld. Subject focus: sexuality. In German (100%). Other holding institution: [Edward G. Miner Library, School of Medicine and Dentistry, University of Rochester, Rochester, NY] (NRU).

| Mem | Jan.-Dec., 1908 | Microforms |
|---|---|---|

1461 Zontian. 1951. Quarterly. $3 for individuals. Marion H. Dudley, editor, Zontain, 35 East Wacker Drive, Chicago, IL 60601. (312) 346-1445. OCLC 1770646. Last issue 22 pages, size 22 x 28. Line drawings, photographs. Published by Zonta International. Subject focus: clubs. Other holding institutions: [University of Minnesota Union List, Minneapolis, MN] (MUL), NR (YQR), WM (GZD).

| | | |
|---|---|---|
| MPL | Current Issues Only | Business and Science Section |
| Mem | v.55, n.2- June, 1975- | Periodicals Room |

# Geographic Index

Numbers following each location refer to specific entries and not page numbers.

ALABAMA

   Birmingham, 640
   Montgomery, 393

ALASKA

   Anchorage, 871

ARIZONA

   Phoenix, 1, 60, 481, 639, 911
   Sun City, 192
   Tucson, 866, 1127

CALIFORNIA

   Albion, 249
   Bakersfield, 685
   Berkeley, 7, 64, 74, 89, 90, 96, 121, 124, 174, 226, 279, 280, 294, 333, 491, 567, 581, 681, 766, 811, 918, 953, 1016, 1018, 1067, 1115, 1142, 1234, 1300, 1338, 1366, 1393, 1412
   Beverly Hills, 51
   Burlingame, 996
   Canoga Park, 696
   Claremont, 721
   Corte Madera, 1394
   Costa Mesa, 724, 876
   Davis, 1235, 1381
   Fairchild, 723
   Fresno, 183, 586, 704
   Frontera, 206
   Fullerton, 16, 156, 805
   Goleta, 965
   Hayward, 934
   Hollywood, 666
   Irvine, 770, 1414
   Isla Vista, 1217
   Kensington, 43
   La Crescenta, 726
   La Jolla, 768
   La Mesa, 168
   Lafayette, 1077
   Laguna Beach, 562
   Livermore, 812, 1155
   Lomita, 365
   Long Beach, 694, 1078
   Los Angeles, 15, 65, 109, 152, 157, 165, 169, 198, 315, 361, 576, 595, 620, 680, 682, 684, 756, 771, 897, 922, 1028, 1074, 1101, 1112, 1113, 1168, 1202, 1231, 1236, 1251, 1258, 1293, 1322, 1335, 1388, 1400, 1423
   Malibu, 684
   Manhatten, 85
   Mill Valley, 452
   Millbrae, 813
   Monterey, 646, 814, 1045
   Monterey Park, 815
   Napa Valley, 742
   Newport Beach, 562
   North Hollywood, 991
   Northridge, 2
   Oakland, 43, 59, 79, 363, 375, 859, 1039, 1412
   Orange, 1323

CALIFORNIA (continued)

   Palo Alto, 720, 882, 1396, 1425
   Palos Verdes Estates, 722
   Pittsburg, 1064
   Playa del Rey, 311
   Riverside, 201, 1046, 1314, 1433
   Rolling Hills Estates, 722
   Sacramento, 116, 170, 171, 178, 223, 303, 356, 669, 697, 774, 986, 987, 1044, 1201
   San Diego, 8, 162, 167, 201, 347, 424, 593, 725, 768, 898, 1007, 1052
   San Francisco, 3, 20, 36, 73, 84, 108, 111, 129, 190, 195, 237, 251, 276, 344, 357, 494, 503, 508, 527, 579, 656, 679, 736, 804, 816, 846, 880, 900, 946, 974, 980, 984, 992, 993, 994, 999, 1006, 1036, 1050, 1142, 1153, 1174, 1244, 1264, 1297, 1309, 1337, 1338, 1360, 1450
   San Jose, 166, 395, 577, 698, 904, 997, 1147
   San Mateo, 1439
   San Pedro, 437
   San Rafael, 705, 1411
   Santa Ana, 16
   Santa Barbara, 706
   Santa Cruz, 263, 417, 445
   Santa Monica, 163
   Seaside, 817
   Sherman Oaks, 696
   South Pasadena, 1358
   Stanford, 150, 933, 1304, 1370
   Stockton, 995
   Sunnyvale, 1090
   Thousand Oaks, 232
   Venice, 643, 644, 1028
   Ventura, 1156
   Walnut Creek, 244, 769
   Whittier, 201
   Woodside, 150

COLORADO

   Boulder, 110, 119, 256, 642, 836, 1014, 1161
   Colorado Springs, 286
   Denver, 95, 267, 603, 707, 1032, 1038
   Fort Collins, 370
   Westminster, 1167

CONNECTICUT

   Bridgeport, 461
   Bristol, 236
   Elmwood, 235
   Greenwich, 1262
   Hartford, 1249
   Middletown, 29, 601, 979
   New Canaan, 955
   New Haven, 1029, 1328, 1454
   Norwalk, 371
   Rowayton, 732
   Stamford, 505, 649, 1352
   Stonington, 1060
   Storrs, 1031
   Stratford, 461
   Wallingford, 212
   Waterbury, 868

## Women's Periodicals and Newspapers

CONNECTICUT (continued)

West Hartford, 188
Westport, 782

DELAWARE

Newark, 243, 781

DISTRICT OF COLUMBIA

Washington, 21, 27, 28, 66, 69, 70, 116, 131, 149, 189, 218, 221, 222, 234, 260, 263, 266, 272, 283, 298, 301, 305, 328, 342, 355, 366, 400, 403, 409, 422, 430, 480, 511, 570, 584, 624, 627, 672, 673, 676, 739, 744, 746, 747, 748, 756, 761, 763, 765, 767, 799, 800, 809, 818, 861, 867, 884, 894, 916, 928, 940, 943, 957, 963, 984, 1011, 1070, 1088, 1159, 1171, 1173, 1180, 1188, 1192, 1193, 1194, 1195, 1197, 1211, 1215, 1245, 1250, 1281, 1303, 1310, 1327, 1336, 1348, 1353, 1355, 1363, 1378, 1406, 1419, 1446

FLORIDA

Boca Raton, 1410
Coconut Grove, 683
Coral Gables, 192
Gainsville, 833
Jacksonville, 1185
Miami, 59, 1458
Miami Beach, 651
Orlando, 803
Palm Beach, 790
Pompano Beach, 1209
Tallahassee, 390, 886, 941, 1035
Tampa, 98, 984, 1110, 1144

GEORGIA

Atlanta, 75, 76, 165, 185, 504, 715, 890, 1062, 1451
Augusta, 56
Savannah, 538

HAWAII

Honolulu, 25, 240, 462, 895, 1072, 1367

ILLINOIS

Alton, 912
Champaign, 406, 1179
Charleston, 230
Chicago, 13, 23, 39, 40, 41, 101, 132, 150, 161, 165, 209, 219, 245, 252, 272, 282, 360, 405, 439, 466, 481, 492, 513, 566, 634, 635, 652, 695, 738, 783, 801, 891, 1023, 1027, 1065, 1075, 1080, 1122, 1124, 1136, 1141, 1163, 1210, 1240, 1253, 1267, 1270, 1279, 1337, 1438, 1458, 1461
Dekalb, 1122
Dubois, 1162
Edwardsville, 133
Elgin, 377
Evanston, 659, 944, 1141, 1375, 1455
Galesburg, 59, 181

ILLINOIS (continued)

Glen Ellyn, 1116
Joliet, 1458
Macomb, 832
Mendota, 481, 885
Moline, 937
Mount Morris, 104, 885
Murphysboro, 515
Northbrook, 714
Palatine, 1077
Parkridge, 419
Peoria, 708
River Forest, 101
Rockford, 481, 667
Skokie, 714
Springfield, 1449
Urbana, 851, 1179, 1416
Worth, 719

INDIANA

Bloomington, 284, 397, 470, 1179, 1382, 1428
Columbus, 19
Connersville, 1204
Evansville, 692
Gary, 1011
Indianapolis, 59, 181, 471, 472, 602, 757, 1255
Middlebury, 931
Muncie, 709
New Albany, 151
Richmond, 590, 1345
West Lafayette, 6, 230, 958, 1107

IOWA

Des Moines, 93, 438, 499, 622, 819, 885, 893, 1120, 1280, 1445
Iowa City, 24, 150
Milo, 19
Mitchellville, 1096
Parkersburg, 440
Rockwell City, 973
Sutherland, 1280
Waterloo, 1280

KANSAS

Buffalo, 440
Girard, 219
Lawrence, 507
Topeka, 139, 509
Wichita, 820, 919

KENTUCKY

Ashland, 1011
Lexington, 618
Louisville, 791, 1256

LOUISIANA

Bastrop, 1011
Baton Rouge, 370, 852
New Orleans, 271, 444, 446
Saint Gabriel, 87, 924
Shreveport, 481, 925

## MAINE

Augusta, 45, 259
Portland, 467, 608, 609

## MARYLAND

Annapolis, 49, 691
Baltimore, 215, 301, 302, 425, 617, 755, 789, 976, 1216, 1296, 1368
College Park, 217, 321, 984
Greenbelt, 1015
Hagerstown, 1191
Hyattsville, 1022
Jessup, 436
Rockville, 394
Silver Spring, 160, 1022
Temple Hills, 727

## MASSACHUSETTS

Allston, 1030
Amherst, 196, 313
Arlington, 319
Beverly, 307
Boston, 92, 114, 181, 211, 270, 304, 310, 314, 324, 334, 412, 455, 459, 527, 540, 547, 549, 585, 607, 638, 777, 821, 822, 839, 841, 879, 928, 954, 984, 1069, 1135, 1138, 1200, 1247, 1260, 1267, 1274, 1282, 1283, 1408
Brookline, 1257
Cambridge, 114, 221, 239, 325, 334, 367, 427, 463. 525, 565, 841, 869, 967, 984, 1008, 1053, 1403
East Sandwich, 177
Lenox, 1295
Lexington, 1181, 1182
Lowell, 546, 875
Martha's Vineyard, 468
Natick, 1453
Newtonville, 1164
Northampton, 255, 399, 1152, 1269
North Dartmouth, 830
Rockport, 307
Salem, 541
Somerville, 31, 841
Springfield, 423, 1199
Wellesley, 1320
Worcester, 175, 1267, 1442

## MICHIGAN

Ann Arbor, 187, 499, 630, 759, 829, 936, 1013, 1071, 1145, 1389
Dearborn, 947
Detroit, 63, 155, 213, 663, 947, 1132, 1254
East Lansing, 464, 572, 828, 1179
Farmington, 1206
Holland, 344
Kalamazoo, 1237
Lansing, 179, 343, 510, 631
Midland, 50

## MINNESOTA

Duluth, 105
Minneapolis, 12, 241, 289, 354, 404, 408, 420, 699, 917, 1025, 1057, 1129, 1130, 1179,

## MINNESOTA (continued)

Minneapolis (continued), 1261, 1361
Rochester, 391
St. Joseph, 1041
St. Paul, 228, 331, 354, 1175
Shakopee, 951

## MISSOURI

Boonville, 107
Kansas City, 192, 447, 527, 667, 1009, 1316
St. Louis, 9, 47, 948, 990, 1055, 1139, 1267, 1272

## MISSISSIPPI

Summit, 1243

## MONTANA

Bozeman, 368
Great Falls, 61
Missoula, 61

## NEBRASKA

Beatrice, 1281
Hastings, 1079
Lincoln, 481, 569, 591, 619, 1026
Omaha, 181, 316

## NEVADA

Las Vegas, 564
Sparks, 48

## NEW HAMPSHIRE

Concord, 425
Portsmouth, 477, 1213
Seabrook, 1374

## NEW JERSEY

Bergenfield, 1456
Cherry Hill, 808
Clifton, 700
Clinton, 476
Dover, 780
East Orange, 26
Fanwood, 1397
Ho-Ho-Kus, 718
Iselin, 632
Jersey City, 505
Maplewood, 193
Martinsville, 1056
Mountainside, 710
Newark, 1424
New Brunswick, 227, 349, 977
Old Bridge, 678
Orange, 369
Paramus, 806
Passaic, 700
Paterson, 497, 837
Plainfield, 505, 1452
Princeton, 711, 731
Red Bank, 645

NEW JERSEY (continued)

    South Orange, 193
    Thorofare, 120
    Trenton, 469, 1123
    Union, 312
    Wayne, 700
    Westfield, 710
    Westwood, 780, 823

NEW MEXICO

    Albuquerque, 91, 500, 712, 1037
    Santa Fe, 370, 998

NEW YORK

    Albany, 53, 1068
    Bronx, 127
    Brooklyn, 128, 231, 281, 332, 346, 434, 518, 840, 984, 1095
    Buffalo, 130, 278, 1437
    Carle Place, 1160
    Delmar, 1333
    Dewitt, 1387
    Far Rockaway, 743
    Floral Park, 454
    Flushing, 1427
    Forestville, 657
    Fredonia, 701, 793
    Great Neck, 824
    Hempstead, 834, 1305
    Hiler, 716
    Ithaca, 269, 425, 984
    Kingston, 322
    Massapequa, 1292
    Middletown, 1021
    Newburgh, 147
    New York, 8, 10, 11, 35, 37, 38, 44, 55, 67, 68, 71, 82, 92, 97, 100, 103, 105, 106, 116, 117, 119, 120, 125, 136, 148, 150, 155, 165, 180, 202, 205, 211, 214, 233, 246, 248, 250, 256, 268, 275, 300, 308, 318, 321, 323, 326, 327, 328, 329, 344, 358, 372, 410, 412, 416, 423, 432, 433, 438, 441, 448, 454, 456, 457, 474, 480, 486, 490, 493, 495, 496, 497, 501, 505, 506, 518, 551, 554, 558, 559, 574, 578, 587, 600, 601, 603, 606, 610, 611, 622, 623, 625, 641, 642, 647, 658, 664, 671, 674, 677, 733, 734, 735, 740, 741, 751, 752, 753, 754, 760, 762, 763, 764, 784, 794, 795, 831, 850, 872, 888, 898, 902, 913, 927, 930, 934, 935, 945, 949, 950, 962, 966, 981, 1010, 1014, 1023, 1024, 1033, 1073, 1089, 1093, 1102, 1108, 1111, 1120, 1125, 1131, 1134, 1158, 1161, 1176, 1184, 1188, 1189, 1190, 1202, 1233, 1239, 1246, 1248, 1262, 1277, 1278, 1286, 1291, 1298, 1301, 1307, 1308, 1309, 1315, 1326, 1329, 1337, 1340, 1349, 1356, 1362, 1372, 1380, 1399, 1424, 1436, 1439, 1440, 1441, 1444, 1445, 1447, 1456
    Old Westbury, 337, 1302, 1431
    Piermont, 927
    Plattsburgh, 150, 153
    Port Washington, 1440
    Poughkeepsie, 1373

NEW YORK (continued)

    Rochester, 246, 287, 373, 792, 1083
    Rush, 1350
    Seneca Falls, 590
    Skaneateles, 702
    Slingerlands, 1333
    Smithtown, 238
    Staten Island, 713
    Suffern, 77
    Stony Brook, 1087
    Syracuse, 414, 702, 749, 983, 1331
    Troy, 412
    West Nyack, 840

NORTH CAROLINA

    Chapel Hill, 6, 185, 341
    Charlotte, 1026, 1109
    Durham, 686, 775
    Fayetteville, 778
    Knightdale, 778
    Raleigh, 843

NORTH DAKOTA

    Fargo, 134
    Grand Forks, 102, 915
    Minot, 844

OHIO

    Cincinnati, 516, 548, 894, 962, 1259, 1266, 1337
    Cleveland, 42, 192, 210, 381, 862, 864, 1126, 1151, 1354
    Cleveland Heights, 1208
    Columbus, 665, 758, 858, 863, 865, 971, 1034, 1054, 1177, 1242, 1313
    Dayton, 261, 1285
    Fairfield, 1149
    Grailville, 426
    Loveland, 426
    Marion, 664
    Mount Vernon, 590
    Oberlin, 220
    Springfield, 602
    Toledo, 749
    Warren, 920
    Yellow Springs, 54

OREGON

    Corvallis, 173
    Eugene, 1420
    Portland, 191, 225, 247, 440, 688, 856, 1281
    Salem, 798, 825

PENNSYLVANIA

    Bethlehem, 571
    Harrisburg, 158, 159, 402, 431, 1359
    Johnstown, 1012
    Lancaster, 563, 889
    Levittown, 675
    Marietta, 550
    Narberth, 763
    Newtown, 1059

## PENNSYLVANIA (continued)

Philadelphia, 62, 79, 83, 145, 154, 184, 242, 337, 411, 420, 475, 478, 534, 537, 543, 552, 553, 555, 575, 598, 633, 779, 788, 797, 807, 826, 835, 860, 903, 905, 909, 910, 920, 956, 982, 1104, 1178, 1186, 1187, 1294, 1448
Pittsburgh, 57, 182, 337, 519, 689, 874, 914, 960, 1241, 1308
Radnor, 1010
Reading, 88
Scranton, 440, 921
Slippery Rock, 435, 959
State College, 1170
Valley Forge, 33
Wallingford, 345
Wellsboro, 218

## RHODE ISLAND

Providence, 539, 544, 737, 970, 1138, 1405

## SOUTH CAROLINA

Charleston, 512, 1114

## TENNESSEE

Knoxville, 380, 655
Memphis, 978, 1407
Nashville, 497, 1273, 1384

## TEXAS

Austin, 265, 370, 621, 1005, 1099, 1100, 1329
Dallas, 648, 690, 1128, 1172, 1321
Fort Worth, 582, 827
Houston, 126, 460, 531, 1042
San Antonio, 1002, 1299

## UTAH

Kaysville, 135
Salt Lake City, 52, 773, 1040, 1084, 1263

## VERMONT

Barre, 218
Battleboro, 458
Burlington, 78

## VIRGINIA

Alexandria, 845, 849, 1215
Arlington, 72, 616
Falls Church, 745, 845, 1238, 1323
Norfolk, 842
Richmond, 629, 1143, 1415
Roanoke, 253
Salem, 662
Virginia Beach, 972

## WASHINGTON

Gig Harbor, 353
Lynnwood, 17
Olympia, 693
Poulsbo, 517
Richland, 1214

## WASHINGTON (continued)

Seattle, 6, 46, 138, 407, 588, 728, 896, 985, 1004, 1105, 1121, 1134, 1205
Tacoma, 353, 717, 1196

## WISCONSIN

Amherst, 80
Appleton, 440
Baraboo, 659
Beloit, 614
Brodhead, 1219
Brookfield, 653
Cato, 1225
Chetek, 659
Chippewa Falls, 659
De Pere, 1220
Eau Claire, 614, 1377
Evansville, 659, 1219
Green Bay, 687, 1218, 1221
Greendale, 1242
Janesville, 80, 614
Kaukauna, 1218
Kenosha, 614
Kewaunee, 1225
La Crosse, 1218
Lake Mills, 1218
Madison, 4, 5, 32, 113, 118, 200, 277, 306, 350, 352, 374, 568, 599, 604, 612, 659, 776, 838, 854, 932, 942, 1003, 1043, 1081, 1111, 1119, 1140, 1166, 1179, 1183, 1212, 1218, 1224, 1226, 1228. 1229, 1230, 1346, 1351, 1365, 1376, 1390, 1409, 1434
Manitowoc, 80, 614, 1221, 1222
Menasha, 284, 425, 893, 1218, 1220
Merrill, 1218
Milton, 34
Milwaukee, 30, 99, 144, 224, 261, 292, 330, 362, 374, 439, 443, 488, 596, 636, 637, 659, 883, 891, 988, 1047, 1058, 1080, 1207, 1218, 1220, 1221, 1418
Neenah, 1223
New London, 1218
Oconto, 926
Oshkosh, 1227
Poynette, 659
Racine, 614, 1219
Rice Lake, 659
Ripon, 659
Sheboygan, 1218
Sinsinawa, 317
Stevens Point, 634, 1218, 1220, 1422
Stoughton, 659
Sturgeon Bay, 1103
Superior, 1131
Tri-City, 614
Turtle Lake, 1017
Two Rivers, 1218
Valders, 1225
Watertown, 1221
Waupaca, 659
Waukesha, 1198, 1219, 1220
Wausau, 80, 929, 1379
West Bend, 1227
Whitewater, 1169
Winneconne, 1334

## Women's Periodicals and Newspapers

WYOMING

   Rawlins, 802


AUSTRALIA

   Brisbane, 442, 1019
   Chippendale, 952
   Glebe, 115, 1133
   Melbourne, 1312
   Sydney, 626, 952, 1094
   Victoria, 497


AUSTRIA

   Frankenburg, 146
   Vienna, 273

BELGIUM

   Antwerp, 451, 1137
   Brussels, 186, 309, 428


CANADA

  Alberta
    Calgary, 164
    Edmonton, 112, 870

  British Columbia
    Aldergrove, 489
    Vancouver, 293, 514, 810, 881, 975, 1203, 1319, 1402
    Victoria, 1091

  Newfoundland
    St. Johns, 796

  Ontario
    Ancaster, 208
    Kingston, 772
    London, 293
    Ottawa, 487, 1150, 1317, 1404
    Thunder Bay, 847
    Toronto, 81, 176, 359, 670, 785, 877, 961, 1076, 1082, 1118, 1154, 1165, 1364, 1417
    Willowdale, 877

  Quebec
    Montreal, 320, 351, 483, 498, 594, 650, 939, 1276

  Saskatchewan
    Regina, 229
    Saskatoon, 1001


CHINA (People's Republic)

   Peking, 199, 1341
   Shanghai, 535

CHINA (Republic of)

   Taipei, 194

CUBA

   Camaguëy, 965

CZECHOSLOVAKIA

   Prague, 254

DENMARK

   Copenhagen, 521, 522, 523

DUTCH INDIES

  see

    INDONESIA

ENGLAND

   Berkhamstead, 1066
   Brighton, 524
   Bristol, 122, 299
   Chingford, 172
   Hemel Hempstead, 1426
   London, 22, 86, 197, 288, 295, 296, 297, 392, 401, 413, 465, 484, 485, 526, 529, 542, 545, 556, 557, 560, 561, 787, 906, 908, 923, 1000, 1020, 1048, 1049, 1066, 1252, 1289, 1347, 1383, 1386, 1398, 1413, 1421, 1426, 1432, 1435, 1443
   Manchester, 1271
   Nottingham, 1050, 1339
   Oxford, 786


FRANCE

   Paris, 14, 18, 106, 137, 143, 204, 291, 339, 364, 396, 848, 887, 901, 969, 1117, 1157
   Versailles, 290

GERMANY (Federal Republic of Germany)

   Berlin, 58, 382, 384, 388, 415, 1343, 1459
   Duesseldorf, 383
   Essen, 386
   Munich, 389

GERMANY (German Democratic Republic)

   Breslau, see POLAND
   Dresden, 146
   Frankenburg, see AUSTRIA
   Gruenwald, see POLAND
   Hanau, 1232
   Leipzig, 146, 385, 387, 429, 1232, 1460
   Weimar, 94

## Women's Periodicals and Newspapers

GREAT BRITAIN

   see

      ENGLAND, SCOTLAND

HOLLAND

   Amsterdam, 274, 613

HONG KONG

   Aberdeen, 482

ICELAND

   Reykjavik, 520

INDIA

   Bombay, 338
   Madras, 1085
   New Delhi, 1344

INDONESIA

   Soerabaja, 257

IRELAND

   Dublin, 336, 376

ITALY

   Milan, 285
   Padova, 938
   Rome, 285

JAPAN

   Tokyo, 873
   Yokosuka, 1324

MAURITANIA

   Nouakchott, 615

MEXICO

   Mexico City, 207

NETHERLANDS

   see

      HOLLAND

NEW ZEALAND

   Auckland, 123
   Dunedin, 216
   Palmerston North, 892
   Wellington, 203

NORWAY

   Christiania (Oslo), 855

PAKISTAN

   Karachi, 1290

POLAND

   Breslau, 146
   Gruenwald, 389

SCOTLAND

   Edinburgh, 1288
   Glasgow, 1275, 1325

SOUTH AFRICA

   Johannesburg, 1385

SWEDEN

   Stockholm, 450

SWITZERLAND

   Geneva, 140, 141, 968, 1318

TANZANIA

   Dar Es Salaam, 857

UNITED KINGDOM

   see

      ENGLAND, SCOTLAND

UNION OF SOVIET SOCIALIST REPUBLICS

   Moscow, 258, 1063

URUGUAY

   Montevideo, 853

VIETNAM

   Hanoi, 1342

# Editors Index

Numbers following each name refer to specific entries and not page numbers.

Abel, Judy, 280
Adams, Mary, 395
Ahooja-Patel, Krishna, 1318
Aklum, Carol, 337
Akram, Mujeeb M., 1290
Albert, Harold, Mrs., 144
Aldrich, Mildred, 607
Aldridge, Ruth, 225
Alexander, Nancy, 7
Alexander, Pricilla, 736
Alford, Brucetta, 719
Algazi, Linda, 1414
Allen, Donna, 624
Allen, Karen Kothman, 621
Allen, Mary Louise, 1277
Allen, Pam, 1142
"Alma," 574
Altman, Ruth, Dr., 248, 674
Ames, Fred, 180
Ames, Lucy, 180
Amram, Hortense L., 432
Anderson, Curtis, 534
Anderson, Genevieve De Brue, 1218
Anderson, Lee Berger, 1337
Anderson, Pat, 272
Anderson, Terri, 1055
Andrews, Marilla, 1219
Angus, Valerie, 1404
Annesen, Anne, 374
Antone, Elaine, 772
Apker, Susan, 1058
Appel, Marcia, 1129
Armentrout, Barbara, 903
Armeson, Karen, 16
Armstrong, Florence A., Dr., 301
Armstrong, Mary, 614
Armstrong, Toni, 891
Arnold, Kathryn Steeg, 757
Angress, Ruth, 897
Arthur, T. S., 62
Ash, Marion, 1044
Asmus, Edna J., 1240
Asserson, Grace P., 1249
Atherton, Robert, 246
Atkins, John, Mrs., 144
Auclert, Hubertine, 204
Aufenkamp, Jane, 28
Augspurg, Anita, 1459
Austin, Jean, 38
Autry, James A., 93
Ayars, Mary Warren, 1274
Ayukawa, Barbara, 13

Babcock, Joan, 306
Bacon, Henry, 549
Baggett, Lucy R., 747
Bailey, Janice, 33
Bailey, Wilma A., 284
Bailie, Stephen, Mrs., 144
Baldauf, Helen J., 374
Baldwin, Barbara, 173
Ball, H. R., Mrs., 569
Ballin, Ada S., 1252
Banerjee, Mukul, 1344
Barba, Sharon, 91

Barnard, Shirley, 724
Barney, Mary, 755
Barr, Kathy, 974
Barron, Craig, Mrs., 629
Barrows, Anna, 314, 445
Barrows, Ethel Duke, 218
Barry, Carol Barner, 833
Barry, Harriet H., 1258
Barschall, Eleanor, 568
Bartella, Frances, 614
Barwick, Joann R., 457
Bascom, Emma C., 659
Batt, Sharon, 112
Bauer, Fredric G., Mrs., 763
Beal, Frances M., 1125
Beals, Janet L., 1359
Beard, Mary R., 1248
Becker, Lydia Ernestine, 1432
Beecher, Henry Ward, 654
Beers, Henry S., Mrs., 1249
Beh, Siew-Hwa, 1300
Beizel, Corrine, 614
Bell, Sherry S., 863
Benjamin, Julliet N., 433
Bennet, Vivian, 1279
Bennett, Janice, 1149
Benson, Carol, 995
Benson, Joanne B., 107
Berge, Irene, 1225
Bernfeld, Lauri Roman, 1391
Berry, Betty, 730, 760
Berry, Caroline Sanderson, 636
Berry, Margaret C., Dr., 746
Berseth, Mary, 951
Betancourt, Isabel Esperanza, 965
Bevoso, Carole, 578
Bick, Barbara, 627
Bidwell, Susan, 12
Bieberdorf, Kay, 1172
Bien, Esther R., 37
Bigelow, William Frederick, 423
Biggs, Caroline A., 297
Biggy, M. Virginia, 284
Bilansky, Lawrence, Mrs., 144
Bingham, Rebecca Saady, 744
Birmingham, Fred A., 180
Birnie, William A. H., 1265
Birr, Carol, 1140
Bishop, Barbara E., 600
Bixler, Genevieve Knight, 284
Bjarnjedinsdottir, Breit, 520
Blackburn, Helen, 297
Blackwell, Alice Stone, 1260, 1267
Blackwell, Betsy Tabbot, 603
Blackwell, Henry B., 1267
Blender, Dorothy, 1337
Block, Virginia Lee, 284
Blount, Alice S., 34
Blue, Janice, 460
Boardman, Barbara, 799
Boeckel, Florence B., 1088
Boehringer, C. Louise, 481
Boggs, Henry P., Mrs., 763
Bok, Edward W., 534
Boles, Denise, 963

Bonsignore, Madelyn, 765
Boole, Ella A., 1141
Boose, Patti A., 849
Borman, Nancy, 733, 743
Boroff, Andrea, 441
Borziller, Eleonora, 92
Bost, Bernice Challenger, 1240
Boswell, Eleanore, 425
Boucher, Violet, 772
Boucherett, Emilia J., 297
Bowles, Louise Cunningham, 636
Boycott, Rosie, 1066
Boyd, Mary Sumner, 97
Brady, James, 438
Brandt, Jane Lewis, 1358
Braverman, Barnet, 219
Bray, Sandra, 1149
Breitinger, Nancy, 163
Brennan, Michael J., Mrs., 1215
Brewer, Ginger, 107
Bridel, Louis, 968
Britton, Susan, 481
Bronson, Minnie, 1245
Brower, Elizabeth, 256
Brown, Donna, 7
Brown, Gleah, 1414
Brown, Helen Gurly, 246
Brown, Helene, 38
Brown, Josephine M., 1337
Brown, Rita Mae, 784
Brown, Tara, 706
Brown-Rowe, Marshallay, 264
Bryan, Miriam M., 284
Bryant, Alice Franklin, 138
Bryant, Nathan F., 459
Buck, Carol, 1404
Budnik, Mary Ann, 1058
Buge, Lois E., 1195
Bull, Gladys V., 181
Bullard, Ethel M., 893
Bullard, Laura Curtis, 966
Burch, Betty Ann, 1361
Burchett, Thomas, Mrs., 1011
Burford, Effie B., 59
Burgess, William J., 212
Burns, Lucy, 1088
Burton, H. P., 246
Bushman, Claudia L., 319
Butenhoff, Jean, 915
Butler, Frank N., Mrs., 1273
Butwin, Miriam, 699

Cain, Mary D., 1243
Callahan, Martha J., 1280
Cameron, Mary C., 218
Campillo, Bona, 207
Canblath, Nancy, 27
Cantwell, Lois, 1456
Capistrant, Pat, 951
Carabillo, Toni (Virginia), 684, 756
Cardiasmenos, Marie, 810
Cardinale, Susan, 217
Carr, Mrs., 478
Carreon, Vera, 157
Carroll, Nola S., 531
Carstensen, Vernon, Mrs., 374
Carter, Anne, 301
Carter, John Mack, 38, 423, 534, 622

Carter, Patricia, 176
Carter, Salley, 1410
Cartwright, W. C., Mrs., 1220
Casey, Lois, 242
Cassell, Kay, 1333
Cassidy, Helen, 126
Cassirer, Sidonie, 337
Cassler, Carla, 441
Cates, J. J., Mrs., 374
Caudle, Marjorie Savage, 1240
Cauer, Minna, 384, 1459
Cechantek, Helen, 614
Cefft, B. F., Rev., 548
Chamberlain, Jean, 16
Chapin, Maria Bowen, 329
Chapman, Carrie Lane, 1280
Charleton, Helen H., 1219
"Charlotte Elizabeth," 197
Chase, Edna Woolman, 1161
Chassler, Sey, 950
Chaudhuri, Nupur, 153
Cheda, Sherrill, 293
Cheney, Marjory, 1249
Child, Abbie B., 585
Childs, Marjorie M., 1337
Chingan, Marj, 727
Chumbley, Joyce, 803
Cipolla, Deborah, 1388
Claflin, Tennie C. (Tennessee), 1441
Clark, John W., 473
Clarke, Mary, 1231
Clarkson, Sherri, 483, 498
Clermont, Jacqueline, 839
Clubb, Barbara, 293
Cobb, Hubbard H., 38, 534
Cobbs, Lisa, 347, 593
Coblentz, Margaret P., 753
Coggeshall, Mary J., 1280
Cohn, Sarah D., 490
Colby, Clara Bewick, 1281
Collin, Jacquelene Aubenas Francoise, 428
Collins, Marjory, 927
Collins, Sheila, 493
Colvin, D. Leigh, 1141
Compere, Moiree, 292
Comstock, Nania, 623
Condon, Evelyn C., 266
Conger-Kancko, Josephine, 219
Connelly, Mary M., 1337
Conners, Joy, 724
Cook, Eliza, 288
Cook, Tracy, 799
Cordova, Jeanne, 576
Cornwell, R. L., Mrs., 659
Corson, Rosalie P., 931
Cortes-Comerer, Nhora, 1111
Corti, Karen, 891
Cortinovis, Irene, 978
Corvalho, Julie A., 799
Coryell, Gladys A., 284
Cosgriff, Gabrielle, 460
Costick, Rita M., 1174
Coulter, Emogene, 1167
Covert, Anne, 1207
Cowl, Margaret, 1447
Coyne, Mary Jeanne, 1337
Crankshaw, Charles W., Mrs., 763
Crannell, Winslow, Mrs., 53

Crater, Flora, 1238
Crossley, David, 460
Crowell, George E., 458
Csida, June Bundy, 684
Currie, Birton W., 534
Curry, Daniel, Rev., 548
Curtis, Emma J., 659
Curtis, Hugh, 93

Dadourian, Ruth McIntire, 1249
Dael, Caroline Wells Healy, 1138
Dague, Linda Clark, 284
Dahl, Howard, Mrs., 374
Daire-Reber, Ginger, 1144
Daldy, Celia, 903
Damin, Anna, 1447
Damon, Gene, 527
Daniels, Arlene, 984
Danish, Max D., 505
Danzig, Ethel B., 1337
Darby, Hugh, 92
Davies, Mary Carolyn, 501
Davis, Enid, 1090
Davis, H. O., 534
Davis, Jessica, 1161
Davis, Major, 639
Davis, Paulina Wright, 1138
Davis, Sue, 82
Davis, Thomas, 534
Dawson, Alison, 1127
Dean, Robert W., Mrs., 80
Deane, Julia F., 1141
De Courcy, Beatrice, 529
De Courcy, Margaret, 529
deGaines, Pamelia, 48
Demetrovie, Zofka Kreder, 502
de Meuron, Alfred, 968
Deming, William H., Mrs., 1249
Derus, Jean, Sister, 317
Desmoines, Harriet, 1026
de Sola Pool, David, Mrs., 433
Deville, Carolyn, 924
Dey, Maryot Holt, 412
Dibner, Nancy Cushman, 609
Dickinson, Hilary, 351
Diehl, Nona M., 598
Dieter, Bert, 93
Dietrich, Charles H., Mrs., 1079
Dietrich, Ira J., Mrs., 763
Dingee, M. P., Mrs., 1219
di Sernia, Pat, 37
Dissard, Clotilde, 969
Dobkowski, Sandy, 20
Doelle, Lynn, 32
Dolan, Merrillee, 712
Dole, Marjorie, 1335
Donnelly, Margarita, 173
Donovan, Catherine, 1337
Donovan, Patricia, 328
Doonan, Lesley, 1405
Dorn, Hanns, 389
Dorr, Rheta C., 1088
Dostert, Candy, 102
Douglas, Angela K., 651
Douglas, Laura, 126
Downey, Rose, 1058
Downing, Camilla, 225
Drake, Kathy, 690

Dramm, Joan, 80
Dredge, Nancy T., 319
Drucker, Elsalyn, 645
Drummond, Veda Mathis, 645
Dudley, Marion H., 1461
Duganne, Phyllis, 501
Dumene, Jeanne A., 1215
Durand, Francis, Dr., 496
Durand, Marguerite, 396
Durken, Daniel, Fr., 1041
Durkin, Kathy, 82
Dyc, Gloria, 663
Dyche, John A., 533
Dyer, Edgar R., Mrs., 201

Eades, Dan, 102
Eades, Joan, 102
Eakes, Mildred, 181
Earwood, Glenda, 342
Eastman, Elaine G., 255
Eaton, Mary, 659
Edelmann, Josef, 439
Edelson, Morris, 460
Edwards, Janet, 614
Ehrlich, Ruth, 1423
Eichler, Margrit, 176, 961
Eiser, Anthony Conrad, Mrs., 902
Ellis, Charlotte, 696
Engler, Ellie, 1302
Englund, Shirley S., 1009
Erickson, Judy, 891
Essary, Helen K., 266
Esser, Jane, 200
Etzi, Ruth, 718
Evans, Jean Smith, 1337
Evans, Marianne, 447
Evers, Dora R., 1378
Evert, Ray, Mrs., 374

Fahmie, Barbara, 759
Fahs, Margaret, 1173
Fair, Ramey, 1144
Fairchild, Stacey M., 26
Fairman, Robert, Mrs., 144
Falk, Ethel Marie, 284
Fannin, Dorothy, 614
Farley, Harriet, 782
Farrington, Laura A., 863
Faulkner, Lulu V., 509
Faust, Pamela, 223
Fedotova, Valentina, 1063
Ferguson, Ann, 527
Ferranti, Lucie, 839
Ferrier, Carole, 442
Ferris, Henry D., Mrs., 1143
Fiedlander, Bernice, 272
Field, Amy Walker, 583
Fielding, Elizabeth, 366, 957
Fields, Daisy B., 799
Fierstein, Laurie, 82
Finch, Myron, 658
Finkel, Mimi, 105
Finn, C. Virginia, 988
Finn, Eugenia T., 1073
Firestone, Shulamith, 850
Fisher, Beverly, 940
Fisher, Elizabeth, 55
Fitch, Louise, 425

Fitzgerald, Anna, 1270
Fitzgerald, J.M.H., Mrs., 218
Flaherty, Etta Lee, 726
Fleming, L.W., Mrs., 181
Flessners, H.A., Rev., 262
Flynn, Eileen, 1337
Flynn, Sharon, 739
Fonk, Barbara, 614
Forbs, Carol, 160
Foreman, Carol T., 1173
Forer, Lois G., 1337
Forrest, Mona, 351
Forsyth, Anne, 1438
Forth, Sarah S., 1359
Foster, Agnes, 1218
Fountain, Kathy, 924
Fox, Jean, 425
Fox, Lauretta E., 107
Fox, Marcha, 7
Frandsen, Alice, 1159
Franklin, S.M., 583
Frederickson, L.E., 137
Freedom, Virginia Star, 301
Fretter, Alice Louise, 1240
Friedlander, Alfred, Mrs., 1259
Fritz, Nancy, 996
Froid-Fleming, Irene, Mrs., 569
Frye, Ruth, 422
Fuetsch, Joan, 48
Fuller, Mary, 799
Furran, Lee J., 757

Gagarina, Zincuda, 1063
Gage, Matilda Joslyn, 749
Gaines, Martha, 890
Gallager, Marie, 192
Gandel, Rhonda, 1227
Garcia, Ezelda, 16
Gates, Theophilus Ransom, 83
Gaulke, Cheri, 1074
Gavigan, Pam, 614
Gawthorpe, Mary, 392
Gaylor, Annie Laurie, 352
Gehman, Mary, 271
Gehrke, Kim, 224
Geib, Eugenia, 497
Geidel, Patti, 1227
Georgeson, Patricia, 374
Geriak, Bonnie, 461
German, Eleanor Miller, 634
Getty, Rita, 977
Gibbs, D., 188
Gibbs, Winifred Stuart, 454
Gibson, Anne, 225
Gibson, Janet, 7
Gilbert, Jane, Miss, 598
Gilbert, Levi, Mrs., 1266
Gilbert, Victoria, 1337
Giles, Barbara, 597
Gillespie, Marcia Ann, 308
Gilman, Charlotte, 372
Gilman, Rhoda, 1175
Girton, Dorothy Felker, 266, 765
Giuseppi, Ellen, 1207
Gittings, Barbara, 527
Gizycki, Lily von, 384
Gladstone, Leslie, 1173
Glass, Estelle, 1218

Gleason, Karen, 1058
Gochberg, Karen, 374
Godey, Louis, 420
Goglick, Kathy, 214
Gohl, Kathryn, 891
Golding, Jeanne, 1414
Goock, Beth, 1240
Goodman, Vera, 780
Goodsitt, William, Mrs., 144
Gordon, Anna A., 1141
Gordon, Arthur, 246
Gordon, Robin, 884
Gordon-Lazareff, Helene, 339
Gould, Beatrice, 534
Gould, Bruce, 534
Grabowski, Virginia, 391
Graff, Andrea (Dede), 1230
Graham, Pamela, 697
Graham, Rubye, 1010
Grant, Teddi A., 1058
Grasso, Rick, 1174
Gray, Mary W., 66
Graziani, Bernice Solomen, 674
Greathouse, Kathy, 1226
Green, Ernestine, 492
Greene, Hattie Bryant Witt, 640
Greene, Louise L., 1263
Gregg, Dawn, 61
Griffin, Donna, 1167
Griffith, Susan, 1227
Grimstad, Kirsten, 198
Gropp, Ann, 158, 159
Gross, David C., 913
Gross, Shelley, 318
Groves, Alma Zola, 1337
Grugett, Sylvia F., 518
Gurling, Elizabeth, 1337
Gunther, Gertrud M., 143
Guyol, Alexander, Mrs., 765

Hack, Sidney, Mrs., 144
Hal, Ester J.W., Dr., 107
Hale, Sarah Josepha, 420, 540
Hall, Mary Rose, 260
Hall, Vivian, 770
Halline, Paul L., Mrs., 1220
Hamilton, Ruth, 374
Hamline, L.L., Rev., 548
Hammerschlag, Meta, 389
Hammond, Gail Winston, 1358
Hammond, Victoria, 667
Hanau, Stella, 97
Hanchett, Maria F., 659
Hanlon, Emily, 82
Hansen, Judy P., 1359
Hanson, Cindy, 404
Happel, Margaret E., 38
Harbert, Elizabeth Boynton, 783
Harding, Bernice, 1393
Hardisty, Barbara, 1015
Harman, Moses, 40
Harman-Brown, Helen S., 955
Harpole, Patricia C., 1175
Harrison, Gene, Mrs., 1220
Hart, Marie, 422
Hartley, Jo, 239
Hartwig, Lise-Lotte, 521
Hasbrouck, Sayer, 1021

Haupt, Emil A., 1010
Havener, Helen, 747
Havriluk, Ann, 188
Hawks, A. Grace, 181
Haycock, Carol-Ann, 293
Haycock, Ken, 293
Hayes, Florence, 1307
Hays, Cecil T., Mrs., 763
Hays, Glenn G., Mrs., 1141
Haywood, Hubert, Mrs., 843
Haywood, Martha Helen, 843
Hazelwood-Brady, Anne, 609
Hecht, Lucille, 481
Heck, D.W., Mrs., 1220
Hedstrom, Susan, 911
Heffernan, Elaine, 808
Hegstedt, Nina, 1197
Heinemann, Marlene, 1428
Heintzelman, Diane, 1177
Helstad, Orvin, Mrs., 374
Henderson, Metta Lou, 107
Henkel, Eloise, 903
Henry, Alice, 583
Henry, Linda, 978
Henry, Troyce, 696
Herb, Carol Marie, 962
Heredeen, Anne, 501
Hershey, Lenore, 534
Hettich, Arthur, 323
Hicks, Julia Margaret, 1249
Higgenson, T.W., 1267
Hilbert, Edwin, Mrs., 1221
Hill, Eliza Trask, 1283
Hill, Janet McKenzie, 92
Hill, Jeanie, 925
Hill, Robert B., 92
Hilliker, Katharine, 501
Hindin, Robert, Mrs., 144
Hinton, Mary Hilliard, 843
Hirsch, Charity, 280
Hirsch, Max, Dr., 58
Hirschfeld, Magnus, Dr., 1460
Hodgkins, Louise Manning, 1274
Hoffman, B., Dr., 505
Hoffman, Nancy, 337
Hoffmann, Angela, 903
Hogan, David, 956
Hogan, Fran, 712
Hoggan, Margaret, 682
Hoier, Juli, 614
Holeckova, Bozena, 254
Holgren, Carol, 690
Holle, Charles G., Mrs., 763
Hollenbeck, Martha Ann, 1218
Holmes, Sherrie, 261
Holzschlag, Phyllis, 632
Holzman, Ellen B., 280
Homnick, Candyce, 1022
Hooker, Edith Houghton, 301, 302
Hooker, F.J., Mrs., 1259
Hoover, Jinks, 646
Horning, H.L., Mrs., 1220
Hornstein, Francie, 361
Horst, Enos A., Mrs., 763
Horwitz, Carole Rosen, 475
Houseman, Robert W., 642
Hosken, Fran P., 1181, 1182
Howe, Florence, 337, 1431

Howe, Julia Ward, 1267
Howe, Kitty, 1231
Hubbs, Harriet L., 145
Huggins, W. Zack, Mrs., 1143
Hughes, Alice A., 614
Hughes, Horace H., 120
Humphrey, Marie E. Ives, 473
Hunt, Janet, 984
Hurst, Willard, Mrs., 374
Husa, Judy, 712
Hutchinson, Barbara, 380
Hutchinson, Julia, Miss, 659
Hutton, Edna Rait, 893

Igler, Chris, 1242
Ingram, Fredrick B., Mrs., 763
Irving, Helen, 551
Irwin, Thomas, 956
Iskin, Ruth, 1293
Israel, Jody, 348

Jackson, Ida May, 636
Jackson, Norliskia A., 264
Jackson, Willda Shaw, 269
Jaffe, Phyllis, 293
James, Dot, 395
Janis, Barbara, 862, 864
Janowski, Joseph, Mrs., 1011
Jenkins, Marty, 1395
Jenkins, Meredith, 173
Jenkins, Patricia, 425
Jensen, Edythe, 911
Jensen, Julie, 107
Jensen, Marlene, 1078
Jett, Eldon M., Mrs., 1143
Johnson, Helen Louise, 410, 412
Johnson, Karen Colaianni, 160
Joice, Lois, 469
Jones, Dorothy M., 1337
Jones, Egbert, Mrs., 629
Jones, Kasey, 461
Jones, Olga Anna, 865
Joyce, Kay, 614
Jtangiani, K.D., Dr., 338
Judd, Kathryn, 891

Kahn, Robert F., Mrs., 144
Kaiser, Ann, 330
Kallowaay, Sheryn, 1018
Kaminski, Margaret, 663
Kane, Aissata, 615
Kane, Kathy, 47
Kanof, Naomi M., 497
Kassell, Paula S., 780
Katz, E.S., 35
Katz, Phyllis, 1014
Kaufer, Nancy, 978
Keener, Randa, 374
Kees, Virginia, 436
Keinmaier, Judie, 568
Keith, Carolyn, 488
Kelley, Marian Booth, 1311
Kelly, Martin, 120
Kelly, Mary, 422
Kendall, Annabel, 113
Kendall, Maude, 1285
Kenna, Dee, 632
Kennedy, Flo, 357

Kennedy, Mary, 501
Kenney, Anne, 978
Kerman, Judith, 278
Kern, Mary Margaret, 481
Kerner, Isabel C., 265
Kerr, Mina, 425
Kettler, J., Mrs., 94
Keyserling, Mary Dublin, 222
Kidder, Dorothy Perry, 1175
King, Larry, 1439
Kisielewski, Julie, 799
Kittredge, Marie A., 422
Klarnet, Betty, 38
Klein, Louanne, 445
Klemm, Dixie, 667
Kling, Sandra Eells, 269
Klingle, Sandra, 269
Knapp, Louisa, Mrs., 534
Knowles, Jane, 1179
Knox, Jessie A., 454
Knoy, Sarah Jane, 1173
Koch, Marion, 1218
Kocdt, Anne, 850
Korn, Eva, 1322
Kowall, Bonnie C., 747
Kramer, Eileen M., 1218
Krauska, Patricia C., 47
Krebs, Magdalene, Sister, 262
Krenkel, Noele, 3
Krents, Irma, 248
Krescanko, Marie, 614
Kresge, Pat, 425
Krody, Nancy, 411
Krog, Gina, 855
Krohn, Barbara, 1134
Kulman, Doris, 645
Kulpa, Lorraine A., 510
Kwik, Gwen, 702
Kyle, Alice M., 585

Lacki, Ruth, 614
Lafontaine, Phyllis Watts, 1054
Lam, Mithan J., 10, 11
Lamson, C.M., Mrs., 585
Landmann, Lynn C., 326
Lane, Ernest Mrs., 144
Lane, Gertrude B., 1265
Lang, Maria, 273
Lange, Helene, 382
Langston, William C., Mrs., 218
Larken, Sally, 92
Larson, Cynthia, 706
Laspier, Tony, 506
Latham, Helen, 1242
Lattimer, Mariagnes, 678
Laub, Edith, 280
Laurie, Jesse Zel, 433
Lauter, Estella, 1119
Lawrence, Linda, 1379
Lawson, W.A., Mrs., 659
Lazin, Brenda, 393
Leadbetter, L.A., Mrs., 1220
Leibenguth, Charla, 107
Leindecker, Pamela, 1346
Leivenberg, Richard, 165
Lemke, June, 614
Lenfest, H.F., 1010
Lennert, Midge, 365

Leonard, Joan, Sister, 317
Leone, Janice, 1430
Lepeska, Jane, 1229
Leskovar, Corinne, 1458
Leslie, Miriam F., 378
L'Esperance, Elise S., 497
Levine, Marcy, 712
Levine, Roz, 1231
Levine, Ruth, 913
Lewis, E.G., 1272
Lewis, Eva C., Mrs., 659
Lewis, H.C., 537
Lewis, Linda, 568
Lieben, Gabriele von, 389
Lincoln, Richard, 327
Lindsey, Martha, 582
Lining, Ida Marshall, 512
Linton, Goerge, Dr., 35
Lipsen, Linda, 160
Livermore, Mary, 1267
Lloyd, Kate Rand, 1445
Locke, Edith Raymond, 603
Lockeretz, Sarah Wernick, 990
Lockeretz, Willie, 990
Loeb, Catherine, 350
Loercher, Donna, 734
Lombard, Mary, 1287
Loignon, Emilye, 1080
Loss, Martha, 1218
Love, Nancy, 38
Lovewell, Irene, 166
Loyd, Edith, 1064
Ludwick, Bernice Collins, 440
Luecke, Susan, 1207
Lyle, Cindy, 1315
Lyon, Dore, 211
Lyon, Phyllis, 527

MacInnes, Deborah, 269
Mack, Eva M., 1337
Mackenzie, Antoinette M., 297
Mackler, Gretchen, 1142
MacLean, Annie Marion, 1285
Madrid, Vicki, 242
Madsen, Dorothy L., 209
Mainardi, Patricia, 346
Makielski, Katherine K., 1337
Malec, Sharon, 568
Malinski, Violet, 1159
Mandel, T., 280
Manley, Kathleen, 370
Manlove, Ruth Lemmer, 481
Mann, Robert, Mrs., 144
Manning, Janet Earley, 780
Manocchia, Lino, 416
Manske, Pat, 80
Manthorne, Jackie, 594
Marschner, P.J., 963
Marcus, Naomi, 903
Marezall, Louise, 387
Marieskind, Helen S., 1301, 1302
Marino, Sara, 285
Marklein, Carol, 1346
Marley, Faye, 747
Marlowe, Leigh, 9, 67, 68
Marner, Mary Antisdel, 636
Marsden, Dora, 392
Marsden, Lorna, 208

Marsh, Beatrice H., 1249
Marshall, F.A., Mrs., 374
Marshall, Mel, Mrs., 144
Marshall, T.C., 473
Marti, Beatriz, 207
Martin, Del, 527
Martin, Gertrude S., 425
Martin, Maria, 204
Martin, Wendy, 1427
Martinson, Sue Ann, 1025
Martyn, S.T., Mrs., 551
Mason, Joyce, 697
Mason-Hohl, Elizabeth, 894
Masselli, Mark, 979
Matles, Victor, Mrs., 144
Mattes, Alvena, 885
Matteson, Connie, 7
Matthews, Tom, 1012
Matthias, Vera, 1048
Maule, Frances, 747
Maxcy, Eaton W., 544
Maxwell, Margaret W., 893
Mayes, Herbert R., 246, 423, 622
Mayhew, William H., Mrs., 374
Mazusech, Veronica, 192
McAdow, Jerry, Mrs., 568
McAllister, Henry, Mrs., 629
McBride, Marion, 443
McCabe, Jewell Jackson, 1340
McClelland, Ruth M., 181
McConnell, Lucius W., Mrs., 763
McCracken, Catherine, 19
McCulloch, Rhoda E., 1277
McCullough, Ann, Sister, 317
McDaniel, Lucy C., 753
McDonough, Frank W., 93
McGlasson, C.E., Mrs., 569
McGraw, Mary E., 1365
McGuigan, Dorothy, 187, 630, 829
McIntyre, Chi, 306
McKay, Eleanor, 978
McKenzie, Carol Ann, 490
McKeown, Pat, 903
McKinstry, Alice, 1240
McLeod, Mary Louise D., 1337
McMaster, Susan, 112
McMichael, Morton, 420
McMurtry, Rosemary, 623
McNamara, Kathleen, 1231
McNulty, Rosemary, 614
Mehlberg, Otis, Mrs., 1220
Melicher, Charles, Mrs., 374
Mercer, Leslie, 1361
Meredity, E.T., 93
Merrill, Effie A., 1274
Merrill, Estelle M.H., 314, 455
Merritt, Jean J., 192
Metcalfe, Ann, 862
Meuli, Judith, 756
Meute, Maria C., 1337
Meyer, Eleanor, 409
Meyer, Marianna, 834
Michaud, G. Ellen, 475
Miglionico, Nina, 1337
Mikkelson, Floria, Rev., 282
Miley, Marjorie, 1218
Milhaupt, V. Rachel, 614
Millard, Ronnie, Mrs., 192

Miller, Anne, 963
Miller, Barbara, 996
Miller, Kathi, 827
Miller, Linda, (Springfield, IL), 729
Miller, Linda, (Seattle, WA), 728
Miller, Mary Agnes, 902
Miller, Meyer, 505
Mills, Leonore M., 218
Milner, Mrs., 296
Milton, Linda, 445
Mines, Libby, 280
Minogue, Ann, 7
Mirabella, Grace, 1161
Mitchell, Carol, 370
Moffitt, E.E., Mrs., 843
Molarsky, Martha, 903
Moon, S. Joan, 1201
Moore, Barbara Jordan, 1108, 1353
Moore, George T., Mrs., 181
Moore, Kitty, 757
Moramarcie, Sheila, 168
Morehead, W.F., Mrs., 598
Morrison, Jane, 311
Morrissy, Carol, 242
Morse, Amy Kellogg, 659
Moser, Nancy, 1072
Moses, Claire D., 321
Moss, Irene, 346
Mouer, Holly, 125
Mountcastle, Amy, 1198
Mozzola, Anthony T., 438
Mueller, Kate Hevner, 746
Muller, Pat, 1229
Murphy, Jane, 1153
Murray, Dali, Mrs., 653
Musken, Byron, Mrs., 1220

"Nancy", 1225
Nasif, Helen G., 1337
Neal, Patsy, 212
Neff, Susie, Miss, 659
Nelson, Harold L., Mrs., 374
Nelson, Nancy, 646
Nemser, Cindy, 346
Nerlien, Alice, Mrs., 659
Newman, Gail, 974
Newman, Lena V., 1219
Newton, Jennifer L., 176, 961
Nichols, Diane, 926
Nichols, R., 577
Nichols, Wade H., 423
Nicholson, Catherine, 1026
Nicholson, Joan, 272
Nickol, Walter, Mrs., 80
Niedzielska, Krystyna, 1343
Nopper, Shelley, 1310
Norderhaug, Kathy, 32
Northrup, Elizabeth C., 1274
Novak, Albina, 1458

Oakes, Helen, 860
O'Brien, Margaret, 765
O'Connell, John, 246
O'Donnell, Gladys, Mrs., 366
Oen, Beng H., 11
Ohlsen, Linda, 102
Olin, Helen, 659
Olson, Judy, 568

O'Malley, Kathy, 47
Oppegard, Sandy, 951
Ordas, Ruth, 697
Orlando, Joe, 1440
Orr, Chris, 918
Orton, Virginia Keating, 1073
Ovsyannikova, Maria, 1063
Owens, Edward J., Mrs., 763

Packard, Dolly, 727
Padik, Saul, Mrs., 1221
Page, Ellen, 925
Pagliaro, Penny, 240
Pankhurst, Sylvia, 1443
Pappas, Mary A., 1337
Paradise, Viola, 674
Park, Margaret Jane, 1218
Parker, J.M., Mrs., 1261
Parker, John R., 638
Parker, John W., 310
Parker, Linda, 350, 776
Parker, R.G., 933
Parlane, J., 1288
Parlane, R., 1288
Pas, Gerry, 1198
Pasternak, Judie, 740
Pasternacki, Amalia, 1337
Paturis, Cleo, 37
Patwardhan, Shirimati Malati, 1085
Paynter, Mary, Sister, 317
Peaks, Deborah J., 264
Penland, Lee, 1337
Perales, Mely, 207
Perkins, Sarah M., Mrs., 1126
Perry, Emily, 301
Peters, Betty, 252
Peterson, Elmer T., 93
Peterson, Grethe B., 319
Peterson, Sarah Webb, 553
Phillips, Mary, 734
Phillips, Micheal J., 596
Phinney, Elizabeth, 425
Pickett, Flo, 694
Pickett, John E., 534
Pidhirnyj, Myroslava, 1364
Pierce, Josephine, 1379
Pierce, Katherine M., 1280
Pierce, Marlene, 614
Pierce, Vivian, 1088
Pierson, Pamela, 306
Pillsbury, Parker, 966
Pingree, Suzanne, Dr., 838
Pisani, Josephine M., 1337
Platt, Allison A., 1053
Pollack, Michael, 505
Poppenheim, Laura B., 512
Poppenheim, Mary B., 512
Porritt, Annie G., 97
Porsak, Bernard, Mrs., 374
Porter, Sonia, 374
Potts, A.F., 1220
Pousland, Edward, Mrs., 1249
Powell, Ernestine Breisch, 1337
Pratt, Elizabeth R., 1218
Prescott, Viviann P., 156
Preston, John, 404
Priestly, Mary, 336
Prior, D'Ann, 1207

Quinton, A.S., Mrs., 473

Rafter, Barbara Benton, 903
Rainsford, M.L., Mrs., 270
Ralston, Isaac, 543
Rankin, Belle, 425
Rantorp, Jette, 521
Ratner, J.E., 93
Raymond, Landon T., Mrs., 1249
Read, Lizzie B., 1280
Reddi, Muthulakshoni, 1085
Redmond, Donna, 842
Redondo, Ana Maria Q.F., 853
Reed, Elizabeth F., 1337
Reeder, Janice Scot, 1209
Reel, S.F. Vincent, 1433
Reeves, Winona Evans, 885
Reinartz, Kay F., 712
Reiter, Robert A., Mrs., 902
Repa, Irene, 13
Replogle, Maxine, 225
Retamal, Evelyn, 696
Reuss, Pat, 1173
Reynolds, Judy, 1227
Reynolds, Minnie, 1248
Rheingans, Ruth, 659
Richards, Lula Greene, 1263
Richardson, Midge Turk, 1010
Ride, Sally, 1077
Reid, Ada Chree, 497
Riggs, Jim, 93
Rightsell, Raymond, Mrs., 1220
Rishel, Virginia, 266
Roach, Margaret, 1425
Roberts, Willa, 1265
Robertson, Edna, 1218
Robins, Raymond, Mrs., 583
Roche, Ann, 732
Roderick, Virginia, 1268
Roerden, Chris, 1198
Romjue, Sharon, 13
Rongone, Christine, 978
Rorke, Lorraine, 1077
Rose, Harriet, 674
Rosebury, A., 505
Rosenfelt, Deborah Silverton, 337
Rosier, Michele, 339
Roth, Barbara, 674
Rothfus, Helen, 1058
Roth-White, Darlene, 890
Rowe, Marsha, 1066
Rowell, Carol, 593
Rozett, Ruth, 823
Rubinstein, Maurice, Mrs., 144
Rubinstein, Sally, 1175
Rueckel, Patricia, Dr. 746
Rusnak, Ann, 48
Russell, Catherine E., 879
Russell, Dorothy M., 301
Russell, Evelyn M., 1280
Russell, G. Gardner, Mrs., 1249
Rutherford, Nancy, 614
Ruttenber, Helen G., 147

Saavedra-Vela, Pilar, 963
Sabella, Pat, 206
Saiger, Maurice, Mrs., 815
Saint James, Margo, 251

Salkind, E., 280
Sanders, Helen, 527
Sandler, Bernice, 867
Sanger, Margaret, 97, 1246
Sarkissian, Eileen, 461
Saunders, Mary Virginia, 481
Saunders, John, 906
Sayler, Sawnie, 1300
Sayre, Mary Ellen, 765
Schelly, Percy Young, Mrs., 763
Schendel, Herman, 292
Scheppele, Kim, 634
Schern, Peggy, 951
Schlafly, Phyllis, 912
Schleret, Barbara, 951
Schneider, Susan Weidman, 587
Schrage, Jennie, 1220
Schramm, Sarah Slavin, 337, 808, 1308
Schreiber, LeAnne, 1439
Schroeder, Sandra, 1430
Schruber, Angela M., 1195
Schuette, Mary Lou, 614
Schuller, Loring A., 534
Schuyler, Margaretta Van Resellaer, 501
Schwartz, Doris A., 678
Schwartz, Sulamith, 433
Schweik, Joanne, 793
Schwenn, Gretchen, 1201
Scott, John W., 956
Scott, Virginia, 1089
Scudder, Antoinette, 1073
Secor, Cynthia, 337
Seemeyer, Mary Alice, 1227
Segal, Bonnie, 402
Sewell, Elizabeth, 658
Shalikov, P.I., Count, 258
Shampanier, Phyllis, 1337
Shannon, Betty, 501
Shannon, Marian H., 59
Shapiro, Jeane, 721
Shapley, Gene D., Mrs., 201
Shearer, Madeline H., 96
Shientag, Florence P., 1337
Showalter, Elaine, 337
Shufro, Cathy, 276
Sickinger, Audrey, 1225
Siegfried, Ginny, 1215
Sigel, Albert J., Mrs., 902
Sigourney, Lydia H., 420
Siley, Mabel L., 902
Silver, Barbara, 706
Simon Leopold K., Mrs., 97
Simpson, Lucy Picco, 1095
Singer, Eve, 409
Siporin, Rae Lee, 337
Sjoo, Monica, 299
Skinner, Beverly, 299
Slocum, Ray Emerson, Mrs., 218
Smith, Charlotte, 1446
Smith, Daniel D., 549
Smith, Dorothy M., 659
Smith, Elizabeth H.W., 1143
Smith, Ellen Kerrigan, 1155
Smith, Fred, 38
Smith, Ida B. Wise, 1141
Smith, Lloyd DeWitt, Mrs., 763
Smith, Lucy C., 1143
Smith, Lynne, 562

Smith, Sandra, 1090
Smith, Terry, 1134
Smith, Victoria, 460
Smokey, George, Mrs., 659
Smolka, Susanne, 1236
Snow, Carmel, 438
Snyder, Margaret, 1218
Sokoloff, Judith A., 913
Soldwedel, Bette J., 746
"Solomon Slender", 956
Somerville, Rose, 1052
Sonneschein, Rosa, 40
Sooci, Annette, 16
Soska, Dolores J., 381
Soule, Chris, 712
Spanks, Clarence, Mrs., 201
Sprague, Victoria, 1129
Stacey, Margaret, 1058
Stafford, Bart Lanier, 1080
Stanhope, Mrs., 557
Stanhope, Charles, Rev., 787
Stanley, Herman, Mrs., 1141
Stanley, Sylvia, 1058
Stanton, Elizabeth Cady, 966
Starnes, Nancy, 107
Starr, Laura B., 275
Steffens, Sharon, 1162
Stein, Leon, 505
Stein, Robert, 622
Steinem, Gloria, 664
Stephens, Ann S., Mrs., 788
Stephens, Vel, Mrs., 763
Stephenson, Bertha, 1266
Stephenson, Marylee, 176, 961
Stern, Ava, 300
Sternberger, Estelle M., 495
Stevens, Lillian M.N., 1141
Stevenson, J.O., 1280
Stewart, Charlotte, 1062
Stewart, Marie Goodwin, 1062
Stief, Helle, 521
Stiller, John G., 35
Stillwell, W.E., Mrs., 1259
Stimpson, Catherine, 1023
Stinsen, George, 467
Stitig, Rob, 712
St. James, see Saint James
Stockwell, Nancy, 121
Stoddard, Agnes Cuyler, 45
Stoffman, Jody, 1364
Stommel, Anne, 799
Stone, Elizabeth, 722
Stone, Lucy, 1267
Stough, Ada Barnett, 765
Stow, Marietta L., 1264
Strada, Lisa, 1231
Strang, Ruth, 746
Stratford, Anne, 503
Strauss, Theodore, 1265
Stromwasser, Sheila, 445
Stuart, Helen K., Mrs., 1223
Stuber, Gloria, 781
Stultz, Deborah, 1175
Sudow, Ellen, 1173
Sullivan, Margaret W., 409
Summer, Ruth, 668
Sutherland, Mary E., 526
Swallow, Marie, 1218

## Women's Periodicals and Newspapers

Swanson, Donna, 271
Sweet, Ellen B., 1362
Swerdlow, Amy, 628, 1349

Tanguay, Pauline, 868
Tanham, Mary, 1378
Tarver, Marie Nero, 59
Tatum, Beulah Benton, 284
Taylor, Emily, Dr., 117
Taylor, Mary Kathleen, 1077
Taylor, Mary McGinn, 409
Taylor-Pierlot, Lucille, 621
Teletzke, Gerald H., Mrs., 80
Temple, Jean, 2
Tenenbaum, Martin, Mrs., 144
Tenenbaum, Susan, 1197
Tennant, B., 799
terHorst-deBoer, T., 257
Terry, Diane, 272
Thatcher, Sharon, 1218
Thomas, Eileen Mitchell, 11
Thomas, Gladys P., 903
Thompson, E., Rev., 548
Thompson, J.C., Miss, 1287
Thompson, M.E.B., Mrs., 659
Thompson, Margaret R., 757
Thompson, Marian, 1081, 1228
Thompson, Mary Lou, 1069
Thompson, Megan, 568
Thompson, Vance, 641
Tilden, Lola S., 747
Tinsley, Adrain, 337
Tober, Barbara D., 119
Tobias, Sheila, 337
Todd, Janet M., 1306
Tombs, Dorothy, 476
Tooze, Fred J., Mrs., 1141
Torr, Joseph, 552
Towle, Dorothy S., 92
Towne, Lucia P., 1307
Townsend, Reginald, 38
Townsend, Virginia F., 62
Trenchard, Nancy, 1159
Tryon, Ruth Wilson, 425
Tucker, Jessie, 1151
Turner, Betty, 698
Turner, Maurice, Mrs., 104
Turpin, Allen, Mrs., 1011
Twing, A.T., Mrs., 202
Tycner, Wanda, 1343
Tyler, Jocelyn, 817
Tyor, Peter, 153

Ueland, Brenda, 501
Ullman, Varda, 1231
Ulrich, Laurel T., 319
Urin, Cecilia, 269
Uwechue, Austa, 22
Uwechue, Raph, 22

Vance, Shirley, 1220
Van Nierop, Henreitte, 344
Van Twest, Pat, 299
Van Wagenen, Pamela, 1439
Velson, Evelyn, 280
Vercheak, Susan, 1424
Vetter, Martha, 568
Victor, Elaine, 291

Viera, Dierdre, 702
Vlisides, Claudia, 306
Volberg, Nancy, 674
Volberg, Naomi, 248
Vollmer, Debbie, 175
Vreeland, Diana, 1161

Wagner, Anne M., 789
Wagner, Ellen D., 38
Wagner, Mary Anthony, Sister, 1041
Walch, Margaret, 35
Walker, Ann S., 486
Walker, Ida M., 509
Walker, John Brisben, 246
Walker, Mary, 1061
Walker, Thomas J., 145
Wallace, Dan A., 331
Wallace, Edith Markham, 885
Waller, Alice, 747
Walter, James, Mrs., 568
Walts, Penny, 963
Ward, Alden, 412
Warren, William F., Mrs., 1274
Warrin, Helen B., 284
Warshaw, Martin, Mrs., 144
Waters, Harriet Bishop, 410, 412
Watkins, Harold A., Mrs., 144
Watkins, Joan Casale, 725
Watson, Archie C., Mrs., 1143
Wauters, Rita, 614
Weaver, Adele T., 1337
Web, Eileen, 574
Webb, Dawn, 924
Weber, Maria, 383
Weibel, Kathleen, 1227
Weideman, Elizabeth, 903
Weidler, Mary B., 393
Weiss, Joanne, 394
Weitz, Alice C., 409
Weitzman, Lenore, 1052
Welch de Llosa, Martha, 35
Weller, Rachel, 1416
Wellisch, Karen, 1075
Wells, Emmeline B., 1263
Wells, Mildred White, 409
Wendt, Diana, 481
Wentworth, E., Rev., 548
Wenzel, Gretchen, 1058
West, Eunice, 304
West, Helen Hust, 301
West, Mary Allen, 1141
Westly, Bruce H., Mrs., 374
Wheat, Valerie, 1174
Wheaton, Esther, 1266
Wheeler, Louise G., 747
Wheelock, Ernestine, 621
Whipple, Merry Mason, 374
Whitaker, Earl L., Mrs., 763
White, Nancy, 438
White, Sue S., 1088
Whitehead, Margaret Harold, 790
Whitehurst, Sara W., 409
Whiting, Frances, 246
Whitney, Mary Traffarn, 324
Whitney, Ruth, 418
Whitney, Sarah Ware, 1280
Whittelsey, A.G., Mrs., 658
Whittier, Helen A., 412

Widmayer, Patricia R., 63
Wierig, Woodrow, 1265
Wiese, Otis Lee, 622
Wigger, Anne, 897
Wilde, Oscar Fingal O'Flahertie Wills, 1289
Wiley, Anna Kelton, 301
Wiley, I. W., Rev., 548
Wilk, Regina, 422
Wilkerson, Marjorie, 1196
Willard, Frances E., 1141
Willard, Mary B., 1141
Williams, Betty, 425
Williams, Henry T., 532
Williams, Mary Theriot, 59
Williams, Sarah R. L., 749
Williamson, Nancy, 918
Willson, Winifred, 747
Wilson, Norma, 365
Wilson, Patricia, 306
Windsor, Herbert T., Mrs., 763
Winner, Vella Alberta, 409
Winslow, Helen M., 211
Winzenz, Karen H., 1119
Wise, Daniel, 546
Wolcott, Imogene, 92
Wold, Clara, 1088
Wood, Mabel Travis, 97
Woodhull, Victoria C., 1441

Woods, Roma W., 1280
Woodworth, Samuel, 536
Woodworth, Valerie, 718
Woolston, Florence, 1248
Wortman, Marlene Stein, 153
Wright, Edna, 374
Wright, Rosalie Muller, 1439
Wychgram, Jacob, Dr., 385
Wynn, James Osgood, Mrs., 629

Xanthes, Samantha Marie, 951

Yancy, Dorothy, 1337
Yanofsky, S., 505
Yarosz, Diane, 645
Youmans, Henry M., Mrs., 1219
Young, Rose, 764, 1268
Youngman, Lenore, 682
Youry, Mary, 765

Zachary, Frank, 1120
Zavitz, Carol, 961
Zerkel, Gaylynn, 7
Zielinska, Helena, 419
Zimmerman, Karen, 1112, 1113
Zipse, Edith, 1218
Zulgervitz, Annelise, 429
Zwickey, Virginia, 1230

# Index of Publishers

Numbers following each publisher refers to specific entries and not page numbers.

AAUW, 32, 425
ABC Needlework and Crafts, 623
AFL-CIO, Committee on Political Education, Women's Activities Department, 511
AFSC, 36
AFSCME, Clerical, Technical, and Professional Employees Local 1695, 294
AIAW Collective, 24
ALA/SRRT Task Force on Women, 1333
AME Church, Women's Missionary Society, 640
Abzug, Bella, Reports, 234
Acorn Educational Press Inc./Helen Oakes, 860
Action Coordinating Council for Comprehensive Child Care, 15
Action Latin America, Women's Caucus, 967
Action Social de la Femme et Association du Livre Francais, 18
Adoration of the Most Blessed Sacrament, United Societies of Polish Women, 921
Advocates for Women, 20
Aertzlichen Gesellschaft fuer Sexualwissenschaft und Konstitutions-forschung, 58
Affiliated Association of California Personnel Guidance Association/California Personnel Guidance Association Women's Caucus 156
Africa Journal Ltd., 22
African Methodist Episcopal, Women's Missionary Society, 640
Alan Guttmacher Institute, 327, 328
Alaska Women's Resource Center, 1060
Alert, Inc., 29
Alexander Hogg, 787
All China Democratic Women's Federation, 1341
All India Congress Committee, Women's Department, 1344
Alliance Against Sexual Coercion, Feminist Alliance Against Rape, National Communication Network, 21
Alpha Kappa Alpha Sorority, 492
Altrusia, 481
Amazon Collective, 30
Amazon-Nation, 252
Amazon Publications, Inc., 1077
Ambitious Amazons, 572
American Association of University Women, 425
American Association of University Women, California Division, 166
American Association of University Women, Educational Foundation, 1378
American Association of University Women, Madison Branch, 32
American Association of University Women, Wisconsin State Division, 80
American Association of Women in Community and Junior Colleges, 1
American Baptist Woman Leaders, 33
American Birth Control League, Inc., 97
American Broadside Corporation, 125
American Committee on Maternal Welfare, Inc., 652
American Council on Education, Commission on the Education of Women, 283
American Educational Research Association, Women's Caucus, 3
American Fashion Co., 39

American Federation of State, County, and Municipal Employees, Local 1695, 294
American Food Journal, Inc., 454
American Friends Service Committee, 36
American Geological Institute, Women Geoscientists Committee, 1323
American Gold Star Mothers, 422
American Home Publishing Co., Inc., 38
American Legion Auxiliary, Burlington, VT, 78
American Legion Auxiliary, Indianapolis, IN, 757
American Legion Auxiliary, Topeka, KS, 139
American Legion Auxiliary, Department of Illinois, 133
American Legion Auxiliary, Department of Kansas, 509
American Legion Auxiliary, Department of Minnesota, 408
American Legion Auxiliary, Department of Nebraska, 569
American Legion Auxiliary, Department of North Dakota, 134
American Legion Auxiliary, Department of Pennsylvania, 807
American Legion Auxiliary, Department of Utah, 135
American Legion Auxiliary, Department of Wyoming, 802
American Library Association Social Responsibility Round Table, 6
American Library Association, Social Responsibilities Round Table-Task Force on Women, 1333
American-Lithuanian Roman Catholic Women's Alliance, 653
American Medical Women's Association, Inc., 497
American Society for Psycho-Prophylaxis in Obstetrics, 7, 96
American Society for Public Administration, 43
American Vigilance Association, 1158
American Women's Club of Paris, Inc., 137
American Woman Suffrage Association, 1247
Anarcho-Feminists, 1027
Anchorage Women's Liberation, 871
An Association of Females/Operatives Magazine, 875
Androgyny Press, 1055
Antioch Women's Liberation, 54
Aphra, Inc., 55
Arizona Women's Political Caucus, 60
Artemis Enterprises, Inc., 300
Ash, Marian, 1044
Asian Women, University of California, Berkeley, 64
Asociacion Feminina de Camaguey, 965
Associated Students of UCLA Communications Board, 1113
Association du Livre Francais, Action Social de la Femme, 18
Association for Children Deprived of Support, 2
Association for Women in Mathematics, 66
Association for Women in Psychology, 9, 67, 68

Association of American Colleges, 69
Association of American Colleges, Project on the Status and Education of Women, 867
Association of American Law Schools, 70
Association of Commissions on Women, Interstate, 117
Association of Faculty Women, 4
Association of Faculty Women and University Community Women, 5
Association of Halfway House Alcoholism Programs of North America, Inc., 228
Association of Libertarian Feminists, 71
Association of Married Women, 72
Association of Women in Science, 8
Association to Repeal Abortion Laws, 73
Atlanta Women's Club, 76
Atlanta Women's Liberation, 504
Auckland Women's Liberation, 123
Austin Women's Liberation Movement, 1005
Australian News and Information Bureau, 1380

B.G. Leubner, 385
Badger, T., 310
Baldwin Street Gallery, 81
Baltimore Women's Center, 1368
Baltimore Women's Liberation, 215
Barnard College, 1023
Barrer and Associates, 1195
Battle-Axes, 83
Bay Area Women's Liberation, 1115
Bay Area Women's Liberation, 84
Bella Abzug Reports, 234
Bergen Community College, Division of Community Services, 806
Berkeley Community YWCA, 74
Berkeley-Oakland Women for Peace, 280
Berkeley-Oakland Women's Union, 89
Berkeley's Women's Liberation, 90
Berkshire Women's Liberation, 1295
Best Friends Poetry Collective, 91
Betsy Hogan Associates, 1257
Big Mama Rag, Inc., 95
Biological Sciences Program, State University of New York, 1302
Black Maria Collective, 101
Bloodroot, Inc., 102
Bloomington Women's Liberation, 397
Blue Collar Press, 1064
Blumenberg Press, 641
B'Nai B'Rith Women's Supreme Council, 104
Board of Missions of the Methodist Episcopal Church, 1273
Board of Missions of the Presbyterian Church in the U.S.A., Woman's Committees, 1307
Bonneville Power Administration, Women's Advisory Group, 225
Born A Woman, 109
Boston/Cambridge Female Liberation, 334
Boston Daughters of Bilitis, 367
Bread and Roses, 114
Breakthrough Publishing Co., 460
Breitinger, Nancy, 163
Briere, E. and V. Giard, 968
Bright Medusa Press, 121
Bristol Women's Liberation, 299
Bristol Women's Liberation Group, 122

Buck's County Community College, Women's Caucus, 1059
Bulmer, W. & Co., 401
Bund Deutscher Frauenvereine, 146
Bureau de la Tribune des Femme Libre, 364
Bureau of Community Health Service, Department of Health, Education and Welfare, Health Medical Service Administration, 326
Bureau of Public Affairs, U.S. Department of State, 1336
Bureau of Scientific Temperance Investigation and Department of Scientific Temperance Instruction of the World's and National Women's Christian Temperance Union, 1098
Butterick Fashion Marketing Co., 148

CCWHP, New Albany, IN, 151
CCWHP, Plattsburgh, NY, 150
CHOICE, 154
CLUW, 155
CLUW, Madison-Janesville, 1140
COPE, Women's Activities Department, AFL-CIO, 511
COYOTE, 251
CUNY, 1427
Calgary Status of Women Action Committee, 164
California Commission on the Status of Women, 171
California Democratic Council, State Women's Caucus, 1423
California Division American Association of University Women, 166
California Fashion Publications, Inc., 165
California Institution for Women, 206
California Personnel Guidance Association Women's Caucus/Affiliated Association of California Personnel Guidance Association, 156
California State University, Hayward Department of Psychology, 934
California State University, Sacramento Feminist News Women's Center, 356
Call Off Your Old Tired Ethics (COYOTE), 251
Calliope Publishing, Inc., 891
Cambridge/Boston Female Liberation, 334
Campus Women's Forum, University of California, Berkeley, 1234
Canada Department of Labour, Women's Bureau, 1317
Canadian Native Sisterhood Organization of Penitentiary Women, 772
Canadian Women's Coalition to Repeal Abortion Laws, 1076
Cape Cod Women's Liberation, 177
Capitol Hill Women's Political Caucus, 305
Carousel, Inc., 180
Carter, Sally, 1410
Cassell & Co., Ltd., 1289
Caucus of Women in History of the Southern Historical Association, 185
Caucus for Women in Statistics, 184
Cell 16/Female Liberation, 841
Center for Women and Family Living Education, University Extension, University of Wisconsin, 1228

Center for Women Policy Studies, 963
Center for Women's Studies and Services, 162, 347, 593
Center for Continuing Education for Women, University of California, Berkeley, League of Associated Women, 567
Center for Continuing Education of Women, University of Michigan, 630
Central Administration, University of Wisconsin System, 1146
Central Committee, Communist Party of the U.S.A. Woman's Department, 1447
Central Council of Trade Unions of the USSR, Soviet Women's Committee, 1063
Central Pennsylvania District, International Ladies' Garment Workers Union, 402
Le Centre des Femmes, 939
Charles B. Slack, Inc., 120
Charlotte Perkins Gilman Chapter of the New American Movement on Socialist Feminism, 775
Charlotte Women's Center, 1109
Charlton Co., 372
Charmian, 620
Chicago Gay Teachers Union, 405
Chicago Women's Liberation Movement, 1163
Chicago Women's Liberation Union, 161, 1253
Chicana Service Action Center, 157
Chinese Women's Anti-Aggression League, 194
Church of God, Seventh-Day, Women's Association, 1167
Church of Jesus Christ of Latter-Day Saints, 1263
Church Women United in Madison, Wisconsin, Inc., 200
Church Women United of Southern California-Southern Nevada, 201
Church Work Association, 202
City Club of Cincinnati, 1259
City University of New York, Queens College, Department of English, 1427
City Wide Women's Liberation, 205
Clarke, John Owen, 288
Clearinghouse for Feminist Media, 208
Clearinghouse International of the Eleanor Association, Women's Forum, 209
Clerical, Technical, and Professional Employees, Local 1695, 294
Cluster Communication Committee, University of Michigan, 1389
Coalition of Labor Union Women, 155
Coalition of Labor Union Women, Madison-Janesville, 1140
Collective of the Center for Women's Studies and Services, 593
Collective for Woman, 216
College of Law, University of Arizona, 866
College Settlements Association, 480
Colonial Dames of America, National Society, 629
Colorado State University, English Department, 370
Comision Femenil Mexicana, 152
Le Comite National d' Action sur le statut de la femme/National Action Committee on the Status of Women, 670
Commission on the Education of Women, American Council on Education, 283
Commission on the Status of Women, Harrisburg, PA, 158, 159
Commission on the Status of Women, Sacramento, CA, 223
Commission on the Status of Women, Washington, DC, 222
Commission on the Status of Women, University of Kansas, 507
Commission on the Status of Women in the Profession, Modern Language Association of America, 601
Committee on Political Education, Women's Activities Department, AFL-CIO, 511
Committee Opposing Racist Practice and Sentiments, 462
Common Woman Collective, Berkeley, CA, 226
Common Woman Collective, New Brunswick, NJ, 227
Communist Party of the U.S.A., Woman's Department, Central Committee, 1447
Community Health Center, 979
Community of Women, 250
Community Women's Centre, 229
Community Women's Newspaper/Woman, 1237
Concern for Health Options, Information, Care, and Education (CHOICE), 154
Concilio Mujeres, 946
Conde Nast Publications, Inc., 119, 418, 603
Conference Group in Women's History, 153
Conference of Indochinese and North American Women, 810
Congress to Unite Women, 233
Congressional Clearinghouse on Women's Rights, 160
Congressional Union for Woman Suffrage, 1088
Connecticut League of Women Voters, 1249
Connections Guidance Center, 237
Conseil National des Femmes Francaises, 14
Convenience Publications, 245
Coordinating Committee on Women in the Historical Profession, New Albany, IN, 151
Coordinating Committee on Women in the Historical Profession, Plattsburgh, NY, 150
Cornell University, University Personnel Service, 269
Correctional Institution for Women, 476
Corson Publishing, Inc., 931
Council for the Continuing Education of Women-Miami Dade Community College, 1457
Council for Women's Equality, 247
Covenant of the Goddess, Susan B. Anthony Coven No. 1, 1101
Craeftgemont Witancoveyne, Inc., 1209
Critic Company, 329
Crowell-Collier Publishing Company, 1265
Czechoslovak Women's Council, 254

DAR
see Daughters of the American Revolution
DC Comics, Inc., 1440
DYK Enterprises, 403
Dallas Area Women's Liberation, 1128
Dane County Chapter Wisconsin Women's Political Caucus, 1230
Darlex Corp., 443
Daughters of American Colonists, National Society, 218
Daughters of Bilitis, Boston, 367

Daughters of Bilitis, Kansas City, MO, 527
Daughters of Bilitis, New Detroit Chapter, 947
Daughters of Bilitis, New York, NY, 574
Daughters of Bilitis, San Francisco, CA, 1036
Daughters of Bilitis/Tide Collective 576
Daughters of Bilitis/Women for Action, 648
Daughters of the American Revolution, New York, NY, 606
Daughters of the American Revolution, Washington, DC, 260
Daughters of the American Revolution, Betsy Allen Chapter, 255
Daughters of the American Revolution, National Society, New York, NY, 753
Daughters of the American Revolution, National Society, Washington, DC, 761
Daughters of the American Revolution, North Carolina Society, 843
Daughters of the American Revolution-Wisconsin, 1223
David Hogan, 956
Davis Women's Forum, University of California, 1235
Dayton Women's Liberation, 261
Deacon and Peterson, 553
Deaconess Movement, 499
Defense Fuel Supply Center, Federal Women's Program Committee, 849
Delta Kappa Gamma Society, 265
Delta Sigma Theta, Inc., 264
Democratic National Committee Women's Division, 266
Denver Women's Liberation, 267
Department of Biology, OML, Yale University, 1328
Department of Employment and Youth Affairs, 1312
Department of English, Douglass College, Rutgers University, 1306
Department of English, University of Nebraska, 619
Department of Health, Education, and Welfare, Health Medical Service Administration, Bureau of Community Health Service, 326
Department of Industrial Relations, Division of Fair Employment Practices, Fair Employment Practice Commission, 804
Department of Geography, Syracuse University, 414, 1331
Department of German, University of Wisconsin, 1332
Department of Illinois, American Legion Auxiliary, 133
Department of Kansas, American Legion Auxiliary, 509
Department of Minnesota, American Legion Auxiliary, 408
Department of Nebraska, American Legion Auxiliary, 569
Department of North Dakota, American Legion Auxiliary, 134
Department of Pennsylvania, American Legion Auxiliary, 807
Department of Utah, American Legion Auxiliary, 135
Department of Wyoming, American Legion Auxiliary, 802

Department of Psychology, California State University, Hayward, 934
Department of Scientific Temperance Instruction of the Worlds and National Women's Christian Temperance Union, Bureau of Scientific Temperance Investigation, 1098
Department of Sociology, Ontario Institute for Studies in Education, 961
Department of the Navy, Print Media Division, 1215
Deutscher Gewerkschaftsbund, 383
Division of Community Services, Bergen Community College, 806
Division of Fair Employment, Fair Employment Practice Commission, Department of Industrial Relations, 804
Dollemina of Antwerp, 451
Doric Publishing, Inc., 35
Douglass College, Department of English, Rutgers University, 1306

E.A. Rice and Company, 546
E. Henderson, 529
East Bay Feminists, 279
East London Federation of Suffragettes, 1443
Earlham College Women's Center, 1345
Ecumenical Women's Center, 282
Eden Press Women's Publications, 483, 498
Editorial Mex Ameris S.A., 207
Edizioni Cooperative Effe, 285
Educational Foundation, American Association of University Women, 1378
Een Dolle Mina Publikatie, 1137
Eleanor Association Women's Forum, Clearinghouse International, 209
Elizabeth Blackwell's Women's Health Center, 289
Eliza Heywood, Mrs., 336
English Woman's Journal Company, Ltd., 295
Enthusiasts' Publications, Inc., 311
Equal Rights Alliance/Sisterhood, 592
Equal Rights, Inc., 302
Equal Rights Project, 303
Equal Suffrage League, 789
Essence Communications, Inc., 308
Etats Generaux de la Femme Conference, 290
Every Woman Press/Women's Study Group, 952
Everywoman Newspaper, 315
Everywoman's Center, Division of Continuing Education, University of Massachusetts, 313

FAAR-Alliance Against Sexual Coercion, National Communication Network, 21
FLIPPIES-Feminist Lesbian Intergalatic Party, 513
FOCAS-Feminist Organization for Communication Action and Service, 611
Fairchild Publications, 1190
Fair Employment Practice Commission, Department of Industrial Relations, Division of Fair Employment Practices, 804
Family Circle, Inc., 323
Fawcett Society and Women's Lobby, 1421
Federal Women's Program Committee, Defense Fuel Supply Center, 849
Federal Women's Program, U.S. Civil Service, 1327

Federally Employed Women, Inc., 799
Federation Abolitionniste Internationale, 140
Federation Britannique, Continentale, et Generale, 141
Federation of Organizations for Professional Women, 28, 1303
Female Liberation/Cell 16, 841
Female Liberation/Second Wave, Inc., 1008
Femina-Illustration, 339
Feminist Alliance Against Rape, Alliance Against Sexual Coercion, National Communication Network, 21
Feminist Art Journal, Inc., 346
Feminist Communication Collective, 351
Feminist Lesbian Intergalatic Party (FLIPPIES), 513
Feminist News Women's Center, California State University, Sacramento, 356
Feminist Organization for Communication, Action and Service (FOCAS), 611
Feminist Press, 337
Feminist Press and the National Women's Studies Association, 1431
Feminist Publications of Ottawa, 1150
Feminist Publishing Alliance, Inc., 918
Feminist Studies, Inc., 321
Feminist Voice Collective, 360
Feminist Women's Health Center, 361
Feminists for Life, 1034
Feminists Writers' Guild, Milwaukee Chapter, 362
51% Publications, 365
Finnish Federation, Inc., 1131
First Catholic Slovak Ladies Association, 381
Florida Free Press, 886
Florida State University-Tallahassee, 941
Foothill College, 882
Fourth World Publications, 375
France Editions et Publications SA, 291
French Women's Liberation, 1117
Fredrika Bremer Association, 450
Free University Women's Center, 1412

Garment Workers Local No. 125, 595
Gay Community Social Services, 1105
Gay People and Mental Health, 404
Gay Women's Caucus, Lavender Women Collective Committee, 566
Gay Women's Liberation Front, 1034
General Federation of Women's Clubs, New York, NY, 211, 410
General Federation of Women's Clubs, Washington, DC, 409
George B. Whittaker, 86
Getting On Women's Collective, 828
Giard, V. and E. Briere, 968
Gibbons, W., 555
Girl Scouts of the Milwaukee Area, 1058
Girl Scouts of the USA, 37, 256
Godey Company, 420
Gold Star Mothers, 422
Goodbye to All That/San Diego Women, 424
Gordon & Breach Science Publishers, Ltd., 1427
Graduate Theological Union Women's Caucus, 1366
Greenwood Reprint Corporation, T.W. Harris, 782

Grist Press, 427
Growing Room Collective, 975
Gruner & Jahr, USA, Inc., Parents Magazine Enterprises, 1456
Grupo Latino-Americano de Mujeres en Paris, 848

HRW, Inc., 430
Hadassah, the Women's Zionist Organization of America, 432, 433
Hal Publications, 1445
Harcourt Brace Jovanovich Merchandising Publications, 105
Harrisburg Women's Center, 431
Harrison, James, and Co., 560
Hartman, Stephanie, 983
Hausfrau, Inc., 439
Hawaii Women's Liberation, 25
Haworth Press, Inc., 1301, 1308
Health Medical Service Administration, Department of Health, Education and Welfare, Bureau of Community Health Service, 326
Healthright, Inc., 441
Hearst Corporation, 246, 423, 438, 457
Helen Oakes/Acorn Educational Press, Inc., 860
Henderson, E., 529
Heresies Collective, Inc., 448
Herself, Inc., 449
Heywood, Eliza, Mrs., 336
High School Women's Group, 452
Hofstra University, School of Law, 1305
Hogan, David, 956
Home Economics Division, Scholastic Magazines, Inc., 214
Home-Maker Co., 456
Hosford and Sons, 654
House Committee on Constitutional Revision and Women's Rights, 179
Human Rights for Women, Inc., 430
Hutchinson and Co., 561

ILGW, 292, 416, 506, 518, 533, 862, 864, 878, 1012
Illinois Association Opposed to the Extension of Suffrage to Women, 132
Illinois Association Opposed to Women Suffrage, 466
Illinois Women's Athletic Club, 1240
Indiana Abortion Law Repeal Coalition, 470
Indiana University-Bloomington, 1428
Indiana University Student Association-Women's Affairs, 1382
Indianapolis Women's Liberation, 471
Industrial Committee of the War Work Council of the Young Women's Christian Association, 474
Infinity Publishing Co., 210
Institute for the Study of Women in Transit, 477
Institute of Education, University of London, 1429
Inter-American Commission of Women, 800
Intercollegiate Association of Women Students, Columbus, OH, 758
Intercollegiate Association of Women Students, East Lansing, MI, 464

Intercollegiate Association for Women
  Students, Lansing, MI, 343
Intercollegiate Association for Women
  Students, Washington, DC, 342
Intercommunications, Inc., 212
Interdepartmental Task Force on Women, 1211
Inter-Municipal Research Committee, 142
International Association of Altrusian Clubs,
  481
International Childbirth Education Association, 96
International Cooperative Women's Guild, 484
International Council of Social Democratic
  Women, 465
International Council of Women, 143
International Federation of Women Lawyers,
  10, 11
International Feminist League of Hong Kong,
  482
International Labor Office, Office for Women
  Workers, 1318
International Ladies' Garment Workers Union,
  Cleveland, OH, 864
International Ladies' Garment Workers Union,
  Milwaukee, WI, 292
International Ladies' Garment Workers Union,
  New York, NY, 416, 506, 533
International Ladies' Garment Workers Union,
  Knitgoods Workers Union, Local 155, AFL-CIO
  518
International Ladies' Garment Workers Union
  Local 91, 878
International Ladies' Garment Workers Union,
  Ohio-Kentucky Region, 862
International Ladies' Garment Workers Union,
  Western Pennsylvania District Council 424-
  445, 1012
International Liaison Network of Women
  Artists, 1202
International Marxist Groups/Socialist Woman
  Groups, 1049
International Sociological Association
  Research Committee on Sex Roles in Society,
  836
International Woman Suffrage Alliance, 485
International Women's Year Secretariat, 487
Interstate Association of Commissions for
  Women, 117
Interstudio Feminist Alliance, 666
Iowa Training School for Girls, 1096
Iowa Woman Suffrage Association, 1280
Ishtar Women's Resource Centre and Transition
  House, 489
Isla Vista Women's Center, 964

J. Menzies & Co., 1288
James Harrison and Co., 560
Jeannette Rankin Brigade, 494
Jensen-Fane Publications, 1078
John Brown Women's Caucus, 737
John Owen Clarke, 288
Johnson, Karen Colaianni, 160
Joint Strategy and Action Committee, Inc.,
  493
Judy, Inc., 501
Junior League of San Francisco, 503
Just Government League of Maryland, 617

Kansas City Women's Liberation Union, 1316
Kappa Beta Pi Legal Sorority, 510
Kappa Epsilon, National Pharmacy Fraternity
  for Women, 107
Karen Colaianni Johnson, 160
Knitgoods Workers' Union, International
  Ladies' Garment Workers Union, Local 155
  AFL-CIO, 518
Know, Inc., 874
Knoxville Lesbian Collective, 655

LDM Publications, 531
Labour Party, 526
Lancaster Women's Center, 563
Last Gasp Ecofunnies, Women's Liberation
  Basement Press, 491
Lavender Women Collective, Committee of the
  Gay Women's Caucus, 566
League of Associated Women, University of
  California, Berkeley, Center for Continuing
  Education for Women, 567
League of Women Voters-Connecticut, 1249
League of Women Voters of Dane County, Inc.,
  568
League of Women Voters of Ohio, 865
League of Women Voters of Pennsylvania, 145
League of Women Voters of the United States,
  765
League of Women Voters of Wisconsin, 374
Legislative Reference Bureau, State of Ohio
  Women's Information Center, 1177
Leubner, B.G., 385
Lewis Publishing Company, 1272
Lesbian-Feminist Liberation, 573
Lesbian Resource Center, 1057
Liaison Committee for Women's Peace Groups,
  172
Liberated Space For the Women of Haight, 579
Librarians for Social Change, 524
Lilith Publications, Inc., 587
Linguistics Department/Stanford University,
  1304
Local 91, International Ladies' Garment
  Workers Union, 878
Local No. 125, Garment Workers, 595
Loewenthal, W. & S., 384, 1459
Louisiana Correctional Institute for Women,
  87, 924
Luna Collective, 597
Lutheran Deaconess Motherhouse, 262

MUCIA-Midwest University Consortium for
  International Activities, Inc., 1179
Mac-A-Nan Press, 955
Madison Branch, American Association of University Women, 32
Madison Coalition for the ERA, 277
Madison-Janesville CLUW (Coalition of Labor
  Union Women), 1140
Madison Rape Crisis Center, 942
Madison Women's News, 1376
Madison Women's Union, 604
Madison YWCA, 605
Maid Library, Ohio State University, 1313
Mail Order News Corporation, 147
Marian Ash, 1044
Marin Women's Publishing Cooperative, 1411
Martha Movement, 616

Maryland Correctional Institute for Women, 436
Massachusetts Association Opposed to the Further Extension of Suffrage, 954
Maternal Information Services, Inc., Voice of Mother's and Children's Liberation, 1444
McGraw-Hill, College Division, 490
Media Center, 565
Media Women, 625
Menzies, J. & Co., 1288
Merritt College Women's Collective, 1039
Methodist Episcopal Church, Board of Mission, 1273
Methodist Episcopal Church, Women's Home Missionary Society, 1266
Miami Dade Community College-Council for the Continuing Education of Women, 1457
Michigan University Center for Continuing Education of Women, University of Michigan, 630
Michigan Women's Commission, 631
Midwest Modern Language Association-Women's Caucus for Modern Languages, 1169
Midwest Sociologists for Women in Society, 634
Midwest University Consortium for International Activities, Inc., (MUCIA), 1179
Midwest Women's Legal Group, 635
Milwaukee Area Girl Scouts, 1058
Milwaukee Chapter, Feminist Writers' Guild, 362
Milwaukee Chapter, Wisconsin Women's Political Caucus, 637
Milwaukee Journal Co., 636
Milwaukee Women's Political Caucus-Wisconsin Women's Political Caucus, 1418
Ming and Young, 558
Minnesota Correctional Institute for Women, 951
Minnesota Historical Society, Women Historians of the Midwest, 1175
Minnesota Planning and Counseling Center for Women, Office of Student Affairs, University of Minnesota, 917
Modern Language Association of America, Commission on the Status of Women in the Profession, 601
Modern Language Association of America, Women's Caucus for Modern Languages, 230, 958
Montana State University-Bozeman, 368
Montreal Women's Liberation, 650
Mormon Sisters, Inc., 319
Mormons, 1263
Mother Publications, 933
Mothers for Fair Child Support, National Chapter, 657
Mountain Moving Day, Inc., 661
Mouvement National des Femmes, 615
Ms. Atlas Press, 577
Mueller and Kiepenhauer, 1232
Multiple Vision, Inc., 668

NAC, 1082
NOW
 see National Organization for Women
NUC, Women's Caucus, 738

N.V. Soerabayasch Handelsblad en Deukkeryen, 257
Nancy Breitinger, 163
Napa Valley Women's Center, 742
Nassau County Department of General Services, 1160
Nassau Herald, 743
National Action Committee on the Status of Women/Le Comite National d'Action sur le statut de la femme, 670
National Action Committee on the Status of Women, 1082
National Ad Hoc Committee for ERA, 745
National American Woman Suffrage Association, New York, NY, 764, 930
National American Woman Suffrage Association, Portland, OR, 1281
National American Woman Suffrage Association, Warren, OH, 920
National Association for Repeal of Abortion Laws, 671
National Association of Commissions for Women, 116
National Association for Women Deans, Administrators and Counselors, 746
National Association of Women Lawyers, 1337
National Association Opposed to Woman Suffrage, 1278
National Board of Young Women's Christian Associations, 1277
National Cash Register, 1285
National Catholic Center for Interracial Justice, 1122
National Coalition for Research on Women's Education and Development, 239
National Committee on Household Employment, 673
National Communication Network, Alliance Against Sexual Coercion, Feminist Alliance Against Rape, 21
National Communications Network for the Elimination of Violence Against Women, 750
National Congress of Mothers, 211
National Council of Jewish Women, Milwaukee, WI, 144
National Council of Jewish Women, New York, NY, 248, 495, 674, 751, 831
National Council of Women of the United States, 752
National Education Association, 672
National Federation of Business and Professional Women's Clubs, 747
National Federation of Republican Women, 131, 189, 366, 676, 957, 1194
National Federation of Republican Women, Comprehensive Advocacy Program, 149
National Information Clearing Office, Women Strike for Peace, 570, 627
National Interim Committee for a Mass Party of the People, 677
National League for Women's Service, 100, 647, 754
National League of Women, Sixth Region, 1079
National Lesbian Information Service, 679

National Organization for Women
  [Entries for this organization are arranged two ways; first by name and thereunder geographically under state, subdivided by city]
  Ann Arbor Chapter, 759
  Anne Arundel County Chapter, 49
  Annapolis Legislative Information Office of Maryland, 691
  Atlanta Chapter, 75, 715
  Beach Cities Chapter, 85
  Bakersfield Chapter, 685
  Baton Rouge Chapter, 852
  Berk County Chapter, 88
  Berkeley Chapter, 681
  Boulder Chapter, 110
  Bronx Chapter, 127
  Brooklyn Chapter, 128
  Buffalo Chapter, 130
  Butler County Chapter, 1149
  California Educational Task Force, 168
  California Statewide Chapter, 169
  Central Connecticut Chapter, 188
  Central New Jersey Chapter, 711
  Central Savannah River Area Chapter, 56
  Chicago Chapter, 13
  Cincinnati Chapter, 703
  Clark Campus Chapter, 175
  Cleveland Chapter, 1354
  Columbus Chapter, 971
  Committee to Promote Women's Studies, 808
  Conejo Valley Chapter, 232
  Connecticut Chapter, 235
  Contra Costa County/Diablo Valley Chapter, 244
  Dade County Chapter, 683
  Dallas County Chapter, 690
  Denver Chapter, 707
  Des Moines Chapter, 819
  Diablo Valley/Contra Costa County Chapter, 244
  DuPage Chapter, 1116
  Durham Chapter, 686
  Eastern Massachusetts Chapter, 821
  Elgin/Fox Valley Chapter, 377
  El Paso County Chapter, 286
  Erie County Chapter, 716
  Essex County Chapter, 193
  Essex County/North Shore Chapter, 307
  Fort Worth Chapter, 582, 827
  Fox Valley/Elgin Chapter, 377
  Fullerton Chapter, 805
  Fresno Chapter, 704
  Genesee Valley Chapter, 373
  Great Falls/Missoula Chapter, 61
  Greater Kansas City Chapter, 447
  Greater Pittsburgh Chapter, 689
  Green Bay Chapter, 687
  Harbor/South Bay Chapter, 437
  Houston Chapter, 126
  Image of Women National Task Force Committee, Rochester Image Committee, 287
  Indianapolis Chapter, 472
  International Chapter/Paris Organization of Women, 887
  Jacksonville Chapter, 1185
  King/Seattle County Chapter, 728
  Kitsap County Chapter, 517
  Laguna Beach Chapter, 562
  Lake Worth Chapter/Northern Palm Beach Chapter, 580
  Las Vegas Chapter, 564
  Legal Defense and Education Fund, Project on Equal Education Rights, 884
  Lehigh Valley Chapter, 571
  Lincoln Chapter, 591
  Livonia/Schoolcraft Chapter, 1206
  Long Beach Chapter, 694
  Long Island/Nassau Chapter, 824
  Los Angeles Chapter, 680
  Los Angeles/Southern California Chapter, 682
  Madison Chapter, 306
  Maine Chapter, 609
  Malibu Chapter, 684
  Manitowoc Chapter, 1222
  Marin County Chapter, 705
  Martha's Vineyard Task Force on the Image of Women, 468
  Michigan Chapter, 63
  Midland Chapter, 50
  Middlesex County Chapter, 632
  Milwaukee Chapter, 1207
  Missoula/Great Falls Chapter, 61
  Monmouth County Chapter, 645
  Monterey Chapter, 1045
  Monterey Peninsula Chapter, 646
  Montgomery Chapter, 393
  Montgomery County Chapter, 394
  Muncie Chapter, 709
  Nassau/Long Island Chapter, 824
  National Federal Communication Commission Task Force, 695
  National Headquarters, 272, 756
  National Task Force-Marriage, Divorce, and Family Relations, 760
  New Mexico Chapter, 712
  New Mexico Chapter, Task Force on Women in Poverty, 1037
  New Orleans Chapter, 446
  New York City Chapter, 733, 734, 735, 784
  New York State Chapter, 702, 793
  Norfolk Chapter, 842
  North Shore/Essex County Chapter, 307
  North Suburban Chapter, 714
  Northeast Bucks County Chapter, 675
  Northern California Regional Chapter, 846
  Northern Chautauqua County Chapter, 701
  Northern Nevada Chapter, 48
  Northern New Jersey Chapter, 718, 823
  Northern Palm Beach/Lake Worth Chapter, 580
  Northern Prince George's County Chapter, 1015
  Northern Virginia Chapter, 845
  Orange County Chapter, 16
  Orlando Chapter, 803
  Palo Alto Chapter, 720
  Pamona Valley Chapter, 721
  Paris Organization of Women/International Chapter, 887
  Passaic County Chapter, 700
  Peninsula Women's Coalition Chapter, 722
  Peoria Chapter, 708
  Philadelphia Chapter, 909
  Phoenix Chapter, 911
  Princeton Chapter, 731

*Women's Periodicals and Newspapers*

National Organization for Women (continued)
  Prince George's County Chapter, 727
  Portland Chapter, 688
  Project on Equal Education Rights, Legal Defense and Education Fund, 884
  Quad Cities Chapter, 937
  Rhode Island Chapter, 970
  Riverside Chapter, 1314
  Roanoke Valley Chapter, 662
  Rochester Chapter, 391
  Rochester Image Committee, Image of Women National Task Force Committee, 287
  Rockford Chapter, 667
  Sacramento Area Chapter, 697
  Sacramento Chapter Legislative Committee, 178
  St. Johns County Chapter, 989
  St. Louis Chapter, 47
  Salem Chapter, 825
  San Antonio Chapter, 1002
  San Diego Chapter, 167, 725
  San Fernando Valley Chapter, 696
  San Francisco Chapter, 1244
  San Gabriel Valley Chapter, 726
  San Joaquin Chapter, 995
  San Jose Chapter, 698
  San Mateo County Chapter, 996
  Santa Barbara Chapter, 706
  Santa Cruz Chapter, 445
  Schoolcraft/Livonia Chapter, 1206
  Seattle/King County Chapter, 728
  Shreveport Caddo-Bossier Chapter, 925
  Snohomish County Chapter, 17
  Springfield Chapter, 729
  Suffolk County Chapter, 1087
  Staten Island Chapter, 713
  Solano County Chapter, 723
  Somerset County Chapter, 1056
  South Bay Chapter, 1090
  South Bay/Harbor Chapter, 437
  Southeastern Connecticut Chapter, 1061
  Southern California/Los Angeles Chapter, 682
  Southwest Cook County Chapter, 719
  Tacoma Chapter, 717
  Task Force on Marriage, Divorce, and Family Relations, 730
  Task Force on Women and the Arts, 732
  Task Force on Women in Poverty, New Mexico Chapter, 1037
  Thurston County Chapter, 693
  Tippecanoe Chapter, 1107
  Trenton Chapter, 1123
  Tri-Cities Chapter, 1214
  Tri-State Chapter, 692
  Tucson Chapter, 1127
  Twin Cities Chapter, 699
  Union County Chapter, 710
  Ventura Chapter, 1156
  Virginia Beach Chapter, 972
  Washington County Chapter, 1191
  Washington, DC Chapter, 1159
  Washington Metro Area Chapter, 1192
  Waukesha Chapter, 1198
  Western Connecticut Chapter, 461
  Western Region Chapter (Costa Mesa, CA), 724
  Western Region Chapter (Seattle, WA), 1205

National Organization for Women (continued)
  Wichita Chapter, 820
  Willamette Valley Chapter, 798

  Alabama
    Montgomery Chapter, 393
  Arizona
    Phoenix Chapter, 911
    Tucson Chapter, 1127
  California
    Bakersfield Chapter, 685
    Berkeley Chapter, 681
    Burlingame
      San Mateo County Chapter, 996
    Canoga Park
      San Fernando Valley Chapter, 696
    Claremont
      Pamona Valley Chapter, 721
    Costa Mesa
      Western Region Chapter, 724
    Fairchild
      Solano County Chapter, 723
    Fresno Chapter, 704
    Fullerton Chapter, 805
    Laguna Beach Chapter, 562
    La Mesa
      California Educational Task Force, 168
    Long Beach Chapter, 694
    Los Angeles
      California Statewide Chapter, 169
      Los Angeles Chapter, 680
      Los Angeles/Southern California Chapter, 682
      Southern California/Los Angeles Chapter, 682
    Malibu Chapter, 684
    Monterey Chapter, 1045
    Monterey Peninsula Chapter, 646
    Palo Alto Chapter, 720
    Palos Verdes Estates/Rolling Hills Estates, Peninsula Women's Coalition Chapter, 722
    Riverside Chapter, 1314
    Sacramento Area Chapter, 697
    Sacramento Chapter Legislative Committee, 178
    San Diego Chapter, 167, 725
    San Francisco
      Northern California Regional Chapter, 846
      San Francisco Chapter, 1244
    San Gabriel Valley Chapter, 726
    San Jose Chapter, 698
    San Pedro
      Harbor/South Bay Chapter, 437
      South Bay/Harbor Chapter, 437
    San Rafael
      Marin County Chapter, 705
    Santa Ana
      Orange County Chapter, 16
    Santa Barbara Chapter, 706
    Santa Cruz Chapter, 445
    Stockton
      San Joaquin Chapter, 995
    Sunnyvale
      South Bay Chapter, 1090
    Thousand Oaks
      Conejo Valley Chapter, 232

National Organization for Women (continued)
  California (continued)
    Ventura Chapter, 1156
    Walnut Creek
      Contra Costa County/Diablo Valley Chapter, 244
      Diablo Valley/Contra Costa County Chapter, 244
  Colorado
    Boulder Chapter, 110
    Colorado Springs
      El Paso County Chapter, 286
    Denver Chapter, 707
  Connecticut
    Bridgeport
      Western Connecticut Chapter, 461
    Elmwood
      Connecticut Chapter, 235
    Greenwich
      Task Force on Marriage, Divorce, and Family Relations, 730
    Rowayton
      Task Force on Women and the Arts, 732
    Stonington
      Southeastern Connecticut Chapter, 1061
    West Hartford
      Central Connecticut Chapter, 188
  District of Columbia
    Washington
      Legal Defense and Education Fund, Project on Equal Education Rights, 884
      National Headquarters, 272, 756
      Metro Area Chapters, 1192
      Project on Equal Education Rights, Legal Defense and Education Fund, 884
      Washington, DC Chapter, 1159
  Florida
    Coconut Grove
      Dade County Chapter, 683
    Jacksonville Chapter, 1185
    Lake Worth
      Lake Worth/Northern Palm Beach Chapter, 580
      Northern Palm Beach/Lake Worth Chapter, 580
    Orlando Chapter, 803
    St. Augustine
      St. Johns County Chapter, 989
  Georgia
    Atlanta Chapter, 75, 715
    Augusta
      Central Savannah River Area Chapter, 56
  Illinois
    Chicago Chapter, 13
    Chicago
      National Federal Communication Commission Task Force, 695
    Elgin
      Elgin/Fox Valley Chapter, 377
      Fox Valley/Elgin Chapter, 377
    Glen Ellyn
      DuPage Chapter, 1116
    Moline
      Quad Cities Chapter, 937

National Organization for Women (continued)
  Illinois (continued)
    Northbrook
      North Suburban Chapter, 714
    Peoria Chapter, 708
    Rockford Chapter, 667
    Springfield Chapter, 729
    Worth
      Southwest Cook County Chapter, 719
  Indiana
    Evansville
      Tri-State Chapter, 692
    Indianapolis Chapter, 472
    Muncie Chapter, 709
    West Lafayette
      Tippecanoe Chapter, 1107
  Iowa
    Des Moines Chapter, 819
  Kansas
    Wichita Chapter, 820
  Louisiana
    Baton Rouge Chapter, 852
    New Orleans Chapter, 446
    Shreveport
      Caddo-Bossier Chapter, 925
  Maine
    Portland
      Maine Chapter, 609
  Maryland
    Annapolis
      Annapolis Legislative Information Office of Maryland, 691
      Anne Arundel County Chapter, 49
    Greenbelt
      Northern Prince George's County Chapter, 1015
    Hagerstown
      Washington County Chapter, 1191
    Rockville
      Montgomery County Chapter, 394
    Temple Hills
      Prince George's County Chapter, 727
  Massachusetts
    Beverly/Rockport
      Essex County/North Shore Chapter, 307
      North Shore/Essex County Chapter, 307
    Boston
      Eastern Massachusetts Chapter, 821
    Martha's Vineyard Task Force on the Image of Women, 468
    Worcester
      Clark Campus Chapter, 175
  Michigan
    Ann Arbor Chapter, 759
    Detroit
      Michigan Chapter, 63
    Farmington
      Livonia/Schoolcraft Chapter, 1206
      Schoolcraft/Livonia Chapter, 1206
    Midland Chapter, 50
  Minnesota
    Minneapolis
      Twin Cities Chapter, 699
    Rochester Chapter, 391
  Missouri
    Kansas City
      Greater Kansas City Chapter, 447
    St. Louis Chapter, 47

National Organization for Women (continued)
  Montana
    Great Falls/Missoula Chapter, 61
    Missoula/Great Falls Chapter, 61
  Nebraska
    Lincoln Chapter, 591
  Nevada
    Las Vegas Chapter, 564
    Sparks
      Northern Nevada Chapter, 48
  New Jersey
    Cherry Hill
      Committee to Promote Women's Studies, 808
    Iselin
      Middlesex County Chapter, 632
    Maplewood
      Essex County Chapter, 193
    Martinsville
      Somerset County Chapter, 1056
    Mountainside
      Union County Chapter, 710
      Passaic County Chapter, 700
    Princeton
      Central New Jersey Chapter, 711
      Princeton Chapter, 731
    Red Bank
      Monmouth County Chapter, 645
    Trenton Chapter, 1123
    Westwood
      Northern New Jersey Chapter, 718, 823
  New Mexico
    Albuquerque
      New Mexico Chapter, 712
      New Mexico Chapter, Task Force on Women in Poverty, 1037
      Task Force on Women in Poverty, New Mexico Chapter, 1037
  New York
    Bronx Chapter, 127
    Brooklyn Chapter, 128
    Buffalo Chapter, 130
    Fredonia
      Northern Chautauqua County Chapter, 701
    Great Neck
      Long Island/Nassau Chapter, 824
      Nassau/Long Island Chapter, 824
    Hiler
      Erie County Chapter, 716
    New York
      National Task Force-Marriage, Divorce, and Family Relations, 760
      New York City Chapter, 733, 734, 735, 784
    Rochester
      Genesee Valley Chapter, 373
      Image of Women National Task Force Committee, Rochester Image Committee, 287
      Rochester Image Committee, Image of Women National Task Force Committee, 287
    Staten Island Chapter, 713
    Stony Brook
      Suffolk County Chapter, 1087
    Syracuse
      New York State Chapter, 702, 793

National Organization for Women (continued)
  North Carolina
    Durham Chapter, 686
  Ohio
    Cincinnati Chapter, 703
    Cleveland Chapter, 1354
    Columbus Chapter, 971
    Fairfield
      Butler County Chapter, 1149
  Oregon
    Portland Chapter, 688
    Salem
      Salem Chapter, 825
      Willamette Valley Chapter, 798
  Pennsylvania
    Bethlehem
      Lehigh Valley Chapter, 571
    Penndel
      Northeast Bucks County Chapter, 675
      Philadelphia Chapter, 909
    Pittsburgh
      Greater Pittsburgh Chapter, 689
    Reading
      Berk County Chapter, 88
  Rhode Island
    Providence
      Rhode Island Chapter, 970
  Texas
    Dallas County Chapter, 690
    Fort Worth Chapter, 582, 827
    Houston Chapter, 126
    San Antonio Chapter, 1002
  Virginia
    Alexandria
      Northern Virginia Chapter, 845
    Norfolk Chapter, 842
    Salem
      Roanoke Valley Chapter, 662
    Virginia Beach Chapter, 972
  Washington
    Lynnwood
      Snohomish County Chapter, 17
    Olympia
      Thurston County Chapter, 693
    Poulsbo
      Kitsap County Chapter, 517
    Richland
      Tri-Cities Chapter, 1214
    Seattle
      King/Seattle County Chapter, 728
      Seattle/King County Chapter, 728
      Western Region Chapter, 1205
    Tacoma Chapter, 717
  Wisconsin
    Green Bay Chapter, 687
    Madison Chapter, 306
    Manitowoc Chapter, 1222
    Milwaukee Chapter, 1207
    Waukesha Chapter, 1198

  France
    Paris
      International Chapter/Paris Organization of Women, 887
      Paris Organization of Women/International Chapter, 887

National Pharmacy Fraternity for Women, Kappa Epsilon, 107
National Political Women's Caucus, 919
National Progressive Woman Suffrage Union, 44
National Secretaries Association, 1009
National Society of Colonial Dames XVII Century, 1011
National Society Colonial Dames of America, 629
National Society Daughters of American Colonists, 218
National Society of the Daughters of the American Revolution, 761
National Society of the Daughters of the Revolution, 753, 902
National Society, United States Daughters of 1812, New York, NY, 762
National Society, United States Daughters of 1812, Washington, DC, 763
National Task Force on Prostitution, 736
National University Extension Association, University of Delaware, 243
National Woman Suffrage Association, 1267
National Woman's Party, 301
National Woman's Relief Corps, 440
National Women's Army Corps Veterans Association, 192
National Women's Employment and Education, Inc., 1299
National Women's Political Caucus, 739, 767, 1419
National Women's Political Caucus, Alameda County-Northern California Chapter, 766
National Women's Political Caucus, Contra Costa County Chapter, 769
National Women's Political Caucus, Los Angeles Metropolitan/Southern California Section, 771
National Women's Political Caucus, Orange County Chapter, 770
National Women's Political Caucus, San Diego Chapter, **768**
National Women's Political Caucus, Texas Chapter, 1100
National Women's Studies Association and the Feminist Press, 1431
National Women's Trade Union League, 1438
National Women's Trade Union League of America, 584
Netherlands Consulante General, Press and Culture Sections, 344
Nevermind Press, 774
New American Movement on Socialist Feminism, Charlotte Perkins Gilman Chapter, 775
New Century Guild of Working Women, 1448
New Detroit Daughters of Bilitis, 947
New Direction's Inc., 780
New England Kitchen Publishing Co., 314
New Feminists, 785
New Haven Women's Liberation, 1454
New Jersey Women's Action League, 678
New Moon Publications, 649, 1352
New Jersey State Commission on Women, Department of Community Affairs, 469
New Peoples Center, 1324
New South Feminist Press, Inc., 271
New University Conference, Women's Caucus, 738

New Woman Inc., 790
New Women's Times, Inc., 792
New Women's Magazine Society, 112
New York Radical Feminist, 740
New York Women, 850
New York Women Strike for Peace/Women Strike for Peace, 741
New York Women's Division, 1340
New York Women's Trade Union, 136
New Yorkers for Abortion Law Repeal, 795
Newark State College, 312
Newberry Library, 325
Newfoundland Status of Women Council, 796
Newsette Publishing Company, 809
9 to 5, Organization for Woman Office Workers, 839
North American Indian Women's Council on Chemical Dependency, 1017
North American Jewish Feminists Organization, 589
North Carolina Society, Daughters of the American Revolution, 843
North Dakota Women's Liberation, 844
Northwestern University, Special Collections Department, 1375
Northwestern University, Women's Caucus, 660
Nottingham Socialist Women's Committee, 1050
Nottingham Women's Liberation Group, 1339

OAS, 298, 479
Oakland Women's Liberation, 859
Off Our Backs, Inc., 861
Office for Women Workers, International Labor Office, 1318
Office of Continuing Education for Women, Temple University, 242
Office of Women in Higher Education, 221
Office of Special Services, University of Tennessee, 380
Office of Women's Studies, Ohio State University, 1054
Office of the Governor, State Capitol, 1390
Ohio Bureau of Employment Service, Women's Services Division, 863
Ohio-Kentucky Region, International Ladies' Garment Workers' Union, 862
Ohio League of Women Voters, 865
Ohio State University, Maid Library, 1313
Ohio State University, Office of Women's Studies, 1054
Ohio State University Women's Liberation, 858
Ohio Women's Information Center, Legislative Reference Bureau, 1177
Ontario Arts Council, 293
Ontario Institute for Studies in Education, Department of Sociology, 176, 961
Ontario Ministry of Labor, Women's Bureau, 1364
Operatives Magazine/An Association of Females, 875
Options for Women Over Forty, 129
Order of the Lead Balloon, Women's Majority Union, 588
Oregon Council for Women's Equality, 856
Organization of American States Inter-American Commission of Women, General Secretariat, 298

## Women's Periodicals and Newspapers

Organization of American States-Office of the General Secretariat, 479
Organization for Woman Office Workers, 9 to 5, 839
Ottawa Women's Liberation Committee, 1404

Pacific Coast Media Center, Women Against Violence Against Women, 1168
Palmerston North Women's Liberation, 892
Pan-American Women's Alliance, 894
Pandora, Inc., 897
Parents Magazine Enterprises, Gruner & Jahr, USA, Inc., 1456
Paxton Press, Ltd., 1347
Penfield Publishing Co., 788
Pennsylvania Commission for Women, 1359
Pennsylvania Commission on the Status of Women, 158, 159
Pennsylvania League of Woman Voters, 145
Pennsylvania Program for Women and Girl Offenders, Inc., 475
Pennsylvanians for Women Rights, 889
People's Journal, 906
Persistence of Vision, Inc., 1300
Philadelphia Area Women's Liberation Movement, 1294
Philadelphia Radical Lesbians Women's Center, 575
Philadelphia Task Force on Women in Religion, 411
Philadelphia Women's Center, 835
Philadelphia Women's Liberation Center, 79
Philadelphia Women's Political Caucus, 910
Pi Lambda Theta, 284
Pittsburgh Radical Women's Union, 57
Plainfield Organization for Women's Equal Rights-Young Women's Christian Association, 1452
Plainswoman, Inc., 915
Planned Parenthood, 916
Planted Breast Collective, 417
Plenum Publishing Co., 1014
Polish Women's Alliance of America, 419
Presbyterian Church in the U.S.A., Woman's Committees of the Board of Missions, 1307
Presbyterian Church Women's Foreign Missionary Society, 1287
Press and Culture Sections of the Netherlands Consulante General, 344
Print Media Division, Department of the Navy, 1215
Professional and Technical Programs, Inc., 1108
Professional Women's Caucus, 888
Project on the Status and Education of Women-Association of American Colleges, 867
Protect Each Other Sisterhood, 885
Portcullis Family, 922
Prime Time, Inc., 927
Pro Se Collective, 928

Queens College, CUNY, Department of English, 1427

R.B. Seeley and W. Burnside, 197
Rankin, Jeanette, Brigade, 494
Red Action Administration, 901

Red Women's Detachment, 949
Redbook Publishing Co., 950
Reichenbach Brothers, 387
Revolution, 966
La Revue Feministe, 969
Rhode Island Women's Liberation Union, 1401
Rice, E.A., and Co., 546
Riverside Women's Chapter, 1046
Roanoke Valley Women's Coalition, 253
Rockland County Feminists, 77
Rosa Sonneschein, Co., 40
Rush Publishing Co., Inc., 1350
Russell and Edes, 538
Rutgers University, Douglass College, Department of English, 1306
Rutgers University Feminist Coalition, 349
Rutgers University, Law School, 1424
Rutgers University Women's Caucus, 977

SFWR, 981
SHE, 203
SUNY, 1302, 1437
SWP, Women's Committee, 1282
S.T. Taylor, 106
Sacramento Women's Center and Bookstore, 987
Sacramento Women's Liberation, 669
St. Benedict's Convent, 1041
Saint Joan's Alliance, 988
St. Louis Organization for Women's Rights, 990
St. Louis Women's Liberation, 948, 1139
Sally Carter, 1410
Sangamon State University, Women's Studies Committee, 1449
San Diego State College Women's Liberation-Women's Union, 898
San Diego State College, Women's Studies Program, 1007
San Diego Women/Goodbye to All That, 424
Sandra Brown Publishing Co., 318
San Fernando Valley Women's Political Caucus, 991
San Francisco Bay Area Women in Technical Trades, 811
San Francisco Vasser Club, 1153
San Francisco Women's Center, 993
San Francisco Women's Liberation, 994
Santa Clara County Women's Political Caucus, 997
Santa Cruz Women's Center, 263
Santa Fe Women's Community, 998
Sapphire, 999
Sappho Publication, Ltd., 1000
Saskatoon Women's Centre, 1001
Saxe, Susan, Defense Committee, 1092
Scarlet Letter Collective, 1003
Scholastic Magazines, Inc., Home Economics Division, 214
School of Law, Hofstra University, 1305
Seattle Women Act for Peace, 1004
Second Page, 1006
Second Wave, Inc.,/Female Liberation, 1008
Seventeen Magazine, 1010
Seventh-Day Adventists, Women's Association, 1167
Shameless Hussy Press, 953, 1016
Sheryn Kallowaay, 1018

Shirley Chisholm for President Campaign Committee, 195
Sibyl-Child Press, Inc., 1022
Sibylline House, 1086
Sigma Alpha Iota, 893
Simplicity Pattern Co., 1024
Sister Courage, Inc., 1030
Sister for Homophile Equality, 203
Sisterhood, Equal Rights Alliance, 592
Sisters for Liberation, 281
Sisters Stand, University of Utah, 1040
Sixth Region of the National League of Women Voters, 1079
Skilled Jobs for Women, Inc., 1043
Slack, Charles B., Inc., 120
Slippery Rock Women's Liberation, 435
Slovenian Women's Union of America, 1458
Social Responsibility Round Table, American Library Association, 6
Social Responsibilities Round Table, American Library Association, Task Force on Women, 1333
Socialist Woman Groups/International Marxist Groups, 1049
Socialist Workers Party-Women's Committee, 1282
Socialist Woman Publishing Company, 219
Society for Humane Abortion, 1051
Society for Women in Philosophy, 832
Society of American Archivists, 978
Society of American Archivists, Women's Caucus, 665
Society of Woman Engineers, United Engineering Center, 1134
Sociologists for Women in Society, 984
Sojourner Truth House Inc., Task Force on Battered Women, 883
South Carolina Federation of Women's Clubs, 512
South New England Conference, United Methodist Church, 1320
Southern California Women Strike for Peace, 1231
Southern California-Southern Nevada, Church Women United, 201
Southern Historical Association Caucus of Women in History, 185
Southeastern Massachusetts University, Women's Center, 830
Soviet Women's Committee and the Central Council of Trade Unions of the USSR, 1063
Spare Ribs, Ltd., 1066
Spartacist League, 1239
Spartacist League, Women's Commission, 1309
Speak Out Sisters, Temple University, 982
Special Collections Department, Northwestern University, 1375
Spectre Collective, 1071
Springfield Women's Liberation, 1199
Standard Fashion Co., 268
Stanford University, Linguistics Department, 1304
Stardust Magazine Agency, Inc., 1080
State of New York, Women's Division, 1340
State of Ohio Women's Information Center, Legislative Reference Bureau, 1177
State Federation of Women's Clubs, 412

State University of New York, Buffalo, Women's Voices, 1437
State University of New York, Old Westbury, Biological Sciences Program, 1302
State Women's Caucus, California Democratic Council, 1423
Status of Women, 514
Stephan Swift and Co., Ltd., 392
Stephanie Hartman, 983
Stewardesses for Women's Rights, 981
Susan B. Anthony Coven No. 1, Covenant of the Goddess, 1101
Susan Saxe Defense Committee, 1092
Sydney Women's Liberation, 1094
Synod of Southern California Task Force on Women, United Presbyterian Church in the United States of America, 1335
Syracuse University Department of Geography, 414, 1331

TCFLCC-Twin Cities Female Liberation Communication Center, 335
T. Badger, 310
T.W. Harris, Greenwood Reprint Corporation, 782
Tallahassee Women's Liberation, 1035
Task Force on Battered Women and Sojourner Truth House, Inc., 883
Taylor, S.T., 106
Temple University Office of Continuing Education for Women, 242
Temple University, Speak Out Sisters, 982
Texas Women's Equity Action League, 1172
Third World Women's Alliance, 1125
13th Moon, Inc., 1102
Tide Collective, Daughters of Bilitis, 576
Tiff-Davis Publishing Company, 642
Times of India Press, 338
Today News Service, Inc., 1353
Toledo Woman Suffrage Association, 749
Toronto Women's Liberation, 1118
Toronto Women's Liberation/Velvet Fist, 1154
Total Repeal of Illinois Abortion Laws, 1124
Tower Press, 1374
Traders Union Auxiliary, Woman's International Union Label League, 1270
Transexual Action Organization, 651
Tribner and Company, 1432
True and Company, 259
Twin Cities Female Liberation Communication Center, TCFLCC, 335
Twin Cities Woman, Inc., 1129

UAW, Women's Department, 1132
UCLA, Associated Students Communications Board, 1113
USSR Central Council of Trade Unions, Soviet Women's Committee, 1063
Union of Soviet Socialist Republic, Central Council of Trade Unions, Soviet Women's Committee, 1063
Union Women's Alliance to Gain Equality, 1142
Unitarian Universalist Women's Federation, 1069, 1135
United Auto Workers, Women's Department, 1132
United Engineering Center, Society of Woman Engineers, 1134
United Lutheran Church in America, 598

United Methodist Church, South New England, 1320
United Methodist Women's Caucus, 1455
United Presbyterian Church in the United States of America, Synod of Southern California Task Force on Women, 1335
United Sisters, 1110
United Societies of the Polish Women of Adoration of the Most Blessed Sacrament, 921
United Society of Friends Women, 19
United States Civil Service Commission, Federal Women's Program, 1327
United States Daughters of 1812, 211
United States Daughters of 1812, National Society, Washington, DC, 763
United States Daughters of 1812, National Society, New York, NY, 762
United States Department of Agriculture, Cooperative Extensions Programs, University of Wisconsin Extension, 854
United States Department of Labor, Office of Information, Publications and Reports, 1310
United States Department of Labor, Women's Bureau, 1070, 1250, 1363
United States Department of State, Bureau of Public Affairs, 1336
United States Department of the Navy, Print Media Division, 1215
United Women's Contingent, 818
University of Arizona, College of Law, 866
University of California, Berkeley, AFSCME, Clerical, Technical, and Professional Employees Local 1695, 294
University of California, Berkeley, Asian Women, 64
University of California, Berkeley, Center for Continuing Education for Women, League of Associated Women, 567
University of California, Berkeley, Campus Women's Forum, 1234
University of California, Davis Women's Forum, 1235, 1381
University of California, Irvine, Crawford Hall, Women's Opportunities Center, 1414
University of California, Los Angeles, Associated Students Communications Board, 1113
University of California, Los Angeles, Women's Resource Center, 1112
University of California, San Diego, 1052
University of Chicago, University Women's Association, 1136
University of Connecticut, Women's Center, 1031
University of Delaware, National University Extension Association, 243
University of Hawaii Continuing Education for Women, 240
University of Houston Women's Liberation Front, 1042
University of Idaho, Women's Center, 1371
University of Kansas Commission on the Status of Women, 507
University of London, Institute of Education, 1429
University of Maryland Women's Studies, 217

University of Massachusetts, Division of Continuing Education, Everywoman's Center, 313
University of Michigan, 187, 829, 1145
University of Michigan, Cluster Communication Committee, 1389
University of Michigan, Michigan University Center for Continuing Education of Women, 630
University of Minnesota, Continuing Education and Extension, 241
University of Minnesota, Minnesota Planning and Counseling Center for Women, Office of Student Affairs, 917
University of Minnesota, Minnesota Women's Center, 1361
University of New Mexico, Women's Coordinating Center, 500
University of New South Wales Women's Liberation, 1133
University of Pennsylvania, Women's Center, 905
University of Pittsburgh, Women's Caucus for the Modern Languages, 960
University of Utah, Salt Lake City, Sister's Stand, 1040
University of Wisconsin-Extension Center for Women and Family Living Education, 1228
University of Wisconsin-Extension, U.S. Department of Agriculture, Cooperative Extensions Program, 854
University of Wisconsin, Madison, Department of French and Italian, 118
University of Wisconsin, Madison, Department of German, 1332
University of Wisconsin, Madison, Women's Studies Research Center, 838
University of Wisconsin System, Central Administration, 1146
University of Wisconsin System, Women's Studies Librarian-at-Large, 350, 776
University Personnel Service at Cornell, 269
University Women's Association, University of Chicago, 1136

V. Giard and E. Briere, 968
Valley Women's Center, 399, 1152, 1269
Vancouver Women's Caucus, 1319
Vancouver Women's Health Collective, 881
Vancouver Women's Liberation Alliance, 1402
Velvet Fist/Toronto Women's Liberation, 1154
Velvet Glove Press, 1155
Verner & Hood, 542
Vietnam Women's Union, 1342
Virgin's Liberation Front, 508
Voice of Mother's and Children's Liberation, Maternal Information Services, Inc., 1444
Voice of Women of New England, 1164
Voice of Women, U.S.A., 1151

W. Bulmer & Co., 401
W. Gibbons, 555
W. & S. Loewenthal, 384, 1459
WAAODA, 1346
WAVAW, 1168
WICCHE, 1178

WILPF
  see Women's International League for Peace and Freedom
WIN, 1182
WISE–Madison, WI, 612
WISE–New York, NY, 1184
WITCH, 1093
WONAAC, Women's National Abortion Action Coalition, Western Regional Office, 1360
WSP
  see Women Strike for Peace
WTA, 1434
Waller Press, 190
War Work Council, Industrial Committee, Young Women's Christian Association, 474
Washington Area Women's Center, 943
Waterbury Area Woman's Center, Inc., 868
Wayne Women's Liberation, Wayne State University, 663
West Coast Art Center–Womanspace, 1293
West Coast Association of Women Historians, 1201
Western Canadian Women's News Service, 1203
Western Pennsylvania District Council 424-445, International Ladies' Garment Workers Union, 1012
Western Service Workers Association, 170
Whirlwind, 1210
Whitney Publications, 92
Whittaker, George B., 86
Whole Woman Catalog, 1213
Wildcat Woman, 1216
Williams and Norgate, 297
Wisconsin Agri-Women, 1225
Wisconsin Association on Alcohol and Other Drug Abuse, 1346
Wisconsin Daughters of the American Revolution, 1223
Wisconsin Federation of Business and Professional Women's Clubs, Inc., 1218
Wisconsin Feminist Project Fund, Inc., 1081
Wisconsin, Office of the Governor, State Capitol, 1390
Wisconsin State Division, American Association of University Women, 80
Wisconsin Woman Suffrage Association, 1219
Wisconsin Women Library Workers, 1227
Wisconsin Women in the Arts, 1226
Wisconsin Women's Political Caucus, Dane County Chapter, 1230
Wisconsin Women's Political Caucus, Madison, WI, 1229
Wisconsin Women's Political Caucus, Milwaukee Chapter, 637
Wisconsin Women's Political Caucus–Milwaukee Women's Political Caucus, 1418
Woman Citizen Corporation, 1268
Woman Citizen Publishing Society, 1383
Woman/Community Women's Newspaper, 1237
Woman–Los Angeles, 1236
Woman Patriot Corporation, 1245
Woman Publishing Co., 1233
Woman Suffrage Party, 1248
Woman's Board of Foreign Missions of the Presbyterian Church, U.S.A., 1286
Woman's Board of Missions of the Interior, 801
Woman's Bulletin Company, 1258
Woman's Centre, 1091

Woman's Committees of the Board of Missions of the Presbyterian Church in the U.S.A., 1307
Woman's Department, Central Committee, Communist Party of the U.S.A., 1447
Woman's Foreign Missionary Society, 1274
Woman's International Union Label League and Traders Union Auxiliary, 1270
Woman's National Industrial League, 1446
Woman's Publishing Co., 1283
Womanspace–West Coast Art Center, 1293
Women Against Violence Against Women, Pacific Coast Media Center, 1168
Women at A.T. & T., 1121
Women for Action (Daughters of Bilitis), 648
Women for Change Center, 1321
Women for Constitutional Government, 1243
Women for Legislative Action, 1322
Women for Peace, 280
Women for the Inclusion of Sexual Expression, 1184
Women Free Women in Prison, 840
Women Geoscientists Committee, American Geological Institute, 1323
Women Historians of the Midwest, Minnesota Historical Society, 1175
Women in Action, 1326
Women in City Government United, 1329
Women in Communications, Inc., 621
Women in San Francisco Women's Liberation, 656
Women in Self-Employment, 612
Women in Technical Trades, San Francisco Bay Area, 811
Women in the Arts, 1176
Women in the Historical Profession, Coordinating Committee, Plattsburgh, NY, 150
Women in the Historical Profession, Coordinating Committee, New Albany, IN, 151
Women Incensed at Telephone Company Harassment, 1093
Women Intercollegiate Sports Club, 1183
Women Library Workers, Wisconsin, 1227
Women Mobilized for Change, 1065
Women of Detroit, 1254
Women of Knightdale, 778
Women of Rochester, 1083
Women of Youth Against War and Fascism, 82
Women Organized Against Rape, 1186, 1187
Women Organized for Employment, 276
Women Strike for Peace
  [Entries for this organization are arranged two ways; first by name and thereunder geographically under state, subdivided by city]
  National Information Clearinghouse, 570, 627
  National Office, New York, NY, 1349
  National Office, Washington, DC, 1348
  New York Branch, 628
  New York Women Strike for Peace, 741
  Philadelphia Branch, 826
  Sacramento Branch, 986
  San Francisco Branch, 980
  Southern California Branch, 1231
  United Nations, 1189
  Urbana Branch, 1416

Women Strike for Peace (continued)
  California
    Los Angeles
      Southern California Branch, 1231
    Sacramento Branch, 986
    San Francisco Branch, 980
  District of Columbia
    National Information Clearinghouse, 570, 627
    National Office, 1348
  Illinois
    Urbana Branch, 1416
  New York
    New York City
      National Office, 1349
      New York Branch, 628
      New York Women Strike for Peace, 741
      United Nations, 1189
  Pennsylvania
    Philadelphia Branch, 826
Women United for Action, 1356
Women Unlimited, 354
Women's Action Alliance, 1362
Women's Action Movement, 1166
Women's Activities Department, AFL-CIO Committee on Political Education, 511
Women's Ad-Hoc Abortion Coalition, 816
Women's Advisory Group to the Bonneville Power Administration, 225
Women's Association, Church of God (Seventh-Day), 1167
Women's Athletic Association of San Jose, 395
Women's Board of Missions, 585
Women's Bureau-Canada, Department of Labour, 1317
Women's Bureau, Ontario Ministry of Labor, 1364
Women's Caucus, Bucks County Community College, 1059
Women's Caucus, California Personnel Guidance Association/Affiliated Association of California Personnel Guidance Association, 156
Women's Caucus, Society of American Archivists, 665
Women's Caucus for Political Science, 833
Women's Caucus for the Modern Languages, 959
Women's Caucus for Modern Languages-Midwest Modern Language Association, 1169
Women's Caucus for the Modern Languages, Modern Language Association of America, 230, 958
Women's Caucus for the Modern Languages, University of Pittsburgh, 960
Women's Caucus of Action Latin America, 967
Women's Caucus of the New University Conference, 738
Women's Centennial Committee, 779
Women's Center, Costa Mesa, CA, 876
Women's Center, Philadelphia, PA, 1104
Women's Center, Poughkeepsie, NY, 1373
Women's Center, San Jose, CA, 1147
Women's Center, Stanford, CA, 1370
Women's Center, Tampa, FL, 1144, 1369
Women's Center, Venice, CA, 1028
Women's Center at Northwestern University, 660
Women's Center, Earlham College, 1345

Women's Center of Richmond, 1415
Women's Center Office, 869
Women's Center, Southeastern Massachusetts University, 830
Women's Center, University of Connecticut, 1031
Women's Center, University of Idaho, 1371
Women's Center, University of Pennsylvania, 905
Women's Choice Clinic, 363
Women's Coalition, Inc., 224
Women's Collective Front de Liberation des Femmes Quebecoises, 320
Women's Commission of the Spartacist League, 1309
Women's Committee-Socialist Workers Party, 1282
Women's Community Center, Inc., 1377
Women's Community, Inc., Los Angeles, CA, 1074
Women's Community, Inc., Wausau, WI, 929
Women's Coordinating Center, University of New Mexico, 500
Women's Coordinating Committee, 182
Women's Department of All India Congress Committee, 1344
Women's Division, Democratic National Committee, 266
Women's Division of the State of New York, 1340
Women's Editorial Collective, 191
Women's Education Equity Communications Network, 1173
Women's Employment Project, 1103
Women's Equity Action League-New Jersey, 678
Women's Equity Action League-State College, PA, 1170
Women's Equity Action League-Texas, 1172
Women's Equity League-Washington, DC, 1171, 1173
Women's Foreign Missionary Society of the Presbyterian Church, 1287
Women's Forum, Clearinghouse Internationl of the Eleanor Association, 209
Women's Group, 1385
Women's Health Center, 1072
Women's History Research Center, 1067
Women's Home Missionary Society of the Methodist Episcopal Church, 1266
Women's Indian Association, 1085
Women's Industrial Journal, 1386
Women's Information Center, 1387
Women's Institute for Freedom of the Press, 624
Women's International Bowling Congress, 1242
Women's International Democratic Federation, 1343
Women's International League for Peace and Freedom (WILPF)
[Entries for this organization are arranged two ways; first by name and thereunder geographically under state, subdivided by city]
Baltimore Branch, 1392
Berkeley-East Bay Branch, 1393
Fanwood Branch, 1397
Fresno Branch, 183
Legislative Office, U.S. Section, 1180

Women's International League for Peace and
   Freedom (continued)
   Livermore Branch, 812
   Madison Branch, 1395
   Marin County Branch, 1394
   Monterey Peninsula Branch, 817
   New England Regional Conference, 822
   Northern California Branch, 814
   Palo Alto Branch, 1396
   Paterson Branch, 837
   Philadelphia Branch, 903
   San Francisco Branch, 992
   San Gabriel Valley Branch, 815
   San Jose Peace Center, 904
   San Mateo Branch, 813
   Seattle Branch, 138
   Washington, DC Branch, 1193
   California
      Berkeley-East Bay Branch, 1393
      Corte Madera
         Marin County Branch, 1394
      Fresno Branch, 183
      Livermore Branch, 812
      Millbrae
         San Mateo Branch, 813
      Monterey
         Northern California Branch, 814
      Monterey Park
         San Gabriel Valley Branch, 815
      Palo Alto Branch, 1396
      San Francisco Branch, 992
      San Jose Peace Center, 904
      Seaside
         Monterey Peninsula Branch, 817
   District of Columbia
      Legislative Office, U.S. Section, 1180
      Washington, DC Branch, 1193
   Maryland
      Baltimore Branch, 1392
   Massachusetts
      Boston
         New England Regional Conference, 822
   New Jersey
      Fanwood Branch, 1397
      Paterson Branch, 837
   Pennsylvania
      Philadelphia Branch, 903
   Washington
      Seattle Branch, 138
   Wisconsin
      Madison Branch, 1395
Women's International Network, 1182
Women's Itinerant Hobo's Union, 111
Women's Labor Zionist Organization of
   America, 913
Women's Law Journal, Inc., 1400
Women's Liberation, Brisbane, Australia, 1019
Women's Liberation, Brooklyn, NY, 332
Women's Liberation, Cambridge, MA, 1403
Women's Liberation, Denver, CO, 1038
Women's Liberation, Glebe, Australia, 115
Women's LibeRATion, New York, NY, 945
Women's Liberation, Seattle, WA, 46
Women's Liberation and Gay Liberation, 390
Women's Liberation Basement Press, Last
   Gasp Ecofunnies, 491
Women's Liberation Center, Evanston, IL, 944
Women's Liberation Center, Norwalk, CT, 371

Women's Liberation Center, Philadelphia, PA,
   797
Women's Liberation Center, Media Workshop,
   1097
Women's Liberation Center of Nassau County,
   834
Women's Liberation Center of New York, 1372
Women's Liberation Coalition, New Orleans,
   LA, 444
Women's Liberation Coalition of Michigan, 213
Women's Liberation, Delaware County, 345
Women's Liberation Media Center, 463
Women's Liberation National Coordinating
   Committee, 1426
Women's Liberation of Ann Arbor, 936
Women's Liberation Union, 1405
Women's Liberation Workshop of Bedfordshire,
   1020
Women's Lobby and Fawcett Society, 1421
Women's Lobby, Inc., 27, 1406
Women's Majority Union (the Order of the
   Lead Balloon), 588
Women's Missionary Society, A.M.E. Church,
   640
Women's Movement for Reform, 1271
Women's Municipal League of Boston, 879, 1408
Women's Municipal League of the City of New
   York, 1311
Women's National Abortion Action Coalition,
   1188
Women's National Abortion Action Coalition-
   WONAAC, Western Regional Office, 1360
Women's National Indian Association, 473
Women's Network International, Inc., 1388
Women's Newspaper Collective, 1256
Women's Newspaper Women, 1413
Women's Opportunities Center, University of
   California Extension, Crawford Hall, 1414
Women's Overseas Service League, 181
Women's Place, 1417
Women's Protective and Provident League, 1435
Women's Resource Center, Stevens Point, WI,
   1422
Women's Resource Center, UCLA, 1112
Women's Reformatory, Rockwell City, IA, 973
Women's Review of Political Research, Inc.,
   1279
Women's Services Division, Ohio Bureau of
   Employment Services, 863
Women's Sports Publications, Inc., 1425
Women's Strike Coalition, 610
Women's Studies Committee, Sangamon State
   University, 1449
Women's Study Group/Every Woman Press, 952
Women's Studies Librarian-at-Large, Univer-
   sity of Wisconsin, 350, 776
Women's Studies Library, 976
Women's Studies Program, San Diego State
   College, 1007
Women's Studies Program, University of
   Colorado, 398
Women's Studies Research Center, University
   of Wisconsin-Madison, 838
Women's Transit Authority, 1434
Women's Tribune, 748
Women's Union, 1032
Women's Union-Women's Liberation, San Diego
   State College, 898

Women's Universal Movement, Inc., 1436
Women's Voices, State University of New York, Buffalo, 1437
WomenSports Publishing Company, 1439
Woodworth and Heustis, 536
Worcester Women's Press-Women's Center, 1442
World's and National Women's Christian Temperance Union, Bureau of Scientific Temperance Investigation and Dept. of Scientific Temperance Instruction, 1098
World's Young Women's Christian Association, 1398

YWCA
   See Young Women's Christian Association
Yale University, Department of Biology, OML, 1328
Young Women's Christian Association
[Entries for this organization are arranged two ways; first by name and thereunder geographically under state, subdivided by city]
  National Board, 1277
  Plainfield Organization for Women's Equal Rights, 1452
  YWCA of Berkeley, 74
  YWCA of Greater Atlanta, 1451
  YWCA of Los Angeles, 65
  YWCA of Madison, 605, 1106
  YWCA of Natick, 1453
  YWCA of Oahu, 1367
  YWCA of San Francisco, 1450
  YWCA of Tacoma and Pierce Counties, 353
  YWCA War Work Council, 103
  YWCA War Work Council, Industrial Committee, 474

Young Women's Christian Association (continued)
  YWCA Women's Center, 369
  California
    Berkeley Association, 74
    Los Angeles Association, 65
    San Francisco Association, 1450
  Georgia
    Greater Atlanta Association, 1451
  Hawaii
    Honolulu
      YWCA of Oahu, 1367
  Massachusetts
    Natick Association, 1453
  New Jersey
    Orange
      Women's Center, 369
    Plainfield Organization for Women's Equal Rights, 1452
  New York
    New York City
      National Board, 1277
      War Work Council, 103
      War Work Council, Industrial Committee, 474
  Washington
    Tacoma/Gig Harbor
      Tacoma and Pierce Counties Association, 353
  Wisconsin
    Madison Association, 605, 1106
Youth Against War and Fascism, 82
Youth Together, Inc., 639

Zeta Phi Beta Sorority, Inc., 59
Zonta International, 1461

# Subject Index

AFL-CIO
see American Federation of Labor-Congress of Industrial Organizations

Abortion (anti), 73, 309

Abortion (pro), 12, 13, 16, 17, 30, 42, 46, 47, 49, 50, 61, 63, 75, 84, 88, 89, 95, 99, 122, 123, 126, 130, 152, 154, 171, 178, 188, 190, 205, 213, 215, 216, 220, 261, 267, 299, 306, 307, 313, 320, 327, 333, 334, 335, 347, 353, 358, 360, 361, 377, 388, 391, 399, 417, 421, 434, 435, 447, 461, 470, 482, 488, 500, 514, 563, 581, 592, 593, 625, 626, 650, 660, 667, 669, 671, 680, 681, 682, 683, 689, 690, 692, 700, 702, 707, 709, 710, 711, 713, 715, 719, 721, 724, 725, 727, 728, 735, 744, 777, 784, 791, 795, 816, 821, 823, 824, 827, 830, 844, 845, 858, 876, 877, 887, 892, 898, 910, 916, 932, 943, 944, 947, 982, 989, 990, 991, 994, 996, 1007, 1015, 1020, 1028, 1031, 1034, 1038, 1042, 1046, 1051, 1068, 1075, 1076, 1081, 1084, 1088, 1090, 1094, 1097, 1107, 1117, 1118, 1123, 1124, 1127, 1130, 1144, 1154, 1159, 1163, 1165, 1166, 1184, 1188, 1195, 1207, 1208, 1235, 1236, 1237, 1244, 1246, 1253, 1291, 1294, 1305, 1316, 1325, 1334, 1354, 1360, 1362, 1370, 1372, 1373, 1381, 1382, 1385, 1401, 1402, 1403, 1405, 1410, 1411, 1424, 1426, 1442, 1444, 1452
see also National Abortion Rights Action League

"Action 218," 388

Advertising
see media, sexism in advertising

Affirmative action, 20, 29, 66, 171, 446, 643, 798, 804, 867, 903, 919, 1030, 1140, 1192, 1229, 1233, 1257, 1371

Affirmative action in education, 5, 69

Afro-Americans, 42, 59, 84, 264, 281, 308, 444, 492, 639, 640, 840, 1105, 1324
see also Black Panthers

Aging, 82, 477, 915, 927, 1442
see also seniors, retirement

Agism, 927

Agriculture, 467, 486, 1162, 1179, 1225
see also farm life

Airline industry, 981

Alcoholism, 140, 228, 899, 1017, 1346
see also drug abuse, halfway houses, temperance

Alternative lifestyles, 321
see also collectives, communes

Alternative literature, 108, 293

Alternative press, 460

American Federation of Labor-Congress of Industrial Organizations, 292, 294, 402, 416, 505, 506, 518, 533, 1012

American Telephone & Telegraph, 1093, 1121

Amnesty, 1322
see also draft

Amusements
see recreation

Anthropology, 669, 1427

Anti-nuclear movement, 1231
see also nuclear power

Anti-vice groups, 1158

Archivists, 665, 978
see also historians, librarians

Art, 31, 37, 55, 64, 81, 91, 101, 106, 121, 173, 177, 196, 206, 207, 227, 249, 254, 271, 278, 332, 333, 337, 339, 346, 360, 365, 377, 379, 400, 410, 420, 435, 442, 448, 449, 450, 467, 503, 521, 523, 527, 530, 546, 548, 551, 553, 566, 573, 577, 578, 579, 581, 586, 597, 608, 620, 641, 650, 661, 663, 664, 667, 681, 773, 774, 786, 806, 834, 850, 869, 887, 900, 913, 915, 918, 924, 927, 931, 936, 951, 974, 976, 994, 998, 1003, 1008, 1016, 1022, 1025, 1026, 1029, 1030, 1036, 1055, 1063, 1064, 1096, 1102, 1138, 1144, 1149, 1159, 1161, 1176, 1210, 1212, 1232, 1236, 1240, 1252, 1261, 1292, 1296, 1298, 1350, 1373, 1381, 1391, 1427, 1437
see also art history

Art history, 1427

Art reviews, 1226, 1298

Artists, 1202, 1232, 1315, 1391

Arts, 45, 62, 275, 593, 623, 660, 788, 946, 975, 1024, 1031, 1074, 1097, 1119, 1129, 1150, 1157, 1202, 1226, 1276, 1293, 1347, 1374, 1387
see also names of individual arts

Asian-Americans, 25, 64, 65

Astrology, 531, 922, 1000

Atheism, 352

Athletics
see sports

Authors
  see writers

Auto industry workers, 1132

Bail bonds, 986

Baptists, 33

Battered women, 21, 224, 883, 979, 1168, 1377, 1390
  see also family violence, women's shelters

Beauty care, 37, 45, 119, 180, 214, 246, 291, 308, 323, 339, 418, 423, 438, 534, 603, 622, 642, 790, 950, 1010, 1062, 1120, 1161, 1252, 1262, 1290

Beauty pageants, 639

Behavior modification, 840
  see also psychology

Bibliographies, 886, 1135

Biographies, 197, 207, 236, 259, 261, 270, 288, 296, 302, 337, 387, 413, 459, 522, 528, 536, 541, 542, 552, 556, 557, 643, 773, 783, 787, 833, 849, 855, 874, 906, 913, 915, 931, 1053, 1060, 1078, 1082, 1095, 1099, 1105, 1134, 1153, 1224, 1232, 1275, 1282, 1289, 1341, 1342, 1374, 1406, 1439
  see also interviews, obituaries

Biologists, 1328

Birth control, 97, 122, 126, 326, 327, 328, 377, 388, 397, 434, 523, 650, 777, 844, 848, 876, 881, 898, 967, 1020, 1051, 1117, 1147, 1166, 1184, 1246, 1325, 1360, 1385, 1404, 1413, 1424, 1426
  see also family planning, sterilization

Black Panthers, 114, 462, 1083
  see also Afro-Americans

Blacks
  see Afro-Americans

Bookstores, 987

Business, 20, 147, 300, 318, 599, 612, 747, 931, 1108, 1218, 1365, 1388
  see also career development, executives

Business education, 1111

Business finance, 612

C-R
  see consciousness raising

California Prisoners' Union, 237

Canadians
  see French-Canadians

Career development, 28, 37, 156, 166, 184, 209, 225, 239, 264, 312, 318, 342, 413, 425, 450, 507, 588, 621, 630, 643, 848, 866, 867, 917, 1082, 1131, 1160, 1234, 1246, 1260, 1268, 1285, 1328, 1414, 1445, 1457

Catholic Church, 317, 381, 419, 499, 614, 653, 921, 988, 1041, 1122
  see also convents, nuns, priests

Catholic Theological Society, 499

Celebrities, 180, 1120, 1456

Centers
  see women's centers

Chicanas, 152, 157, 453, 595, 742, 848, 946, 967, 1100
  see also Puerto Ricans

Child advocacy, 15, 1105

Child care, 6, 15, 19, 36, 46, 47, 60, 63, 69, 77, 79, 84, 123, 124, 126, 128, 130, 152, 191, 199, 205, 213, 216, 233, 237, 240, 247, 261, 274, 307, 319, 320, 331, 333, 334, 397, 399, 421, 424, 431, 435, 445, 450, 456, 461, 471, 489, 514, 519, 525, 562, 563, 591, 600, 611, 625, 626, 643, 644, 652, 657, 662, 681, 682, 683, 688, 689, 693, 694, 698, 702, 707, 710, 711, 712, 715, 718, 725, 727, 728, 740, 780, 784, 823, 841, 849, 851, 852, 856, 868, 871, 889, 892, 898, 905, 911, 917, 919, 948, 952, 964, 971, 985, 987, 989, 994, 995, 1001, 1006, 1007, 1020, 1041, 1083, 1087, 1107, 1112, 1130, 1132, 1135, 1139, 1152, 1154, 1159, 1215, 1217, 1237, 1251, 1294, 1309, 1314, 1316, 1321, 1324, 1370, 1373, 1381, 1384, 1401, 1405, 1410, 1417, 1424, 1426, 1444, 1455

Child labor, 1270

Child rearing, 194, 249, 423, 455, 458, 610, 658, 847, 1030, 1167, 1253, 1258, 1265, 1296, 1319, 1411, 1420
  see also non-sexist children's materials

Child sexual abuse, 942

Child support, 2, 657
  see also divorce

Child welfare, 15, 72, 172
  see also child advocacy, child care, child labor

Childbirth, 96, 285, 1237
  see also Lamaze technique, midwifery, pregnancy

Childbirth education, 7, 96

Childrearing
  see child rearing

Children, 146, 233, 287, 526, 562, 636, 643, 656, 712, 782, 823, 858, 901, 998, 1062, 1090, 1128, 1146, 1165, 1342, 1343, 1344, 1456
see also pediatrics

Children's literature, 169, 459, 952, 1159
see also non-sexist children's materials

Children's rights
see child advocacy

Chisholm, Shirley, 195

Christian missions
see missions

Christianity, 197, 296, 539, 548, 585, 598, 640, 659, 855, 962, 1141, 1167, 1266, 1273, 1274, 1286, 1287, 1307, 1320, 1367, 1398, 1450, 1451, 1452, 1453
see also church workers, missions, names of specific denominations, e. g., Baptists, Catholic Church, Church of Christ, etc.

Church of Christ, 200, 201

Church workers, 202

Citizenship, 761

Civic services
see social services, volunteer work

Civil service, 410, 799, 1317, 1327, 1329, 1340, 1407, 1408

Class consciousness, 1246
see also middle-class women, poor people, socialites, upper classes

Clerical workers
see office workers, secretaries

Clinics, 363

Clothes, 35, 105, 165, 246, 268, 454, 518, 1021
see also fabrics, fashion, garment industry

Clubs, 34, 76, 78, 104, 133, 134, 135, 137, 139, 144, 211, 218, 248, 255, 260, 329, 408, 409, 410, 412, 419, 440, 481, 495, 503, 509, 512, 569, 605, 606, 614, 629, 674, 676, 747, 752, 757, 761, 762, 763, 802, 807, 885, 893, 902, 921, 957, 1080, 1106, 1143, 1153, 1183, 1218, 1220, 1223, 1240, 1259, 1261, 1271, 1461
see also sororities

Coaching, 212
see also sports

Collectives, 114, 738, 1316
see also alternative lifestyles, communes

College education
see higher education

College students, 64, 65, 69, 175, 342, 343, 464
see also students, sororities

College teachers, 4, 5, 32, 80
see also teachers, teaching

Colleges
see college students, college teachers, community colleges, higher education

Comics, 26, 491, 1440

Commissions on women, 116, 117, 158, 159, 171, 222, 223, 469, 479, 777, 829

Communes, 321, 508
see also alternative lifestyles, collectives

Communications, 351, 355, 1018, 1100, 1182, 1330, 1376
see also language, linguistics, media, sexism in media, libraries

Communism, 1443, 1447
see also socialism

Community colleges, 1

Community health planning, 154, 410
see also health

Consciousness raising, 56, 98, 110, 238, 249, 263, 345, 356, 377, 500, 524, 563, 564, 661, 723, 785, 803, 821, 834, 937, 944, 970, 1086, 1214, 1294, 1368, 1372, 1385

Consumerism, 25, 316, 386, 526, 720, 778, 923, 1034, 1356, 1358, 1445

Continuing education, 80, 187, 240, 241, 242, 243, 283, 313, 567, 630, 829, 860, 977, 1381, 1389, 1414, 1457

Convents, 1041
see also Catholic Church, nuns

Cooking, 92, 207, 314, 344, 379, 787
see also food

Cooperatives, 508, 599, 1179, 1225
see also collectives, communes

Counseling, 157, 404, 407, 675, 905, 917, 1136, 1186, 1187, 1321, 1345, 1373

Counselors, 156

Crafts, 45, 62, 93, 147, 256, 275, 323, 330, 331, 379, 420, 429, 439, 532, 553, 623, 788, 950, 1024, 1031, 1097, 1262, 1265, 1276, 1374, 1387
see also flower arrangement, needlework

Credit, 990, 1197

Crime
see criminal justice system, offenders

Crimes against women, 72, 1442
see also battered women, family violence, rape, sexual harrassment, incest, violence

Criminal justice system, 475, 1105
see also judicial reform, offenders

Criminals
see offenders

Criticism
see art reviews, film reviews, literary criticism, periodical reviews, record reviews, television reviews, theatre reviews

Dance, 1391

Dane County Project on Rape, 942

Day care
see child care

Decorating
see interior decoration

Defense policy, 255, 753
see also nuclear weapons, peace movement, disarmament

Democratic party, 266, 1423

Diplomat Tie Co., 1216
(Baltimore, MD)

Disarmament, 143, 1343, 1348, 1349
see also defense policy, peace movement

Discrimination, 430
see also racism, school integration, sexism, sexism in employment, stereotypes

Displaced homemakers, 929
see also employment re-entry, vocational rehabilitation

Divorce, 2, 210, 730, 760, 777, 1014, 1373
see also child support

Doctors, 497, 894
see also gynecology, health, medicine, pediatrics

Domestic workers, 673

Draft, 280, 741, 1348, 1396
see also amnesty

Drama, 636
see also plays, theatre, theatre reviews

Drug abuse, 65, 503, 899, 973, 1017, 1346, 1382
see also alcoholism

ESP, 931

Ecology, 183, 280, 471, 667, 927, 1028, 1155, 1165, 1291

Economic conditions
see employment, poverty, wages

Economics, 386, 809, 901, 931, 968, 1035, 1253, 1277, 1427

Ecumenism, 200, 282, 499

Education, 1, 4, 28, 32, 46, 59, 64, 66, 94, 110, 128, 130, 154, 157, 158, 166, 167, 168, 169, 175, 176, 177, 193, 199, 216, 222, 232, 233, 239, 247, 265, 274, 284, 286, 287, 290, 296, 305, 312, 313, 319, 320, 342, 343, 347, 353, 377, 385, 394, 405, 410, 432, 435, 437, 445, 447, 461, 464, 465, 477, 484, 492, 495, 504, 522, 525, 538, 557, 563, 583, 602, 632, 645, 672, 681, 682, 683, 692, 694, 696, 700, 702, 703, 707, 710, 715, 716, 718, 725, 727, 728, 735, 738, 743, 751, 755, 758, 761, 781, 784, 785, 806, 808, 820, 821, 823, 824, 829, 831, 833, 845, 854, 856, 858, 860, 866, 867, 871, 873, 882, 884, 885, 889, 898, 903, 905, 917, 928, 946, 947, 948, 952, 958, 960, 968, 982, 986, 988, 1028, 1061, 1075, 1085, 1095, 1100, 1112, 1113, 1116, 1118, 1122, 1133, 1136, 1139, 1147, 1159, 1160, 1165, 1169, 1187, 1191, 1199, 1201, 1202, 1206, 1233, 1257, 1277, 1313, 1328, 1330, 1344, 1347, 1350, 1354, 1369, 1370, 1371, 1378, 1402, 1412, 1417, 1421, 1422, 1426, 1437, 1449, 1453
see also affirmative action in education, business education, childbirth education, teaching, community colleges, continuing education, fellowships, higher education, public schools, reading, religious education, scholars, sex education, sexism in education, law schools

Educational research, 3, 430

Educators, 746, 838, 1431
see also college teachers, teachers, non-sexist teaching materials

Employment, 17, 20, 28, 29, 66, 94, 115, 116, 123, 125, 128, 130, 157, 166, 170, 190, 209, 213, 225, 230, 232, 247, 249, 253, 254, 282, 285, 305, 312, 313, 318, 343, 351, 353, 357, 358, 376, 383, 391, 403, 414, 425, 443, 445, 446, 447, 450, 507, 519, 522, 563, 571, 611, 626, 632, 666, 672, 679, 681, 682, 685, 688, 694, 697, 699, 702, 703, 709, 711, 715, 718, 725, 726, 727, 728, 729, 735, 777, 779, 780, 792, 798, 799, 804, 811, 820, 821, 824, 832, 835, 839, 845, 853, 856, 863, 867, 888, 889, 890, 909, 923, 938, 946, 966, 987, 1006, 1019, 1020, 1043, 1054, 1066, 1068, 1075, 1088, 1097, 1099, 1103, 1121, 1132, 1142, 1159, 1175, 1191, 1197, 1239, 1251, 1257, 1284, 1291, 1299, 1310, 1312,

Employment (continued)
1318, 1321, 1325, 1328, 1329, 1330, 1332, 1350, 1354, 1361, 1378, 1379, 1381, 1389, 1414, 1426, 1445, 1455, 1457
see also self-employment, sexism in employment, unemployment, affirmative action, career development, job training, labor unions, skills, volunteer work, wages, war work, workers

Employment re-entry, 941
see also displaced homemakers, vocational rehabilitation

Engineers, 1134

Entertaining, 38, 93, 534, 622

Equal pay for equal work, 673, 1132, 1251, 1310, 1402
see also, wages

Equal Rights Amendment (anti), 912

Equal Rights Amendment (pro), 6, 8, 13, 15, 16, 17, 42, 46, 47, 48, 49, 50, 60, 61, 63, 88, 109, 110, 124, 178, 184, 193, 210, 223, 232, 240, 244, 251, 253, 272, 277, 286, 303, 306, 313, 357, 369, 377, 391, 393, 394, 437, 445, 446, 447, 471, 472, 517, 519, 564, 571, 580, 582, 591, 592, 608, 609, 611, 625, 632, 635, 637, 645, 660, 662, 675, 680, 681, 682, 683, 684, 685, 686, 687, 688, 689, 690, 691, 692, 693, 694, 695, 696, 697, 698, 699, 700, 701, 702, 703, 704, 705, 706, 707, 708, 709, 710, 711, 712, 713, 714, 715, 716, 717, 718, 719 thru 735, 739, 745, 756, 758, 760, 766, 767, 771, 777, 778, 781, 784, 793, 796, 799, 803, 805, 819, 820, 823, 825, 827, 842, 846, 852, 887, 903, 909, 910, 911, 917, 925, 937, 944, 970, 971, 972, 988, 989, 990, 991, 995, 996, 1002, 1015, 1037, 1045, 1056, 1068, 1075, 1087, 1107, 1108, 1123, 1127, 1135, 1149, 1156, 1160, 1172, 1185, 1191, 1192, 1195, 1198, 1205, 1206, 1207, 1213, 1222, 1238, 1243, 1244, 1253, 1308, 1314, 1338, 1353, 1354, 1355, 1415, 1423, 1457

Etiquette, 197, 336

Eugenics, 41, 392

Executives, 318
see also business

Extra sensory perception
see ESP

FOCAS (Feminists Organization for Commission, Action, and Service), 1184

Fabrics, 35, 105, 165, 268
see also clothing, interior decorating, fashion

Family, 46, 132, 146, 180, 194, 199, 299,

Family (continued), 324, 325, 384, 439, 563, 630, 658, 674, 697, 711, 712, 760, 784, 854, 897, 949, 1052, 1133, 1244, 1350

Family planning, 154, 326, 327, 328, 500, 643, 671, 871, 939
see also birth control

Family relations
see psychology, marriage

Family services
see counseling, social services

Family violence, 21, 942, 963, 979, 1081
see also battered women, women's shelters

Farm life, 330, 331, 1225, 1272
see also agriculture, ranchers, rural life

Farm women
see rural women

Farmers
see agriculture

Farming
see agriculture

Fascism, 182

Fashion, 35, 37, 38, 39, 45, 62, 86, 105, 106, 117, 165, 180, 207, 214, 246, 254, 258, 259, 268, 291, 308, 323, 331, 339, 378, 401, 413, 418, 420, 423, 438, 439, 443, 450, 456, 459, 467, 503, 529, 534, 536, 542, 553, 602, 603, 622, 642, 787, 788, 907, 950, 1010, 1024, 1046, 1062, 1111, 1120, 1129, 1157, 1161, 1190, 1262, 1265, 1272, 1275, 1289, 1290, 1445, 1456
see also clothing, fabrics

Fellowships, 1175

Feminism, 30, 56, 61, 63, 75, 77, 84, 85, 88, 90, 95, 110, 113, 115, 126, 127, 128, 130, 167, 168, 169, 174, 175, 177, 178, 188, 193, 198, 210, 215, 232, 234, 235, 244, 263, 272, 279, 286, 287, 299, 306, 332, 333, 334, 335, 337, 345, 346, 347, 348, 349, 350, 351, 352, 353, 354, 355, 356, 358, 359, 360, 361, 363, 371, 373, 378, 382, 390, 391, 394, 397, 400, 421, 428, 435, 437, 444, 445, 446, 447, 448, 461, 468, 471, 472, 482, 488, 504, 513, 515, 517, 519, 521, 535, 562, 563, 564, 571, 573, 580, 582, 589, 591, 592, 609, 610, 611, 613, 626, 632, 645, 646, 650, 656, 662, 663, 664, 666, 667, 668, 675, 680, 681, 682, 683, 684, 685, 686, 687, 688, 689, 690, 691, 692, 693, 694, 695, 696, 697, 698, 699, 700, 701, 702, 703, 704, 705, 706, 707, 708, 709, 710, 711, 712, 713, 714, 715, 716, 717, 718, 719 thru 735, 756, 759, 760, 776, 784, 785, 793, 796, 798, 803, 804, 819, 820, 842, 844, 856, 852, 872, 887, 900, 909, 911, 914, 925, 937, 940, 970, 971, 972, 983, 989,

*Women's Periodicals and Newspapers*

Feminism (continued), 995, 996, 1002, 1015, 1037, 1045, 1056, 1059, 1081, 1087, 1092, 1107, 1117, 1123, 1127, 1149, 1150, 1156, 1185, 1191, 1192, 1198, 1205, 1206, 1207, 1214, 1222, 1244, 1245, 1409
see also libertarian feminism, radical feminism, socialist feminism

Feminist Lesbian Intergalactic Party, 513

Feminists Organization for Commission, Action and Service
see FOCAS

Fertility
see population policy

Fiction, 26, 39, 40, 62, 92, 101, 102, 111, 112, 121, 137, 173, 194, 196, 199, 207, 210, 211, 214, 231, 245, 246, 256, 258, 259, 268, 270, 288, 295, 308, 311, 315, 331, 338, 339, 341, 360, 372, 378, 379, 387, 413, 420, 423, 424, 436, 439, 449, 456, 458, 459, 463, 476, 478, 496, 501, 502, 512, 528, 530, 531, 534, 537, 538, 540, 541, 542, 543, 544, 545, 546, 547, 548, 549, 550, 552, 553, 554, 555, 558, 559, 561, 577, 578, 589, 581, 587, 590, 594, 597, 602, 603, 607, 618, 622, 638, 641, 658, 663, 664, 755, 772, 782, 783, 786, 788, 794, 841, 852, 875, 897, 906, 908, 918, 923, 924, 950, 951, 956, 965, 974, 975, 1005, 1010, 1016, 1022, 1025, 1026, 1030, 1047, 1053, 1054, 1057, 1062, 1066, 1099, 1102, 1110, 1113, 1114, 1141, 1148, 1157, 1200, 1204, 1210, 1232, 1233, 1241, 1255, 1263, 1265, 1269, 1272, 1277, 1289, 1290, 1296, 1351, 1425, 1440, 1456

Film, 174, 1407

Film reviews, 527, 564, 593, 603, 660, 664, 740, 821, 848, 861, 870, 882, 918, 999, 1000, 1028, 1029, 1053, 1066, 1082, 1161, 1163, 1212, 1255, 1300, 1316, 1384, 1411, 1427

Filmmaking, 1097, 1300

Finance
see business finance, investments, personal finance

Flight attendants, 981

Flippies, 513

Flower arrangement, 532

Folklore, 370

Food, 37, 38, 92, 93, 191, 246, 256, 291, 308, 323, 331, 418, 423, 429, 454, 455, 458, 534, 603, 622, 790, 935, 950, 1010, 1129, 1254, 1262, 1264, 1265, 1352, 1374, 1445
see also cooking, health food, nutrition, restaurants

France, 14, 18, 86

Free Church of Scotland, 1288

Free love, 1441
see also sexuality

Freemasonry, 618

French-Canadians, 320, 939

Fund raising, 771
see also philanthropy

Gardening, 38, 93, 314, 323, 456, 532, 1272, 1275

Garment industry, 165, 292, 402, 416, 505, 506, 518, 533, 595, 862, 864, 878, 1012, 1190
see also clothes

Gay rights, 30, 84, 95, 114, 122, 203, 281, 306, 367, 390, 403, 421, 449, 513, 514, 577, 588, 679, 861, 918, 945, 947, 1030, 1060, 1086
see also lesbianism, lesbians

Gay teachers, 405

Gay women
see lesbians

Genealogy, 218, 260, 606, 762, 763, 843, 1011, 1143
see also marriage announcements, obituaries

Geographers, 1331

Geoscientists, 1323

Germanists, 1332

Germany, 146

Girl Scouts, 37, 256, 1058

Government workers
see civil service

Gynecology, 649

Haiku, 1035
see also poetry

Halfway houses, 228

Handicrafts
see crafts

Health, 13, 30, 45, 58, 65, 77, 82, 93, 95, 120, 123, 128, 154, 164, 177, 186, 191, 194, 198, 199, 201, 205, 214, 229, 236, 254, 261, 267, 271, 285, 289, 290, 291, 308, 313, 315, 319, 323, 331, 338, 341, 353, 360, 363, 388, 393, 394, 397, 417, 418, 423, 424, 429, 431, 432, 434, 438, 441, 444, 449, 454, 455, 456, 458, 476,

322

Health (continued) 488, 490, 502, 514, 534, 535, 556, 563, 571, 587, 592, 600, 603, 610, 611, 631, 652, 660, 661, 664, 667, 675, 678, 680, 681, 746, 759, 780, 781, 790, 792, 830, 844, 847, 851, 859, 861, 868, 877, 881, 882, 887, 895, 899, 909, 915, 922, 927, 931, 943, 944, 951, 985, 990, 1001, 1021, 1028, 1029, 1030, 1040, 1060, 1072, 1075, 1079, 1091, 1113, 1118, 1120, 1125, 1133, 1144, 1148, 1150, 1152, 1159, 1161, 1181, 1197, 1208, 1235, 1236, 1237, 1240, 1252, 1253, 1254, 1262, 1264, 1275, 1284, 1290, 1301, 1302, 1303, 1319, 1334, 1347, 1350, 1357, 1358, 1362, 1370, 1384, 1403, 1411, 1420, 1421, 1425, 1437, 1442, 1445, 1449
  see also community health planning, hospital services, Medicaid, medicine, mental health, nursing, nutrition, occupational health and safety, venereal disease

Health care, 484, 497, 894
  see also clinics, hospital services

Health clinics
  see clinics

Health foods, 1316
  see also nutrition

Health planning
  see community health planning

Heraldry, 843
  see also genealogy

High school students, 452
  see also students, teenagers

Higher education, 977, 984, 1007, 1039, 1054, 1136, 1146, 1174, 1234, 1321, 1344, 1381, 1382, 1389, 1431, 1454
  see also education, law schools

Hispanics
  see Chicanas

Historians, 150, 185, 1175, 1201
  see also archivists

History, 77, 90, 137, 146, 150, 151, 153, 185, 218, 260, 296, 297, 301, 315, 321, 325, 334, 372, 384, 389, 397, 483, 496, 538, 545, 552, 556, 557, 606, 629, 669, 761, 762, 763, 843, 850, 879, 902, 952, 1011, 1066, 1143, 1150, 1181, 1201, 1233, 1261, 1289, 1296, 1339, 1350, 1390, 1427, 1453
  see also art history, genealogy, heraldry

Hobbies
  see crafts, recreation

Hobos, 111

Home economics, 38, 39, 45, 92, 245, 259, 268, 314, 379, 410, 429, 439, 443, 454, 455, 456, 457, 458, 467, 516, 520, 532,

Home economics (continued) 536, 636, 654

Homemakers, 142, 180, 526, 616, 654, 1265, 1272, 1283, 1356
  see also displaced homemakers

Homemaking
  see cooking, entertaining, home economics

Homesteading, 249

Horticulture
  see gardening

Hospital services, 262
  see also health care

Hospital volunteers, 1221

Housing, 222, 727, 835, 948, 1372

Housewives
  see homemakers

Human rights, 8, 36, 484, 493, 633, 1135
  see also rights

Human services
  see community health services, counseling, family services, social services

Humor, 258, 311, 501, 733, 905, 985, 999, 1006, 1062, 1113, 1114, 1358, 1411
  see also satire

Immigration, 751, 753, 831

Imperialism, 1125
  see also militarism, war

Incest, 942

Indians
  see Native Americans

Intellectuals, 969

Interior decoration, 38, 92, 93, 119, 214, 246, 323, 339, 418, 423, 429, 457, 458, 603, 622, 642, 950, 1120, 1262
  see also fabrics, flower arrangement

International General Assembly of the Grail, 426

International law, 10, 11

International relations, 143, 465, 837, 903, 1048, 1125, 1165, 1189, 1193, 1436
  see also United Nations

Internationalism, 1443

Interviews, 102, 113, 123, 124, 137, 174, 227, 346, 428, 587, 660, 891, 1161
  see also biographies

Investments, 809
see also personal finance

Israel, 104, 248, 674

Jeanette Rankin Brigade, 1231

Jews, 40, 104, 248, 432, 433, 495, 589, 674, 751, 831, 913
see also Judaism, Zionism

Job training, 1310

Journalism, 621
see also newspapers

Judaism, 40, 104, 248, 432, 433, 495, 831, 913
see also Jews, sexism in Judaism

Judicial reform, 865, 1081
see also criminal justice system

Junior colleges
see community colleges

Justice
see criminal justice system, judicial reform, law, lawyers, law schools

Labor law, 1257, 1317
see also child labor, labor unions

Labor unions, 46, 89, 136, 147, 155, 291, 294, 333, 383, 402, 416, 505, 506, 511, 518, 526, 533, 583, 584, 595, 604, 610, 796, 811, 861, 862, 864, 878, 896, 1012, 1019, 1049, 1050, 1060, 1066, 1070, 1132, 1140, 1142, 1208, 1216, 1246, 1248, 1250, 1270, 1386, 1415, 1424, 1438
see also American Federation of Labor-Congress of Industrial Organizations, labor law

Labor Zionism, 913

Lamaze technique, 7, 882
see also childbirth

Language, 601, 1347
see also communication, linguistics, sexism in language

Latin America, 298, 479, 800

Latinas
see Chicanas

Law, 3, 87, 112, 113, 179, 198, 206, 215, 222, 223, 233, 234, 273, 290, 304, 315, 321, 341, 345, 348, 373, 374, 383, 388, 444, 450, 469, 479, 482, 487, 502, 514, 568, 590, 610, 635, 662, 669, 670, 682, 777, 778, 780, 795, 796, 803, 804, 816, 824, 847, 855, 866, 871, 895, 928, 948, 968, 1005, 1029, 1037, 1044, 1076, 1085, 1094, 1110, 1159, 1197, 1228, 1238, 1254, 1291, 1305, 1310, 1312, 1337, 1341, 1352, 1353, 1362, 1364, 1384, 1399, 1400,

Law (continued) 1421, 1424, 1427
see also international law, judicial reform, labor law, lobbying, rights, sexism in law

Law reform
see judicial reform

Law schools, 70

Lawyers, 10, 11, 70, 510, 928, 1337, 1400

Legal aid, 1110, 1399

Legal services, 2, 229, 430, 635

Legal status
see law, child advocacy

Legislation, 287, 683, 728, 1193
see also law, lobbying, Medicaid, social legislation, suffrage, taxation

Legislators
see politicians

Lesbianism, 26, 1346

Lesbians, 30, 31, 75, 95, 203, 231, 250, 251, 252, 281, 334, 341, 347, 356, 360, 367, 400, 403, 404, 405, 406, 407, 417, 429, 448, 513, 514, 527, 565, 566, 572, 573, 574, 575, 576, 577, 581, 588, 594, 608, 619, 648, 655, 663, 679, 740, 840, 872, 876, 877, 922, 933, 935, 936, 945, 947, 985, 998, 1000, 1001, 1003, 1026, 1033, 1036, 1057, 1060, 1071, 1086, 1092, 1144, 1178, 1212, 1413
see also gay rights

Libertarian feminism, 71
see also feminism

Librarians, 6, 108, 293, 524, 1333, 1338
see also archivists

Libraries, 350, 975, 1227, 1333, 1338, 1375

Lifestyles, 922
see also lesbianism

Linguistics, 958, 959, 960, 1169, 1304
see also communication, language

Linguists, 230

Literature, 31, 55, 106, 113, 198, 208, 333, 400, 410, 467, 483, 521, 527, 530, 536, 551, 620, 663, 681, 834, 872, 875, 944, 999, 1035, 1063, 1067, 1074, 1252, 1269, 1306, 1350, 1382, 1427
see also alternative literature, children's literature, drama, fiction, plays, poetry, writers

Literary criticism, 258, 498, 557, 586, 641, 966, 1261, 1306

Lithuanian-Americans, 653

Lobbying, 21, 25, 28, 29, 32, 42, 47, 48, 51, 56, 60, 63, 66, 80, 85, 88, 110, 117, 123, 126, 127, 131, 149, 154, 158, 159, 160, 168, 169, 178, 210, 213, 232, 235, 244, 261, 272, 305, 348, 353, 356, 360, 369, 373, 374, 388, 393, 394, 402, 409, 410, 430, 431, 432, 437, 445, 446, 447, 451, 461, 462, 470, 471, 472, 493, 515, 517, 562, 563, 566, 567, 568, 570, 571, 580, 582, 591, 592, 593, 601, 604, 608, 609, 611, 625, 627, 628, 631, 637, 645, 646, 648, 662, 667, 670, 671, 672, 673, 675, 678, 679, 680, 681, 682, 683, 684, 685, 686, 687, 688, 689, 690, 691, 692, 693, 694, 695, 696, 697, 698, 699, 700, 701, 702, 703, 704, 705, 706, 707, 708, 709, 710, 711, 712, 713, 714, 715, 716, 717, 718, 719, 720, 721, 722, 723, 724, 725, 726, 727, 728, 729, 730, 731, 732, 733, 734, 735, 741, 744, 745, 756, 759, 760, 765, 767, 768, 769, 770, 771, 780, 781, 784, 793, 798, 799, 803, 805, 816, 819, 820, 823, 825, 827, 831, 833, 837, 842, 846, 852, 856, 858, 867, 887, 890, 898, 902, 903, 904, 909, 910, 911, 912, 915, 916, 925, 928, 937, 943, 963, 970, 971, 972, 979, 981, 989, 991, 992, 995, 996, 997, 1001, 1002, 1004, 1015, 1034, 1037, 1039, 1044, 1045, 1049, 1051, 1056, 1060, 1061, 1068, 1075, 1082, 1087, 1094, 1100, 1103, 1107, 1119, 1123, 1124, 1127, 1130, 1132, 1140, 1142, 1147, 1149, 1154, 1156, 1159, 1170, 1171, 1172, 1173, 1174, 1177, 1180, 1185, 1186, 1187, 1188, 1191, 1192, 1193, 1195, 1196, 1198, 1203, 1205, 1206, 1207, 1214, 1222, 1228, 1229, 1238, 1243, 1244, 1248, 1257, 1279, 1295, 1303, 1314, 1316, 1317, 1322, 1334, 1335, 1337, 1340, 1353, 1354, 1355, 1359, 1360, 1390, 1393, 1394, 1396, 1402, 1405, 1406, 1411, 1422, 1423, 1452, 1457

Love, 596

Lutherans, 262, 598

Marriage, 85, 132, 199, 210, 273, 290, 697, 730, 760, 854, 909, 1191, 1244, 1341
see also divorce, monogamy, polygamy, weddings, wives

Marriage announcements, 541, 555, 558, 794

Married women
see wives

Marxism
see communism, socialism

Mass media
see media

Mathematicians, 66

Media, 16, 47, 49, 57, 85, 89, 110, 177, 208, 215, 240, 261, 281, 287, 355, 357, 377,

Media (continued) 463, 468, 525, 563, 567, 621, 624, 625, 645, 666, 672, 682, 688, 689, 695, 712, 732, 738, 740, 785, 795, 821, 823, 824, 825, 835, 845, 846, 852, 868, 872, 876, 882, 909, 918, 971, 986, 1000, 1066, 1067, 1090, 1096, 1159, 1168, 1169, 1181, 1182, 1244, 1316, 1321, 1407, 1426
see also comics, communications, sexism in media, television, film

Medicaid, 916
see also legislation, Social Security

Medical clinics
see clinics

Medicine, 199, 490, 497, 894, 1262, 1301, 1302
see also health, pediatrics, pharmacists, sexism in medicine

Mental health, 404, 407, 669, 870
see also psychology

Methodism, 1320, 1455

Middle age, 129

Middle class women, 336
see also class consciousness

Midwifery, 124
see also childbirth

Migrants, 1019

Militarism, 837
see also imperialism, soldiers, war

Military families, 1215
see also soldiers

Minimum wage, 1250
see also equal pay for equal work, wages

Minorities, 43, 69, 87, 375, 630, 655, 698, 767, 851, 867, 1165, 1415
see also Afro-Americans, Asian-Americans, Chicanas, Native Americans, Jews, Lithuanian-Americans, French-Canadians, Polish-Americans, Slovenian-Americans, Latinas

Minority women
see minorities

Missing persons, 72

Missions, 19, 801, 962, 1266, 1273, 1274, 1286, 1287, 1288, 1307

Monogamy, 949

Morality, 1441
see also anti-vice groups

Mormonism, 1263
see also polygamy

Mormons, 319

Motherhood, 398, 422, 455, 488, 656, 657, 658, 838, 929, 1008, 1167, 1254, 1256, 1319, 1351
see also single mothers, unwed mothers

Museums, 1298

Music, 40, 62, 270, 310, 410, 449, 521, 529, 530, 532, 536, 540, 546, 549, 553, 554, 558, 602, 636, 663, 787, 891, 956, 1007, 1030, 1157, 1216, 1456
see also songs

National Abortion Rights Action League, 12

National Organization for Women, 247, 261, 263, 271

National Security
see defense policy

National Women's Political Caucus, 353

Native Americans, 473, 772, 839, 1017, 1105, 1224

Natural childbirth
see Lamaze technique

Needlework, 423, 623
see also sewing

Neo-paganism, 1209

The Netherlands, 344

New Right, 912

New York City, 1311

Newspapers, 636
see also journalism

Non-sexist children's materials, 108, 293, 1061

Non-sexist teaching materials, 1013

Nuclear power, 51, 280
see also anti-nuclear movement

Nuclear weapons, 980, 986, 1004, 1165, 1348, 1349
see also anti-nuclear movement, defense policy, disarmament, peace movement

Nuns, 1122
see also convents, Catholic Church

Nursing, 881
see also health

Nutrition, 199, 490
see also health foods

Obituaries, 541, 555, 558, 794

Occult
see astrology, ESP

Occupational health and safety, 155, 981
see also working conditions

Offenders, 222, 475
see also prisoners

Office workers, 839
see also secretaries

Old people
see seniors

Organizations
see clubs, sororities, and names of specific groups, e.g., National Organization for Women

Organized labor
see labor unions

Paganism
see neo-paganism

Pageants, beauty
see beauty pageants

Parenting
see child rearing

Parents
see single parents

Parks, 1311

Patriotism, 1245

Peace movement, 51, 82, 114, 138, 172, 182, 183, 226, 280, 386, 389, 399, 471, 494, 570, 627, 628, 633, 741, 751, 812, 813, 814, 815, 817, 818, 826, 831, 837, 869, 885, 903, 904, 980, 986, 992, 1004, 1007, 1065, 1067, 1084, 1109, 1151, 1163, 1164, 1165, 1189, 1193, 1231, 1294, 1314, 1322, 1342, 1343, 1348, 1349, 1357, 1392, 1393, 1394, 1395, 1396, 1397, 1416
see also disarmament, nuclear weapons, utopianism

Pediatrics, 120

Periodical reviews, 1128

Personal beauty
see beauty care

Personal finance, 323, 443, 773, 860, 1446
see also investments

Personal histories
see biographies

Pharmacists, 107

Philadelphia Centennial Exhibition, 779

## Women's Periodicals and Newspapers

Philosophy, 786, 832

Photography, 81, 360, 375, 1022, 1026, 1055, 1292

Physicians
see doctors

Plays, 340, 501
see also drama, theatre

Poetry, 26, 30, 31, 36, 37, 39, 56, 62, 65, 77, 81, 91, 92, 98, 101, 102, 111, 112, 121, 129, 137, 161, 173, 177, 191, 196, 203, 206, 211, 213, 215, 227, 229, 231, 237, 249, 250, 252, 253, 258, 261, 263, 265, 270, 271, 273, 278, 288, 295, 296, 299, 311, 315, 316, 322, 332, 334, 335, 341, 346, 348, 351, 353, 356, 360, 365, 367, 372, 375, 376, 378, 379, 380, 387, 397, 399, 400, 407, 413, 417, 420, 421, 424, 427, 436, 439, 442, 448, 449, 452, 453, 456, 458, 459, 463, 471, 476, 478, 482, 496, 501, 502, 504, 512, 515, 516, 523, 527, 528, 529, 530, 531, 536, 537, 538, 539, 540, 541, 542, 543, 544, 545, 546, 547, 548, 549, 550, 551, 552, 553, 554, 555, 556, 557, 558, 559, 560, 561, 565, 566, 573, 574, 575, 576, 577, 578, 579, 581, 582, 585, 586, 587, 588, 590, 594, 596, 597, 602, 607, 608, 618, 620, 626, 638, 641, 648, 650, 655, 656, 658, 661, 663, 664, 669, 712, 738, 742, 754, 759, 772, 773, 774, 778, 779, 780, 782, 783, 785, 786, 787, 788, 794, 796, 828, 834, 841, 844, 847, 857, 861, 868, 869, 874, 875, 876, 877, 882, 897, 900, 905, 906, 908, 915, 918, 922, 924, 925, 926, 933, 935, 936, 937, 939, 945, 947, 951, 952, 953, 956, 965, 966, 967, 973, 974, 975, 985, 988, 994, 998, 1000, 1001, 1003, 1005, 1007, 1008, 1016, 1019, 1020, 1021, 1022, 1025, 1026, 1027, 1028, 1031, 1032, 1033, 1034, 1035, 1036, 1038, 1040, 1041, 1045, 1046, 1055, 1057, 1060, 1062, 1064, 1065, 1068, 1073, 1083, 1086, 1089, 1093, 1094, 1096, 1097, 1099, 1102, 1104, 1109, 1110, 1114, 1118, 1138, 1141, 1144, 1147, 1148, 1154, 1155, 1166, 1167, 1178, 1199, 1200, 1208, 1210, 1212, 1217, 1232, 1237, 1241, 1248, 1253, 1254, 1255, 1256, 1269, 1273, 1275, 1277, 1289, 1292, 1296, 1316, 1319, 1324, 1342, 1344, 1352, 1358, 1382, 1384, 1411, 1413, 1420, 1427, 1435, 1437, 1448
see also haiku

Poets, 362

Polish-Americans, 419, 921

Political parties, 357, 358, 359, 366, 465, 513, 676, 957, 1194, 1423
see also names of individual parties

Political science, 1427

Politicians, 145, 164, 210, 234, 266, 465,

Politicians (continued), 1418

Politics, 12, 145, 152, 159, 172, 177, 178, 182, 191, 195, 199, 213, 215, 216, 224, 232, 233, 234, 239, 247, 263, 271, 272, 285, 286, 290, 301, 304, 305, 307, 352, 391, 517, 564, 664, 670, 672, 674, 675, 676, 677, 679, 685, 688, 690, 693, 697, 698, 702, 704, 709, 710, 712, 713, 714, 715, 718, 725, 726, 729, 734, 738, 739, 741, 753, 756, 765, 766, 767, 768, 769, 770, 771, 777, 781, 785, 789, 791, 792, 795, 796, 820, 822, 825, 833, 841, 845, 850, 851, 852, 858, 865, 868, 869, 876, 877, 882, 892, 896, 901, 903, 909, 910, 912, 913, 918, 919, 923, 925, 931, 935, 936, 939, 940, 945, 949, 957, 967, 970, 971, 980, 985, 986, 991, 992, 995, 997, 998, 1001, 1003, 1004, 1006, 1007, 1008, 1027, 1028, 1031, 1034, 1035, 1039, 1049, 1050, 1056, 1059, 1063, 1065, 1066, 1067, 1068, 1069, 1072, 1075, 1076, 1081, 1082, 1084, 1086, 1087, 1088, 1090, 1091, 1100, 1104, 1112, 1115, 1116, 1118, 1125, 1127, 1139, 1140, 1149, 1159, 1163, 1165, 1166, 1180, 1185, 1191, 1194, 1195, 1196, 1203, 1205, 1207, 1211, 1212, 1214, 1219, 1230, 1236, 1238, 1243, 1244, 1245, 1249, 1253, 1255, 1258, 1277, 1279, 1281, 1291, 1294, 1296, 1308, 1313, 1321, 1322, 1334, 1344, 1347, 1348, 1349, 1353, 1354, 1360, 1370, 1384, 1393, 1396, 1397, 1403, 1410, 1415, 1418, 1419, 1420, 1421, 1437, 1438, 1442, 1446, 1447, 1450, 1452
see also conservatism, lobbying, political parties, politicians, New Right, radicalism, suffrage

Polygamy, 52
see also Mormons

Poor people, 82, 167, 1299
see also class consciousness, legal aid, poverty, social services, welfare

Population policy, 316, 328, 399, 1018
see also eugenics

Pornography, 205, 883, 1168, 1297
see also sexual deviation

Poverty, 365, 462, 694, 827, 845, 1037, 1424
see also poor people

Pregnancy, 96, 120, 326, 327, 582, 600, 652, 1028, 1372
see also childbirth, pre-natal care

Prejudice
see discrimination

Pre-natal care, 490
see also pregnancy

Presbyterianism, 1335

Press, alternative
see alternative press

Priests, 1122
see also Catholic Church

Prison reform, 89, 162, 237, 475, 948

Prisoners, 87, 124, 206, 237, 436, 475, 476, 772, 924, 951, 973, 1096, 1105, 1424, 1450
see also offenders

Prisons, 741, 861

Pro-choice movement
see abortion (pro)

Professionals, 147, 166, 217, 239, 240, 414, 425, 483, 497, 503, 507, 567, 621, 624, 665, 672, 725, 743, 746, 747, 799, 832, 833, 851, 888, 931, 978, 984, 1014, 1054, 1108, 1134, 1159, 1234, 1257, 1260, 1328, 1378, 1414, 1431, 1445
see also individual professions, e. g., artists, etc.

Prohibition
see temperance

"Pro-life" movement
see abortion (anti)

Prostitution, 140, 141, 251, 376, 611, 736, 740, 873, 877, 949, 985, 1324

Psychologists, 9, 67, 68

Psychology, 488, 730, 897, 934, 1427
see also behavior modification, mental health

Psychotherapy, 9, 68, 263

Public health
see community health planning, occupational health and safety

Public schools, 860, 1283, 1311
see also education

Public service projects
see social service

Puerto Ricans, 1105
see also Chicanas

Quakers, 19

Racism, 42, 219, 356, 462, 608, 810, 980, 1007, 1105, 1125, 1147
see also discrimination

Radical feminism, 46, 57, 79, 82, 190, 226, 424, 575, 740, 1008, 1027, 1144, 1264
see also feminism

Radicalism, 442, 625, 633, 661, 869, 877, 901, 935, 936, 945, 949, 967, 985, 1067, 1084, 1086, 1125, 1239, 1309, 1326, 1403
see also communism, revolution, socialism

Ranchers, 1162
see also farm life

Rape, 57, 73, 253, 263, 351, 391, 393, 437, 475, 489, 500, 582, 690, 692, 716, 725, 750, 770, 803, 820, 910, 942, 944, 1014, 1028, 1034, 1046, 1072, 1107, 1244, 1382, 1412
see also crimes against women

Rape prevention, 21, 1168, 1186, 1187, 1434
see also self-defense

Reading, 976

Record reviews, 1099

Recreation
see crafts, hobbies, sports, travel

Religion, 83, 270, 282, 394, 411, 426, 428, 436, 493, 557, 582, 700, 702, 725, 900, 951, 1101, 1277, 1347, 1350, 1354, 1455
see also atheism, Christianity, ecumenism, neo-paganism, religious education, spirituality, witches
see also specific denominations

Religious education, 317, 1370

Reproduction
see abortion, birth control, childbirth, gynecology, pregnancy

Reproductive rights
see abortion (pro)

Republican Party, 131, 149, 189, 366, 676, 957, 1194
see also New Right

Research, 90, 117, 150, 151, 153, 176, 179, 187, 217, 221, 320, 350, 414, 469, 477, 630, 634, 836, 934, 952, 958, 960, 961, 984, 1023, 1054, 1145, 1165, 1304, 1328, 1351, 1428, 1429, 1430
see also educational research, scholars, women's studies

Restaurants, 599
see also food

Retirement, 1082
see also aging, agism, seniors

Reviews
see art reviews, film reviews, periodical reviews, record reviews, television reviews, theatre reviews

Revolution, 841, 857, 949, 967, 1217, 1239, 1403
see also radicalism

Rights, 14, 16, 17, 18, 36, 54, 71, 75, 79, 80, 82, 99, 113, 115, 116, 117, 123, 125, 152, 158, 161, 171, 179, 188, 190, 194, 199, 204, 209, 216, 221, 223, 224, 226,

Rights (continued), 237, 251, 261, 267, 271, 272, 273, 274, 280, 285, 293, 295, 298, 301, 302, 303, 304, 306, 315, 341, 347, 348, 359, 360, 372, 373, 375, 382, 383, 396, 400, 411, 415, 421, 424, 430, 434, 444, 449, 451, 460, 477, 479, 487, 502, 513, 514, 515, 521, 535, 562, 565, 587, 593, 608, 610, 615, 624, 626, 631, 636, 660, 664, 665, 670, 678, 679, 680, 681, 682, 683, 684, 685, 686, 687, 688, 689, 690, 691, 692, 693, 694, 695, 696, 697, 698, 699, 700, 701, 702, 703, 704, 705, 706, 707, 708, 709, 710, 711, 712, 713, 714, 715, 716, 717, 718, 719, 720, 721, 722, 723, 724, 725, 726, 727, 728, 729, 730, 731, 732, 733, 734, 735, 740, 742, 743, 746, 747, 756, 759, 760, 769, 772, 780, 784, 785, 791, 792, 793, 796, 798, 800, 803, 805, 814, 818, 819, 820, 822, 823, 825, 827, 828, 841, 842, 846, 847, 849, 850, 852, 855, 856, 863, 870, 880, 884, 887, 889, 896, 898, 903, 909, 911, 915, 917, 918, 925, 928, 933, 937, 938, 939, 945, 952, 962, 966, 970, 971, 972, 980, 981, 984, 988, 989, 995, 996, 1002, 1003, 1004, 1005, 1015, 1019, 1021, 1028, 1029, 1030, 1037, 1045, 1053, 1056, 1060, 1065, 1069, 1071, 1081, 1082, 1085, 1087, 1088, 1095, 1097, 1104, 1107, 1109, 1110, 1115, 1123, 1127, 1128, 1132, 1137, 1138, 1142, 1148, 1149, 1150, 1156, 1162, 1163, 1170, 1171, 1172, 1173, 1185, 1188, 1191, 1192, 1193, 1195, 1198, 1203, 1205, 1206, 1207, 1208, 1212, 1213, 1214, 1219, 1222, 1224, 1229, 1235, 1241, 1244, 1246, 1253, 1254, 1255, 1256, 1267, 1268, 1270, 1281, 1293, 1295, 1296, 1305, 1309, 1314, 1316, 1317, 1319, 1325, 1326, 1329, 1334, 1339, 1343, 1344, 1354, 1362, 1364, 1371, 1377, 1393, 1395, 1402, 1404, 1405, 1406, 1411, 1419, 1420, 1421, 1423, 1424, 1438, 1444, 1446, 1447, 1454, 1455, 1459
see also abortion (pro), equal pay for equal work, Equal Rights Amendment (pro), gay rights, human rights, suffrage

Rural life, 249, 338
see also farm life

Rural women, 486

Safety
see occupational health and safety, working conditions

Satire, 191, 252, 316, 365, 371, 400, 446, 472, 491, 566, 579, 611, 733, 740, 873, 985, 999, 1000, 1006, 1358, 1411
see also humor

Scholars, 838
see also college students, education, research

School integration, 860
see also discrimination

Science, 339, 467, 535, 538, 1181, 1204, 1252

Science (continued)
see also technology, names of specific sciences

Scientists, 8
see also biologists, geographers, geoscientists, mathematician, psychologists

Secretaries, 1009, 1111
see also office workers

Self-defense, 21, 279, 334, 356, 397, 399, 400, 471, 650, 711, 721, 723, 724, 726, 750, 785, 823, 868, 871, 874, 876, 922, 1028, 1186, 1187, 1217
see also rape prevention, sexual harassment

Self-employment, 612
see also employment

Self-help, 77, 156, 201, 215, 229, 263, 279, 330, 361, 375, 451, 489, 649, 655, 742, 881, 927, 1149, 1213, 1237, 1319, 1370, 1374, 1384, 1387, 1411, 1417, 1422

Seniors, 129, 523, 927
see also aging, agism, retirement

Sewing, 38, 45, 105, 148, 378, 623, 1024
see also needlework

Sex-change surgery, 651

Sex education, 152, 274, 738, 1019, 1051
see also education

Sex roles, 463, 836, 860, 961, 968, 1014, 1350

Sexism, 13, 16, 17, 36, 42, 110, 126, 128, 159, 220, 235, 274, 333, 430, 431, 435, 447, 451, 482, 499, 592, 626, 635, 651, 661, 672, 681, 683, 705, 706, 711, 715, 740, 785, 810, 824, 827, 833, 845, 852, 871, 873, 910, 918, 944, 945, 1031, 1084, 1090, 1094, 1125, 1127, 1128, 1139, 1155, 1159, 1308, 1325, 1328, 1370, 1371, 1442, 1444
see also discrimination

Sexism in advertising, 743, 1404

Sexism in education, 69, 399, 500, 702, 867, 877, 990, 1013, 1014, 1059, 1099, 1174, 1308, 1389, 1454

Sexism in employment, 6, 230, 276, 804, 839, 1108, 1121, 1132
see also discrimination

Sexism in Judaism, 587
see also Judaism

Sexism in language, 1304
see also language

Sexism in law, 1424
see also law

Sexism in media, 666
see also media

Sexism in medicine, 649
see also medicine

Sexual deviation
see child sexual abuse, incest, pornography, rape, transsexuals, transvestites

Sexual harassment, 21
see also self-defense

Sexuality, 58, 220, 316, 327, 392, 417, 579, 643, 663, 725, 848, 881, 927, 993, 1000, 1018, 1019, 1139, 1184, 1441, 1460
see also free love, venereal disease

Shelters
see women's shelters

Single mothers, 643, 644
see also motherhood, unwed mothers

Single parents, 299, 854

Skills
see arts, crafts, job training

Slovenian-Americans, 1458

Social change, 880, 1336

Social conditions
see discrimination, housing, poverty

Social legislation, 831, 1211
see also legislation

Social Security, 760, 863
see also Medicaid

Social services, 19, 409, 674, 751, 754, 831, 1286, 1287, 1307, 1359
see also volunteer work, welfare

Social work, 480, 851

Socialism, 372, 396, 442, 465, 502, 526, 677, 1048, 1049, 1050, 1245, 1282, 1309, 1344, 1421, 1443
see also communism, radicalism

Socialist feminism, 89, 219, 604, 775
see also feminism

Socialites, 1120
see also class consciousness, upper classes

Sociologists, 634, 984

Sociology, 738, 984, 1427

Soldiers, 1324
see also draft, militarism, veterans, WACs, war

Soldier services, 181

Songs, 231, 826
see also music

Sorcery
see witchcraft

Sororities, 59, 107, 264, 265, 492
see also college students

South America
see Latin America

Spirituality, 324
see also religion

Sports, 198, 212, 339, 341, 395, 398, 576, 605, 610, 781, 834, 867, 1077, 1078, 1113, 1150, 1183, 1191, 1240, 1242, 1350, 1425 1433, 1439
see also coaching

Statisticians, 184

Status of Women commissions
see Commissions on women

Stereotypes, 435, 437, 463, 468, 630, 901
see also discrimination

Sterilization, 482, 1352, 1360
see also birth control

Stewardesses
see flight attendants

Students, 242, 283, 689, 746, 758, 838, 858, 866, 871, 898, 905, 917, 928, 1039, 1112, 1113, 1212, 1298, 1345, 1371, 1382, 1400, 1414, 1454
see also college students, education, high school students, scholars

Suffrage (anti), 53, 132, 466, 954, 955, 1245, 1247, 1278

Suffrage (pro), 14, 44, 204, 219, 364, 484, 485, 522, 617, 748, 749, 764, 783, 789, 855, 920, 930, 966, 969, 1085, 1126, 1219, 1248, 1252, 1258, 1260, 1263, 1267, 1268, 1271, 1280, 1383, 1432, 1443, 1459

Taxation, 612
see also legislation

Teachers, 265, 284, 860, 1332
see also college teachers, educators, gay teachers

Teaching, 435, 738, 984
see also education

Technology, 486
see also science

Teenagers, 1010, 1354, 1456
see also high school students

Telephone industry workers, 1093, 1121

Television, 1407
   see also media

Television reviews, 1066

Temperance, 590, 659, 1098, 1126, 1141, 1264

Theatre, 106, 205, 346, 557, 907, 1029, 1030, 1038
   see also drama, plays

Theatre reviews, 547, 610, 786, 1240

Theology
   see religion

Therapy
   see psychotherapy

Third world, 1020, 1048, 1125, 1343

Transsexuals, 651

Transvestites, 651

Travel, 93, 111, 119, 339, 418, 438, 508, 642, 931, 1120, 1161,

UNICEF
   see United Nations International Children's Emergency Fund

Unemployment, 863
   see also employment

Unions
   see labor unions

Unitarian Universalist Association, 1069, 1135

United Nations, 10, 11, 486, 752, 1189, 1436

United Nations International Children's Emergency Fund, 200

University education
   see higher education

Unwed mothers, 73, 274, 844
   see also motherhood, single mothers

Upper classes, 86
   see also socialites

Utopianism, 636
   see also peace movement

Venereal disease, 376, 874
   see also health, sexuality

Veterans, 192, 422, 757
   see also soldiers

Vietnam, 1109, 1342

Vietnamese, 1109, 1342

Violence, 1181, 1297
   see also crimes against women

Vocational rehabilitation, 924
   see also displaced homemakers, employment re-entry

Vocational training
   see career development, job training

Volunteer work, 443, 616, 754, 757, 879, 1258, 1259
   see also hospital volunteers, social services

WACs
   see Women Army Corps

Wages, 6, 147, 170, 209, 318, 507, 923, 1318
   see also equal pay for equal work, minimum wage

War
   see disarmament, draft, imperialism, militarism, nuclear weapons, peace movement, soldiers, war work, World War I, World War II

War work (World War I), 100, 103, 415, 647, 754, 1070, 1250
   see also World War I

War work (World War II), 1380
   see also World War II

Weddings, 119, 642
   see also marriage

Welfare, 46, 128, 162, 170, 237, 356, 399, 643, 644, 681, 724, 778, 827, 871, 949, 987, 991, 1027, 1037, 1040, 1081, 1199, 1254, 1256, 1314, 1405
   see also poor people, social services

West German Women for Peace and Freedom, 386
   see also peace movement

Witches, 1101, 1209
   see also neo-paganism, religion

Wives, 72, 330, 331, 439, 458, 1199, 1215
   see also marriage

Women Strike for Peace, 986
   see also peace movement

Women's Army Corps, 192
   see also World War II

Women's centers, 65, 152, 263, 313

Women's movement
   see feminism, rights

Women's shelters, 21, 1377
   see also battered women, family violence

*Women's Periodicals and Newspapers*

Women's studies, 6, 117, 150, 151, 176, 217, 263, 313, 321, 333, 337, 342, 350, 368, 370, 398, 424, 464, 483, 498, 519, 630, 737, 776, 808, 838, 849, 851, 961, 982, 1007, 1054, 1112, 1145, 1174, 1175, 1212, 1255, 1333, 1361, 1427, 1428, 1429, 1430, 1431, 1449

Work
see employment

Workers, 79, 82, 90, 95, 155, 164, 170, 171, 213, 220, 269, 276, 290, 299, 302, 319, 329, 338, 415, 474, 526, 583, 584, 608, 631, 773, 779, 780, 790, 796, 811, 849, 869, 873, 929, 941, 1006, 1017, 1050, 1070, 1131, 1137, 1140, 1142, 1146, 1148, 1154, 1208, 1216, 1228, 1246, 1248, 1251, 1270, 1275, 1285, 1312, 1317, 1318, 1341, 1363, 1435, 1442, 1443, 1446, 1447, 1448
see also affirmative action, auto industry workers, child labor, church work, employment, garment workers, government workers, homemakers, labor unions, office workers,

Workers (continued) professionals, secretaries, telephone industry workers, wages, war work, working women

Working conditions, 1285
see also occupational health and safety

Working women, 329, 338, 382, 383, 415, 474, 502, 505, 1285, 1444

World War I, 100, 103, 474, 1438
see also war work (World War I)

World War II, 1380
see also war work (World War II), Women's Army Corps

Writers, 362, 1306
see also literature

Yale Non-Faculty Action Committee, 1454

Zionism, 432, 433, 913
see also Jews, Judaism

# Foreign Language Materials Index

Arabic, 615
Chinese, 194, 199, 535
Danish, 521, 522, 523
Dutch, 257, 274, 451, 613, 1137
Finnish, 1131
French, 11, 14, 18, 106, 118, 140, 141, 186, 204, 291, 309, 339, 340, 359, 364, 396, 428, 487, 496, 615, 670, 787, 901, 907, 939, 968, 969, 1082, 1117, 1150, 1157, 1165, 1342, 1343
German, 58, 94, 146, 273, 383, 384, 385, 386, 387, 388, 389, 415, 429, 439, 1232, 1343, 1459, 1460
Hebrew, 913
Hindi, 1085
Icelandic, 520
Italian, 285, 416, 533, 938
Lithuanian, 653
Norwegian, 855
Polish, 419, 921
Portuguese, 848
Russian, 258, 505
Serbo-Croatian, 502
Slovenian, 381, 1458
Spanish, 10, 11, 207, 271, 453, 506, 518, 595, 742, 848, 853, 878, 965, 1125, 1455
Swedish, 450
Tamil, 1085
Telugu, 1085
Yiddish, 533

# Catchword and Subtitle Index

AAUW, Madison Branch Bulletin, 32
AFSC Women's Newsletter, 36
Abolitionniste, 140
Abortion Coalition, 1360
Abortion Law Repeal, 1076
Abortion Law Repeal Coalition Newsletter, 470
Abortion Law Repeal Newsletter, 795
Abortion Rights, 932
Accion Fememina, 853
Activist, 1238
Acts, 684
Ad Hoc Committee for ERA, 745
Administrative Women in Education News, 672
Advocate, 1361
Afternoon Visitor, 528
Against Woman Suffrage, 954
Agenda, 1362
Ain't I A Woman!, 46
Alliance Newsletter, 988
Alternatives, 668
Amaranth, 552
American Agri-Woman, 1162
American Association of University Women - California Division, 166
American Food Journal, 454
American Housewife, 458
American Journal of Maternal Child Nursing, 600
American Law Schools Newsletter, 70
American Medical Women's Association Journal, 497
and N.O.W., 445, 446, 447
Annee Internationale de la Femme, 487
Apparel News, 165
Apple Cart, 56
Arbeit und Frauen, 383
Archivist, 665
Art and Women, 1298
Association for Women Deans, Administrators, and Counselors, 746
Association for Women in Psychology Newsletter (St. Louis Edition), 9
Association of Women in Science Newsletter, 8
Athletic, 1240

Bag, 1202
Ballot Box, 747
Baptist Woman 33
Bars and Belles, 87
Bazaar, 438
Beauties of British Poetry, 560
Beautiful House, 457
Becoming Woman, 1241
Bella Abzug Reports, 234
Bench of the Women's Athletic Association of San Jose, 395
Berkeley Community Y.W.C.A., 74
A Berkshire Women's Liberation Newsletter, 1295
Black U.S.A. Magazine, 639
Books on Women and Feminism, 776
Bookstore Newsletter, 987
Bowler, 1242
Breakthrough, 460
Bride, 642
Brooklyn Newsletter, 434

The Broom, 777
Brule, 1117
Bucks N.O.W. Newsletter, 675
Bulletin, 1048
Bulletin (International Socialist Women's Secretariat), 465
Bulletin d'Information Canadien - Recherches sur la Femme, 176
Bulletin of the National League for Woman's Service, 647
Bulletin of the Women's Municipal League of Boston, 1408
Business News, 1365
Business Woman, 747, 1218
By and For Gay Women, 1036

Cabinet of Fashion, 529
Cain, 943
California Personnel and Guidance Association Women's Caucus Newsletter, 156
Canadian Women's News Service, 1203
Capital Alert, 178
Casket, 1204
Cassandra, 252
Cauliflower, 508
Cell Biology Women, 1328
Center for Continuing Education of Women Newsletter, 630
Center for Women's Studies and Services Newsletter, 162
Century for Woman, 779
Changes, 668
Charity Edition, Milwaukee Journal, 636
Chicago Women's Liberation Union News, 161
Chicana Service Action Center News, 157
Chinese Women, 1341
Christian Mothers' Miscellany, 296
Chromosome Chronicle, 1449
Chung-hua fu nu, 194
Circle, 323
Citizen and Ballot Box, 749
City Club Bulletin, 1259
City Government Women, 1329
City's Work, 1311
Claflin's Weekly, 1441
Clarion, 163
Clearinghouse on Women's Issues in Congress, 160
Club Woman, 34
Clubwoman, 410, 957, 1220
Coalition Newsletter, 349
Coalition of Labor Union Women News, 155
Column, 1260
Comision Femenil Mexicana Report, 152
Commission Newsletter, 601
Commission of Women Informational Bulletin, 479
Commission on the Status of Women - Career Newsletter, 507
Commission on the Status of Women News, 158
Commission on the Status of Women Report, 159
Common Cause, 1271
Communication Network, 1376
Communicator, 941
Community Center Newsletter, 1377
Community Women's Newspaper, 449

Companion, 530
Comprehensive Advocacy Program Alert, 149
Concern for Health Options, Information, Care, and Education, 153
Conference Group in Women's History Newsletter, 153
Constitutionalist, 1243
Continuing Education of Women Newsletter, 187
Cook's Journal, 288
Coordinating Committee on Women on the Historical Profession Newsletter, 150, 151
Cornell Women at Work Newsletter, 269
Council of Jewish Women Newsletter, 751
Council of Women of the United States Bulletin, 752
Courrior des Dames, 907
Court and Fashionable Magazine, 86
Current Issues of Women's Equality, 1081

DAR Magazine, 606
DOB'R Monthly, 648
Dane County Newsletter, 1230
Daughters of 1812 Bulletin, 762
Daughters of 1812 News-Letter, 763
Daughters of the Confederacy Magazine, 1143
The Dawn, 1458
Defense Bulletin, 753
Delight Magazine, 531
Deutscher Frauenvereine, 146
Directions for Women, 780
Dreadnought, 1443
Dyke, 513

The Eagle, 964
Education, 1378
Educational Task Force - California N.O.W., 168
Elevation of Women, 1138
Elgin N.O.W., 377
Employment and Women, 1299
Employment Opportunity Program, 1379
Ending Violence Against Women Magazine, 21
Entertaining Companion for the Fair Sex, 556
Equal Times, 1192
Essex County Chapter News, 193
Experimental and Communal Family-Oriented People, 322
Exponent, 1263

Fabrics and Fashions, 35
Fact Bulletin, 1380
Fair Child Support, 657
Fair Employment Practice Commission News, 804
Family Culture, 324
Family Journal, 96
Fashion Gallery, 401
Fashion Magazine, 1024
Federally Employed Women, 799
Feminist League of Hong Kong Newsletter, 482
A Feminist Newsletter, 1059
Feminist Research/Documentation Sur la Recherche Feministe, 961
Feminist Studies, 321
Fight Back, 575
Film and Women, 1300
Fist, 1154
Floral Cabinet, 532
Focus, 342, 343

Fogcutter, 503
Footnotes on Maternity Care, 120
For Women Only, 849
Forum, 353, 1381, 1382
Franchise, 1383
Frauenfrage, 94
Frauenkunde und Konstitutions-forschung, 58
Frauenzeitung Gewerkschaftliche, 415
Frauen-Stimmrecht, 1459
Free Express, 1384
Free Woman, 392
Freewoman, 786
FreeWoman, 1198
Freewoman's Herald, 608
Frieden und Frau, 386
Friend, 553
From the Basement, 1147
From Under, 1148
Fu Nu Tsa Chih, 535

Garment Worker, 533, 595
Glove, 1155
Goldflower, 421

Harrisburg Women's Rights Movement Newsletter, 431
Headlines, 432
Health and Women, 1301, 1302
Health and Women Roundtable, 1303
Health Care of Women, 490
Health Right, 441
Hear This..., 688, 689, 690
Heathen Lands Work, 1288
Herald of Industry, 1264
Historical Perspective, 325
Home Companion, 1265
Home Journal, 534
Home Magazine, 39
Home Missions, 1266
Homes and Gardens, 93
Horizons, 284
Hospital Assocation Auxiliaries, 1221
Household Magazine, 467, 654
Housekeeping, 314
Howitt's Journal, 906
Human Rights for Women Newsletter, 430
Humane Abortion Newsletter, 1051
Hussy Review, 1016

IACWI Bulletin, 479
ICS Quarterly, 480
In Motion, 1450
In Touch, 511
Independent Feminst Weekly, 302
Indochinese and North American Women, Vancouver, British Columbia, Canada, 810
Industrial News, 1386
Information Center Newsletter, 1387
Information Network, 1388
Information Network Bulletin, 1389
Initiatives, 1390
Interart Center Newsletter, 1391
Intercollegiate Association of Women Studies, 464
International Quarterly, 1398
Inter-Studio Feminist Alliance Newsletter, 666
Intimate Apparel, 105
An Irregular Periodical, 649

*Women's Periodicals and Newspapers*

Jacksonville Women's Movement, 1185
Jam, 1121
Jeopardy, 1125
Joint Strategy and Action Committee Grapevine, 493
A Journal of Anarcho-Feminism, 1027
Journal of Communication, 872
Journal of Eugenics, 41
A Journal of Female Liberation, 841
A Journal of Feminism and Film Theory, 174
A Journal of Liberation, 1296
Journal of the National Council of Jewish Women, 674
A Journal of Women Studies, 398
Journal of Women's Studies, 483

Kappa Epsilon, 107
Kentucky-Ohio News, 862

Label League Journal, 1270
Labor and Life, 583
Labor and Life Bulletin, 584
Ladies' Casket, 1204
Ladies Gazette, 310
Ladies' Journal, 378
Ladies' Literary Magazine, 618
Ladies' Miscellany, 1200
Ladies' Spectator, 270
Ladies' Tea Tray, 478
Ladies Weekly Museum, 956
Lady's Emporium, 755
Lady's Magazine, 197, 379
Language and Women News, 1304
Law and Women, 1305
Law Center, 1399
Law Journal, 1400
Law Reporter, 1424
Lawyer's Journal, 1337
League for Women's Service Weekly Bulletin, 754
Legal Group Newsletter, 635
Legionette, 509
A Legislative Newsletter for Massachusetts Women, 777
A Lesbian/Feminist Journal of Communication, 872
Letter, 574
Liberation News, 1401, 1402
Liberation Newsletter, 1403, 1404
Librarians for Social Change, 524
Library Workers, 1338
Light and Life for Women, 585
Like A Woman, 504
Literary Cabinet, 536
Literary Gazette, 540
Literary Museum, 537
Literary Pieces Principally Designed for the Amusement of the Ladies, 1114
Lobby Quarterly, 1406
The Looking Glass, 1104
The Looking Glass, A Women's & Children's Newsletter, 1105

A Magazine About Women, 1449
A Magazine of the New Feminism, 1008
Maid, 1140
Majority, 1159
Mama Rag, 95

Manhattan Tribune, 734
Marriage, Divorce, and Family Relations, 730
Marriage, Divorce, and Family Relations Newsletter, 760
Maternity Care Footnotes, 120
Media Project, 1407
Media Project Newsletter, 355
Medical Women's Journal, 894
Medusa, 121
La Mestiza, 946
A Midwest Journal for Women, 30
Mill Girl's Magazine, 782
Milwaukee/Her, 443
Mirror, 1047
Miscellany, 558, 618
Miss, 1456
Missionary Advocate, 1273
Missionary Friend, 1274
Missions and Women, 1307
Modern Life, 413
Le Moniteur de la Mode, 106
Monitor, 303, 559
Monthly Information Exchange for All Women's Peace Groups, 1416
Monthly Museum, 542
A Monthly Report on Gay People and Mental Health, 404
Moon Shadow, 651
Morale Sociale, 968
Mother for Peace, 51
Motherhood, 455
Moving Mountains, 660
Moving Mountains Day, 661
Muse, 1025
Museum, 543, 544, 545
Musical Intelligencer, 310
Musical Repository, 554

NOW Letter, 852
N.O.W. On, 393, 394
N.O.W. Times, 756
National Action Committee Memo, 670
National Association for Repeal of Abortion Laws, News, 671
National Committee on Household Employment News, 673
National Council of Jewish Women, 831
National Interim Committee for a Mass Party of the People Women's Newsletter, 677
National Law Women's Newsletter, 928
National Lesbian Information Service Newsletter, 679
Near and Far, 329
Needlework and Crafts, 623
Negro Woman, 42
Network News & Notes, 1174
Never Mind, 774
New Directions, 668
New Getting on Women's Collective, 828
The New Woman, 364
New York Mlle., 641
New York Times, 733
New York Woman, 734, 735
New York Women, 1340
News, 1409, 1430
News and Views, 799
News Exchange, 1410
News from the Women's Services Division of

the Ohio Bureau of Employment Services, 863
News Journal, 1411
News on Women, 1211
Newsletter, 1412
Newsletter from Women in Japan, 873
Newsletter of Research on Women, 176
Newsletter of the Association of Women in Science, 8
Newsletter of the Bread and Roses Women's Health Center, 488
Newspaper, 1413
Newspaper/Magazine for Single Mothers, 643
Nifty Newsletter, 1018
Notes, 715, 716, 717
Nothing Less, 47
Nous les Femmes, Nous Pensons, 186
Nouvelles du Parti Feministe du Canada, 359

On Scene, 666
On the March, 1344
Only Just Begun, 1206
Opportunities Center Newsletter, 1414
Opposed to Woman Suffrage Bulletin, 466
or Never, 719
Organizacao Da Muhler de Angola, 857
Our Fire, 953
Ourselves, 882
Outlook, 1275
Outside/Inside, 475

Paper of Joyful Noise for the Majority Sex, 365
Papers in Women's Studies, 1145
Party News, 358
Patriot, 1245
Peace and Freedom, 633
Peace Movement Bulletin, 1416
Peaceletter, 741
Pearl, 546
Periodical Essays, 908
Peer Perspective, 884
Peterson Magazine, 788
Poetical Magazine, 560
Polek, 419
A Polish Women's Magazine, 921
Polite Companion for the Fair Sex, 557
Polite Repository of Amusement and Instruction, 542, 794
Polite, Useful, and Entertaining Monthly for the Fair Sex, 787
Political Times, 1419
Population Reporter, 328
Port Folio, 547
Press, 723
Prison Newsletter, 840
The Private Weekly Letter for Women, 809
Project on the Status and Education of Women, 69
Protest Against Woman Suffrage, 1278
Protect Each Other Record, 885
Proud and Free, 390
Public School Champion, 1283
Publicity Committee Bulletin, 761

Quai, 1017

Radicalesbians Journal, 936
Rankin Brigade Newsletter, 494

Reaching Women Newsletter, 1346
Realm, 561
Rebel, 1246
Recherche et d'Information Feministes, 428
Recherches sur la Femma - Bulletin d'Information Canadien, 176
Regional News West, 724
Religious Studies Newsletter, 1366
Repeal Abortion Laws Newsletter, 73
Report, 1421
Report to Women, 624
Repository, 548, 549
Repository of Entertaining Knowledge, 555
Repository, Religious and Literary Magazine for the Home Circle, 549
Research/Action About Wo/Men, 221
Review of Political Research, 1279
Review of Social and Industrial Questions, 297
A Review of the Tastes, Errors, and Fashions of Society, 1021
Revolution and Women, 1309
Ribbon, 1455
Rights Law Reporter, 1424
Rights Newsletter, 1423
Roses & Bread, 113
Roses and Bread Newsletter, 114, 115
Roundtable on Women and Health, 1303

SJW, Inc., Newsletter, 1043
SRRT/ALA Task Force on Women Newsletter, 6
Samfundet, 522
Sappho, 281
Saxe Defense Committee Newsletter, 1092
Schoe and Foote, 371
Schoene Geschlecht, 1232
Service Worker, 170
Sew Biz, 864
Sewing World, 148
Sex Roles in Society, 836
Sexualwissenschaft Zeitschrift, 1460
She Wants, 1208
Sigma Alpha Iota Pan Pipes, 893
Single Mothers Magazine, 643
Sisterhood, 772
Sisterhood Week, 743
Sisters in Social Work, 851
Sisters Magazine, 1144
Social Science Cooperator, 1264
Society for Women in Philosophy Newsletter, 832
Sociologists for Women in Society Newsletter, 634
Sofia Perouskaya and Andrei Zhelyabou, 1067
Southern Illinois Women's Newsletter, 515
Spectator, 336
Spiegel-Frauen, 387
Sports, 1425
Staatsbuergerliche Bildung der Frau, 1459
Standard, 1280
Star, 569
State News, Church Women United, 201
Status of Women Council Newspaper, 796
Struggle, 500, 1426
Stephanie's Office Service, 983
Study of Women in Transition Newsletter, 477
Suffrage Journal, 1432
Suffrage Leaflet, 1247

Suffrage News, 617, 764
Suffragette, 44
Switchboard, 1032

Task Force on the Status of Women and Minorities - Bay Area, 43
Task Force on Women Newsletter, 6
Temple University Continuing Education for Women, 242
Tide, 576
To, By, Of, For and About Women, 1352
Today's Women, 1353
Top Women, 1345
Track World, 1433
Transit Home Companion, 1434
Triangle, 1106
Tribal Women's News, 1224
Tribune, 1281

UCW/AFW Newsletter, 5
Union Journal, 1435
Union Newsletter, 604
Universal Movement, 1436
University of Delaware Continuing Education for Women, 243
Unite Women, 233
United N.O.W. Women, 1354
United Women, 1355, 1356
United Women for November 6 Newsletter, 1357

Verlag fuer die Frau, 429
Vietnam Women, 1342
Vignettes of the Netherlands, 344
Violence and Sexual Abuse in the Family, 963
Violence Against Women, 750
Vision, 565
Visiter, 550
Voice, 1282
Voice and Public School Champion, 1283
Voices, 577, 1437
La Voix des Femmes, 1165
Voter, 789, 1248
The Voter, 765
Voters' Bulletin, 1249

W.A.G.E., 1142
W.E.A.L.er, 678
War and Work, 1438
Way, 1284
We See It, 1199
Weapons of War, 83
Weekly Repository, 537
The Weekly Visitor, 558
Welfare, 1285
West Women, 1358
Western Women, 1358
Whole World, 1343
Wisconsin Women in the Arts Newsletter, 1119
Witch Way, 1209
A Woman Born, 109
Woman Catalog, 1213
Woman Co-operator, 484
Woman Engineer, 1134
Woman Graduate, 425
Woman Power, 1257
Woman Smith, 1292
Woman Socialist, 1049
Woman Suffrage News, 485

Woman Voter, 865
Womankind, 791
Woman/Love, 596
Woman's Handi-Work, 275
Woman's Institute News, 806
The Woman's Magazine, 268
Woman's Missionary Society Magazine, 640
Woman's Work, 598
Women Act for Peace, 1004
Women & Arts Task Force Newsletter, 732
Women for Agriculture Newsletter, 1225
Women for Peace Newsletter, 980, 986
Women Historians Newsletter, 1201
Women in Culture and Society, 1023
Women in Delaware, 781
Women in History Newsletter, 185
Women in Japan Newsletter, 874
Women in Mathematics Newsletter, 66
Women in Psychology Newsletter, 67
Women in Psychology Newsletter (San Francisco Branch), 68
Women in Statistics, 184
Women in the Arts, 1176
Women in the Arts Newsletter, 1226
Women Liberation Newsletter, 858
Women Library Workers Newsletter, 1227
Women News, 1359
Women of the Haight, 579
Women on Campus, 867
Women Sports, 1439
Women's Achievement Newsletter, 414
Women's Action Movement Newsletter, 1166
Women's Association News Digest, 1167
Women's Athletics, 212
Women's Caucus for Political Science, 833
Women's Clubs Magazine, 412
Women's Communication, 370
Women's Community Magazine, 998
Women's Culture, 1074
Women's Department Special Bulletin, 1132
Women's Equality Newsletter, 247
Women's Health Center Newsletter, 289
Women's Health Center Report, 361
Women's Health Centers, 363
Women's International Network, 1182
Women's Legislative Review, 29
A Women's Literary Journal, 974
Women's Monthly, 625
Women's News, 1359
Women's News (Downtown), 276
Women's Newsletter on Socialist Feminism, 775
Women's Political Caucus, 766, 767
Women's Political Caucus Newsletter, 768
Women's Political Caucus of Contra Costa County, 769
Women's Political Caucus - Orange County Chapter, 770
Women's Political Caucus - Southern California Section, 771
Women's Press, 1442
Women's Prison Newsletter, 840
Women's Representative, 1197
Women's Sports, 1439
Women's Studies Abstracts, 1350
Women's Studies in Literature, 498
Women's Studies Library Resources in Wisconsin, 350
Women's Studies Newsletter, College Press, 217

Women's Studies Research Center Newsletter, 1351
Women's Task Force Newsletter - Communication and Services Newsletter, 228
Women's Times, 792
Women's Union Newsletter: A Socialist-Feminist Organization, 89
Women's World, 104
Work, 1286
Work and War, 1438
Work and Women, 1310
Work and Women Newsletter, 1312
Work for Woman, 1287
Work in Heathen Lands, 1288
Worker, 1250, 1251

Workers Voice, 518
A Working Woman's Newspaper, 190
World, 1289, 1290, 1291
World Population Washington Memo, 916
World Women, 1343
Wreath, 551

Your Old Lady, 1057

Zeitschrift fuer die gesamten Interessen des weiblichen Unterrichtswesens, 385
Zeitung Frauen, 388
Zena, 502
Zenska Jednota, 381
Zukunft-Frauen, 389

# Chronological Index

```
      1746  1747  1748  1749  1750  1751  1752  1753  1754  1755  1756  1757  1758  1759  1760  1761
336    x-x
557                                                                          o---------x-xo-o+


      1762  1763  1764  1765  1766  1767  1768  1769  1770  1771  1772  1773  1774  1775  1776  1777
557   +o----------------------x-x
556                                                x------------------------------------------x+


      1778  1779  1780  1781  1782  1783  1784  1785  1786  1787  1788  1789  1790  1791  1792  1793
556   +x------------------------------------------------------------------------------------x+
1232        x-x
560                     x------x
908                                             x------x
787                                             x------------------------------x+
794                                                         o------------------------x--------x+
555                                                                     x------x


      1794  1795  1796  1797  1798  1799  1800  1801  1802  1803  1804  1805  1806  1807  1808  1809
556   +x----------------------------------------------------------------------------------x+
787   +x------x
794   +x----------------------------------------------------------------------------------x+
401    x----------------------------------------x
542                           x----------------------------------------------------------x+
543                                 x-xo------------------------------------------------o+
956                                 x----------------------------------------x
1114                    x-x
554                     x------x
559                     x------x
558                           x------------------------------------------------------x+
528                                                         x------x
86                                                          x--------------------x+


      1810  1811  1812  1813  1814  1815  1816  1817  1818  1819  1820  1821  1822  1823  1824  1825
556   +x------x
558   +x------------x
794   +x----------------------------xo-----o
543   +o----------------------------------------------------o
542   +x----------------------------------------------------------------------------x+
496    x-x
478                     x------x
907                     o------------------------------------------------------------o+
1200                          x--------------xo--------------------------ox-x
537                                 x------x
```

## Women's Periodicals and Newspapers

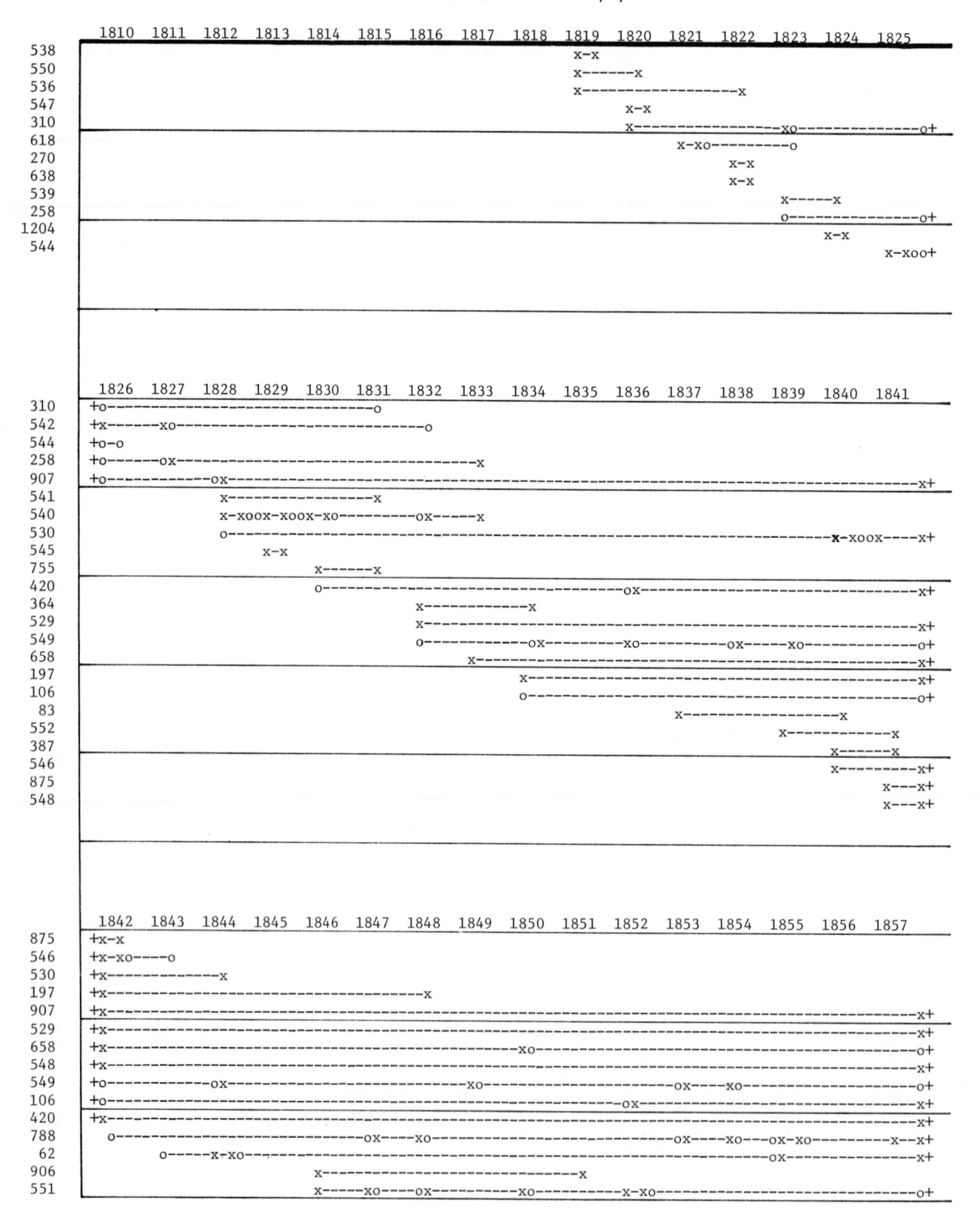

|      | 1810 | 1811 | 1812 | 1813 | 1814 | 1815 | 1816 | 1817 | 1818 | 1819 | 1820 | 1821 | 1822 | 1823 | 1824 | 1825 |
|------|------|------|------|------|------|------|------|------|------|------|------|------|------|------|------|------|
| 538  |      |      |      |      |      |      |      |      |      | x-x  |      |      |      |      |      |      |
| 550  |      |      |      |      |      |      |      |      |      | x------x |   |      |      |      |      |      |
| 536  |      |      |      |      |      |      |      |      |      | x-----------------x |    |      |      |
| 547  |      |      |      |      |      |      |      |      |      |      | x-x  |      |      |      |      |      |
| 310  |      |      |      |      |      |      |      |      |      |      | x---------------xo-------------o+ |
| 618  |      |      |      |      |      |      |      |      |      |      |      | x-xo--------o |   |      |      |      |
| 270  |      |      |      |      |      |      |      |      |      |      |      |      | x-x  |      |      |      |
| 638  |      |      |      |      |      |      |      |      |      |      |      |      | x-x  |      |      |      |
| 539  |      |      |      |      |      |      |      |      |      |      |      |      |      | x-----x |    |      |
| 258  |      |      |      |      |      |      |      |      |      |      |      |      |      | o--------------o+ |
| 1204 |      |      |      |      |      |      |      |      |      |      |      |      |      |      | x-x  |      |
| 544  |      |      |      |      |      |      |      |      |      |      |      |      |      |      |      | x-xoo+ |

|      | 1826 | 1827 | 1828 | 1829 | 1830 | 1831 | 1832 | 1833 | 1834 | 1835 | 1836 | 1837 | 1838 | 1839 | 1840 | 1841 |
|------|------|------|------|------|------|------|------|------|------|------|------|------|------|------|------|------|
| 310  | +o--------------------------o |
| 542  | +x------xo-----------------------o |
| 544  | +o-o |
| 258  | +o-------ox----------------------------x |
| 907  | +o----------ox------------------------------------------------------x+ |
| 541  |      |      | x----------------x |
| 540  |      |      | x-xoox-xoox-xo---------ox----x |
| 530  |      |      | o------------------------------------------------------x-xoox----x+ |
| 545  |      |      |      | x-x  |
| 755  |      |      |      |      | x------x |
| 420  |      |      |      |      | o-------------------------------ox------------------------x+ |
| 364  |      |      |      |      |      |      | x----------x |
| 529  |      |      |      |      |      |      | x-----------------------------------------------------x+ |
| 549  |      |      |      |      |      |      | o----------ox---------xo---------ox----xo-----------o+ |
| 658  |      |      |      |      |      |      |      | x-----------------------------------------------x+ |
| 197  |      |      |      |      |      |      |      |      | x--------------------------------------x+ |
| 106  |      |      |      |      |      |      |      |      | o---------------------------------------o+ |
| 83   |      |      |      |      |      |      |      |      |      |      | x-----------------x |
| 552  |      |      |      |      |      |      |      |      |      |      | x-----------x |
| 387  |      |      |      |      |      |      |      |      |      |      |      | x------x |
| 546  |      |      |      |      |      |      |      |      |      |      |      | x---------x+ |
| 875  |      |      |      |      |      |      |      |      |      |      |      | x---x+ |
| 548  |      |      |      |      |      |      |      |      |      |      |      | x---x+ |

|      | 1842 | 1843 | 1844 | 1845 | 1846 | 1847 | 1848 | 1849 | 1850 | 1851 | 1852 | 1853 | 1854 | 1855 | 1856 | 1857 |
|------|------|------|------|------|------|------|------|------|------|------|------|------|------|------|------|------|
| 875  | +x-x |
| 546  | +x-xo----o |
| 530  | +x-----------x |
| 197  | +x-------------------------x |
| 907  | +x---------------------------------------------------------------------x+ |
| 529  | +x---------------------------------------------------------------------x+ |
| 658  | +x------------------------------------xo------------------------------o+ |
| 548  | +x---------------------------------------------------------------------x+ |
| 549  | +o----------ox--------------------xo----------------ox----xo-----------o+ |
| 106  | +o---------------------------------------------ox-------------------x+ |
| 420  | +x---------------------------------------------------------------------x+ |
| 788  |      | o------------------------ox----xo----------------------ox----xo--ox-xo---------x--x+ |
| 62   |      |      | o-----x-xo------------------------------------------ox--------------x+ |
| 906  |      |      |      |      | x---------------------------x |
| 551  |      |      |      |      | x------xo----ox-----------xo----------x-xo-----------------o+ |

342

## Women's Periodicals and Newspapers

```
         1842 1843 1844 1845 1846 1847 1848 1849 1850 1851 1852 1853 1854 1855 1856 1857
  296                         o-----------------ox---------------------x
 1120                         o-----------------------------------------------------o+
  782                              x-----------x
  288                                   x--------------------------x
  590                                   x-------------------xo------ox------------xo------o+
 1138                                             x----------x
  379                                             o-----------------------------------o+
 1021                                                            x--------x+
  331                                                            o---o+

         1858 1859 1860 1861 1862 1863 1864 1865 1866 1867 1868 1869 1870 1871 1872 1873
  551   +o--------------------o
 1021   +x-----------------------------x
  907   +x--------------------------------------------x
  529   +x-------------xo----------------------------------o
  658   +o--------------------------------------------------------o
  548   +x----------------------------------------------------------x+
  549   +o---------------------------------ox-----------------------xo--o+
  379   +o----------ox----------------xo-----------------------------o+
  106   +x--------------------------------------------xo---ox----xo------o+
  590   +o---------------------------------------------------------------o+
  788   +x----------------------------------------------------------x+
  420   +x----------------------------------------------------------x+
   62   +x----------------------------------------------------------x+
  331   +o----------------------------------------------------------o+
 1120   +o----------------------------------------------------------o+
  459    x----------x
  295    x-----------------------x
  553                    o------------------------------x-xo---------⊖
  297                         x-------------------------------------x+
  438                              x--------------------------------x+
  966                                        x-------------xo----o
  458                                        o------------------------x+
   23                                             x-x
  654                                             x-x
  585                                             x------------------x+
 1274                                             x------------------x+
 1441                                                  x-------------x+
 1267                                                  x-------------x+
 1432                                                  o----ox-------x+
  378                                                       x--------x+
 1263                                                            o------x---x+
  532                                                            o---------o+
 1265                                                            o---o+

         1874 1875 1876 1877 1878 1879 1880 1881 1882 1883 1884 1885 1886 1887 1888 1889
 1441   +x-----------x
  548   +x-----------x
  549   +o--------------------o
  378   +x---------------------------------------x
  379   +o------------------------------------------o
  532   +ox---------------------------------------------------x
  458   +x---------------------------------------------------x
 1432   +x-------------------------------------------------------x+
  106   +o-------------------------------------------------------o+
  590   +o-------------------------------------------------------o+
```

343

## Women's Periodicals and Newspapers

```
      1874 1875 1876 1877 1878 1879 1880 1881 1882 1883 1884 1885 1886 1887 1888 1889
 788  +x---------------------xo----------ox-xo------ox-xo-------ox------------x+
 420  +x-----------------------------------------------------------------------x+
  62  +x-----------------------------------------------------------------------x+
 297  +x-----------------------------------------------------------------------x+
1263  +x-----------------------------------------------------------------------x+
1267  +x-----------------------------------------------------------------------x+
 585  +x-----------------------------------------------------------------------x+
 331  +o-----------------------------------------------------------------------o+
1274  +x-----------------------------------------------------------------------x+
1265  +o-----------------------------------------------------------------------o+
1120  +o-----------------------------------------------------------------------o+
 438  +x-----------------------------------------------------------------------x+
1287       x-------------------------------------------x
 141       x-----------------------------------------------------------------x+
1141       o----------------------------ox----------xo----------ox-----xo-------o+
 779            x-x
 749            x-----------------------x
1435            o-------------------------------ox-----------------------------x+
 622            o-----------------------------------------------------------------o+
 467                      o----------ox-----x
  52                           x----------------x
1273                           x-----------------------------------------------x+
1264                                x--------------x
 516                                x--------------------------------------x
 204                                x-----------------------------------------x+
 425                                     o------------------------------------o+
1288                                     x------------------------------------x+
1281                                     x------------------------------------x+
 534                                     o----ox------------------------------x+
 275                                          x------x
 783                                               x-x
 522                                               x---------------------------x+
 202                                               x-------------------------x
1286                                               x---------------------------x+
 423                                               o---------------------------o+
 259                                                    x----------------------x+
1280                                                    x----------------------x+
1158                                                    x----------------------x+
 246                                                    x----------------------x+
 659                                                    x----------------------x+
  19                                                    o----------------------o+
1233                                                    x------x
1446                                                    x-xo----------o+
 855                                                    x----------------------x+
1219                                                    x----------------------x+
1289                                                         x---------x+
  94                                                         x---------x+
1247                                                         x---------x+
 473                                                         x---------x+
1260                                                         o---------o+
1448                                                         o---------o+
 456                                                              x---x+
 885                                                              o---o+


      1890 1891 1892 1893 1894 1895 1896 1897 1898 1899 1900 1901 1902 1903 1904 1905
1432  +x-x
 106  +ox-x
1435  +x-x
 204  +x-x
1288  +x-x
```

344

## Women's Periodicals and Newspapers

|      | 1890 1891 1892 1893 1894 1895 1896 1897 1898 1899 1900 1901 1902 1903 1904 1905 |
|------|---|
| 1289 | +x-x |
| 1446 | +ox-xo-x-x |
| 94   | +x------------------x |
| 456  | +x------------------x |
| 590  | +o----------------------o |
| 259  | +x----------------------x |
| 1448 | +o-----------------------ox-x |
| 788  | +x----------xo-----------------------------o |
| 420  | +x----------------------------------x |
| 62   | +x----------------xo-----------------o |
| 522  | +x--------------------------------------x |
| 141  | +x------------------------------------------------x |
| 1247 | +x--------------------------------------------------------x |
| 1281 | +x-----------------------------------------------------------------x+ |
| 297  | +x-----------------------------------------------------------------x+ |
| 1273 | +x-----------------------------------------------------------------x+ |
| 1280 | +x-----------------------------------------------------------------x+ |
| 1263 | +x-----------------------------------------------------------------x+ |
| 1158 | +x-----------------------------------------------------------------x+ |
| 1267 | +x-----------------------------------------------------------------x+ |
| 1219 | +x-----------------------------------------------------------------x+ |
| 585  | +x-----------------------------------------------------------------x+ |
| 1286 | +x-----------------------------------------------------------------x+ |
| 855  | +x-----------------------------------------------------------------x+ |
| 331  | +o-----------------------------------------------------------------o+ |
| 1274 | +x-----------------------------------------------------------------x+ |
| 1260 | +o------ox-----------------------------------------------xo------o+ |
| 473  | +x-----------------------------------------------------------------x+ |
| 1265 | +o----------------------------------x-----xo---------ox-----------x+ |
| 885  | +o-----------------------------------------------------------------o+ |
| 1120 | +o-----------------------------------------------------------------o+ |
| 438  | +x-----------------------------------------------------------------x+ |
| 1141 | +o------------ox----------xo--------ox-----------------------------x+ |
| 622  | +o-----------------------------------------------------------------o+ |
| 425  | +o-----------------------------------------------------------------o+ |
| 534  | +x-----------------------------------------------------------------x+ |
| 423  | +o---------------------------------------------------------ox----x+ |
| 246  | +x-----------------------------------------------------------------x+ |
| 659  | +x-----------------------------------------------------------------x+ |
| 19   | +o-----------------------------------------------------------------o+ |
| 329  | x---------------------x |
| 1283 | x------------------------------------------------------------------x+ |
| 954  | x------------------------------------------------------------------x+ |
| 413  | o------------------------------------------ox---------------------x+ |
| 748  | x----------------------------x |
| 1126 | x---------------------------------------------------------------x |
| 607  | x-x |
| 1161 | x----------------------------------------------------------------x+ |
| 260  | x----------------------------------------------------------------x+ |
| 45   | o================================================================o+ |
| 1047 | x-----------x...... |
| 606  | x-------------x |
| 382  | o----------------------------------------------------------------o+ |
| 894  | o----------------------------------------------------------------o+ |
| 1261 | x-----------x |
| 455  | x---------------------------------------------------xo-------o+ |
| 314  | x--------------------------------------------------------------x+ |
| 268  | o----ox---------------------------------------------------------x+ |
| 1272 | o-----------------------------------------ox--------------------x+ |
| 636  | x-x |
| 969  | x----------x |
| 40   | x----------------xo-----o |
| 641  | x-----xo---------ox-xo---o |
| 146  | x-xo-------------ox-xo------ox-xo----------------ox----x |
| 384  | x--------------------------------------------------------------x+ |

345

## Women's Periodicals and Newspapers

## Women's Periodicals and Newspapers

```
       1906 1907 1908 1909 1910 1911 1912 1913 1914 1915 1916 1917 1918 1919 1920 1921
 520   +x--------------------------------------------------xo----o
 585   +x-------------------------------------------------------------x+
1270   +o----------------------------------------ox-----------------x+
 385   +x-----------------------------------------------------------x+
1286   +x-----------------------------------------------------------x+
 268   +x-----------------------------------------------------------x+
 413   +x-----------------------------------------------------------x+
 843   +x-----------------------------------------------------------x+
 855   +x-xo---------------------------------------------------------o+
 140   +x-----------------------------------------------------------x+
 396   +x-----------------------------------------------------------x+
 331   +o-----------------------------------------------------------o+
1274   +x-----------------------------------------------------------x+
  18   +x-----------------------------------------------------------x+
 382   +o---------------ox----xo-------------------------------------o+
  92   +o---------------------------ox------------------------------x+
1260   +o-----------------------------------------------------------o+
 473   +x-----------------------------------------------------------x+
 894   +o-----------------------------------------------------------o+
 339   +o-----------------------------------------------------------o+
1265   +x--------------xo---------------------------------ox---------x+
 885   +o-----------------------------------------------------------o+
  70   +o-----------------------------------------------------------o+
1120   +o-----------------------------------------------------------o+
 438   +x-----------------------------------------------------------x+
1141   +x-----------------------------------------------------------x+
 622   +o-----------------------------------------------------------o+
 425   +o------------------------------------------------ox-----x+
 534   +x-----------------------------------------------------------x+
 423   +x-----------------------------------------------------------x+
 246   +x-----------------------------------------------------------x+
 659   +x-----------------------------------------------------------x+
  19   +o-----------------------------------------------------------o+
1161   +x-----------------------------------------------------------x+
 260   +x-----------------------------------------------------------x+
 457   +o------------------------------------------------ox---------x+
 950   +o-----------------------------------------------------------o+
1111   +o-----------------------------------------------------------o+
 418   +o-----------------------------------------------------------o+
 439   +x-----------------------------------------------------------x+
 257        x-------------------x
 454        o------------------------------------------------------o+
1383             x-----------x
  41             x---------------x
 219             x-------------------------------x
1459             x-----------------------------------------------x
 763             x-----------------------------------------------------x+
1277             o---------ox-xo-------------------ox-xo--x---------xo--o+
 485             x---------------------------------------------x
1460                  x-x
  53             x-------------------x
 598                  o-----------------------------------------------o+
 893                  o-----------------------------------------------o+
  44                  x-----------x
 132                  x-----------------x
 466                  x-----------------x
  14                  x---------------------------x
 372                  x---------------------------x
1271                  x-----------------------------------------------------x+
 389                       x------x
 789                       x------x
1098                       x---------------------------x
1248                       x---------------------------x
1408                       x---------------------------x
 533                       x---------------------------------x
```

347

## Women's Periodicals and Newspapers

## Women's Periodicals and Newspapers

```
         1922 1923 1924 1925 1926 1927 1928 1929 1930 1931 1932 1933 1934 1935 1936 1937
  585    +x--x
 1270    +x--x
  415    +ox-x
  385    +x-------x
 1311    +x-------x
 1286    +x-------------x
 1443    +x-------------x
  145    +o-------------x-x
  268    +x------------------------x
  413    +x------------------------x
  843    +x------------------------x
  965    +o-------ox--------------x
 1275    +x------------------------x
  855    +o--------------------------------x
  408    +o-------ox----------------------x
  140    +x------------------------------x
  454    +o----------------------ox----x
  396    +x--------------------------------x
 1240    +o------------------ox--------------------x
 1277    +ox-xo--------------------------------------ox-x
  495    +x--------------------------------------------x
 1268    +x--------------------------------------------x
 1245    +x----------------------------------------xo----o
 1271    +x----------------------------------------------------x
   58    +x----------------------------------------------------x
 1085    +o-------------------------ox----------------------------------x
  331    +ox---------------------xo-------------------------------------------------o+
 1249    +x-------------------------------------------------------------------------x+
 1274    +x-------------------------------xo----------------------------------------o+
   18    +x-------------------------------------------------------------------------x+
 1266    +x-------------------------------------------------------------------------x+
   97    +x-------------------------------------------------------------------------x+
 1250    +o-------------------------------------------------------------------------o+
  382    +o-------------------------------------------------------------------------o+
   92    +x-------------------------------------------------------------------------x+
 1260    +o-------------------------------------------------------------------------o+
  473    +x-------------------------------------------------------------------------x+
  894    +o-------------------------------------------------------------------------o+
  339    +o-------------------------------------------------------------------------o+
 1265    +x-------------------------------------------------------------------------x+
  598    +o-------------------------------------------------------------------------o+
  885    +x-------------------------------------------------------------------------x+
  526    +o--------------------------------------------------------ox---------x+
   70    +o-------------------------------------------------------------------------o+
  510    +o-------------------------------------------------------------------------o+
  433    +o-----------------------------------------ox------------------------------x+
 1363    +x-------------------------------------------------------------------------x+
   37    +o-------------------------------------------------------------------------o+
 1120    +o-------------------------------------------------------------------------o+
  438    +x-------------------------------xo----------------------------------------o+
 1141    +x-------------------------------------------------------------------------x+
  622    +x-------------------------------------------------------------------------x+
  425    +x-------------------------------------------------------------------------x+
  534    +x-------------------------------------------------------------------------x+
  423    +x-------------------------------------------------------------------------x+
  246    +x-------------------------------------------------------------------------x+
  659    +x-------------------------------------------------------------------------x+
   19    +o-------------------------------------------------------------------------o+
 1161    +x-------------------------------------------------------------------------x+
  260    +x-------------------------------------------------------------------------x+
  457    +x-------------------------------------------------------------------------x+
  950    +o-------------------------------------------------------------------------o+
 1111    +o---------------------------+---------------------------------------------o+
  418    +o-------------------------------------------------------------------------o+
  439    +x-----------------------------------------xo------------------------------o+
```

## Women's Periodicals and Newspapers

```
           1922 1923 1924 1925 1926 1927 1928 1929 1930 1931 1932 1933 1934 1935 1936 1937
  763     +x--------------------------------------------------------------------x+
  893     +o--------------------------------------------------------------------o+
 1190     +o--------------------------------------------------------------------o+
  419     +o--------------------------------------------------------------------o+
 1337     +o--------------------------------------------------------------------o+
  381     +o--------------------------------------------------------------------o+
  450     +o--------------------------------------------------------------------o+
  621     +o--------------------------------------------------------------------o+
 1220     +x--------------------------------------------------------------------x+
  747     +o------------------------ox-----------------------------------------x+
  653     +x--------------------------------------------------------------------x+
  505     +x--------------------------------------------------------------------x+
  416     +o--------------------------------------------------------------------o+
  506     +o--------------------------------------------------------------------o+
  409     +o----------------------------ox----xo--------------ox---------------x+
  374     +x--------------------------------------------------------------------x+
  284     +o--------------------------------------------------ox---------------x+
  865      x-x
  801      x----------------------x
  181      x-xo-ox-xo-ox-xo-ox------------------------------------------------x+
  584      x-----------------------------------------------------------------x+
   93      x-----------------------------------------------------------------x+
  135           x-x
 1079           x-x
  133           x------x
  139           x------x
  802           x------x
 1106           x------xo--ox-xo-ox-xo-ox-x
  301           x----------------------------------------------------------x+
   78           o------ox---------x
  134           o------ox-xo--ox----x
  143           o--------------------------------ox-x
  762                x-x
 1307                x----------------------------------------------------x+
  481                o-------------ox-------------------------------------x+
  569                     x-------------------------------------x
  509                     o-----ox------------------------------------------x+
  807                          x-x
  879                          x-x
  266                          o-------------------ox-----------------------x+
  913                          o-----------------------------------------o+
 1218                               x--------------------------------------x+
  757                               o-----------------------ox------------x+
  895                                   x-x
  255                                   x------x
   38                                   x------------------------------x+
  137                                        o-----ox---------------------x
 1458                                        o------------------------------o+
 1447                                        x------------------------x
 1041                                        o------------------------------o+
 1131                                             x-----xo---------ox--------x
  262                                             x-----------------------x+
  245                                              x-x
  629                                                 x-xo-ox-xo-ox-xo-ox-xo-ox-xo------o+
  323                                                 o-----------------------o+
   80                                                  o----------------------o+
  761                                                       x------x
  751                                                       x------------x
  831                                                       x------------x
  753                                                       x-------------x+
  119                                                            o---------o+
  440                                                       x-------------x+
 1073                                                            o-----x-x
   59                                                            o---------o+
  302                                                                 x------x
```

350

## Women's Periodicals and Newspapers

```
           1922  1923  1924  1925  1926  1927  1928  1929  1930  1931  1932  1933  1934  1935  1936  1937
  292                                                                              x-xo---x--------x+
  603                                                                              o---------------o+
  265                                                                              o---------------o+
  921                                                                              o---------------o+
 1242                                                                                 o---------o+
 1223                                                                                       x---x+
 1262                                                                                       o---o+
  120                                                                                       o---o+
   32                                                                                       o---o+

           1938  1939  1940  1941  1942  1943  1944  1945  1946  1947  1948  1949  1950  1951  1952  1953
  753     +x--x
  331     +o-------o
 1249     +x-------x
 1223     +x-------x
 1274     +o-------------x
   18     +x-------------x
 1266     +x-------------x
   97     +x-------------x
  440     +x-------------x
 1250     +ox--------------------x
  382     +o-----------------------x
 1307     +x-----------------------xo---------o
   92     +x-------------------------------------------x
  629     +oox-xo-------ox-xo-------ox-xo----------------------ox-x
  292     +x-------------------------------------------------------x
 1260     +o----------------------------------------------------------o
  584     +x-----------------------------------------------------------x
  473     +x---------xo------------------------------------------------------o
  894     +o-------------------ox---------------------------------------------x
  301     +x-------------------------------------------------------------------x+
  339     +o-------------------------------------------------------------------o+
 1265     +x-------------------------------------------------------------------x+
  598     +oox-xo-----------------------------------------------------xo-------o+
  266     +x-------------------------------------------------------------------x+
  885     +x-------------------------------------------------------------------x+
  526     +x-------------------------------------------------------------------x+
   70     +o-------------------------------------------------------------------o+
  510     +o-------------------------------------------------------------------o+
  433     +x-------------------------------------------------------------------x+
  262     +x-------------------------------------------------------------------x+
  265     +o-------------------------------------------------------------------o+
 1363     +x-------------------------------------------------------------------x+
   38     +x-------------------------------------------------------------------x+
   59     +o---------------------------------------------------ox-xo-----------o+
   37     +o-------------------------------------------------------------------o+
 1120     +o-------------------------------------------------------------------o+
  438     +o----------------------------------------------------------------ox--x+
 1141     +x-------------------------------------------------------------------x+
  622     +o-------------------------------------------------------------------o+
  425     +x-------------------------------------------------------------------x+
  534     +x-------------------------------------------------------------------x+
  423     +x-------------------------------------------------------------------x+
  246     +x-------------------------------------------------------------------x+
  659     +x-------------------------------------------------------------------x+
   19     +o-------------------------------------------------------------------o+
 1161     +x-----------------------------------------------xo-------------ox--x+
  260     +x-------------------------------------------------------------------x+
  457     +x-------------------------------------------------------------------x+
  950     +o-------------------------------------------------------------------o+
 1111     +o-------------------------------------------------------------------o+
```

## Women's Periodicals and Newspapers

*Women's Periodicals and Newspapers*

## Women's Periodicals and Newspapers

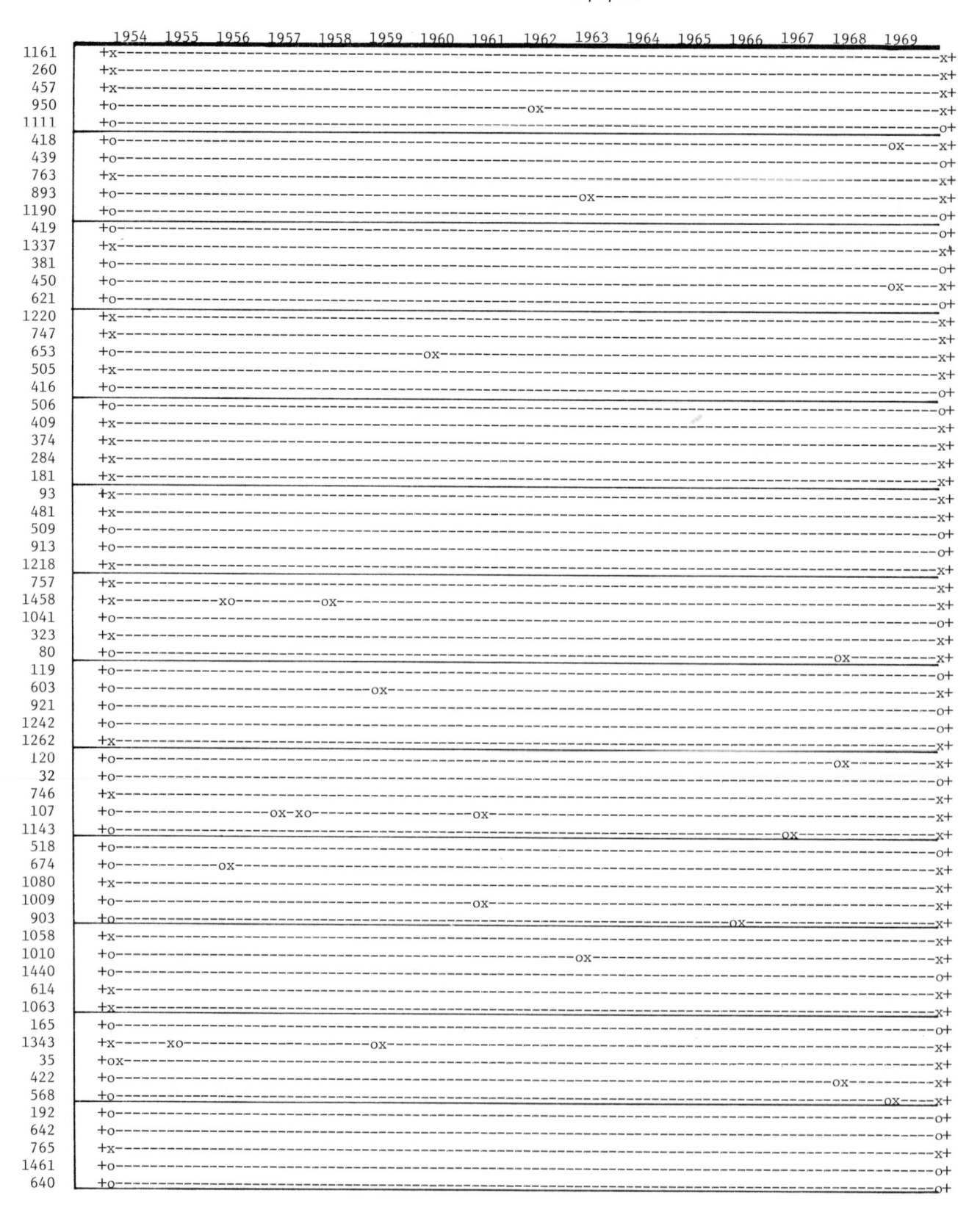

## Women's Periodicals and Newspapers

## Women's Periodicals and Newspapers

```
        1954  1955  1956  1957  1958  1959  1960  1961  1962  1963  1964  1965  1966  1967  1968  1969
294  ─────────────────────────────────────────────────────────────────────────────────────────────
980                                                                            x─────────────x+
992                                                                            x─────────────x+
1044                                                                           x─────────────x+
1393                                                                           x─────────────x+
298  ─────────────────────────────────────────────────────────────────────────x─────────────x+
1180                                                                           x─────────────x+
1231                                                                           x─────────────x+
912                                                                            x─────────────x+
351                                                                            o─────────────o+
1433 ─────────────────────────────────────────────────────────────────────────o─────────────o+
826                                                                            o─────────────o+
180                                                                               x─x
205                                                                               x──────x
588                                                                               x──────x
1163 ────────────────────────────────────────────────────────────────────────────x──────x
248                                                                               x──────x
366                                                                               x────────x+
841                                                                               x────────x+
945                                                                               x────────x+
853  ────────────────────────────────────────────────────────────────────────────x────────x+
684                                                                               x────────x+
1159                                                                              x────────x+
615                                                                               x─xo──────o+
784                                                                               x─xo──────o+
623  ───────────────────────────────────────────────────────────────────────────o─────ox──x+
272                                                                               o────────o+
630                                                                               o────────o+
1330                                                                              o────────o+
756                                                                               o────────o+
54   ─────────────────────────────────────────────────────────────────────────────o────────o+
138                                                                                  x─x
175                                                                                  x─x
235                                                                                  x─x
390                                                                                  x─x
451  ───────────────────────────────────────────────────────────────────────────────x─x
625                                                                                  x─x
671                                                                                  x─x
813                                                                                  x─x
815                                                                                  x─x
953  ───────────────────────────────────────────────────────────────────────────────x─x
983                                                                                  x─x
1067                                                                                 x─x
1093                                                                                 x─x
1392                                                                                 x─x
73   ───────────────────────────────────────────────────────────────────────────────x─x
90                                                                                   x────x+
233                                                                                  x────x+
436                                                                                  x────x+
689                                                                                  x────x+
917  ────────────────────────────────────────────────────────────────────────────────x────x+
1115                                                                                 x────x+
1403                                                                                 x────x+
2                                                                                    x────x+
335                                                                                  x────x+
850  ────────────────────────────────────────────────────────────────────────────────x────x+
1050                                                                                 x────x+
1454                                                                                 x────x+
462                                                                                  x────x+
1096                                                                                 x────x+
13   ────────────────────────────────────────────────────────────────────────────────x────x+
715                                                                                  x────x+
785                                                                                  x────x+
1020                                                                                 x────x+
16                                                                                   x────x+
```

## Women's Periodicals and Newspapers

|      | 1954 1955 1956 1957 1958 1959 1960 1961 1962 1963 1964 1965 1966 1967 1968 1969 |
|------|---|
| 681  | x---x+ |
| 682  | x---x+ |
| 702  | x---x+ |
| 711  | x---x+ |
| 824  | x---x+ |
| 1244 | x---x+ |
| 1394 | x---x+ |
| 1319 | x---x+ |
| 1327 | x---x+ |
| 55   | x---x+ |
| 317  | x---x+ |
| 327  | x---x+ |
| 799  | x---x+ |
| 962  | x---x+ |
| 951  | x---x+ |
| 1296 | x---x+ |
| 1166 | o---o+ |
| 680  | o---o+ |
| 493  | o---o+ |
| 117  | o---o+ |
| 772  | o---o+ |
| 221  | o---o+ |
| 744  | o---o+ |

|      | 1970 1971 1972 1973 1974 1975 1976 1977 1978 1979 1980 1981 CIO date |
|------|---|
| 172  | +x--x |
| 738  | +x--x |
| 814  | +x--x |
| 73   | +x--x |
| 90   | +x--x |
| 233  | +x--x |
| 436  | +x--x |
| 689  | +x--x |
| 917  | +x--x |
| 1115 | +x--x |
| 1403 | +x--x |
| 526  | +x-------x |
| 1193 | +x-------x |
| 254  | +ox-------x |
| 1290 | +x-------x |
| 1348 | +x-------x |
| 1051 | +x-------x |
| 494  | +xo-------o |
| 1122 | +x-------x |
| 248  | +x-------x |
| 366  | +x-------x |
| 841  | +x-------x |
| 945  | +x-------x |
| 784  | +x-------x |
| 2    | +x-------x |
| 335  | +x-------x |
| 850  | +x-------x |
| 1050 | +x-------x |
| 1454 | +x-------x |
| 344  | +ox------------x |
| 527  | +x------------x |
| 343  | +x------------x |
| 853  | +x------------x |
| 462  | +x------------x |
| 1096 | +x------------x |

## Women's Periodicals and Newspapers

```
           1970  1971  1972  1973  1974  1975  1976  1977  1978  1979  1980  1981  CIO date
   1096   +x--------------x
   1166   +o-ox-----------x
     70   +o-------------ox-----x
    510   +o-------ox----------x
    386   +o------ox-xo-------x-x
   1221   +x--------------------x
    201   +x--------------------x
     11   +x--------------------x
   1457   +x--------------------x
    684   +x--------------------x
     13   +x--------------------x
    715   +x--------------------x
    785   +x--------------------x
   1020   +x--------------------x
    433   +o------------------------o
    262   +x--------------------------x
    265   +o-ox-----------------------x
    497   +x--------------------------x
    672   +x------------xo----ox----x
    800   +x--------------------------x
   1165   +x--------------------------x
    741   +x-------xo----------ox----x
   1004   +x--------------------------x
      7   +x--------------------------x
   1342   +x-------xo---ox-xo------ox-x
     51   +x--------------------------x
    294   +x------xo----------ox----x
    980   +x--------------------------x
    992   +x--------------------------x
   1044   +x--------------------------x
   1393   +x--------------------------x
    351   +o---------------ox----x
   1159   +o-ox-----------------------x
     16   +x--------------------------x
    681   +x--------------------------x
    682   +x--------------------------x
    702   +x--------------------------x
    711   +x--------------------------x
    824   +x--------------------------x
   1244   +x--------------------------x
   1394   +x--------------------------x
    117   +o---------ox----------x
   1363   +x-----------------------------x
    902   +x-----------------------------x
    402   +o-----------ox-xo--------ox-----x
   1319   +x-----------------------------x
    194   +o-ox------------------xo-----o
    298   +x-----------------------------x
    615   +o------ox------------xo----ox----x
    772   +o---------------------ox---------x
   1344   +o-------------------ox----------------x
    272   +o-------ox------------------------------x
     38   +x------------------------------------x
     59   +o-------------------ox-----xo----ox-xo-ox-x
    144   +x----------------------------------------x
    383   +x----------------------------------------x
    465   +x----------------------------------------x
    430   +o-ox-------------------------------------x
   1327   +x----------------------------------------x
    680   +o-----ox---------------------------------x
    221   +o-----------------ox-xo------ox-xo------ox-x
     37   +x-----------------------------------------------x
   1167   +o--------------------------------ox----------x
   1120   +o-----------------------------------------ox---------------------x
    438   +x-------------------------------------------------------------------x
```

358

## Women's Periodicals and Newspapers

|      | 1970 | 1971 | 1972 | 1973 | 1974 | 1975 | 1976 | 1977 | 1978 | 1979 | 1980 | 1981 | CIO date |
|------|------|------|------|------|------|------|------|------|------|------|------|------|----------|
| 1141 | +x---------------------------------------------------------------------------x |
| 622  | +x---------------------------------------------------------------------------x |
| 425  | +x---------------------------------------------------------------------------x |
| 534  | +x---------------------------------------------------------------------------x |
| 423  | +x---------------------------------------------------------------------------x |
| 246  | +x---------------------------------------------------------------------------x |
| 659  | +x---------------------------------------------------------------------------x |
| 19   | +o---------------------------------------ox----------------------------------x |
| 1161 | +x---------------------------------------------------------------------------x |
| 260  | +x---------------------------------------------------------------------------x |
| 457  | +x---------------------------------------------------------------------------x |
| 950  | +x---------------------------------------------------------------------------x |
| 1111 | +o-ox------------------------------------------------------------------------x |
| 418  | +x---------------------------------------------------------------------------x |
| 439  | +o---------------------------------------------------------------------------o |
| 763  | +x---------------------------------------------------------------------------x |
| 893  | +x---------------------------------------------------------------------------x |
| 1190 | +o-ox------------------------------------------------------------------------x |
| 419  | +o---------------------------ox----------------------------------------------x |
| 1337 | +x---------------------------------------------------------------------------x |
| 381  | +o-------------------------------ox------------------------------------------x |
| 450  | +x-------------------xo------------------------------------------------------o |
| 621  | +o------------ox-------------------------------------------------------------x |
| 1220 | +x---------------------------------------------------------------------------x |
| 747  | +x---------------------------------------------------------------------------x |
| 653  | +x---------------------------------------------------------------------------x |
| 505  | +x---------------------------------------------------------------------------x |
| 416  | +o-------------------------------------ox------------------------------------x |
| 506  | +o--------------------------------------------ox-----------------------------x |
| 409  | +x---------------------------------------xo-----------ox---------------------x |
| 374  | +x---------------------------------------------------------------------------x |
| 284  | +x---------------------------------------------------------------------------x |
| 181  | +x---------------------------------------------------------------------------x |
| 93   | +x---------------------------------------------------------------------------x |
| 481  | +x---------------------------------------------------------------------------x |
| 509  | +o---------------------------------------------------------------------------o |
| 913  | +o-----------------ox-xo-----------------------ox-xo-ox----------------------x |
| 1218 | +x---------------------------------------------------------------------------x |
| 757  | +x-----------------------xo-------------------ox-----------------------------x |
| 1458 | +x---------------------------------------------------------------------------x |
| 1041 | +o-ox------------------------------------------------------------------------x |
| 323  | +x---------------------------------------------------------------------------x |
| 80   | +x---------------------------------------------------------------------------x |
| 119  | +o-----------------------------ox--------------------------------------------x |
| 603  | +x---------------------------------------------------------------------------x |
| 921  | +o-------------------------------------ox------------------------------------x |
| 1242 | +o------------ox-------------------------------------------------------------x |
| 1262 | +x---------------------------------------------------------------------------x |
| 120  | +x---------------------------------------------------------------------------x |
| 32   | +o---------------------------------ox----------------------------------------x |
| 746  | +x---------------------------------------------------------------------------x |
| 107  | +x---------------------------------------------------------------------------x |
| 1143 | +x---------------------------------------------------------------------------x |
| 518  | +o-----------------------------------------------------ox--------------------x |
| 674  | +x---------------------------------------------------------------------------x |
| 1080 | +x---------------------------------------------------------------------------x |
| 1009 | +x---------------------------------------------------------------------------x |
| 903  | +x---------------------------------------------------------------------------x |
| 1058 | +x---------------------------------------------------------------------------x |
| 1010 | +x---------------------------------------------------------------------------x |
| 1440 | +o----------------------------------------------------------------ox-----x |
| 614  | +x---------------------------------------------------------------------------x |
| 1063 | +x---------------------------------------------------------------------------x |
| 165  | +o----------------------------------------------------------------ox-----x |
| 1343 | +x---------------------------------------------------------------------------x |

## Women's Periodicals and Newspapers

```
            1970  1971  1972  1973  1974  1975  1976  1977  1978  1979  1980  1981  CIO  date
    35     +x-----------------------------------------------------------------------------x
   422     +x-----------------------------------------------------------------------------x
   568     +x-----------------------------------------------------------------------------x
   192     +o---------ox----------------------------------------------------------------x
   642     +o-------------------------------------------------------------ox-----------x
   765     +x-----------------------------------------------------------------------------x
  1461     +o--------------------------ox------------------------------------------------x
   640     +o------------------------------------------ox-xo-ox-xo-ox-------------------x
    10     +oox-xo-------------------------------------------------------------------o
  1456     +o-----------------------------------------------------------ox------------x
  1134     +o----------ox----------xo---------------------------------------------------o
   492     +o---------------------------ox----------------------------------------------x
   218     +x-------xo-----------------------------------ox----------------------------x
   214     +o--------------ox------------------------------------------------------------x
  1374     +o-------------------------ox-------------------xo------------------o
    33     +x-----------------------------------------------------------------------------x
  1011     +x-----------------------------------------------------------------------------x
  1347     +x---------------------xo----ox---------------------------------------------x
   338     +x-----------------------------------------------------------------------------x
   280     +x------------------xo---------------------------ox-------------------------x
  1243     +x-----------------------------------------------------------------------------x
   342     +o------------------------------------ox-xo----------ox--------------------x
   862     +o----------ox-xo-ox-xo----------ox-------------------------------------------x
   207     +o---------------------------ox-------------------xo------------------------o
   878     +o-----------------------------------------------------ox-------------------x
   752     +o---------------------------------------------------ox--------------------x
  1180     +x-----------------------------------------------------------------------------x
  1231     +x-----------------------------------------------------------------------------x
   912     +o---------ox----------------------------------------------------------------x
  1433     +o------------------------------------------------------------ox----x
   623     +oox-------------------------------------------------------------------------x
   630     +o---------------ox-----------------------------------------------------------x
  1330     +o----------------------------------------ox--------------------------------x
   756     +o------------------------------------------------ox-------------------------x
    55     +x----------------xo---------ox------------------------------------------------x
   317     +x-----------------------------------------------------------------------------x
   327     +x-----------------------------------------------------------------------------x
   799     +x-----------------------------------------------------------------------------x
   962     +x-----------------------------------------------------------------------------x
   951     +x-----------------------------------------------------------------------------x
  1296     +x-----------------------------------------------------------------------------x
   744     +o-------------------------------------------------ox------------------------x
    25       x-x
    99       x-x
   267       x-x
   279       x-x
   290       x-x
   299       x-x
   320       x-x
   354       x-x
   504       x-x
   650       x-x
   669       x-x
   811       x-x
   817       x-x
   822       x-x
   857       x-x
   898       x-x
   901       x-x
   936       x-x
   986       x-x
  1018       x-x
 =1035       x-x
  1042       x-x
  1083       x-x
```

360

## Women's Periodicals and Newspapers

|      | 1970 | 1971 | 1972 | 1973 | 1974 | 1975 | 1976 | 1977 | 1978 | 1979 | 1980 | 1981 | CIO date |
|------|------|------|------|------|------|------|------|------|------|------|------|------|----------|
| 1108 | x-x |
| 1124 | x-x |
| 1136 | x-x |
| 1139 | x-x |
| 1164 | x-x |
| 1195 | x-x |
| 1199 | x-x |
| 1251 | x-x |
| 1282 | x-x |
| 1294 | x-x |
| 1329 | x-x |
| 1352 | x-x |
| 1358 | x-x |
| 1381 | x-x |
| 1404 | x-x |
| 114  | x------x |
| 125  | x------x |
| 126  | x------x |
| 130  | x------x |
| 161  | x------x |
| 183  | x------x |
| 213  | x------x |
| 444  | x------x |
| 463  | x------x |
| 491  | x------x |
| 574  | x------x |
| 596  | x------x |
| 709  | x------x |
| 733  | x------x |
| 734  | x------x |
| 777  | x------x |
| 778  | x------x |
| 823  | x------x |
| 886  | x------x |
| 949  | x------x |
| 1005 | x------x |
| 1007 | x------x |
| 1128 | x------x |
| 1217 | x------x |
| 1256 | x------x |
| 1401 | x------x |
| 1402 | x------x |
| 1423 | x------x |
| 206  | x------------x |
| 315  | x------------x |
| 471  | x------------x |
| 833  | x------------x |
| 924  | x------------x |
| 1037 | x------------x |
| 1154 | x------------x |
| 237  | x------------------x |
| 240  | x------------------x |
| 424  | x------------------x |
| 435  | x------------------x |
| 592  | x------------------x |
| 620  | x-xo-ox-xo---------x-x |
| 628  | x------------------x |
| 673  | x------------------x |
| 795  | x-xo---------ox------x |
| 994  | x------------------x |
| 1349 | x-----xo-----ox------x |
| 1372 | x------------------x |
| 6    | x--------------------------x |
| 24   | x--------------------------x |
| 63   | x--------------------------x |

## Women's Periodicals and Newspapers

```
        1970   1971   1972   1973   1974   1975   1976   1977   1978   1979   1980   1981   CIO date
  46     x-----xo---------ox-----x
  47     x------------------------x
  82     x------------------------x
 261     x------------------------x
 312     x------------------------x
 334     x------------------------x
 397     x------------------------x
 447     x------------------------x
 461     x------------------------x
 499     x------------------------x
 696     x-xo--------ox-----------x
 697     x------------------------x
 705     x------------------------x
 712     x------------------------x
 721     x------------------------x
 821     x------------------------x
 845     x------------------------x
 860     x------------------------x
 909     x------------------------x
 911     x------------------------x
 988     x------------------------x
1036     x------------------------x
1065     x------------------------x
1069     x------------------------x
1090     x------------------------x
1094     x------------------------x
1201     x------------------------x
1396     x------------------------x
1436     x------------------------x
1006     x-------------------------------x
1028     x-------------------------------x
1420     x---------------------xo----------------------------o
1207     x---------------------xo-----------------ox---------x
 150     x-----------------------------------------------------------------x
 337     x-----------------------------------------------------------------x
 367     x-----------------------------------------------------------------x
 519     x-----------------------------------------------------------------x
 861     x-----------------------------------------------------------------x
 896     x-----------------------------------------------------------------x
1075     x-----------------------------------------------------------------x
1228     x-----------------------------------------------------------------x
 508     o-----ox-x
 190     o-----ox------------x
1185     o-----ox-----------------x
 116     o-----ox-----------------------------------------------------------x
 308     o-----ox-----------------------------------------------------------x
1334     o-----ox-----------------------------------------------------------x
 166     o-----------ox-x
 187     o-----------ox-xo--------ox-xo-ox-----------xo-ox----x
 503     o-----------------ox-x
 479     o---------------------------ox-----------------x
 341     o---------------------------ox-------------------------------------x
1024     o---------------------------------------------------------ox----x
   9           x-x
  57           x-x
  64           x-x
  79           x-x
  84           x-x
 109           x-x
 115           x-x
 186           x-x
 226           x-x
 247           x-x
 274           x-x
 287           x-x
```

## Women's Periodicals and Newspapers

|      | 1970 | 1971 | 1972 | 1973 | 1974 | 1975 | 1976 | 1977 | 1978 | 1979 | 1980 | 1981 | CIO date |
|------|------|------|------|------|------|------|------|------|------|------|------|------|----------|
| 332  |      | x-x  |      |      |      |      |      |      |      |      |      |      |          |
| 333  |      | x-x  |      |      |      |      |      |      |      |      |      |      |          |
| 375  |      | x-x  |      |      |      |      |      |      |      |      |      |      |          |
| 426  |      | x-x  |      |      |      |      |      |      |      |      |      |      |          |
| 434  |      | x-x  |      |      |      |      |      |      |      |      |      |      |          |
| 453  |      | x-x  |      |      |      |      |      |      |      |      |      |      |          |
| 468  |      | x-x  |      |      |      |      |      |      |      |      |      |      |          |
| 470  |      | x-x  |      |      |      |      |      |      |      |      |      |      |          |
| 565  |      | x-x  |      |      |      |      |      |      |      |      |      |      |          |
| 601  |      | x-x  |      |      |      |      |      |      |      |      |      |      |          |
| 683  |      | x-x  |      |      |      |      |      |      |      |      |      |      |          |
| 724  |      | x-x  |      |      |      |      |      |      |      |      |      |      |          |
| 728  |      | x-x  |      |      |      |      |      |      |      |      |      |      |          |
| 737  |      | x-x  |      |      |      |      |      |      |      |      |      |      |          |
| 743  |      | x-x  |      |      |      |      |      |      |      |      |      |      |          |
| 758  |      | x-x  |      |      |      |      |      |      |      |      |      |      |          |
| 810  |      | x-x  |      |      |      |      |      |      |      |      |      |      |          |
| 816  |      | x-x  |      |      |      |      |      |      |      |      |      |      |          |
| 818  |      | x-x  |      |      |      |      |      |      |      |      |      |      |          |
| 819  |      | x-x  |      |      |      |      |      |      |      |      |      |      |          |
| 825  |      | x-x  |      |      |      |      |      |      |      |      |      |      |          |
| 827  |      | x-x  |      |      |      |      |      |      |      |      |      |      |          |
| 828  |      | x-x  |      |      |      |      |      |      |      |      |      |      |          |
| 844  |      | x-x  |      |      |      |      |      |      |      |      |      |      |          |
| 858  |      | x-x  |      |      |      |      |      |      |      |      |      |      |          |
| 874  |      | x-x  |      |      |      |      |      |      |      |      |      |      |          |
| 876  |      | x-x  |      |      |      |      |      |      |      |      |      |      |          |
| 899  |      | x-x  |      |      |      |      |      |      |      |      |      |      |          |
| 904  |      | x-x  |      |      |      |      |      |      |      |      |      |      |          |
| 948  |      | x-x  |      |      |      |      |      |      |      |      |      |      |          |
| 959  |      | x-x  |      |      |      |      |      |      |      |      |      |      |          |
| 964  |      | x-x  |      |      |      |      |      |      |      |      |      |      |          |
| 1002 |      | x-x  |      |      |      |      |      |      |      |      |      |      |          |
| 1019 |      | x-x  |      |      |      |      |      |      |      |      |      |      |          |
| 1033 |      | x-x  |      |      |      |      |      |      |      |      |      |      |          |
| 1040 |      | x-x  |      |      |      |      |      |      |      |      |      |      |          |
| 1045 |      | x-x  |      |      |      |      |      |      |      |      |      |      |          |
| 1084 |      | x-x  |      |      |      |      |      |      |      |      |      |      |          |
| 1104 |      | x-x  |      |      |      |      |      |      |      |      |      |      |          |
| 1109 |      | x-x  |      |      |      |      |      |      |      |      |      |      |          |
| 1118 |      | x-x  |      |      |      |      |      |      |      |      |      |      |          |
| 1121 |      | x-x  |      |      |      |      |      |      |      |      |      |      |          |
| 1133 |      | x-x  |      |      |      |      |      |      |      |      |      |      |          |
| 1135 |      | x-x  |      |      |      |      |      |      |      |      |      |      |          |
| 1137 |      | x-x  |      |      |      |      |      |      |      |      |      |      |          |
| 1153 |      | x-x  |      |      |      |      |      |      |      |      |      |      |          |
| 1184 |      | x-x  |      |      |      |      |      |      |      |      |      |      |          |
| 1213 |      | x-x  |      |      |      |      |      |      |      |      |      |      |          |
| 1254 |      | x-x  |      |      |      |      |      |      |      |      |      |      |          |
| 1298 |      | x-x  |      |      |      |      |      |      |      |      |      |      |          |
| 1314 |      | x-x  |      |      |      |      |      |      |      |      |      |      |          |
| 1357 |      | x-x  |      |      |      |      |      |      |      |      |      |      |          |
| 1413 |      | x-x  |      |      |      |      |      |      |      |      |      |      |          |
| 1038 |      | x-xo---o |  |      |      |      |      |      |      |      |      |      |          |
| 77   |      | x------x |  |      |      |      |      |      |      |      |      |      |          |
| 122  |      | x------x |  |      |      |      |      |      |      |      |      |      |          |
| 234  |      | x------x |  |      |      |      |      |      |      |      |      |      |          |
| 360  |      | x------x |  |      |      |      |      |      |      |      |      |      |          |
| 513  |      | x------x |  |      |      |      |      |      |      |      |      |      |          |
| 661  |      | x------x |  |      |      |      |      |      |      |      |      |      |          |
| 851  |      | x------x |  |      |      |      |      |      |      |      |      |      |          |
| 882  |      | x------x |  |      |      |      |      |      |      |      |      |      |          |
| 931  |      | x------x |  |      |      |      |      |      |      |      |      |      |          |
| 933  |      | x------x |  |      |      |      |      |      |      |      |      |      |          |
| 947  |      | x------x |  |      |      |      |      |      |      |      |      |      |          |

## Women's Periodicals and Newspapers

| ID | 1970 | 1971 | 1972 | 1973 | 1974 | 1975 | 1976 | 1977 | 1978 | 1979 | 1980 | 1981 | CIO date |
|---|---|---|---|---|---|---|---|---|---|---|---|---|---|
| 947  | | x------x | | | | | | | | | | | |
| 982  | | x------x | | | | | | | | | | | |
| 1003 | | x------x | | | | | | | | | | | |
| 1071 | | x------x | | | | | | | | | | | |
| 1086 | | x------x | | | | | | | | | | | |
| 1155 | | x------x | | | | | | | | | | | |
| 1269 | | x------x | | | | | | | | | | | |
| 1291 | | x------x | | | | | | | | | | | |
| 1339 | | x------x | | | | | | | | | | | |
| 1355 | | x------x | | | | | | | | | | | |
| 1385 | | x------x | | | | | | | | | | | |
| 1450 | | x------x | | | | | | | | | | | |
| 8    | | x------------x | | | | | | | | | | | |
| 67   | | x------------x | | | | | | | | | | | |
| 91   | | x------------x | | | | | | | | | | | |
| 152  | | x------------x | | | | | | | | | | | |
| 193  | | x------------x | | | | | | | | | | | |
| 230  | | x------------x | | | | | | | | | | | |
| 307  | | x------------x | | | | | | | | | | | |
| 656  | | x------------x | | | | | | | | | | | |
| 852  | | x------------x | | | | | | | | | | | |
| 856  | | x------------x | | | | | | | | | | | |
| 958  | | x------------x | | | | | | | | | | | |
| 1027 | | x------------x | | | | | | | | | | | |
| 1188 | | x------------x | | | | | | | | | | | |
| 1253 | | x------------x | | | | | | | | | | | |
| 1370 | | x------------x | | | | | | | | | | | |
| 1444 | | x------------x | | | | | | | | | | | |
| 820  | | x-xo---------o | | | | | | | | | | | |
| 798  | | x-----xo-----o | | | | | | | | | | | |
| 253  | | o-----ox-----x | | | | | | | | | | | |
| 1160 | | o---------x-x | | | | | | | | | | | |
| 15   | | x-----------------x | | | | | | | | | | | |
| 17   | | x-----------------x | | | | | | | | | | | |
| 66   | | x-----------------x | | | | | | | | | | | |
| 110  | | x-----------------x | | | | | | | | | | | |
| 128  | | x-xo--------ox-----x | | | | | | | | | | | |
| 162  | | x-----------------x | | | | | | | | | | | |
| 178  | | x-----------------x | | | | | | | | | | | |
| 185  | | x-----------------x | | | | | | | | | | | |
| 188  | | x-----------------x | | | | | | | | | | | |
| 191  | | x-----------------x | | | | | | | | | | | |
| 411  | | x-----------------x | | | | | | | | | | | |
| 517  | | x-----------------x | | | | | | | | | | | |
| 563  | | x-----------------x | | | | | | | | | | | |
| 566  | | x-----------------x | | | | | | | | | | | |
| 611  | | x-----------------x | | | | | | | | | | | |
| 613  | | x-----------------x | | | | | | | | | | | |
| 626  | | x-----------------x | | | | | | | | | | | |
| 678  | | x-----------------x | | | | | | | | | | | |
| 688  | | x-----------------x | | | | | | | | | | | |
| 706  | | x-----------------x | | | | | | | | | | | |
| 707  | | x-----------------x | | | | | | | | | | | |
| 710  | | x-----------------x | | | | | | | | | | | |
| 714  | | x-----------------x | | | | | | | | | | | |
| 718  | | x-----------------x | | | | | | | | | | | |
| 725  | | x-----------------x | | | | | | | | | | | |
| 735  | | x-----------------x | | | | | | | | | | | |
| 766  | | x-----------------x | | | | | | | | | | | |
| 767  | | x-----------------x | | | | | | | | | | | |
| 771  | | x-----------------x | | | | | | | | | | | |
| 804  | | x-----------------x | | | | | | | | | | | |
| 829  | | x-----------------x | | | | | | | | | | | |
| 869  | | x-----------------x | | | | | | | | | | | |
| 871  | | x-----------------x | | | | | | | | | | | |

## Women's Periodicals and Newspapers

```
             1970 1971 1972 1973 1974 1975 1976 1977 1978 1979 1980 1981  CIO  date
 943              x------------------x
 995              x------------------x
 996              x------------------x
1049              x------------------x
1238              x------------------x
1316              x------------------x
1321              x------------------x
1354              x------------------x
1412              x------------------x
1414              x------------------x
1426              x------------------x
 403              o-----ox-----------x
1125              x-----------------------x
 151              x---------------------------x
 101              x-------------------------------x
 927              x-------------------------------x
 928              x-------------------------------x
1400              o---------------------ox-xo---o
 576              x-----------------------------------x
1148              x-----------xo---------------------------o
1257              x-----------xo-----------------------o
 421              x-------------------------------x
 278              x-----------------------------------------------------x
 663              x-----------------------------------------------------x
 739              x-----------------------------------------------------x
 839              x-----------xo------------------ox-------------x
 867              x-----------------------------------------------------x
 984              x-----------------------------------------------------x
1000              x-----------------------------------------------------x
1008              x-----------------------------------------------------x
1309              x-----------------------------------------------------x
1353              x-----------------------------------------------------x
1424              x-----------------------------------------------------x
1142              x-----------xo----------------------------ox-xo---o
1173              x---------------xo---ox-xo-ox-----xo------------------ox-xo---o
 610              o-----------ox-----------------------------------------x
1333              o-----------------------ox-----------------------------x
 347              o-----------------------------ox-----------------------x
 790              o-----------------------------------ox-----------------x
 330              o-----------------------------------------------ox-xo---o
  20                        x-x
  81                        x-x
  98                        x-x
 127                        x-x
 195                        x-x
 220                        x-x
 325                        x-x
 358                        x-x
 376                        x-x
 399                        x-x
 404                        x-x
 407                        x-x
 452                        x-x
 575                        x-x
 586                        x-x
 635                        x-x
 644                        x-x
 657                        x-x
 679                        x-x
 687                        x-x
 695                        x-x
 699                        x-x
 717                        x-x
 731                        x-x
 768                        x-x
```

## Women's Periodicals and Newspapers

```
        1970  1971  1972  1973  1974  1975  1976  1977  1978  1979  1980  1981  CIO date
 797                 x-x
 805                 x-x
 832                 x-x
 835                 x-x
 873                 x-x
 914                 x-x
 935                 x-x
 867                 x-x
 973                 x-x
 985                 x-x
1039                 x-x
1076                 x-x
1117                 x-x
1170                 x-x
1235                 x-x
1369                 x-x
1387                 x-x
1391                 x-x
1410                 x-x
1452                 x-x
  69                 x------x
 177                 x------x
 232                 x------x
 243                 x------x
 345                 x------x
 369                 x------x
 395                 x------x
 400                 x------x
 406                 x------x
 414                 x------x
 431                 x------x
 582                 x------x
 675                 x------x
 910                 x------x
 938                 x------x
 989                 x------x
 990                 x------x
1052                 x------x
1068                 x------x
1202                 x------x
1335                 x------x
1360                 x------x
1366                 x------x
1389                 x------x
 356                 o-----x-x
 730                 o-----x-x
  29                 x-----------x
  36                 x-----------x
  49                 x-----------x
  60                 x-----------x
 123                 x-----------x
 158                 x-----------x
 159                 x-----------x
 184                 x-----------x
 208                 x-----------x
 215                 x-----------x
 216                 x-----------x
 225                 x-----------x
 239                 x-----------x
 244                 x-----------x
 313                 x-----------x
 353                 x-----------x
 365                 x-----------x
 373                 x-----------x
 394                 x-----------x
```

## Women's Periodicals and Newspapers

|      | 1970 | 1971 | 1972 | 1973 | 1974 | 1975 | 1976 | 1977 | 1978 | 1979 | 1980 | 1981 | CIO date |
|------|------|------|------|------|------|------|------|------|------|------|------|------|----------|
| 394  |      |      | x----------x |
| 437  |      |      | x----------x |
| 445  |      |      | x----------x |
| 446  |      |      | x----------x |
| 472  |      |      | x----------x |
| 567  |      |      | x----------x |
| 591  |      |      | x----------x |
| 643  |      |      | x----------x |
| 645  |      |      | x----------x |
| 649  |      |      | x----------x |
| 667  |      |      | x----------x |
| 685  |      |      | x----------x |
| 690  |      |      | x----------x |
| 700  |      |      | x----------x |
| 703  |      |      | x----------x |
| 719  |      |      | x----------x |
| 720  |      |      | x----------x |
| 740  |      |      | x----------x |
| 834  |      |      | x----------x |
| 877  |      |      | x----------x |
| 937  |      |      | x----------x |
| 939  |      |      | x----------x |
| 970  |      |      | x----------x |
| 971  |      |      | x----------x |
| 991  |      |      | x----------x |
| 993  |      |      | x----------x |
| 1031 |      |      | x----------x |
| 1034 |      |      | x----------x |
| 1087 |      |      | x----------x |
| 1097 |      |      | x----------x |
| 1116 |      |      | x----------x |
| 1127 |      |      | x----------x |
| 1172 |      |      | x----------x |
| 1212 |      |      | x----------x |
| 1239 |      |      | x----------x |
| 1241 |      |      | x----------x |
| 1295 |      |      | x----------x |
| 1313 |      |      | x----------x |
| 1322 |      |      | x----------x |
| 1356 |      |      | x----------x |
| 1373 |      |      | x----------x |
| 1405 |      |      | x----------x |
| 1417 |      |      | x----------x |
| 1437 |      |      | x----------x |
| 1455 |      |      | x----------x |
| 281  |      |      | x-----xo-----o |
| 524  |      |      | o----ox-xo---o |
| 28   |      |      | o-----ox-----x |
| 26   |      |      | o-----ox-----x |
| 282  |      |      | o-----ox-----x |
| 326  |      |      | x---------------x |
| 581  |      |      | x---------------x |
| 1300 |      |      | x---------------x |
| 1411 |      |      | x---------------x |
| 31   |      |      | x-----xo----------o |
| 346  |      |      | x---------------------------x |
| 449  |      |      | x---------------------------x |
| 500  |      |      | x-----xo--------------------x |
| 1016 |      |      | o------------------ox----------x |
| 176  |      |      | x-----------------------xo------------------------------o |
| 12   |      |      | o-------------------ox------------------------------x |
| 30   |      |      | x----------------------------------------------------x |
| 189  |      |      | x----------------------------------------------------x |
| 306  |      |      | x----------------------------------------------------x |
| 321  |      |      | x----------------------------------------------------x |

## Women's Periodicals and Newspapers

```
         1970  1971  1972  1973  1974  1975  1976  1977  1978  1979  1980  1981  CIO  date
 328                 x-------------------------------------------------------------x
 514                 o-----------------------------ox------------------------------x
 624                 x-------------------------------------------------------------x
 664                 x-------------------------------------------------------------x
 780                 x-----------xo----ox-----------------------------------------x
 863                 x-----------xo-----------------------ox-----------------------x
1066                 x-----------xo-------------------------------------ox-xo---o
1119                 o-------------------------------------------------ox-xo---o
1229                 x-------------------------------------------------------------x
1306                 x-------------------------------------------------------------x
1310                 o-----ox-----------------------------------------------------x
1350                 x-------------------------------------------------------------x
1427                 x-------------------------------------------------------------x
1431                 x-------------------------------------------------------------x
   3                       x-x
  43                       x-x
  72                       x-x
 124                       x-x
 163                       x-x
 169                       x-x
 170                       x-x
 236                       x-x
 252                       x-x
 286                       x-x
 309                       x-x
 316                       x-x
 322                       x-x
 371                       x-x
 377                       x-x
 380                       x-x
 388                       x-x
 405                       x-x
 417                       x-x
 515                       x-x
 573                       x-x
 580                       x-x
 609                       x-x
 655                       x-x
 665                       x-x
 722                       x-x
 774                       x-x
 775                       x-x
 791                       x-x
 830                       x-x
 859                       x-x
 866                       x-x
 872                       x-x
 880                       x-x
 888                       x-x
 889                       x-x
 890                       x-x
 892                       x-x
 916                       x-x
 922                       x-x
 977                       x-x
 999                       x-x
1015                       x-x
1046                       x-x
1057                       x-x
1061                       x-x
1099                       x-x
1100                       x-x
1112                       x-x
1169                       x-x
1171                       x-x
```

## Women's Periodicals and Newspapers

|      | 1970 | 1971 | 1972 | 1973 | 1974 | 1975 | 1976 | 1977 | 1978 | 1979 | 1980 | 1981 | CIO date |
|------|------|------|------|------|------|------|------|------|------|------|------|------|----------|
| 1178 |      |      |      | x-x  |      |      |      |      |      |      |      |      |          |
| 1182 |      |      |      | x-x  |      |      |      |      |      |      |      |      |          |
| 1196 |      |      |      | x-x  |      |      |      |      |      |      |      |      |          |
| 1205 |      |      |      | x-x  |      |      |      |      |      |      |      |      |          |
| 1216 |      |      |      | x-x  |      |      |      |      |      |      |      |      |          |
| 1234 |      |      |      | x-x  |      |      |      |      |      |      |      |      |          |
| 1236 |      |      |      | x-x  |      |      |      |      |      |      |      |      |          |
| 1237 |      |      |      | x-x  |      |      |      |      |      |      |      |      |          |
| 1276 |      |      |      | x-x  |      |      |      |      |      |      |      |      |          |
| 1293 |      |      |      | x-x  |      |      |      |      |      |      |      |      |          |
| 1345 |      |      |      | x-x  |      |      |      |      |      |      |      |      |          |
| 1367 |      |      |      | x-x  |      |      |      |      |      |      |      |      |          |
| 1453 |      |      |      | x-x  |      |      |      |      |      |      |      |      |          |
| 564  |      |      |      | x-xo---o |  |      |      |      |      |      |      |      |          |
| 571  |      |      |      | x-xo---o |  |      |      |      |      |      |      |      |          |
| 579  |      |      |      | x-xo---o |  |      |      |      |      |      |      |      |          |
| 1176 |      |      |      | x-xo---o |  |      |      |      |      |      |      |      |          |
| 89   |      |      |      | o---ox-x |  |      |      |      |      |      |      |      |          |
| 168  |      |      |      | o---ox-x |  |      |      |      |      |      |      |      |          |
| 870  |      |      |      | o---ox-x |  |      |      |      |      |      |      |      |          |
| 1442 |      |      |      | o---ox-x |  |      |      |      |      |      |      |      |          |
| 4    |      |      |      | x------x |  |      |      |      |      |      |      |      |          |
| 48   |      |      |      | x------x |  |      |      |      |      |      |      |      |          |
| 50   |      |      |      | x------x |  |      |      |      |      |      |      |      |          |
| 61   |      |      |      | x------x |  |      |      |      |      |      |      |      |          |
| 65   |      |      |      | x------x |  |      |      |      |      |      |      |      |          |
| 68   |      |      |      | x------x |  |      |      |      |      |      |      |      |          |
| 74   |      |      |      | x------x |  |      |      |      |      |      |      |      |          |
| 76   |      |      |      | x------x |  |      |      |      |      |      |      |      |          |
| 85   |      |      |      | x------x |  |      |      |      |      |      |      |      |          |
| 87   |      |      |      | x------x |  |      |      |      |      |      |      |      |          |
| 88   |      |      |      | x------x |  |      |      |      |      |      |      |      |          |
| 157  |      |      |      | x------x |  |      |      |      |      |      |      |      |          |
| 167  |      |      |      | x------x |  |      |      |      |      |      |      |      |          |
| 179  |      |      |      | x------x |  |      |      |      |      |      |      |      |          |
| 203  |      |      |      | x------x |  |      |      |      |      |      |      |      |          |
| 210  |      |      |      | x------x |  |      |      |      |      |      |      |      |          |
| 223  |      |      |      | x------x |  |      |      |      |      |      |      |      |          |
| 242  |      |      |      | x------x |  |      |      |      |      |      |      |      |          |
| 250  |      |      |      | x------x |  |      |      |      |      |      |      |      |          |
| 263  |      |      |      | x------x |  |      |      |      |      |      |      |      |          |
| 305  |      |      |      | x------x |  |      |      |      |      |      |      |      |          |
| 318  |      |      |      | x------x |  |      |      |      |      |      |      |      |          |
| 348  |      |      |      | x------x |  |      |      |      |      |      |      |      |          |
| 355  |      |      |      | x------x |  |      |      |      |      |      |      |      |          |
| 357  |      |      |      | x------x |  |      |      |      |      |      |      |      |          |
| 391  |      |      |      | x------x |  |      |      |      |      |      |      |      |          |
| 393  |      |      |      | x------x |  |      |      |      |      |      |      |      |          |
| 469  |      |      |      | x------x |  |      |      |      |      |      |      |      |          |
| 482  |      |      |      | x------x |  |      |      |      |      |      |      |      |          |
| 489  |      |      |      | x------x |  |      |      |      |      |      |      |      |          |
| 507  |      |      |      | x------x |  |      |      |      |      |      |      |      |          |
| 525  |      |      |      | x------x |  |      |      |      |      |      |      |      |          |
| 562  |      |      |      | x------x |  |      |      |      |      |      |      |      |          |
| 589  |      |      |      | x------x |  |      |      |      |      |      |      |      |          |
| 594  |      |      |      | x------x |  |      |      |      |      |      |      |      |          |
| 632  |      |      |      | x------x |  |      |      |      |      |      |      |      |          |
| 646  |      |      |      | x------x |  |      |      |      |      |      |      |      |          |
| 651  |      |      |      | x------x |  |      |      |      |      |      |      |      |          |
| 666  |      |      |      | x------x |  |      |      |      |      |      |      |      |          |
| 686  |      |      |      | x------x |  |      |      |      |      |      |      |      |          |
| 693  |      |      |      | x------x |  |      |      |      |      |      |      |      |          |
| 694  |      |      |      | x------x |  |      |      |      |      |      |      |      |          |
| 698  |      |      |      | x------x |  |      |      |      |      |      |      |      |          |
| 704  |      |      |      | x------x |  |      |      |      |      |      |      |      |          |

## Women's Periodicals and Newspapers

```
       1970  1971  1972  1973  1974  1975  1976  1977  1978  1979  1980  1981  CIO  date
 708                     x------x
 713                     x------x
 716                     x------x
 723                     x------x
 726                     x------x
 727                     x------x
 729                     x------x
 742                     x------x
 760                     x------x
 770                     x------x
 781                     x------x
 803                     x------x
 836                     x------x
 837                     x------x
 868                     x------x
 887                     x------x
 905                     x------x
 919                     x------x
 925                     x------x
 944                     x------x
 960                     x------x
 972                     x------x
 976                     x------x
 987                     x------x
 997                     x------x
1032                     x------x
1059                     x------x
1078                     x------x
1107                     x------x
1113                     x------x
1123                     x------x
1130                     x------x
1147                     x------x
1149                     x------x
1156                     x------x
1284                     x------x
1317                     x------x
1320                     x------x
1325                     x------x
1328                     x------x
1371                     x------x
1399                     x------x
1407                     x------x
1451                     x------x
 271                     x-----------x
1144                     x-----------x
 981                     x-----------------x
1186                     x-----xo----ox-----x
 108                     x-------------------------------x
 952                     x-----xo---------ox------------x
 608                          o-----ox------------------------x
1077                          o-----------------ox----xo------o
 251                     x-xo-----------------------ox------------x
1029                          o-----ox---------------------------------x
1421                          o-----------------------ox-----------x
 249                     x---------------------------xo----------------o
  95                     x---------------------------------------------------------------x
 112                     x---------------------------------------------------------------x
 200                     x---------------------------------------------------------------x
 285                     x-xo-ox-xo--------ox-xo-ox-xo--------------------------------o
 370                     x---------------------------------------------------------------x
 428                     x---------------------------------------------------------------x
1082                     x---------------------------------------------------------------x
1102                     x---------------------------------------------------------------x
1175                     x---------------------------------------------------------------x
```

## Women's Periodicals and Newspapers

```
         1970  1971  1972  1973  1974  1975  1976  1977  1978  1979  1980  1981  CIO  date
1208                       x------------------------------------------------------x
1230                       x------------------------------------------------------x
1361                       x------------------------------------------------------x
 961                       o-----------------------ox------------------------------x
 633                       o-------------------------------------ox----------------x
 105                       o-------------------------------------------------ox-xo---o
   1                             x-x
  42                             x-x
 154                             x-x
 156                             x-x
 217                             x-x
 222                             x-x
 229                             x-x
 238                             x-x
 241                             x-x
 289                             x-x
 349                             x-x
 361                             x-x
 363                             x-x
 443                             x-x
 648                             x-x
 662                             x-x
 691                             x-x
 692                             x-x
 701                             x-x
 732                             x-x
 759                             x-x
 769                             x-x
 793                             x-x
 806                             x-x
 808                             x-x
 842                             x-x
 848                             x-x
 881                             x-x
 900                             x-x
 923                             x-x
 946                             x-x
 998                             x-x
1001                             x-x
1056                             x-x
1072                             x-x
1089                             x-x
1091                             x-x
1152                             x-x
1191                             x-x
1206                             x-x
1210                             x-x
1214                             x-x
1324                             x-x
1331                             x-x
1336                             x-x
1368                             x-x
1376                             x-x
1382                             x-x
1384                             x-x
1397                             x-x
1415                             x-x
 487                             o----ox-x
1406                             x------x
 269                             x-----------x
1203                             x-----------x
1224                             x-----------x
 475                             o-ox-------------x
 578                             x---------------x
1145                             x----------------------x
```

371

## Women's Periodicals and Newspapers

```
         1970  1971  1972  1973  1974  1975  1976  1977  1978  1979  1980  1981  CIO  date
1439                                   x-----------------------x
 196                                   x-----------------------------x
 849                                   o-----------------------ox----xo-----o
 160                                   o--------------------ox---------------x
  21                                   o-----------ox-------------------------------------x
  26                                      o-----ox--------------------------------------x
  96                                      o------------------ox-xo--------ox----------------x
 293                                   x-------------------------------------------------x
 319                                   x-------------------------------------------------x
 796                                   x-------------------------------------------------x
 891                                   x-------------------------------------------------x
 918                                   x-xo----------------ox----------------------------x
 926                                   x-------------------------------------------------x
 940                                   x-------------------------------------------------x
1146                                   x-------------------------------------------------x
1215                                   x-xo-ox-xo-------------ox-------------------------x
1225                                      o---------ox-----------------------------------x
1301                                      o---------------ox--------------------------x
1323                                   x-------------------------------------------------x
1375                                   x-------------------------------------------------x
1434                                   x-------------------------------------------------x
  27                                         x-x
 677                                         x-x
1110                                         x-x
1140                                         x-x
   5                                         x------x
 303                                         x------x
 639                                         x------x
1013                                         x------x
1409                                         x------x
 300                                            o-----ox-----x
 477                                         x------------x
 577                                         x------------x
 604                                         x------------x
1183                                            o-----ox-----x
1198                                         x------------x
1292                                         x-xo---------o
 427                                         x---------------x
 634                                         x---------------x
1030                                         x---------------x
  22                                            x-xo-ox-------------------------------x
 153                                         x----------------------------------------x
 155                                         x----------------------------------------x
 164                                         x----------------------------------------x
 212                                            o----------ox--------------------------x
 228                                         x----------------------------------------x
 256                                            o----------ox--------------------------x
 276                                            o-----ox-xo-----------------ox---------x
 368                                            o-----ox------------------------------x
 398                                         x----------------------------------------x
 572                                            o-----ox------------------------------x
 597                                         x----------------------------------------x
 792                                         x----------------------------------------x
 847                                         x----------------------------------------x
 884                                         x----------------------------------------x
 975                                         x----------------------------------------x
 978                                         x----------------------------------------x
1014                                         x----------------------------------------x
1022                                         x----------------------------------------x
1023                                         x----------------------------------------x
1053                                            o------------------ox-----------------x
1054                                            o-----ox------------------------------x
1060                                         x----------------------------------------x
1105                                            o-----ox-xo---------------ox----------x
1162                                            o----------ox-------------------------x
```

## Women's Periodicals and Newspapers

```
       1970 1971 1972 1973 1974 1975 1976 1977 1978 1979 1980 1981 CIO  date
 1181                                x-------------------------------------x
 1332                                o-----ox----------xo----ox------------------x
 1395                                x-------------------------------------x
 1428                                o-----------------------ox------------------x
  441                                o-----------------------------------ox-xo---o
  442                                o-----------------------------------ox-xo---o
 1315                                o-----------------------------------ox-xo---o
  476                           x-x
  854                           x-x
  121                           x------x
  209                           o----x-x
  676                           x------x
  974                           x------x
 1092                           x------x
 1222                           x------x
 1055                           x-----------x
 1362                           x-----------x
   75                           o----ox-xo----ox----------x
  198                           x----------------------x
  460                           o----ox-xo-------------ox----x
   71                                x-------------------------------------x
  102                                x-------------------------------------x
  118                                x-------------------------------------x
  173                                x-------------------------------------x
  174                                x-------------------------------------x
  224                                o-----------ox-------------------------x
  264                                x-------------------------------------x
  486                                o----ox-------------------------------x
  587                                o----ox-------------------------------x
  600                                x-------------------------------------x
  660                                x-------------------------------------x
  934                                x-------------------------------------x
  963                                x-------------------------------------x
 1026                                x-------------------------------------x
 1197                                x-------------------------------------x
 1226                                x-------------------------------------x
 1227                                x-------------------------------------x
 1302                                x-------------------------------------x
 1304                                x-------------------------------------x
 1338                                x-------------------------------------x
 1340                                x-xo--------ox-------------------------x
 1364                                x----xo-----ox-------------------------x
 1377                                o-------------------ox-----------------x
 1419                                x-xo-ox-xo---------ox------------------x
 1430                                x-xo--------------ox-------------------x
 1445                                o----ox-------------------------------x
  304                                o---------------------------ox-xo--o
  227                                     x-x
 1043                                     x-x
 1379                                     x-x
  111                                     x------x
  616                                     x------x
  750                                     x------x
 1012                                     x-----------x
 1129                                     x-----------x
 1150                                     o-----ox-----------x
  448                                     x-xo--ox------------------------x
  113                                     x-------------------------------x
  171                                     x-------------------------------x
  231                                     x-------------------------------x
  523                                          o-----------ox-------------x
  593                                          x-------------------------x
  619                                          x-------------------------x
  631                                          x-------------------------x
  883                                          x-------------------------x
```

373

## Women's Periodicals and Newspapers

```
       1970 1971 1972 1973 1974 1975 1976 1977 1978 1979 1980 1981 CIO  date
  915                                        x-------------------------x
 1064                                        x-------------------------x
 1168                                        x-------------------------x
 1174                                        x-------------------------x
 1187                                        o-----ox------------------x
 1255                                        x-------------------------x
 1297                                        o-----ox------------------x
 1303                                        x-------------------------x
 1318                                        x-------------------------x
 1359                                        x-------------------------x
 1449                                        o-----ox-x
 1388                                        o-----ox-----x
  129                                        x-------------------------x
  149                                        x-------------------------x
  277                                        o-----ox------------------x
  483                                        x-------------------------x
  490                                        x-------------------------x
  521                                        x-------------------------x
  599                                        x-------------------------x
  773                                        x-xo-ox-------------------x
  864                                        x-------------------------x
  929                                        x-------------------------x
  941                                        x-------------------------x
  979                                        x-------------------------x
 1025                                        x-------------------------x
 1095                                        x-------------------------x
 1103                                        x-xo-ox-------------------x
 1177                                        x-------------------------x
 1192                                        o-----ox-xo-ox------------x
 1299                                        x-------------------------x
 1305                                        x-------------------------x
 1312                                        o-----ox------------------x
 1422                                        x-------------------------x
 1429                                        x-------------------------x
  148                                        o-----------------ox-xo--o
  736                                             x-x
  199                                             x--------------------x
  359                                             x--------------------x
  429                                             x--------------------x
  488                                             x--------------------x
  498                                             x--------------------x
  776                                             x--------------------x
  838                                             x--------------------x
  840                                             o-----ox-------------x
  932                                             x--------------------x
 1017                                             x--------------------x
 1048                                             x--------------------x
 1074                                             x-xo--ox-------------x
 1081                                             x--------------------x
 1101                                             x--------------------x
 1209                                             x-----xo-------------o
 1211                                             x--------------------x
 1346                                             o-----ox-------------x
 1351                                             x--------------------x
 1365                                             o-----ox-------------x
 1425                                             x--------------------x
  350                                                  x---------------x
  352                                                  x---------------x
  362                                                  x---------------x
  605                                                  x---------------x
  612                                                  x---------------x
  637                                                  x---------------x
  668                                                  x---------------x
  670                                                  x---------------x
  942                                                  x---------------x
```

374

## Women's Periodicals and Newspapers

```
       1970  1971  1972  1973  1974  1975  1976  1977  1978  1979  1980  1981  CIO  date
1308                                                              x----------------x
1390                                                              x----------------x
1418                                                              x----------------x
1179                                                              o--------ox-xo---o
```

# About the Contributors

JAMES P. DANKY is Newspapers and Periodicals Librarian at the State Historical Society and the author/compiler of many publications including Women's History: Resources at the State Historical Society of Wisconsin, fourth edition revised, 1981 as well as union lists of newspapers and periodicals for Hispanic Americans, blacks, and Asian Americans. A former columnist on alternative periodicals for Wilson Library Bulletin, Danky was co-director of the U.S. Office of Education-supported Alternative Acquisitions Project, Temple University, Philadelphia and co-editor of Alternative Materials in Libraries, Metuchen, New Jersey, Scarecrow Press, 1981.

MAUREEN E. HADY received both a B.A. in English and an M.A. in Library Science from the University of Wisconsin-Madison. She was employed in the Newspapers and Periodicals Unit of the State Historical Society of Wisconsin for three years. Hady is the co-compiler, with Neil E. Strache, James P. Danky, Susan Bryl and Erwin Welsch, of Black Periodicals and Newspapers: A Union List of Holdings in Libraries of the University of Wisconsin and the Library of the State Historical Society of Wisconsin, second edition revised, 1979. She also co-compiled, with James P. Danky, Asian American Periodicals and Newspapers: A Union List of Holdings in the Library of the State Historical Society of Wisconsin and the Libraries of the University of Wisconsin-Madison, 1979.

MARGARET E. McGUIGAN is a resident of Spring Green, Wisconsin where she formerly owned and operated a bakery and cafe. A mother of nine children, McGuigan is now employed as a Project Assistant in the Newspapers and Periodicals Unit of the State Historical Society of Wisconsin, where she typed this manuscript among many other tasks.

BARRY CHRISTOPHER NOONAN is a native of Milwaukee, Wisconsin and is currently an undergraduate at the University of Wisconsin-Madison, majoring in history. He is also a professional genealogical indexer and was a major contributor to the recently completed 1905 Wisconsin State Census Index. Noonan contributes to the annual index to the Wisconsin Magazine of History and his current project is an index to all extant Wisconsin Newspapers for the period 1833-1850.

NEIL E. STRACHE is an undergraduate at the University of Wisconsin-Madison, majoring in political science. He is originally from Clyman, Wisconsin and is employed in the Newspapers and Periodicals Unit of the State Historical Society of Wisconsin. In addition to his work on Black Periodicals and Newspapers Held by the Library of the State Historical Society of Wisconsin and the Libraries of the University of Wisconsin-Madison, 1979, Neil co-compiled with James P. Danky, Hispanic Americans in the United States: A Union List of Periodicals and Newspapers Held by the Library of the State Historical Society of Wisconsin and the Libraries of the University of Wisconsin-Madison, 1979.